NEURAL NETWORKS
for
PERCEPTION

Volume 1
Human and Machine Perception

NEURAL NETWORKS
for
PERCEPTION

Volume 1

Human and Machine Perception

Edited by

Harry Wechsler

George Mason University
Fairfax, Virginia

ACADEMIC PRESS, INC.
Harcourt Brace Jovanovich, Publishers
Boston   San Diego   New York
London   Sydney   Tokyo   Toronto

Cover design by Elizabeth E. Tustian

ACADEMIC PRESS, INC.
1250 Sixth Avenue, San Diego, CA   92101

United Kingdom Edition published by
ACADEMIC PRESS LIMITED
24–28 Oval Road, London NW1   7DX

Library of Congress Cataloging-in-Publication Data

Neural Networks for perception / edited by Harry Wechsler.
        p.   cm.
    Includes bibliographical references and index.
    Contents: v. 1. Human and machine perception — v. 2. Computation,
learning, and architecture.
    ISBN 0-12-741251-4 (v. 1). — ISBN 0-12-741252-2 (v. 2)
    1. Neural networks (Computer science)   2. Perception.
I. Wechsler, Harry.
QA76.87.N485   1991
006.3—dc20   91-24207
                                                                  CIP

Printed in the United States of America
91 92 93 94   9 8 7 6 5 4 3 2 1

To my daughter, Gabriela Anya

Contents

Contents of Volume 2: Computation, Learning, and Architectures ix

Contributors xiii

Foreword xvii

PART I

Human Perception

I.Introduction 3
  H. Wechsler

I.1 Visual Cortex: Window on the Biological Basis of Learning and
  Memory 8
  L.N. Cooper

I.2 A Network Model of Object Recognition in Human Vision 25
  S. Edelman

I.3 A Cortically Based Model for Integration in Visual Perception 41
  L.H. Finkel, G.N. Reeke, and G.M. Edelman

I.4 The Symmetric Organization of Parallel Cortical Systems for
  Form and Motion Perception 64
  S. Grossberg

I.5 The Structure and Interpretation of Neuronal Codes in the Visual
  System 104
  B.J. Richmond and L.M. Optican

I.6 Self-Organization of Functional Architecture in the
  Cerebral Cortex 120
  S. Tanaka

I.7 Filters versus Textons in Human and Machine Texture
  Discrimination 145
  D. Williams and B. Julesz

I.8 Two-Dimensional Maps and Biological Vision: Representing
  Three-Dimensional Space 176
  G.L. Zimmerman

PART II

Machine Perception

II.Introduction 195
 H. Wechsler

II.1 WISARD and Other Weightless Neurons 202
 I. Aleksander

II.2 Multi-Dimensional Linear Lattice for Fourier and Gabor Transforms,
 Multiple-Scale Gaussian Filtering, and Edge Detection 214
 J. Ben-Arie

II.3 Aspects of Invariant Pattern and Object Recognition 234
 T. Caelli, M. Ferraro, and E. Barth

II.4 A Neural Network Architecture for Fast On-Line Supervised
 Learning and Pattern Recognition 248
 G.A. Carpenter, S. Grossberg, and J. Reynolds

II.5 Neural Network Approaches to Color Vision 265
 A.C. Hurlbert

II.6 Adaptive Sensory-Motor Coordination Through
 Self-Consistency 285
 M. Kuperstein

II.7 Finding Boundaries in Images 315
 J. Malik and P. Perona

II.8 Compression of Remotely Sensed Images Using Self-Organizing
 Feature Maps 345
 M. Manohar and J.C. Tilton

II.9 Self-Organizing Maps and Computer Vision 368
 E. Oja

II.10 Region Growing Using Neural Networks 386
 T.R. Reed

II.11 Vision and Space-Variant Sensing 398
 G. Sandini and M. Tistarelli

II.12 Learning and Recognizing 3D Objects from Multiple Views in a
 Neural System 426
 M. Seibert and A.M. Waxman

II.13 Hybrid Symbolic-Neural Methods for Improved Recognition
 Using High-Level Visual Features 445
 G.G. Towell and J.W. Shavlik

II.14 Multiscale and Distributed Visual Representations and Mappings
 for Invariant Low-Level Perception 462
 H. Wechsler

II.15 Symmetry: A Context Free Cue for Foveated Vision 477
      Y. Yeshurun, D. Reisfeld, and H. Wolfson
II.16 A Neural Network for Motion Processing 492
      Y.T. Zhou and R. Chellappa
Index 517

Contents of Volume 2

PART III

Computation and Learning

III.Introduction
H. Wechsler

III.1 Learning Visual Behaviors
D.H. Ballard and S. D. Whitehead

III.2 Nonparametric Regression Analysis Using Self-Organizing
Topological Maps
V. Cherkassky and H. Lari-Najafi

III.3 Theory of the Backpropagation Neural Network
R. Hecht-Nielsen

III.4 Hopfield Model and Optimization Problems
Behrooz Kamgar-Parsi and Behzad Kamgar-Parsi

III.5 DAM, Regression Analysis, and Attentive Recognition
W. Pölzleitner

III.6 Intelligence Code Machine
V.M. Stern

III.7 Cycling Logarithmically Converging Networks That Flow Information
to Behave (Perceive) and Learn
L. Uhr

III.8 Computation and Learning in the Context of Neural
Network Capacity
S.S. Venkatesh

PART IV

Architectures

IV.Introduction
H. Wechsler

IV.1 Competitive and Cooperative Multimode Dynamics in Photorefractive Ring Circuits
D.Z. Anderson, C. Benkert, and D.D. Crouch

IV.2 Hybrid Neural Networks and Algorithms
D. Casasent

IV.3 The Use of Fixed Holograms for Massively-Interconnected, Low-Power Neural Networks
H. Jeon, J. Shamir, R.B. Johnson, H.J. Caulfield, J. Kinser, C. Hester, and M. Temmen

IV.4 Electronic Circuits for Adaptive Synapses
J. Mann and J. Raffel

IV.5 Neural Network Computations on a Fine Grain Array Processor
S.S. Wilson

Contributors

Numbers in parentheses indicate pages on which the authors' contributions begin.

Igor Aleksander (202), Department of Electrical Engineering, Imperial College of Science, Technology, and Medicine, Exhibition Road, London SW7 2BT, England

Erhardt Barth (234), Department of Computer Science, School of Information Technology and Electrical Engineering, The University of Melbourne, Parkville, Victoria 3052, Australia

Jezekiel Ben-Arie (214), Department of Electrical and Computer Engineering, Illinois Institute of Technology, Chicago, Illinois 60616

Terry Caelli (234), Department of Computer Science, School of Information Technology and Electrical Engineering, The University of Melbourne, Parkville, Victoria 3052, Australia

Gail A. Carpenter (248), Center for Adaptive Systems and Graduate Program in Cognitive and Neural Systems, Boston University, 111 Cummington Street, Boston, Massachusetts 02215

R. Chellappa (492), Electrical Engineering Department, University of Maryland, College Park, Maryland 20742

Leon N. Cooper (8), Department of Physics and Center for Neural Science, Brown University, Providence, Rhode Island 02912

Gerald M. Edelman (41), Neurosciences Institute and Rockefeller University, New York, New York 10021

Shimon Edelman (25), Applied Mathematics, Weizmann Institute of Science, Rehovot, Israel

Mario Ferraro (234), Dipartimento di Fisica Sperimentale, Universita' di Torino, Italy

Leif H. Finkel (41), Department of Bioengineering, 220 S. 33rd Street, University of Pennsylvania, Philadelphia, Pennsylvania 19104

Stephen Grossberg (64, 248), Center for Adaptive Systems and Graduate Program in Cognitive and Neural Systems, Boston University, 111 Cummington Street, Boston, Massachusetts 02215

Anya C. Hurlbert (265), Department of Physiology, Oxford University, Oxford, England

Bela Julesz (145), Laboratory of Vision Research, 41 Gordon Road, Kilmer Campus, Rutgers University, New Brunswick, New Jersey   08903

Michael Kuperstein (285), Neurogen Laboratories, Inc., 325 Harvard Street, Suite 202, Brookline, Massachusetts   02146

Jitendra Malik (315), Electrical Engineering and Computer Science, University of California, Berkeley, California   94720

M. Manohar (345), Universities Space Research Association, Greenbelt, Maryland   20771

Erkki Oja (368), Information Technology, Lappeenranta University of Technology, P.O. Box 20, SF-53851 Lappeenranta, Finland

Lance M. Optican (104), Laboratory of Sensorimotor Research, National Eye Institute, Bethesda, Maryland   20892

Pietro Perona (315), California Institute of Technology, Department of Electrical Engineering, Pasadena, California   91125

Todd R. Reed (386), Department of Electrical and Computer Engineering, University of California, Davis, California   95616

George N. Reeke, Jr. (41), Neurosciences Institute and Rockefeller University, New York, New York   10021

Daniel Reisfeld (477), Department of Computer Science, Tel Aviv University, Tel Aviv, Israel

John Reynolds (248), Center for Adaptive Systems and Graduate Program in Cognitive and Neural Systems, Boston University, 111 Cummington Street, Boston, Massachusetts   02215

Barry J. Richmond (104), Laboratory of Neuropsychology, National Institute of Mental Health, Building 9, Room 1N-107, 9000 Rockville Pike, Bethesda, Maryland   20892

G. Sandini (398), Dipartimento di Informatica, Sistemistica e Telematica, University of Genoa, Genoa, Italy

Michael Seibert (426), Machine Intelligence Technology Group, MIT Lincoln Laboratory, Lexington, Massachusetts   02173

Jude W. Shavlik (445), Computer Sciences Department, University of Wisconsin, Madison, Wisconsin   53706

Shigeru Tanaka (120), Fundamental Research Lab, NEC Corporation, Miyukigaoka 34, Tsukuba, Ibaraki 305, Japan

J.C. Tilton (345), NASA Goddard Space Flight Center, Greenbelt, Maryland   20071

M. Tistarelli (398), Dipartimento di Informatica, Sistemistica e Telematica, University of Genoa, Genoa, Italy

Geoffrey G. Towell (445), Computer Sciences Department, University of Wisconsin, Madison, Wisconsin   53706

Allen M. Waxman (426), Machine Intelligence Technology Group, MIT Lincoln Laboratory, Lexington, Massachusetts 02173

Harry Wechsler (462), Department of Computer Science, George Mason University, Fairfax, Virginia 22030

Douglas Williams (145), Laboratory of Vision Research, 41 Gordon Road, Kilmer Campus, Rutgers University, New Brunswick, New Jersey 08903

Haim Wolfson (477), Department of Computer Science, Tel Aviv University, Tel Aviv, Israel

Yehezkel Yeshurun (477), Department of Computer Science, Tel Aviv University, Tel Aviv, Israel

Y.T. Zhou (492), HNC, Inc., 5501 Oberlin Drive, San Diego, California 92121

G. Lee Zimmerman (176), Department of Electrical Engineering, Tulane University, New Orleans, Louisiana 70118

Foreword

Neural Networks for Perception explores perception and the recent research in neural networks that has advanced our understanding of both human and machine perception. Perception is a major facet of our senses and provides us with the essential information needed to broaden our horizons and to connect us to the surrounding world, enabling safe movement and advantageous manipulation. Far beyond being merely a scientific challenge, the possibility of emulating the human sense of perception would revolutionize countless technologies, such as visual tracking and object recognition, robotics and flexible manufacturing, automation and control, and autonomous navigation for future space missions. As Aristotle noted,

> "All men, by nature, desire to know. An indication of this is the delight we take in our senses, for even apart from their usefulness they are loved for themselves and above all others the sense of sight. For not only with a view to action, but even when we are not going to do anything we prefer seeing to everything else. The reason is that this, most of all senses, makes us know and brings to light many differences between things."

Indeed, reflecting the intricate connection between perception and purposeful activity, many of the papers in this book deal with meaningful tasks.

Meanwhile, we are witnessing the rapid growth of neural networks research as a novel and viable approach to emulating intelligence in general and to achieving the recognition and perceptual learning functions of vision. Neural network research is a synergetic endeavor that draws from cognitive and neuro-sciences, physics, signal processing, and pattern recognition. Neural networks (NN), also known as artificial neural systems (ANS), are implemented as parallel and distributed processing (PDP) models of computation consisting of dense interconnections among computational processing elements (PE or "neuron"). The competitive processes that take place among the PEs enable neural networks to display fault-tolerance and robustness with respect to noisy and/or incomplete sensory inputs, while allowing graceful degradation with respect to faulty memory storage and internal processing.

Neural Networks for Perception showcases the work of preeminent practitioners in the field of neural networks and enhances our understanding of what neural networks are and how they can be gainfully employed. It is organized into two volumes: The first, subtitled *Human and Machine Perception*, focuses on models for understanding human perception in terms of distributed computation and examples of PDP models for machine perception. The second, subtitled *Computation, Learning, and Architectures*, examines computational and adaptation problems related to the use of neuronal systems, and the corresponding hardware architectures capable of implementing neural networks for perception and of coping with the complexity inherent in massively distributed computation.

Perception is just one of the capabilities needed to implement machine intelligence. The discussion on perception involves, by default, the full range of dialectics on the fundamentals of both human and machine intelligence. Normal science and technological development are always conducted within some predefined paradigm and this work is no exception. The paradigms attempt to model the everlasting dichotomy of brain and matter using specific metaphors. One of the metaphors for neural networks is statistical physics and thermodynamics; nonetheless, some thoughts on the feasibility and future use of evolution and quantum mechanics are contemplated as well. NN advancements parallel those underway in artificial intelligence toward the development of perceptual systems. Consequently, the possibility of hybrid systems, consisting of NN and AI components, is also considered.

Many have postulated possible arguments about what intelligence is and how it impinges on perception. Apparently, recognition is a basic biological function crucial to biological systems in recognizing specific patterns and responding appropriately: antibodies attack foreign intruders; our ears capture sound and speech; animals have to locate edible plants; and sensory–motor interactions involved in navigation and manipulation are predicated on adequate recognition capabilities. Failure to recognize can be fatal; recognition should therefore be the ultimate goal of the perceptual system, and indeed, it probably underlies much of what is intelligence.

Albert Szent-Gyorgi said that

> "The brain is not an organ of thinking but an organ of survival, like claws and fangs. It is made in such a way as to make us accept as truth that which is only advantage. It is an exceptional, almost pathological constitution one has, if one follows thoughts logically through, regardless of consequences. Such people make martyrs, apostles, or scientists, and mostly end on the stake, or in a chair, electric or academic."

The concepts of recognition and reasoning by analogy underlie recent views on both planning and learning as espoused by the case-based reasoning methodology.

Perception involves information processing, and one has to address those descriptive levels along which visual tasks of varying complexity can be analyzed and explained. Marr argued earlier that the specific levels are those of function and strategy, process (in terms of representation and algorithm), and mechanism (hardware implementation). At the first level is computational theory, which specifies the task, its suitability, and the strategy needed to carry it out. The second level, that of the process, specifies the computational approach in terms of input and output representations, and the corresponding transformational algorithms. The last level, the hardware, specifies the actual implementation. Consequently, the computational task determines the mix of representations and algorithms, with a good match among the three levels critical to the outcome. Among the basic computational tasks being examined are those involved in optimization and adaptation towards eventual recognition.

The role of representation in both human and machine perception cannot be overestimated. According to Herb Simon,

> "All mathematical derivation can be viewed simply as change of representation, making evident what was previously true but obscure. This view can be extended to all of problem-solving — solving a problem then means representing (transforming) it so as to make the solution transparent. In other words, knowledge has to be made explicit if and when needed."

A basic issue underlying neural networks in general and self-organization in particular is that of determining which principles, if any, lead to the development of neural circuitry. The principles behind such development seem to preserve, in a multilevel fashion through successive representations, the information contents, and to indicate the link between information and energy.

Complexity issues are broad and pervasive in the development of a computational theory that models perception. According to McClelland and Rumelhart, "the time and space requirements of any cognitive theory are important determinants of the theory's (biological) plausibility," while, at the same time, Tsotsos remarks "complexity satisfaction provides a major source of constraints on the solution of the problem."

Active perception is essential for decreasing the computational load on the perceptual system. Active perception leads naturally to exploration and mobility. It is this very mobility that provides people with complex stimulations and demands, which eventually lead to human evolution. There is more to active perception than just exploration, and the word *active* could be rewritten as "ACTive" to emphasize the role activity plays in our interactions with the environment. We are more than simple observers and our perceptual activities are task-dependent.

Current computer usage is predicated largely on rationalistic assumptions and bias toward the mind-and-matter dualism. That dichotomy assumes an objective world of physical reality and a subjective mental world. The interpreted and the interpreter, however, do not exist independently: existence is interpretation and interpretation is existence. Observers cannot be objective in their interpretation of the world and, by default, have to bring their whole background to the very act of interpretation.

Active perception can be redefined as throwness, i.e., our condition of understanding in which our actions find some resonance or effectiveness in the world. We usually become aware of objects and their properties when they break down. The process of things or activities breaking down is thus essential to make them concrete to us. Indeed, it suggests that perceptual activities are task-dependent and that their functionality is related to us acting on our environment.

Directed perception enhances active perception and implements a many (information)-to-one(object properties) mapping. This allows the possibility of being selective about which information source one should use. Different invariants can then be selected for use in different tasks based on their specific information efficacy. According to Cutting, directed and active perception underspecify process but overspecify interpretation. The perceiver has the choice of which information to pick up; both adaptation and task functionality can further enhance the ultimate visual performance.

Exploration, which is characteristic of active perception, is clearly an essential ingredient, because it allows the observer to attend only to those affordances most likely to be successful in sifting through the information available in the optical array. As a consequence, directed perception provides a mobile and intelligent observer with the capability of deciding which and how much one needs to be exposed to, and from that experience which and how much information to "intelligently" pick up and process, so it can correctly interpret the surrounding world. Directed perception builds upon low-level invariants and mappings and is the model-driven counterpart of the data-driven scale space (multiscale and distributed) low-level visual representations.

This book addresses both theoretical and practical issues related to the feasibility of both explaining human perception and implementing machine perception in terms of neural network models. To that end, the reader will find many examples of perceptual functional models, and hardware architectures suitable for realizing neural networks for machine perception. It is only through successful applications that a particular scientific paradigm or technology can eventually become accepted. Computational and learning issues involved in neural modeling are also addressed to understand the limitations of neural networks for machine perception and to suggest possible remedies.

The possibility of focusing on a major behavioral task, that of perception, makes the publication of this book timely in terms of the current interest in exploiting neural networks for perceptual tasks. This work is truly an international effort, with participation from contributors whose institutional affiliations span the globe. Each chapter covers a major aspect of neural modeling and is representative of state-of-the art research. The contents go beyond merely reporting recent research results to discuss the major issues facing neural network research and to suggest future trends. I would like to express my gratitude to all the contributors who made this book a reality. Many thanks go to Sari Kalin, of Academic Press, for her patience and support in facilitating the publication of this book.

Harry Wechsler
Washington, DC

PART I

Human Perception

I. Introduction

The first part of the book, dedicated to human perception, illustrates how biologically-inspired neural systems implement fundamental elements of neural networks processing and could account for some of the perceptual behavior displayed by humans. Each chapter elucidates the mysteries of the human visual system (HVS) and suggests ways to build artificial visual systems (AVS) from the vantage point of experts in signal processing, physics, psychophysics (a branch of psychology that measures the relationship between perceived and physical attributes of a stimulus), neurophysiology, and cognitive sciences. It has indeed been the case that machine perception has drawn much from the workings of James Gibson in psychophysics, and Hubel and Wiesel in neurophysiology, among others. This is not to say that the only way to build machine perception is to copy human perception. Evolving and successful biological systems provide clues that go a long way towards speeding up our understanding of what drives perception. Furthermore, it is also worth remembering that perceptual development probably has underlying general principles that should apply across the whole spectrum of biological existence. Consequently, we should heed Bertrand Russell, who back in 1921 said that "in attempting to understand the elements out of which mental phenomena are compounded, it is of greatest importance to remember that from protozoa to man there is nowhere a very wide gap either in structure or in behavior. From this fact it is a highly probable inference that there is also nowhere a very wide mental gap." The rest of this introduction describes briefly the contents of each chapter and its contribution to the understanding of perception.

The first chapter, written by Leon Cooper, a Nobel laureate in physics, proposes the study of the visual cortex with a combination of statistical and single cell methods so that the detailed evolution of some LGN synapses can be examined in a mean-field produced by clusters of related cortical cells. Such a theory has significant implications for neural networks research where "the whole is more than the sum of its parts," and where emerging perceptual Gestalts have been explained in terms of statistical mechanics whose task is to integrate local and global constraints through specific optimization techniques. Experiments, carried out on classical visual deprivation cases, indicate quantitative agreement between theory and experiment in both the final equilibrium states and the kinetics by which these states are reached. The theory developed by Cooper suggests a molecular basis for learning and memory storage regarding the development of selectivity (and plasticity) and ocular dominance.

Shimon Edelman addresses the problem of object recognition in human vision, where the appearance of an object depends on the observer's point of view. One of the reasons for perception's high degree of computational complexity is this inherent variability of input. Such variability can be the result of noise, occluded data, and geometric or topological changes. Vision systems must not only perceive the identity of objects despite such variability but explicitly characterize it, because the variability in the image formation process (particularly that due to geometric distortion and varying incident illumination) inherently carries valuable information about the image. Theories that have been advanced to explain the phenomena of size and shape constancy and to understand how the recognition system avoids storing a possibly infinite number of object occurrences, usually involve the concepts of canonical views embedded in some visual potential and alignments such as mental rotation. Mental rotation has been disputed recently, however, by Irwin Rock and his colleagues. The experiments they report claim that subjects are unable to perform mental rotation unless they "make use of strategies that circumvent the process of visualization." They further suggest that "the linear increase in time required to succeed in mental rotation tasks as a function of the angular discrepancy between the figures compared is the result of increasing difficulty rather than of the time required for rotation." Reported experimental results on mental rotation could then be explained in terms of familiarity with the figure and practice, i.e., learning, and availability of landmarks for recognition, while at the same time question if an object-centered representation is achieved. The research carried out by Edelman replicates the central features of human performance and supports the notion that at least one of the pathways to recognition in the human visual system relies on relatively few viewpoint-specific canonical representations and limited anisotropic generalization (learning) of novel views.

The third chapter, due to Leif Finkel, George Reeke, and Gerald Edelman--another Nobel laureate (in medicine) who like Leon Cooper (see first chapter) became interested in perception--considers how the viewer can construct a coherent scene, despite (or just because of) the fact that in higher mammals, the visual cortex comprises multiple, independent areas, each of which is functionally specialized for particular visual tasks. This problem is of interest not only to those working on human perception but on machine perception, where it is treated under data fusion and multisensory perception. The solution for cortical integration suggested in this chapter, coined as the Reentrant Cortical Integration (RCI), addresses the binding problem through dynamic, temporally ongoing, parallel and recursive process of signaling between two or more neural maps. The maps are retinotopically organized so responses in these maps relate to positions in space and achieve spatial coherence.

The next chapter, written by Stephen Grossberg, addresses the same issue of cortical integration, by proposing that object discrimination depends upon two separate but interconnected systems. The first, the Static Boundary Contour System (SBCS), generates emergent boundary segmentations whose outputs are insensitive to direction-of-contrast and to direction-of-motion, whereas the second system, the Motion Boundary Contour System (MBCS), generates emergent boundary segmentations whose outputs are insensitive to direction-of-contrast but sensitive to direction-of-motion. Complementary to the BCS system, is the Feature Contour System (FCS), whose output signals are sensitive to direction-of-contrast and which is responsible for visibility. The underlying principle behind the development of theses parallel cortical systems is a symmetry principle. Symmetry is known to suggest attention, and its underlying feature integration further subserve shifts of spatial attention. The Form-And-Color-And-DEpth (FACADE) unifies the BCS and FCS circuits and explains how multiplexing several key properties of the scenic representation can cooperatively generate an unambiguous 3-dimensional representation. The themes of uncertainty, complementarity, symmetry, and resonance, which permeate the FACADE theory, show the inadequacy of modular and rule-based vision theories and suggest how context-sensitive interactions overcome such computational uncertainties. It is also interesting to note that the same themes also lie in the foundations of quantum mechanics.

The traditional and accepted view that all that is relevant about the neuron's response lies in its strength (number of spikes) has been challenged by Richmond and Optican. The hypothesis they advance in the fifth chapter is that the spike train has a temporal dimension that allows individual neurons to encode local stimulus features. From information theory and physiological studies, they found that the efficiency of encoding visual information while using the temporal-modulation hypothesis is about twice that of the traditional mean-firing rate. Multiple messages are carried simultaneously by or are multiplexed onto the spike train. Such a hypothesis still requires some decoding mechanism to unscramble the stimulus features that have been multiplexed together--such decoding still waits to be found. The use of temporally modulated messages could provide the basis for feature binding, cortical integration and pattern recognition using the mechanisms of Associative Memory (AM).

Self-organization involves unsupervised training and leads to an advanced type of learning when compared to supervised training. Research by Hubel and Wiesel has uncovered a regular interconnection pattern for early visual processing stages. The pattern, or cytoarchitecture, has as its main processing unit a hypercolumn that detects edges within a 3-dimensional "hardware" (Receptive Field - RF - position, orientation and size). An alternative interpretation of the same cytoarchitecture has been suggested recently in terms of conjoint spatial/spatial-frequency image representations such as the Gabor distribution.) The sixth chapter, written by Shigeru Tanaka, addresses the development of how the columnar organization of the visual cortex, thought to provide the functional units needed in information processing such as feature detection. The same question was addressed earlier by Ralph Linsker, who has suggested that such development is predicated on the preservation of information when signals are transformed at each processing stage, and on multi-layer networks with feed-forward connections, linear summation response and Hebbian learning. Tanaka attempts to elucidate the specific form of Hebbian mechanism and build a general theory underlying synaptic stabilization. Towards that end, he draws analogies from thermodynamics, and expresses the synaptic connection density in local equilibrium in terms of the Potts spin variables. Furthermore, the Langevin equation and the Lyapunov function of the RFs are obtained by combining the RFs with the thermodynamic theory of self-organization of synaptic connections.

The seventh chapter, written by Williams and Julesz, is concerned with the human ability to distinguish between textures and accounts for the known asymmetry in discrimination, where for certain texture pairs the ease of discrimination changes when the role of figure and ground are reversed. Standing behind such asymmetry are three properties of texture perception: subjective closure, perceptual distortion, and fill-in. The authors conclude that because edge detection and boundary segmentation are lacking and visual information processing is object based, fill-in between edges and boundaries is required. Interestingly enough, the fill-in property is also one of the characteristics behind the BCS and FCS systems discussed by Stephen Grossberg in chapter four.

The first part of the book closes with a chapter written by Lee Zimmerman and describes joint research with Harry Wechsler on how 2-dimensional retinal information can be effectively used towards 3-dimensional object recognition using distributed computation. The distributed computation concept, with its treatment of representations, processing and strategies, could advance our understanding of fault-tolerant and invariant 3-dimensional object recognition. Parallel and distributed processing (PDP) is implemented using distributed associative memories (DAMs), while distributed strategies take the form of active perception and influence the formation of the depth map and its reprojection (flattening) so it can be matched against canonical views stored in the DAM.

I.1

Visual Cortex: Window on the Biological Basis of Learning and Memory

LEON N. COOPER

*Department of Physics and
Center for Neural Science
Brown University
Providence, RI*

I. Introduction

The idea that so complicated a portion of the brain as visual cortex could be understood well enough to provide a model for further detailed, experimental and theoretical studies seems, at first, far-fetched. Visual cortex, just as the rest of cortex of all primates, is a highly complex structure composed of many layers and columns, many different types of cells interconnected with one another with an almost bewildering variety of synaptic contacts and receptors and numerous different transmitters. If we add to this, non-linearities and time delays as well as noise and the erratic behavior of individual neurons, we arrive at a problem of such complexity, one could be inclined to leave it for those of our descendants who might populate our planet (assuming that our planet still exists) several centuries hence.

Response to this possibly depressing situation, for those of us too impatient to wait for our descendants, is varied. One can, if one wishes, write down a

8

description of the problem as a set of equations that include every conceivable complexity - those observed as well as those imagined. The result is a set of rules that may, in fact, contain the true behavior of the system, but is perhaps no more informative than the statement that in somewhere among the solutions of the Schrodinger equation, for a sufficent number of electrons and protons exists a living creature. At the other extreme, one can simplify so much that one is no longer describing anything of serious interest. As Albert Einstein instructed, one must make the problem as simple as possible - but no simpler.

Perhaps the simplest problem is that of a single idealized cell. We have previously described work concerning the evolution of such single cells under various learning rules. The next seeming complexity would be to extend what has been learned for single cells to systems of several cells. But it often happens that the next simplest problem is, in fact, a problem involving very large numbers of individual units. For one then has the possibility of introducing statistical methods. In Physics the statistical mechanics of many body systems such as gases and some solids provide famous examples.

What we propose is that visual cortex (and this, possibly could be generalized to other regions of cortex) can be treated by a combination of statistical and single cell methods so that the detailed evolution of some of the synapses (in this case LGN - cortical synapses) can be studied in a mean-field produced by clusters of related cortical cells.

SUMMARY OF SINGLE CELL THEORY

Cortical neurons receive afferents from many sources. In visual cortex (layer 4, for example) the principle afferents are those from the lateral geniculate nucleus and from other cortical neurons. This leads to a complex network that we have analyzed in several stages. In the first stage we consider a single neuron with inputs from both eyes (Figure 1).

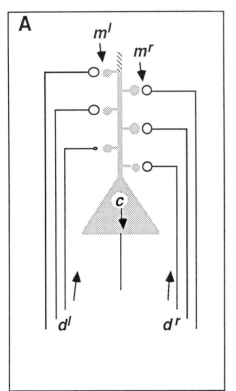 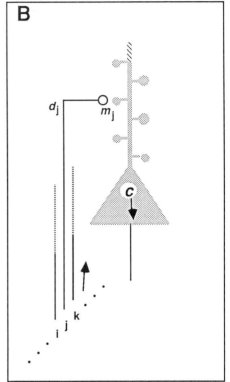

Fig. 1. Illustrated schematically are pyramidal shaped cortical neurons and the proximal segments of their apical dendrites. The shaded circles attached to the dendrites represent dendritic spines. In the first stage of the theoretical analysis we consider only the inputs to the cell from the lateral geniculate nucleus (A). The signals conveyed along these afferents arise either from the left retina (d^l) or the right retina (d^r) and are transfered to the cortical neuron by the synaptic junctions m^l and m^r. The output of the cortical neuron, as measured by the firing rate or the dendritic depolarization, is represented as c which is the sum of $d^l \cdot m^l$ and $d^r \cdot m^r$. The central question is how one of these afferent synapses, m_j, modifies in time as a function of both its level of presynaptic activity d_j and the level of postsynaptic depolarization (B).

The output of this neuron (in the linear region) can be written

$$c = m^l \cdot d^l + m^r \cdot d^r \qquad (1)$$

This means that the neuron firing rate (in the linear region) is the sum of the inputs from the left eye multiplied by the appropriate left-eye synaptic weights plus the inputs from the right eye multiplied by the appropriate right-eye synaptic weights. Thus the neuron integrates signals from the left and right eyes. According to the theory presented by Bienenstock, Cooper and Munro (BCM, 1982), these synaptic weights modify as a function of local and global variables. To illustrate we consider the synaptic weight m_j (Figure 2).

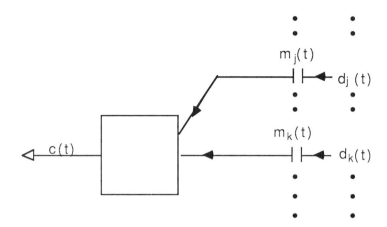

Fig. 2. Local and Quasi-Local Variables

Its change in time, $\dot{m}_j$, is given below:

$$\dot{m}_j = F(d_j \ldots m_j; d_k \ldots c; \bar{\bar{c}}; X, Y, Z). \qquad (2)$$

Here variables such as $d_j \ldots m_j$ are designated local. These represent information (such as the incoming signal, d_j, and the strength of the synaptic junction, m_j) available locally at the synaptic junction, m_j. Variables such as d_k $\ldots$c are designated quasi-local. These represent information (such as c, the firing rate of the cell, or d_k, the incoming signal to another synaptic junction) that is not locally available to the junction m_j but is physically connected to the junction by the cell body itself--thus necessitating some form of internal communication

between various parts of the cell and its synaptic junctions. Variables such as $\bar{\bar{c}}$ (the time averaged output of the cell) are averaged local or quasi-local variables. Global variables are designated X,Y,Z... These latter represent information (e.g. presence or absence of neurotransmitters such as norepinephrine or the average activity of large numbers of cortical cells) that is present in a similar fashion for all or a large number of cortical neurons (distinguished from local or quasi-local variables presumably carrying detailed information that varies from synapse to synapse).

In a form relevant to this discussion, BCM modification can be written

$$\dot{m}_j = \phi(c,\bar{\bar{c}};X,Y,Z...)d_j \tag{3}$$

so that the jth synaptic junction, m_j, changes its value in time as a function of quasi-local and time-averaged quasi-local variables, c and $\bar{\bar{c}}$, as well as global variables X,Y,Z, through the function,f, and a function of the local variable d_j . The crucial function,f, is shown in Figure 3.

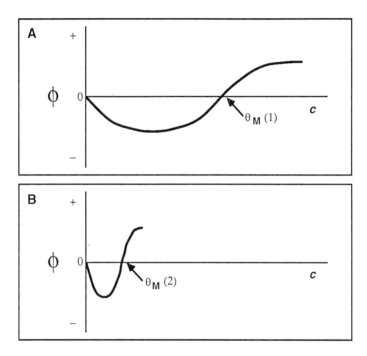

Fig. 3. The f function at two values of the modification threshold, q_M. According to BCM, active synapses (d > 0) are strengthened when f is positive and are weakened when f is negative. f is positive when c, the postsynaptic depolarization, is greater than q_M. The modification threshold, where f changes sign, is a non-linear function of the average activity of the postsynaptic neuron (c). Hence, in this example, q_M (1) would be expected when cortical neurons have experienced a normal visual environment (A) while q_M (2) would result from a prolonged period of binocular deprivation (B).

What is of particular significance is the change of sign of,f, at the modification threshold and the non-linear variation of θ_M with the average output of the cell $\bar{\bar{c}}$. In the form originally proposed by BCM, this was written

$$\theta_M = (\bar{\bar{c}})^2 \tag{4}$$

Detailed simulations that have allowed us to investigate precise time evolution for various experimental paradigms have enabled us to refine this relation and to begin an investigation of their various subtle consequences.as well as their quite different physiological basis. (Clothiaux, Bear and Cooper, to be published).
The occurrence of negative and positive regions for f drives the cell to selectivity in a 'normal' environment. This is so because the response of the cell is diminished to those patterns for which the output, c, is below threshold (f negative) while the response is enhanced to those patterns for which the output, c, is above threshold (f positive). The non-linear variation of the threshold with the average output of the cell, $\bar{\bar{c}}$, places the threshold so that it eventually separates one pattern from all of the rest. Further it provides the stability properties of the system.

EXTENSION TO NETWORKS

To better confront these ideas with experiment the single neuron discussed above must be placed in a network with the anatomical features of the region of interest. For visual cortex this suggests a network in which inhibitory and excitatory cells receive input from the lateral geniculate nucleus (LGN) and from each other. Such a network is a highly complex non-linear system. Some of the key questions concern the necessary levels of connectivity, the importance of instantaneous signalling, stochastic behavior as well as the approach to equilibrium. For example, the amount of connectivity is of significance both from a theoretical point of view as well as for the possible embodiment of neural networks in electronic circuitry.In various recent approaches such as those of Hopfield (1982), Hinton and Sejnowski (1983,1986) and Geman and Geman (1984), a very high degree of connectivity is assumed as well as a stochastic approach to equilibrium. In their work, as well as that of von der Malsburg (1973), it is essentially assumed that cortical activity reaches equilibrium rapidly. An alternative is to assume that non-equilibrium information is essential. We have taken this latter point of view in our work to date; thus one does not have to wait for equilibrium to obtain useful information.
In a network generalization of Eq. 1, we may therefore write

$$c_i = m_i^l \cdot d^l + m_i^r \cdot d^r + \sum_j L_{ij} c_j \tag{5}$$

where m_i^l and m_i^r are the synaptic junctions between left and right eye and the cortical neuron as in Eq. 1 while L_{ij} are the intracortical connections. A model network that is a first-order representation of the anatomy and physiology of layer IV of cat visual cortex (Figure 4) has been studied by Scofield and Cooper, 1985.

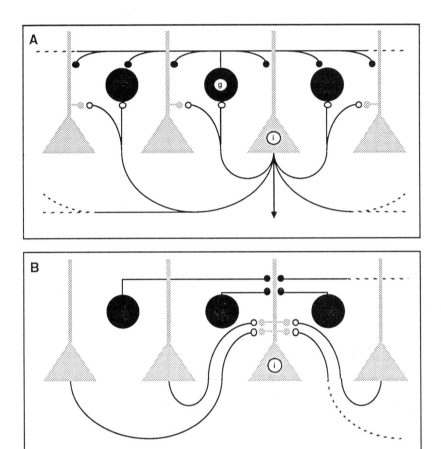

Fig. 4. In the second stage of the theoretical analysis, the neurons of Figure 1 are placed in a cortical network in which the inhibitory and excitatory cells receive input from the LGN and from each other. Illustrated in (A) are the efferent intracortical connections of two neurons in the network. The ith neuron is excitatory, the gth is inhibitory, and both synapse upon every other cell in the network. Illustrated in (B) are the intracortical inputs to the ith neuron. Thus, in addition to the geniculate afferents (d^l and d^r, shown in Figure 1A), each neuron in the network receives excitatory and inhibitory intracortical inputs. In a network generalization of

Eq. 1, the integrated output of the ith neuron may be written:

$$c_i = m_i^l \cdot d^l + m_i^r \cdot d^r + \sum_{ij} L_{ij} \, c_j$$

where the term $\sum_{ij} L_{ij} \, c_j$ is the sum of the output from other cells in the network multiplied by the weight of their synapses on the ith cell.

Analysis by Scofield and Cooper of the network along lines similar to that of the single cell analysis described above shows that under proper conditions on the intracortical synapses, the cells converge to states of maximum selectivity with respect to the environment formed by the geniculate signals. In addition, it can be shown that within a region all cells will prefer the same pattern; this defines an orientation column. Under proper conditions, the network will evolve to a state in which orientation preference is a piecewise continuous function of cortical distance. Our conclusions are therefore similar to those of BCM with explicit further statements concerning the independent effects of excitatory and inhibitory neurons on selectivity and ocular dominance. For example, shutting off inhibitory cells lessens selectivity and alters ocular dominance, (masked synapses). These inhibitory cells may be selective but there is no theoretical necessity that they be so. Further the intracortical inhibitory synapses do not have to be very responsive to visual experience. Most of the learning process can occur among the excitatory LGN-cortical synapses.

MEAN FIELD THEORY OF THE NEURAL NETWORK

We have previously described a mean field approximation to the complex neural network discussed above that captures in a fairly transparent manner the qualitative, and many of the quantitative results of the full network theory (Cooper and Scofield (CS, 1988)). In what follows, we give a brief description of the main results. We focus attention on the input from LGN and intracortical interactions. Input from other regions of cortex are considered part of a background excitation or inhibition contributing to the spontaneous activity of the cell. In addition, the various time delays that result in structure in the psth are assumed to be integrated over periods of the order of a second for purposes of synaptic modification.

The output of the cells of the full network can be written

$$c = c^*(Md + Lc) \tag{6}$$

where

$$c = (c_1 \ldots c_N)^T. \tag{6a}$$

c_i is the output firing rate of the ith cortical cell and

$$M = (M_{ia}^l, M_{ia}^r)$$ (6b)

where M_{ia}^l and M_{ia}^r are the ath LGN 'synapses' from the left and right eye to the ith cortical cell.

$$d = (d^l, d^r)^T \text{ and } d^{l,r} = (d_1^{l(r)} \quad ... \quad d_N^{l(r)})^T$$ (6c)

are the time averaged inputs from the left and right eye as described in BCM, and

$$L = (L_{ij})$$ (6d)

is the matrix of cortical-cortical synapses and L_{ij} is the synapse from the jth cell to the ith cell. (Notice that italicized symbols always contain left and right eye components.) We set $L_{ii} = 0$, thus allowing no feedback from a cell to itself, and c^* is the sigmoidal function illustrated in Figure 5.

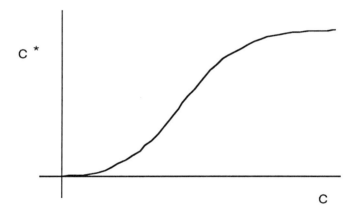

Fig. 5. c^* as a function of $M d$ +Lc.

In the monotonically increasing region above threshold and below saturation, in a linear approximation,

$$c = Md + Lc.$$ (7)

We consider a region of cortex for which the neural mapping of the input from the visual field is constant (all of the cells, in effect, look at a given region of the visual field.) Under these conditions, for an input d constant in time, the equilibrium state of this network would be

$$c = (1-L)^{-1}Md. \tag{8}$$

Mean Field Approximation

For a given LGN-cortical vector of synapses, m_i, and for a given input from both eyes, d, the firing rate of the ith cortical cell is given by

$$c_i = m_i d + \sum_j L_{ij} c_j \tag{9}$$

where the first term is the input from LGN and the second represents intracortical input to the cell. We define $\bar{c}$ as the average firing rate of all of the cortical cells under the conditions above:

$$\bar{c} = (1/N) \sum_i c_i. \tag{10}$$

The mean field approximation is obtained by replacing c_j in the sum in Eq. 9 by its average value so that c_i becomes

$$c_i = m_i d + \sum_j L_{ij} \bar{c}. \tag{11}$$

Here, in a manner similar to that in the theory of magnetism, we have replaced the effect of individual cortical cells by their average effect (as though all other cortical cells can be replaced by an 'effective' cell). This leads to:

$$c_i = m_i d + \bar{c} \sum_j L_{ij} = m_i d + \bar{c} L(i). \tag{12}$$

Since

$$\bar{c} = (1/N) \sum_i c_i = \bar{m}d + \bar{c}L_o, \tag{13}$$

where

$$L_o = (1/N) \sum_i L(i) \tag{13a}$$

and

$$\bar{m} = (1/N) \sum_i m_i, \tag{13b}$$

we obtain

$$\bar{c} = (1-L_0)^{-1} \bar{m}d. \tag{14}$$

This yields

$$c_i = (m_i + (L(i)/(1-L_0))\bar{m})d. \tag{15}$$

If we assume that the lateral connection strengths are a function only of i-j (not dependent on the absolute position of a cell in the network, therefore dependent only on the distance of two cells from one another), L_{ij} becomes a circular matrix so that

$$\sum_i L_{ij} = \sum_j L_{ij} = L_c = \text{constant} \tag{16a}$$

and

$$L_0 = (1/N) \sum_j L(i) = (1/N) \sum_j L_c = L_c. \tag{16b}$$

We then obtain

$$c_i = (m_i + (L_0/(1-L_0))\bar{m})d. \tag{17}$$

In the mean field approximation we can therefore write

$$c_i = (m_i^l - a^l) \cdot d^l + (m_i^r - a^r) \cdot d^r, \tag{18}$$

where

$$a^l = -(L_0/(1-L_0)) \bar{m}^l \tag{18a}$$

and

$$a^r = -(L_0/(1-L_0)) \bar{m}^r \tag{18b}$$

are vectors each of whose components is positive; a^l and a^r are the mean background inhibition.

The Cortical Network

The behavior of visual cortical cells in various rearing conditions suggests that some cells respond more rapidly to environmental changes than others. In monocular deprivation (MD), for example, some cells remain responsive to the closed eye in spite of the very large shift of most cells to the open eye (Hubel & Wiesel 1962). Singer et. al. (1977) found, using intracellular recording, that geniculo-cortical synapses on inhibitory interneurons are more resistant to monocular deprivation than are synapses on pyramidal cell dendrites. In dark rearing some cells become non-responsive to visual stimuli while most cells retain some responsiveness. Recent work suggests that the density of inhibitory GABAergic synapses in kitten striate cortex is also unaffected by MD during the cortical period (Bear et. al.; Mower, et al 1985).

These results suggest that some LGN-cortical synapses modify rapidly, while others modify relatively slowly, with slow modification of cortico-cortical synapses. Excitatory LGN-cortical synapses into excitatory cells may be those that modify primarily. (Since these synapses are formed exclusively on dendritic spines, this raises the possibility that the mechanisms underlying synaptic modification exist primarily in axo-spinous synapses.) To embody these facts we introduce two types of LGN-cortical synapses: those (m_i) that modify (according to the modification rule discussed in BCM) and those (z_k) that remain relatively constant. In a simple limit we have

$$\dot{m}_i = f(c_i, \bar{\bar{c}}_i)d$$

and $\hspace{8cm}$ (19)

$$\dot{z}_k = 0.$$

(In what follows $\bar{c}$ denotes an average over all cortical cells, while $\bar{\bar{c}}_i$ denotes the time averaged activity of the ith cortical cell). The function f discussed in BCM has the form shown in Figure 3. We assume for simplicity and consistent with the above physiological interpretation that these two types of synapses are confined to two different classes of cells and that both left and right eye have similar synapses (both m_i or both z_k) on a given cell. We therefore can write

$$c_i(m_i) = m_i d + \sum_j L_{ij} c_j$$

and $\hspace{8cm}$ (20)

$$c_k(z_k) = z_k d + \sum_j L_{kj} c_j.$$

In a cortical network with modifiable and non-modifiable LGN-cortical synapses, M and Z, and non-modifiable cortico-cortical synapses L_{ij}, the synaptic evolution equations become

$$\dot{m}_i = f(c_i, \bar{\bar{c}}_i)d$$

$$\dot{z}_k = 0 \tag{21}$$

$$\dot{L}_{ij} = 0.$$

This leads to a very complex set of coupled non-linear stochastic evolution equations that have been simulated and partially analyzed elsewhere (Scofield, 1984; Scofield & Cooper, 1988).

The mean field approximation permits dramatic simplification of these equations leading to analytic results and a fairly transparent understanding of their consequences in various conditions. In the mean field approximation they become

$$c_i(m_i) = m_i d + L_c \bar{c}$$

and   (22)

$$c_k(z_k) = z_k d + L_c \bar{c}.$$

These become

$$c_i(a) = (m_i^l - a^l) \cdot d^l + (m_i^r - a^r) \cdot d^r$$

and   (23)

$$c_k(a) = (z_k^l - al) \cdot dl + (z_k^r - ar) \cdot dr,$$

where now $a^{l(r)}$ contain terms from modifiable and non-modifiable synapses:

$$a^{l(r)} = -(L_0/(1-L_0))(\bar{m}^{l(r)} + \bar{z}^{l(r)}), \tag{23a}$$

$$\bar{m}^{l(r)} = N^{-1} \sum_{i=1}^{N_m} m_i^{l(r)}, \tag{23b}$$

and

$$\bar{z}^{l(r)} = N^{-1} \sum_{k=1}^{N_{nm}} z_k^{l(r)}. \tag{23c}$$

($N = N_m + N_{nm}$, where N_m is the number of cells with modifiable synapses and N_{nm} is the number of cells with non-modifiable synapses.) Since it is assumed that neither L nor z change as the network evolves, we can write

$$a^{l(r)} = a\,(\bar{m}^{l(r)} + \bar{z}^{l(r)}), \tag{24}$$

where

$$a = |L_o|\,(1 + |L_o|)^{-1} \tag{24a}$$

is a positive number since we assume that $L_o < 0$ (the network is inhibitory on average) and only $\bar{m}^{l(r)}$ is time dependent.

As is discussed in CS the position and stability of the fixed points of the mean field network can be related to those of the a = 0 network. For every fixed point of $m_i(a=0)$ there exists a corresponding fixed point for $m_i(a)$ with the same selectivity and stability properties. Therefore, just as for the $a = 0$ theory, for arbitrary a only selective fixed points are stable. Further, at corresponding fixed points we obtain the same cell output.

II. Discussion

A detailed and quantitative comparison of the theory outlined above with classical visual deprivation experiments: normal rearing, monocular deprivation, reverse suture, normal rearing after monocular deprivation, binocular deprivation and strabimus has been carried out. (Clothiaux, Bear and Cooper). Their results indicate quantitative agreement between theory and experiment in both the final equilibrium states and the kinetics by which these states are reached.

Now we are in a position to turn our attention to various pharmacological manipulations. These present problems of interpretation, but they also offer extraordinary opportunities to investigate fundamental molecular mechanisms underlying learning and memory storage, as well as the interaction of the various neurotransmitters in controlling these events.

In addition, recent experiments, Stanton and Sejnowski (1989), Staubli and Lynch (1988) and Artola, Brocher and Singer (in Print) have provided a striking confirmation of an essential assumption underlying our theory. Afferent input accompanied by insufficient postsynaptic deplorization leads to long-term depression (LTD) whereas the same input with sufficient post-synaptic deplorization leads to well-known long-term potentiation (LTP). This critical effect (first proposed by us over ten years ago to explain the development of selective responses of visual cortex neurons) is one key component of our theory. Experimental work is in progress to check a second critical assumption - that of the moving modification threshold.

One of our longer term goals is to construct a molecular model for the synaptic changes postulated in our theory. While this goal seemed unrealistic a few years ago, recent findings have opened an exciting new avenue of research we are now actively pursuing.

For example, it has been recently shown that (Bear, 1988; Bear and Dudek, 1990) the critical period for synaptic modification in kitten visual cortex is characterized by an enhanced ability of excitatory amino acids (EAA's) to stimulate the breakdown of phosphoinostides (PI). Since PI hydrolysis leads to the formation of at least two second messengers, diacyl glycerol and insositol triphosphate, we conclude that excitatory synaptic transmission is unique during the time when cortex is most susceptible to lid closure. Together with the second messenger activity associated with NMDA receptors, EAA-stimulated PI turnover could serve as a biochemical mechanism for synaptic plasticity in the developing visual cortex. It has been proposed that the strengthening of some synapses in striate cortex during development depends on the poststynaptic Ca^{++} conductance mediated by NMDA receptors. Synaptic modifications of the type now observed in striate cortex and postulated in our theory could be explained if the second messenger systems linked to PI turnover specifically were to promote the weakening of synaptic relations during development. According to this hypothesis, input activity that is coincident with strong postsynaptic depolarization ($c>q$), is a favorable condition for postsynaptic strength. Input activation coincident with relative postsynaptic inactivity ($c<q$) would lead only to the stimulation of PI turnover via non-NMDA receptors and a subsequent decrease in synaptic efficacy.

In summary, the single cell theory for the development of selectivity and ocular dominance in visual cortex has been generalized to incorporate more realistic neural networks that approximate the actual anatomy of small regions of cortex. In particular, we have analyzed a network consisting of excitatory and inhibitory cells, both of which may receive information fronm LGN. These two cortical cell types then interact through intracortical connections that are either excitatory or inhibitory. Our investigation of the evolution of a cell in this mean field network indicates that many of the results on existence and stability of fixed points that have been obtained previously in the single cell theory can be successfully generalized here. We can, in addition, make explicit further statements concerning the independent effects of excitatory and inhibitory neurons on selectivity and ocular dominance. For example, shutting off inhibitory cells lessens selectivity and alters ocular dominance (masked synapses). These inhibitory cells may be selective but there is no theoretical necessity that they be so. Further, the intracortical inhibitory synapses do not have to be very responsive to visual experience. Most of the learning process can occur among the excitatory LGN-cortical synapses. A further test of our theory is provided by the predicted relation between the development of selectivity and ocular dominance in kittens with monocular visual experience during the critical period.

Several experimental investigations on global controls, including the importance of activity in the norepinephrine system for learning during the critical period have been completed, as has been a study of the organization of GABAergic and cholinergic circuitry in kitten striate cortex. In addition, experiments on the effect of visual experience on the inhibitory circuitry in visual cortex, have yielded the important result that one measure of cortical inhibition is relatively constant even during dramatic manipulations of the visual environment, in agreement with the network theory mentioned above.

We, thus claim to have achieved a theoretical description of a very complex region of the brain - visual cortex - that is consistent with many experiments done and has been able to predict new results. One of the two underlying assumptions of this theory seems to have been confirmed experimentally, while the other is being tested. In addition a possible molecular basis for these assumptions now exists. We believe that we have uncovered at least one part of the molecular basis for learning and memory storage and can reasonably expect important further progress in the next few years. In addition the understanding thus provided can make possible the use of visual cortex as a preparation for the study of the molecular basis for learning and memory storage as well as various complex interactions between neurotransmitters and receptors.

References

1.   Artola, A., S. Brocher, and W. Singer, "Different Voltage Dependent Thresholds for the Induction of Long-Term Depression and Long-Term Potenation in Slices of Rat Visual Cortex", *Nature* (In Print).
2.   Bachmann, C.M., "Learning and Generalization in Neural Networks", Ph.D. Thesis, Brown University (1990).
3.   Bear, M.F. (1988), "Involvement of Excitatory Amino Acid Receptor Mechanisms in the Experience-dependent development of visual cortex," in Frontiers in Excitatory Amino Acid Research, pp. 393-401.
4.   Bear, M.F. and Dudek S.M. (1990)
5.   Bienenstock, E., L.N Cooper, and P. Munro (1982), "On the Development of Neuron Selectivity: Orientation Specificity and Binocular Interaction in Visual Cortex," *J. of Neuroscience* 2:32-48.
6.   Clothiaux, E., M.F. Bear, and L.N Cooper (1990) to be published.
7.   Cooper, L.N and C.L. Scofield (1988), "Mean-field Theory of a Neural Network," *Proc. Nat. Acad. Science* 85:1973-1977.
8.   Dudek, S.M., W.D. Bowen and M.F. Bear (1989), "Postnatal Changes in Glutamate Stimulated Phosphoinositide Turnover in Rat Neocortical Synaptoneurosomes," *Developmental Brain Research* 47:123-128.
9.   Geman and Geman (1984), "Stochastic Relaxation, Gibbs Distributions, and the Bayesian Restoration of Images," *IEEE Trans. on Pattern Anal. Machine Intelligence* 6:721-741.
10. Hinton, G.E. and Sejnowski, T.J. (1983), "Optimal Perceptual Inference," in *Proceedings IEEE Conf. on Comput. Vision Pattern Recognition.*
11. Hinton, G.E. and Sejnowski, T.J. (1986), "Learning and Relearning in Boltzmann Machines," in *Parallel Distributed Processing, Explorations in the Microstructure of Cognition, Vol. 1: Foundations* (Rumelhart, D.E. and McClelland, J.L., eds.) MIT Press, Cambridge, Ma.

12. Hopfield, J.J. (1982), "Neural Networks and Physical Systems with Emergent Collective Computational Abilities," *Proc. Natl. Acad. Sci.* **79**:2554-2558.

13. Hubel, D.H. and T.N. Wiesel (1961), "Integrative Action in the Cat's Lateral Geniculate Body," *J. Physiol.* **155**: 385-398.

14. Hubel, D.H. and T.N. Wiesel (1962), "Receptive Fields, Binocular Interaction and Functional Architecture in the Cat's Visual Cortex. *J. Physiol.* **160**: 106-154.

15. Mower, G.D., et. al. (1985), *J. Comp. Neurology* **235**:448.

16. Scofield, C.L. (1984) "The Development of Selectivity and Ocular Dominance in a Neural Network," Ph.D. Thesis, Brown University.

17. Scofield, C.L., and L.N Cooper (1985), "Development and Properties of Neural Networks," in *Contemporary Physics* **26**:125-145.

18. Singer, W. (1977), "Effects of Monocular Deprivation on Excitatory and Inhibitory Pathways in Cat Striate Cortex," *Experimental Brain Research* **134**:508-518.

19. Stanton, P.K. and T. J. Sejnowski (1989), "Associative Long-Term Depression in the Hippocampus Induced by Hebbian Covariance," *Nature* **339**:215-218.

20. Staubli, U. and G. Lynch (1988) Society for Neurosciences Abstracts 225:16 (1990) "Stable Depression of Potentiated Synaptic Responses in the Hippocampus with 1-5 H_z Stimulation," *Brain Research* **513**:113-118.

21. Von der Malsburg, C. (1973), "Self-organization of Orientation Sensitive Cells in the Striate Cortex," *Kybernetik* **14**:85.

22. Wiesel T.N. and D.H. Hubel (1963), "Single-cell Responses in Striate Cortex of Kittens Deprived of Vision in One Eye," *J. Neurophysiol.* **26**: 1003-1017.

I.2

A Network Model of Object Recognition in Human Vision

S. EDELMAN

The Weizmann Institute of Science
Rehovot, Israel

Abstract

Unlike basic-level categorization, which is largely viewpoint-invariant, object recognition at the subordinate levels depends on the observer's point of view in several ways. The first part of this article surveys three viewpoint-dependent aspects of human performance in recognition: canonical views, mental rotation, and limited anisotropic generalization to novel views. The second part offers a detailed but informal computational account of these phenomena, obtained by analyzing the functioning of an implemented network model of recognition. The success of the model in replicating central features of human performance supports the notion that at least one of the available pathways to recognition in the human visual system relies on viewpoint-specific representations.

1   Introduction

The human visual system excels at recognizing three-dimensional objects despite wide variation in the appearance of their retinal projections, caused by changes in illumination and vantage point. For many object classes (for example, human figures and faces) recognition does not break down even when the shape of the object undergoes nonrigid deformation. To a large extent, this performance is made possible by the extreme versatility of vision. In addition to the shape-based pathway to recognition, the existence of which is apparent, e.g., in our ability to identify objects in line drawings and cartoons, there are many other pathways, some of which rely on cues such as characteristic color or texture, others on top-down influences of prior scene knowledge and reasoning. Ready availability of these cues in everyday situations tends to mask certain peculiarities of the shape-based pathway, the study of which in isolation can yield insights into mechanisms of vision.

The same stimulus can engage different processes within the shape-based pathway, depending on the precise specification of the task at hand. For example, if asked to classify a stimulus at the basic category level (see [1]), subjects' performance is essentially viewpoint-invariant [2]. In contrast, at the subordinate levels recognition is markedly dependent on the viewpoint of the observer relative to the object [3,4,5,6]. The present article deals with viewpoint effects in recognition. The next section reviews three major psychophysical characterizations of the shape-based viewpoint-dependent pathway to recognition. The rest of the paper offers a computational account of the psychophysical findings and describes an implemented model whose performance in simulated experiments parallels that of human subjects.

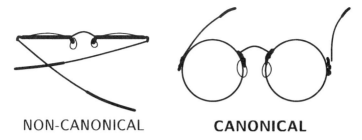

NON-CANONICAL   **CANONICAL**

Figure 1: Canonical views: certain views of 3D objects are consistently easier to recognize or process in a variety of visual tasks. For example, a front view of a pair of spectacles is bound to yield lower response time and error rate and to receive higher subjective "goodness" score than a top view of the same object. Such differences may exist even among views that are seen equally often.

2   Shape-Based Recognition Performance in Human Vision

Three basic characteristics of human performance in tasks in which recognition is viewpoint-dependent are illustrated schematically in figures 1 through 3 (detailed accounts of the relevant experiments can be found in the references cited below). These are the phenomena of canonical views [7,5], mental rotation (analogous to the "classical" mental rotation of [8]; see [4,9]), and limited generalization [3,10,6,11]. Following is a brief account of the relevant psychophysical findings.

2.1   Canonical Views

Three-dimensional objects are more easily recognized when seen from certain viewpoints, called canonical, than from other, random, viewpoints (Figure 1). The advantage of canonical views is manifested in consistently shorter response time, lower error rate and higher subjective "goodness" rating [7]. Moreover, this advantage cannot depend solely on the variation in the subject's prior exposure to the different views, since canonical views

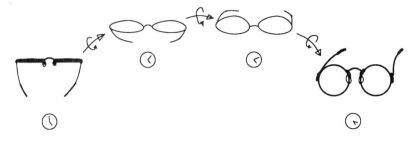

Figure 2: Recognition time for an object grows monotonically with its misorientation relative to a canonical view, as if the object is mentally rotated to match an internal representation. Rates of "rotation" range between 40 and 550 degrees per second, depending on the stimuli and the task. This effect tends, however, to disappear with practice.

are found for synthetic novel objects under controlled exposure conditions, when each view is shown equally often [5].

While uniform initial exposure does not preclude the formation of canonical views, repeated presentation of the same stimulus eventually increases the uniformity of response time over different views of the stimulus. Thus, practice affects the response time aspect of the canonical views phenomenon: after only a few trials, the differences in response time between canonical and random views diminish significantly, even in the absence of any feedback to the subject [5]. Notably, the differences in error rate remain fairly constant.

2.2   Mental Rotation

Transition from a canonical to a non-canonical view of an object does not merely increase the expected recognition time: response latency depends on the viewpoint in an orderly fashion, growing monotonically with misorientation relative to the nearest canonical view ([4,6]; see Figure 2). This dependency of response time on misorientation resembles the celebrated finding by Shepard and Metzler [8] of a class of phenomena that became known as mental rotation (see [12] for an overview).[1]

---

[1]In Shepard's experiments the task was to determine whether two simultaneously

The explanation of mental rotation in terms of an analog process involving continuous transformation of internal representations, offered by Shepard and his coworkers, has been incorporated into the foundations of the current paradigm in vision [13]. At present, monotonic dependency of response time on orientation is still widely accepted as evidence for 3D object-centered representations that can be subjected to analog transformations such as rotation, at will.

Caution regarding such an interpretation of the mental rotation phenomena is well-advised in view of recent findings that show the dependency of mental rotation phenomena in recognition on the subject's familiarity with the stimuli. For example, Tarr and Pinker [4] have found that repeated exposure to the same stimulus causes an apparent shift in the subject's strategy: while naming time for novel test views grows monotonically with misorientation relative to the nearest training view, familiar test views yield essentially constant response times (this is consistent with a changeover from time-consuming rotation-based strategy to a faster memory-intensive approach that saves time by storing all frequently occuring views). A similar effect has been reported by Edelman et al. [5,9], who show how both the initial manifestation of mental rotation and its disappearance with exposure can be replicated by a model that does not rely on 3D object-centered representations and, a fortiori, has no means for rotating such representations (see section 3).

2.3   Limited Anisotropic Generalization

The limited ability of the visual system to generalize recognition to novel views of a stimulus (previously seen from a narrow range of viewpoints) is perhaps the most counterintuitive characteristic of human performance in recognition. When asked to give a relatively broad classification of an object seen from an odd viewpoint (that is, when the task requires basic-level categorization), people virtually never err (except when the object appears

---

shown images were projections of the same 3D object, or of different objects related by a mirror transformation. In this respect, classical mental rotation is different from recognition, where the comparison is made, presumably, between an image of an object and its internal representation.

training view

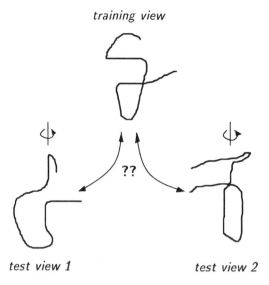

test view 1   *test view 2*

Figure 3: Limited generalization to novel views: error rate for views never seen before by the subject deteriorates rapidly with misorientation relative to a familiar view. If asked which of the bottom two images of wire-like objects matches the one at the top, subjects perform essentially at chance level when the rotation in depth is as small as 40°.

severely foreshortened; see [2]). In comparison, when the task can only be solved through relatively precise shape matching, the error rate reaches chance level already at misorientation of about 40° relative to a familiar attitude ([3,6]; see Figure 3). The detrimental effect of misorientation persists in the presence of depth cues such as binocular disparity, which reduces somewhat the mean error rate, but does not cancel the dependency of error rate on viewpoint [6].

The increase in the error rate depends on the arrangement of familiar views with respect to each other, and not just on the distance between the test view and the nearest familiar view. Specifically, interpolation among familiar views obtained by rotating the object in a fixed plane appears to be easier than extrapolation, which, in turn, is easier than recognition of views that lie outside the plane of rotation [11,6]. Furthermore, under interpolation conditions, not all directions of rotation away from a familiar view are equivalent: subjects tolerate about three times as much misorientation in the horizontal than in the vertical plane before recognition is reduced to guessing. Note that this anisotropy is ecologically understandable: creatures confined to the horizontal plane have more use for information about what an object looks like from the side than from above.

2.4 Summary of Human Performance

From the preceding review it appears that at least one of the routes to recognition available to the human visual system can be jointly characterized by a cluster of phenomena — canonical views, mental rotation and limited anisotropic generalization — whose common denominator is *viewpoint dependency*. As the following section shows, accepting viewpoint dependency as the basic premise in computational modeling of recognition allows one to replicate all three central characteristics of human performance discussed above.

3 The CLF Model

3.1 An Overview

Computational accounts of vision describe recognition in terms of a *comparison* between an appropriately encoded and processed input image and an internal *representation* [13]. Different representations thus require different comparison procedures and are bound to result in different recognition performance. In particular, viewpoint-dependent performance can be rather easily obtained with viewpoint-specific representations and a simple comparison method based on template matching. The model proposed in this section does precisely that. What follows is an intuitive description; details can be found in [9].

The model, called CLF (standing for Conjunctions of Localized Features), encodes specific views of objects by recording the co-occurence of arbitrary features at certain locations in (two-dimensional) input images. The CLF framework places no constraints on the type of features that it

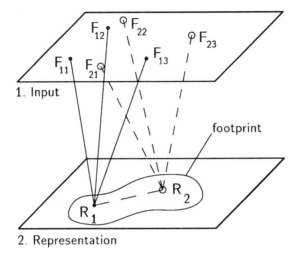

1. Input

2. Representation

Figure 4: The CLF model represents an object by a collection of its views. Each view is encoded as a conjunction of several features, occuring at well-defined locations in the 2D image. The views are tied together in the order of their original presentation to the system (e.g., in the order of appearance during rotation of the object), forming a characteristic *footprint* of the object. In this schematic example, the first view activates feature units F_{11}, F_{12} and F_{13} in the input layer, and is represented by unit R_1 in the second layer. The second view activates F_{21}, F_{22} and F_{23}, and is represented by R_2.

can use. While the lower levels of recognition are assumed to rely on simple visual events such as individual edge elements or corners, progressively more complex features may be built from these in a hierarchical fashion (for example, a CLF recognizer for a face may use eyes, nose and mouth as features).

The main requirement imposed on the representation of an individual view in the CLF model is that of compactness. In principle, there is no reason why a view should not be jointly represented by a substantial proportion of the second-layer units (see Figure 4). In practice, however, views are better represented by grandmother units, since these can be linked together more efficiently to form representations of entire objects.

3.2   Learning Object Representations

The CLF model acquires the representation of a novel object as follows. The very first view of the object is allocated a representation unit in the second layer through projection convergence, followed by non-maximum suppression. First, each input unit projects activation to an area in the second layer defined by a bell-shaped point spread function, with many inputs converging on the same representation unit. Next, a non-maximum suppression or winner-take-all mechanism selects the most active representation unit and allocates it. Once an R-unit is allocated, its input weights and threshold are adjusted according to a Hebbian rule to ensure future selectivity to the view it encodes.

When a new view is shown to the system, it attempts to recognize it by looking at the activation levels of allocated R-units. If the new view is sufficiently different from any of the old ones (i.e., none of the allocated R-units passes the threshold), a new R-unit is recruited from the pool of free units. At the same time, a lateral link is established between the two R-units in the representation layer, again by a Hebbian rule. Eventually, a chain of R-units standing for the entire object — the object's *footprint* — is formed in this fashion. By definition, a snapshot of the activity of all the units participating in a footprint (rather than mere connection pattern of these units) constitutes the representation of the object.

3.3   Replicating the Canonical Views Phenomenon

This is what happens when activation is injected at a specific point of a footprint as a result of exposing the system to a test view (assume for the moment that the test view is familiar to the system from the training period; the question of generalization to novel views will be treated later). First, activation is allowed to spread through the lateral links to the footprint-neighbors of the R-unit corresponding to the test view. After a fixed period of time, the activity of the entire footprint is compared to the snapshot stored during training. The degree of similarity between the

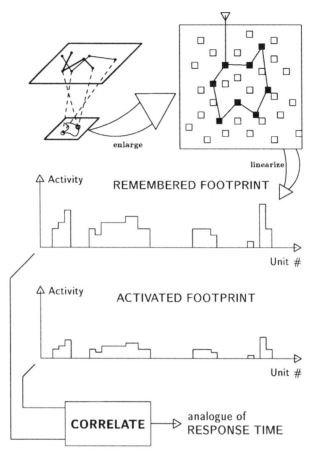

Figure 5: *Top:* a schematic illustration of a footprint. Solid and hollow squares stand for allocated and free R-units, respectively. *Bottom:* R-units comprising a footprint become active when the system is exposed to one of the familiar views, at a level that decreases with their distance along the footprint from the excitation point (because of the imperfect efficacy of the lateral links). The gradation in the spread of activity causes the correlation between actual and stored footprint snapshots to be less than ideal. The dependency of this correlation on the excitation point parallels a similar dependency of response time on viewpoint, known as mental rotation.

two patterns of activity, measured by their (2D) correlation, is then interpreted as the model's analog of response time (see Figure 5). The variation of this measure with viewpoint (that is, with the initial locus of activation) is the counterpart of the canonical views phenomenon.

3.4 Replicating Mental Rotation and Its Disappearance with Practice

The simulated response time not only varies with viewpoint: because of the sequential structure of the footprint, it depends on the viewpoint in an orderly fashion, resembling the typical pattern of mental rotation (see Figure 6, top). When the same views on which the model has been trained appear in a different order, the original sequential structure of the footprint is weakened, because of the emergence of new lateral links between different R-units that are not necessarily adjacent to each other in the footprint (see Figure 6, middle). Eventually, the interconnection pattern of the participating R-units becomes amorphous, causing mental rotation signs, which are epiphenomenal to the structure of the footprint, to disappear (see Figure 6, bottom).

3.5 Replicating Limited Anisotropic Generalization

The generalization capability of the CLF model is explored by training it on sets of views of several objects, presented separately in succession. Quite understandably, the model performs perfectly when tested on any of the training views, provided that the footprints do not overlap (that is, if the representation capacity is not exceeded). Even in that simple situation, the model yields a useful insight into possible mechanisms of generalization of recognition.

Generalization in the CLF model is made possible by the bell shape of the point spread function that governs the pattern of projection from first-layer to second-layer units (see section 3.2). Intuitively, the blurring of the input activity distribution caused by the point spread function increases the chances that moderate distortion of the input view (due, e.g., to a rotation of the object away from a training attitude) will be tolerated

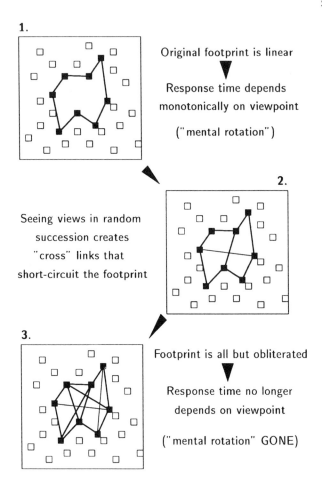

1. Original footprint is linear

▼

Response time depends
monotonically on viewpoint

("mental rotation")

Seeing views in random
succession creates
"cross" links that
short-circuit the footprint

2.

3.

Footprint is all but obliterated

▼

Response time no longer
depends on viewpoint

("mental rotation" GONE)

Figure 6: Three stages in the development of object representation with practice, as implemented in the CLF model. *Top:* Immediately after training with an orderly sequence of views that arises, e.g., when the object is rotating, its footprint (see Figure 4) is highly structured. The sequential spread of activation through the footprint following exposure to one view creates a semblance of mental rotation. *Middle:* Two shortcuts across the footprint are created, e.g., because of practice-induced association between non-neighbor views. *Bottom:* The dependency of "response time" on viewpoint is lost due to the weakening of the original footprint structure.

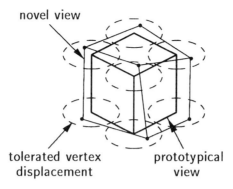

Figure 7: Generalization capability of the CLF model may be attributed to the fact that it tolerates feature displacements caused, e.g., by the object's rotation because of the diffuse projections from the feature to the representation layer. The anisotropy of generalization can be accounted for by asymmetries in the shape of the tolerance regions centered at the average positions of features. Here the tolerance regions are elongated in the horizontal direction, to replicate the better generalization in the horizontal plane found in human data.

when the correlation between its representation and the proper footprint is computed. Thus, test views that are close to more than one familiar view are easier to recognize, because of superposition of the contributions of the feature detectors corresponding to those views, achieved by blurring the input. This may explain why human subjects are better at interpolation than at extrapolation to a novel view. Furthermore, the anisotropy of generalization with respect to the horizontal/vertical distinction may be accounted for by postulating an asymmetrical point spread function (see Figure 7). An analysis of the generalization capability of the CLF model, along with a discussion of functional similarities between blurred template matching and nonlinear interpolation by regularization networks [14,15], can be found in [9].

4   Discussion

The CLF approach to the modeling of recognition, described in this article, has three key characteristics. A version of the first one, which states that conjunctions of features are important, has been advocated in the past by Barlow, who also has been a long-time proponent of the grandmother cell dogma [16,17]. The second ingredient of CLF, namely, the achievement of constancy over a group of transformations (such as rotations in 3D) through exhaustive coverage of the resulting configuration space, can be traced back to Pitts and McCulloch [18]. Both these ideas used to draw criticism on the grounds of excessive memory requirements. It is not too surprising, therefore, that the third key ingredient of CLF, blurred template matching, is designed to permit it to store relatively few views, while maintaining adequate generalization performance. Poggio and Girosi have recently used techniques from approximation theory to show why such an approach works [14].

To date, the CLF model has achieved a degree of success in replicating several basic findings in the psychology of three-dimensional object recognition (see [9,11,19,6]). Some of the issues currently under investigation are modeling of the influence of depth cues, and extension to recognition and classification of complex objects on various categorical levels. Already at this stage, however, the available simulation results prompt one to consider seriously the possibility that a major recognition pathway in human vision relies on two-dimensional view-specific representations (see also [20]). The amenability of the model to implementation in an adaptive network architecture which complies with general rules of cortical organization (see the discussion in [9,21]) lends further support to this possibility.

References

[1] E. Rosch, C. B. Mervis, W. D. Gray, D. M. Johnson, and P. Boyes-Braem. Basic objects in natural categories. *Cognitive Psychology*, 8:382–439, 1976.

[2] I. Biederman. Human image understanding: Recent research and a

theory. *Computer Vision, Graphics, and Image Processing*, 32:29–73, 1985.

[3] I. Rock and J. DiVita. A case of viewer-centered object perception. *Cognitive Psychology*, 19:280–293, 1987.

[4] M. Tarr and S. Pinker. Mental rotation and orientation-dependence in shape recognition. *Cognitive Psychology*, 21:233–282, 1989.

[5] S. Edelman, H. Bülthoff, and D. Weinshall. Stimulus familiarity determines recognition strategy for novel 3D objects. A.I. Memo No. 1138, Artificial Intelligence Laboratory, Massachusetts Institute of Technology, July 1989.

[6] S. Edelman and H. H. Bülthoff. Viewpoint-specific representations in 3D object recognition. A.I. Memo No. 1239, Artificial Intelligence Laboratory, Massachusetts Institute of Technology, 1990.

[7] S. E. Palmer, E. Rosch, and P. Chase. Canonical perspective and the perception of objects. In J. Long and A. Baddeley, editors, *Attention and Performance IX*, pages 135–151. Erlbaum, Hillsdale, NJ, 1981.

[8] R. N. Shepard and J. Metzler. Mental rotation of three-dimensional objects. *Science*, 171:701–703, 1971.

[9] S. Edelman and D. Weinshall. A self-organizing multiple-view representation of 3D objects. *Biological Cybernetics*, 64:209–219, 1991.

[10] I. Rock, D. Wheeler, and L. Tudor. Can we imagine how objects look from other viewpoints? *Cognitive Psychology*, 21:185–210, 1989.

[11] H. H. Bülthoff and S. Edelman. Psychophysical support for a 2D interpolation theory of object recognition, 1990. submitted.

[12] R. N. Shepard and L. A. Cooper. *Mental images and their transformations*. MIT Press, Cambridge, MA, 1982.

[13] D. Marr. *Vision*. W. H. Freeman, San Francisco, CA, 1982.

[14] T. Poggio and F. Girosi. Regularization algorithms for learning that are equivalent to multilayer networks. *Science*, 247:978–982, 1990.

[15] T. Poggio and S. Edelman. A network that learns to recognize three-dimensional objects. *Nature*, 343:263–266, 1990.

[16] H. B. Barlow. Cerebral cortex as model builder. In D. Rose and V. G. Dobson, editors, *Models of the visual cortex*, pages 37–46. Wiley, New York, 1985.

[17] H. B. Barlow. The role of single neurons in the psychology of perception. *Quart. J. Exp. Psychol.*, 37A:121–145, 1985.

[18] W. Pitts and W. S. McCulloch. How we know universals: the perception of auditory and visual forms. In *Embodiments of mind*, pages 46–66. MIT Press, Cambridge, MA, 1965.

[19] S. Edelman and H. H. Bülthoff. Generalization of object recognition in human vision across stimulus transformations and deformations. In Y. Feldman and A. Bruckstein, editors, *Proc. 7th Israeli AICV Conference*, pages 479–487. Elsevier, 1990.

[20] S. Edelman. Features of recognition. In *Proc. Intl. Workshop on Visual Form, Capri, Italy*, New York, 1991. Plenum Press.

[21] S. Edelman and T. Poggio. Bringing the Grandmother back into the picture: a memory-based view of object recognition. A.I. Memo No. 1181, Artificial Intelligence Laboratory, Massachusetts Institute of Technology, 1990.

I.3

A Cortically Based Model for Integration in Visual Perception

LEIF H. FINKEL
University of Pennsylvania

GEORGE N. REEKE, JR. and
GERALD M. EDELMAN
The Neurosciences Institute and
The Rockefeller University

I. Introduction

A. Background

It is a commonplace observation that when we look at the world around us, at a rustic landscape or a flock of birds in flight, we perceive a coherent *scene* composed of discrete objects against a background. Neuroanatomical and neurophysiological studies have recently begun to clarify how processes in the visual system lead to the generation of this scene. In higher mammals, the visual cortex comprises multiple, independent areas (approaching two dozen in some species), each of which is functionally specialized for particular visual tasks (Zeki 1978; Van Essen 1985). Each cortical area undoubtedly participates in several tasks and conversely, each task requires the joint action of

41

several areas. However, it is a fair generalization that visual attributes such as color, shape, and motion largely give rise to responses in different sets of visual cortical areas (Mishkin *et al.* 1983; Maunsell and Newsome 1987; Livingstone and Hubel 1988; DeYoe and Van Essen 1988; Zeki and Shipp 1988).

One of the most difficult aspects of the construction of visual scenes to understand is how regions of space having common attributes are linked to form objects. This "binding problem" arises, for example, in linking the motion, color, shape, and depth of each bird in a flock with that particular bird, and not with another bird or a background object. Several investigators have discussed this problem (e.g. Ballard *et al.* 1983; Damasio 1989; Crick and Koch 1990), but a definitive solution has not yet emerged. It has been proposed that recently discovered 40 Hz oscillations in cat striate cortex (Eckhorn *et al.* 1988; Gray and Singer 1989) could serve to link neurons in the same and different cortical areas, and thus bind the attributes to which they are selective. A model based on the theory of neuronal group selection (Edelman 1978; Edelman 1987) has been constructed that shows how these oscillations might arise and provide binding in environments with multiple objects and complex figure-ground relationships (Sporns *et al.* 1989; Sporns *et al.* 1990). A variety of other models for cortical oscillators has also been proposed (e.g. Eckhorn *et al.* 1989; Kammen *et al.* 1989; Schillen and König 1990; Wang *et al.* 1990).

Any full treatment of the problem must have both spatial and temporal aspects, inasmuch as objects can be localized in both space and time. Schemes based on cortical oscillations implicitly depend on the underlying neuroanatomy—the cells in question must be anatomically connected in order to communicate with their oscillating partners (Edelman and Finkel 1984). In this chapter, we present a model of cortical integration which emphasizes this spatial and anatomical aspect. The key components of this model are an *anatomical* system of cortico-cortical connections between areas and a *physiological* process which we call reentry (Edelman 1978; Edelman 1981; Edelman 1987) that mediates real-time signalling between areas along the anatomical connections.

The basic idea of our proposal, which is called the Reentrant Cortical Integration (RCI) model, is that reentrantly interconnected neural maps are critical to solving the binding problem. Reentry is defined as a dynamic, temporally ongoing, parallel and recursive process of signaling between two or more mapped regions (Edelman 1987; Finkel and Edelman 1989). (Several explicit examples will be detailed below.) Since most early visual maps are topographically organized, responses in these maps are related to positions in space. Connections between different maps mainly respect this topographic organization, hence activity in the maps is largely linked in a spatially coherent fashion. The attributes of an object are thus linked by the coactivation of groups of neurons in different cortical regions. It is well known (Gibson 1979; Marr 1982) that visual processes such as depth perception and motion perception are interdependent (e.g. closer objects appear to move faster). We propose that this physical interdependence places important constraints upon the connections between different cortical areas.

B. Psychophysical Evidence

The most compelling evidence for the role of cortical interconnections in integrating visual perception comes from visual psychophysics, in particular, from a set of visual illusions known as subjective contours. The use of illusions allows the intrinsic operations of the visual system to be elicited in the absence of direct external stimulation. In fact, as Ramachandran (1986) and others have pointed out, these types of illusions are not "illusory" at all; rather, they reflect the same operations that are normally carried out in response to "real" stimuli. Thus, illusions can provide a deep insight into the fundamental workings of the visual system.

Figure 1 shows an illusion known as the Kanizsa triangle (Kanizsa 1979). We see what appears to be a white triangle, vertex upward, and the triangle appears to be both closer and brighter than the background of the page. Inspection or actual measurement reveals that the borders, apparent depth, and apparent brightness of the triangle are all illusory. Kanizsa and others have developed many similar illusions, all of which confirm the same point. Namely, our visual systems, in response to such stimuli, construct an object and this object is endowed with several mutually-consistent attributes. In the case of Figure 1, the visual system constructs a triangle in which the discontinuities in apparent depth and brightness exactly coincide with the locations of the illusory object borders.

Figure 1. The Kanizsa Triangle (from Kanizsa 1979).*

Given the underlying anatomy, with separate areas dedicated to shape, brightness, and depth, such a consistency in object generation implies a strong degree of consistency in the operations of the different cortical areas. Moreover, each area must be able to use the responses of other areas as input.

Ramachandran has demonstrated a number of illusions which illustrate this point in an even more compelling fashion (Ramachandran and Cavanaugh 1985; Ramachandran 1986). In a phenomenon called "motion capture", an illusory square undergoes apparent motion over a background of regularly spaced dots. As the square moves, those background dots lying behind appear to move with the square. Thus, the motion of the illusory square is "attributed" to the stationary background dots, i.e., the motion of the background dots is "bound" to that of the illusory square in the foreground. Ramachandran interprets such phenomena as reflecting a process in which operations by one cortical center are used by another. He proposes that cortico-cortical connections may subserve this transfer, and suggests that the return connections from area V2 to area V1 may be instrumental.

Some recent physiological evidence bears on this point. Responses to illusory contours have been recorded in cells of areas V1 and V2 of macaque monkeys (von der Heydt *et al.* 1984; von der Heydt and Peterhans 1989; Peterhans and von der Heydt 1989). While a sizable proportion of cells in V2 respond in an orientation-selective manner to illusory lines, no such cells are found in V1. The authors propose an anatomical model for such responses that involves a dual projection from V1 to V2: one from endstopped cells and the other from simple or complex cells.

We propose that reentrant signalling along cortico-cortical connections mediates the integration of multiple cortical areas. Towards justifying this claim, we will describe a computer simulation of three interconnected cortical areas of the macaque monkey, and will show how such a system can generate integrated responses to illusory contours and other related illusions. We will present the results of this model in detail; first, however, to set the context, we will briefly review several related models of visual integration.

C. Other Models

Marr (1982) was among the first to propose a model of visual processing based on neural properties. He emphasized the importance of illusory contours and structure-from-motion in understanding how integration across modalities takes place. Ullman (1976) produced the first computational model of illusory contour formation. His model was based on the idea of minimizing curvature at intermediate points along an illusory contour which coincides with two colinear edges of an inducing object (see Figure 1). Stevens (1981), Richards (1988), and many others have continued to analyze vision in computational terms. In particular, Poggio (1989) has recently proposed a "vision machine" which has separate modules for color, stereopsis, texture, and shape discrimination. These modules are integrated by an algorithm based on Markov random fields. While it is unlikely that the brain uses such a statistical procedure for integration, the vision machine illustrates how multiple modules can work together to produce a powerful system.

Grossberg and his colleagues have taken a different approach which is closer in spirit to that taken here (Grossberg and Mingolla 1985; Grossberg 1987). They propose that object discrimination depends upon two separate but interconnected systems, one concerned with boundary properties, the other with surface properties (with analogies to the magnocellular and parvocellular systems in visual cortex). They do not attempt explicitly to model particular brain regions, but to produce a network system with properties resembling, to some degree, those of the visual system. They provide accounts for a large number of different illusions, including illusory contours and structure-from-motion. The mechanism of Grossberg and Mingolla for generating illusory contours is an alternative to that presented here. They propose that illusory contours must arise at all line endings due to an uncertainty in the location and orientation of the border at such endings. When several line endings are in close proximity, and arranged such that they could be connected by a simple curve, such a curve is generated by excitation of the intermediate points. An attractive feature of the model is that the relative contrast of the inducing edges is rendered irrelevant due to the type of local contrast detectors which form the first stage of the network.

In comparison to the models cited, the RCI model puts a greater emphasis on the known cortical anatomy and physiology. Like the model of Grossberg and Mingolla, RCI embeds the mechanism for integration directly into the network architecture, rather than imposing it as an additional step. However, RCI goes on to postulate reentry as the physiological process responsible for integration. The model does not attempt to cover a broad range of visual performance, restricting its attention to motion, occlusion, and shape. Finally, it attempts to make a series of experimental predictions which can be tested in the physiological laboratory. We now turn to a description of the model.

II. The RCI Model

A. General Description

Figure 2 shows a schematic of the network architecture of the RCI model. Visual stimuli are generated on an Input Array which projects through a network modelled after the lateral geniculate nucleus (LGN) to the cortically

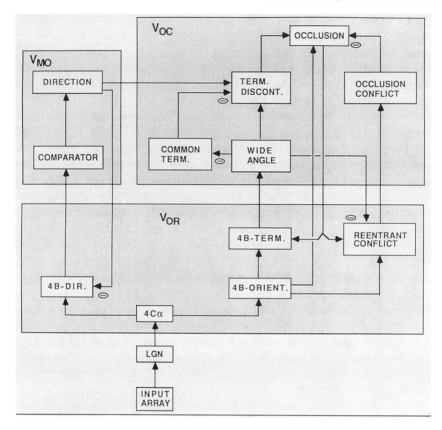

Figure 2. Schematic of network connectivity, indicating major connections between simulated unit types. The three shaded boxes indicate the simulated areas, V_{OR}, V_{OC}, and V_{MO}, which are specialized for orientation, occlusion, and motion, respectively. Unit types (white boxes) are named either according to their dominant function or their closest analogue in the CNS. Abbreviations: Dir. = Direction, Discont. = Discontinuity, Orient. = Orientation, Term. = Termination. Reentrant connections are indicated, e.g. from Direction units of V_{MO} to 4B-Dir units of V_{OR}, from Occlusion units of V_{OC} to 4B-Term and Reentrant-Conflict units of V_{OR}, and from Direction units of V_{MO} to Termination-Discontinuity units of V_{OC}. Each arrow indicates multiple, parallel connections between many units. All connections are excitatory unless indicated by a (-) sign. (Figs. 2-7 are from Finkel and Edelman 1989.)

based networks. Three functionally specialized cortical areas are modelled: V_{OR} (specialized for orientation), V_{MO} (specialized for motion), and V_{OC} (specialized for occlusion). These areas are modeled, with considerable simplification and abstraction, after the properties of areas V1, MT, and V3, respectively, in the macaque monkey. Anatomically, these three areas constitute a simply connected cortical trio in which a single cortical layer in area V1, layer 4B, provides both the source and termination of the majority of connections.

In the model, each area contains multiple networks which represent different physiological cell types within the cortical areas. V_{OR}, for example, contains orientation-selective, directionally selective, and endstopped units (these categories are not exclusive). The figure also indicates the major pathways of connectivity between the networks. Note that there are ascending, descending, and cross connections between areas. As we shall show, each of these pathways subserves an important function in integrating the responses of the three areas.

In the simulations presented here, there are a total of 222,208 units with 8,521,728 synaptic connections. Each network contains a multiple of 1024 units (32x32), which is the size of the visual input array. There are eight preferred orientations and directions of motion (spaced at 45° intervals), thus, each network with orientation or directional selective cells has eight similar variants of each type of cell. Only very short simulations are run, on the order of 100 milliseconds of real time, and thus the synaptic connections are not plastic.

The physiological properties of the individual units are controlled by six parameters according to the following equation:

$$s_i(t) = [\Sigma_k \, w_k \, \{\Sigma_j \, c_{ij}(s_j(t) - \Theta_k)\}_{MINk}^{MAXk} - \Theta_k'] \tag{1}$$

where $s_i(t)$ is the output of unit i at time t. The first summation (over k) is over the different classes of connections received by a unit (a class of connections is defined as those that come from the same type of unit in the same network), and the second summation (over j) is over all the connections of class k. w_k is a weighting factor on the relative efficacy of connections of class k. c_{ij} is the synaptic weight of the connection from unit j to unit i. Θ_k and Θ_k' are thresholds on presynaptic and postsynaptic activity, respectively. The square brackets [ ] denote a thresholding scheme by which [x]=0 if x<0 and [x]=x otherwise. The curly brackets { } denote a separate threshold that is applied to the sum of all inputs from a given class of connections: $\{x\}^{MAX}$=MAX if x>MAX, and $\{x\}^{MAX}$=x otherwise. Likewise, $\{x\}_{MIN}$=0 if x<MIN, and $\{x\}_{MIN}$=x otherwise. These thresholding schemes are a simple

computational means of representing some of the inherent nonlinearities involved in neuronal processing.

Only a few combinations of different values of the six parameters given in equation 1 (w_k, c_{ij}, Θ_k, Θ_k', MIN_k, and MAX_k) were used in the simulations, and the values of the last four were mutually dependent. In fact, only five distinct classes of units were used, each with a clearly recognizable functional role. For example, cells of one class performed simple weighted summations of their inputs, those of a second class compared different types of inputs, while those of a third carried out multiple-input AND operations. Thus, despite the large numbers of cells and the multiplicity of potential parameters, only a modest number of physiological cell types were actually used. T h e simulations were carried out on IBM 3090 and 4331 computers using CNS, a network simulation program (Reeke and Edelman 1987). A complete description of the anatomical, physiological, and technical details of the simulations has been provided elsewhere (Finkel and Edelman 1989). The simulations can be divided into three main groups concerned with the ability of the network to discriminate occlusion relationships, motion, and more complex combined phenomena. These will now be considered in turn.

B. Occlusion System

1. Construction

Occlusion is one of the major monocular cues to depth. It refers to the obscuration from view by nearer objects of parts or all of more distant objects. While not as powerful a depth cue as stereopsis in normal individuals, it is easier to simulate due to its monocular nature. In addition, occlusion relations provide the basis for several classes of visual illusions which will serve as the main stimuli used to test the network.

Figure 3 shows the provisional definition of occlusion used to construct the RCI network architecture. A presumptive occlusion boundary (indicated in Figure 3A) can be identified as a line or curve along which other lines or curves of various orientations terminate. As shown in Figure 3B, the saliency of this termination cue to occlusion is much stronger if lines terminate along the occlusion boundary from both sides, rather than from a single side (as occurs along the outer edges of the figure). In fact, Figures 3B and 3C show that this definition of occlusion provides the basis for an explanation of the emergence of illusory contours (Kanizsa 1979). In Figure 3B, the central vertical illusory contour is simply an occlusion border by our definition. In Figure 3C, the edges of the Kanizsa triangle are occlusion borders induced by the combination of terminations of the lines forming the mouths of the "pac-man" figures and terminations of the circular curves of these figures (these terminations are indicated by dots in the bottom figure). In this view, illusory contours arise due to the presence of cues to occlusion boundaries.

The network architecture designed to detect occlusion boundaries is based upon this definition. It shares several points in common with a scheme proposed by Peterhans *et al.* (1986). As shown in Figure 2, there are both direct and indirect pathways from V_{OR} to V_{OC}. The indirect pathway, which is the major feedforward path, begins in V_{OR} with units selective for line orientation. The 4B-Orient units (so named to reflect their site of origin in layer 4B of area V1) project to 4B-Term units which are endstopped, and thus

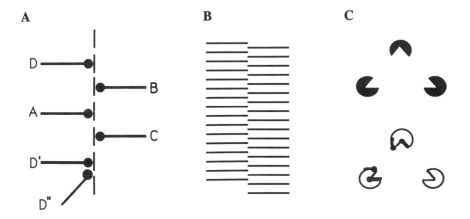

Figure 3. Network Mechanism for Discriminating Occlusion.

(A) Working definition of an occlusion boundary. Dashed vertical line is the presumptive occlusion boundary, circles indicate line terminations. Occlusion boundary requires collinear terminations of at least three lines approaching border from both sides, e.g. Line A and at least two of {Lines B, C, and (D or D′)}. Lines approaching the boundary at an angle (Line D″) are also allowed. These same conditions are used by the model to generate responses to illusory contours.

(B) Two abutting grids, one half cycle out of phase, give rise to a vertical illusory contour at their border. The line terminations fulfill the conditions for occlusion given in (A). Note that the extreme left and right borders of the figure do not give rise to vivid illusory contours.

(C) (Above) The Kanizsa triangle as in Figure 1. (Below) Line terminations (circles with stems) giving rise to the illusory contour forming one side of the Kanizsa triangle. Corresponding terminations generate responses to the other two sides. In this case, terminations of both lines and arcs are used—a generalization of the scheme in (A).

are selective for line terminations. However, unlike the majority of hypercomplex cells in V1, 4B-Term units are polarized, i.e., they respond to oriented lines which terminate at one end even if the line continues in the other direction.

4B-Term units project to Wide-Angle units in V_{OC}. These units are so named because they receive inputs from units with orientation preferences spanning 90°, allowing line terminations at presumptive occlusion boundaries to have a wide range of orientations. The pathway next leads to Termination-Discontinuity units, which respond to line terminations distributed along a presumptive occlusion boundary. This is accomplished by choosing the MAX_k parameters to allow a unit to fire only if inputs are received from several Wide-Angle units distributed along a line. The final units in the pathway, Occlusion units, interpolate responses between those detected by the Termination-Discontinuity units and fill in responses to complete occlusion boundaries. These units also receive a direct projection from the 4B-Orient units which allows them to respond to real (luminance-defined) lines as well as occlusion boundaries. These responses can be seen in the results described below.

The V_{OR}-V_{OC} system also includes several reentrant pathways. Occlusion units project back to layer 4B where they excite 4B-Term units. This allows responses to occlusion borders which have been generated by the system to be cycled back and treated in the same way as luminance borders detected peripherally. One potential danger of this scheme is that a loss of distinction between "reality" and "interpretation" will occur. This danger is offset by the back-projection of Occlusion units to the so-called Reentrant-Conflict units which serve to detect conflicts between real borders and generated occlusion borders. There are a number of logical relationships which must hold among occlusion borders, for example, an occlusion border can not cross a real border, and Reentrant-Conflict units are designed to detect such meaningless configurations. In the event that they occur, the units activate Occlusion-Conflict units which in turn veto the response of Occlusion units to the presumptive occlusion boundary.

2. Results

Figure 4 shows some results of the operations of the occlusion system. Figure 4A shows the responses of occlusion units to an illusory contour stimulus. The arrangement of the eight boxes of occlusion units signifies the orientation selectivity of the units, e.g., the box in the upper right corner contains units selective for 45° lines. The box marked "Occl. Displ." shows the superposed responses of all eight orientations of occlusion units; it is intended for display purposes only (to show how the units line up) and is not used by the network for any operations. The responses shown were generated on the first cycle after exposure to the stimulus. They remain constant for as long as the stimulus is maintained. Note that responses are generated both to the luminance-defined horizontal lines (by means of the direct V_{OR}-V_{OC} pathway) as well as to the vertical occlusion boundary (by means of the multi-stage feedforward pathway). The detection of this occlusion boundary agrees with human subjective perception of a vertical illusory contour.

Figure 4B shows a control stimulus in which the lines of the horizontal gratings are interposed, destroying the subjective perception of an illusory contour (in agreement with the definition of occlusion given above which requires lines to terminate along a common border). As shown, the network responds to the real horizontal lines, but does not generate a response to an occlusion boundary.

Finally, Figure 4C shows the responses to an illusory square. Note that the system responds both to the real edges present and to the four illusory occlusion borders of the square. Again, all these responses arise on the first

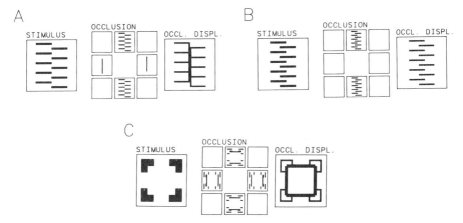

Figure 4. Network Generation of Illusory Contours.

(A) Response of occlusion units (center panels) to an abutting grid stimulus (shown at left) after one cycle of stimulation. Panels of occlusion units are arranged such that position of panel indicates orientation preference of unit (e.g. units in upper right panel prefer 45° lines). Occlusion Display (Occl. Displ.) panel shows at a larger scale the superposed responses of all eight types of Occlusion units. Note responses to both the real (horizontal) lines as well as to the illusory (vertical) contour.

(B) Responses to a control stimulus in which terminations of the grids overlap. There are no illusory contour responses.

(C) Responses to an illusory square stimulus. On first cycle of presentation, responses are generated to the edges of the four corner stimuli, as well as to the four illusory contours making up the square.

cycle of operation due to the feedforward nature of the pathways. The system responds in an appropriate fashion to more complicated stimuli as well as to stimuli which contain intrinsic conflicts between real and occlusion boundaries. See Finkel and Edelman (1989) for more details.

These results show that, based on our simple definition of occlusion, a network architecture based on plausible cortical anatomy and physiology can be designed to respond appropriately to a range of normal and illusory contour stimuli. The most interesting capabilities of the system, however, involve the reentrant sharing of information between the occlusion and motion systems. Before turning to these studies, we briefly consider the operations of the motion system.

C. Motion System

1. Construction

Like most models of directional selectivity, the present scheme relies on time-delayed inhibition in the null direction as first proposed by Barlow and Levick (1965) for the rabbit retina and by Reichardt et al. (1983) for the fly. However, the present scheme is more complicated due to its goal of modelling some of the properties of area MT (V5) in the monkey. As shown by Movshon et al. (1985) and others, MT cells are capable of responding to the direction of motion of a line regardless of its orientation. This property, which implies a solution of the so-called aperture problem (Marr 1982; Hildreth and Koch 1987), requires, in our view, the use of population principles. In other words, no single cell can overcome the aperture problem, but a population of cells can do so. Thus the basic operation carried out by the V_{OR}-V_{MO} pathway is a series of convergent comparisons used to cull information about the motion of lines of different orientation and then to determine the direction of maximum response.

A degree of directional selectivity first emerges in the orientation-selective $4C\alpha$ units of V_{OR}. These units receive two projections from the LGN units; both are composed of an excitatory center and an inhibitory surround, but one projection arises from a spatially displaced location, is temporally delayed, and acts through an inhibitory interneuron.

As shown in Figure 2, $4C\alpha$ units project to 4B-Dir units in layer 4B. This projection involves several components: three sets of spatially displaced, temporally delayed excitatory inputs from cells in $4C\alpha$ whose directional selectivities lie within 90° of the preferred direction, and a large-field inhibitory input from $4C\alpha$ cells with directional preferences in the null direction. There are thus two stages of spatially displaced, temporally delayed inputs (LGN to $4C\alpha$ and $4C\alpha$ to 4B-Dir). The effect of this double process is to prevent 4B-Dir cells from responding to stimuli of reverse contrast moving in the null direction. There are other possible ways to reach this result, but the present one is particularly simple.

4B-Dir units project to area V_{MO}, which is modelled after the function of cortical area MT. For each direction of motion, e.g. North, there are four sets of Comparator units which serve respectively to compare the amount of excitation in the 4B-Dir units preferring northward motion with those preferring motion in the four adjacent directions (Northeast, Northwest, East, and West). This is accomplished by assigning a slightly larger weight to the inhibitory inputs (from adjacent directions, NE, NW, etc.) than to the excitatory inputs (from the preferred direction, North). The activities of the four sets of comparator units are then summed by Direction units. These units are configured using the MAX_k parameter described above such that a Direction unit is activated only if at least three of the four sets of Comparator units are active. This represents a majority vote decision that motion in the preferred direction is greater than in any adjacent direction.

Finally, there is a major reentrant pathway from the Direction units back to the 4B-Dir units (in accord with the anatomical pathway from MT to layer 4B in cortex). This pathway effects a widespread inhibition on all 4B-Dir units with common receptive fields (to the Direction unit in question) *except* those with the same preferred direction. This pathway has a profound effect on the accuracy and speed with which the network determines the correct direction of motion as will be seen in the results to be presented next.

2. Results

Figure 5 shows the responses of the network to a field of moving, randomly placed one-pixel dots. As indicated in the box labelled "dot motion", the random dots in the central third of the display move southward, while those in the outer two thirds move northward. The central column of panels (labelled "with reentry") shows the responses of three stages of the motion system after four cycles of presentation of the stimulus. As in Figure 4, individual boxes are arranged to indicate the directional selectivity of their units (e.g., the upper right box contains cells responding preferentially to northeasterly motion). Each box contains $32 \times 32 = 1024$ cells, the activity of which is indicated by small dots. The $4C\alpha$ cells respond to the direction of motion in that northward-preferring cells do not respond to the central third of the display, and southward preferring cells do not respond to the outer two thirds of the display. However, there is a vigorous response by cells tuned for the orthogonal and oblique directions. This is because dots excite cells tuned for all orientations, and the first stage of delayed inhibition only vetoes motion in the null direction.

However, after the second stage of delayed excitation in 4B-Dir, the responses are essentially perfect. There is no response to motion in other than

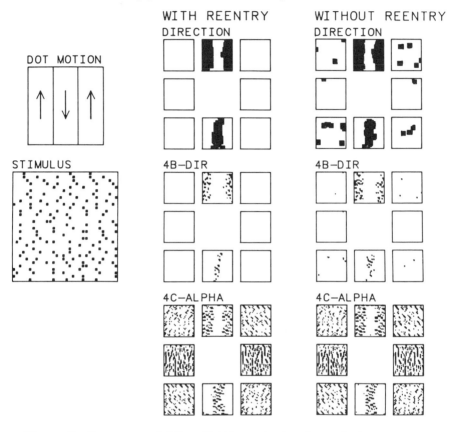

Figure 5. Responses of 4Cα, 4B-Dir, and Direction units in the presence and absence of reentry after four cycles of a moving random-dot pattern. Dots in center third of stimulus display were moved southward, those in outer thirds were moved northward (see panel labelled "Dot Motion") at 1 pixel/cycle. Panels are arranged by directional preference according to convention in Figure 4A. The larger receptive fields of Direction cells are manifested by the number of cells responding to a single stimulus dot. 4Cα units show a degree of directional selectivity, but 4B-Dir and Direction units respond much more selectively to the direction of motion. Reentry leads to more accurate directional discrimination. Without reentry (right) a number of Direction units respond inappropriately to dot motion. The responses of units in 4Cα are nearly identical with or without reentry, since 4Cα does not receive reentrant connections from V_{MO}.

the preferred direction. This accurate response is also seen in the highest level of the system, the Direction units.

The functioning of the system, however, relies very strongly upon the presence of the reentrant pathway from Direction units back to 4B-Dir. The rightmost panel of boxes shows the effects of cutting this reentrant pathway. Responses in $4C\alpha$ are not affected as the pathway projects only as far back as 4B-Dir. In 4B-Dir and Direction units, however, it is now seen that many spurious responses are present. In fact, as the simulation continues to run, these spurious responses can grow and come to degrade the responses to the true direction of motion. Thus, in this case, the retrograde reentry plays an important role in stabilizing and controlling the gain of multiple coupled networks.

The motion system also responds in an appropriate fashion to other moving stimuli such as lines, objects, etc. In fact, it can be shown to be overcoming the aperture problem in that it responds correctly to the direction of motion of lines regardless of their orientations. Thus, the motion system displays an interesting division of function. Units in V_{OR} and V_{MO} are selective for both orientation and motion. However, in V_{OR} the primary selectivity is for orientation, while in V_{MO} the primary selectivity is for motion. It is as if, in the specialization of higher cortical areas for different modalities, some degree of de-specialization must also occur.

D. Motion Segmentation and Combined Illusions

As we described at the outset, the goal of the present studies was not to make detailed models of particular cortical areas but rather to try to envisage how a small set of coupled areas might operate together to perform a kind of psychophysical integration. Now that the functions of the occlusion and motion systems have been described, we can explore the ability of the two systems to cooperate in analyzing more complex stimuli.

The first test involves motion segmentation, which in this case is tested with a two-dimensional structure-from-motion task. Figure 6 shows the stimulus which again is a moving random-dot display, this time with a central square region of dots moving eastward and the rest of the display moving westward (see panel labelled "dot motion"). The system responds to this stimulus as follows: The motion system detects the motion of individual dots moving, generating a fairly accurate motion map in the Direction units (panels at lower left; note that the same conventions apply to relative position of boxes as in earlier figures). There are some spurious direction responses, but these come and go as the simulation continues.

Referring to Figure 2, note that there is a reentrant pathway which connects the Direction units of V_{MO} with the Termination-Discontinuity units of V_{OC}.

Recall that the Termination-Discontinuity units serve to detect discontinuities in line terminations consistent with an occlusion boundary. The inputs received from Direction units allow an identical operation to be carried out on motion discontinuities. Units respond to occlusion boundaries signalled by an abrupt change in the direction of motion. These responses are displayed in Figure 6 in the panels labelled "Dir. Disc." for directional discontinuity units. The panel labelled "Occl. Displ." superposes these responses (this panel is for diagnostic purposes only) and shows that the occlusion system has discerned

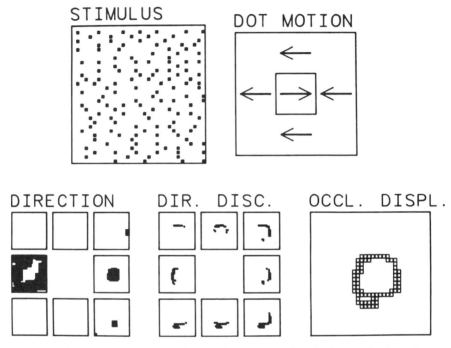

Figure 6. Motion Segmentation. Stimulus consisted of one-pixel random dots moving eastward within a central square region and westward elsewhere in the array (see "Dot Motion") at 1 pixel/cycle. Responses of the Direction and Direction-Discontinuity units are shown after five cycles of activity (panels arranged by direction preference according to convention of Figure 4A). Direction units preferring eastward and westward motion respond to appropriate regions of dot motion. Direction-Discontinuity units generate borders between regions that contain differentially moving objects. Occlusion display shows (at larger scale) the superposed responses of the eight Direction-Discontinuity repertoires. The exact positions of the motion segmentation borders vary from cycle to cycle depending on variations in the gaps between random dots.

the presence of the central square. In this case, the occlusion was due to motion segmentation rather than line terminations, but the same cortical machinery handles both tasks due to convergent inputs from different cortical areas.

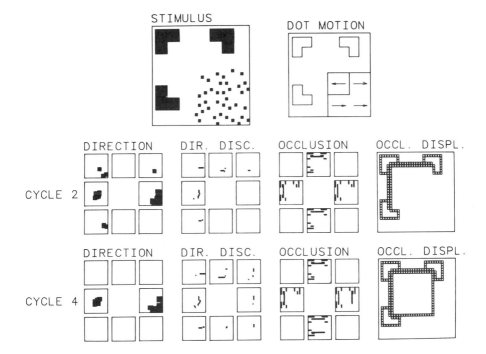

Figure 7. Recursive Synthesis of a Combined Illusion. Responses of Direction, Direction-Discontinuity, and Occlusion units to a combined illusory contour and motion segmentation stimulus. Stimulus consists of three of the four corner elements of Figure 4C. In place of the bottom right corner element is a random-dot stimulus in which dots are moved at 1 pixel/cycle in the directions shown in panel labelled "Dot Motion". By the second cycle (intermediate row of panels), the Occlusion units have generated illusory contours between the corner elements (see Occlusion Display), the Direction units have begun to respond to the directions of dot motion, and the Direction-Discontinuity units have begun to generate motion segmentation borders. By the fourth cycle (bottom row), the responses to motion segmentation borders have been reentered back to V_{OR} (see text), and their terminations have been detected and used by the ascending V_{OC} system to construct responses to the two remaining sides of the illusory square. The construction of these illusory contours thus requires the prior construction of borders based on motion segmentation.

A more formidable task for the network involves the synthesis of responses to a complex combined illusion. The actual illusion used involves motion and can only be perceived on the computer screen, however, some indication of the effect is given in Figure 7. The stimulus features three of the four corners of the illusory square stimulus of Figure 4C, but in place of the bottom right corner there is a moving random-dot display. The dots are moved, as shown in the box labelled "Dot Motion", such that motion segmentation generates an "inverse-L"-shaped occlusion boundary that precisely lines up with the edges of the illusory square. When shown to human subjects on the computer screen, an illusory square "pops out". Figure 7 shows that, by four cycles of operation, the network also generates a response to the illusory square (see bottom box labelled "Occl. Displ."). The manner in which this integrated response emerges offers a deep insight into the reentrant nature of network processing.

On the first cycle of simulation, the normal feedforward pathway from V_{OR} to V_{OC} detects the oriented lines in the three corner "bracket" stimuli. Terminations of these lines determine the positions of two occlusion boundaries running along the top and left side of the illusory square (see Figure 7, cycle 2, panel labelled "Occl. Displ."). Over the next few cycles, the motion system pathway from V_{OR} to V_{MO} picks up the direction of motion of the moving random dots and through its feedback pathway generates a clean response to the eastward and westward moving pixels (see panels labelled "Direction").

The next stage of processing involves motion segmentation in which the Direction units of V_{MO} activate units in V_{OC} via the reentrant pathway (see Figure 2). This causes a response to the occlusion borders generated through motion discontinuities in the random-dot display (see panels labelled "Dir. Disc."). At this point (cycles 2 & 3) Occlusion units have been activated by (1) direct inputs from oriented units in V_{OR}, (2) indirect inputs via the main feedforward pathway between V_{OR} and V_{OC}, and (3) inputs derived from motion signals to V_{MO}. Once active, however, the Occlusion units show no trace of their source of activation, and all reentrantly project back down to V_{OR} where they excite the hypercomplex-type cells in layer 4B. Now, the entire process begins another cycle along the feedforward path from V_{OR} to V_{OC}. However, due to the combination of real (luminance-defined) lines, termination-induced occlusion boundaries, and motion-induced occlusion boundaries, there are now sufficient cues to generate the two missing sides of the illusory square. Thus, by the fourth cycle (lower panels), the system responds to all four sides of the illusory square. Once generated, these responses are stable as long as the stimulus is presented.

III. Implications for Perception

This last example shows the power of reentrant connectivity in integrating the responses of different cortical modules. Three different integrative processes can be identified: (1) *Resolution of conflicts* occurs due to the veto power exercised by certain units, such as the Reentrant Conflict units described above. Since different modules receive information from a variety of sources, some sort of conflict resolution is necessary. This resolution can be effected through winner-take-all networks, cyclical sampling networks, or other means. (2) *Cross-modal interaction* refers to the use by modules of inputs from other sources for their own operations—the key example here being motion segmentation, in which V_{OC} determines occlusion boundaries based on motion information from V_{MO}. Given the multiplicity of connections between cortical areas, such cross-modal interactions are likely to play important roles in integrating cortical responses. (3) The most intriguing integrative process is illustrated by the final example. *Recursive synthesis* describes the recycling of responses from higher level areas (which in turn can have responses derived through cross-modal interactions) to lower level areas, from which they can again ascend through feedforward pathways. However, unlike simple feedback loops, such synthetic loops, with the constant input of additional information at each stage, allow responses to increasingly complex stimuli to be synthesized. It is as if the response is being successively sewn together through successive response cycles, while at each step, all necessary checks and balances are applied to prevent internal interpretation from departing too far from external reality.

Several experimental predictions based on the current studies have been made (Finkel and Edelman 1989), but one is particularly trenchant. It should be possible to detect distinct differences in post-stimulus time delay for higher area cells responding to stimuli perceived through different cortical pathways. For example, a cell in area V2 or V3 which responds to a moving line could be stimulated with lines created by a luminance difference, an illusory contour, motion segmentation, texture difference, or various other sets of cues. The RCI model predicts that certain of these stimuli (e.g. motion segmentation) which require preliminary processing by additional cortical areas will take longer to activate the cell in question. The time delays should be measurable and on the order of at least 10 milliseconds (Sereno 1988). Such an experiment is currently feasible, and would provide a sharp test of the underlying assumptions of the model. All of the processes described in this chapter can occur quite rapidly, probably within the first 50 to 100 milliseconds after stimulation in primates. More complex perceptions and higher cognitive tasks most likely require more extensive reentry and the contributions of higher cortical areas. It is quite likely that cortical oscillations play a role in these processes (Sporns *et al.* 1989; Sporns *et al.* 1990).

The present modelling studies are limited in a number of ways that may be overcome by future work. The networks, though roughly based on cortical anatomy and physiology, are not as rich in cellular detail as might be desired. The design of individual circuits is, to some degree, arbitrary and based upon a largely functional approach. The model as a whole is extremely large, and thus extensive computer analysis of possible dynamic behaviors is precluded. Most importantly, the model only addresses the very earliest stages of visual discrimination—there is no object recognition or even appreciation of surfaces, only the ability to respond to motion and borders which arise from several different types of cues.

However, the RCI model does demonstrate, for the first time, that a self-contained set of cortically-based neural networks can operate in a consistent and complex fashion *as a system*. This system can deal with a range of stimuli and generate responses to implicit regularities in the stimulus which are, in fact, not physically present, but which represent a kind of internal logic about the physical world. Illusions serve as an excellent instrument for uncovering the characteristics of such network behaviors, and the most promising aspect of the model is thus that it provides an example of how modelling may play a role in the ongoing synthesis of physiology and psychophysics.

Acknowledgements

    This work was carried out under The Neurosciences Institute's research program in theoretical neurobiology, which is supported by the Neurosciences Research Foundation in part through grants from the John D. and Catherine T. MacArthur Foundation, the Lucille P. Markey Charitable Trust, The Pew Charitable Trusts, the van Ameringen Foundation, the Charles and Mildred Schnurmacher Foundation, and the Office of Naval Research. Key simulations were conducted using the Cornell National Supercomputer Facility, a resource of the Cornell Theory Center, which receives major funding from the National Science Foundation and IBM Corporation, with additional support from New York State and members of its Corporate Research Institute. LHF would like to thank the Office of Naval Research, The Whitaker Foundation, and the McDonnell-Pew Program in Cognitive Neuroscience for support of his ongoing research in this area.

References

Ballard, D.H., Hinton, G.E., Sejnowski, T.J. 1983. Parallel visual computation. *Nature* 306:21-26.

Barlow, H.B., Levick, R.W. 1965. The mechanism of directional selectivity in the rabbit's retina. *J. Physiol. (Lond.)* 173:477-504.

Crick, F., Koch, C. 1990. Towards a neurobiological theory of consciousness. *Seminars in the Neurosciences* 2:263-275.

Damasio, A.R. 1989. The brain binds entities and events by multiregional activation from convergent zones. *Neural Comp.* 1:123-132.

DeYoe, E.A., Van Essen, D.C. 1988. Concurrent processing streams in monkey visual cortex. *Trends Neurosci.* 11:219-226.

Eckhorn, R., Bauer, R., Jordan, W., Brosch, M., Kruse, W., Munk, M., Reitboeck, H.J. 1988. Coherent oscillations: A mechanism of feature linking in the visual cortex? Multiple electrode and correlation analyses in the cat. *Biol. Cybern.* 60:121-130.

Eckhorn, R., Reitboeck, H.J., Arndt, M., Dicke, P. 1989. A neural network for feature linking via synchronous activity: Results from cat visual cortex and from simulations. In *Models of Brain Function*, ed. Cotterill, R.M.J., pp. 255-272. Cambridge, UK: Cambridge University Press.

Edelman, G.M. 1978. Group selection and phasic reentrant signaling: A theory of higher brain function. In *The Mindful Brain: Cortical Organization and the Group-Selective Theory of Higher Brain Function*, eds. Edelman, G.M., Mountcastle, V.B., pp. 51-100. Cambridge, Mass.: MIT Press.

Edelman, G.M. 1981. Group selection as the basis for higher brain function. In *The Organization of the Cerebral Cortex*, eds. Schmitt, F.O., Worden, F.G., Adelman, G., Dennis, S.G., pp. 535-563. Cambridge, Mass.: MIT Press.

Edelman, G.M. 1987. *Neural Darwinism: The Theory of Neuronal Group Selection*. New York: Basic Books.

Edelman, G.M., Finkel, L.H. 1984. Neuronal group selection in the cerebral cortex. In *Dynamic Aspects of Neocortical Function*, eds. Edelman, G.M., Gall, W.E., Cowan, W.M., pp. 653-695. New York: Wiley.

Finkel, L.H., Edelman, G.M. 1989. The integration of distributed cortical systems by reentry: A computer simulation of interactive functionally segregated visual areas. *J. Neurosci.* 9:3188-3208.

Gibson, J.J. 1979. *The Ecological Approach to Visual Perception*. Boston: Houghton-Mifflin.

Gray, C.M., Singer, W. 1989.   Stimulus-specific neuronal oscillations in orientation columns of cat visual cortex.   *Proc. Natl. Acad. Sci. USA* 86:1698-1702.

Grossberg, S. 1987.   Cortical dynamics of three-dimensional form, color, and brightness perception: I. Monocular theory.   *Perception & Psychophysics* 41:87-116.

Grossberg, S., Mingolla, E. 1985.   Neural dynamics of form perception: boundary completion, illusory figures, and neon color spreading.   *Psychol. Rev.* 92:173-211.

Hildreth, E.C., Koch, C. 1987.   The analysis of visual motion: From computational theory to neuronal mechanisms.   *Annu. Rev. Neurosci.* 10:477-533.

Kammen, D.M., Holmes, P.J., Koch, C. 1989.   Cortical architecture and oscillations in neuronal networks: Feedback versus local coupling.   In *Models of Brain Function*, ed. Cotterill, R.M.J., pp. 273-284. Cambridge UK: Cambridge University.

Kanizsa, G. 1979. *Organization in Vision.* New York: Praeger.

Livingstone, M., Hubel, D. 1988. Segregation of form, color, movement, and depth: Anatomy, physiology, and perception. *Science* 240:740-749.

Marr, D. 1982. *Vision.* San Francisco: W.H. Freeman.

Maunsell, J.H.R., Newsome, W.T. 1987.   Visual processing in monkey extrastriate cortex. *Ann. Rev. Neurosci.* 10:363-401.

Mishkin, M., Ungerleider, L.G., Macko, K.A. 1983.   Object vision and spatial vision: Two cortical pathways. *Trends Neurosci.* 6:414-417.

Movshon, J.A., Adelson, E.H., Gizzi, M.S., Newsome, W.T. 1985.   The analysis of moving visual patterns. In *Pattern Recognition Mechanisms*, eds. Chagas, C., Gattass, R., Gross, C., pp. 117-151. Exp. Brain Res. Suppl. 11.

Peterhans, E., von der Heydt, R. 1989. Mechanisms of contour perception in monkey visual cortex. II. Contours bridging gaps. *J. Neurosci.* 9:1749--1763.

Peterhans, E., von der Heydt, R., Baumgartner, G. 1986. Neuronal responses to illusory contour stimuli reveal stages of visual cortical processing. In *Visual Neuroscience*, eds. Pettigrew, J.D., Sanderson, K.J., Levick, W.R., pp. 343-351. Cambridge, England: Cambridge University Press.

Poggio, T. 1989. A parallel vision machine that learns. In *Models of Brain Function*, ed. Cotterill, R.M.J., pp. 51-88. Cambridge: Cambridge University Press.

Ramachandran, V.S. 1986. Capture of stereopsis and apparent motion by illusory contours. *Percept. Psychophys.* 39:361-373.

Ramachandran, V.S., Cavanaugh, P. 1985. Subjective contours capture stereopsis. *Nature* 317:527-530.

Reeke, G.N., Jr., Edelman, G.M. 1987. Selective neural networks and their implications for recognition automata. *Int. J. Supercomputer. Appl.* 1:44-69.

Reichardt, W., Poggio, T., Hausen, K. 1983. Figure-ground discrimination in the visual system of the fly. II. Towards the neural circuitry. *Biol. Cybern. (Suppl.)* 46:1-30.

Richards, W., ed. 1988. *Natural Computation.* Cambridge, Mass.: MIT Press.

Schillen, T.B., König, P. 1990. Coherency detection by coupled oscillatory responses--synchronizing connections in neural oscillator layers. In *Parallel Processing in Neural Systems and Computers*, eds. Eckmiller, R., Hartmann, G., Hauske, G., pp. 139-142. Amsterdam: Elsevier.

Sereno, M.I. 1988. The visual system. In *Organization of Neural Networks*, eds. Von Seelen, W., Shaw, G., Leinhos, U.M., pp. 167-184. New York: VCH Publishers.

Sporns, O., Gally, J.A., Reeke, G.N., Jr., Edelman, G.M. 1989. Reentrant signaling among simulated neuronal groups leads to coherency in their oscillatory activity. *Proc. Natl. Acad. Sci. USA* 86:7265-7269.

Sporns, O., Tononi, G., Edelman, G.M. 1990. Dynamic interaction of neuronal groups and the problem of cortical integration. In *Nonlinear Dynamics of Neural Networks*, ed. Schuster, H.G. Weinheim: VCH (in press).

Stevens, K.A. 1981. Evidence relating subjective contours and interpretations involving occlusion. AI Memo No. 637. Cambridge, Mass.: MIT Artificial Intelligence Laboratory.

Ullman, S. 1976. Filling in the gaps: The shape of subjective contours and a model for their generation. *Biol. Cybern.* 25:1-6.

Van Essen, D.C. 1985. Functional organization of primate visual cortex. In *Cerebral Cortex, Vol. 3, Visual Cortex*, eds. Peters, A., Jones, E.G., pp. 259-329. New York: Plenum.

von der Heydt, R., Peterhans, E. 1989. Mechanisms of contour perception in monkey visual cortex. I. Lines of pattern discontinuity. *J. Neurosci.* 9:1731-1748.

von der Heydt, R., Peterhans, E., Baumgartner, G. 1984. Illusory contours and cortical neuron responses. *Science* 224:1260-1262.

Wang, D., Buhmann, J., von der Malsburg, C. 1990. Pattern segmentation in associative memory. *Neural Comp.* 2:94-106.

Zeki, S., Shipp, S. 1988. The functional logic of cortical connections. *Nature* 335:311-317.

Zeki, S.M. 1978. Functional properties in visual cortex of rhesus monkey. *Nature* 274:423-428.

I.4

THE SYMMETRIC ORGANIZATION OF PARALLEL CORTICAL SYSTEMS FOR FORM AND MOTION PERCEPTION

STEPHEN GROSSBERG†

Center for Adaptive Systems and
Graduate Program in Cognitive & Neural Systems
Boston University
111 Cummington Street
Boston, MA 02215

I. Introduction: Why Do Parallel Cortical Systems Exist for the Perception of Static Form and Moving Form?

This chapter analyses computational properties that clarify why the parallel cortical systems $V1 \to V2$, $V1 \to MT$, and $V1 \to V2 \to MT$ exist for the perceptual processing of static visual forms and moving visual forms. The chapter describes a symmetry principle, called FM Symmetry, that is predicted to govern the development of these parallel cortical systems by computing all possible ways of symmetrically gating sustained cells with transient cells and organizing these sustained-transient cells into opponent pairs of on-cells and off-cells whose output signals are insensitive to direction-of-contrast. This symmetric organization explains how the Static Boundary Contour System, that models the $V1 \to V2$ static form system, generates emergent boundary segmentations whose outputs are insensitive to direction-of-contrast and insensitive to direction-of-motion, whereas the Motion Boundary Contour System, that models the $V1 \to MT$ motion form system, generates emergent boundary segmentations whose outputs are insensitive to direction-of-contrast but sensitive to direction-of-motion. The theory also suggests how the $V1 \to V2 \to MT$ cortical stream helps to compute moving-form-in-depth and how this stream may generate a percept of long-range apparent motion of illusory contours.

FM Symmetry clarifies why the geometries of static and motion form perception differ; for example, why the opposite orientation of vertical is horizontal (90°), but the opposite direction of up is down (180°). Opposite orientations and directions are embedded in gated dipole opponent processes that are capable of antagonistic rebound. Negative afterimages, such as the MacKay and waterfall illusions, are hereby explained, as are aftereffects of long-range apparent motion. These antagonistic rebounds help to control a dynamic balance between complementary perceptual states of resonance and reset. Resonance cooperatively links features into emergent boundary segmentations via positive feedback in a CC Loop, and reset terminates a resonance when the image changes, thereby preventing massive smearing of percepts.

These complementary preattentive states of resonance and reset are related to analogous states that govern attentive feature integration, learning, and memory search in Adaptive Resonance Theory. The mechanism used in the $V1 \rightarrow MT$ system to generate a wave of apparent motion between discrete flashes may also be used in other cortical systems to generate spatial shifts of attention.

These results collectively argue against vision theories that espouse independent processing modules. Instead, specialized subsystems interact to overcome computational uncertainties and complementary deficiencies, to cooperatively bind features into context-sensitive resonances, and to realize symmetry principles that are predicted to govern the development of visual cortex.

II. The Motion BCS and the Static BCS

The Motion Boundary Contour System, or Motion BCS, constitutes a new theory of biological motion perception. The theory was outlined in Grossberg (1987b) and quantitatively developed in Grossberg and Rudd (1989a, 1989b, 1990a, 1990b) and in Grossberg and Mingolla (1990a, 1990b, 1990c). The Motion BCS consists of several parallel copies, such that each copy is activated by a different range of receptive field sizes. Each copy is further subdivided into hierarchically organized subsystems: a *Motion Oriented Contrast Filter*, or *MOC Filter*, for preprocessing moving images; and a Cooperative-Competitive Feedback Loop, or CC Loop, for generating coherent emergent boundary segmentations of the filtered signals. This theory suggests a computational explanation for the cortical stream $V1 \rightarrow V2$ that joins the areas V1 and MT of visual cortex.

A previous model of static form perception, called the Static BCS, modeled aspects of the parallel $V1 \rightarrow V2$ cortical stream. The Static BCS model also consists of several parallel copies, such that each copy is activated by a different range of receptive field sizes, as in the Motion BCS. Also as in the Motion BCS, each Static BCS copy is further subdivided

BOUNDARY CONTOUR SYSTEM (BCS)

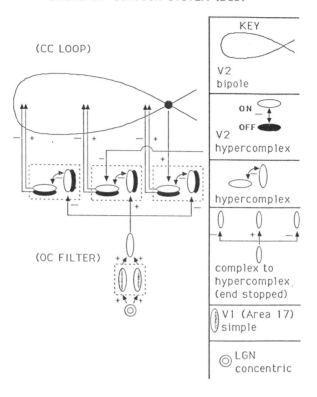

Figure 1. The static Boundary Contour System circuit described by Grossberg and Mingolla (1985b). The circuit is divided into an oriented contrast-sensitive filter (SOC Filter) followed by a cooperative-competitive feedback network (CC Loop). Multiple copies of this circuit are used, each corresponding to a different range of receptive field sizes of the SOC Filter. The depicted circuit has been used to analyse data about monocular vision. A binocular generalization of the circuit has also been described (Grossberg, 1987b; Grossberg and Marshall, 1989).

into two hierarchically organized systems (Figure 1): a *Static Oriented Contrast Filter*, or *SOC Filter*, for preprocessing quasi-static images (the eye never ceases to jiggle in its orbit); and a Cooperative-Competitive Feedback Loop, or CC Loop, for generating coherent emergent boundary segmentations of the filtered signals. Thus the Motion BCS and Static BCS models share many common design features. This important fact, which is not evident in other form and motion theories, enables us to view both models as variations on a common architectural design for visual cortex. A great conceptual simplification is afforded by the fact that variations on a common design can now be used to explain large data bases about form

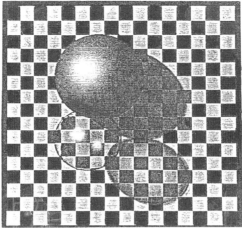

Figure 2. Long vertical and horizontal boundaries are detected despite regular contrast reversals in defining the grid of alternating black and white squares. (Figure by Ennio Mingolla. Reprinted with permission.)*

Figure 3. A reverse-contrast Kanizsa square: The BCS is capable of completing illusory boundaries between the vertical dark-light and light-dark contrasts of the pac man figures. This boundary completion, or emergent segmentation, process enables the BCS to detect boundaries along contrast reversals, as in Figure 2.

and motion perception that have heretofore been treated separately.

III. Joining Sensitivity to Direction-of-Motion with Insensitivity to Direction-of-Contrast

Given the similarity of these two systems, why is one of them not

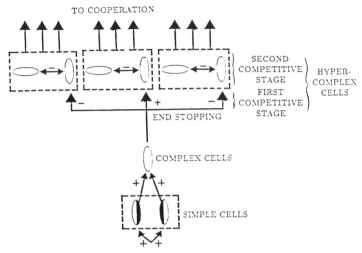

Figure 4. Early stages of SOC Filter processing: At each position exist cells with elongated receptive fields (simple cells) of various sizes which are sensitive to orientation, amount-of-contrast, and direction-of-contrast. Pairs of such cells sensitive to like orientation but opposite directions-of-contrast (lower dashed box) input to cells (complex cells) that are sensitive to orientation and amount-of-contrast but not to direction-of-contrast (white ellipses). These cells, in turn, excite like-oriented cells (hypercomplex cells) corresponding to the same position and inhibit like-oriented cells corresponding to nearby positions at the first competitive stage. At the second competitive stage, cells corresponding to the same position but different orientations (higher-order hypercomplex cells) inhibit each other via a push-pull competitive interaction.

sufficient to process both static form and motion form? Analysis of the SOC Filter design revealed that one of its basic properties made it unsuitable for motion processing; namely, the output of the SOC Filter cannot effectively process the direction-of-motion of a moving figure. This deficiency arises from the way in which the SOC Filter becomes insensitive to direction-of-contrast at its complex cell level. Insensitivity to direction-of-contrast of the SOC Filter's complex cells enables the CC Loop of the Static BCS, which involves feedback interactions between hypercomplex cells and bipole cells (Figure 1), to generate boundary segmentations along scenic contrast reversals (Figures 2 and 3).

The simple cells at the first BCS level are, however, sensitive to direction-of-contrast (Figure 4). The activities of like-oriented simple cells that are sensitive to opposite directions-of-contrast are rectified before they generate outputs to their target complex cells. Because the complex cells pool outputs from both directions-of-contrast, they are themselves insensitive to direction-of-contrast.

Figure 4 shows a single pair of simple cells generating inputs to each complex cell. Such an arrangement is not sufficient in general. For ex-

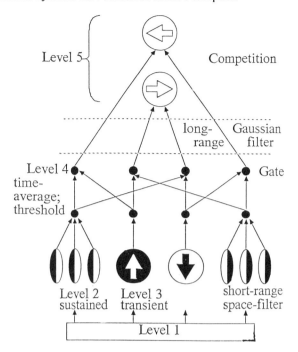

Figure 5. The MOC Filter: Level 1 registers the input pattern. Level 2 consists of sustained response cells with oriented receptive fields that are sensitive to direction-of-contrast. Level 3 consists of transient response cells with unoriented receptive fields that are sensitive to direction-of-change in the total cell input. Level 4 cells combine sustained cell and transient cell signals to become sensitive to direction-of-motion and sensitive to direction-of-contrast. Level 5 cells combine Level 4 cells via a long-range filter to become sensitive to direction-of-motion and insensitive to direction-of-contrast.

ample, Grossberg (1987b) and Grossberg and Marshall (1989) have shown that multiple simple cells may input to each complex cell. The number of converging simple cells is predicted to covary in a self-similar manner with the size of the simple cell receptive fields, and then to trigger nonlinear contrast-enhancing competition at the complex cell level, in order to explain basic data about binocular vision such as the size-disparity correlation and binocular fusion and rivalry.

Inspection of the (simple cell)-to-(complex cell) interaction in Figure 4 shows that a vertically-oriented complex cell could respond, say, to a dark-light vertical edge moving to the right *and* to a light-dark vertical edge moving to the left. Thus the process whereby complex cells become insensitive to direction-of-contrast has rendered them insensitive to direction-of-motion in the SOC Filter.

Table 1. Levels of Motion OC Filter

Level 1:	Input Pattern
Level 2:	**Sustained Response Cells** Time-averaged and shunted signals from rectified outputs of spatially filtered oriented receptive fields
Level 3:	**Transient Response Cells** Rectified outputs of time-averaged and shunted signals from unoriented change-sensitive cells
Level 4:	**Local Motion Detectorsg** Pairwise gating of sustained and transient response combinations Sensitive to direction-of-contrast Sensitive to direction-of-motion
Level 4→5:	**Long-Range Gaussian Filter**
Level 5:	**Motion-Direction Detectors** Contrast-enhancing competition Insensitive to direction-of-contrast Sensitive to direction-of-motion

The main design problem leading to a MOC Filter is to make the minimal changes in the SOC Filter that are needed to model an oriented, contrast-sensitive filter whose outputs are insensitive to direction-of-contrast—a property that is just as important for moving images as for static images—yet is also *sensitive* to direction-of-motion—a property that is certainly essential in a motion perception system. The MOC Filter, summarized in Figure 5 and Table 1, is rigorously defined below.

Although this modification of the Static BCS is computationally modest, it is based upon a conceptually radical departure of our vision theory from previous vision models. Insensitivity to direction-of-contrast could be articulated within the BCS because all boundary segmentations within the BCS are perceptually invisible. Visibility is a property of the Feature Contour System, or FCS, whose output signals are sensitive to direction-of-contrast. In particular, the FCS compensates for variable illumination conditions and fills-in surface properties of brightness, color, and depth among multiple spatial scales (Cohen and Grossberg, 1984; Grossberg, 1987a, 1987b, 1990; Grossberg and Mingolla, 1985a; Grossberg and Todorović, 1988; Grossberg and Wyse, 1990). A vision theory built up from the usual type of independent processing modules could not articulate the heuristics or the mechanisms of the Motion BCS because it could not articulate the fact that the BCS and FCS are computationally *complementary* subsystems of a single larger-system, rather than being independent modules for the processing of form and color (Grossberg, Mingolla, and Todorović, 1989).

IV. Why is not a Motion Form Perception System Sufficient?

A further analysis of the Static BCS and Motion BCS poses a new puzzle. This puzzle arises because it seems that the Motion BCS has stronger computational properties than the Static BCS. Why, then has Nature not used only a Motion BCS? Why has not the Static BCS atrophied due to disuse? In particular, if Nature could design a MOC filter that is sensitive to direction-of-motion and insensitive to direction-of-contrast, then why did the SOC Filter evolve, in which insensitivity to direction-of-contrast comes only at the cost of a loss of sensitivity to direction-of-motion? This question is perplexing given the facts that animals are usually in relative motion with respect to their visual environment, and that simple cells in V1 are already sensitive to direction-of-motion.

An answer to this question can be derived by first noting that the SOC Filter design that was described by Grossberg and Mingolla (1985b), Grossberg (1987b), and Grossberg and Marshall (1989) is incomplete. This design omits the processes that would be needed to make the SOC Filter sensitive to transient changes in the input pattern, as also occurs *in vivo* (DeValois, Albrecht, and Thorell, 1982; Heggelund, 1981; Hubel and Wiesel, 1962, 1968, 1977; Tanaka, Lee, and Creutzfeldt, 1983). An analysis of how to correct this omission leads herein to a unified theory in which the Static BCS and the Motion BCS may be viewed as parallel subsystems of a single total system. I have predicted (Grossberg, 1991a, 1991b) that this total system unfolds during the development of the visual cortex as an expression of an underlying symmetry principle, called FM Symmetry (F = form, M = motion). This prediction suggests that the static form perception and motion form perception systems are not independent modules that obey different rules. Rather, they express two sides of a unifying organizational principle that is predicted to control the development of visual cortex.

V. A Symmetry Principle for Cortical Development: Sustained-Transient Gating, Opponent Processing, and Insensitivity to Direction-of-Contrast

This symmetry principle is predicted to control the simultaneous satisfaction of three constraints; namely,

(1) multiplicative interaction, or gating, of all combinations of sustained cell and transient cell output signals to form four sustained-transient cell types;

(2) symmetric organization of these sustained-transient cell types into two opponent on-cell and off-cell pairs, such that

(3) output signals from all the opponent cell types are independent of direction-of-contrast.

Multiplicative gating of sustained cells and transient cells is shown
below to generate change-sensitive receptive field properties of oriented
on-cells and off-cells within the Static BCS, and direction-sensitive cells
within the Motion BCS. The constraint that output signals be independent
of direction-of-contrast enables both the Static BCS and the Motion BCS to
generate emergent boundary segmentations along image contrast reversals.

The previous discussion suggests how the static form and motion form
systems may both arise. This discussion does not, however, disclose how
these systems control different perceptual properties whose behavioral usefulness has preserved their integrity throughout the evolutionary process.
The following behavioral implications of the symmmetry principle will be
explained herein:

VI. Different Geometries and Afterimages for Perception of Static Form and Motion Form

We take for granted that the opposite *orientation* of "vertical" is "horizontal," a difference of 90°; yet the opposite *direction* of "up" is "down,"
a difference of 180°. Why are the perceptual symmetries of static form and
motion form different? These symmetries reflect an opponent organization whereby orientations that differ by 90° are grouped together, whereas
directions that differ by 180° are grouped together.

Negative aftereffects illustrate a key property of this opponent organization. For example, after sustained viewing of a radial input pattern, looking at a uniform field triggers a percept of a circular afterimage (MacKay,
1957). The orientations within the input and the circular afterimage differ
from each other by 90°. After sustained viewing of a downwardly moving
image, looking at a uniform field triggers a percept of an upwardly moving afterimage, as in the waterfall illusion (Sekuler, 1975). The directions
within the downward input and the upward afterimage differ from each
other by 180°. In summary, the geometries of both static form perception
and motion form perception include an opponent organization in which offset of the input pattern after sustained viewing triggers onset of a transient
antagonistic rebound, or activation of the opponent channel.

VII. Resonance versus Reset: Cooperative Feature Linking without Destructive Smearing

Antagonistic rebound within opponent channels is needed to control
the complementary perceptual processes of *resonance* and *reset*. Within

the CC Loop (Figure 1), positive feedback signals between the hypercomplex cells and bipole cells can cooperatively link similarly oriented features at approximately colinear locations into emergent boundary segmentations (Grossberg and Mingolla, 1985a, 1985b, 1987; Grossberg and Somers, 1990). Several neurophysiological laboratories (Eckhorn *et al.*, 1988; Gray *et al.*, 1989) have supported the prediction that such cooperative linking occurs between cortical representations of similarly oriented features.

These positive feedback interactions selectively amplify and sharpen the globally "best" cooperative grouping and provide the activation for inhibiting less favored groupings. The positive feedback interactions also subserve the coherence, hysteresis, and structural properties of the emergent segmentations. The positive feedback can, however, maintain itself for a long time after visual inputs terminate. Thus the very existence of cooperative linking could seriously degrade perception by maintaining long-lasting positive afterimages, or smearing, of every percept.

Although some smearing can occur, it is known to be actively limited by inhibitory processes that are triggered by changing images (Hogben and DiLollo, 1985). I suggest that antagonistic rebounds between opponently organized on-cells and off-cells can actively inhibit CC Loop resonances when the input pattern changes. This inhibitory process *resets* the resonance and enables the CC Loop to flexibly establish new resonances in response to rapidly changing scenes.

In summary, the symmetry principle that is predicted to control the parallel development of the static form and motion form systems enables these systems to rapidly reset their resonant segmentations in response to rapidly changing inputs.

VIII. Combining Rapid Reset and Spatial Impenetrability Predictions

The network design that controls rapid reset of a CC Loop resonance also constrains which combinations of features can resonate together, and thereby helps to structure the geometry of perceptual space. In particular, rapid reset of a resonating segmentation uses on-cells and off-cells of a given orientation that generate excitatory inputs and inhibitory inputs, respectively, to bipole cells of the same orientation (Figure 1). When on-cells lose their input, an antagonistic rebound activates off-cells that inhibit bipole cells and terminate the resonance.

Grossberg and Mingolla (1985b) have shown that the same mechanism can also generate the property of *spatial impenetrability* whereby emergent segmentations, during the resonance phase, are prevented from penetrating figures whose boundaries are built up from non-colinear orientations. This property suggests a solution to the problem of why emergent segmentations, which are capable of completing boundaries between pairs of colinear inducers, do not penetrate all intervening forms, which would prevent percepts from separating figures from each other and their backgrounds. In particular, in a cartoon drawing of a person standing in a grassy field, the horizontal contours where the ground touches the sky do not generate horizontal emergent boundaries that cut the person's vertical body in half. This property follows from the fact that vertical hypercomplex on-cells inhibit vertical hypercomplex off-cells, which disinhibit horizontal hypercomplex off-cells (Figure 1). The horizontal off-cells, in turn, inhibit horizontal bipole cells, and thereby undermine horizontal segmentations that might otherwise have penetrated the vertical figure.

IX. Perception of Moving-Form-in-Depth: The $V1 \rightarrow V2 \rightarrow MT$ Pathway

The FM Symmetry principle clarifies how parallel $V1 \rightarrow V2$ and $V1 \rightarrow MT$ cortical streams may develop and realize their computational properties. With these properties in mind, we can focus on one of the perceptual tasks that requires both of these cortical streams, in addition to an indirect cortical pathway $V1 \rightarrow V2 \rightarrow MT$ that exists from V1 to MT (DeYoe and van Essen, 1988). Outputs from the MOC Filter sacrifice a measure of orientational specificity in order to effectively process direction-of-motion. However, precisely oriented binocular matches are important in the selection of cortical cells that are tuned to the correct binocular disparities (von der Heydt, Hänny, and Dürsteler, 1981). The Static BCS can carry out such precise oriented matches; the Motion BCS cannot. This fact suggests that a pathway from the Static BCS to the Motion BCS exists in order to help the Motion BCS to generate its motion segmentations at correctly calibrated depths.

Such a pathway needs to arise after the level of BCS processing at which cells capable of binocular fusion are chosen and binocularly rivalrous cells are suppressed. This occurs within the hypercomplex cells and bipole cells of the Static BCS (Grossberg, 1987b; Grossberg and Marshall, 1989), hence within the model analog of prestriate cortical area V2 (Figure 6). Thus the existence of a pathway from V2 and/or V4 to MT is consistent with the different functional roles of the Static BCS and the Motion BCS.

According to this reasoning, the $V2 \rightarrow MT$ pathway should occur at a processing stage prior to the one at which several orientations are pooled into a single direction-of-motion within each spatial scale. Thus, the pathway ends in the MOC Filter at a stage no later than Level 4 in Figure 5. Such a pathway would join like orientations within like spatial scales between the Static BCS and the Motion BCS. It could thereby enhance the

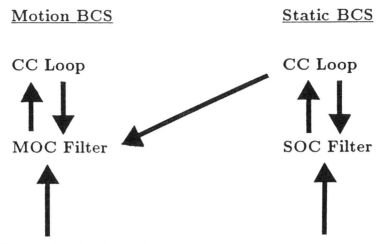

Motion BCS   Static BCS

CC Loop   CC Loop

MOC Filter   SOC Filter

Figure 6. Model analog of $V1 \rightarrow V2 \rightarrow MT$ pathway: Stereo-sensitive emergent segmentations from the Static CC Loop help to select the depthfully correct combinations of motion signals in the MOC Filter.

activation within the Motion BCS of those spatial scales and orientations that are binocularly fused within the Static BCS.

X. Apparent Motion of Illusory Figures

This interpretation of the $V2 \rightarrow MT$ pathway helps to explain the percept of apparent motion of illusory figures—a type of "doubly illusory" percept. Ramachandran, Rao, and Vidyasagar (1973) and Ramachandran (1985) have, for example, studied this phenomenon using the display summarized in Figure 7. Frame 1 of this display generates the percept of an illusory square using a Kanizsa figure. Frame 2 generates the percept of an illusory square using a different combination of image elements. When Frame 2 is flashed on after Frame 1 shuts off, the illusory square is seen to move continuously from its location in Frame 1 to its location in Frame 2. Because matching of image elements between the two frames is impossible, the experiment demonstrates that the illusory square, not the image elements that generate it, is undergoing apparent motion.

This phenomenon can be explained using the pathway from the CC Loop of the Static BCS to Level 4 of the MOC Filter. The CC Loop is capable of generating an illusory square in response to Frame 1 and Frame 2 (Grossberg and Mingolla, 1985b; Van Allen and Kolodzy, 1987). Successive inputs to Level 4 of the MOC Filter can induce continuous apparent motion if they are properly timed and spatially arranged (Grossberg and Rudd, 1989c, 1990b), as I will indicate below in Section 15. When this happens,

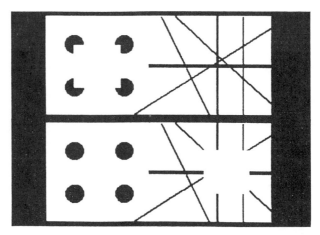

Figure 7. Images used to demonstrate that apparent motion of illusory figures arises through interactions of the static illusory figures, not from the inducing elements. Frame 1 (row 1) is temporally followed by Frame 2 (row 2). Reprinted with permission from Ramachandran (1985).*

the two static illusory squares can induce a continuous wave of apparent motion at Level 5 of the MOC Filter.

This explanation of apparent motion of illusory figures can be used to test whether the $V2 \to MT$ pathway plays the role suggested above. One possible approach is to train a monkey to respond differently when the two illusory figures appear to move and when they do not. Then a (reversible) lesion of V2 or of the $V2 \to MT$ pathway should abolish the former behavior but not the latter.

XI. Design of a MOC Filter

This section suggests a solution to the problem raises in Section 3. The equations for a one-dimensional MOC Filter were described in Grossberg and Rudd (1989c). The MOC Filter's five processing levels are described qualitatively below for the more general two-dimensional case. The equations used for the 1-D theory are also described to provide a basis for rigorously defining the FM Symmetry principle.

Level 1: Preprocess Input Pattern

The image is preprocessed before activating the MOC Filter. For example, it is passed through a shunting on-center off-surround net to compensate for variable illumination, or to "discount the illuminant" (Grossberg and Todorović, 1988).

---

* Reprinted with permission from Pion, Limited. Ramachandran, V.S., *Perception*, **14**, 127–273 (1985).

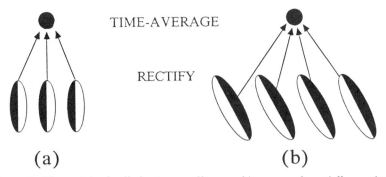

Figure 8. The sustained cell short-range filter combines several spatially contiguous receptive fields of like orientation via a spatial filter with a fixed directional preference. The orientation perpendicular to the direction is preferred, but non-orthogonal orientations can also be grouped in a prescribed direction.

In the 1-D theory, I_i denotes the input at position i.

Level 2: Sustained Cell Short-Range Filter

Four operations occur here, as illustrated in Figure 8.

(1) Space-Average: Inputs are processed by individual sustained cells with oriented receptive fields.

(2) Rectify: The output signal from a sustained cell grows with its activity above a signal threshold.

(3) Short-Range Spatial Filter: A spatially alligned array of sustained cells with like orientation and direction-of-contrast pool their output signals to activate the next cell level. This spatial pooling plays the role of the short-range motion limit D_{max} (Braddick, 1974). The breadth of spatial pooling scales with the size of the simple cell receptive fields (Figures 8a and 8b). Thus "D_{max}" is not independent of the spatial frequency content of the image (Anderson and Burr, 1987; Burr, Ross, and Morrone, 1986; Nakayama and Silverman, 1984, 1985), and is not a universal constant.

The direction of spatial pooling may not be perpendicular to the oriented axis of the sustained cell receptive field (Figure 8b). The target cells are thus sensitive to a movement *direction* that may not be perpendicular to the sustained cell's preferred orientation.

(4) Time-Average: The target cell time-averages the directionally-sensitive inputs that it receives from the short-range spatial filter. This

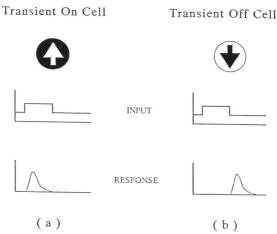

Transient On Cell   Transient Off Cell

(a)   (b)

Figure 9. The transient cell filter consists of on-cells which react to input increments and off-cells which react to input decrements.

operation has properties akin to the "visual inertia" during apparent motion that was reported by Anstis and Ramachandran (1987).

In the 1-D theory, only horizontal motions are considered. It therefore suffices to consider two types of such cells that filter the input pattern I_i, one of which responds to a light-dark luminance contrast (designated by L, for left) and the other of which responds to a dark-light luminance contrast (designated by R, for right). Output pathways from like cells converge (Figure 10) to generate inputs J_{iL} and J_{iR} at each position i. The activity x_{ik} of the ith target cell at Level 2 obeys a membrane equation

$$\frac{d}{dt}x_{ik} = -Ax_{ik} + (1 - Bx_{ik})J_{ik},\tag{1}$$

where $k = L, R$, which performs a time-average of the input J_{ik}.

Level 3: Transient Cell Filter:

In parallel with the sustained cell filter, a transient cell filter reacts to input increments (on-cells) and decrements (off-cells) with positive outputs (Figure 9). This filter uses four operations too:

(1) Space-Average: This is accomplished by a receptive field that sums inputs over its entire range.

(2) Time-Average: This sum is time-averaged to generate a gradual growth and decay of total activation.

(3) Transient Detector: The on-cells are activated when the time-average increases (Figure 9a). The off-cells are activated when the time-average decreases (Figure 9b).

(4) Rectify: The output signal from a transient cell grows with its activity above a signal threshold.

In the 1-D theory, the activities of the transient cells were computed as the rectified time derivatives of an unoriented space-time average x_i of the input pattern I_i. The time derivative is given by the membrane equation

$$\frac{d}{dt}x_i = -Cx_i + (D - Ex_i)\sum_j I_j F_{ji}, \qquad (2)$$

where F_{ji} is the unoriented spatial kernel that represents a transient cell receptive field.

Positive and negative half-wave rectifications of the time derivative were performed independently by defining

$$y_i^+ = \max\left(\frac{d}{dt}x_i - \Gamma, 0\right), \qquad (3)$$

and

$$y_i^- = \max\left(\Omega - \frac{d}{dt}x_i, 0\right), \qquad (4)$$

where Γ and Ω are constant thresholds. The activity y_i^+ models the response of a transient on-cell; and the activity y_i^- models the response of a transient off-cell.

Level 4: Sustained-Transient Gating Yields Direction-of-Motion Sensitivity and Direction-of-Contrast Sensitivity

Maximal activation of a Level 2 sustained cell filter is caused by image contrasts moving in either of two directions that differ by 180°. Multiplicative gating of each Level 2 sustained cell output with a Level 3 transient cell on-cell or off-cell removes this ambiguity (Figure 10). For example, consider a sustained cell output from vertically oriented light-dark simple cell receptive fields that are joined together in the horizontal direction by the short-range spatial filter (Figure 8a). Such a sustained cell output is maximized by a light-dark image contrast moving to the right or to the left. Multiplying this Level 2 output with a Level 3 transient on-cell output generates a Level 4 cell that responds maximally to motion to the right.

In the 1-D theory, there are two types of sustained cells (corresponding to the two antisymmetric directions-of-contrast), and also two type of transient cells (the on-cells and the off-cells). Consequently, there are four types of gated responses that can be computed. Two of these produce cells that are sensitive to local rightward motion: the $(L, +)$ cells that respond to $x_{iL}y_i^+$, and the $(R, -)$ cells that respond to $x_{iR}y_i^-$. The other two produce cells which are sensitive to local leftward motion: the $(L, -)$ cells that

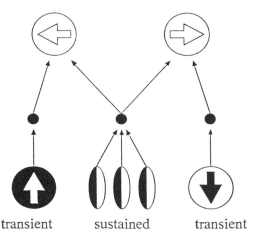

transient   sustained   transient

Figure 10. Sustained-transient gating generates cells that are sensitive to direction-of-motion as well as to direction-of-contrast.

respond to $x_{iL}y_i^-$, and the $(R,+)$ cells that respond to $x_{iR}y_i^+$. All of these cells inherit a sensitivity to the direction-of-contrast of their inputs from the Level 2 sustained cells from which they are constructed.

The cell outputs from Level 4 are sensitive to direction-of-contrast. Level 5 consists of cells that pool outputs from Level 4 cells which are sensitive to the same direction-of-motion but to opposite directions-of-contrast.

Level 5: Long-Range Spatial Filter and Competition

Outputs from Level 4 cells sensitive to the same direction-of-motion but opposite directions-of-contrast activate individual Level 5 cells via a long-range spatial filter that has a Gaussianly profile across space (Figure 11). This long-range filter groups together Level 4 cell outputs that are derived from Level 3 short-range filters with the same directional preference but different simple cell orientations. Thus the long-range filter provides the extra degree of freedom that enables Level 5 cells to function as "direction" cells, rather than "orientation" cells.

The long-range spatial filter broadcasts each Level 4 signal over a wide spatial range in Level 5. Competitive, or lateral inhibitory, interactions within Level 5 contrast-enhance this input pattern to generate spatially sharp Level 5 responses. A winner-take-all competitive network (Grossberg, 1973, 1982) can transform even a very broad input pattern into a focal activation at the position that receives the maximal input. The winner-take-all assumption is a limiting case of how competition can restore positional localization. More generally, we suggest that this com-

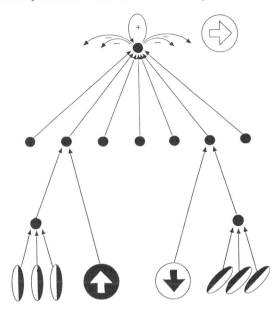

Figure 11. The long-range spatial filter combines sustained-transient cells with the same preference for direction-of-motion, including cells whose sustained cell inputs are sensitive to opposite directions-of-contrast and to different orientations.

petitive process partially contrast-enhances its input pattern to generate a motion signal whose breadth across space increases with the breadth of its inducing pattern. A contrast-enhancing competitive interaction has also been modeled at the complex cell level of the SOC Filter (Grossberg, 1987b; Grossberg and Marshall, 1989). The Level 5 cells of the MOC Filter are, in other respects too, computationally homologous to the SOC Filter complex cells.

In the 1-D theory, we define the transformation from Level 4 to Level 5 by letting

$$r_i = x_{iL}y_i^+ + x_{iR}y_i^-, \tag{5}$$

and

$$l_i = x_{iL}y_i^- + x_{iR}y_i^+, \tag{6}$$

be the total response of the local right motion and left motion detectors, respectively, at position i of Level 4. Signal r_i increases if either a light-dark or a dark-light contrast pattern moves to the right. Signal l_i increases if either a light-dark or a dark-light contrast pattern moves to the left.

These local motion signals are assumed to be filtered independently by a long-range operator with a Gaussian kernel

$$G_{ji} = H \ \exp \ [-(j-i)^2/2K^2], \tag{7}$$

which defines the input fields of the Level 5 cells. Thus, there exist two types of direction sensitive cells at each position i of Level 5. The activity at i of the right-motion sensitive cell is given by

$$R_i = \sum_j r_j G_{ji}, \tag{8}$$

and the corresponding activity of the left-motion sensitive cell is given by

$$L_i = \sum_j l_j G_{ji}. \tag{9}$$

We assume that contrast-enhancing competitive, or lateral inhibitory, interactions within Level 5 generate the activities which encode motion information. In the simplest case, the competition is tuned to select that population whose input is maximal, as in

$$x_i^{(R)} = \begin{cases} 1 & \text{if } R_i > R_j, j \neq i \\ 0 & \text{otherwise,} \end{cases} \tag{10}$$

and

$$x_i^{(L)} = \begin{cases} 1 & \text{if } L_i > L_j, j \neq i \\ 0 & \text{otherwise.} \end{cases} \tag{11}$$

In the simulations summarized below, the above assumption was made for simplicity. The functions $x_i^{(R)}$ and $x_i^{(L)}$ change through time in a manner that idealizes parametric properties of many apparent motion phenomena. See Grossberg and Rudd (1989c, 1990b) for details. More generally, we suggest that the competitive process idealized by (10) and (11) performs a partial contrast enhancement of its input pattern and thereby generates a motion signal whose breadth across space increases with the breadth of its inducing pattern.

The total MOC Filter design is summarized in Figure 5.

XII. Continuous Motion Paths from Spatially Stationary Flashes

The model equations listed in Section 11 provide an answer to long-standing questions in the vision literature concerning why individual flashes do not produce a percept of long-range motion, yet long-range interaction between spatially discrete pairs of flashes can produce a spatially sharp percept of continuous motion. Such apparent motion phenomena are a

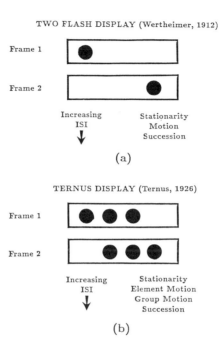

TWO TYPES OF APPARENT MOTION
DISPLAYS

TWO FLASH DISPLAY (Wertheimer, 1912)

(a)

TERNUS DISPLAY (Ternus, 1926)

(b)

Figure 12. Two types of apparent motion displays in which the two frames outline the same region in space into which the dots are flashed at successive times: In (a), a single dot is flashed, followed by an interstimulus interval (ISI), followed by a second dot. At small ISI's, the two dots appear to flicker in place. At longer ISI's, motion from the position of the first dot to that of the second is perceived. (b) In the Ternus display, three dots are presented in each frame such that two of the dots in each frame occupy the same positions. At short ISI's, all the dots appear to be stationary. At longer ISI's the dots at the shared positions appear to be stationary, while apparent motion occurs from the left dot in Frame 1 to the right dot in Frame 2. At still longer ISI's, the three dots appear to move from Frame 1 to Frame 2 as a group.

particularly useful probe of motion mechanisms because they describe controllable experimental situations in which nothing moves, yet a compelling percept of motion is generated. For example, two brief flashes of light, separated in both time and space, create an illusion of movement from the location of the first flash to that of the second when the spatiotemporal parameters of the display are within the correct range (Figure 12a).

Another well-known apparent motion display, originally due to Ternus

(1926/1950), illustrates the fact that not only the existence of a motion percept, but also its figural identity, may depend on subtle aspects of the display, such as the interstimulus interval, or ISI, between the offset of the first flash and the onset of the second flash (Figure 12b). In the Ternus display, a cyclic alternation of two stimulus frames gives rise to competing visual movement percepts. In Frame 1, three elements are arranged in a horizontal row on a uniform background. In Frame 2, the elements are shifted to the right in such a way that the positions of the two leftward-most elements in Frame 2 are identical to those of the two rightwardmost elements in Frame 1. Depending on the stimulus conditions, the observer will see either of two bistable motion percepts. Either the elements will appear to move to the right as a group between Frames 1 and 2 and then back again during the second half of a cycle of the display or, alternatively, the leftwardmost element in Frame 1 will appear to move to the location of the rightwardmost element in Frame 2, jumping across two intermediate elements which appear to remain stationary. The first percept is called "group" motion, and the second percept "element" motion. At short ISI's there is a tendency to observe element motion. At longer ISI's, there is a tendency to observe group motion.

Formal analogs of these and many other motion phenomena occur at Level 5 of the motion MOC Filter in response to sequences of flashes presented to Level 1. Intuitively, a signal for motion will arise when a continuous wave of activation connects the locations corresponding to the flashes; that is, when a connected array of the functions $x_i^{(R)}$, $x_{i+1}^{(R)}$, $x_{i+2}^{(R)}$, ... are activated sequentially through time, or alternatively the functions $x_i^{(L)}$, $x_{i-1}^{(L)}$, $x_{i-2}^{(L)}$, ... are activated sequentially through time. Each activation $x_i^{(R)}$, or $x_i^{(L)}$, represents the peak, or maximal activity, of a broad spatial pattern of activation across the network.

The broad activation pattern (Figure 13b) is generated by the long-range Gaussian filter G_{ji} in (7) in response to a spatially localized flash to Level 1 (Figure 13a). The sharply localized response function $x_i^{(R)}$ is due to the contrast-enhancing action of the competitive network within Level 5 (Figure 13c). A stationary localized $x_i^{(R)}$ response is hereby generated in response to a single flashing input.

In contrast, suppose that two input flashes occur with the following spatial and temporal separations. Let the positions of the flashes be $i = 1$ and $i = N$. Let the activity $r_1(t)$ in (5) caused by the first flash start to decay as the activity $r_N(t)$ in (5) caused by the second flash starts to grow. Suppose, moreover, that the flashes are close enough that their spatial

SPATIAL RESPONSE TO A
SINGLE FLASH

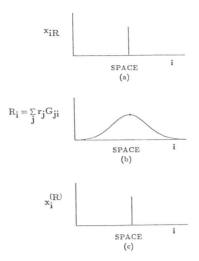

Figure 13. Spatial response of the MOC Filter to a point input. (a) Sustained activity of a Level 2 cell. (b) Total input pattern to Level 5. (c) Contrast-enhanced response at Level 5. Reprinted with permission from Grossberg and Rudd (1989c).*

patterns r_1G_{1i} and r_NG_{Ni} overlap. Then the total input

$$R_i = r_1G_{1i} + r_NG_{Ni} \qquad (12)$$

to the ith cell in Level 5 can change in such a way that the maximum value of the spatial pattern $R_i(t)$ through time, namely $x_i^{(R)}(t)$ in (10), first occurs at $i = 1$, then $i = 2$, then $i = 3$, and so on until $i = N$. A percept of continuous motion from the position of the first flash to that of the second will result.

This basic property of the MOC Filter is illustrated by the computer simulations from Grossberg and Rudd (1989c) summarized in Figures 14–16. Figure 14 depicts the temporal response to a single flash at position 1 of Level 1. The sustained cell response at position 1 of Level 2 undergoes a gradual growth and decay of activation (Figure 14b), although the position of maximal activation in the input to Level 5 does not change through time (Figure 14c). The temporal decay of activation in Figure 14b may be compared with the "visual inertia" discovered by Anstis and Ramachandran (1987, Figure 17) during their experiments on apparent motion.

* Copyright 1984 by the American Psychological Association.

TEMPORAL RESPONSE TO A
SINGLE FLASH

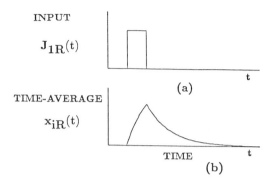

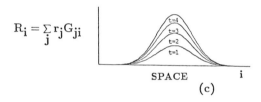

Figure 14. Temporal response of sustained response cells to a point input: (a) The input is presented for a brief duration at location 1. (b) The activity of the sustained response cell gradually builds up after input onset, then decays after input offset. (c) Growth of the input pattern to Level 5 through time with transient cell activity held constant. The activity pattern retains a Gaussian shape centered at the location of the input. Reprinted with permission from Grossberg and Rudd (1989c).*

Figure 15 illustrates an important implication of the fact that the Level 2 cell activations persist due to temporal averaging after their Level 1 inputs shut off. If a flash at position 1 is followed, after an appropriate delay, by a flash at position N, then the sustained response to the first flash [e.g., $x_{1R}(t)$] can decay while the response to the second flash [e.g., $x_{NR}(t)$] grows.

Assume for simplicity that the transient signals defined by equations (3) and (4) are held constant and consider how the waxing and waning of sustained cell responses control the motion percept. Then the total input pattern R_i to Level 5 can change through time in the manner depicted in Figure 16. Each row of Figure 16a illustrates the total input to Level 5 caused, at a prescribed time t, by $x_{1R}(t)$ alone, by $x_{NR}(t)$ alone, and

* Copyright 1984 by the American Psychological Association.

TEMPORAL RESPONSE TO
TWO SUCCESSIVE FLASHES

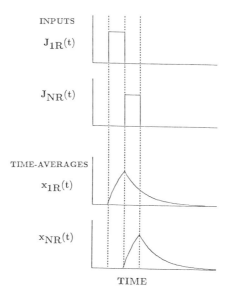

Figure 15. Temporal response of the sustained response cells at Level 2 to two successive point inputs. One input is presented briefly at location 1, followed by a second input at location N. For an appropriately timed display, the decaying response at position 1 overlaps the rising response at position N. Reprinted with permission from Grossberg and Rudd (1989c).[*]

by both flashes together. Successive rows plot these functions at equally spaced later times. As $x_{1R}(t)$ decays and $x_{NR}(t)$ grows, the maximum value of $R_i(t)$ moves continuously to the right. Figure 16b depicts the position $x_i^{(R)}(t)$ of the maximum value at the corresponding times.

XIII. Feature Integration and Spatial Attention Shifts

The conditions under which such a travelling wave of activation can occur are proved in Grossberg and Rudd (1989c) to be quite general. The phenomenon can arise whenever a decaying trace of one activation adds to an increasing trace of a second activation via spatially long-range Gaussian receptive fields before the sum is contrast-enhanced. Such a travelling wave may, for example, subserve certain shifts in spatial attention (Eriksen and Murphy, 1987; LaBerge and Brown, 1989; Remington and Pierce, 1984). It remains for future analyses to determine whether discrete jumps of spatial attention and continuous shifts of attention may receive a unified analysis in terms of the same formal constraints that explain how discrete flashes

* Copyright 1984 by the American Psychological Association.

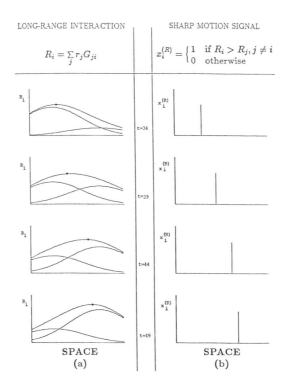

Figure 16. MOC Filter simulation in response to a two flash display. Successive rows correspond to increasing times: (a) The two lower curves in each row depict the total input to Level 5 caused by each of the two flashes. The input due to the left flash decreases while the input due to the right flash increases. The total input due to both flashes is a travelling wave whose maximum value moves from the location of the first flash to that of the second flash. (b) Position of the contrast-enhanced response at Level 5. Reprinted with permission from Grossberg and Rudd (1989c). *

or continuous apparent motion are perceived.

XIV. Augmenting the Static BCS

The design of the Motion BCS, and the symmetry principle which combines the Static BCS and Motion BCS into a unified theory, both came into view by noting and correcting incomplete features of the Static BCS model that was introduced by Grossberg and Mingolla (1985b, 1987). These features can be understood by inspecting Figure 1.

* Copyright 1984 by the American Psychological Association.

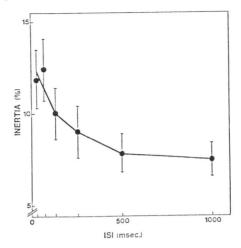

Figure 17. Strength of visual inertia as a function of the timing of dots that prime the direction of a subsequent apparent motion. Reprinted with permission from Anstis and Ramachandran (1987).*

A. Insensitivity to Input Transients

In Figure 1, the simple cells of the SOC Filter are modelled as oriented sustained-response cells. Sustained-response cells can respond with a constant output to a constant input. In contrast, simple cells *in vivo* are sensitive to transient changes in input patterns, including changes due to moving images.

When the SOC Filter is modified to be sensitive to image transients, it may be compared with the MOC Filter, which is obviously also sensitive to image transients. Such a comparison led to the discovery of FM Symmetry, and to the realization that both filters may be viewed as parallel halves of a larger system design.

The answer to how the SOC Filter computes image transients was suggested by another incomplete feature of the original SOC Filter model:

B. No Simple and Complex Off-Cells

The simple cells and complex cells in Figure 1 are all on-cells; they are activated when external inputs turn on. No simple or complex off-cells are represented. In contrast, the hypercomplex cells in Figure 1 include both on-cells and off-cells. This asymmetry in the network raises the question of how to design simple off-cells and complex off-cells to interact with the hypercomplex off-cells.

It turns out that problems (A) and (B), which seem to be two distinct

* Copyright 1984 by the American Psychological Association.

problems, have the same solution. Multiplicative coupling of transient on-cells and transient off-cells with oriented sustained on-cells define simple on-cells and off-cells, as well as complex on-cells and off-cells, that are sensitive to image transients.

In summary, including off-cells and the property of sensitivity to image transients in the SOC Filter leads to a more symmetric SOC Filter model which, when compared with the MOC Filter model, reveals a deeper principle of symmetric design. The remainder of this chapter shows how problems (A) and (B) may be solved, and describes how these solutions lead to the data implications summarized in Sections 1–10.

XV. Design of Simple On-Cells and Off-Cells in the SOC Filter

This section suggests a solution to the problems raised in Sections 14A and 14B. In Figures 1 and 4, pairs of like-oriented simple cells that are sensitive to opposite directions-of-contrast input to a single complex cell, which is insensitive to direction-of-contrast. Our task is to preserve this fundamental property while rendering the simple cells sensitive to image transients and defining both on-cells and off-cells of simple and complex type. To define simple on-cells that are sensitive to image transients, let a transient on-cell, as defined in equation (3), multiply each sustained cell in the pair of like-oriented cells depicted in Figures 1 and 4. This gives rise to a pair of like-oriented simple on-cells (Figure 18a) that are sensitive to opposite directions-of-contrast and are activated when properly oriented and positional inputs are turned on. In the 1-D model notation of equations (1) and (2), these cell responses are defined by $x_{iL}y_i^+$ and $x_{iR}y_i^+$, rather than x_{iL} and x_{iR} alone. As in Figures 1 and 4, a pair of simple on-cells with like-orientation but opposite direction-of-contrast inputs to a complex on-cell, as in Figure 18a. The complex on-cell is defined by summing the rectified outputs of the simple on-cells, as in the equation

$$c_i^+ = x_{iL}y_i^+ + x_{iR}y_i^+. \tag{13}$$

Likewise, a pair of simple off-cells can be defined by gating the pair of like-oriented sustained cells in Figure 1 with a transient off-cell, as defined in equation (4). The pair of simple off-cell responses is thus defined by $x_{iL}y_i^-$ and $x_{iR}y_i^-$, rather than x_{iL} and x_{iR} alone. The off-cells are activated when properly oriented and positioned inputs shut off. Such a pair of simple off-cells is depicted in Figure 20b, where it gives rise to a complex off-cell through the interaction

$$c_i^- = x_{iL}y_i^- + x_{iR}y_i^-. \tag{14}$$

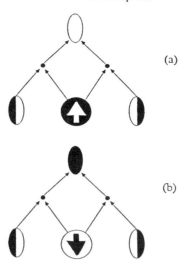

Figure 18. (a) A complex/orientation/on cell: Pairs of rectified sustained cells with opposite direction-of-contrast are gated by rectified transient on-cells to generate simple sustained-transient on-cells before the gated responses are added. (b) A complex/orientation/off cell: Pairs of rectified sustained cells with opposite direction-of-contrast are gated by rectified transient off-cells to generate simple sustained-transient off-cells before the gated responses are added.

By construction, both complex on-cells and off-cells are insensitive to direction of contrast.

Let the complex on-cell in Figure 18a input to hypercomplex on-cells as in Figure 1. In a similar fashion, let the complex off-cell in Figure 18b input to the hypercomplex off-cells in Figure 1. The process of gating sustained cells by transient cells to generate on-cells and off-cells in the Static BCS thus makes the overall design of this architecture more symmetric by showing how simple and complex on-cells and off-cells fit into the scheme.

XVI. FM Symmetry

The above refinement of the SOC Filter merely adds sensitivity to image transients in a manner consistent with Figure 1. Having done so, a comparison of the modified SOC Filter with the MOC Filter reveals the FM Symmetry principle that was introduced in Section 5. FM Symmetry is embodied in the following set of four equations, the first two from the MOC Filter, and the last two from the enhanced SOC Filter.

Left-Direction Motion Complex On-Cell

$$r_i = x_{iL} y_i^+ + x_{iR} y_i^- \tag{5}$$

Right-Direction Motion Complex On-Cell

$$l_i = x_{iL} y_i^- + x_{iR} y_i^+ \tag{6}$$

Vertical-Orientation Static Complex On-Cell

$$c_i^+ = x_{iL} y_i^+ + x_{iR} y_i^+ \tag{13}$$

Vertical-Orientation Static Complex Off-Cell

$$c_i^- = x_{iL} y_i^- + x_{iR} y_i^- \tag{14}$$

These equations describe all possible ways of symmetrically gating an opponent pair (x_{iL}, x_{iR}) of sustained cells with transient cells to generate two opponent pairs, (c_i^+, c_i^-) and (r_i, l_i), of output signals that are insensitive to direction-of-contrast. One opponent pair of outcomes (c_i^+, c_i^-) contains cell pairs that are insensitive to direction-of-motion, but sensitive to either the onset or the offset of an oriented contrast difference. These cells may be called complex/orientation/on cells and complex/orientation/off cells, respectively, as in equations (13) and (14). They belong to the SOC Filter.

The other opponent pair of outcomes (r_i, l_i) contains the MOC Filter cell pairs, schematized in Figure 19, that are sensitive to opposite directions-of-motion. These cells may be called complex/direction/left cells and complex/direction/right cells, as in equations (5) and (6). When both sets of pairs are combined into a single symmetric diagram, the result is shown in Figure 20. Figure 20 suggests that parallel, but interdependent, streams of static form and motion form processing arise in visual cortex because the cortex develops by computing all possible sustained-transient output signals that are independent of direction-of-contrast and organized into opponent on-cells and off-cells. Experimental tests of this prediction will require a coordinated analysis of cell types and processing levels.

XVII. 90° Orientations: From V1 to V2

An important consequence of the abstract symmetry described in Figure 20 is the familiar fact from daily life that opposite static orientations are 90° apart, whereas opposite motion directions are 180° apart, as summarized in Section 6.

The 90° symmetry of opposite orientations may be explained by the way in which perpendicular *end cuts* are generated at the hypercomplex cells of the Static BCS, as analysed in Grossberg and Mingolla (1985b). This perpendicularity property arises from the fact that the opponent feature of a complex/orientation/on cell is a complex/orientation/off cell. This mechanism is reviewed below for completeness. For those familiar with the end cut concept, the 90° symmetry may tersely be summarized as follows: Suppose that a vertical line end excites a complex/vertical/on cell in

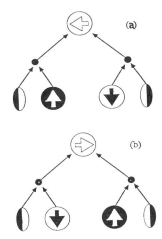

Figure 19. (a) A complex/direction/left cell: Pairs of rectified sustained cells with opposite direction-of-contrast are gated by pairs of rectified transient on-cells and off-cells, before the gated responses are added. (b) A complex/direction/right cell: Same as in (a), except sustained cells are gated by the opposite transient cell.

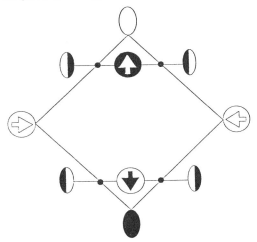

Figure 20. FM Symmetry: Symmetric unfolding of pairs of opponent orientation cells and opponent direction cells whose outputs are insensitive to direction-of-contrast. The gating combinations from Figures 20 and 21 are combined to emphasize their underlying symmetry.

Figure 1. Suppose that the end stopped competition inhibits hypercomplex/vertical/on cells at positions beyond the line end. Hypercomplex/horizontal/on cells at these positions are thereby activated, and generate a horizontally oriented end cut. In addition, hypercomplex/horizontal/off cells at these positions are inhibited by the opponent interaction. As a result, a net excitatory input is generated from the horizontally oriented hypercomplex cells to the horizontally oriented bipole cells of the CC Loop at that position. These excitatory end cut inputs cooperate across positions to generate a horizontal emergent segmentation, that is perpendicular to the vertical line, along the entire line end.

XVIII. 180° Opponent Directions from V1 to MT

The fact that opponent directions differ by 180°, rather than 90°, follows from the fact, summarized in Figure 19, that the opposite feature of a complex/direction cell is another complex/direction cell whose direction preference differs from it by 180°. When this latter property is organized into a network topography, one finds the type of direction hypercolumns that were described in MT by Albright, Desimone, and Gross (1984). A schematic explanation of how direction hypercolumns in MT may be generated from the orientation hypercolumns of V1 is shown in Figure 21. This explanation suggests that the pathways from V1 to MT combine signals from sustained cells and transient cells, as in Figure 19, in a different way than the pathways from V1 to V2, as in Figure 18.

XIX. Opponent Rebounds: Rapid Reset of Resonating Segmentations

A final refinement of the SOC Filter and MOC Filter design assumes that the opponent cell pairs shown in Figures 18 and 19 are capable of *antagonistic rebound*; that is, offset of one cell in the pair after its sustained activation can trigger an antagonistic rebound that transiently activates the opponent cell in the pair. A minimal neural model of such an opponent rebound, illustrated in Figure 22, is called a *gated dipole* (Grossberg, 1972, 1982, 1988). Such an antagonistic rebound, when appropriately embedded in an SOC Filter or MOC Filter, can reset a resonating segmentation in response to rapid changes in the stimulus, as discussed in Section 7. For example, suppose that horizontally oriented hypercomplex cells in the SOC Filter are cooperating with horizontally oriented bipole cells to generate a horizontal boundary segmentation in the CC Loop (Figure 1) when the input pattern is suddenly shut off. In the absence of opponent processing, the positive feedback signals between the active hypercomplex on-cells and bipole cells could maintain the boundary segmentation for a long time after input offset, thereby causing massive smearing of the visual percept in response to rapidly changing scenes.

Suppose, however, that due to opponent processing by gated dipoles, offset of the horizontal complex on-cells can trigger an antagonistic rebound

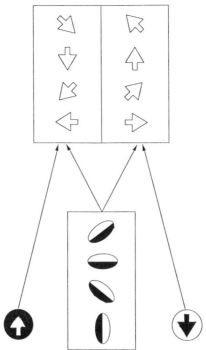

Figure 21. Orientation and direction hypercolumns: A single hypercolumn of orientation cells (say in $V1$) can give rise to a double hypercolumn of opponent direction cells (say in MT) through gating with opponent pairs of transient cells.

that activates the horizontal hypercomplex off-cells. The horizontal hypercomplex off-cells would then generate inhibitory signals to the horizontal bipole cells, as in Figure 1. These inhibitory signals would actively shut off the resonating segmentation, thereby preventing too much smearing from occurring. Such inhibitory signals from hypercomplex cells to bipole cells are predicted to be one of the inhibitory processes that control the amount of smearing caused by a moving image in the experiments of Hogben and DiLollo (1985).

This analysis of how antagonistic rebounds can reset a resonating segmentation leads to the prediction that gated dipoles occur at the complex cell level or the hypercomplex cell level (Figure 23) in the Static BCS and Motion BCS.

XX. MacKay Afterimages, the Waterfall Effect, and Long Range Motion Aftereffects

The previous sections argued that some positive aftereffects may be partly due to a lingering resonance in a CC Loop, and some negative af-

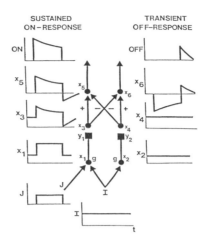

Figure 22. Example of a feedforward gated dipole: A sustained habituating on-response (top left) and a transient off-rebound (top right) are elicited in response to onset and offset, respectively, of a phasic input J (bottom left), when tonic arousal, I (bottom center), and opponent processing (diagonal pathways) supplement the slow gating actions (square synapses).

tereffects may be partly due to an antagonistic rebound that resets such a resonance. Within the Static BCS, negative aftereffects tend to activate perpendicular segmentations via the same 90° symmetry of the SOC Filter that generates perpendicular end cuts (Section 17). Due to this symmetry, sustained inspection of a radial image can induce a circular aftereffect if a blank field is subsequently inspected (MacKay, 1957). In a similar fashion, it follows from the 180° symmetry of the MOC Filter, summarized in Figure 21, that sustained inspection of a waterfall can induce an upward-moving motion aftereffect (MAE) if a blank field is subsequently attended (Sekuler, 1975).

The assumption that a level of gated dipoles occurs at, or subsequent to, Level 5 of the MOC Filter also provides an explanation of how a long-range MAE can occur between the locations of two flashes that previously generated apparent motion between themselves (von Grünau, 1986). As discussed in Section 12, a wave of apparent motion is synthesized at Level 5 due to interactions of the flashes through the long-range Gaussian filter described in equations (5)–(11). The gated dipoles at, or subsequent to, Level 5 will habituate to the wave of apparent motion much as they would in response to a "real" motion signal expressed at Level 5.

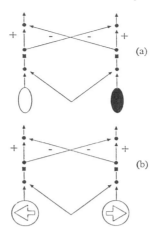

Figure 23. Opponent rebounds: When orientationally tuned complex cells in the SOC Filter are organized into gated dipole opponent circuits, as in (a), offset of a complex on-cell can transiently activate like-oriented complex off-cells, as well as perpendicular hypercomplex on-cells at the second competitive stage (see text). Offset of directionally tuned complex cells within the MOC Filter, as in (b), can transiently activate complex cells tuned to the opposite direction.

XXI. Concluding Remarks: FACADE Principles of Uncertainty, Complementarity, Summetry, and Resonance as a Foundation for Biological Vision Theories

The above results clarify that, whereas specialization of function surely exists during visual perception, it is not the type of specialization that may adequately be described by independent neural modules for the processing of edges, textures, shading, depth, motion, and color information. This is true because independent modules do not map well onto the perceptual demands of naturally occurring scenes. Each part of a visual scene often contains locally ambiguous information about edges, textures, shading, depth, motion, and color, all overlaid together. Humans and other seeing creatures are capable of using these multiple types of visual information cooperatively to generate an unambiguous 3-dimensional representation of Form-And-Color-And-DEpth; whence the term FACADE Theory as a name to unify all BCS and FCS circuits. The hyphens in "Form-And-Color-And-DEpth" emphasize the well-known fact that changes in perceived color can cause changes in perceived depth and form, changes in perceived depth can cause changes in perceived brightness and form, and so on. Every stage of visual processing *multiplexes* together several key properties of the scenic representation. It is a central task of biological vision theories to understand how the organization of visual information processing regulates which properties are multiplexed together at each processing stage, and how the stages interact to generate these properties.

FACADE Theory became possible through the discovery of several new principles of uncertainty, complementarity, symmetry, and resonance. Uncertainty principles show what combinations of visual properties cannot, in principle, be computed at a single processing stage (Grossberg, 1987a; Grossberg and Mingolla, 1985b). The theory has by now described how to design hierarchical and parallel interactions that can resolve these uncertainties using several processing stages. Hierarchical interactions are illustrated by the interactions of simple cells, complex cells, and hypercomplex cells to overcome, using hypercomplex end cuts, the computational uncertainties implied by the fact that the receptive fields of simple cells are oriented (Section 17). Parallel interactions occur between two subsystems, the Boundary Contour System (BCS) and the Feature Contour System (FCS), in order to be able to carry out computations that are computationally complementary. Principles of symmetry seem to govern the organization of these various subsystems, as FM Symmetry illustrates. Resonance principles are also operative, as in the design of the CC Loop.

The themes of uncertainty, complementarity, symmetry, and resonance show the inadequacy of modular and rule-based vision theories from an alternative computational perspective. Although the BCS, FCS, and their individual processing stages are computationally specialized, their *interactions* overcome computational uncertainties and complementary deficiencies to generate useful visual representations, rather than properties that may be computed by independent processing modules. Context-sensitive interactions also determine which combinations of positions, orientations, disparities, spatial scales, and the like will be cooperatively linked through resonance. Likewise, the FM Symmetry principle that integrates static form and motion form properties cannot be stated as a property of independent modules for form or motion perception, because the Static BCS and the Motion BCS each process aspects of both form and motion, and the design of each of these networks can best be understood as parts of a single larger system, as in Figure 20.

Such an interactive theory precludes the sharp separation between formal algorithm and mechanistic realization that Marr (1982) proposed. How computational uncertainties can be overcome, how complementary processing properties can be interactively synthesized, and how particular combinations of multiplexed properties may resonate or be symmetrically organized are all intrinsic properties of particular classes of mechanistic realizations, not conceptually separate instantiations.

Principles of uncertainty, complementarity, symmetry, and resonance also lie at the foundations of quantum mechanics and other physical theories. Mammalian vision systems are also quantum systems in the sense that they can generate visual percepts in response to just a few light quanta. The types of uncertainty, complementarity, symmetry, and resonance that have been articulated in FACADE Theory seem to be disclosing how the brain has adapted its design to harmoniously interact with the physical world of light.

References

1. Albright, T.D., Desimone, R., and Gross, C.G. (1984). Columnar organization of directionally sensitive cells in visual area MT of the macaque. *Journal of Neurophysiology*, **51**, 16–31.

2. Anderson, S.J. and Burr, D.C. (1987). Receptive field size of human motion detection units. *Vision Research*, **27**, 621–635.

3. Anstis, S. and Ramachandran, V.S. (1987). Visual inertia in apparent motion. *Vision Research*, **27**, 755–764.

4. Braddick, O.J. (1974). A short range process in apparent motion. *Vision Research*, **14**, 519–527.

5. Burr, D.C., Ross, J., and Morrone, M.C. (1986). Smooth and sampled motion. *Vision Research*, **26**, 643–652.

6. Cohen, M.A. and Grossberg, S. (1984). Neural dynamics of brightness perception: Features, boundaries, diffusion, and resonance. *Perception and Psychophysics*, **36**, 428–456.

7. DeValois, R.L., Albrecht, D.G., and Thorell, L.G. (1982). Spatial frequency selectivity of cells in macaque visual cortex. *Vision Research*, **22**, 545–559.

8. DeYoe, E.A. and van Essen, D.C. (1988). Concurrent processing streams in monkey visual cortex. *Trends in Neuroscience*, **11**, 219–226.

9. Eckhorn, R., Bauer, R., Jordan, W., Brosch, M., Kruse, W., Munk, M., and Reitboeck, H.J. (1988). Coherent oscillations: A mechanism of feature linking in the visual cortex? *Biological Cybernetics*, **60**, 121–130.

10. Eriksen, C.W. and Murphy, T.D. (1987). Movement of attentional focus across the visual field: A critical look at the evidence. *Perception and Psychophysics*, **42**, 29–305.

11. Gray, C.M., Konig, P., Engel, A.K., and Singer, W. (1989). Oscillatory responses in cat visual cortex exhibit inter-columnar synchronization which reflects global stimulus properties. *Nature*, **338**, 334–337.

12. Grossberg, S. (1972). A neural theory of punishment and avoidance, II. Quantitative theory. *Mathematical Biosciences*, **15**, 253–285.

13. Grossberg, S. (1973). Contour enhancement, short-term memory, and constancies in reverberating neural networks. *Studies in Applied Mathematics*, **52**, 217–257.

14. Grossberg, S. (1982). **Studies of mind and brain: Neural principles of learning, perception, development, cognition, and motor control.** Boston: Reidel Press.

15. Grossberg, S. (1987a). Cortical dynamics of three-dimensional form, color, and brightness perception, I: Monocular theory. *Perception and Psychophysics*, **41**, 87–116.

16. Grossberg, S. (1987b). Cortical dynamics of three-dimensional form, color, and brightness perception, II: Binocular theory. *Perception and Psychophysics*, **41**, 117–158.

17. Grossberg, S. (Ed.) (1988). **Neural networks and natural intelligence.** Cambridge, MA: MIT Press.

18. Grossberg, S. (1990). 3-D vision and figure-ground separation by visual cortex. Submitted for publication.

19. Grossberg, S. (1991a). Neural FACADES: Visual representations of static and moving Form-And-Color-And-DEpth. *Mind and Language*, in press.

20. Grossberg, S. (1991b). Why do parallel cortical systems exist for the perception of static form and moving form? *Perception and Psychophysics*, in press.

21. Grossberg, S. and Marshall, J. (1989). Stereo boundary fusion by cortical complex cells: A system of maps, filters, and feedback networks for multiplexing distributed data. *Neural Networks*, **2**, 29–51.

22. Grossberg, S. and Mingolla, E. (1985a). Neural dynamics of form perception: Boundary completion, illusory figures, and neon color spreading, *Psychological Review*, **92**, 173–211.

23. Grossberg, S. and Mingolla, E. (1985b). Neural dynamics of perceptual grouping: Textures, boundaries, and emergent segmentations, *Perception and Psychophysics*, **38**, 141–171.

24. Grossberg, S. and Mingolla, E. (1987). Neural dynamics of surface perception: Boundary webs, illuminants, and shape-from-shading. *Computer Vision, Graphics, and Image Processing*, **37**, 116–165.

25. Grossberg, S. and Mingolla, E. (1990a). Neural dynamics of motion segmentation: Direction fields, apertures, and resonant grouping. In M. Caudill (Ed.), **Proceedings of the international joint conference on neural networks**, January, **I**, 11–14. Hillsdale, NJ: Erlbaum Associates.

26. Grossberg, S. and Mingolla, E. (1990b). Neural dynamics of motion segmentation. In **Proceedings of Vision Interface '90**, Halifax, Nova Scotia, May 14–18.

27. Grossberg, S. and Mingolla, E. (1990c). Neural dynamics of motion segmentation: Direction fields, apertures, and resonant grouping. Submitted for publication.

28. Grossberg, S., Mingolla, E., and Todorović, D. (1989). A neural network architecture for preattentive vision. *IEEE Transactions on Biomedical Engineering*, **36**, 65–84.

29. Grossberg, S. and Rudd, M.E. (1989a). A neural architecture for visual motion perception: Group and element apparent motion. In M. Caudill (Ed.), **Proceedings of the international joint conference on neural networks**, June, I, 195–199. Piscataway, NJ: IEEE.

30. Grossberg, S. and Rudd, M.E. (1989b). Neural dynamics of visual motion perception: Group and element apparent motion. *Investigative Ophthalmology Supplement*, **30**, 73.

31. Grossberg, S. and Rudd, M.E. (1989c). A neural architecture for visual motion perception: Group and element apparent motion. *Neural Networks*, **2**, 421–450.

32. Grossberg, S. and Rudd, M.E. (1990a). Cortical dynamics of visual motion perception: Short- and long-range motion. *Investigative Ophthalmology Supplement*, **31**, 529.

33. Grossberg, S. and Rudd, M.E. (1990b). Cortical dynamics of visual motion perception: Short-range and long-range motion. Submitted for publication.

34. Grossberg, S. and Somers, D. (1990). Synchronized oscillations during cooperative feature linking in a cortical model of visual perception. Submitted for publication.

35. Grossberg, S. and Todorović, D. (1988). Neural dynamics of 1-D and 2-D brightness perception: A unified model of classical and recent phenomena. *Perception and Psychophysics*, **43**, 241–277.

36. Grossberg, S. and Wyse, L. (1990). Invariant recogntion of cluttered scenes by a self-organizing ART architecture: Figure-ground separation. *IEEE Expert*, in press.

37. Heggelund, P. (1981). Receptive field organization of simple cells in cat striate cortex. *Experimental Brain Research*, **42**, 89–98.

38. Hogben, J.H. and DiLollo, V. (1985). Suppression of visual persistence in apparent motion. *Perception and Psychophysics*, **38**, 450–460.

39. Hubel, D.H. and Wiesel, T.N. (1962). Receptive fields, binocular interaction and functional architecture in the cat's visual cortex. *Journal*

of Physiology, **160**, 106–154.

40. Hubel, D.H. and Wiesel, T.N. (1968). Receptive fields and functional architecture of monkey striate cortex. *Journal of Physiology*, **195**, 215–243.

41. Hubel, D.H. and Wiesel, T.N. (1977). Functional architecture of macaque monkey visual cortex. *Proceedings of the Royal Society of London (B)*, **198**, 1–59.

42. LaBerge, D. and Brown, V. (1989). Theory of attentional operations in shape identification. *Psychological Review*, **96**, 101–124.

43. MacKay, D.M. (1957). Moving visual images produced by regular stationary patterns. *Nature*, **180**, 849–850.

44. Marr, D. (1982). **Vision**. San Francisco: Freeman.

45. Nakayama, K. and Silverman, G.H. (1984). Temporal and spatial characteristics of the upper displacement limit for motion in random dots. *Vision Research*, **24**, 293–299.

46. Nakayama, K. and Silverman, G.H. (1985). Detection and discrimination of sinusoidal grating displacements. *Journal of the Optical Society of America*, **2**, 267–273.

47. Ramachandran, V.S. (1985). Apparent motion of subjective surfaces. *Perception*, **14**, 127–134.

48. Ramachandran, V.S., Rao, V.M., and Vidyasagar, T.R. (1973). Apparent motion with subjective contours. *Vision Research*, **13**, 1399–1401.

49. Remington, R. and Pierce, L. (1984). Moving attention: Evidence for time-invariant shifts of visual selective attention. *Perception and Psychophysics*, **35**, 393–399.

50. Sekuler, R. (1975). Visual motion perception. In E.C. Carterette and M.P. Friedman (Eds.), **Handbook of perception, Volume V: Seeing**. New York: Academic Press.

51. Tanaka, M. Lee, B.B., and Creutzfeldt, O.D. (1983). Spectral tuning and contour representation in area 17 of the awake monkey. In J.D. Mollon and L.T. Sharpe (Eds.), **Colour vision**. New York: Academic Press, 1983.

52. Ternus, J. (1926/1950). Experimentelle Untersuchungen über phänomenale Identität. *Psychologische Forschung*, **7**, 81–136. Abstracted and translated in W.D. Ellis (Ed.), **A sourcebook of Gestalt psychology**. New York: Humanities Press, 1950.

53. van Allen, E.J. and Kolodzy, P.J. (1987). Application of a boundary contour neural network to illusions and infrared sensor imagery. In M. Caudill and C. Butler (Eds.), **Proceedings of the IEEE first inter-**

national conference on neural networks, IV, 193–197. Piscataway, NJ: IEEE Press.

54. von der Heydt, R., Hänny, P., and Dürsteler, M.R. (1981). The role of orientation disparity in stereoscopic perception and the development of binocular correspondence. In E. Grastyán and P. Molnár (Eds.), **Advances in physiological sciences, volume 16: Sensory functions**. Elmsford, NY: Pergamon Press.

55. von Grünau, M.W. (1986). A motion aftereffect for long-range strobo-scopic apparent motion. *Perception and Psychophysics*, **40**, 31–38.

†Supported in part by the Air Force Office of Scientific Research (AFOSR 90-0175), DARPA (AFOSR 90-0083), and Hughes Research Labs (S1-903136).

I.5

The Structure and Interpretation of Neuronal Codes in the Visual System

BARRY J. RICHMOND
Laboratory of Neuropsychology
National Institute of Mental Health
Bethesda, MD 20892

LANCE M. OPTICAN
Laboratory of Sensorimotor Research
National Eye Institute
Bethesda, MD 20892

Physiological studies of vision generally assume that only the strength of the responses of visual system neurons matters. According to current interpretation, the neuron's functional role in vision is to signal how closely a stimulus falling on its receptive field matches some preferred stimulus (Barlow, 1972; Barlow, 1985). Work from our laboratory shows that neurons throughout the visual system actually use a much more complex code to carry information than has been generally assumed. We have found that these neurons show stimulus-dependent modulation of both the pattern and strength of their responses, Figure 1. We infer from these complex temporal codes that visual system neurons function more like information processors than feature encoders. The same neuron can participate in developing many different visual percepts, rather than just reporting similarities between current and preferred stimuli. This paper discusses how temporally modulated neuronal codes may areas in the visual system, and how they may be used in solving some computational tasks essential in visual perception.

Neural Networks for Perception   104   ISBN 0–12–741251–4
Volume 1
Human and Machine Perception

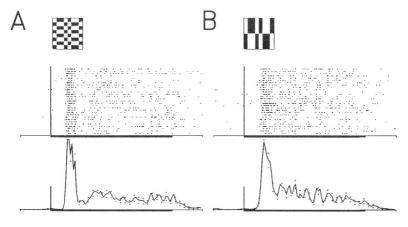

Figure 1. Responses of one striate cortical complex cell to two different stimulus patterns (upper row), each two degrees square, and presented centered on the receptive field. In the middle row, the responses are displayed as rows of dots in spike impulse diagrams, with time increasing from left to right and each row representing a different trial. The vertical line indicates the time of stimulus appearance and the dots show relative times of impulses. The heavy bar at the bottom indicates the 320 ms duration of stimulus presentation. Spike density diagrams (lower row) represent the probability that a neuronal impulse will occur. These were constructed by convolving the response with a Gaussian kernel, and then averaging these across the stimulus presentations (Richmond & Optican, 1987; Richmond *et al.*, 1990). The of the vertical line at stimulus onset represents a probability of 0.1/ms, or 100 spikes/trial/sec. This illustration shows a difference in firing pattern that depends on the stimulus presented. The response at the left shows a distinct pause after the initial burst of firing that is not present for the example at the right.

1. Defining the stimulus-response relation.

The responses of single visual system neurons can be interpreted correctly only if the representation of stimulus features in the neuronal responses is correctly identified, i.e., the complete stimulus-response relation must be characterized. We implemented an approach that treats each neuron as an information channel. Our goal has been, first, to characterize the input-output relation, seen here as the stimulus-response relation, and then to infer the functions carried out by the neurons.

To achieve the needed characterization, neurons must be tested with a set of stimuli that is adequate to derive the stimulus-response relation. Visual stimuli can be broken down into multiple, simple elements. These simple elements can be considered as axes in a stimulus space. Some of these such as luminance or color can be easily represented in physical terms, whereas others such as shape

Figure 2. The set of stimuli based on Walsh functions. The complete set included the same pictures with black and white exchanged. These stimuli form a complete basis for pictures of resolution 8x8, or less. This set can be extended to any resolution that increases as a power of two (Ahmed & Rao, 1975; Richmond *et al.*, 1987).

or texture are more difficult to define. For analytic purposes, pictures can be represented as sets of basic features constructed from complete, orthogonal basis sets. Pictures constructed from these sets can be considered as basic picture features. Such a set of stimuli should allow one to infer the stimulus-response relation, and from this, it should be possible to predict the neuronal response to any stimulus that can be made up from the basic set.

The stimulus set we used to investigate how picture features are represented, was a two-dimensional set of black and white patterns derived from complete, two-dimensional Walsh functions, Figure 2 (Ahmed & Rao, 1975; Richmond *et al.*, 1987). Although any orthogonal set would do, the Walsh functions have two particularly useful properties. First, they are defined to take values of 1 and -1 only, so they can be produced on relatively inexpensive hardware, and second, each single picture element, a pixel, is uncorrelated with any of the other pixels, i.e., whether surrounding elements are black or white can not be predicted by knowing the value of the pixel under consideration. This latter property makes the Walsh set a good one for stimulating nonlinear components of the stimulus-response relation.

To correctly characterize the stimulus-response relation, the aspects of responses that depend on the stimulus must be correctly identified. Because examining responses across stimuli showed that they varied in pattern, i.e., temporal modulation, as well as the strength across stimuli we chose a method that characterizes the responses completely, a complete linear decomposition

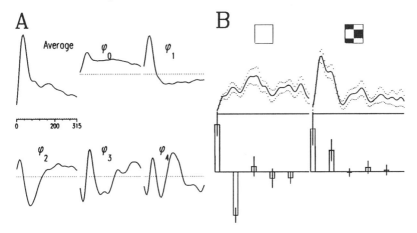

Figure 3. A. The average response and the first 5 principal components, ϕ_0-ϕ_4 derived from all of the responses to all of the Walsh patterns from one neuron. The average was subtracted from each response before the principal components were extracted. The principal components, which are the eigenvectors of the data domain covariance matrix, are ordered so that each successive principal component represents progressively smaller amounts of variance across the data set. Thus, truncation of the set provides the optimal linear representation of the data, in the least mean squared error sense, for any given number of transform elements. B. The line spectral representation of two responses in terms of principal components. The spike densities of the responses to two stimuli are shown above and the relative amounts of each principal component needed to reconstruct the responses is shown below. These two examples show the decomposition for the responses to two patterns given by the neuron whose the principal components are shown in panel A. The obvious difference in the firing pattern is quantified by the difference in the value of the second principal component.

into principal components, Figure 3. Conveniently, the first principal component, ϕ_0, correlates highly with response strength (Richmond & Optican, 1987; Richmond & Optican, 1990).

This approach can fail to identify the stimulus-responses relationship if the neurons under study only respond to stimuli that are off these axes, i.e., the neurons respond to other stimuli, but none of the ones in the basis set. So far the neurons we have studied responded well to a large number of the Walsh patterns, Figure 4.

Although our representations in the input space and the output space are linear, i.e., simple addition of the basic elements will reconstruct the original pattern, there is no requirement that a linear transformation describe the functional relation between the inputs or Walsh patterns, and the outputs or principal components. The input-output mapping can be examined statistically (Richmond & Optican, 1987), or, alternatively, with Shannon's information theory (Shannon, 1948; Abramson, 1963; Optican & Richmond, 1987). To apply information theory, we defined the Walsh patterns as an input or picture

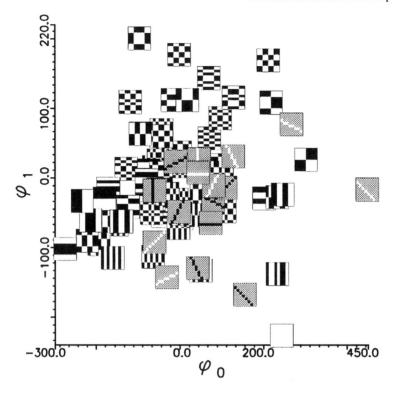

Figure 4. Plot of responses to the Walsh patterns and a set of oriented bar-like stimuli. The Walsh pattern is placed at the location of the response to that pattern as determined by the weights of the first two principal components. The horizontal axis shows the response strength as represented by the first principal component, and the vertical axis is one aspect of the temporal modulation as represented by the second principal component. The responses to the bars and Walsh patterns are largely intermingled. In addition, the responses to the Walsh patterns cover a larger proportion of this response plane than the responses to the bars. Thus, the responses to the Walsh patterns span the classical response space in a continuous and extensive manner. This demonstrates that the Walsh set is an adequate set to study the stimulus-response relation for this neuron.

code, and we utilized the principal components as a response code. We then quantified the mutual or transmitted information (Optican & Richmond, 1987; Gawne *et al.*, 1989).

Using this approach we compared the information transmitted about the Walsh patterns in several brain regions; parvocellular lateral geniculate neurons, complex cells in primary visual cortex, pulvinar neurons, and inferior temporal neurons. These brain regions were studied because they are part of a pathway considered to subserve functions related to complex visual pattern recognition (Mishkin, 1982; Ungerleider & Mishkin, 1982).

TABLE I.			
Region	Information(bits)		Ratio
	Strength Code	Temporal Code	T3/T1
Ganglion Cell Fibers	.52	.67	1.29
Lateral Geniculate Nucleus	.47	.67	1.42
Pulvinar	.35	.60	1.70
Striate Cortex	.32	.67	2.10
Inferior Temporal Cortex	.20	.46	2.30

Table I. The average amount of information conveyed by neurons based on codes derived from the response strength, and the first 3 principal components, along with their ratios (Optican & Richmond, 1987; Gawne et al., 1989; Richmond & Optican, 1990; McClurkin et al., 1988a; McClurkin et al., 1988b).

The average amount of information transmitted about the stimulus set in each of the areas ranges between 0.4 and 0.7 bits, showing that neurons in each of these regions carry similar amounts of information. However, the relative amounts of information carried in the temporally modulated part of the code, increases for neurons that are further from the retina, Table I. Thus, the temporally modulated part of the code becomes more important in the responses of neurons further along in the processing stream.

2. Stimulus parameter interactions.

Because neurons are sensitive to changes in several stimulus parameters such as luminance and pattern, the responses contain a mixture of information about the variables. For example, complex cells in primary visual cortex were envisioned by Hubel and Wiesel as extracting orientation independent of stimulus contrast or position. However, the responses of a neuron to a bar often depend on the contrast sign of the stimulus, Figure 5. Thus, the messages contained in the responses of single neurons are ambiguous because the response can only be interpreted correctly when other stimulus parameters are known (Hubel & Wiesel, 1962; Richmond et al., 1990).

Presumably, these ambiguities could be resolved by selective activation of neurons in a large population. In this view the stimulus is represented by the subpopulation of active neurons. Encoded information about different stimulus variables is represented across further subdivisions of the population representing the stimulus. Decoding the values of different stimulus variables such as brightness and pattern could only be carried out by decoding the information from the neuronal population if the neurons have different relative sensitivities to different stimulus variables.

Our discovery that there is more stimulus-related information in a multivariate temporal code than in a response strength code raises the possibility that information about different stimulus parameters can be decoded from the responses of a single neuron. Thus, in the example in Figure 5, the

Figure 5. Orientation tuning curves made from the responses of a supragranular striate cortical complex cell to white (heavy line) and dark (light line) bars presented on a grey background. The distance from the center indicates the response strength, and the angle represents the orientation of the bar. The bars were centered on the receptive field and were 0.25° in width (Richmond *et al.*, 1990; Richmond & Optican, 1990).

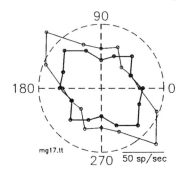

neuron is unsuitable for defining orientation based on a response strength code because the orientation of a stimulus can only be decoded if other information, here the contrast sign, is available (Richmond *et al.*, 1990). However, the pattern of the responses elicited by white bars was frequently different from the pattern elicited by black bars, Figure 6. Thus, it seems possible to decode the information about different stimulus variables, here orientation and contrast sign, from the responses of a single neuron (Richmond & Optican, 1990).

It would be especially convenient if information about individual stimulus parameters were related to individual temporal patterns as represented by the principal components, e.g., stimulus pattern might be represented by the response strength, and luminance information might be represented in the temporal code as represented by the second principal component. Unfortunately, that hope is not realized, Figure 7 (Gawne *et al.*, 1987). Nonetheless, because this analysis shows that the information has been independently encoded it could be separably decoded from just a few neurons if the code were known.

For the population decoding scheme outlined above, neurons would have to have different sensitivities, i.e., different tuning curves. In that case the responses could presumably be decoded from the population. However, this decoding would be sensitive to changes in the relative sensitivities of the neurons, so effects such as differential habituation could be devastating to the decoding process. With a multivariate code, it is possible for neurons to represent different stimulus characteristics by combining different messages in a single response. In this case, changes in sensitivity due to processes such as habituation might affect all of the messages simultaneously, thus interfering less with decoding.

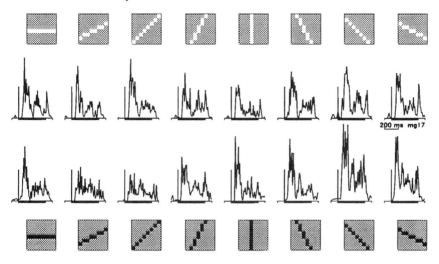

Figure 6. Responses of one neuron to bar-like stimuli at 8 orientations. The upper row shows the responses to a white bar, and the lower row shows the responses to a black bar, both on a grey background. These responses are taken from a complex cell in either layer 2 or 3 of primary visual cortex. The responses to the white bar show weak directional tuning in terms of response strength, whereas there is sharp tuning to the black bar. The response pattern elicited by the white and black bars often differs.

3. The multiplex-filter hypothesis.

The results from our experiments in inferior temporal cortex showed that several patterns of response were related to the stimuli, and the informational analysis showed that these temporal patterns each carried independent information. Thus, we proposed a multiplex-filter hypothesis: each neuron can be considered as if it multiplexed information from several independent channels, each carrying out a spatial-to-temporal transformation (Optican & Richmond, 1987).

A simple model can be formed based on this multiplex-filter hypothesis, Figure 8. The specific form of the model will depend on the data being modeled. To accurately model data taken from parvocellular neurons in the lateral geniculate, a simple nonlinearity compressing luminance values is needed early in each channel, labeled nonlinearity in Figure 8. In all other respects the model is linear. Although this model contains a nonlinearity it describes a very well-behaved relation. To extend this model so that it can simulate the input-output relation of complex cells in striate cortex, a small amount of cross-linking needs to be added between the channels, after the spatial filter, and before generating the temporal waveforms, Figure 9.

Figure 7. Average amount of information carried about pattern and luminance by the spike count, solid bars, and the first three principal components, hollow bars. The stimuli were made up of 8 one-dimensional Walsh patterns (bottom row of Figure 2) and their contrast reversed mates presented at 7 different pairs of luminances, The information was calculated as if the stimuli varied in pattern only, luminance only, and both. Comparing the height of the black and white bars shows that more than half of the information about pattern in the three part temporal code is carried by the first principal component, whereas substantially less than half of the information carried about luminance is carried by the first principal component. Thus, there is information about both pattern and luminance is carried by all of the principal components, although in different proportions.

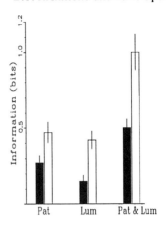

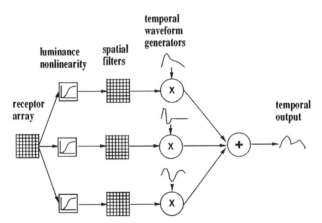

Figure 8. Diagramatic representation of the multiplex-filter model. The principal components are taken as basic temporal waveforms. If the weights for the nonlinearity and the pixels in the spatial filter are adjusted so that the model's output gives the best least-squared error estimate of the responses to the Walsh patterns presented at the input, the model will predict the responses to arbitrary patterns, i.e., patterns not in the Walsh set (Optican & Richmond, 1986; Gawne *et al.*, 1988).

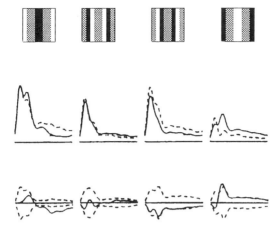

Figure 9. Predicted, dotted lines middle row, and actual responses, solid lines middle row, for one striate cortical complex cell using the model in Figure 8. The parameters of the model were adjusted to give the lowest mean squared error between the predicted and the actual responses to 8 one-dimensional Walsh patterns (taken from the lower row of Figure 2), and their contrast reversed mates. All of the Walsh patterns were presented at 7 different sets of luminances that varied widely in both contrast and mean luminance. The test stimuli were constructed by combining two 1-dimensional Walsh patterns, here the seventh and second from the left, combined in the four possible combinations, i.e., positive contrast for both, positive for the first and negative for the second, and their contrast reversed combinations. These test patterns are schematically illustrated above the responses. The lower row of traces (solid lines) shows the residual error at each point in time. The 95% confidence interval is also shown (dotted line) (Richmond *et al.*, 1989; Richmond & Optican, 1986; Optican & Richmond, 1986).

4. Decoding multiplex messages.

To decode this multidimensional neuronal code the rules about how the stimulus variables are mapped into the responses must be discovered. The results illustrated in Figure 7 show that stimulus dimensions are not simply assigned to different basic response patterns, i.e., different principal components. In an experiment where the luminance as well as the stimulus pattern was varied, the responses of striate cortical complex cells to each different stimulus pattern were found to lie in a squashed ellipsoidal region within a multidimensional response space spanned by the first three principal components. The planes used to approximate these squashed ellipsoids were observed to be different in orientation and extent for many different stimulus patterns. In the classical feature model, the code is the pattern of activity in the population, and the stimulus pattern is represented as a subset of active neurons. Our results suggest that information about stimulus pattern could be decoded from a small group, perhaps as few as three, of neurons by determining the plane of their activity in the neuronal response space (Richmond *et al.*, 1989).

Discovering the structure of a neuronal code is one step in learning how to build a visual system. Another step is to learn whether the extra information carried in the temporally modulated signal increases the decodability of neuronal responses. To examine the decodability a simple neural network was trained using back propagation to signal a one if a neuronal signal was elicited by one pattern and a zero if the neuronal signal was elicited by another pattern (Hertz *et al.*, in press). There were two observations. When the first five principal components were used as the input the network converged in about one-half the time needed when the response strength alone was the input. Second, the network classified the patterns correctly significantly more often when the principal component code was used as the input. Thus, this simple network showed better performance at classifying patterns when it used the temporally modulated responses of the neurons.

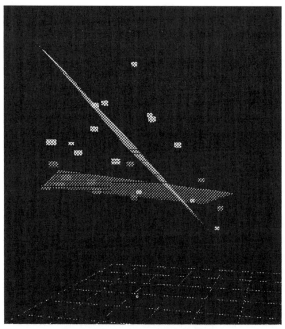

Figure 10. Responses to two Walsh patterns, each presented at 7 different luminances. The responses to each Walsh pattern at 7 different luminances were plotted in a 3 dimensional space whose axes are the weights of the first three principal components. The average response to a Walsh pattern at a particular luminance is shown as a small cube. The responses all lie in a small volume of this space, and the planes leaving the smallest residual error have been placed in the figure. The responses to the Walsh patterns defined planes with a different orientation in this space.

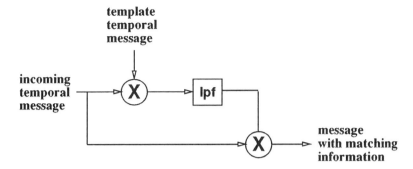

Figure 11. A simple scheme for weighting temporal messages by the degree of correlation with the template of the desired signal. The mechanism requires that messages be temporally modulated. In the case of neurons with colateral axonal terminations, the responses from a neuron could be correlated against different templates at different terminations. The lpf is a low pass filter.

5. Feature selection.

To function properly the visual system must associate patterns that occur at different locations, so that they may be recognized as part of a single object. This problem has recently received wide attention when it was discovered that neurons separated by several millimeters in visual cortex intermittently show oscillations that have the same frequency. It was proposed that the oscillations represented selection of feature detecting neurons that were binding a shared feature (Eckhorn *et al.*, 1988; Eckhorn *et al.*, 1989; Gray *et al.*, 1989; Gray *et al.*, 1990). Our discovery that neurons carry several temporally modulated messages multiplexed into the response suggests an alternative mechanism wherein these temporally modulated signals could be compared through correlation. The degree of correlation between messages could be used to determine how much emphasis to give their common message in the output, Figure 11. Such a mechanism would always be active and therefore it would be used by all neurons at all times. This mechanism would also have other advantages. The receptive fields of neurons grow as information converges at each subsequent stage of processing. If neurons at each successive processing stage simply summed their inputs, a loss of spatial resolution would occur. The nonlinear mechanism used here would preserve spatial resolution because when messages correlate, the resulting new message has all of the features of the original messages, preserving its description of the stimulus. Since this can happen for any message, resolution has been preserved.

A similar temporal correlation mechanism could also be used for recognition of remembered images. Whereas in the spatial correlation the template would be present at the time it was needed, in a recognition system the template to be matched would have to be stored, and then recalled when messages for observed stimuli arrived. The output of the correlation could be integrated as shown in the upper path in Figure 12, and then compared to a threshold, which if crossed would trigger one decision, and if not crossed would trigger another. At the stage where the multiplication takes place the response to the current stimulus should contain information about the remembered stimulus.

We have found evidence that is consistent with this prediction. Monkeys were trained to signal whether a test stimulus was the same as or different from a sample stimulus presented a few hundred milliseconds earlier. We have found that inferior temporal neurons carry information about the current stimulus, and its experimental significance, i.e., whether it is presented in the sample, or test condition, and whether the test stimulus matches or doesn't match the sample stimulus. In addition, two-thirds of the neurons carry significant amounts of information about the sample stimulus in the response to the test stimulus, a result consistent with the correlation matching hypothesis (Eskandar et al., 1991; Optican et al., 1991).

6. Feature linking.

The brain is organized into a sequence of processing regions. Each region contains a complete representation of the visual field. In general, as the neurons located in regions further from the retina are studied, the optimal stimuli become more complex. In the traditional model, the lateral geniculate nucleus neurons represent spots, primary visual cortex neurons represent bars or edges at particular orientations, and in inferior temporal cortex, the neurons represent complex stimuli such as brushes, hands, and faces. It is assumed that the percept of a complicated pattern is built up from the conjunction of messages across the different processing regions (Gross et al., 1972; Ungerleider & Mishkin, 1982). A complete percept includes information that is emphasized in many of these areas.

To form a complete percept, information about stimulus attributes that are quite dissimilar must be associated. The temporal messages that best represent different attributes almost certainly arise in different brain regions, each of which emphasizes a different stimulus feature (Ungerleider & Mishkin, 1982). The several different temporal messages that emphasize different stimulus features could be brought together in associative memories. For example, a high resolution message about stimulus location coming from a brain region emphasizing that information would be accompanied by a low resolution message about stimulus pattern, and vice versa. Regions that receive these complementary message sets from different regions, could integrate them through use of associative memories, Figure 12.

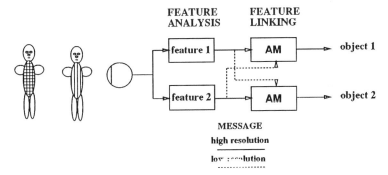

Figure 12. Mechanism to associate patterns from two different areas of cortex using associative memory elements and temporally modulated message tags. In this example, the two cartoons could be discriminated by the textures of their torsos, or their locations. If information about texture was processed in a different region or pathway from information about location, then to form an accurate percept requires that information about texture and location be associated. Using temporally modulated messages, some location information would be carried in a low resolution message in the area analyzing the texture, whereas some texture or pattern information would be carried in low resolution message in the areas analyzing the location. Feeding the outputs from these high resolution analytic regions through associative memories would provide a mechanism to link the correct messages based on the lower resolution messages acting as tags. The AM is an associative memory using temporal correlation.

7. Interpreting Neuronal Codes.

In the past, the responses of neurons in the visual system have been interpreted in terms of their strengths. Because neurons have been considered to represent different stimulus features, e.g., different orientations, the description of the stimulus has been assumed to to be encoded in the population distribution of activity in the different brain regions. Our results show that neurons carry information about several stimulus aspects in their responses. Thus, the response of a single neuron can be regarded as a description, not an abstraction, of the stimulus. As the number of neurons used increases, the estimate of the stimulus properties improves. Thus, the responses of many neurons are needed to develop an accurate stimulus description. In this new interpretation, it is *not* necessary to examine the entire population of neurons to interpret the message that has been encoded. The message can be decoded from *any* subset of active neurons. The penalty for using too small a subset would a loss of accuracy in decoding the message. The prediction from this hypothesis is that a loss of neurons used to perform a particular function would lead to decreased accuracy in the ability to perform that function. Thus, when a brain region that carries out a high resolution analysis loses function entirely, through damage or disease, the information about that parameter carried in other pathways could still preserve some degraded function.

8. Conclusion.

Previous hypotheses about the role of single neurons in vision have been based on the connection between a single optimal feature or receptive field structure and the strength of neuronal responses. However, temporal encoding of visual information is a fundamental property of neurons throughout the visual system. To account for the stimulus-dependent temporal modulation we proposed the multiplex-filter hypothesis which forms the basis for successful models of neuronal function. In addition, the use of temporally modulated messages provides a basis for mechanisms to carry out higher functions such as featural binding and pattern recognition. Thus, a single principle can be used to derive many properties necessary to explain visual function.

REFERENCES:

Abramson, N. (1963): *Information theory and coding*, New York: McGraw-Hill.

Ahmed, N. and Rao, K. R. (1975): *Orthogonal Transforms for Digital Signal Processing*, Berlin: Spring-Verlag.

Barlow, H. B. (1972): Single units and sensation: A neuron doctrine for perceptual psychology. *Perception* 1, 371-394.

Barlow, H. B. (1985): The role of single neurons in the psychology of perception. *Quarterly Journal of Experimental Pschology* 37A, 121-145.

Eckhorn, R., Bauer, R., Jordan, W., Brosch, M., Kruse, W., Munk, M., and Reitboeck, H. J. (1988): Coherent oscillations: A mechanism of feature linking in visual cortex?. *Biol. Cybern.* 60, 121-130.

Eckhorn, R., Reitboeck, H. J., Arndt, M., and Dicke, P. (1989): Feature linking via stimulus-evoked oscillations: Experimental results form cat visual cortex and functional implications from a network model. *Abstr. International Conference on Neural Networks* 1, 723-730.

Eskandar, E. N., Richmond, B. J., and Optican, L. M. (1991): Role of inferior temporal neurons in visual pattern recognition: I. Temporal encoding of current and recalled information. *Investigative Ophthalomology and Visual Science, ARVO Abstr. Supp.* in press.

Gawne, T. J., McClurkin, J. W., Optican, L. M., and Richmond, B. J. (1988): Lateral geniculate neurons in awake behaving primates: III. Successful predictions of a multi-channel model. *Soc. Neuroscience Abstr.* 14, 309.

Gawne, T. J., Optican, L. M., and Richmond, B. J. (1989): Estimating information transmitted by neurons.. *Soc. Neuroscience; Abstr.* 15, 1054.

Gawne, T. J., Richmond, B. J., and Optican, L. M. (1987): Striate cortex neurons do not confound pattern, duration, and luminance. *Soc. Neurosci. Abs.* 13, 631.

Gray, C. M., Engel, A. K., König, P., and Singer, W. (1990): Stimulus-dependent neuronal oscillations in cat visual cortex: Receptive field properties and feature dependence. *Europeon J. Neuroscience* 2, 607-619.

Gray, C. M., König, P., Engel, A., and Singer, W. (1989): Oscillatory responses in cat visual cortex exhibit inter-columnar synchronization which reflects global stimulus poperties. *Nature* 338, 334-337.

Gross, C. G., Rocha-Miranda, C. E., and Bender, D. B. (1972): Visual properties of neurons in inferotemporal cortex of the macaque. *J. Neurophysiol.* 35, 96-111.

Hertz, J. A., Richmond, B. J., Hertz, B. G., and Optican, L. M. (in press): Neural decoding. In *Proceedings of the NATO Advanced Workshop on Visual Processes*, ed. B. Lee and A. Valberg, eds., London: Plenum.

Hubel, D. H. and Wiesel, T. N. (1962): Receptive fields, binocular interaction and functional architecture in the cat's visual cortex. *J. Physiol. (Lond.)* **160**, 106-154.

McClurkin, J. W., Gawne, T. J., Richmond, B. J., Optican, L. M., and Robinson, D. L. (1988a): Lateral geniculate neurons in awake behaving primates: I. Responses to B&W 2-D patterns. *Soc. Neuroscience Abstr.* **14**, 309.

McClurkin, J. W., Optican, L. M., Richmond, B. J., and Robinson, D. L. (1988b): Encoding of visual stimuli in the pulvinar of the monkey. *Investigative Ophthalomology and Visual Science, ARVO Abstr. Supp.* **29**, 295.

Mishkin, M. (1982): A memory system in the monkey. *Philos. Trans. R. Soc. Lond.* **298**, 85-95.

Optican, L. M. and Richmond, B. J. (1986): Temporal encoding of pictures by striate neuronal spike trains. II. Predicting complex cell responses. *Society for Neuroscience; Abstract* **12**, 431.

Optican, L. M. and Richmond, B. J. (1987): Temporal encoding of two-dimensional patterns by single units in primate inferior temporal cortex. III. Information theoretic analysis. *J. Neurophysiol.* **57**, 162-178.

Optican, L. M., Richmond, B. J., and Eskandar, E. N. (1991): Role of inferior temporal neurons in visual pattern recognition: II. Temporal correlation of current and recalled information. *Investigative Ophthalomology and Visual Science, ARVO Abstr. Supp.* in press.

Richmond, B. J. and Optican, L. M. (1986): Temporal encoding of pictures by striate neuronal spike trains. I. The multiplex-filter hypothesis. *Society for Neuroscience; Abstract* **12**, 431.

Richmond, B. J. and Optican, L. M. (1987): Temporal encoding of two-dimensional patterns by single units in primate inferior temporal cortex: II. Quantification of response waveform. *J. Neurophysiol.* **57**, 147-161.

Richmond, B. J. and Optican, L. M. (1990): Temporal encoding of two-dimensional patterns by single units in primate primary visual cortex: II. Information transmission. *J. Neurophysiol.* **64**, 370-380.

Richmond, B. J., Optican, L. M., and Gawne, T. J. (1989): Neurons use multiple messages encoded in temporally modulated spike trains to represent pictures. In *Seeing Contour and Colour*, ed. J. J. Kulikowski and C. M. Dickinson, pp. 701-710. Oxford: Pergamon Press.

Richmond, B. J., Optican, L. M., Podell, M., and Spitzer, H. (1987): Temporal encoding of two-dimensional patterns by single units in primate inferior temporal cortex: I. Response characteristics. *J. Neurophysiol.* **57**, 132-146.

Richmond, B. J., Optican, L. M., and Spitzer, H. (1990): Temporal encoding of two-dimensional patterns by single units in primate primary visual cortex: I. Stimulus-response relation. *J. Neurophysiol.* **64**, 351-369.

Shannon, C. E. (1948): A mathematical theory of communication. *Bell Syst. Tech. J.* **27**, 379-423.

Ungerleider, L. G. and Mishkin, M. (1982): Two cortical visual systems. In *Analysis of Visual Behavior*, ed. D. J. Ingle, M. A. Goodale, R. J. W. Mansfield, pp. 549-586. Cambridge: MIT Press.

I.6

Self-Organization of Functional Architecture in The Cerebral Cortex

SHIGERU TANAKA
NEC Corporation
Tsukuba, Ibaraki, Japan

I. Introduction

Columnar organizations of the visual cortex which were discovered by Hubel and Wiesel (1962, 1977) are thought to serve as the functional units in visual information processing such as feature detection. The discovery of the columnar organizations has stimulated theoretical research as well as experimental investigation. Theoreticians have proposed various mathematical models to clarify the mechanisms of information processing and the formation of the columnar organizations. However, despite the accumulation of mathematical models, a unified picture of the columnar organizations, namely functional architecture, has yet to be established. The word "functional architecture" implies that there is mutual regulation between neural activity related to brain functions and neural network structures. In other words, neural activity is generated in the neural networks, and these neural networks are, at the same time, modified by the neural activity. Considering the importance of such functional-structural relationships, we have conducted research on activity-dependent self-organization of neural networks in order to obtain a better understanding of functional architecture.

As noted above, many mathematical models were proposed for the activity-dependent self-organization of the ocular dominance column (ODC) (Von der Malsburg, 1979; Miller et al., 1989; Tanaka, 1989, 1990a, 1990c), orientation column (Von der Malsburg, 1973; Bear et al., 1987; Linsker, 1986;

120

Tanaka, 1990a), and topographic map (Willshaw & Von der Malsburg, 1976; Amari, 1980). All of these models were basically built on the assumption of learning rules which are classified into the Hebbian mechanism of synaptic plasticity (Hebb, 1949). From a theoretical viewpoint, we may say that the Hebbian mechanism is essential to the activity-dependent self-organization of neural networks. Recently, biologists have been revealing molecular mechanisms of synaptic plasticity (Collingridge & Bliss, 1987; Kleinschmidt, et al., 1987) which seem to support the Hebbian mechanism hypothesis. The problem for theoreticians is to elucidate what type of Hebbian mechanism is used in early developmental processes. It is necessary to build a realistic and mathematically elaborated general theory for such synaptic plasticity which would explain and predict experimental observations.

II. Self-Organization of Synaptic Connections

A. Basic Hypothetical Mechanisms

In order to describe the activity-dependent self-organization of neural connections, three basic mechanisms are postulated (Tanaka, 1990a,b):
(1) modifiable synapses are stabilized due to a postsynaptic factor released from the dendrites of the target cells;
(2) stability of the synapses is also regulated by a presynaptic factor which might be synthesized in presynaptic cell bodies and transported through axons to presynaptic terminals;
(3) if presynaptic spike activity coincides with postsynaptic local membrane depolarization (hyperpolarization), the synapse is stabilized (destabilized).

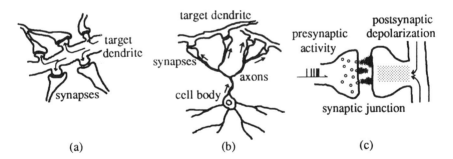

Fig. 1. Three basic mechanisms for synaptic stabilization.
(a) The postsynaptic factor is secreted from the target cell to the presynaptic buttons through the dendrites. (b) The presynaptic factor is sent from the presynaptic cell to the synapses by the axonal transport. (c) When the presynaptic activity coincides with the postsynaptic membrane depolarization, the synapse is stabilized.

Let us now discuss the biological meanings of the above-mentioned mechanisms in more detail.

Mechanism (1) predicts the competition among synapses for the limited amount of the postsynaptic factor which is secreted from the target neurons. If there is a small number of synapses within a region whose size is determined by the diffusion length of the factor, each synapse takes a sufficient amount of the factor to become stabilized. On the other hand, if there is a large number of synapses within the region, the amount of the factor which one neuron can take decreases. This mechanism is important in the sense that it gives rise to a winner-take-all process together with mechanism (3) (Fig.1(a)).

Mechanism (2) describes stabilization by the presynaptic factor which is synthesized in a presynaptic cell body and sent through its axon to terminals. It is thought that the synaptic stabilization attributed to the presynaptic factor occurs only within a limited region in which terminals of the axon from the presynaptic cell body arborize because the factor cannot be transported to the outside of this region. (Fig.1(b))

Mechanism (3) implies that if the neurotransmitter is released from the presynaptic side synchronously with the occurrence of the postsynaptic membrane depolarization, then the synapse receives a reward which promotes its stabilization. On the other hand, if the release of the neurotransmitter and the postsynaptic membrane hyperpolarization take place synchronously, a penalty is imposed on the synapse, causing the synapse to destabilize. We shall call this synaptic stabilization mechanism a local Hebbian rule. This hypothetical mechanism is a likely model for explaining experimentally observed synaptic plasticity (Collingridge & Bliss, 1987). (Fig.1(c))

B. Mathematical Formulation

Based on the three hypothetical mechanisms, we can express a basic equation describing the formation of stable synaptic connections between two neuronal layers as follows:

$$
\frac{d}{dt}\rho_{j,k,\mu}(t) = \rho_{j,k,\mu}(t)\left[\kappa_0 - \kappa_1\sum_{\mu'}\sum_{k'}\rho_{j,k',\mu'}(t)\right] + \varepsilon_{j,k,\mu}
$$

$$
+ \frac{g}{\tau_s}\int_{t-\tau_s/2}^{t+\tau_s/2}\zeta_j(t')\eta_{k,\mu}(t')\rho_{j,k,\mu}(t')dt' , \qquad (2.1)
$$

where $\rho_{j,k,\mu}(t)$ represents the density of modifiable connections from the presynaptic cell body at position k to position j on the dendrite in the postsynaptic layer. Symbol μ stands for the type of presynaptic cells or that of afferent pathways. If we take the geniculocortical projection as an example, the types of pathways correspond to the ipsilateral or contralateral pathway, parvocellular or magnocellular pathway, on-center or off-center pathway, and so on.

The first term on the right-hand side of Eq. (2.1) stands for the stabilization rate due to the postsynaptic factor. The summation of synaptic connection densities with respect to k' and μ' in this term means that the amount of the available postsynaptic factor is only determined by the synaptic terminal density, which leads to the saturation effect in the synaptic connection density.

$\varepsilon_{j,k,\mu}$ in the second term is a nonnegative-valued function of j, k and μ, which represents the stabilization rate by the presynaptic factor. Outside of the region where $\varepsilon_{j,k,\mu} > 0$, the birth-and-death process of stable synapses cannot take place.

The third term is a mathematical description of the local Hebbian mechanism. $\zeta_j(t)$ and $\eta_{k,\mu}(t)$ are the membrane potential on the dendrite at position j, and the firing frequency elicited from the cell body of type μ at position k. The coefficients κ_0 and κ_1 are positive constants. The coefficient g stands for the effectiveness of the Hebbian mechanism, and takes a positive value. The relevant Hebbian term should be averaged over the time course for synaptic stabilization τ_s. Since the time course for synaptic stabilization is longer than that for electrical activities, the synaptic connection density can be taken outside the integration.

For a complete description of activity-dependent self-organization of neural networks, we need other equations concerning the time evolution of electrical activities $\zeta_j(t)$ and $\eta_{k,\mu}(t)$. Hereafter, $\eta_{k,\mu}(t)$ is assumed to be a Gaussian stochastic process specified by the average value $\eta_{k,\mu}^{AV}$ and the correlation function $\langle \delta\eta_{k,\mu}(t)\delta\eta_{k',\mu'}(t')\rangle$. On the other hand, the membrane potential in the cortical cell $\zeta_j(t)$ is generated by the input of the firing frequency $\eta_{k,\mu}(t)$. Therefore, the third term behaves in a probabilistic manner. If we write the term as $W_{j,k,\mu}(t)\rho_{j,k,\mu}(t)$ and express $W_{j,k,\mu}(t)$ by the sum of its average $\overline{W}_{j,k,\mu}(t)$ and fluctuation $\delta W_{j,k,\mu}(t)$, the basic equation can be re-expressed in the following way:

$$\frac{d}{dt}\rho_{j,k,\mu}(t) = \rho_{j,k,\mu}(t)\left[\kappa_0 - \kappa_1 \sum_{\mu'}\sum_{k'} \rho_{j,k',\mu'}(t) + \overline{W}_{j,k,\mu}(t) + \delta W_{j,k,\mu}(t)\right] + \varepsilon_{j,k,\mu} \quad .$$

$$(2.2)$$

This equation describes the population dynamics of the system in which an enormous number of species compete for their survival. The averaged term related to the activity dependence, $\overline{W}_{j,k,\mu}(t)$, is expressed as follows:

$$\overline{W}_{j,k,\mu}(t) = g\zeta_j^{AV}\eta_{k,\mu}^{AV} + \frac{g}{\tau_S}\int_{t-\tau_s/2}^{t+\tau_s/2} \langle \delta\zeta_j(t')\delta\eta_{k,\mu}(t')\rangle dt' \quad . \quad (2.3)$$

By expressing the fluctuation of the membrane potential $\delta\zeta_j(t)$ in the postsynaptic layer in terms of the fluctuation of firing frequency $\delta \eta_{k,\mu}(t)$, the time-averaged cross-correlation function is given as follows:

$$\frac{1}{\tau_s} \int_{t-\tau_s/2}^{t+\tau_s/2} \langle \delta \zeta_j(t') \delta \eta_{k,\mu}(t') \rangle dt' = \sum_j' \sum_k' \sum_\mu' V_{j;j'}^{\text{post}} \Gamma_{k,\mu;\ k',\mu'}^{\text{pre}} \rho_{j',k',\mu'}(t) , \quad (2.4)$$

where $V_{j;j'}^{\text{post}}$ represents the synaptic interaction function in the postsynaptic layer. $\Gamma_{k,\mu;\ k',\mu'}^{\text{pre}}$ denotes the spatial part of the correlation function of the presynaptic activities as follows:

$$\Gamma_{k,\mu;\ k',\mu'}^{\text{pre}} = \int_{-\infty}^{+\infty} \langle \delta \eta_{k,\mu}(t+t') \delta \eta_{k',\mu'}(t) \rangle dt' . \quad (2.5)$$

Function $V_{j;j'}^{\text{post}}$ consists of three types of interactions: one is the interaction between two synapses on the same neuron's dendrites, another is the indirect interaction via excitatory neurons, and the other is the indirect interaction via inhibitory neurons. There is possibility that these interactions depend upon the morphology of indivisual neurons. However, such dependence on neuronal morphology is omitted as the first-order approximation. The synaptic interaction function $V_{j;j'}^{\text{post}}$ is assumed to be calculated by the use of the immutable intracortical connections averaged over the possible arborization of axons and dendrites.

The fluctuation term is expressed as follows:

$$\delta W_{j,k,\mu}(t) = \frac{g}{\tau_s} \int_{t-\tau_s/2}^{t+\tau_s/2} \left[\eta_{k,\mu}^{AV} \delta \zeta_j(t') + \zeta_j^{AV} \delta \eta_{k,\mu}(t') \right] dt' . \quad (2.6)$$

Synaptic stabilization can be affected by this fluctuation. The higher-frequency modes of the fluctuation, however, do not have much influence on the slowly varying process of the synaptic stabilization. Therefore, the variance of this fluctuation can be roughly evaluated as follows:

$$\langle [\delta W_{j,k,\mu}(t)]^2 \rangle = \frac{\tau_c}{\tau_s} \gamma^2 O(\overline{W^2}) , \quad (2.7)$$

where γ is a rough estimate for the ratio of the standard deviation to the average firing frequency elicited from the presynaptic neurons.

C. Reformulation Based on Thermodynamics

Now, we limit ourselves to the case of sufficiently small positive $\varepsilon_{j,k,\mu}$. From detailed analyses of the local and global stabilities of Eq. (2.2), which were discussed in depth elsewhere (Tanaka, 1990b), it is found that Eq. (2.2) describes a winner-take-all process of synaptic connections and that it shows the global stability of its solutions. That is, for any j, when $W_{j,k,\mu}$ is the maximum of all the $W_{j,k',\mu'}$'s, there is only one stable fixed point for the synaptic configuration such that only $\rho_{j,k,\mu}$ takes a large positive value and the others take much smaller values of the order of $\varepsilon_{j,k,\mu}$. Let us define $\sigma_{j,k,\mu}$ as the normalized synaptic connection density in the local equilibrium configuration of synapses. $\rho_{j,k,\mu}$ scales with the total synaptic density $\bar{\rho}$ as follows:

$$\rho_{j,k,\mu} = \bar{\rho}\,\sigma_{j,k,\mu} \quad . \tag{2.8}$$

As a result of the winner-take-all process, $\sigma_{j,k,\mu}$ satisfies the following:

$$\sigma_{j,k,\mu} = 0 \text{ or } 1 \text{, for any } j, k \text{ and } \mu , \tag{2.9}$$

$$\sum_{\mu, k} \sigma_{j,k,\mu} = 1 \text{, for any } j . \tag{2.10}$$

These are the same properties that the Potts spin variable satisfies (Wu, 1982). Therefore, we shall hereafter refer to $\sigma_{j,k,\mu}$ as the Potts spin.

Now, the time axis can be discretized with the time course for the synaptic stabilization τ_s, which corresponds to the nonlinear relaxation time for synaptic connection density from one locally stable state to another during development. The transient behavior of synaptic connection densities $\rho_{j,k,\mu}$'s, is omitted and $\rho_{j,k,\mu}$'s are replaced by the discrete Potts spins. The Potts spin configuration changes into a new configuration during τ_s after $W_{j,k,\mu}(t)$'s change.

The probability of transition from one spin configuration to another can be written by the error function and the variance given by Eq. (2.7). Since the error function can be approximated by the logistic function, the final form of the transition probability is expressed as:

$$P(\sigma_{j,k,\mu} = 1 \rightarrow \sigma_{j,k',\mu'} = 1) = \left\langle \Theta(W_{j,k',\mu'} - W_{j,k,\mu}) \right\rangle_{\{\delta W_{j,k,\mu}\}}$$

$$\cong \left[1 + exp\left\{ (\overline{W}_{j,k',\mu'} - \overline{W}_{j,k,\mu}) / T \right\} \right]^{-1} , \quad (2.11)$$

where T gives the width of the transition region and is given by

$$T \cong \frac{\sqrt{\pi}}{2} \gamma \sqrt{\frac{\tau_c}{\tau_s}} \quad . \tag{2.12}$$

By the use of this sigmoid function and the detailed balance condition whose validity is guaranteed by the global stability of Eq.(2.2), the equilibrium distribution function of Potts spins can be derived.

Finally, we obtain the equilibrium distribution function $\pi_{eq}(\{\sigma_{j,k,\mu}\})$, the Hamiltonian H:

$$\pi_{eq}(\{\sigma_{j,k,\mu}\}) = \frac{1}{Z} exp\left[-\frac{H(\{\sigma_{j,k,\mu}\})}{T}\right], \tag{2.13}$$

$$H = -sgn(\zeta^{AV}) \sum_j \sum_\mu \sum_{k \in B_{j,\mu}} \varphi_{k,\mu} \sigma_{j,k,\mu}$$

$$-\frac{q}{2} \sum_{j,j'} \sum_{\mu,\mu'} \sum_{\substack{k \in B_{j,\mu} \\ k' \in B_{j',\mu'}}} V_{j:j'}^{post} \Gamma_{k,\mu;k',\mu'}^{pre} \sigma_{j,k,\mu} \sigma_{j',k',\mu'}, \tag{2.14}$$

where $\varphi_{k,\mu}$ represents the averaged firing frequency elicited from the neuron specified by k and μ. The parameter T defined by Eq. (2.12) turns out to be the effective temperature, comparing the functional form of $\pi_{eq}(\{\sigma_{j,k,\mu}\})$ given by Eq. (2.13) with that of the equilibrium distribution function in the conventional statistical thermodynamics. The normalization factor Z also corresponds to the partition function and is given by the following equation:

$$Z = \sum_{\{\sigma_{j,k,\mu}=1,0\}} exp\left[-\frac{H(\{\sigma_{j,k,\mu}\})}{T}\right]. \tag{2.15}$$

Coefficient q in the second term of the Hamiltonian is given by

$$q = \frac{2\zeta_{SP}^{AV}}{|\zeta^{AV}|}. \tag{2.16}$$

The set $B_{j,\mu}$ is defined by

$$B_{j,\mu} = \{k \mid \varepsilon_{j,k,\mu} > 0\}. \tag{2.17}$$

This set represents a group of the presynaptic neurons which can project their axons to the postsynaptic position j. Therefore, this may play a role similar to that of the arbor function used in the model proposed by Miller et al. (1989).

Let us summarize the above discussion. In order to discuss the activity-dependent self-organization of afferent neural connections during development, we have only to consider the thermodynamics in the Potts spin system whose behavior is determined by the Hamiltonian H. This theory, however, is mainly concerned with a structural aspect of functional architecture. A functional aspect is thought to be describable by the RFs of neurons. The subsequent section will be devoted to the mathematical description of the RFs.

III. Receptive Fields

In formulating the RF which describes the neural response to input stimuli from the environment around animals, we will limit ourselves to a two-layer system in which the presynaptic layer corresponds to the sensory receptor layer.

The input-output relation of neural activity may take the following form:

$$(Output\ activity) = \Re \bullet (Input\ stimulus) , \qquad (3.1)$$

where " $\bullet$ " represents an operation which reflects the nonlinearity inherent in the neuronal input-output relationship. However, if we focus on the fluctuation of input and output activity, we can expect Eq. (3.1) to be reduced to a linear equation. In some sense, the RF can be looked upon as the response function. Thus, the RF function $\Re_{j,k,\mu}(t - t')$ is defined by the following:

$$\delta\eta_j(t) = \int_{-\infty}^{t} \sum_{\mu} \sum_{k} \Re_{j,k,\mu}(t - t')\delta S_{k,\mu}(t')dt' , \qquad (3.2)$$

where $\delta S_{k,\mu}(t)$ represents fluctuation in input stimuli from the environment to the sensory neuron specified by position k and cell type μ. The fluctuation in output activity of the neuron at position j is denoted by $\delta\eta_j(t)$

The RF function $\Re_{j,k,\mu}(t - t')$ can describe the response properties to the stimuli which convey temporal information as well as spatial information. For simplicity, however, the subsequent discussions of the RF function will be restricted to the static properties. As a result, the following static RF function is adopted:

$$R_{j,k,\mu} = \int_{-\infty}^{+\infty} \Re_{j,k,\mu}(t')dt' . \qquad (3.3)$$

Equation (3.2) is reduced to

$$\delta\eta_j(t) = \sum_{\mu} \sum_{k} R_{j,k,\mu}\delta S_{k,\mu}(t) . \qquad (3.4)$$

Since the input stimulus to the presynaptic neuron (k,μ) is propagated to other neurons through the lateral connections, the output activity of the neuron is given by

$$\delta\eta_{k,\mu}(t) = \sum_{\mu'} \sum_{k'} V^{pre}_{k,\mu;\ k',\mu'}\delta S_{k',\mu'}(t) . \qquad (3.5)$$

The propagation of the stimulus is described by the interaction function in the presynaptic layer $V^{pre}_{k,\mu;\,k',\mu'}$. By the use of this expression, the fluctuation in output activity of the postsynaptic neuron at j is given by

$$\delta\eta_j(t) = \sum_{j'} \sum_{\mu'} \sum_{k'} V^{post}_{j;\,j'} \sigma_{j',k',\mu'} \delta\eta_{k',\mu'}(t)$$

$$= \sum_{\mu} \sum_{k} \sum_{j'} \sum_{\mu'} \sum_{k'} V^{post}_{j;\,j'} \sigma_{j',k',\mu'} V^{pre}_{k',\mu';\,k,\mu} \delta S_{k,\mu}(t) \ . \tag{3.6}$$

Therefore, we obtain the formula of the static RF as follows:

$$R_{j,k,\mu} = \sum_{j'} \sum_{\mu'} \sum_{k'} V^{post}_{j;\,j'} \sigma_{j',k',\mu} V^{pre}_{k',\mu';\,k\mu} \ . \tag{3.7}$$

If the input stimulus is assumed to be Gaussian white noise, the above expression can be rewritten as the cross-correlation function:

$$R_{j,k,\mu}\delta(t-t') = \left\langle \delta\eta_j(t)\delta S_{k,\mu}(t') \right\rangle . \tag{3.8}$$

This implies that the RF function can be looked upon as the response function when the Gaussian white noise is applied to sensory receptors. Hereafter, we will use the expression for the RF given by Eq. (3.7).

Although the nonlinearity is thought to play an essential role in the nervous system, it is possible to deal with the neural activity as a minimal nonlinear system. That is, the fluctuation of activity is treated within the linear mathematics, while the nonlinearity is retained in the averaged activity. As shown in author's previous paper (1990b), the averaged activity is included in the postsynaptic interaction function $V^{post}_{j;\,j'}$ and works as a gate for signal transmission. If the averaged membrane potential in the cortex is positive, the interaction takes a finite value. On the other hand, if the averaged membrane potential is much hyperpolarized, the magnitude of the interaction decreases. Hence, the RF is also regulated by the averaged activity since it depends on the interaction function (Eq. (3.7)). Thus, in the minimal nonlinear system, information is mainly included in activity fluctuation while the gate function is performed by the averaged activity.

Now, the correlation function $\Gamma^{pre}_{k,\mu;\,k',\mu'}$ can be rewritten so that the theory of RF self-organization will be easier to discuss. $\Gamma^{pre}_{k,\mu;\,k',\mu'}$ includes the correlation of input stimuli from the environment and the neural connectivity within the sensory input layer. The latter intrinsic effect is included by the synaptic interaction function in the input layer $V^{pre}_{k,\mu;\,k',\mu'}$. In order to see the factorization of the correlation function into the experience-dependent factor and the intrinsic one, Eq. (3.5) is substituted for $\delta\eta_{k,\mu}(t)$ in Eq. (2.5). As a result, the static correlation function $\Gamma^{pre}_{k,\mu;\,k',\mu'}$ is transformed into

$$\Gamma^{pre}_{k,\mu;\,k',\mu'} = \sum_{\mu_1,\,k_1} \sum_{\mu'_1,\,k'_1} V^{pre}_{k,\mu;\,\mu_1,\,k_1} G_{k_1,\mu_1;\,\mu'_1,\,k'_1} V^{pre}_{k'_1,\mu'_1;\,k',\mu'} \qquad (3.9)$$

$$\text{with } G_{k,\mu;\,k',\mu'} = \int_{-\infty}^{+\infty} \langle \delta S_{k,\mu}(t+t')\,\delta S_{k',\mu'}(t)\rangle dt' \,, \qquad (3.10)$$

where $G_{k,\mu;\,k',\mu'}$ represents the correlation function of input stimuli from the environment. This stimulus correlation function can offer a mathematical basis for discussing experience dependence in self-organization. Therefore, when the postnatal development is mathematically analyzed, the function $G_{k,\mu,\,k',\mu'}$ which is suitable for rearing conditions should be modeled.

IV. Self-Organization of Receptive Fields

A. Derivation of Lyapunov Functional

The theory based on the thermodynamics in the Potts spin system excellently describes the experimental observations, for example, those of ODC formation under various rearing conditions (Tanaka, 1989, 1990a, c). However, it does not offer a way to directly analyze the electrophysiological response properties of neurons to light stimuli. In order to obtain the response properties of each neuron from a configuration of the Potts spins representing synaptic connections, we need a mathematical transformation from anatomical quantities to electrophysiological ones. When we attempt to discuss the development of RFs of cortical neurons, it will be convenient to directly obtain the RF functions without any such transformation. To this end, it is necessary to derive a theory of RF self-organization from the theory of the self-organization of synaptic connections.

In this section, auxiliary variables are first introduced. The Hamiltonian of the system is re-expressed in terms of these variables and their Lyapunov function is obtained. Next, the auxiliary variables are shown to represent the RF at low temperature. The mathematical transformation used here is a *dual* transformation from the synaptic connections to the RFs. By approximating the nonlinear term included in the Lyapunov function, we can derive an equation which is almost the same as the dynamical equation used in the Rayleigh-Bénard convective roll pattern.

Now, we adopt the following identity equation in order to transform the Hamiltonian which describes the self-organization of synaptic connections:

$$exp[\frac{1}{2}\sum_{i,\,j=1}^{N} x_i A_{i,j} x_j] = (2\pi)^{-N/2}[det\mathbf{A}]^{-1/2}\int d^N u$$

$$\times exp\left\{-\frac{1}{2}\sum_{i,\,j=1}^{N} u_i(\mathbf{A}^{-1})_{i,j}u_j + \sum_{i=1}^{N} u_i x_i\right\}. \qquad (4.1)$$

This equation is applied to the calculation of the partition function Z defined by Eq. (2.15) with the Hamiltonian H given by Eq.(2.14). When j, x_j and A_{ij} in the expression (4.1) are replaced with (j,k,μ), $\sum_{k',\mu'} (\mathbf{G V}^{\text{pre}})_{k,\,\mu;\,k',\mu'}\sigma_{j,k',\mu'}$, and $V_{j;j'}^{\text{post}}(\mathbf{G}^{-1})_{k,\mu;\,k'\mu'}$ in the Hamiltonian, respectively, another expression for the partition function is obtained as follows:

$$Z = (2\pi qT)^{-NM/2}[det(\mathbf{V}^{\text{post}}\mathbf{G}^{-1})]^{-1/2} \sum_{\{\sigma_{j,k,\mu}=1,\,0\}} \int d^{NM}\phi$$

$$\times exp\Big[-\frac{1}{2qT}\sum_{j,\,j'}\sum_{\mu,\,\mu'}\sum_{k,\,k'} (\mathbf{V}^{\text{post}\,-1})_{j;\,j'}G_{k,\mu;\,k'\mu'}\phi_{j,k,\mu}\phi_{j',k',\mu'}$$

$$+\frac{1}{T}\sum_{j,k,\mu} (\phi_{j,k,\mu} + sgn(\zeta^{AV})\varphi_{k,\mu})\sum_{k',\mu'} (\mathbf{G V}^{\text{pre}})_{k,\,\mu;\,k',\mu'}\sigma_{j,k',\mu'}\Big]. \qquad (4.2)$$

The summation with respect to all the spin configurations in Eq.(4.2) can be carried out, with the result that

$$Z = \int D[\phi]exp\left\{-\frac{F[\phi]}{T}\right\}, \qquad (4.3)$$

where the Lyapunov function $F[\phi]$ is given by

$$F[\phi] = \frac{1}{2q}\sum_{j,\,j'}\sum_{\mu,\mu'}\sum_{k,\,k'} (\mathbf{V}^{\text{post}\,-1})_{j;\,j'}G_{k,\mu;\,k',\mu'}\phi_{j,k,\mu}\phi_{j'k'\mu'}$$

$$-T\sum_{j} \log\left[\sum_{\mu}\sum_{k\in \mathbf{B}_{j,\mu}} exp\left\{\sum_{\mu',\,k'} (\mathbf{G V}^{\text{pre}})_{k,\mu;\,k',\mu}\left[\phi_{j,k',\mu'} + sgn(\zeta^{AV})\varphi_{k',\mu'}\right]/T\right\}\right].$$

$$\qquad (4.4)$$

$D[\phi]$ symbolically denotes $(2\pi qT)^{-NM/2}[det(\mathbf{V}^{\text{post}}\mathbf{G}^{-1})]^{-1/2}d^{NM}\phi$. The second nonlinear term on the right-hand side of Eq. (4.4) originates in the summation with respect to the Potts spin variables.

The obtaining of the Lyapunov functional $F[\phi]$ is simply a result of mathematical transformations. To see the physiological meaning of variables

$\{\phi_{j,k,\mu}\}$, the thermal average of $R_{j,k,\mu}$ is calculated. It is given by the following:

$$\langle R_{j,k,\mu}\rangle = \frac{1}{Z} \sum_{\{\sigma_{j,k,\mu}=1,\,0\}} R_{j,k,\mu} \exp\left(-\frac{H[\sigma]}{T}\right) . \tag{4.5}$$

The right-hand side of Eq. (4.5) can be rewritten by the use of the derivative with respect to $\sum_{k',\mu'} (\mathbf{GV}^{\text{pre}})_{k,\mu;\,k',\mu'}\sigma_{j,k',\mu'}$ as follows:

$$\frac{1}{Z} \sum_{\{\sigma_{j,k,\mu}=1,\,0\}} \left[T\frac{\delta}{\delta \sum_{k',\mu'} (\mathbf{GV}^{\text{pre}})_{k,\,\mu;\,k',\,\mu'}\sigma_{j,k',\,\mu'}} - sgn(\zeta^{AV})\varphi_{k,\mu} \right] \exp\left(-\frac{H[\sigma]}{T}\right) . \tag{4.6}$$

This can be further transformed in terms of $\{\phi_{j,k,\mu}\}$ into

$$\frac{1}{Z}\int D[\phi] \sum_{\{\sigma_{j,k,\mu}=1,\,0\}} \left[T\frac{\delta}{\delta \sum_{k',\mu'} (\mathbf{GV}^{\text{pre}})_{k,\,\mu;\,k',\,\mu'}\sigma_{j,k',\,\mu'}} - sgn(\zeta^{AV})\varphi_{k,\mu} \right]$$

$$\times \exp\left[-\frac{1}{4qT}\sum_{j,\,j'}\sum_{\mu,\,\mu'}\sum_{k,\,k'} (\mathbf{V}^{\text{post-}1})_{j;\,j'}G_{k,\mu;\,k',\mu'}\phi_{j,k,\mu}\phi_{j',k',\mu'}\right.$$

$$\left. +\frac{1}{T}\sum_{j}\sum_{\mu,\,k}\left\{\phi_{j,k,\mu} + sgn(\zeta^{AV})\varphi_{k,\mu}\right\}\sum_{\mu'}\sum_{k'} (\mathbf{GV}^{\text{pre}})_{k,\,\mu;\,k',\,\mu'}\sigma_{j,\,k',\,\mu'}\right] . \tag{4.7}$$

The derivative only operates the linear term with respect to $\sigma_{j,k,\mu}$ in the argument of the exponential function. Finally we obtain the following relation:

$$\langle R_{j,k,\mu}\rangle = \frac{1}{Z}\int D[\phi]\,\phi_{j,k,\mu}\,\exp\left(-\frac{F[\phi]}{T}\right)$$

$$= \langle\phi_{j,k,\mu}\rangle . \tag{4.8}$$

This indicates that the thermal average of the auxiliary variable $\phi_{j,k,\mu}$ is the same as the average of the RF, $R_{j,k,\mu}$.

Similarly, higher-order correlation functions with respect to $\{R_{j,k,\mu}\}$ can be calculated. For example, we can easily obtain

$$\langle R_{j,k,\mu}R_{j',k',\mu'}\rangle = \langle\phi_{j,k,\mu}\phi_{j',k',\mu'}\rangle - TqV_{j;\,j'}(\mathbf{G}^{-1})_{k,\mu;\,k',\mu'} . \tag{4.9}$$

This means that $\phi_{j,k,\mu}$ is not completely equivalent to $R_{j,k,\mu}$ so long as the second term remains. However, columnar organizations emerge only when T takes a small value. Thus, one can approximately identify $\phi_{j,k,\mu}$ as $R_{j,k,\mu}$ when the RFs of cortical neurons in the columnar organizations are discussed. Hereafter, we shall call $\phi_{j,k,\mu}$ as well as $R_{j,k,\mu}$ the RF of the neuron j.

B. Langevin Equation of Receptive Field Functions

If we want to describe the relaxation of variables $\{\phi_{j,k,\mu}\}$ with a Lyapunov function $F[\phi]$, we have only to use the Langevin equation:

$$\frac{d\phi_{j,k,\mu}}{dt} = - \frac{\delta F[\phi]}{\delta \phi_{j,k,\mu}} + \xi_{j,k,\mu}(t) \qquad (4.10)$$

with $\langle \xi_{j,k,\mu}(t) \rangle = 0$, and $\langle \xi_{j,k,\mu}(t) \xi_{j',k',\mu'}(t') \rangle = T \delta_{j,j'} \delta_{k,k'} \delta_{\mu,\mu'} \delta(t-t')$. (4.11)

The first term on the right-hand side of Eq. (4.10) is given by the derivative of the Lyapunov function with respect to $\phi_{j,k,\mu}$. The use of the Langevin equation (4.10) in describing the dynamic process of RF self-organization is justified by the fact that the equilibrium distribution function of $\{\phi_{j,k,\mu}\}$, $exp(-F[\phi]/T)/Z$, can be obtained from the equilibrium solution to the Fokker-Planck equation equivalent to (4.10). The calculation of this derivative leads to the following dynamical equation which describes the self-organization process of the RFs of cortical neurons:

$$\frac{d\phi_{j,k,\mu}}{dt} = -\frac{1}{q} \sum_{j'} \sum_{\mu'} \sum_{k'} (\mathbf{V}^{post-1})_{j;j'} G_{k,\mu; k',\mu'} \phi_{j',k',\mu'}$$

$$+ \frac{\sum_{\mu''} \sum_{k'' \in B_{j,\mu''}} (\mathbf{GV}^{pre})_{k,\mu; k'',\mu''} \, exp\left[\frac{1}{T}\left\{\sum_{k',\mu'} (\mathbf{GV}^{pre})_{k'',\mu''; k',\mu'}\left[\phi_{j,k',\mu'} + sgn(\zeta^{AV})\varphi_{k',\mu'}\right]\right\}\right]}{\sum_{\mu''} \sum_{k'' \in B_{j,\mu''}} exp\left[\frac{1}{T}\left\{\sum_{k',\mu'} (\mathbf{GV}^{pre})_{k'',\mu''; k',\mu'}\left[\phi_{j,k',\mu'} + sgn(\zeta^{AV})\varphi_{k',\mu'}\right]\right\}\right]}$$

$$+ \xi_{j,k,\mu}(t) \ . \qquad (4.12)$$

The first term describes a damping process of RFs by the interaction due to intracortical neuronal connections and by the stimulus correlation. Roughly speaking, the self-organized RFs are determined by the slowest damping mode. In contrast, the self-organized synaptic strengths in the Miller's model (1989) are determined by the fastest growing mode. However, considering that the RFs interact by the inverse matrix of the synaptic interaction while the synaptic strengths in Miller's model interact by the synaptic interaction, the basic mode selection mechanism of Eq. (4.12) is expected to be similar to that of the model.

The second term represents the growth rate which reflects the nonlinearity inherent in the Potts spin variables. Because of this nonlinearity, the divergence of the variable $\phi_{j,k,\mu}$ can be avoided. Therefore, the constraint for synaptic strengths in Miller's model can be interpreted as a substitute for this nonlinear term.

The third term represents the thermal noise which originates in the synaptic stabilization caused by the presynaptic factor. The finiteness of the temperature is necessary to explain the birth-and-death process of stable functional synapses. In general, this noise term is also important in discussing the behavior of the system in the vicinity of a phase transition point. For example, in the ODC segregation, there is a transition point which divides a stripe phase from a uniform phase (Tanaka, in preparation). Just below the transition point, stripe patterns with fluctuating band width can be seen because of thermal noise. Based on these considerations, Miller's equation is found to describe the development of sharply delimitated ODC patterns since it does not include the noise term. It should be noted that such noise effect cannot be derived only from the information-theoretical approaches such as Linsker's infomax principle (1989).

The RF functions $\phi_{j,k,\mu}$'s describe the electrophysiological response properties, while the Potts spin variables $\sigma_{j,k,\mu}$'s represent the distribution of stable synaptic connections. Therefore, these two should be clearly distinguished from each other. On the other hand, we may say that they describe different aspects of functional architecture. That is, there is a *duality* in the relationship between $\phi_{j,k,\mu}$ and $\sigma_{j,k,\mu}$.

V. Simple Application

A. Langevin Equation of Ocular Dominance

Having so far discussed a general theory of RF self-organization, we will now focus on applying the theoretical method described in the preceding section to the problem of ODC formation.

We assume here that retinotopic order is already completed and well defined before ODC formation begins. The Hamiltonian H appropriate for ODC formation (Appendix 1) is given by

$$H = -\frac{q(1-r)}{2}\sum_{j}\sum_{j'\neq j} U_{j\,;j'}s_j s_{j'}. \tag{5.1}$$

The parameter r denotes the correlation strength in activity between the left and right retinas.

Ocular dominance for neural response to monocular light stimuli is one type of substructure of the RF. Since the response of the neuron at position j may be induced by the afferent projection more effectively than by the lateral input from other posysynaptic neurons, we will obey the following definition of the ocular dominance of the neuron at position j, O_j, by using the Potts spin with regard to retinotopic order $\sigma_{j,k}^R$ (Appendix 1):

$$O_j = \sum_\mu \sum_k \mu \sigma_{j,k}^R R_{j,k,\mu} \ . \tag{5.2}$$

Therefore, it follows that

$$O_j = \sum_\mu \sum_k \mu \sum_j \sum_{\mu'} \sum_{k'} V_{j,j}^{post} \Gamma_{k,\mu;k',\mu'}^{pre} \sigma_{j',k',\mu'}$$

$$= q(1 - r) \sum_{j'} U_{j\,;\,j'} s_{j'} \ . \tag{5.3}$$

The auxiliary variable at position j, ψ_j, is now introduced through the calculation of Eq.(4.1) for the Hamiltonian (5.1). As already described for the relations between $R_{j,k,\mu}$ and $\phi_{j,\,k,\,\mu}$, the average value of the ocular dominance O_j can then be proven to be the average value of ψ_j. As a result, ψ_j will hereafter also be referred to as ocular dominance. The Langevin equation of ψ_j can also be derived in the same manner as discussed in Section IV:

$$\frac{d\psi_j}{dt} = - \frac{1}{q(1- r)} \sum_{j' \neq j} (\mathbf{U}^{-1})_{j,\,j'} \psi_{j'} + tanh(\psi_j/T) + \xi_j(t) \tag{5.4}$$

with $\langle \xi_j(t) \rangle = 0$, and $\langle \xi_j(t)\xi_{j'}(t') \rangle = T\delta_{j,\,j'}\delta(t-t')$. \tag{5.5}

Further discussions on Eqs. (5.4) and (5.5) lead to the following partial differential equation (Appendix 2):

$$\frac{d\psi(\mathbf{x},t)}{dt} = \varepsilon\psi(\mathbf{x},t) - (\nabla^2 + Q_0^2)^2 \psi(\mathbf{x},t) - B[\psi(\mathbf{x},t)]^3 + \xi(\mathbf{x},t) \tag{5.6}$$

with $\langle \xi(\mathbf{x},t) \rangle = 0$, and $\langle \xi(\mathbf{x},t)\xi(\mathbf{x}',t') \rangle = \frac{T}{A}\delta(\mathbf{x}- \mathbf{x}')\delta(t-t')$, \tag{5.7}

where the parameter ε is as follows:

$$\varepsilon = - \frac{8\tilde{U}_{Q_0}}{\tilde{U}_{Q_0}^{''} Q_0^2} \cdot \frac{T_0 - T}{T} \cdot Q_0^4 \tag{5.8}$$

$$\text{with } T_0 = q(1 - r)\widetilde{U}_{Q_0} \ . \tag{5.9}$$

Parameters A and B are positive constants.

Equation (5.6) takes the same form as the dynamical equation which describes the time evolution of the vertical element of the velocity vector representing the liquid flow in the Rayleigh-Bénard convection (Greenside et al., 1982) if the noise $\xi(\mathbf{x},t)$ is omitted. According to the theory of the convection, the roll pattern appears for $\varepsilon \geq 0$. Therefore, the temperature T_0 in this system is analogous to the critical Rayleigh number of the convective system.

The Lyapunov functional $F[\psi(\mathbf{x},t)]$ for Eq. (5.6) becomes

$$F[\psi(\mathbf{x},t)] = \int \left\{ -\frac{1}{2}\psi(\mathbf{x},t)\left[\varepsilon - (\nabla^2 + Q_0^2)^2\right]\psi(\mathbf{x},t) + \frac{B}{4}[\psi(\mathbf{x},t)]^4 \right\}d\mathbf{x} \ . \tag{5.10}$$

This is essentially the same as the free energy functional which describes the behavior of the domain structure of magnetic thin films (Garel and Doniach, 1982). This equivalence suggests that there are common mechanisms between ODC formation and domain structure formation in the magnetic thin films, as noted before (Tanaka, 1990a, c). The emergence of stripe patterns can be mainly attributed to the competition subserving the phenomena. In fact, the domain structure in magnetic thin films can also be described by the Ising spin model with competition between the short-range ferromagnetic interaction and the long-range magnetic dipole interactions (Garel & Doniach, 1982).

B. Origin of Straight Parallel Stripes in Monkey ODC

Several mathematical models (Swindale, 1980; Miller et al., 1989; Tanaka, 1990a) were able to reproduce spatially segregated patterns. However, these were usually labyrinth-like patterns in which the direction of each band is irregular and the patterns include many branches and end points even though the bands maintain a constant width. On the other hand, the monkey ODC pattern has a specific feature in that it shows a straight parallel stripe (Hubel & Wiesel, 1977), which should be distinguished from the labyrinth-like pattern as found in simulated results of the mathematical models. To understand the reason why the monkey ODC stripe pattern is straight and parallel, we will analyze the mathematical form of the synaptic interaction function on the basis of the theory developed so far.

Two typical interaction functions will be adopted. One is the short-range positive and long-range negative stepwise interaction function (S) (Eq. (A3.1)). The other is the mexican-hat-type interaction function (M) which is given as the sum of short-range positive and long-range negative Gaussian functions (Eq. (A3.2)). The major difference between the two interaction functions is the distribution of axon terminals of inhibitory interneurons. That is, the tail of interaction function (M) spreads to infinity even though the value of the interaction becomes infinitesimal. On the other hand, interaction function (S) suddenly vanishes at a finite length. The cutoff of this interaction function gives rise to the oscillatory behavior of the Fourier-transformed interaction function. When the interaction strength of only the inhibitory part increases (the value of κ increases), the maximum height of the Fourier-transformed function for the stepwise interaction increases while that for the mexican-hat-type interaction decreases. This leads to a different κ-dependence of the transition temperature T_0 (Eq. (5.9)) between the two interactions.

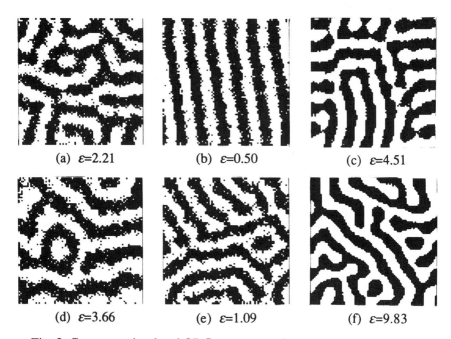

(a) $\varepsilon=2.21$ (b) $\varepsilon=0.50$ (c) $\varepsilon=4.51$

(d) $\varepsilon=3.66$ (e) $\varepsilon=1.09$ (f) $\varepsilon=9.83$

Fig. 2. Computer-simulated ODC patterns on the square panel composed of 80×80 pixels; (a), (b) and (c) with a stepwise interaction function (S), and (d), (e) and (f) with a mexican-hat-type interaction function (M). (a) and (d) were obtained with weak lateral inhibition ($\kappa=1.0$), while (b), (c), (e) and (f) were obtained with strong lateral inhibition ($\kappa=10.0$). Simulations were carried out at $T=T_0/2$ for (a), (b), (d) and (e) and at $T=T_0/10$ for (c) and (f). For all the results here, other parameters are as follows: $q_{ex}=1.0$, $\lambda_{ex}=0.15$ and $\lambda_{inh}=1.0$. The values of ε evaluated from Eqs.(5.11) and (5.12) are indicated in the parentheses. Only (b) with the smallest ε value shows a straight parallel stripe pattern.

Figures 2(a), (b), (d) and (e) were obtained by Monte Carlo simulations (Tanaka, 1990c) based on the Hamiltonian (5.1) for $\delta \equiv \lambda_{ex}/\lambda_{inh}=0.25$ at $T=T_0/2$, where δ and T_0 stand for the ratio of interaction lengths and the transition temperature between the stripe and uniform phases, respectively. For weak lateral inhibition ($\kappa \equiv q_{inh}/q_{ex}=1$), both interactions produced labyrinth-like patterns although the ODC bands did not have sharp borders (Figs 2(a) and (d)). For strong lateral inhibition (κ=10), interaction function (S) produced a straight parallel stripe (Fig. 2(b)) while interaction function (M) yielded again a labyrinth-like pattern (Fig. 2(e)).

By using the computer simulation based on the same deterministic equation as Eq. (5.6) without the noise term, Greenside et al. (1982) have demonstrated that a pattern of convective rolls undergoes a drastic change from a straight parallel stripe to a labyrinth-like pattern when the value of the Rayleigh number increases. (The increase of the Rayleigh number corresponds to the decrease of the temperature in Eq. (5.8).) Such a change was shown to occur between ε=0.1 and ε=0.9 for $|Q_0|$ = 1. Although the details of the mechanism have not been fully understood, the change in patterns is thought to be connected with the change in the complexity of the landscape of the Lyapunov functional. Therefore, the situation is similar to that found in the emergence of spin glass states which has many metastable local minima due to the complexity of the energy landscape.

The emergence of straight parallel stripes is expected to be a common mechanism between monkey ODCs and Rayleigh-Bénard convective rolls because both processes are described by almost the same equation. Based on this expectation, we will examine the behavior of ε when the values of κ and T are varied. Parameters ε^S and ε^M for the two interaction functions can be obtained (Appendix 3) as follows:

$$\varepsilon^S = \frac{8}{c^2}\left[\frac{-J_1(c)}{J_3(c)} + \frac{J_1(c\delta)}{J_3(c)}\frac{1}{\kappa\delta}\right]\cdot\frac{T_0 - T}{T}, \qquad (5.11)$$

$$\varepsilon^M = 2\left(\frac{1}{\delta} - \delta\right)^2\left[log\left(\frac{\kappa}{\delta^2}\right)\right]^{-2}\cdot\frac{T_0 - T}{T}, \qquad (5.12)$$

where the value of $|Q_0|$ is set to be 1. The function $J_n(x)$ is the nth order Bessel function of x. The value of c is given as the first zero of the second order Bessel function; c=5.13562.

Both ε^S and ε^M for δ =0.25 are shown to be decreasing functions of κ in Fig. 3. The reasonable range of κ was taken to be between 0 and 15 since strong lateral inhibition leads to hyperpolarization of the averaged membrane potential in the cortex. The curve of ε^S is always below that of ε^M. This means that interaction function (S) can give rise to straight parallel stripes more easily than interaction function (M). Only the pattern whose value of ε is smaller than 0.9 (Fig. 2(b); ε=0.50) is found to be a straight parallel stripe. Thus, the dependence of parameter ε on κ is consistent with the formation of ODC patterns obtained from simulations.

The above discussion suggests that interaction function (S) is more appropriate than interaction function (M) with regard to ODC formation in the monkey visual cortex. Therefore, the distribution of axon terminals of inhibitory neurons is suggested to be sharply limited to a finite range since the form of the synaptic interaction function reflects the morphology of axonal arborization.

synaptic interaction function reflects the morphology of axonal arborization.

Moreover, the finite temperature effect is also important because the temperature can manipulate the value of ε according to Eqs. (5.11) and (5.12). At zero temperature, ε always tends to infinity regardless of the form of the interaction function. The computer simulations for both interaction functions at very low temperatures ($T = T_0 / 10$) produced labyrinth-like patterns in spite of strong lateral inhibition ($\kappa=10$) (Figs. 2(c) and (f)). Therefore, we can say that finite temperatures are also necessary to obtain straight parallel ODC patterns.

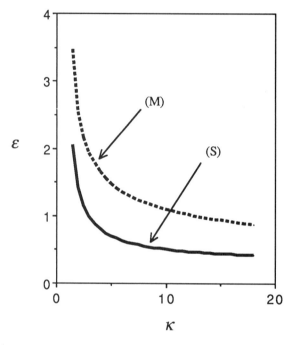

Fig. 3. The dependence of ε on κ for the two interaction functions (S) and (M) at $T=T_0/2$. All the values of ε for (S) are smaller than those for (M). This shows that the interaction function (S) is more likely to make the pattern straight than the function (M).

VI. Summary

The idea of synaptic stabilization has been first introduced by Changeux and Danchin (1976). The theory of the self-organization of specific synaptic connections was constructed by adding three microscopic mechanisms to this idea. The mathematical formulation of synaptic stabilization yielded the basic equation of the synaptic connection density which couples with electrical activities through the Hebbian mechanism. According to properties of the solution to this equation, the synaptic connection density in local equilibrium was expressed in terms of the Potts spin variable. Moreover, the self-organization of synaptic connections was reformulated within the framework of the thermodynamics in the Potts spin system. Thus, this theory describes the development of structural aspects of functional architecture.

Next, the RF function was introduced as a linear response function of neural activity to input stimuli. This RF function is well defined when we consider only the relation between the fluctuations of the stimulus and response. The RFs can be calculated by using the results obtained from the self-organization theory of synaptic connections. In general, it is, however, difficult to directly examine the properties of the RFs. To avoid this difficulty, the Langevin equation and the Lyapunov function of the RFs were obtained by combining the RFs with the thermodynamic theory of self-organization of synaptic connections. This equation and function allows us to directly discuss the development of the RFs. We can say that this RF self-organization theory describes the development of functional aspects of functional architecture while the theory of synaptic connection self-organization is useful in discussing the development of their structural aspects.

By applying this theory to the simplest version of ODC formation, we were able to explain that the straightness of the monkey ocular dominance bands is closely related to the form of the intracortical inhibitory connections. In other words, if the axon terminal distribution of the inhibitory neurons spreads over the cortex with slowly decreasing behavior, the bands are likely to be labyrinth-like. On the other hand, if the axon terminal distribution has a sharp cutoff at a certain distance, the bands are likely to be straight parallel stripes. Based on the simulated results and mathematical analysis, it is suggested that axon terminals of inhibitory neurons in the primary visual cortex of monkeys suddenly vanish after reaching a certain diameter.

Our theoretical framework is unique in that it allows the development of various columnar organizations to be systematically discussed and it possesses a wide applicability brought about by basic mechanisms which do not seem to have any specificity. Therefore, this framework can offer explanation and prediction regarding anatomical and physiological observations. Based on its application to the self-organization of various forms of functional architecture in the cerebral cortex, information processing mechanisms of the brain may be better understood. Finally, we expect such theoretical research to provide strong feedforward and feedback connections to technologists and biologists.

Appendix 1

In deriving the function which describes the correlation between firing frequencies from retinal ganglion cells (RGCs) in the left and right retinas, it is assumed that the lateral geniculate nucleus (LGN) plays only the role of a relay nucleus which transmits neural activity from RGCs to the primary visual cortex without any additional information processing.

We can obtain an appropriate mathematical description for the correlation function of the RGC activities by assuming two firing mechanisms, spontaneous firing and visually stimulating firing (Tanaka, 1990a, c). When

$C_{k;k'}$ represents the spatial correlation between any pair of neurons at positions k and k' in the retinas, the correlation function $\Gamma^{\text{pre}}_{k,\mu;k',\mu'}$ is given by.

$$\Gamma^{\text{pre}}_{k,\mu;k',\mu'} = \left[r + (1\text{-}r)\delta_{\mu,\mu'} \right] C_{k;k'} \ , \tag{A1.1}$$

where parameter r describes the degree of correlation between firings elicited from the left RGCs and the right. $\delta_{\mu,\mu'}$ is Kronecker's delta.

   If there are only spontaneous firings, there is no correlation between left and right RGCs' firings ($r=0$). On the other hand, in the presence of visual stimulation, firings from the left and right eyes correlate ($0<r\leq1$) since in normal animals any pair of RGCs with retinotopic correspondence in the respective retinas receive almost the same image. The effects of the imbalanced activity is not taken into account in this paper and hence the first term in the Hamiltonian (2.14) will be neglected hereafter.

   Here, we adopt the following factorization (Tanaka, 1990c) in order to separate the ocular dominance and the retinotopic order:

$$\sigma_{j,k,\mu} = \sigma^R_{j,k} \cdot \sigma^{OD}_{j,\mu} \ . \tag{A1.2}$$

where $\sigma^R_{j,k}$ and $\sigma^{OD}_{j,\mu}$ are the Potts spin variable for the retinotopic order and that for the ocular dominance, respectively. The latter Potts spin can be rewritten in terms of the Ising spin s_j which can take only the values of $+1$ or -1.

$$\sigma^{OD}_{j,\mu} = \frac{1 + \mu s_j}{2} \ . \tag{A1.3}$$

   By using this Ising spin variable, the Hamiltonian of this system can be reduced to

$$H = -\frac{q(1\text{-}r)}{2} \sum_j \sum_{j \neq j} U_{j;j'} s_j s_{j'} \ , \tag{A1.4}$$

where $U_{j;j'}$ is the interaction between two Ising spins, s_j and $s_{j'}$. The interaction $U_{j;j'}$ includes the effect of retinotopic order since it can be written as

$$U_{j;j'} = V^{\text{post}}_{j;j'} \sum_{k \in B_j} \sum_{k' \in B_j'} C_{k;k'} \sigma^R_{j,k} \sigma^R_{j',k'} \ . \tag{A1.5}$$

Appendix 2

Let us assume that the interaction $U_{j;j'}$ can be written as a function of $d_{j,j'}$, the distance between j and j'. The first term on the right-hand side of Eq. (5.4) can be simplified by considering its Fourier transformation:

$$- \frac{1}{q(1-r)} \sum_Q \frac{1}{\tilde{U}_Q} \tilde{\psi}_Q \qquad (A2.1)$$

$\tilde{A}_Q$ and Q represent the Fourier transformation of A_j and the wave number, respectively.

If the interaction $U_{j,j'}=U(d_{j,j'})$ is given by the sum of the short-range excitatory and long-range inhibitory interactions, there is the maximum value of $\left(- 1/\tilde{U}_Q\right)$ at $Q = Q_0$. Therefore, $\left(- 1/\tilde{U}_Q\right)$ can be expanded with respect to $(Q - Q_0)$. By considering the role of the first term on the right hand side of Eq.(5.4), this Fourier component $\tilde{\psi}_{Q_0}$ is found to be the fastest growing mode if $\left(- 1/\tilde{U}_{Q_0}\right)$ takes a positive value. Since the second term of Eq.(5.4), reflecting the winner-take-all property, may allow the fastest growing mode to survive, only modes $\tilde{\psi}_Q$'s in the vicinity of $Q = Q_0$ determine the behavior of the system. Therefore, we will focus on $\left(- 1/\tilde{U}_Q\right)$ near $Q = Q_0$ and approximate it as follows:

$$- \frac{1}{\tilde{U}_Q} \cong - \frac{1}{\tilde{U}_{Q_0}} + \frac{\tilde{U}''_{Q_0}}{2\tilde{U}^2_{Q_0}} (Q - Q_0)^2 \; , \qquad (A2.2)$$

where $\tilde{U}''_{Q_0}$ stands for the second derivative of $\tilde{U}_Q$ at $Q = Q_0$. The first derivative of $\tilde{U}_Q$ should be zero at $Q = Q_0$:

$$\left[\frac{d}{dQ} \tilde{U}_Q\right]_{Q = Q_0} = 0 \; . \qquad (A2.3)$$

The right-hand side of Eq. (A2.2) can be further approximated to

$$- \frac{1}{\tilde{U}_{Q_0}} + \frac{\tilde{U}''_{Q_0}}{8\tilde{U}^2_{Q_0}Q^2_0} (Q^2 - Q^2_0)^2 \; . \qquad (A2.4)$$

Next, if we calculate the Fourier inverse transformation of (A2.4), we obtain the expression:

$$\left[- \frac{1}{\tilde{U}_{Q_0}} + \frac{\tilde{U}''_{Q_0}}{8\tilde{U}^2_{Q_0}Q^2_0} (\nabla^2 + Q^2_0)^2\right]\delta_{j,j'} \; . \qquad (A2.5)$$

Consequently, the Langevin equation (4.12) is reduced to the equation:

$$\frac{d\psi(\mathbf{x},t)}{dt} = -\left[A(\nabla^2 + Q_0^2)^2 + \frac{1}{T_0}\right]\psi(\mathbf{x},t) + tanh\{\psi(\mathbf{x},t)/T\} + \xi(\mathbf{x},t) \quad \text{(A2.6)}$$

$$\text{with } A = -\frac{\widetilde{U}_{Q_0}''}{8q(1-r)\widetilde{U}_{Q_0}^2 Q_0^2} \quad \text{(A2.7)}$$

$$\text{and } T_0 = q(1-r)\widetilde{U}_{Q_0} . \quad \text{(A2.8)}$$

In Eq. (A2.6), the variable representing ocular dominance is redefined in the continuum space and replaced by $\psi(\mathbf{x},t)$ since the equation includes the spatial derivative.

By using the expansion $tanh\{\psi(\mathbf{x},t)/T\} \cong \frac{1}{T}\psi(\mathbf{x},t) - \frac{1}{3T^3}\psi(\mathbf{x},t)^3$, we finally obtain

$$\frac{d\psi(\mathbf{x},t)}{dt} = \varepsilon\psi(\mathbf{x},t) - (\nabla^2 + Q_0^2)^2\psi(\mathbf{x},t) - B[\psi(\mathbf{x},t)]^3 + \xi(\mathbf{x},t) , \quad \text{(A2.9)}$$

where the scale transformation concerning time t, $t \to t/A$, and replacements $\varepsilon = (T_0 - T)/AT_0T$ and $B = 1/3AT^3$ are used.

Appendix 3

Two models of the effective interaction function $U(d_{j,j'})$ are assumed by the following:

$$U^S(d_{j,j'}) = \frac{q_{ex}}{4\pi\lambda_{ex}^2}\Theta(2\lambda_{ex} - d_{jj'}) - \frac{q_{inh}}{2\pi\lambda_{inh}^2}\Theta(2\lambda_{inh} - d_{jj'}) , \quad \text{(A3.1)}$$

$$U^M(d_{j,j'}) = \frac{q_{ex}}{2\pi\lambda_{ex}^2}exp(-\frac{d_{jj'}^2}{2\lambda_{ex}^2}) - \frac{q_{inh}}{2\pi\lambda_{inh}^2}exp(-\frac{d_{jj'}^2}{2\lambda_{inh}^2}) . \quad \text{(A3.2)}$$

where λ_{ex} and λ_{inh} represent the extent of excitatory and inhibitory lateral connections, respectively. Parameters q_{ex} and q_{inh} are strengths of excitatory and inhibitory lateral interactions.

Equation (5.8) and the above models lead to the following equations:

$$q_{ex} J_2(2\lambda_{ex}Q) - q_{inh} J_2(2\lambda_{inh}Q) = 0 , \quad \text{(A3.3)}$$

$$q_{ex}\lambda_{ex}^2 exp(-\frac{\lambda_{ex}^2 Q^2}{2}) - q_{inh}\lambda_{inh}^2 exp(-\frac{\lambda_{inh}^2 Q^2}{2}) = 0 . \quad \text{(A3.4)}$$

The wave number Q_0 is obtained by solving these equations. From (A3.4),

$\left(Q_0^M\right)^2 = \dfrac{2\log\left(\kappa/\delta^2\right)}{\lambda_{inh}^2(1-\delta^2)}$, where $\kappa = q_{inh}/q_{ex}$ and $\delta = \lambda_{ex}/\lambda_{inh}$ .On the other hand, Q_0 for
(A3.4) is approximately given by the first zero of $J_2(2\lambda_{inh}Q)$ in the case of $\delta \ll 1$
to which our discussion is confined. Therefore, we find that $Q_0^S \cong c/(2\lambda_{inh})$ for
$c \cong 5.13562$. The substitution of the expressions of Q_0^S and Q_0^M for Q_0 in $\left(-\dfrac{8\widetilde{U}_{Q_0}}{\widetilde{U}_{Q_0}''Q_0^2}\right)$
gives rise to Eqs. (5.11) and (5.12), respectively.

References

Amari S. (1980) Topological organization of nerve fields, Bulletin of Mathematical Biology. **42**: 339-364.

Bear M. F., Cooper L. N. and Ebner F. F. (1987) A physiological basis for a theory of synapse modification. Science **237**: 42-47.

Changeux W. H. and Danchin A. (1976) Selective stabilization of developing synapses as a mechanism for the specification of neuronal networks. Nature **264**: 705-712.

Collingridge G. L. and Bliss T. V. P. (1987) NMDA receptors - their role in long-term potentiation. Trends in Neurosci.**10**: 288-293.

Garel T. and Doniach S. (1982) Phase transitions with spontaneous modulation - the dipolar Ising ferromagnet. Phys. Rev. B **26**: 325-329.

Greenside H. S., Coughran Jr. W. H. and Schryer N. L. (1982) Nonlinear pattern formation near the onset of Rayleigh-Bénard convection. Phys Rev Letts **49**: 726-729.

Hebb D. O. (1949) The Organization of Behavior. Wiley.

Hubel D. H. and Wiesel T. N. (1962) Receptive fields, binocular interaction and functional architecture in the cat's visual cortex. J Physiol **160**: 106-154.

Hubel D. H. and Wiesel T. N. (1977) Functional architecture of macaque monkey visual cortex. Proc R Soc Lond B**198**: 1-59.

Kleinschmidt A., Bear M. F. and Singer W. (1987) Blockade of "NMDA" receptors disrupts experience-dependent plasticity of kitten striate cortex. Science **238**: 355-358.

Linsker R. (1986) From basic network principles to neural architecture: Emergence of spatial-opponent cells. Proc. Natl. Acad. Sci. USA **83**: 7508-7512.

Linsker R. (1989) An application of the principle of maximum information preservation to linear systems. In Advances in Neural Information Processing System 1, (Touretzky, D.S. (Ed.), Morgan Kaufmann Inc.),186-194.

Miller K. D., Keller J. B. and Stryker M. P. (1989) Ocular dominance column development: Analysis and simulation. Science **245**: 605-615.

Swindale N. V. (1980) A model for the formation of ocular dominance stripes. Proc. R. Soc. Lond. B**208**: 243-264.

Tanaka S. (1989) Theory of self-organization of cortical maps. In Advances in Neural Information Processing System 1, (Touretzky D. S. (Ed.), Morgan Kaufmann Inc.), 451-458.

Tanaka S. (1990a) Experience-dependent self-organization of biological neural networks. NEC Research and Development No.98: 1-14.

Tanaka S. (1990b) Theory of self-organization of cortical maps: mathematical framework. Neural Networks **3**:625-640.

Tanaka S. (1990c) Theory of ocular dominance column formation -mathematical basis and computer simulation-. Biol. Cybern. (in press).

Von der Malsburg C. (1973) Self-organization of orientation selective cells in the striate cortex. Kybernetik **14**: 85-100.

Von der Malsburg C (1979) Development of ocularity domains and growth behavior of axon terminals. Biol. Cybern. **32**: 49-62.

Willshaw D. J. and Von der Malsburg C. (1976) How patterned neural connections can be set up by self-organization. Proc. R. Soc. Lond. B **194**: 431-445.

Wu F. Y. (1982) The Potts model. Review of Modern Physics **54**: 235-268.

I.7

Filters Versus Textons in Human and Machine Texture Discrimination

DOUGLAS WILLIAMS and BELA JULESZ

Laboratory of Vision Research
Rutgers University
New Brunswick, NJ 08903

I. Abstract

A fundamental property of human visual perception is our ability to distinguish between textures. A concerted effort has been made to account for texture segregation in terms of linear spatial filter models and their nonlinear extensions. However, for certain texture pairs the ease of discrimination changes when the role of figure and ground are reversed. This asymmetry poses a problem for both linear and nonlinear models. We have isolated three properties of texture perception which account for this asymmetry in discrimination: subjective closure, perceptual distortion, and fill-

145

in. These properties, which are also responsible for visual illusions, appear to be explainable by early visual processes alone. Our results force a re-examination of the process of human texture segregation and of some recent models that were introduced to explain it.

II. Introduction

Humans have the remarkable ability to distinguish between textures occurring routinely in nature - such as different areas of bark on a tree, grass or plowed fields viewed from a distance and textiles, to name only a few - as well as artificial 2-D arrays of repeated or randomly thrown elements like wallpaper. The fact that textures are devoid of recognizable global forms provides a reason for using such stimuli to determine primitive features of visual information processing.

A. Historical Perspective

The systematic investigation of texture discrimination was pioneered by one of the authors (Julesz, 1962). An immediately discovered and robust property of texture discrimination is that it can easily be divided into two categories - either effortless (texture differences "pop out" at the observer) or requiring scrutiny (differences are only revealed by a systematic serial search of the patterns).

Tasks requiring scrutiny utilize attention to search the textures in a serial manner and detect differences. Conversely, effortless texture discrimination tasks are processed in parallel, and do not require attention (i.e., they are "pre-attentive"). These two processes are illustrated in Figure 1 (from Julesz and Bergen, 1983). Here, two orthogonal line segments form elements of textural arrays. The Xs pop-out from the Ls as a parallel process, almost instantaneously, independent of the number of elements. However, it requires time-consuming element-by-element scrutiny to detect the array composed of Ts among Ls. These serial shifts of focal attention underlying scrutiny can take place rapidly without eye-movements (Helmholtz, 1896; Posner, 1980).

Because of the stochastic nature of texture, initial efforts concentrated on global differences between texture pairs. In particular, the statistical difference in the luminance profile of the texture pairs was studied. Efforts were made to determine the highest N for which it was possible for texture pairs to have identical N^{th}-order statistics and yet remain discriminable. Texture pairs with identical first-order statistics have the property that any point thrown on these textures has an equal probability of falling on the same colors in each. Texture pairs with the same first-order statistics can be effortlessly segregated based on differences in the tonal quality of the textures. Iso-second-order textures have the property that any dipole placed

Figure 1 Preattentive (parallel) texture discrimination versus serial scrutiny by focal attention. The Xs among the Ls pop-out effortlessly, while finding the Ts among the Ls requires element-by-element search. From Julesz and Bergen (1983).*

on these textures has equal probability that its end points will fall on the same colors in both textures. It initially appeared that iso-second-order textures (which also have identical first-order statistics and Fourier power spectra) were so severely constrained globally that the visual system could not tell them apart. Such indiscriminable iso-second-order texture pairs are depicted in Figs. 2 and 3. However, in 1978, Julesz, Caelli, Gilbert, and Victor invented stochastic texture pairs with global constraints of identical second- (and even identical third-) order statistics that yielded preattentive texture discrimination based on some local conspicuous features, later called textons. In Figs. 4A, B, and C, some iso-second-order texture pairs are depicted that are preattentively discriminable based on the local features termed respectively "quasi-collinearity", "corner", and "closure" (Caelli et al., 1978). Figure 4D shows iso-third-order textures with the property that any triangle thrown on these textures has the same probability that the vertices of the triangles will fall on the same colors (however the vertices of probing polygons with four vertices will have different probabilities) (Julesz, Gilbert, and Victor, 1978). For these iso-third-order textures, discrimination is effortless and is obviously not due to computing differences in fourth-order statistics, but rather due to elongated blobs of different aspect ratios and orientations. In essence, it was found that texture segmentation is not

* Reprinted with permission. © 1983, AT&T.

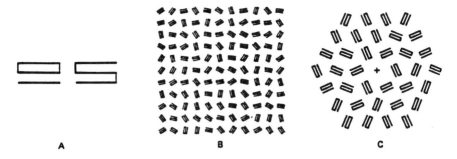

Figure 2 Demonstration of an indistinguishable texture pair composed of S (⊆) and 10 (⊆) shaped elements as shown in A) even though the elements in isolation are discriminable as shown in A). C) is similar to B), except only one target is presented, and to detect this target element-by-element scrutiny is required. From Julesz (1981).*

governed by global (statistical) rules, but rather depends on local features (textons), such as color, orientation, flicker, motion, depth, elongated blobs and collinearity.

B. Linear Spatial Filter Models

Simultaneous with this investigation of texture perception was the investigation of spatial luminance perception. The principle culmination of this research was that spatial luminance information is initially processed by local center-surround linear size-tuned filters followed by some form of nonlinear

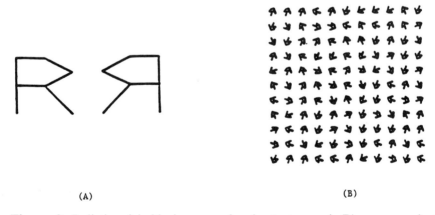

Figure 3 Indistinguishable iso-second-order texture pair B), composed of Rs and their mirror image duals, that in isolation A) appear discriminable. From Julesz (1981).*

* Reprinted with permission from *Nature* **290** 91–97. ©1981 by Macmillan Magazines Ltd.

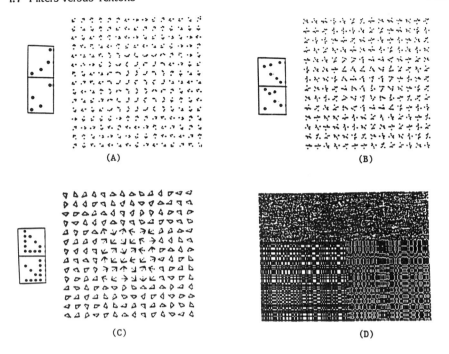

Figure 4 Preattentively discriminable iso-second and iso-third-order texture pairs. A) Iso-second-order texture pair that is discriminable due to the local conspicuous feature (texton) of "quasi-collinearity". B) Iso-second-order texture pair that is discriminable due to the local conspicuous feature (texton) of "corner". C) Iso-second-order texture pair that is discriminable due to the local conspicuous feature (texton) of "closure". From Caelli et. al. (1978). D) Iso-third-order texture pair that is discriminable due to the local conspicuous feature (texton) of "elongated blobs of specific orientation, width, and length". From Caelli et al. (1978).

detection (Campbell and Robson, 1968; Blakemore and Campbell, 1969; Graham and Nachmias, 1971; Sachs, Nachmias and Robson, 1971; and Wilson and Bergen, 1979). The first attempt to apply a linear localized spatial filter model to texture segregation is depicted in Fig. 5 which illustrates how a Kuffler unit (a spatial filter of 2x2 pixel center addition with a 2 pixel wide surround angulus of subtraction, as shown in the inset) acts on the iso-third order texture pair of Fig. 4D, followed by a threshold taking device (Julesz and Bergen, 1983). In 1988, several texture segmentation algorithms were developed based on linear spatial filters followed by squaring or some other non-linear operation (Voorhees and Poggio, 1988; Bergen and Adelson, 1988). Julesz and Kröse (1988) provided the first counterexample demonstrating that such linear spatial filters models are not sufficient to

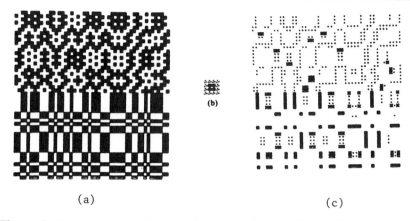

(a)   (c)

Figure 5 Demonstration of how a simple local linear filter followed by a non-linearity (threshold-taking) can segment the iso-third-order texture pair of Fig. 4D. From Julesz and Bergen (1983).*

segment textures. A second is supplied by us and shown in Figure 6, in which two texture elements; an **L** and a tilted **m** form easily discriminated texture pairs. However if the identical small **L** element is added to the two ends of the **L** and tilted **m**, the resulting texture pair is no longer distinguishable. This example violates the superposition property of linear theories.

Fogel and Sagi (1989) and, independently, Malik and Perona (1990) developed nonlinear extensions of the spatial filter models. Both texture segmentation algorithms are based on local spatial filters (oriented Gabor-

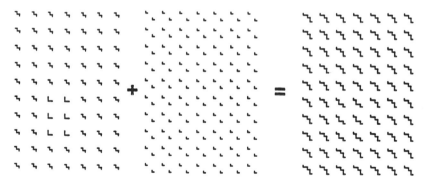

Figure 6 Demonstration of the nonlinearity of human texture discrimination. When to the highly discriminable texture pair (left array) a uniform, nondiscriminable array of small **L** s (middle array) is added, a nondiscriminable texture pair (right array) is obtained. Thus the law of superposition is violated.

filters) followed by a quasi-local non-linear operation (simple squaring and a second spatial filter by Fogel and Sagi, and nonlinear inhibition between neighboring elements by Malik and Perona). Both models provide respectable qualitative fits to human texture discrimination performance as measured by Kröse (1987).

C. The Asymmetry Problem

A relevant recent result in texture perception is that for certain texture pairs, the ease of discrimination changes when the role of figure and ground are switched (Julesz, 1981; Gurnsey and Browse, 1987; Treisman and Gormican, 1988). For example, it is far more difficult to detect an intact circle in a field of circles each of which contains a gap in its circumference than it is to detect a gapped circle in a field of intact ones as shown in Figure 7. The existence of such perceptual asymmetries has been taken to imply that the element which is easier to detect contains an emergent feature (Treisman and Gormican, 1988). The models of Fogel and Sagi (1989) and Malik and Perona (1990) are not able to account for these perceptual asymmetries. Rubenstein and Sagi (1990) extended the model of Fogel and Sagi (1989) by incorporating the variances of the local filter responses, particularly the variation in the orientation responses. With this addition, their model could account for approximately 60% of textural pair asymmetries reported by Gurnsey and Browse (1987). The present extensions of the linear filter models do not appear sufficient to account for the asymmetry property of texture perception.

A complete understanding of texture segregation certainly requires a resolution to this asymmetry problem. The remainder of our chapter is devoted to the investigation of this asymmetry. To anticipate our findings, our results do not support the interpretation that spatial filter models as presently formulated are sufficient to account for the asymmetry, nor the hypothesis that these asymmetries represent emergent features. Indeed as discussed in the next section, our results suggest that texture discrimination and the observed asymmetry crucially depend on fundamental properties of the visual system which produce illusions in visual processing.

III. Perceptual Asymmetries

It is well documented that a perceived visual image can differ from the actual scenic image. For example, incomplete boundaries in a scene can be completed by illusory or subjective contours. Illusory feature "fill-in" can also occur - for example, our completion of the visual field over the blind spot where the optic nerve exits the retina. Our results suggest that these properties of visual processing play a crucial role in texture discrimination and can account for the perceptual asymmetries described above. Specifically, three different properties which contribute to asymmetry have been identified:

(1) subjective contour and closure, (2) perceptual distortion, and (3) fill-in. Each will be considered in a separate section below.

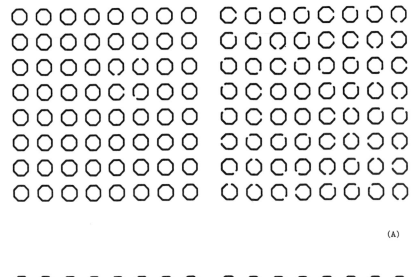

(A)

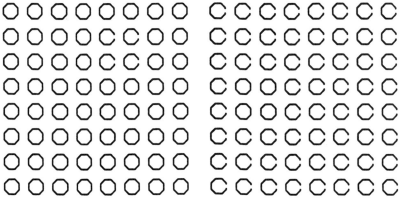

(B)

Figure 7 (a) An example of asymmetry is shown here for texture pairs composed of intact circles and open circles. The perception of a gapped circles in the field of closed circles yields stronger discrimination than vice versa. (b) An example of asymmetry for texture pairs composed of intact circles and open circles for the case in which the orientation of the gap is not randomized. The perception of a gapped circles in closed circles again produces stronger discrimination than vice versa.

A. Subjective Contour and Closure

As shown on the left of Figure 7a, we can effortlessly perceive a group of four open circles in a field of closed ones. However to detect a group of four closed circles in a field of open ones is much more difficult and requires scrutiny. Although the orientation of the gaps have been randomized in the figure the asymmetry is still observed if the all gaps have the same orientation (see Figure 7b). [We note this, because Rubenstein and Sagi (1990) explain asymmetry as the result of randomized orientations.] The fact that a gapped circle is more easily detected has been taken to imply that line ends (terminators) marking the gap are a more significant feature for perception than connectedness (closure) (Treisman and Souther, 1985).

To investigate the contribution of the gap and closure to segregation, we used a simplified version of the stimulus in Figure 7a. This simplified stimulus contained only two elements; a single target and a single distractor. Elements were presented on the circumference of a ring which had a radius of 3 degrees. The diameter of each element was 1 degree. Elements could occur in any location on the ring and the orientation of the gap was randomized. Observers fixated the center of the ring. The stimulus was presented for 48 msec. Each element was then masked by an element composed of both the target and distractor elements. The masking pattern had a stimulus onset asynchrony (SOA) of 112 msec and a duration of 48 msec. Four observers participated in the study. One was one of the authors and the other three observers were naive as to the purposes of the experiments.

A novel research paradigm was devised to determine the effect of reversing the role of target and distractor. For this paradigm the results of two experimental conditions are compared. In the first experimental condition an open circle served as the target. There were two different stimuli. One stimulus consisted of a target open circle and a distractor closed circle. The second stimulus consisted of two closed circles. During an experimental session, presentation of the two stimuli were randomly intermixed. On half the trials which were chosen at random the first stimulus was presented. For the remaining trials the second was presented. Observers were required to determine if at least one of the circles was open on each presentation. The second stimulus consisting of two closed circles provided a measure of the frequency for which the observer falsely reported that a target open circle was present when in fact it was not. In the second experimental condition the target was the closed circle. As was the case for the first experimental condition, two different stimuli were again used. One stimulus consisted of a target closed circle and a distractor open circle. The second stimulus consisted of two open circles. In this condition, the observers were required to determine if one or more of the circles on each presentation was closed.

This research paradigm was generalized and used throughout these studies. For the general case consider the texture element pair A and B. The first experimental condition will comprise the two stimuli AB and AA. For this condition the observer will be required to determine if B is present on each presentation. The second experimental condition consists of the two stimuli AB and BB, and the observer will be required to determine if A is present on each presentation.

Results for the texture element pair of a closed circle and open circle are presented in Figure 8. Those for the first condition are on the left and for the second condition on the right. For the first condition, with a target open circle and distractor closed circle the percent correct for detection is 73%. For two closed circle distractors the percent correct is 86%. If the role of target and distractor are reversed then the percent correct for a target and distractor is 87%. In comparison the percentage correct for two open circles is considerably less (57%). In fact this is near chance (50%). This high false alarm rate for detecting at least one closed circle in a stimulus consisting of just two open circles suggests that open circles are being perceptually closed by subjective contours (Schumann, 1904 and Kanizsa, 1976). Another way of demonstrating this point is made if we take the proportion of incorrect responses for the one open and one closed stimulus in condition 1 (27%) to be the probability that one open circle is being perceptually closed. Then the probability that at least one of two open circles is being perceptually closed (approximately 52%) is shown by the arrow in the right figure[1]. There is reasonable agreement between data and theory.

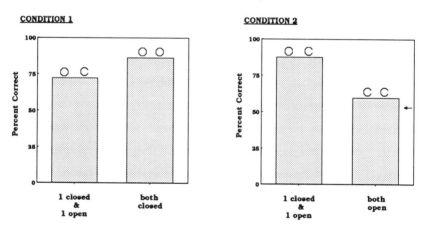

Figure 8 Results shown for the two stimulus conditions used to studied the asymmetry for a open and closed circle. Those for condition 1 are at the left and for condition 2 at the right. For the first condition, on half the trials the stimulus consisted of an open and closed circle. For the remaining trials both circles were closed. The percent of correct responses for each stimulus is denoted by a bar. In the second condition, on half of the trials an open and closed circle was presented just as for the first condition but on the remaining trials the stimulus consisted of two open circles.

Subjective closure of the open circles would explain the search asymmetry observed for an open circle in a field of closed circles compared to a closed circle in a field of open circles. Because of subjective closure some elements in a field of open circle elements will be perceived as closed. Therefore, searching for a closed circle in a field of open ones is equivalent to searching for a closed circle in a field of both open and closed circles. This is far more difficult than searching for a single open circle in a field of closed ones. Thus rather than the gap being an emergent feature it is its closure which leads to the asymmetry. This subjective closure would also explain why discrimination becomes more symmetric as the gap is widened (Treisman and Souther, 1985). As the gap size is increased the likelihood of subjectively closing the gap diminishes and closed and open circles become equally detectable.

Another element pair for which a gap figures prominently is the elongated **S** (⊆) and **10** (⊏). These elements consist of the same three horizontal line segments and same two vertical line segments. The aspect ratio of vertical length to horizontal length is approximately 1/3. The difference between the elements is the location of the vertical gaps. As shown in Figure 2 these texture elements are indistinguishable (Julesz 1981). It was proposed that the failure to segregate the textures results from the fact that both elements have the same number of terminators. To determine if there is subjective closure at the terminators of the contour we carried out an experiment analogous to the two element experiment with the gapped and intact circle. The discriminability of each of the elements **S** and **10** were separately tested against an **8** (⊟) element which contains no gaps.

First consider the case for the **S** and **8**. As with the gapped and intact circles we considered two stimulus conditions. For the first condition, on half the trials chosen at random the stimulus consisted of a target **S** and a distractor **8**s. For the remaining trials both elements were **8**. Observers were required to determine if at least one of the elements contained a gap or gaps on each presentation. In the second condition the role of target and distractor was reversed. On half of the trials a target **8** and distractor **S** was presented. On the remaining trials the stimulus consisted of two **S**s. In this condition, the observers were required to determine if one or more of the elements on each presentation was completely closed. For the first condition, with a target **S** and distractor **8** the percent correct for detection is approximately 63%. For two **8** distractors the percent correct is 83%. If the role of target and distractor are reversed then the percent correct for a target and distractor is 80% while

---

[1]To determine the probability that at least one of two open circles is perceived as closed, let **p** be the probability that one circle with a gap appears to be closed. Then the probability that for two open circles at least one appears to be closed is $1-(1-p)(1-p)$.

that for two distractors drops to 51%. The high false alarm rate for detecting at least one **8** in a stimulus consisting of just two **S** suggests that the gaps are being perceptually closed by subjective contours as was the case for the gapped and intact circles.

The analogous experiment for the **10** and **8** gave similar results. With a target **10** and distractor **8** the percent correct for detection is approximately 58%. For two **8** distractors the percent correct is 88%. If the role of target and distractor are reversed, then the percent correct for a target and distractor is 79% while that for two distractors drops to 44%. Again the high false alarm rate for detecting at least one **8** in a stimulus consisting of just two **10** suggests that the gaps are being perceptually closed.

Thus results suggest that the reason that the **10** and **S** are not discriminable is that the gaps are being closed by subjective contours and the elements become perceptually indistinguishable. This is also consistent with the result of Julesz (1986) that if the aspect ratio of the line lengths is changed to 1, these elements can be discriminated since the gap is less likely to be closed by subjective closure. Two element experiments like the ones described above confirm that the gaps are no longer perceived as closed for such elements. Thus the explanation that the failure to discriminate the **S** and **10** is due to having an equal number of terminators holds if the gaps created by the terminators are sufficiently small to permit subjective contours to occur.

To further investigate the property of closure in texture segregation we examined segregation with an element pair for which one has a closed contour. The elements were a triangle and an arrow. Both the triangle and arrow are constructed of the same three line segments and angles. As can be seen in Figure 9, each can be effortlessly detected in a field of the others. We sought to determine if the closed nature of the triangle is critical for segregation. To do so we introduced gaps in the three line segments of each element to disrupt the perception of closure. As with the previous experiments, elements were restricted to a ring, which has a radius of 3

Figure 9   Distinguishable iso-second-order texture pair composed of triangles and arrows.

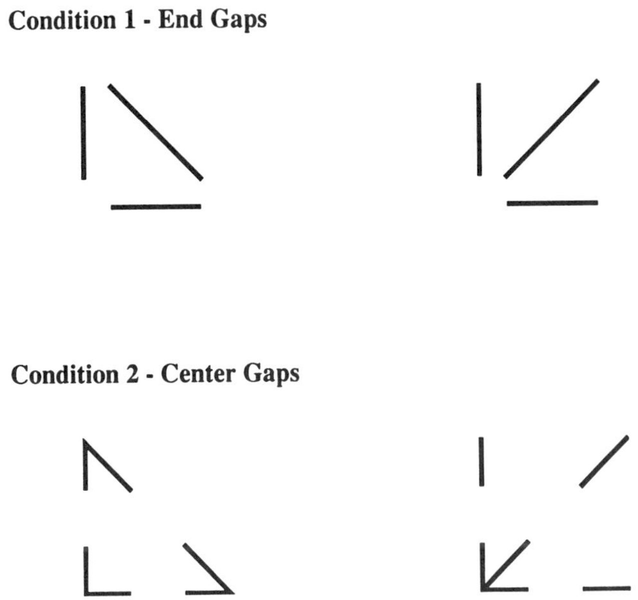

Condition 1 - End Gaps

Condition 2 - Center Gaps

Figure 10 Two conditions for the location of the gaps in the triangle and arrow. Gaps are inserted in the center of the line segments in Condition 1 while the gaps occur at the ends of the line segments in Condition 2.

degrees. The short side of the triangle and arrow subtends 1 degree of visual angle. Measurements were made for the case in which the triangle served as the target and arrow as distractor as well as for the reverse case with the arrow as target and triangle as distractor. In each experiment, for half the trials chosen at random, both the target and distractors were presented. On the remaining trials only the distractors were presented. The subject was required to identify trials on which the target appeared.

Two conditions for the location of gaps were considered (see Figure 10). In the first condition, gaps were introduced at the end of each of the line segments. For the second condition, gaps were placed in the center of the line segments. The different locations of the gaps were used to determine if geometric properties such as corners may be critical or if only closure is relevant. To monitor the detectability of the gaps we also measured discriminability for an intact element compared to the same element with gaps introduced.

For condition 1 (gaps at the ends of lines) results are presented in the top two graphs of Figure 11 and those for the second condition (gaps in the center of line segments) are presented at the bottom. On the left is the case for which the triangle was the target; on the right the arrow served as the target. Consider the case with the triangle as the target. If the target is a

Condition 1 - End Gaps

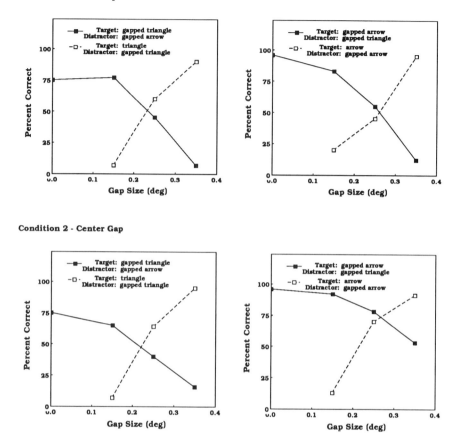

Condition 2 - Center Gap

Figure 11 Results for condition 1 (gaps at the ends of lines) are presented in the top two graphs and those for the second condition (gaps in the center of line segments) are presented at the bottom. On the left is the case for which the triangle was the target and on the right for which the arrow served as the target.

gapped triangle and the distractor is a gapped arrow increasing gap size decreases discriminability (solid squares in upper left graph of Figure 11). If the target is an intact triangle and the distractor is a gapped triangle discrimination increases as gap size increases (open squares in upper left graph of Figure 11). Failure to discriminate an intact triangle from a gapped one is consistent with the subjective closure of the lines comprising the gapped triangle. Comparison of the two data curves for this graph demonstrates that it is more difficult to discriminate a triangle and arrow as the closure of the triangle decreases. As seen in the lower left hand graph, similar results were obtained when the gaps were placed in the center of the line segments. Taken together, the results suggest that the geometric properties of the triangle due to gap position are not critical but that closure is important.

Results were different when the arrow was the target as shown in the graphs on the right hand side of Figure 11. Note first that, comparing the two top graphs it is clear that there is a search asymmetry for the arrow and triangle even without a gap present. It is easier to detect a target arrow than a target triangle. We will return to this asymmetry below. In general, the results in the graph are similar to those for which the triangle is the target. However, as seen in the lower right hand graph, if the gap was placed in the center of the line segments, discriminability of an arrow and triangle was less affected by gap size (decreasing only to 50% at the largest gap size compared to approximately 10% for the other conditions). This is true despite the fact that discriminability of an intact and gapped arrow is as strongly affected by gap size as in the previous conditions. For the arrow, simple closure does not necessarily facilitate discriminability. However, for the triangle which is closed, results suggest that this closure is significant.

As pointed out above, there is an asymmetry for discrimination of intact arrows and triangles. It is easier to detect an target arrow in a field of distractor triangles than the reverse. Two element experiments demonstrate that the asymmetry can be attributed to the subjective closure of the open side of the arrow. Subjective closure of the side of the arrow would account for the result that discriminability between an arrow and triangle is diminished if the aspect ratio of the elements (the ratio between the lengths of the perpendicular lines in each element) is increased (Julesz, 1986). The change in aspect ratio decreases one of the gaps in the arrow and the probability of subjective closure is increased, rendering the arrow and triangle less discriminable.

In summary, the results suggest that closure, including subjective closure, is important for texture segregation.

B. Perceptual Distortion

In general, for the texture element pairs considered in the previous section one member of the pair was constructed from the other by adding and/or deleting a portion of the other. The addition and deletion either closed or opened a gap in the element. For the texture pairs considered in this section one member of the pair is constructed by deforming the other. For example we will consider the pair consisting of a straight line and a curved line (Figure 12). Another pair examined is a circle and an ellipse (Figure 13). In both cases the more asymmetric member of the pair is more easily detected in a

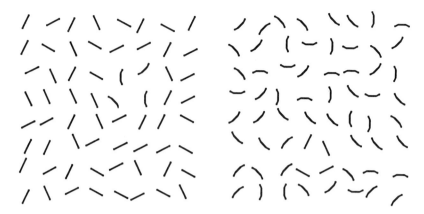

Figure 12 Perceptual asymmetry is shown for texture pairs composed of curved lines and straight lines. The perception of the curved lines in a field of straight lines yields stronger discrimination than vice versa.

field of the symmetric element than the reverse (Treisman and Gormican, 1988).

To investigate this perceptual asymmetry we used the two element paradigm described in the previous section. We first examined the pair consisting of a straight line and a curved line. As with the previous experiments two experimental conditions were compared. For the first condition, on half the trials chosen at random the stimulus consisted of a target curved line and a distractor straight line. For the remaining trials both elements were straight lines. Observers were required to determine if at least one of the elements was curved on each presentation. In the second condition, on half of the trials the target was a straight line and the distactor was a curved line. On the remaining trials the stimulus consisted of two

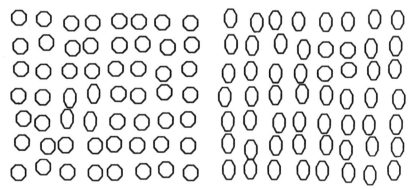

Figure 13 Perceptual asymmetry is shown for texture pairs composed of ellipses and circles. Segregation is stronger if the ellipses are the target and the circles the distractors, than if the roles are reversed.

curved lines. In this condition, the observers determined if one or more of the elements on each presentation was straight. For the first condition, with a target curved line and distractor straight line the percent correct for detection is 74%. For two straight line distractors the percent correct is 85%. If the role of target and distractor are reversed then the percent correct for a target and distractor is 87% while that for two distractors drops to 54%. The high false alarm rate for detecting at least one straight line in a stimulus consisting of just two curved lines suggests that the curvature is not reliably perceived. Failure to detect the curvature would explain the search asymmetry observed for one straight line in a field of curved lines compared to one curved line in a field of straight lines. Because of lack of reliable detection of curvature, searching for a straight line in a field of curved ones amounts to searching for a straight line in a field of both curved and straight lines. This is far more difficult than searching for a single curved line in a field of straight ones.

The line curvature in this experiment was very slight. Treisman and Gormican (1988) found that if the curvature is increased sufficiently the search becomes symmetric when the role of target and distractor are switched. Unreliable perception of curvature would explain why discrimination becomes more symmetric with increased curvature. As the curvature is increased the likelihood of detecting the curve increases and a straight and a curved line become equally detectable.

Results for the texture pair of a circle and an ellipse are similar. In two element experiments the false alarm rate for detecting a circle in a stimulus consisting of two ellipses is high relative to the other stimulus conditions. The failure to detect the difference in length of the major and minor axis of an ellipse would account for the search asymmetry for the circle and ellipse texture pair.

The final texture pair tested in this section was a pair of parallel line

Figure 14 Perceptual asymmetry is shown for texture pairs composed of convergent pairs of lines and parallel pairs of lines. The perception of the convergent pairs in a field of parallel pairs yields easier segregation.

segments versus a pair of convergent line segments for which line separation at one end was greater than at the other (Figure 14). As with the other texture pairs, the more asymmetric member (i.e. the convergent lines) is more easily detected in a field of the symmetric element than the reverse. Two element experiments confirmed a high false alarm rate for a stimulus composed of two convergent lines. These results suggest that the unequal separation of the endings of the lines for the convergent element is not reliably detected.

Taken together the results suggest that for the texture pairs for which one member of the pair is constructed by deforming the other, the search asymmetry is probably the result of a failure to detect the deformation of the more asymmetric element rather than an emergent feature. This is also supported by the evidence that if the deformation is made sufficiently large so that it is reliably detected, the search asymmetry disappears.

C. Spatial Fill-in

For texture pairs considered in this section, search asymmetry is present if there are many distractors and one or more targets but not if there is only a single target and a single distractor. For these texture pairs, search asymmetry does not depend on a change in perception of the elements.

The simplest element pair which shows this property of asymmetry is a long line (1 degree of visual angle) and a short line (1/2 degree). If a set of target long lines are presented in a field of distractor short lines, then it will be easier to detect the target than if the role of target and distractor are reversed (Figure 15). With only a single target and distractor, discrimination is the same at approximately 90% when the role of target and distractor are reversed. This perceptual symmetry is present even if the SOA is decreased to 80 msec. The percentage correct for this SOA is approximately 70%

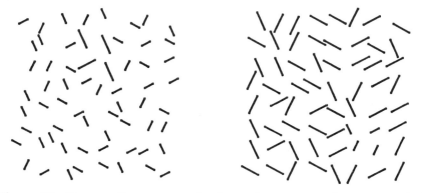

Figure 15 Perceptual asymmetry is shown for texture pairs composed of short line segments and long line segments. It is easier to detect the target long lines in the field of short lines than the reverse.

irrespective of whether the long or short line was the target. Therefore, the asymmetry is not due to a change in the perception of these elements. Since this asymmetry is not due to the elements themselves, we decided to examine if it depended on the relationship between elements.

To examine the precise relationship between these elements, we measured the effect of spacing between them. The results for two conditions were compared (see Figure 16). In one case, six elements were equally spaced over half the circumference of a circle which was three degrees in radius. The portion of the circumference on which the elements occurred varied randomly over trials. For the second case, elements were spaced at twice the separation of the first condition. Six elements were equally spaced over the entire circumference of the circle. For both conditions, there was one target and five distractors.

In the first condition, performance critically depended on whether the short or the long line served as the target. If the target was a long line and the distractors were all short lines, the percent correct for discrimination was 87%. Performance fell to 52% if the roles were reversed; i.e., if the target was a short line and the distractors were long lines.

For the second condition, there was no evidence of asymmetry in discrimination. Whether the short line or the long line served as the target stimulus, performance was constant at approximately 70%. Increasing the spacing reduced discrimination from 87% to 72% correct when the target was a long line, but increased it from 52% to 71% correct if the target was a short line. Thus, the closer spacing has two opposing effects, depending on which stimulus was designated as the target: 1) enhancing performance (target - long line); or 2) diminishing performance (target - short line).

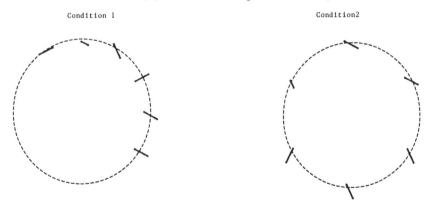

Condition 1   Condition2

Figure 16 The two stimulus presentation conditions for measuring the effects of inter-element spacing are shown. In Condition 1, six elements are evenly spaced over half the circumference of the circle. In Condition 2, the spacing between elements is double in comparison to the first condition. For this case the six elements are equally spaced over the entire circumference.

To further investigate element interactions on texture segregation, we examined performance for three elements traditionally used in texture (**T**, **L**, and **+**). All three elements consist of the same two line segments oriented at right angles to each other. The elements differ only by the exact location at which the two line segments meet (Figure 1).

1. Texture Element Pair "T" and "L"

First consider the element pair, **T** and **L**. As with the other element pairs (discussed previously), performance significantly changes if the role of target and distractor is switched. However, role reversal was not the only factor which determined the direction of the asymmetry. The geometric configuration of figure and ground also altered discriminability. For example, if the figure consists of a rectangle of target elements embedded in a larger background rectangle of distractor elements, performance is higher for the target **L** than the target **T** (Gurnsey & Browse, 1986). The direction of the asymmetry is reversed if all elements are presented on the circumference of a circle. Percent discrimination for a target **T** in a circular field of **L**s is 60% correct. With the role of target and distractor reversed (i.e., target **L** and distractor **T**) performance drops to 30%.

The condition with elements on a circle can be considered the one-dimensional (1-D) analogue of the two-dimensional (2-D) embedded rectangle. Elements are first presented on a one-dimensional line which has been wrapped into a circle. In this context, the differences between the two conditions is that for the embedded rectangles (two-dimensional) each element, except for the border elements, is completely surrounded by other elements. Conversely, on the circle (which is one-dimensional) an element is never completely surrounded; it has neighboring elements only on either side.

This change in asymmetry with geometric configuration places constraints on any models proposed to account for texture segregation. The mere existence of target asymmetries implies that a linear model is inadequate, since element response under such a model would remain constant if the role of target and distractor are switched. The change of asymmetry with geometric configuration implies that texture segregation cannot be explained by the canonical form of the elements, nor by considering the effect of randomized orientation of the elements as proposed by Sagi and Fogel (1989). Under these models, effects of orientation should be the same in 2-D and 1-D cases, and one would expect the same direction for the asymmetry.

The change in the direction of the asymmetry with geometric configuration suggests that the relationship between the elements is critical for segregation. To investigate the effects of inter-element relationships on texture segregation, we compared discriminability for a target **T** in a circular field of distractor **L**s for two conditions, each of which generates different inter-element spacing around the target **T**. The conditions depended on the orientation of the target **T**.

The **T** is not rotationally symmetric for a 90 degree rotation. On the other hand, the **+** is rotationally symmetric and the **L** is mirror symmetric under a rotation of 90 degrees. In the experiments, the **T** could take eight possible orientations which sampled 360 degrees of rotation in steps of 45 degrees. In one condition, the orientation of the **T** was chosen at random from one of the four possible orientations for which the top cross bar is oriented more tangentially to the circumference of the circle, rather than normal to it. In the other condition, the possible orientations consisted of those for which the top cross bar is oriented more normally to the circumference of the circle, rather than tangential to it (Figure 17). Of course the four possible orientations for a particular target **T** which are more tangential or normal to the circumference will depend on the location of the **T** on the circumference of the circle. Thus for both of the conditions all eight possible orientations will occur during the

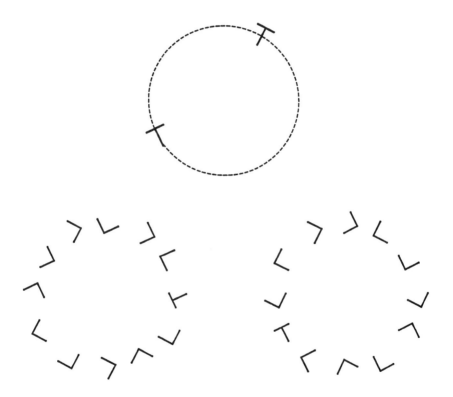

Figure 17 Examples of the two categories of orientation of **T** relative to the circumference of the circle are shown at the top. For one category the cross bar of the **T** is more tangential to the circumference. In the other category it is more normal. At the bottom are examples of the two categories of orientation in a circle of distractor **L**s.

Figure 18 The canonical form of the texture element pairs of a **T** and a half -
T.

experiment as they did for the original experiment. Results revealed that
discrimination is better if the cross bar is oriented more tangentially to the
circumference of the circle, rather than more normal. With the cross bar
tangential in orientation, discrimination was 84%. With the bar normal,
discriminability is reduced to 43%. However, from this paradigm it is not
possible to determine if the change in performance is due to the difference in
the shape of the spaces between elements for the two orientations, or is only
due to the line segments of the **T** being more easily perceived in the
tangential case.

To carefully examine the contribution of the shape of the space between
elements we need a pair of elements which are themselves different, but will
generate the same inter-element spaces. Two elements which fit these
requirements are a **T**, and a **T** with one side of the cross bar removed (short
top, or half-**T**) (Figure 18). For elements presented on a circle, the long stem
of the half-**T** from which the top half was removed will appear similar to the
top of a normal **T** to a neighboring element.

As a control, we were careful not to use vertical or horizontal orientations of
these elements so that the top of the half-**T** with the short line segment
would not be directly exposed to the neighboring element. Thus, when
utilizing the **T** and the half-**T** as stimuli, the elements are different, but the
shape of the inter-element spaces in a circle configuration are the same.

We found that for this element pair, it is virtually impossible to correctly
discriminate the target - regardless of which element is the target (Figure
19). For the target **T** with the distractor half-**T**s, correct discrimination is
only 12%. Similarly, in the obverse condition correct discrimination is only
14%. In both conditions, performance is very close to chance performance
(0%).

The results for this element pair place further constraints on any model of
texture segregation. Since the two elements contain line segments of
different lengths, the elements have different luminances and different first-
order statistics. This strongly suggests that texture segregation is not
necessarily based on luminance differences. Additionally, the different
lengths of the line segments in the two elements produces different convex

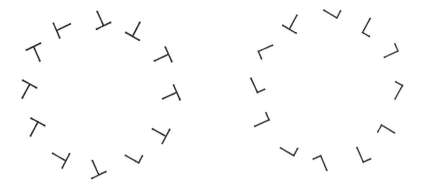

Figure 19 On the left is shown an example of a target half -T in a circle of distractor Ts. On the right is a target T in a circle of distractor half -Ts.

hulls for the two elements. Gurnsey and Browse (1986) have proposed that texture segregation is accounted for by the difference in convex hulls between target and distractor. Our results using a T and a half-T argue against this explanation.

We still need to account for the reversal in the direction of the asymmetry for the elements T and L as their geometric configuration is changed from rectangular to circular. Inter-element spacing may be the crucial factor, but a complete explanation rests on the geometric properties of the T and L. The T is rotationally invariant along the vertical axis, while the L is not rotationally invariant for either the vertical or horizontal axis. As a result of the lack of rotational invariance for the L, the size of the inter-element spaces among Ls is more diverse than among Ts. If the concave edges of two Ls are juxtaposed, the space is very large compared to the case where the two convex sides face each other. The convex portion of an L next to the concave side of a neighboring L will result in a space similar in size and shape to the space produced by juxtaposing the sides of two Ts. It may be argued that discrimination asymmetry using these elements is related to this greater diversity among inter-element spaces for Ls. In particular, for a target rectangle of Ts the inter-element spaces will all be represented within the distractor rectangle of Ls (Figure 20). This logically leads to our observed result for this stimulus configuration: it is difficult to distinguish target Ts from the distractor Ls. In contrast, a target rectangle of Ls can possess inter-element spaces that are larger than, smaller than, and equivalent to those contained in the distractor field of Ts. These inter-element spaces, which are unique to the target rectangle of Ls, provide a means to distinguish this target from the background of distractor Ts.

For these same elements in a circular configuration, a seemingly paradoxical result occurs: the asymmetry reverses direction, with the target T more easily detected than a target L. Upon closer inspection, however, the reason for this reversal becomes clear. For a target L, one arm of the element will

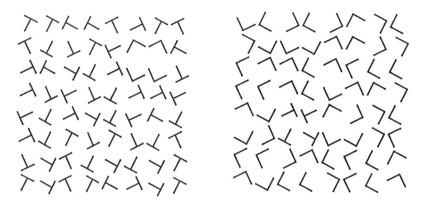

Figure 20 Perceptual asymmetry is shown for texture pairs composed of **T** elements and **L** elements. The perception of the **L** elements in a field of **T** elements produces stronger texture segregation than vice versa.

always be more normal to the circumference of the circle and the other arm more tangential to it. With respect to the neighboring elements, the more normal arm of the **L** will be perceptually indistinguishable from the top of a **T**. Conversely, the arm which is more tangential will be perceptually indistinguishable from the stem of the **T**. Therefore, the inter-element spaces produced between a target **L** and neighboring **T**s on a circle will be very similar to the spaces produced between the other distractor **T**s. This similarity of inter-element spacing will in effect serve to camouflage the **L** in the circle of **T**s.

To account for the detectability of the target **T** in a circle of distractor **L**s, it is necessary to separately consider two orientations of the target **T**; when the top bar is more normal to the circumference of the circle, and when it is more tangential. With respect to the neighboring elements on the circle, the top bar of the target **T** is perceptually indistinguishable from the bottom of any given distractor **L**. Analogously, the bottom of a target **T** will be identical perceptually to the top of an **L** to neighboring elements. For the condition when the top bar of the **T** is more normal to the circumference of the stimulus circle, these will be the parts of the **T** facing neighboring elements. Therefore, the **T** is perceptually identical to an **L** to the neighboring element on each side. It is not surprising that detection is difficult in this condition. For the case where the target **T** is oriented tangentially to the circumference of the circle, it is necessary to consider the sides of the **T**, since these will face neighboring distractor **L**s. The **T** is symmetrical about the vertical axis. However, the **L** is not symmetric about either the vertical or the horizontal axis. Therefore, the inter-element space created by the tangentially oriented target **T** is unique compared to the distractor **L**s. As a result, the tangentially oriented target **T** is easily discriminated from the distractor **L**s in this case.

2. Texture element pair "T" and "+"

Further investigation of the importance of inter-element spacing in texture perception was carried out using the element pair **T** and **+** (Figure 21). Similarly to that described for the elements **T** and **L**, there is a performance asymmetry with this pair. However, this asymmetry does not reverse direction when the geometric configuration of the stimulus is changed from rectangular to circular. For both configurations, discrimination was easier for the detection of a target **T** with a distractor **+** rather than the obverse. Specifically for a circular arrangement of elements, the target **T** was correctly discriminated from **+** distractors 83% of the time, while correct discrimination was only 56% when **+** served as the target.

Before analyzing inter-element spaces in texture patterns composed of **T**s and **+**s, it is instructional to consider a similar texture pair which differs in a crucial aspect; a **+**, and a **+** with one of the four arms missing (partial **+**). Previously we demonstrated that with a **T** and a half-**T** the elements are different but the inter-element spacings were the same. A similar case can be made for the **+** and the partial **+**. If **+** is the target in a circle of partial **+** distractors, it is virtually impossible to detect the target (percent correct is 10%). Observation of the inter-element spaces in this condition reveals a logical explanation. An intact **+** will present right angles to each of its neighboring elements. One side of the partial **+** is also composed of right angles. With respect to any neighboring partial **+**, the **+** will be indistinguishable from one side of a partial **+**. Thus the shape of the inter-element space between a **+** and a partial **+** can always be duplicated between two neighboring partial **+**s. Similarity of inter-element spaces

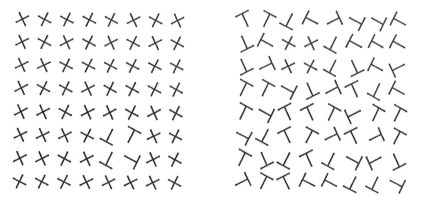

Figure 21 Perceptual asymmetry is shown for texture pairs composed of **T** elements and **+** elements. The perception of the **T** elements in a field of **+** elements produces stronger texture segregation than vice versa.

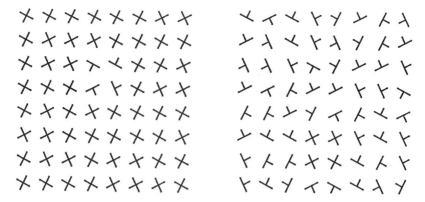

Figure 22 Perceptual asymmetry is shown for texture pairs composed of **+** elements and partial **+** elements.   It is easier to detect the partial **+** elements in the field of **+** elements than the reverse.

renders the target indistinguishable from the distractors.

Performance improved to 30% if the role of target and distractor were switched. In other words, although the task is still difficult, it is easier to distinguish a target partial **+** from distractors which are intact **+**s. This improvement is expected when inter-element spaces are examined. The inter-element spacing between neighboring distractor **+**s consists of regions bordered by right angles. The target partial **+** can, for certain orientations, present a flat line segment to the neighboring element. The inconsistency of the exact shape of the inter-element space between target and distractor in this condition enables the detection of the partial **+** for these trials.

As just demonstrated, segregation based on inter-element spacing can account for the results observed using the element pair **+** and partial **+** (Figure 22). A similar analysis can be used to account for the asymmetry between a **+** and a **T**. For example in Figure 21, since the **+** is symmetric the field of **+**s forms regular spaces between elements. The **T** however is not symmetric, so the four target **T**s form irregular inter-element spaces and are easily discriminated from the **+**s. In comparison, the field of **T**s form both regular and irregular spaces between elements. The four target **+**s form regular spaces, but these are not unique. They are therefore more difficult to detect.

IV.   Conclusions

We have identified three properties of visual processing which account for the perceptual asymmetries associated with texture segregation. These results have forced us to re-examine the process of texture segregation in general. In particular, it appears that more attention must be dedicated to the spaces within texture elements (closure and subjective closure) and between texture elements (spatial fill-in). Although current models of texture segregation are not equipped to deal with these concepts, extensions of these models are possible.

A. Extension of subjective contour and spatial fill-in

By considering the properties of subjective contour and fill-in we can provide a more parsimonious explanation of texture segregation and related phenomena. For example, a fundamental issue in texture perception is why texture elements which segregate in isolation become less and less discriminable as the number of elements in the aggregates increases. Consider the texture pair T and L. When they are presented together as a single pair, at most only one side of each element will form a space with the other element. All other sides are surrounded by empty space, emphasizing the unique aspects of the element. But for this same pair encompassed in a field of elements, each side of nearly every element interacts with up to four other elements to form a variety of inter-element spaces. Thus, as the number of elements increases, the number of indistinguishable inter-element spaces will also increase.

Re-examination of the theory of textons in light of the shape of inter-element spaces suggests why textons lead to effortless discrimination. For example, in Figure 4A the shape of the inter-element spaces between the collinear elements is much different (in this case larger) than for distractor elements. This is also true for other textures; the closure of elements shown in 4B and 4C divide the inter-element space in a unique manner and leads to easy detectability. Perhaps the nature of how these textons divide inter-element space results in their role as the basic perceptual units of texture discrimination. In a system such as the visual system which consists of both on-center and off-center neurons, inter-element space does not represent a null response. For such a system one could consider the inter-element space to be an *anti-texton*. This duality between the element and inter-element space in defining the texton was originally proposed by Julesz (1986). In particular on page 246 of Julesz (1986) it states:

> Another, often misunderstood aspect of the texton theory should also be clarified. Even when the stimulus is restricted to drawings composed of line segments, these line segments often form (outline) blob shaped areas, and these outlined blobs behave like textons.

The findings of the present article clarifies many problems of the texton theory and could extend its explanatory powers. In particular, a critical aspect in defining texture are the neighborhood measurements: the ε-neighborhood and the Δ-neighborhood (Julesz, 1986). The ε-neighborhood is the separation between the line segments which form the elements while the Δ-neighborhood is the inter-element distance in a texture. The results of

experiments on closure and subjective closure demonstrate that ε
-neighborhood is the distance over which subjective contours can be
established.   The Δ-neighborhood is the neighborhood constraint for
determining the shape of inter-elements spaces.

Inter-element spacing can provide an explanation for yet another
phenomenon in visual perception - *perceptual grouping*, initially investigated
by Pomerantz in 1974. In these experiments, the same microelements in
different arrangements can group to form unique objects in certain cases but
not in others.   Consider the example shown in Figure 23, where the
microelements are two curved lines. For each set (A and B) subjects are
asked to sort cards containing the top two pairs from cards showing the lower
two. In Figure 23A, all lines are parallel to each other. When the lines face
each other (as in the lower left pair), they group into a entity which is easily
discriminated from the other three arrangements of these same lines, as
evidenced by relatively fast reaction times. On the other hand, when the
lines are perpendicular to each other (as seen in Figure 23B), no pair results
in perceptual grouping and cannot be distinguished from each other without
scrutiny.

This result becomes intuitively sensible when one considers the spaces
between the microelements, as well as the spaces between the stimuli. In
Figure 23A, the inter-element space between the two curved lines in the
lower left pair is much larger than for the other pairs, resulting in easy
discriminability. Conversely, in Figure 23B the inter-element spaces - and
even the interstimulus spaces - are all quite similar, accounting for the
increased time required to discriminate between these pairs.

The shape of inter-element spacing may also provide an alternative, and

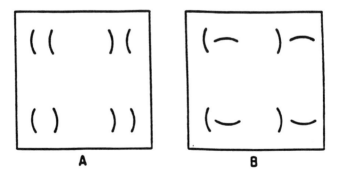

Figure 23 In (A) are four stimuli created by combining two possible curved
elements on the left with two on the right. The stimuli exhibit perceptual
grouping. In (B), the same four stimuli as in (A) but with the right hand
element rotated 90 degrees. These stimuli do not show perceptual grouping.
(From Pomerantz,1981).*

* Reprinted with permission from M. Kubovy and J.R. Pomerantz,
Perceptual Organization, 1981, by Erlbaum Associates, Inc.

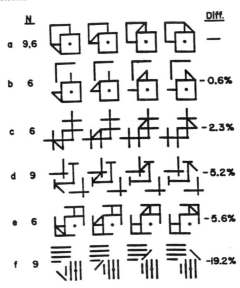

Figure 24 Example of object superiority. Relative accuracy in identifying diagonal line segments when briefly flashed with various context patterns. *Diff* is the mean deficit in accuracy with each context as compared to the overlapping squares (row a). (From Weisstein and Harris, 1974).*

less cognitively based, explanation for the *object superiority effect* described by Harris and Weisstein (1974). They observed that it was easier to distinguish the orientation of a line segment within a group of other line segments if the set of lines formed a recognizable 2-D object, or the 2-D projection of a 3-D object. This is illustrated in Figure 24. Discrimination of the single diagonal line improves as the lines form a cognitively recognizable object. However, note that as the lines are encompassed in a more recognizable object, the shape of the inter-element spaces becomes more unique. If discrimination is based on the differences in the shape of inter-element spaces, it is logical to assume that performance would also increase as the lines are segregated to form closed spaces.

Recently, researchers in the areas of artificial intelligence and computer vision have stressed the need to develop edge detectors which mimic humans' ability to perceive the edges of objects (Walters, 1987). The efficacy of these edge detectors have been tested using the segmentation of line drawn cartoons. It is true that the human visual system is extremely good at edge detection, as well as the segmentation and recognition of line drawn cartoons and caricatures. However, successful navigation about the typical human environment requires more than just the detection of a collection of edges and boundaries. Visual information processing is object based, which requires fill-in between edges and boundaries. For example, detecting the edges of a closed versus an open doorway is useless without the ability to detect the door itself. Our results strongly imply that human texture discrimination depends on the shape of the inter-element space, suggesting that cartoon and caricature segmentation is dependent on the fill-in process. Perhaps the emphasis of research in computer vision should be shifted toward the spatial fill-in within edges, rather than solely the edges.

B. Summary

In conclusion, our results point to the need to consider closure and subjective closure within elements, and fill-in between elements when investigating the nature of human texture perception. These findings have application to future research in human perception, as well as suggesting more appropriate computer models of texture detection.

References

Bergen, J.R. and Adelson, E.H., 1988, "Early vision and texture perception," *Nature*, **333**: 363-364.

Blakemore C. and F.W. Campbell, 1969, "On the existence of neurones in the human visual system selectivity sensitive to the orientation and size of retinal images," *J. Physiol., Lond.* **203**, 237-260.

Caelli, T. and B. Julesz, 1978, "On perceptual analyzers underlying visual texture discrimination: part I," *Biol, Cybernetics*, **28**, 167-175.

Caelli, T., B. Julesz and E. Gilbert, 1978, "On perceptual analyzers underlying visual texture discrimination: Part II," *Biol, Cybernetics*, **29**, 201-214.

Campbell, F.W. and J. G. Robson, 1968, "Applications of Fourier analysis to the visibility of gratings," *J. Physiol., Lond.* **197**, 551-566.

Fogel, I. and D. Sagi, 1989, "Gabor filters as texture discriminators," *Biol. Cybern.* **61**, 103-113.

Graham, N. and J. Nachmias, 1971, "Detection of grating patterns containing two spatial frequencies: a comparison of single-channel and multiple-channel models," *Vision Res.* **11**, 251-259.

Gurnsey, R. and R. Browse, 1987, "Micropattern properties and presentation conditions influencing visual texture discrimination," *Perception and Psychophys.* **41**, 239-252.

Helmholtz, H. von, 1896, *Handbuch der Physiologischen Optik. Dritter Abschnitt, Zweite Auflage* (Voss, Hamburg). [English translation: *Helmholtz's Treatise on Physiological Optics* by J.P.C. Southall, 1924, (The Optical Soc. Am.), republished by Dover Publications, 1962.]

Julesz, B., 1962, "Visual pattern discrimination," *IRE Trans. Info. Theory* **IT-8**, 84-92.

Julesz, B., 1981, "Textons, the elements of texture perception and their interactions," *Nature* **290**, 91-97.

Julesz, B., 1986, Texton gradients: The texton theory revisited," *Biol. Cybernetics* **54**, 245-251.

Julesz, B. and J.R. Bergen, 1983, "Textons, the fundamental elements in preattentive vision and perception of textures," *Bell Syst. Tech. Jour.* **62**(6), 1619-1645.

Julesz, B., E.N. Gilbert and J.D. Victor, 1978, "Visual discrimination of textures with identical third-order statistics," *Biol. Cybern.* **31**(3), 137-40.

Julesz, B. and B. Kröse, 1988, "Visual texture perception:Features and spatial filters," *Nature* **333**, 302-303.

Kanizsa, G., 1976, "Subjective contours," *Scientific American*, **234**, 48-52.

Kröse, B.J.A., 1987, "Local structure analyzers as determinants of preattentive pattern discrimination," *Biol. Cybern.* **55**, 289-298.

Kröse, B.J.A. and B. Julesz, 1989, "The control and speed of shifts of attention," *Vision Res.* **29**(11), 1607-1619.

Malik, J.M.A. and P. Perona, 1990, "Preattentive texture discrimination with early vision mechanisms," *J. Opt. Soc. Am.* **7**(5), 923-932.

Pomerantz, J.R., 1974, "Perceptual organization in information processing," In M. Kubovy and J.R. Pomerantz (eds.), *Perceptual organization.* Hillsdale, NJ.: Erlbaum, 141-180.

Posner, M.I., 1980, "Orienting of attention," *Quarterly Journal of Experimental Psychology* **32**, 3-25.

Rubenstein, B. and D. Sagi, 1990, "Spatial variability as a limiting factor in texture discrimination tasks: implications for performance asymmetries," *J.Opt.Soc.Am.A.* **9**:1632-1643.

Sachs, M.B., J. Nachmias and J. G. Robson, 1971, "Spatial frequency channels in human vision," *J. opt. Soc. Am.* **61**, 1176-1186.

Schatz, B.R., 1977, "The computation of immediate texture discrimination," *MIT A.I. Lab Memo 426.*

Schumann, F., 1904, "Einige Beobachtungen über die Zusammenfassung von Gesichtseindrucken zu Einheiten," *Psychol. Stud.* **1**, 1-32.

Treisman, A. and G. Gelade, 1980, "A feature integration theory of attention," *Cognitive Psychology* **12**, 97-136.

Treisman, A. and S. Gormican., 1988, "Feature analysis in early vision: Evidence from search asymmetries," *Psychological Reviews* **95**, 15-48.

Treisman, A. and J. Souther, 1985, "Search Asymmetry: A diagnostic for preattentive processing of separable features," *Journal of Experimental Psychology: General* **114** 285-310.

Voorhees, H. and T. Poggio, 1988, "Computing texture boundaries from images," *Nature* **333**, 364-367.

Walters, D., 1987, "Selection of image primitives for general-purpose visual processing," *Computer Vision, Graphics, and Image Processing* **37**, 261-298.

Weisstein, N. and C.S. Harris, 1974, "Visual detection of line segments: An object-superiority effect," *Science* **186**,752-755.

Wilson, H.R. and J.R. Bergen, 1979, "A four mechanism model for threshold spatial vision," *Vision Res.* **19** 19-32.

I.8

Two-Dimensional Maps and Biological Vision: Representing Three-Dimensional Space

G. Lee Zimmerman

Department of Electrical Engineering
Tulane University
New Orleans, LA

1. Introduction

This chapter concentrates on two-dimensional spatial transformations of biological and machine vision systems for performing visual tasks such as recognition, path planning, navigation, obstacle avoidance, or tracking. Re-mapping is a very powerful tool for manipulating information contained in a two-dimensional signal such as an image. It has been underexplored by machine vision systems using neural networks. This is unfortunate since these processing methods are easily implemented in neural networks. Biological vision systems are full of examples of two-dimensional re-mapping, at all levels of the neural hardware. This chapter will attempt to show both the strength and necessity of re-mapping for machine vision systems and systems modeling biological vision systems.

The chapter begins with a review of the early part of the human visual system concentrating on the possibilities created by a foveated sampling system and multiple functional streams of processing on visual perception. The processes occur early in the visual system and will greatly alter the flow of information to higher centers of the visual cortex. The last half of the chapter is a demonstration of a machine vision system which incorporates re-mapping to perform three-dimensional recognition. The machine vision system uses many of the transformations found in the human visual system. In vision, it may be critically important that we use the spatial properties of the image as a tool in systems using neural networks.

2. Biological Vision

The light captured by the lens of the eye is sensed on the two-dimensional surface of the retina. The photoreceptors, rods and cones, sample the intensity of the light. The rods and cones respond to light intensity over a broadly tuned spectral range. These intensity signals are transferred along the optic nerve to the LGN and on to the visual cortex. Under conditions of normal daylight viewing the rods are saturated so they add no information to the signals transmitted to the visual cortex. Therefore, in any discussion of photoreceptors, the reader should assume that I mean the cones alone.

The light falling on the retina is initially modified by the lenses of the eye. The human eye consists of a two lens imaging system. The cornea is the outer lens of the eye. It is the major refractive surface. The crystaline lens is behind the pupil of the eye. Muscles stretch the crystaline lens changing its shape which changes its refractive power. The crystaline lens can accommodate or rather bring light into focus on the retina over a range of 10 diopters. This range of accommodation decreases with age.

Another critical optical component of our eyes is the pupil. It acts as an aperture, limiting the amount of light which can reach the retina. As the ambient light in the world increases the pupil contracts. The contracting pupil increases the depth of field bringing more of the scene into focus while decreasing the amount of light reaching the photoreceptors. Squinting is one way of producing an artificial pupil and increasing the depth of field.

What part of the scene will be in focus depends on both the size of the pupil and the state of the lensing system. Even before the light has managed to reach the retina, it has been filtered by the optical system of the eye. We can see that immediately the creation of the image is controlled to a large degree by properties not of the scene but of the imaging system. These modifications are two-dimensonal and effect the image as a whole.

The light in the filtered image is sampled at discrete points on the retina. The sampling position of those points are tightly packed centrally and become more widely spaced as we move eccentrically from the fovea. The non-linear sampling displayed on the retina forces a structure on the future possible processing which can be performed. First, the central part of the retinal image is sampled at a higher resolution than the rest. This non-linear sampling strongly suggests that one part of the image, the fovea, is receiving a disproportionate share of neural processing. This implies that the eye must move to bring interesting surfaces into the higher resolution area. Second, within the fovea the sampling of the photoreceptors is regular due to the dense packing, but away from the fovea this sampling pattern becomes more random as well as more widely spaced. Processes which critically depend on an even sampling grid will not be good models for biological functioning in the periphery. Both of these features hint at a vision system which is really two systems. One concentrates neural resources on the two-dimensional features of a small portion of the retinal image. The other captures information of a more global scale. Such as the movement of the background as we move through a scene.

The sampling in the fovea is almost regular. The photoreceptors are closely packed. This regularity is lost at more eccentric portions of the retina. There is evidence that random sampling acts as an anti-aliasing filter for the retinal image. What ever the case may be sampling the image in this way has profound consequences on the processing which can be carried out at higher stages in the brain. Any information processing being carried out must either account for this randomness in the sampling or be immune to its consequences.

There are approximately one hundred million photoreceptors spread around the retina. There are about one million ganglion cells reporting the image information from the retina to the cortex. These two facts alone require that there must be at least a 100:1 compression of the retinal image information (Tsotsos, 1982). Lateral connections and various spectral response characteristic combine to produce the encoded information necessary for further processing in the visual cortex. The signals transmitted to the visual cortex by the ganglion cells are equivalent to a weighted sum of the portion of the image falling on the ganglion cells receptive field and the response characteristic of the cell itself.

A cells' receptive field is made of two parts: the center and the surround. The total response is the sum of the response to these two components. For example, a given ganglion cell will respond to a small spot of light which exactly fills its center region. This response will diminish if the light extends into the surround. This cell would be called on-center, off-surround. There are off-center, on-surround ganglion cells. Both types of response seem to exist with even probability throughout the brain (Kuffler 1953) .

Ganglion cell response is determined by the given light pattern and its own response properties and can be predicted if those properties are known. The response will be the convolution of the pattern with a difference of Gaussians pattern which matches the center surround characteristic of the cell. This convolution will elicit a strong response to differences in luminance of a size which matches the cell. The response is essentially a local band pass filtered version of the retinal image. The spatial frequency band which is enhanced is determined by the size of the center response of the cell (Enroth-Cugell and Robson, 1966). This can also be modeled as the convolution of the image with a "del squared G" function as outlined in Marr (1982).

The receptive field of a ganglion cell increases in size as we move eccentrically away from the fovea on the retina. This produces a response from the ganglion cells which simulates a space variant filtering of the retinal image. The portion of the image falling on the eccentric portion of the retina is processed by a filter with a pass band which is quite different than that processing the portion of the image falling on the fovea. This space variant filtering will have a dramatic effect on the information being conveyed to the visual cortex.

The ganglion cells map samples from the retina back to the visual cortex. The mapping is not straight forward. The image in each eye is essentially divided in half. The left half of the left eye and the left half of the right eye are mapped to the left hemisphere of the visual cortex. This means that the right half of the visual field is mapped from the two eyes into the same hemisphere of the visual cortex. These binocular differences remain distinct through a significant portion of the early visual processing.

The mapping of the information from the retina to the cortex takes on many twists along its route. Schwartz (1980) suggests re-mapping of the image from the retina to the cortex is equivalent to a log-polar transformation. The log-polar re-mapping of the retinal image has a very interesting property. Items which are rotated in the image will translate in the log-polar domain. This property is very important because it transforms a search of an item which is rotated and scaled into a translational search.

The discussion so far has been centered on results from physiology about the re-mapping and filtering of the early visual processing. Much of this information has been derived from single cell recordings. There seems to be fairly one-to-one correspondence between a light on a portion of the retina and the location of the responding cells in the visual cortex in the early stages. In later stages this one-to-one correspondence begins to break down and cells respond to more complex patterns of light. The discussion of biological vision and retinotopic maps will shift from physiological to psychophysical phenomena.

There are many psychophysiological experiments which reinforce the properties of visual structure found in physiology. For example, our ability to resolve letters in the periphery decreases with eccentricity. This is exactly what would be predicted for a camera system which sampling like the retina. In fact, the resolution change corresponds well to the known cortical magnification factor between the retina and the visual cortex (Kelly, 1984) .

The retina provides a space-variant filtered response image to the visual cortex via the ganglion cells. There is a significant amount of evidence of the existence of spatial frequency channels early in visual processing. Low spatial frequency patterns are apparently processed relatively independently of high spatial frequency patterns (Blakemore and Campbell, 1969, De Valois K. K., 1977, Legge and Foley, 1980). Subjects can adapt to a given spatial frequency pattern. They will show an increase discrimination threshold for patterns close to the adapting spatial frequency pattern. Patterns with spatial frequency content an octave away from the adapting pattern will show no effects. The existence of spatial frequency channels are evidence that the visual system processes multiple full iconic maps independently – essentially maps of many spatial frequency bands.

Another demonstration of the role of independent processing of iconic information is found in the phenomenon of equiluminance (Cavanagh, 1988). Visual stimuli is processed along the dimensions of luminance, R/G chromatic, and B/Y chromatic channels. When a moving pattern of light is presented such that all of the luminance differences in the pattern are minimized leaving only color, three interesting things happen to the perception. First the pattern becomes less distinct because because the chromatic pathways are have a lower resolution. Second, the color pattern loses itself in space and will tend to attach itself to any nearby surface with stronger depth cues. Third and most strikingly the motion of the pattern will appear to slow. If the pattern was moving at three degrees per second at equiluminance it will appear to be moving at two degrees per second. These perception are strong evidence for the existence of pathways determined by the spectrum of light falling on the retina.

The existence of spatial frequency channels and achromatic/chromatic pathways show that for early vision the single image projected on the retina is processed in as many different iconic maps. The reason for maintaining these maps throughout the cortex may be simply to aid in fusing the information back together into a single perception of the scene. The iconic mapping of the retina would be the glue which binds these extracted properties together.

This review of early visual processing, though brief and incomplete, demonstrates the prevalence of re-mapping and filtering taking place in the brain. The retinal image is filtered both by the optics of the eye and by lateral inhibition of cells on the retina. The processed information is carried back to the visual cortex introducing a crossover to keep the halves of the visual field together in the same hemisphere of the visual cortex and a possible unwrapping of the rotational component in the image. The image is processed along multiple pathways. Spatial frequency channels and chromatic/achromatic pathways demonstrate the existence of many iconic maps being processed simultaneously for many different types of information.

What does this mean in terms of image processing? What are the crucial functions these iconic maps are performing for vision? Transforming, filtering, and re-mapping are primary to early visual processing. The next section will examine visual processing from a different angle. Vision will be examined through the design and construction of a machine vision system using iconic transformations and multiple streams of processing.

3. Computational Vision

Two-dimensional images are difficult to interpret because they can be confounded by sensor noise, uneven illumination, occlusion, uncertain camera position and more. This section concentrates on problems created by uncertain camera position for the task of object recognition. I fundamentally assume the three-dimensional surface area of an object visible to the imaging system will remain invariant to small changes in viewpoint, although the area of the projection on the image may change dramatically. This assumption requires a computer vision system which concentrates its efforts on object surface area. The approach will remove matching restrictions due to viewpoint changes and create a data structure in which changes in the perceived layout of space are immediately reflected in the recognition process.

Changing camera position leads to two kinds of changes in the projected images: metric and non-metric. Metric transformations are changes in scale, orientation, or translation of the two-dimensional shape of the object projections. Under metric transformations, the projected shape is an invariant property. For example, let a camera be pointed at a cube such that only one surface of the cube is visible and the line-of-sight of the camera is perpendicular to the surface. If the camera moves along the line-of-sight, the image of the object will simply get larger or smaller. If the camera rotates about the line-of-sight, the image of the object will rotate. If the camera translates along an axis parallel to the plane of the surface, the image of the object will translate. In all these cases the two-dimensional shape of the object's image remains the same: a square.

Non-metric transformations create much more difficulty for computational vision systems. I concentrate on three specific non-metric transformations: occlusion, foreshortening, and perspective projection. Occlusion occurs when one surface in the scene hides another surface from view. Foreshortening occurs when the surface being viewed slants away from the viewer. In perspective projection, parts of the object's surface far from the lens will be projected smaller than closer parts of the object's surface.In each case, viewpoint is inextricably tied to changes in the projected shape of the object in the image. Occlusion, foreshortening and perspective projection are very common in everyday scenes and present the most difficult problems for computational vision modeling.

A common form of occlusion and a problem with direct impact on the design of the machine vision system is called self-occlusion. Self-occlusion arises when part of an object's surface is obscured by other parts of its surface. All opaque objects exhibit self-occlusion. As an observer travels around an object, new surfaces become visible while other surfaces pass from view. Self-occlusion makes the construction of three-dimensional models from multiple views is a very difficult prospect. This fact raises some issues with models of visual perception which rely heavily on stored three-dimensional object models (Roberts, 1966, Brookes, 1981, Lowe, 1987). My fundamental assumption is that the stored object models are two-dimensional entities which are invariant to small changes in the observers viewpoint. A three-dimensional object is then a collection of these entities. These ideas are similar to those proposed by Chakravaty and Freeman (1982) and Koenderink and Van Doorn (1979), and are beginning to find support from psychophysical study of human perception (Biederman, 1987) .

The other non-metric transformations, foreshortening and perspective projection, are at the heart of the problems surrounding three-dimensional object recognition. A square planar surface, when slanted away from the imaging system, will not be projected as a square in the image. Projected distances on the planar surface perpendicular to the axis of rotation will become smaller due to foreshortening. Projected distances parallel to the axis of rotation will be expanded or contracted depending on the distance between the surface and the imaging system due to perspective projection. Both of these occur simultaneously in the image and can cause dramatic changes in the two-dimensional projected shape of the square. In order to discover whether the projection is a square, the vision system must have some information about the spatial layout and the imaging process. The core of the proposed computational vision theory is a process which uses distance information collected from other image sources to invert these non-metric transformations to enhance recognition.

The three-dimensional object recognition system described in this chapter is called ZEEL. A block diagram of ZEEL is shown in Figure 1. The approach assumes access to a dense map of observer-centered distances. Each point in the depth map contains the distance from the observer to the surface being viewed. These distances can be obtained through the measurement of depth cues. The information contained in the depth map is used by a re-projection system which distorts the image to maintain both connectedness and relative three-dimensional area of the object surfaces viewed in the scene. The re-projection system flattens the surfaces depicted in the image, factoring out distortions of shape due to relative viewer orientation. The re-projected images are recognized using a rotational/scale invariant memory system. This means that the information used for matching is no longer a strict function of the projection parameters of the lens system doing the imaging. Instead recognition is accomplished using an invariant vector which incorporates the visions system's instantaneous interpretation of the surrounding spatial structure.

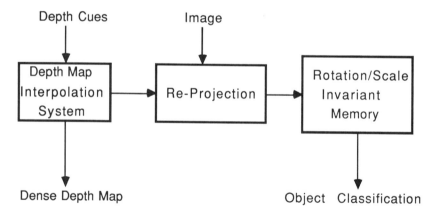

Figure 1. Block Diagram of ZEEL

Orientation changes in the plane of the image due to object or camera rotation and scale changes due to the movement of the camera along the line of sight are common transformations in an image. These produce metric transformations in the image. The memory subsystem of ZEEL is able to recognize memorized two dimensional views regardless of scale and orientation changes. The following is a brief description of the memory system. The memory system is described more completely in (Wechsler and Zimmerman 1988),.

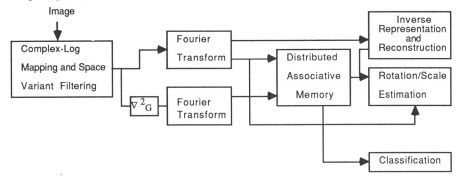

Figure 2. Block Diagram of Rotation/Scale Invariant Memory System

The block diagram which describes the various functional units involved in obtaining an invariant image representation is shown in Figure 2. The image is complex-log conformally mapped so that rotation and scale changes become translation in the transform domain. Along with the conformal mapping, the image is also filtered by a space variant filter to reduce the effects of aliasing. The conformally mapped image is then processed through a Laplacian in order to solve problems associated with the conformal mapping. The Fourier transform of both the conformally mapped image and the Laplacian processed image produce the four output vectors. The magnitude output vector $|\Diamond|_1$ is invariant to linear transformations of the object in the input image. The phase output vector F_2 contains information concerning the spatial properties of the object in the input image. Matching is performed using a distributed associative memory (Kohonen, 1984) indexed by the magnitude output vector $|\Diamond|_1$ The resulting output from the distributed associative memory is a least-squares classification of the unknown image with respect to a set of stored views.

The crucial component of the memory system is the complex-log conformal mapping. By transforming rotation and scale into translation, any correlation technique can be used for matching. A problem associated with the complex-log mapping is sensitivity to center misalignment of the sampled image. ZEEL, therefor, must assume the object is centered in the image frame. Slight misalignments are considered noise. Large misalignments are considered as translations and must be accounted for by changing the gaze in such a way as to bring the object to the center of the frame. An example of the complex-log conformal mapping of an image is shown in Figure 3.

Figure 3. The image on the right is the complex-log mapping of the image on the left.

The key assumption of the rotation/scale invariant memory is that the two-dimensional projected shape of the object in the image does not change with rotation or scale. Objects imaged from real scenes are not restricted to simple rotations in the plane or translations along the line of sight. A three-dimensional object can slant away from the observer, introducing foreshortening and perspective distortion into the two-dimensional projected shape of the object. The re-projection system partially inverts these non-metric transformations enhancing ZEEL's response to changes in camera viewpoint.

The following requirements are placed on the re-projection system. Flat surfaces should re-project to flat frontal surfaces without distorting the shape of the surface markings. Minimizing the distortion of the surface markings may be critical for visual tasks such as reading. Adjacent equal area visible surfaces on an object should be adjacent and equal area in the re-projected image. This requirement retains the spatial relations between adjoining parts of an object. Distortion of surface markings, if they occur, should be smallest in the center of the re-projected image. This last requirement is desirable because of the foveal nature of the memory system.

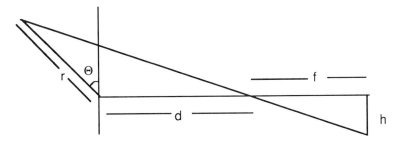

Figure 4. Schematic description of Re-Projection

The re-projection system receives as input a dense depth map and the intensity image. The depth map is in register with the image. Therefore, each pixel of the image is seen by the re-projection system as the intensity value of a point in space which exists on the surface of the object. Let the input information to the re-projection system be from a single plane slanted in space about the horizontal axis. This is shown graphically in figure 4. The slanted plane is vertically foreshortened in the image. If the plane were vertical, the distance r on the objects surface that projects to a unit distance h in the image is given by

$$r = d/f \qquad (1)$$

where f is the focal length and d is the distance from the lens to the surface. When the plane is slanted by an angle θ, the distance on the surface, r ,projects to the same distance h in the image according to the equation

$$r = d/(f cos(\theta) - sin(\theta)) \qquad (2)$$

The magnitude of θ cannot be greater than the $\tan^{-1}(f)$. The equation says the distance r is larger than h for positive θ, smaller than h for negative θ, and equal to h for θ equal zero. To rotate the plane to a frontal position the image needs to be expanded or contracted according to the ratio r/h.

This simple expansion would work fine if we were strictly limiting the camera to rotations about the horizontal axis using orthographic projection to produce the image. Since this is not the general case, the re-projection system must expand the image first along the horizontal axis and then along the vertical axis. Pixels in the image are expanded according to the equation

$$r = \sqrt{\left(\frac{z_i h_i}{f} - \frac{z_{i+1} h_{i+1}}{f}\right)^2 + (z_i - z_{i+1})^2} \qquad (3)$$

where z_i and z_{i+1} are the distances to the surface measured on the coordinate axis centered at the observer as shown in figure 5. The result is the relative expansion of the area covered by the pixel in the image with respect to the size of the surface area of the object.

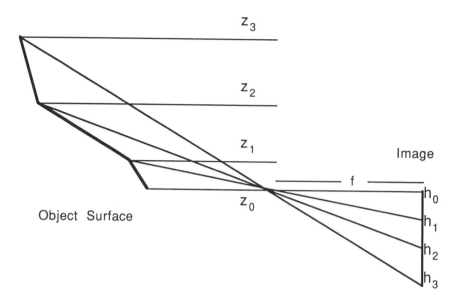

Figure 5. Re-Projection

The re-projection system, as it has been developed so far, will expand the image such that the surface area of the plane will be maintained. We would also like the adjacent surface areas on the object to be adjacent in the re-projected image. To accomplish this, the expansion must link neighboring pixels. In ZEEL, the re-projection system expands from the center outward. Beginning at the x-axis, each pixel is expanded vertically according to the three-dimensional distance between them. The end of the first expanded pixel is the beginning of the second and so on. When the expansion is completed for the entire image, the process is repeated starting at the y-axis and expanding horizontally.

The fundamental language of vision is space. All vision systems, biological or computational, must represent the spatial layout of the environment. In some computational systems this may be done implicitly through the use of data structures such as directed graphs or explicitly through lists of vertices and world positions. ZEEL maintains a representation of space explicitly in the form of a dense depth map. The depth map is a two-dimensional function of observer centered distances in register with the image. Each point in the depth map is the distance between the observer's eye and the portion of the visible surface in the scene producing the projected point in the image. The coordinate system used to describe the location of a point in the scene is centered at the observer with the z-axis directed along the line of sight. The depth map structure is very similar to the 2 1/2D sketch of Marr (1982).

The depth map can be derived from depth cues in the image. For the purposes of this discussion, I assume the depth cues are a measure of disparity between multiple images as is the case for motion or binocular parallax. There exists computational techniques for extracting disparity information from images. Several of these techniques are reviewed in Rosenfeld (1984). Output from the disparity system is assumed to be available to the depth map formation system, although the method for extracting this information is not explicitly formulated. In disparity and many other cues to depth , the resulting measurements are sparse and irregularly placed in the field of view. This problem is entirely due to the nature of the cues and not the extraction method. For systems measuring disparity, there will always be areas in the image where no matchable features exist. Depth estimates at these points are impossible.

Disparity is not a direct measure of distance. Additional information, such as the vergence angle of the cameras and the baseline distance traveled, is needed to transform disparity into a measurement of absolute distance from the camera. In the absence of the necessary additional information, the disparity measures are inversely proportional to the measurement of relative distances in the scene. If one point has a larger disparity value than another point then it is closer to the camera, which is a relative, not an absolute distance measure.

The re-projection system does not need absolute distance information to perform its function satisfactorily. The attention point parameter function controls the two-dimensional size of the re-projected object by changing the perceived absolute distance. Since absolute distances from the depth map can be dynamically altered without drastically changing the overall system performance, it can be shown that relative distance estimates are sufficient. The disparity measures can be used directly to create a dense depth map. If other cues become available, then this information could be incorporated into the relative information to reflect the absolute distances in the scene.

The input information to the depth map formation system is relative observer centered distance estimates which are sparse and irregularly spaced across the field of view. This is the natural form of the depth information available from a variety of disparity cues, such as stereo or motion parallax. The output from the depth map formation system is a dense two-dimensional function of observer-centered distances to surfaces in the scene. Many researchers have been involved in constructing a dense depth map from sparse data (Rosenfeld, 1984,, Grimson, W. E. L., 1983, and Poggio, Torre, and Koch, 1985). To create the dense information from sparse samples, the depth map formation system of ZEEL performs a very simple interpolation by fitting the input data with a mathematically defined thin membrane.

The thin membrane forms a smooth full surface across the area being interpolated. The depth map is a grid of samples of the distances to visible surfaces. The grid points have the following relationship. If a distance estimate is available then the estimate of the grid point is a function of the distance estimate. The estimate of the grid point is also influenced by neighboring grid points. The structure of the distances in a neighborhood of the point corresponds to a flat surface imbedded in the scene. The membrane consists of a collection of data points in which an energy function is minimized, satisfying the constraints placed on the system.

The energy function used to enforce the constraints among the grid points is

$$E = \Sigma(u_{i,j} - d_{i,j})^2 - \lambda^2 \left| u_{i,j}'' \right| \qquad (11)$$

The first term in the energy function enforces the constraint that the derived two-dimensional function, $u_{i,j}$, should be close to the input data from the locality systems, $d_{i,j}$. This is a non-hallucinatory term forcing the resulting depth map to contain some correspondence with the scene. the second term tries to find the flattest function which will do the job. The parameter, λ, balances the effect of these constraints. If λ is large, then the flattening term will dominate and the resulting membrane will be stiff, refusing to bend around the available data. If λ is small then the resulting membrane will follow the input locality data very closely, only searching for flat surfaces at points where none of the sparse data is available. The component energy function which determines the flatness of the surface created by the distance estimates at the grid points, can take a number of different forms depending on the area under inspection, and the tesselation of the grid points. Flatness, for the square tesselation, is measured by the square Laplacian, a form of the second spatial derivative of the data. The depth map formation system minimizes

$$u_{i,j}'' = u_{xx}^2 + u_{yy}^2 \qquad (12)$$

where u_{xx} is the second spatial derivative in the horizontal direction and u_{yy} is the second spatial derivative in the vertical direction. The square Laplacian uses the four nearest neighbors to derive the estimates from the data. All of the measures required to minimize the energy function are local. the locality of the measurements reinforces the idea that the membrane formation can take place in a completely parallel fashion. The minimization process uses successive over-relaxation to perform the membrane fit. This process is outlined thoroughly in Blake and Zisserman (1987) .

The solution to the problem of interpolation presented here are not novel or unique to this system. The primary purpose for this discussion is to address the requirement imposed by the re-projection system of creating a dense depth map from sparse data and to demonstrate that the re-projection and memory system could produce respectable results given an interpolated depth map.

Figure 6 is an example of the whole system working. The upper right image is the original memorized object. The upper right picture is the reconstructed depth map. The reconstruction came from a depth map of a rotated object with more than 50% of the information deleted. The lower left is the reprojected image which is sensed by the memory system. The lower right shows a bar graph demonstrating the response of the memory system. The cube was the first object in the memory and elicits the strongest response.

Figure 6. Example of recall through ZEEL.

4. Conclusion

The beginning of this chapter was a review of early visual processing. The review demonstrated the prevalence of re-mapping and filtering that takes place in the brain. The retinal image is filtered both by the optics of the eye and by lateral inhibition of cells on the retina. The processed information is carried back to the visual cortex, re-mapping the retinal image through binocular crossover an unwrapping of the rotational component in the image. The image is processed along multiple pathways – spatial frequency channels and chromatic/achromatic pathways.

The rest of the chapter is dedicated to the description of a specific implementation of invariant processing. The computational vision system begins with sparse observer-centered distance information extracted from depth cues using locality systems The sparse distance information is interpolated to produce a dense depth map. The depth map is a two-dimensional representation of visible surfaces in the scene. The depth map is used to modify the image -- forcing planar surfaces to be frontal and creating an equal area projection of the scene. This equal area re-projection of the image partially inverts distortions due to projection and foreshortening. The resulting "flattened" image is projected onto a rotation and scale invariant memory system. The memory system combines complex-log conformal mapping with distributed associative memory to store and recall two-dimensional views under metric transformations.

Two ideas guided the design and construction of the machine vision system. First that the important invariant part of an object in the scene is the surface area and not the projected image area. Second, throughout the early processing it is important to perform the image processing functions iconically, maintaining a link with the projected image information. I demonstrated how a machine vision system could be constructed which uses re-mapping and the analysis of the image along multiple pathways. The resulting computer vision system is not complete in any way, but it does demonstrate the power of these techniques drawn from our understanding of biological vision.

References

Biederman, I., (1987) *Recognition-by-components: a theory of human image understanding,* **Psychological Review,** 84, 413-451

Blake, A and Zisserman, (1987) **Visual Reconstruction,** MIT Press, Cambridge

Blakemore, C. and F. W. Campbell (1969) *On the existence of neurones in the human visual system selectively sensitive to orientation and size of retinal images,* **J. Physiol. (Lond.)** 203, 237-260.

Brookes, R. (1981), *Symbolic reasoning among 3-D models and 2-D images,* **Artificial Intelligence,** 17, 1-3.

Cavanagh, P. (1988), *Visual pathways,* **in Computational Processes in Human Vision,** Zenon Plyshyn (ed.) ABLEX Puublishing Corp.

Chakravaty, I. and H. Freeman (1982), *Characteristic views as a basis for three-dimensional object recognition,* **Proceedings of the SPIE Conference on Robot Vision** (Arlington, Ba., May), Vol.336, 37-45.

De Valois K. K. (1977) *Spatial frequency adaptation can enhance contrast sensitivity,* **Vis. Res.** 17, 1057-1065.

Enroth-Cugell, C and J. G. Robson (1966) *The contrast sensitivity of retinal ganglion cells of the cat,* **J. Physiol. (Lond.)** 187, 517-552.

Grimson, W. E. L. (1983), *An implementation of a computational theory of visual surface interpolation,* **Computer Graphics and Image Processing,** 22, 39-69.

Kelly, D. H. (1984) *Retinal inhomogeneity I. Spatiotemporal contrast sensitivity*, **J. Opt. Soc. AM. A.** 1, 107-113.

Koenderink, J. J., and A. Van Doorn (1979), *Internal representation of solid shape with respect to vision*, **Biol. Cybern.**, 32, 4,211-216.

Kohonen, T. (1984) **Self-Organization and Associative Memories,** Springer-Verlag.

Kuffler, S. W. (1953) *Discharge patterns and functional organization of mammillian retina*, **J. Neurophysiol.** 16, 37-68.

Legge, G. E. and J. M. Foley (1980) *Contrast Masking of human vision*, **J. Opt. Soc. Am. A.** 70, 1458-1471.

Lowe, D. G., (1987), *Three-dimensional object recognition from two-dimensional images*, **Artificial Intelligence**, 31, 355-395.

Marr, D. (1982) **Vision**, W.H. Freeman, San Fransisco, CA.

Poggio, T., V. Torre, and C. Koch (1985),.*Computational vision an regularization theory*, **Nature**, 317, 314-319.

Roberts, L. G. (1966) *Machine perception of three-dimensional solids*, **Optical and Eletro-optical Information Processing**, J. Tippitt (ED.), MIT Press, Cambridge MA., 159-197.

Rosenfeld, A. (1984), *Image analysis: problems, progress, and prospects*, **Pattern Recognition,** 17(1):3-12.

Schwartz, E. L. (1980) *Computational anatomy and functional architecture of striate cortex: a spatial mapping approach to perceptual coding*, **Vis. Res.** 20, 645-669.

Tsotsos, J. K. (1982) *Knowledge of the visual process: content, form, and use*, **Proc. 6th. Int. Conf. on Pattern Recognition**, Munich, Germany, 654-669.

Wechsler, H. and G. L. Zimmerman (1988), *2-D Invariant Object Recognition Using Distributed Associative Memories*, **IEEE Transactions on Pattern Analysis and Machine Intelligence**, 10, 811-821.

PART II

Machine Perception

II. Introduction

This second part of the book considers the relevance of neural networks for machine perception. The underlying challenge for machine perception is the sheer complexity of the visual task. Most visual tasks are complex because they are underconstrained--or in mathematical terms are ill-posed; however, the human visual system display robustness (to noise and/or missing data) and fault-tolerance (to memory faults) despite stringent constraints on what can be accomplished and does that with relatively limited computational resources. Neural networks for perception in general, and for machine perception in particular, facilitate the development of an integrated goal-driven theory of distributed computation over space, time and function. Distributed computation goes beyond mere processing to include image representations and processing strategies. Distributed strategies account for active perception and our symbiotic link to the surrounding environment. They are functional if flexible processing is allowed, or exploratory when we engage the environment to interpret it better. The perceptual system casts most visual tasks as optimization problems and solves them using neural networks techniques and enforcing nonaccidental, natural constraints. The constraints are either prewired or evolve through system adaptation and learning. Such a computational theory is embedded within the general framework of intelligent integrated architectures, known generically as the Perception-Control-Action-Learning (PCAL) model. The model is motivated by the fact that perception is directed and primed under the guidance of memory structures.

The first chapter, written by Igor Aleksander, describes WISARD, an adaptive pattern recognition system. The storage traces are implemented as Random-Access Memory (RAM), which stores the learned responses to patterns defining its address terminals. The network can be augmented so that the memory contents could stand for firing probabilities. Such networks lend themselves to generalization and their use of firing probabilities for cost-optimization relates them to genetic algorithms. Generalization occurs across the RAM as the patterns belonging to the same class define a (limited) range of address terminals.

The second chapter, by Jezekiel Ben-Arie, explores the computation of possibly localized spectral image representations. High resolution, an indication of the degree of localization, is achieved through the distributed aspect of image representations, applies to the spatial and spatial/frequency domains, and leads to the concept of conjoint spatial/spectral image representations. Examples of such image representations includes the spectrogram (windowed Fourier transform) and the Gabor transform. The actual derivation of conjoint representations illustrates the relationship between parallel and distributed representations (PDR) and their computation using PDP. As an example, John Daugman has shown how to derive the coefficients of the 2-dimensional Gabor transform using a three-layer neural network via minimization of energy landscapes. Neural computing is relevant in this case because the base of the discrete Gabor transform is not orthogonal and the set of coefficients can be quite useful for data compression applications. Ben-Arie addresses the same problem and brings an elegant solution. Specifically, he has shown how linear web-lattices using the central limit theorem can be used to derive both the difference-of-Gaussians (DOG) and the Fourier and Gabor transforms. Each layer of the web performs only simple repetitive averaging, but the multilayered result converges into exact Gaussian convolution. Hence, each layer of the web generates Gaussian averaging of different scale--the higher the layer in the web the larger the widths of the blurring Gaussian kernels.

Image invariants are crucial for robust and efficient perception in terms of performance and resource utilization, respectively. Retinotopic mappings, discussed in the context of human perception, preserve the topology of the field of view (FOV) and must be followed by appropriate mappings leading to spatiotemporal invariance. Terry Caelli, Mario Ferraro, and Erhard Barth describe in the third chapter a 4-dimensional perceptual image representation, which is "encapsulated in a set of filtered images, each containing the original Cartesian coordinates of the image and indexed in terms of the orientation and scale-specific filters used to produce them. The result of this scheme is that a change in position, scale, or orientation of the input pattern has the effect of shifting the distribution of filters outputs within (position) and between (orientation and scale) columns." Such a distributed representational scheme is implemented through filters defined by specific scale and orientation characteristics. The corresponding Fourier transform of such filters are Gaussian, are sufficient to reconstruct the input image, and their spectral position and bandwidth define the scale and orientation sensitivity range. The net result is an enhanced cytoarchitecture in terms of invariance to linear transformations.

The fourth chapter by Gail Carpenter, Stephen Grossberg, and John Reynolds describes a novel neural network architecture called ARTMAP, which learns to classify arbitrarily many, arbitrarily ordered vectors into recognition categories based on predictive success. The internal architecture is built up from a pair of ART (Adaptive Resonance Theory) modules that are capable of self-organizing stable recognition categories. The ART modules are linked by an associative learning network and an internal controller that ensures autonomous system operation.

The fifth chapter, written by Anya Hurlbert, considers the problem of color constancy and illustrates the link between neural networks and classical techniques of estimation and image reconstruction. As an example, the algorithm suggested for lightness (reflectance) computation starts by separating the brightness into reflectance and illumination as would be the case for homomorphic filtering. Classical conditioning then correlates the brightness of the image with its reflectance. The corresponding look-up table is implemented using the DAM (distributed associative memory) mechanism, which amounts to a space-invariant filter with a narrow positive peak and a broad, shallow, negative surround. The corresponding Fourier transform of such a filter approximates a band-pass filter that eliminates low frequencies from slow gradients of illumination and retains the other frequencies corresponding to steep changes in reflectance.

The sixth chapter, due to Michael Kuperstein, treats the sensory-motor coordination problem. Such coordination involves locating stationary targets with movable sensors, reaching arbitrarily positioned and oriented targets in 3-dimensional space with multi-joint arms, and positioning an unforseen payload with accurate and stable movements despite unknown sensor feedback delay. The controller described in this chapter, called INFANT, learns visual-motor coordination without any knowledge of the geometry of the mechanical system and without a teacher. Ego-centered coordinates are represented by neural topographies and allow unsupervised adaptive sensory-motor calibrations. The controller is designed to learn self-consistency between sensory and motor signal and operates in a two-phased process called circular reaction. The current use of circular reaction comes from an infant development stage described by Jean Piaget. In the first phase, sensory-motor relations are learned via correlations between object sensation and self-produced movement signals. In the second phase, the controller uses the learned correlations to transform the sensation of an object into a movement that reaches the object. A set of weight signals modulate the signals emitted by the input maps are modulated by to produce target signals. The weights constitute the global association between all possible images of an object and the arm motor signals. The target map outputs are compared with the random outputs that generated the arm posture to produce error signals. These error signals update the weight signals, which improves the reaching performance.

The seventh chapter written by Jitendra Malik and Pietro Perona concerns the computation of boundaries. The discussion explores how biological and artificial processors could utilize cues such as luminance (brightness), color, texture, stereoscopic disparity and motion towards image segmentation. They suggest that early visual processing starts by convolving the image with a very redundant bank of linear or quasi-linear filters and that this representation be the basis for the parallel processing of brightness, color, texture, stereopsis and motion. In each of these pathways, significant discontinuities (boundary curves) can be detected. For signal-to-noise ratio considerations, having the different modules cooperate in detecting boundaries using reconstruction techniques such as the Markov Random Field (MRF) framework, offers significant advantages. The filtering approach, embedded within a massive invariant cytoarchitecture, is further discussed by Harry Wechsler in chapter 14.

Chapter eight, written by M. Manohar and James Tilton. describes work undertaken at NASA Goddard on the compression of remotely sensed images using a self-organizing feature map (SOFM). The feature map, originally described by Teuvo Kohonen and known to those working in signal processing as vector quantization (VQ), implements the equivalent of a k-nearest neighbor classifier or a Parzen density estimation with an accompanying degree of dimensionality reduction. The VQ approach compresses certain NASA images by factors of 10 to 20, at a data rate of approximately 10 Megabits/second.

The SOFM is also the topic of the nineth chapter written by Erkki Oja. The author, based on the degree of data parallelism, suggests that the intermediate level of computer vision is the most suitable for neural networks. Oja discusses the role of the SOFM in feature detection and data compression. The stage of feature detection can be further enhanced to correspond to what is known about bandpass filters and early vision and can build up a hierarchical structure, called the coded feature pyramid. Texture segmentation and curve detection are suggested applications.

The tenth chapter, offered by Todd Reed, deals with image segmentation. Segmentation derives from a region growing algorithm modeled as a relaxation scheme and implemented as a simple perceptron network. Relaxation occurs as a function of the similarity shown by neighboring pixels with respect to their gray-levels or low-level features.

The eleventh chapter, the contribution of Giulio Sandini and Massimo Tistarelli, considers the data acquisition stage and low-level image representations. Note that the neural network aspect in this case is related to the distributed nature of the visual representation and that space-variant sensing could be enhanced by coupling it to space-variant filtering to account for the blurred nature characteristic of peripheral and preattentive vision. The chapter discusses the advantages of space-variant sensing to maintain a good balance between resolution and the visual field amplitude with a corresponding and significant degree of data compression. This can be achieved through visuo-motor coordination and requires strong interaction between visual and motor processes to direct the high resolution, equivalent of a fovea, towards points of interest. Visual modules that exploit the advantages of space-variant sensing include target tracking for active gaze control, vergence control, and estimation of collision (time-to-impact).

The twelfth chapter, written by Michael Seibert and Allen Waxman, addresses learning and recognizing 3-dimensional objects from multiple views, an issue also treated by Shimon Edelman in the second chapter of Human Perception. 3-dimensional objects are modeled as visual potentials, and the recognition system exploits the information in observed sequences during learning and recognition. The visual potential models a 3-dimensional object using viewer-centered (canonical) representation rather than object-centered volumetric models. The links connecting the viewer-centered representations comprise the motions needed to take an observer from one view to another one. Learning takes place through ART-2 unsupervised training on an invariant feature vector generated by processing modules.

The thirteenth chapter, due to Geoffrey Towell and Jude Shavlik, answers a question often raised on the status of neural networks vis-a-vis AI. The answer points to hybrid systems, where neural networks could manage the early levels of numerical processing, while AI handles the conceptual and symbolic processing characteristic of high-level vision. It also becomes apparent that neural networks could provide the needed interface with the real world and, at the same time, be primed by AI. Hybrid systems thus bridge low- and high-level vision in support of object recognition. Illustrations include recognizing a cup or a chair.

The fourteenth chapter, the contribution of Harry Wechsler, redefines scale space in terms of multiscale, distributed, and conjoint (spatial/spectral) image representations across spatial and temporal dimensions. The scale space architecture allows compact image representations and data compression, facilitates alignment, and helps with the derivation of middle-level intrinsic image representations, such as optical flow, depth and depth of focus, and 3-dimensional structure (shape), from shade or texture information. The scale-space properly mapped resonates against properly encoded ecological constraints essential for survival (e.g., avoiding collision), and against adaptive memory structures, leading to object recognition. The multiscale, distributed, and conjoint visual representations and mappings are characteristic of invariant low-level vision and provide a cytoarchitecture that facilitates image analysis and understanding using bottom-up and top-down processes suitable for the traditional analysis and synthesis (prediction) interpretation cycle.

The fifteenth chapter, written by Yehezkel Yeshurun, Daniel Reisfeld and Haim Wolfson, addresses the issue of attention and foveated vision. As discussed by Sandini and Tistarelli in the eleventh chapter, space-variant sensing requires strong interaction between visual and motor processes to direct the high resolution equivalent of a fovea towards points of interest. The corresponding points of fixation are located using interest detection operators. The authors suggest an operator based on the intuitive notion of symmetry that is implemented using a simple feed forward network of orientation selective cells and layers of AND/OR cells.

The second part of the book closes with a chapter written by Y. T. Zhou and Rama Chelappa on the use of additive neural networks for motion processing. Batch and recursive algorithms compute optical flow and recover depth from a sequence of monocular images. The batch algorithm simultaneously integrates information from all images by embedding them into the bias inputs of the network, while the recursive algorithm uses a recursive least squares (RLS) method to update the bias inputs of the network. The corresponding CAN (crossbar associative/additive network) defines an energy function whose minimization ensures that the spatiotemporal gradient constraint is fulfilled and that the optical flow is smooth.

II.1

WISARD and other Weightless Neurons

IGOR ALEKSANDER

Imperial College of Science,
Technology and Medicine,
London, UK

I. Introduction

The word "weightless" is used in this discussion to draw attention to the fact that, although the approach is undoubtedly "neural", it is within a somewhat different paradigm from that which is contemporarily seen as the standard approach. As the word suggests, the weightless neural node achieves its learning by means other than weight variation in the connection between two nodes. The node is a Random-Access Memory (RAM), which stores the learnt responses to patterns occurring at its address terminals. This is not a new approach, and dates back to 1965 (Aleksander,1965). In 1981, with the advent of inexpensive silicon RAM, it led to the design of an adaptive pattern recognition system called the WISARD (after its designers: Bruce WIlkie, John Stonham, Igor Aleksander, [Recognition Device])(Aleksander et al. 1984). With the current revival of interest in neural computing, it has been possible to show that the RAM approach fully covers the achievements of standard weighted approaches, with the added properties of direct implementability with conventional VLSI techniques and sufficient generality to represent the increasingly complex descriptions of real neurons and which go beyond that which can be done with weighted models (Aleksander and Morton, 1990 a,b). The discussion contains a review of the work in this area from a perspective of

202

systems that are capable of discerning visual signals: that is, systems that could be said to carry out perceptual tasks.

II. The RAM Node

A. Functional Description

In biological systems, the words "node" and "neuron" are often used synonymously. But not so in artificial systems, and this is particularly true in the weightless paradigm. The atomic unit of weighless sytems is the RAM node, which as we shall see, mostly has no inherent generalization (i.e. it regurgitates that which has been learnt, and makes little sense of unseen inputs). Also, as we shall see, this does not prevent ta neural system designer from "instilling" generalisation into the RAM. But a worse characteristic of the RAM is that its cost increases exponentially with size of input. Ways of overcoming the disadvantage will be discussed.

The real neurons of a weightless system are made up of RAM nodes. This will be discussed in the next section. In this section it is the RAM node that comes under scrutiny. So, in the weightless paradigm, the RAM node is a device which serves a purpose somewhere between a weight and a neuron. The symbol for a RAM node is shown in fig 1.

The input to the node, $i1, i2, ... iN$ are the address terminals of of the RAM. That is, there are 2^N locations that can be addressed within the RAM, each being a B-bit word. In earlier uses of RAMs in neural systems, each of the B bits could be seen as a firing/not firing store, and the node as B binary nodes with inputs connected in parallel (Aleksander and Morton 1990a). More recently however, the B bits have been considered to store a number in the interval from 0 to 1 which represents the "firing probability", $P(1)$, of the neuron. The way in which hardware can be added to an electronic RAM to achieve this has been discussed eldewhere (Aleksander 1989a). Others (Gorse and Taylor 1989) have indeed assumed that B is so large as to allow them to analyse their node (which they called a p-RAM) as storing continuous values of firing probability.

RAM systems with $M=2^B$ well-defined probabilistic states have been called M-PLNs: M-valued Probabilistic Logic Nodes (Myers, 1990). The crucial difference between M-PLNs and p-RAMS, is that the former can be cost-optimized by selecting appropriate values of B and the way that training causes the message stored in the B

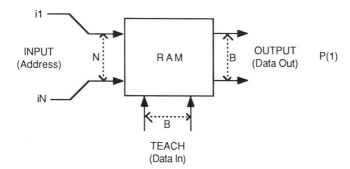

Figure 1. A RAM node

bits to change . In p-RAMs, B is made large enough to allow the theoretical analysis, rooted in continuous mathematics, to hold. Our approach is more closely wedded to discrete system analysis as found in probabilistic automata theory.

B. Training

It is assumed that a RAM node (the discourse is restricted here to M-PLNs) receives global training signls of a "reinforcement" kind. That is, a reward or punish signal is distributed globally to a prescribed section of the system, and every node in that section receives the same signal. It is assumed that the set of M values has at least three elements:

$$P(1)=0, P(1)=1 \text{ and } P(1)=0.5$$

It is further assumed that at the commencement of training all nodes for all inputs store $P(1)=0.5$. As a final assumption, a clocked timing system is required. At the arrival of every clock signal each node will either fire or not fire (i.e. output a 1 or a 0 respectively). Over a stretch of many clock periods the node will have fired with a frequency approaching $P(1)$. At the arrival of a reinforcement signal, each node "knows" whether at the last clock point it fired or not. If the reinforcement is positive (i.e. a reward) the stored probability is increased by a preslected amount amout $dP(1)$ if the last output was 1, or decreased by another selected amount if the last output was 0. In other words, the last firing is encouraged. Should the reinforcement signal be negative, the action is reversed: a 1 is decreased by the incremental amount and a 0 is increased. In other words, the last firing value is discouraged. Myers (1990) has shown the following interesting results:

* The training procedure converges
* $dP(1)$ can profitably be made a function of $P(1)$ controlling the rate
  at which the node learns and forgets and making this control
  dependent on the current level of $P(1)$.
* A value of B between 3 and 4 is sufficient for accuracy and ensures
  a reasonably rapid convergence.

Many users of RAM techniques have adopted the simple 3-state PLN and shown it to be sufficiently accurate, while much of the early work on the WISARD system used RAMs in a totally non-probabilistic sense (i.e. with B=1).

To summarise so far, the **advantages** of the RAM node over the conventional weighted node are:

1. The RAM is a product of conventional silicon technology and therefore brings the design of neural systems closer to immediate implementation than is done by weighted systems for which the technology of making weights is still badly defined and may be shown to be wasteful in silicon (Aleksander, 1989a)

2. The RAM node is capable of performing all possible functions of its input and is therefore capable of modelling the ever increasing complexity of behaviour that is being ascribed to living neurons (Gorse and Taylor 1989).

However, against this there are some **disadvantages**:

1. The RAM as such posesses no generalization, while the powers of generalization of the weighted node are well-known and useful.

2. The memory cost (and hence use of silicon area) scales up as 2^N with the number of inputs to the node, whereas the weighted node scales up as N^2, assuming digital weights.

The next two sections will describe the way in which the disadvantages may be overcome, while still retaining most of the advantages.

III. Generalizing RAM Nodes

There are two ways in which generalisation may be added to a single RAM node: the use of noise during training and the addition of communication paths between the storage locations.

A. Noisy Training.

The name speaks for itself: noise may be introduced during training so that not only a specific set of addresses is updated, but noisy versions of these addresses too. For example, take an 8-input RAM with three states per location. Say that is trained to output a 1 for the all-1 input and a 0 for the all-0 input. Normally only two locations corresponding to these two inputs would be set (to 1 and 0 respectively, all the others being at 0.5). Say that 5% noise is introduced in the setting of the addresses while the training signals are present, that is, it becomes probable that during training, address inputs will become changed. So when 11111111 is being trained the probability of this input being undistorted is 0.95^8 . That is, if the training were repeated say 100 times, the 11111111 input is most likely to have been entered 66 times, each of the addresses with a single 0 among 7 1s will have been addressed about 3 times, while only about 5 of the 28 addresses with two 0s will have been set to 1. So the less is the input like the target address is the storage location, the less likely it its address to have been set to 1. Clearly, the same diffusion in storage locations will occur for the 0 settings. The process is controlled by the amount of noise and the number of training exposures used under noisy conditions. Were the shaped updating procedures mentioned earlier used (Myers 1990), the actual probability of firing would be altered in a manner which depends, in a descending way on the difference from the target state.

B. The Generalising RAM

As an alternative to the use of noise, a modified RAM which generalizes internally has been suggested - the G-RAM (Aleksander 1990c). This (to date, hypothetical) device operates in three phases. Two of them are the usual learning phase and operating phase during which the device records the addresses with their required response and uses the stored information, respectively. The third phase is unusual: it is called the "spreadiing" phase.

Spreading refers to a process of affecting the content of storage locations, not addressed during training, by the use of a suitable algorithm which may be implemented on-chip or through appropriate actions in the control machinery. Whatever the implementation, spreading is something that can be done "off line", that is, between the time that training information has to be captured (which may have to be done in some kind of "real time") and the time that the nodes have to use what has to be learnt (which, too, may have to be done at speed.

A simple example of a spreading algorithm is (for a RAM with three-state locations):

> "Training results in a three-set partition the location set: L0 is the set of locations that record a 0 output,P(1)=0, L1 is the set of locations that record P(1)=1 and L.5 is the set that contains the P(1)=0.5 messages. Select each location in the L.5 set in turn and examine the locations in the other two sets. If there exists a location in either set which is distinctly closer to the chosen location in terms of the Hamming distance of its address, then copy the content of this found location into the chosen one at the end of the search process".

For example say that locations 1111 and 1100 constitute the L1 set, and 0000 and 0011 the L0 set, all others being in the L.5 set. Then location 1110 would be allocated a 1 during spreading as 1111 has a Hamming distance of 1 and is distinctly less than 0000 which has a Hamming distance of 3 and 0011 which is also 3. On the other hand an input such as 0110 is at Hamming distance 2 from all the training patterns and therefore retains the $P(1)=0.5$ message.

C. Characterizing the Level of Generalization

It may be seen that the two methods of generalisation discussed above are very similar, in the sense that whatever noise training regime is applied through the first method, a spreading algorithm can be found that is equivalent in the sense that the same firing messages end up in the same storage locations.So a characterisation of the generalizing RAM can simply refer to these stored messages. Two forms of generalization are defined: partial and full.

Partial generalization, in terms G-RAM terminology, occurs after the system has been subjected to a limited amount of spreading only. For example, say that N=8 and the RAMs use 3-state messages, spreading could be allowed to those locations that differ from the L0 an L1 sets by only two address bits. So, if the trained patterns were the all-0 and the all-1 addresses, set to 0 and 1 respectively, the above limited spreading would place a 0 in all of the 28 addresses with just two 1s and a 1 in all of the 28 addresses with just two 0s. All other addresses remain at the $P(1)=0.5$ state. Partial generalization is therefore characterised by the "degree of spread" in terms of the maximum Hamming distance involved in the spread.

The degree of spread in the above example is 2 out of 8.Full generalization on the other hand, is the application of the notion of spreading to the entire L.5 set. So if for the above RAM the training patterns were 00000000 set to 0 and 11110000 set to 1, only addresses that are equidistant from these two patterns (such as 00110011) would be left with $P(1)=0.5$, while others such as 00001110 and 10000000 would both be set to 0 as they are distinctly nearer to the 00000000 pattern.

IV. Large Neurons
So far in this discussion, we have only looked at the "atoms" of systems that may be used in perceptual tasks. But, as such tasks generally require reactions to large amounts of data, it is necessary to direct the discourse towards systems with reasonable cost growth characteristics of the memory required as a function of the number of inputs. As has been said, the memory of a single RAM grows exponentially with the number of inputs and would therefore be unsuitable. So, in this section we discuss two circuit strategies that have been used to produce neuron-like devices from structures of RAM nodes. The first of these involves using a layer of RAM nodes whose outputs are summed (the WISARD discriminator) while the second is a pyramid of RAM nodes.

A. The WISARD discriminator (WD)

This arrangement is shown in in fig. 2. It was the major building block of the WISARD machine. In the original machine, the RAMs had binary locations (B=1) and were only trained from 0 to 1 (all RAMs starting at 0). Here we shall look at these bearing in mind the probabilistic RAM specifications considered earlier in the paper. The operation of the non-probabilistic discriminator may be found in considerable detail in Chapter 5 of Aleksander and Morton, 1990a and will be assessed here only in passing.Returning to fig. 2, it is assumed that the input of the RAMs is connected at random to some binary input field. The function of the summing device in the discriminator may be defined as follows. Let there

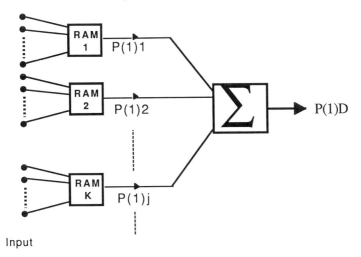

Input

Figure 2. The WISARD discriminator

be R RAMs in the input of the discriminator outputing P(1)j for the jth of the R RAMs. The function of the summer is

$$P(1)D = R^{-1}\sum_j P(1)j$$

where P(1)D is the probability of outputting a 1 for the entire discriminator. From here on we shall assume that the probabilistic RAM is of the three-state kind.

Initially, to indicate that nothing has as yet been learned, all the locations in the RAMs are set to P(1)=0. Clearly the output of the summing device, that is, the output of the discriminator itself is P(1)D=0.

To provide a simple mental model of the "perceptual" function of the discriminator, the case where it is trained on just one pattern, T1, is considered. The global signal received by all the RAMs in this situation is not of the reinforcement kind, but one that requires each addressed RAM to output a 1. This shifts the addressed storage location in each of the RAMs from 0 to 1 without involving the 0.5 message. Consider now the presentation of another, unkown, pattern U1 and imagine that it overlaps with T1 in a proportion $a1$ of the entire image area. The only way in which a RAM can respond with a 1 is for all its N address inputs to be connected to the overlap area. For a random connection this probability is $a1^N$ and this, through the law of large numbers, translates easily into an output firing probability of $P(1)D = a1^N$

Training on more than one pattern has a similar effect (as detailed in Chapter 5 of Aleksander and Morton 1990a) but can be simply stated as follows. "Given a WD trained on set T={T1, T2, ... Tt}, and given an unknown test pattern U1, an approximation to the response of the discriminator is $P(1)D = am^N$ where, $am=\max(a1, a2, ... at)$, aj being the proportional overlap area between U1 and Tj."

It is now seen that it is the whole WISARD discriminator which has neuronal properties broadly of the same kind as the weighted McCulloch and Pitts representation. This is said in the sense that the output (which could be thresholded as in the weighted case) responds strongly to trained patters and generalizes to others with a high overlap area with these

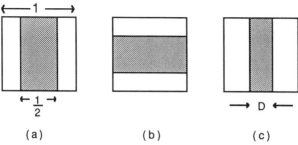

Figure 3. A simple illustrative task

training patterns. However, there is an important difference which can be illustrated by a simple example.

A WD is assumed to have just two, four-input (N=4) RAMs. It is trained to fire fully for the patterns 00000000 and 11111111. (It is assumed that one RAM receives the leftmost four bits and the other the rightmost ones). It is further required that a small departure from these two patterns, that is, a single 1 among all zeros or a single 0 among all 1s should be detected. Clearly this is simply achieved, as the departure would cause one of the RAMs to fire with $P(1)D=0$, making the summed total $P(1)D = 0.5$. Thresholding between $P(1)D = 0.5$ and just below 1 would complete the task. It is clear that this task could not be achieved with a single weighted neuron as it is not linearly separable. Formally, the WD is sensitive to the occurrence of N-tuples in the input, where the conventional weighted model of the neuron is sensitive to 1-tuples only.

B. A single-layer array of WDs

In the WISARD system, discriminators are used to respond to one class of pattern and are therefore used in groups for detecting several classes. Each discriminator is connected to the same pattern interface. So to detect the letters of the alphabet 26 discriminators would be used. In an array of this kind, thresholding of the discriminator outputs is not applied. Rather, these outputs are compared to one another and the identification decision is determined by the discriminator with the strongest response. This decision is accompanied by two confidence factors. The first is CA, the "absolute confidence factor" which is merely the $P(1)D$ of the discriminator with the strongest response. The second is CR, the "relative confidence factor" which takes the difference of the maximum discriminator, and the second strongest candidate as a proportion of the maximum response. These confidence factors play an important role in the use of the WISARD in practical situations, as they allow the user to reject weak decisions made by the system. As an illustration of these concepts consider the two images shown in Fig. 3.

The system has two discriminators, one trained on a vertical bar (a) and the other on a horizontal bar (b). The dark area is precisely 1/2 of the entire area of the image. The overlap area of the two training patterns is 1/2 of the entire image. From previous considerations therefore, were one of the training patterns presented to the system, one of the discriminators would have a response of 1, while that of the other would be $(0.5)^N$. This demonstrates that N is a crucial parameter in determining the relative confidence of the system. which, in, this case, is: $CR = (1 - (0.5)^N)$. (The absolute confidence is always unity in the presentation of a member of the training set).

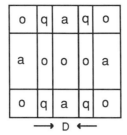

Figure 4. Significant image areas

As a further example (fig. 3 c), given a central vertical bar of width D in the range 0 to 1/2, given that the width of the entire image is unity,and assuming that the bar is situated within the dark area of the training pattern the response of the two discriminators is:
P(1)D vertical $= (D+0.5)^N = 0.32$
P(1)D horizontal $= 0.5^N = 0.0625$
For the above figures, the absolute confidence is only 32% but the relative confidence is 80.5% which means that the system could be used effectively as a "perceiver" of the verticality of dark bars.

C. The WISARD machine

While this has been described in some detal in several other publications, some of its parameters are quoted here to put the above theoretical notions into context. The WISARD was built as a laboratory prototype in 1981 and then taken up by a UK company that produced the first fully engineered version in 1984. This contains 2 megabytes of memory, specially structured to allow the user can structure into WDs. For example face recognition has been done with WDs with input images of 128x128 bits and N=6 (Wilkie 1983). Facial expressions can be recognised with similarly sized WD neurons, and intruder detection experiments have been done with neurons with 512x512 inputs with N=4. These showed that, training a discriminator on a background scene under different lighting conditions, and another with intruders of various kinds present, intruders could be detected in conditions of 45% noise. The key point that is being made here is that the RAM-node technology provides opportunities for making systems (related to single-layer Perceptrons, but less constrained) that contain large neurons with costs scaling more or less linearly with the size of the input field.

D. Probabilistic WD Neurons (Dichotomizers)

It is noted that in the previous section no use was made of the probabilistic property of the RAM node. This comes in useful when a single neuron has to distinguish between two classes, for one of which it is required to have a high P(1)D, and a low one for the other.Such a WD is rewarded, P(1)= 1, when one class is being trained and punished when the other is present. It is best to illustrate this directly with the example used earlier in fig. 3.
   The outlines of the two training patterns and the vertical test bar are redrawn in fig. 4. There are several areas of interst that have been marked:"o" are the areas where the two training images are the same; "a" are the areas where the test image is the same as the vertical training image; "q" are the areas where the test image is different from the vertical training image. Any RAM could be connected to these areas in one of seven ways each with a probability determined by the size of the areas and each resulting in a different P(1). These

are listed below, where the notation a,q, or o is used to indicate the relative area of these parts of the image (total area being unity).

All N in o: probability $p(o) = o^N$,

P(1)=0.5 because RAMs will have received both positive and negative reinforcement for the same address (0000..and 1111... in this case).

All N in q: probability $p(q) = q^N$,

P(1)=0 because RAMs will have received only negative reinforcement.

All N in a: probability $p(a) = a^N$,

P(1)=1 because RAMs will have received only positive reinforcement.

Some N in o and rest in q: $p(o,q) = (o+q)^N - o^N - q^N$,

P(1)=0 because those parts of N in q define addresses that are the same as for the horizontal training pattern.

Some N in o and rest in a: $p(o,a) = (o+a)^N - o^N - a^N$

P(1)=1 because those parts of N in a define addresses that are the same as for the vertical training pattern.

Some N in a and rest in q: $p(a,q) = (a+q)^N - a^N - q^N$

P(1)=0.5 because the RAMs see an address not seen during training.

Some N in o some in q and the rest in a:

$$p(o,q,a) = 1 - (o+q)^N - (o+a)^N - (a+q)^N + o^N + a^N + q^N,$$

P(1)=0.5 because the RAMs see an address not seen during training.

From this it is easily shown that the proportion of RAMs firing with a 1 (including half of the ones with P(1)=0.5) and hence P(1)D is:

$$P(1)D = 0.5[1 + (o+a)^N - (o+q)^N]$$

To compare this with the 2-WD arrangement in section C, the same width of the verical bar in the test pattern (0.25) and N=4 are assumed. From this: a=0.375, q=0.125, o=0.5 so P(1)D vertical = 0.72.

For a similar bar, placed centrally in a horizontal position it is easily calculated that the response is

$$P(1)D \text{ horizontal} = 0.28.$$

There is only one value of confidence for this kind of system and that is an absolute confidence which stems from the realisation that a firing of 50% expresses zero confidence. So a suitable formulation for a "dichotomizer confidence" CD, is

$$CD = abs(P(1)D - .5)/0.5$$

This is 0.44, in this case. This provides an effective way of dichotomizing two training sets so as to assess an unknown probabilistically. This type of system is useful in cases where a large number of classes can be mapped into a binary code with each dichotomizer supplying a distinct binary partition of the classes.

E. Pyramids

This alternative way of using RAM nodes to build a neural module with a large number of inputs is shown in a typical configuration in fig. 5. The major parameters are the input size of the RAMs, N, the height of the pyramid H and the overall number of inputs, W (width). The relationship between these is simple: $W = N^H$. In fig. 5 W=16, N=4 and H=2. The number of RAMs in this type of arrangement is $S = (N^{(H+1)} - 1)/N - 1$ and the cost of the node is $Sx2^N$. To a first approximation, the cost growth of this type of neuron is the same as that of the WD, as the largest number of nodes is in the lowest layer of the pyramid and this number is the same as that of a WD with the same number of overall inputs. Training of the pyramid is of the reinforcement kind. Again assuming that 3-state messages are stored in the RAMs, all the RAMs start in P(1)=0.5 state (for training with more sophisticated RAM content see: Myers 1990).

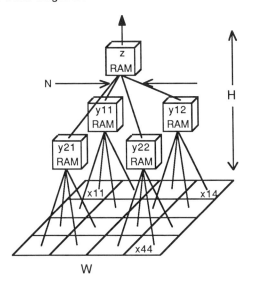

Figure 5. A pyramid.

A target output is known for a given overall image. Say that this is 1. The pyramid is allowed to run (it will output random signals with 50% probability for 0 and 1). As soon as the target output is produced, the system is "frozen" and reinforced as follows. For every RAM, the current output is stored at the current address. Only when the output z is consistently wrong (and this is defined as not reaching the target output for a predetermined number of steps) is the neuron negatively reinforced. This entails making the contents of all the current addresses P(1)=0.5. Due to the presence of hidden units as an inherent part of the pyramidal neural model, the question of training the "hidden" units arises. Indeed, this methodology has been shown to converge more rapidly than the conventional error back-propagation technique (Aleksander 1989b) in the well-known parity detection function. The ability to perform such "difficult" functions is the central advantage of the pyramid over the WD and, indeed, the conventional weighted neuron. To ilustrate this we shall work through a simple example.

In fig. 5, the 16-input device is required to detect an all-0 pattern and an all-1 pattern by outputting P(1)P=1. (P(1)P is the notation used for the probabilistic response as P(1)D was the notatiion used for the WD). Patterns with one bit different from the rest (a single 1 among all 0s, or a single 0 among all 1s) are to be detected by P(1)P=0. This is the type of problem that often occurs in industrial inspection tasks where the "passable" items can differ a great deal from one another while faulty items differ only in small detail from the good ones (e.g. inspection of printed circuit-board assemblies). Using the labels shown in fig. 5, training starts with the all-0 pattern at the x11 to x44 inputs the system is positively reinforced as soon as the output z is 1. The pattern present at the hidden layer is arbitrary and we refer to it as <y11,y12,y21,y22> where each of these symbols assumes a value of either a 0 or a 1. As has been shown by those working with such pyramids (e.g. Myers 1990), if training can proceed by a process of presenting counterexamples, much more rapid convergence occurs.

So the next training pattern is (say) with x11 set to 1 and the other inputs at 0. This allows only y11 to differ, and z can only become free to output a 1 as required when y11 is the opposite to its previously trained value (call this y11'). That is, a hidden layer pattern

<y11',y12,y21,y22> is mapped into a 0 by the output unit. All other 16 single-1 patterns may be handled in the same way. If the all-1 pattern is subsequently presented, the hidden layer will change randomly between all the possible 16 bit patterns. The target output is a 1, and only the patterns with one of y11, y12, y21 and y22 negated will cause a 0 to be output consistently. Therefore any hidden pattrn outside of these four can become trained to output the required 1 from z.

Say that this pattern is <y11',y12',y21',y22> then the final presentation of single-0 patterns causes the following hidden patterns to output a 0 at z.

<y11,y12',y21',y22>   <y11',y12,y21',y22>
<y11',y12',y21,y22>   <y11',y12',y21',y22'>

Clearly, the training has been accepted and the trainig set will provide the proper responses.

However, the training set uderspecifies the task in required, and a pattern such as all 1 but a 0 in x11 and x13 would stimulate <y11,y12,y21',y22> which was trained to output a 0. On the whole, however, it is clear that this arrangement can perform the task completely (if the all 0 and the all 1 pattern stimulate <y1,y12,y21,y22> and the single departures stimulate only the single bit change hidden patterns such as <y11',y12,y21,y22>). It is equally clear that WDs cannot perform this task with any degree of confidence, and weighted neurons not at all as the task is not linearly separable. So while much work remains to be done on pyramids as described here, they can be seen to be a useful tool in the armoury of neural devices used for perceptual tasks.

V. Associative Networks: A Memorandum

This chapter has been largely about systems that are combinational. But much of the excitement of the current revival of interest in neural networks comes from the discovery that a cluster of interconnected neurons has, as an emergent property, the ability to enter stable firing patterns, stimulated by the presentation of parts of these patterns (Hopfield 1982, Aleksander 1983, Hinton Sejnowsky and Ackley 1984). The associative property has a crucial role to play in any perceptual system: it enables the system to store retrievable knowledge in a way that a layered system cannot. In visual perception it can answer the question "what does x look like?" where in a layered system the process only says "the data I have before me looks like x". Put another way, where layered systems are suited to early processing functions such as the identification of objects in a window, associative systems are useful for knowledge-based analysis of more complex scenes. But this cannot be done with one single associative net, and the philosophy central to our current work is that sophisticated perceptual systems need to be constructed from many neural modules that have different degrees and modes of association. It is not possible to enter a discussion of this here, suffice it to say that this theme is tackled in a companion paper to be published concurrently with this one (Aleksander 1991)

References

1. Aleksander, I.(1965) "Fused Adaptive Circuit which Learns by Example," Electronics Letters 1(6).
2. Aleksander, I., Thomas, W.V. and Bowden, P.A.(1984). "WISARD, a Radical Step Forward in Image Recognitio," Sensor Review 4(3), 120-124.
3. Aleksander I. and Morton H.B.(1990a). An Introduction to Neural Computing London: Chapman and Hall.
4. Aleksander, I. and Morton H B (1990b). An Overview of Weightless Neural Systems," International Joint Neural Networks Conference, Washington .

5. Aleksander, I.(1989a). "Are special chips necessary for neural computing?" In Delgado-Frias and Moore (Eds), VLSI for Artificial Intelligence, Norwell, Mass.: Kluwer.

6. Gorse, D. and Taylor, J. G.(1989). "An analysis of noisy RAM and neural nets," Physica D, **34**, 90-114.

7. Myers, C.(1990). *Learning with Delayed Reinforcement in an Exploratory, Probabilistic Logic Neural Network.* PhD thesis, University of London (Imperial College).

8. Wilkie, B.(1983) *A Stand-Alone, High Resolution Adaptive Pattern Recognition System,* PhD Thesis, Brunel University, Uxbridge, UK.

9. Aleksander,I.(1990c). "Ideal neurons for neural computers," Proceedings ICNC Dusseldorf, , Springer Verlag.

10. Aleksander, I.(1989b). "The Logic of Connectionist Systems", in Aleksander, I. (Ed.) *Neural Computing Architectures* , London: Chapman and Hall, Boston MIT Press.

11. Hopfield, J.J.(1982). "Neural networks and physical systems with emergent collective properties, *Proc. Nat. Acad. Sci. USA,* **79,** 2554-2558.

12. Aleksander, I.(1983). "Emergent Intelligent Properties of Progressively Structured Pattern Recognition Nets," Pattern Recognition Letters 1, 375-384

13. Hinton, G. E., Sejnowski , T. J., and Ackley, D.(1984),"Boltzmann Machines: Constraint Satisfaction Networks that Learn," (Tech. Rep. CMU CS 84, 111. Carnegie-Mellon Univ.)

14. Aleksander, I.(1991)."Weightless Neural Tools: Towards Cognitive Macrostructures," To be published.

II.2

Multi-Dimensional Linear Lattice for Fourier and Gabor Transforms, Multiple-Scale Gaussian Filtering, and Edge Detection

JEZEKIEL BEN-ARIE

Dept. of Electrical & Computer Engineering
Illinois Institute of Technology,
Chicago IL 60616

I. Introduction

This chapter describes a novel artificial neural-network that has a novel multi-layered neural-architecture called: **Web-lattice** (in short we call it web). Our web, which is entirely linear, diverges considerably from the common non-linear structures used for neural networks. Unlike other neural networks, the web's **principle of operation** is based on **the central limit theorem.** Each layer of the web performs only simple repetitive averaging , but the multilayered result rapidly evolves into **exact Gaussian convolution.** Hence, each layer of the web generates Gaussian averaging of different scale, the higher the layer in the web the larger the widths of the

214

Gaussians. The successive convolution architecture of the web can be extended to any dimension: 1D data arrays are processed by 2D webs, 2D arrays by 3D webs, etc. .

In addition, other multiple-scale operators such as Gaussian-smoothed-Laplacians, Canny's edge detectors, and even **multi-dimensional Fourier, Cosine, Sine, and Gabor transforms** are also derived from the web in real-time, simply by vertical and/or lateral linear combinations of different processing elements. Such operations are essential parts of many contemporary algorithms in image and speech processing and in various applications in computer vision. Image analysis at multiple-scales is necessary for vision algorithms since each scale reveals structures with different size in the image. Our network generates in parallel all the required scales, and thus they can be combined together to generate the variety of multiple-scale operators mentioned above.

The central limit theorem roughly states, that the sum of many independent random variables (RVs) will have approximately Gaussian distribution, if each summand has high probability of being small. Since the composite distribution of the sum of two independent RVs is equal to their convolved distributions, a repetitive convolution by a constant kernel, tends always to generate a Gaussian distribution. Our neural network which has a novel lattice structure, does exactly that !. Hence we are able to generate quite accurate Gaussian averaging with inaccurate analog components, at any required scale (which is equivalent to the Gaussian's standard deviation). Furthermore, the web is capable of convolving multi-dimensional data structures that are fed to the lowest layer of the web as input arrays, with a complete set of multiple-scaled Gaussians.

To implement the central limit theorem, the web has a novel lattice structure which is composed of multiple layers with repetitive standard processing elements. The basic processing element (PE), and the web's architecture is different from the common structure used for other neural networks. Unlike the perceptron-driven few-layer structure with adjustable synaptic weights, our network may have many more layers, but with interconnections which are identical for each layer. Instead of the nonlinear perceptron we are using simple **linear** analog summers with input weights that are constant for every layer. Thus, our network does not require any kind of training or adjustable components. The number of inputs for every PE is much smaller and also differs from common neural network design. These differences alleviate many of the difficulties that exist in VLSI implementation of common neural networks.

The basic structure of the lattice provides a multi-scale Gaussian averaging of its input array. As shown in following sections, the standard deviation of the averaging Gaussians at each layer is proportional to the square-root of the layer's height in the web. Thus, the higher the layer, the wider its averaging curve. If one examines the structures of the web and the lattice in figs. 1A, 1B, and 2A, one may find that each layer of the lattice performs only simple rectangular convolution, but the multilayered result is a an exact Gaussian shaped averaging. The accuracy of the averaging process increases with the number of layers used, as demonstrated in fig. 2B , but only few layers are necessary to produce quite accurate Gaussian averaging. The theoretical foundations of these results are explained in more detail in section II.

An important advantage of our neural structures is that they produce their multiple-scale outputs in real-time and in parallel. Since the outputs are available simultaneously, we can aggregate various outputs with simple linear combinations to produce more intricate image processing operators. For example, the Gaussian-smoothed-Laplacian (GSL), is generated simply by extracting the difference of two Gussians with different scales from two layers in the network.

These operators and transforms have many applications. It is well known that low-level operators such as Gaussian-smoothed edge detectors and Laplacians, are essential parts of many image analysis algorithms. [Canny 86] found that the edge detector which optimizes the localization and detection criteria of step edges has a simple approximate implementation by a Gaussian smoothed gradient operator. In practice, these operators are implemented by hardware convolution operators which are relatively slow and require separate convolution for every scale.

The multiplicity of scales available in the web, allows to derive all the scales in parallel. With additional lateral and vertical interconnections the web also can provide multiple-scale Canny edge detectors (CED) [Canny 86], and even multi-dimensional Fourier (MDFT) and Gabor transforms (GT). The CED, the MDFT and the GT are derived in the lattice employing new approximations to the CED function and to the sine and cosine functions.

Following the footsteps of [Marr 82] that approximated the GSL by a difference of Gaussians, we found new approximations to the CED by a difference of two Gaussians, and to a sine and cosine functions using a series of shifted Gaussians with equal widths. As shown in following sections, these approximations are quite exact. Employing these approximations, we can derive from the web multi-scaled edge detectors and multi-dimensional Fourier and Gabor transforms. To generate the required sine and cosine basis functions, we use linear combinations of shifted Gaussians with equal standard deviations that are available at each layer of the web. Since each layer of the web produces another size of Gaussian convolution, each layer can approximate another scale of CED, GSL and another spatial frequency of Fourier or Gabor transforms. An obvious advantage of this approach is that these multiple-scale outputs are available simultaneously in real-time.

Another application for multiple scale convolutions arises from the scale space analysis originated by [Witkin 84]. Since each scale reveals structures of different size, [Witkin 84] introduced the scale-space method that is used to analyze images using varying scale Gaussian smoothing. Again, the conventional smoothing-by-convolution requires here a separate convolution for each scale. This can not be accomplished by conventional hardware in reasonable time. The web , on the other hand, has the advantage that it smoothes the image and also can provide explicit Gaussian convolutions that correspond to every scale in parallel.

In addition to the multiple scaled filtering described above, we claim that central limit principle can be extended to any dimension. To substantiate this claim, we develop in this article a generalized approach that can deal with data-structures of any dimension. Hence, different versions of the network are suitable for speech processing (1D), image processing (2D), or temporal scene analysis (3D). The simplest version is a two-dimensional web-lattice that can process one-dimensional arrays. Similar three-dimensional webs can process 2D arrays. We also describe in the following sections a 4D webs that may be used for applications that require 3D arrays, such as temporal scene analysis, and outline the general method to obtain even higher dimensions.

In addition to the dimensional variety of the webs, we also outline in this article a structural variety expressed in the web's order. A d-dimensional web of order n , has n^d inputs for every PE. Increased order results in larger averaging Gaussians.

We believe that the striking resemblance between the lattice's outputs to actual measurements of biological vision systems [Hubel 74][Daugman 80], also entails a large degree of structural similarity between the two. We argue, that the natural way in which this regular repetitive lattice structure provides all of these results, must have a severe impact upon current theories which mainly manifest very complex and irregular models for biological signal processing. The web has one outstanding feature that is absent from other biological models: it does not require any training. Since it is inconceivable that biological systems used for early vision require training, we argue that the web structure bears closer resemblance to the actual networks.

Scanning the available literature, we do not find any networks similar to our lattice. Our web-lattice has a pyramidal multilayered structure. But unlike the common pyramidal structures [Tanimoto 80] that are created by a hierarchical reduction of 4 elements of a level into one element of the next level, our web-lattice does not reduce the resolution at all !. Each layer of our web-lattice has the same number of elements as its predecessor-layer. This is not of any disadvantage, since our basic goal is not to achieve a hierarchical data structure, but to receive multi-scaled Gaussian-averaging.

An interesting approach to produce the GT by a neural network was introduced by [Daugman 88]. He transformed the image into a 1D vector and than processed it with a 3-layer neural network. The number of adjustable coefficients in his network is very large and have to be calculated separately. The network produces an implicit description of the image which is suitable mainly for image compression.

An electronic circuit that generates the Discrete Hartley (DHT) and Fourier transforms is presented by [Culhane 89]. The network structure consists of two main blocks. The first block generates the DHT and the second block is a bank of adders that converts the DHT to the DFT. The first block has a structure of a Hopfield net [Tank 86]. This net seeks to minimize an energy function that is manipulated to produce the DHT. This architecture is completely different from ours. Our network has multilayered structure with constant number of connections between every PE to its predecessors in the lower layer, whereas the Hopfield network has only one layer and every PE is directly connected to the others with different weights that has to be adjusted by a training procedure. For normal sized images, this implies a very large number of interconnections that are extremely inconvenient for implementation on VLSI chips.

A neural network that performs 2D Gaussian smoothing is described by [White 88][Kobayashi 90]. This network has the structure of an active resistive mesh , containing both positive and negative resistors to implement a Gaussian convolution in two dimensions. With an embedded array of photoreceptors, this network may be used for image detection and smoothing. The Gaussian width was controlled within the range of 2:1 , which is considered as a very small range of scales. The network is incapable of producing multiple-scale smoothing simultaneously , and is not suited for other dimensions.

Other lattice structures (also called ladder networks) in the literature, are completely dissimilar. They are used for different operations such as: sequential filtering [Strobach 90], or for simulation of biological neural networks such as the silicon retina [Mead 89] that used for this purpose, a single layer of hexagonal lattice of resistors and processing elements.

In conclusion, scanning the available literature we see that the web has many advantages over the systems and networks described above.

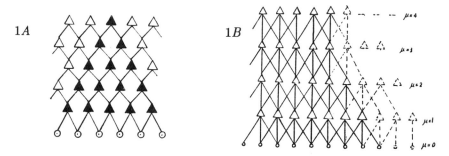

Fig.1: shows 2-D Web-Lattice of orders 2 and 3 (1A and 1B respectively). Each triangle denotes a PE (analog summer).

II. Successive Convolution in terms of the Central Limit Theorem

In this section we shall prove that according to the central limit theorem, successive convolution by a constant kernel produces a Gaussian convolution. Since we can describe the averaging process of the web-lattice as **repetitive discrete convolution with a constant kernel** , the web generates a Gaussian averaging of its input array. Lets start with the simplest kind of 2D web-lattice: the second order web, which averages 1D arrays. This web is described in detail in section III. Referring to fig. 1 , we see that in 2-order web each PE sums up two outputs of PEs that belong to the next lower layer in the web. This operation is equivalent to a convolution with a constant discrete kernel of the form: [1,1]. This kernel generates the PE outputs of layer μ by convolving the kernel with the outputs of layer $\mu-1$. For the sake of simplicity, we set to 1 all the synaptic weights q_μ (anyway, the weights influence only the heights of the averaging curves). The averaging curves in this case will assume the shape of **Pascal triangle (binomial numbers):**

```
               1
            1     1
         1     2     1
      1     3     3     1
   1     4     6     4     1
1     5    10    10     5     1
1  6   15    20    15    6    1
                        .... etc.
```

Here we can use the DeMoivre-Laplace Theorem [Papoulis 84] that shows that if $npq \gg 1$ then:

$$\begin{bmatrix} n \\ k \end{bmatrix} \approx \frac{1}{\sqrt{2\pi npq}} \; \exp^{\frac{-(k-np)^2}{2npq}} \tag{1}$$

Where p+q=1 , k and n are integers and k is in the $\sqrt{npq}$ neighborhood of np. In our case, n corresponds to the layer number μ. We see from (1) that the set of binomial numbers that describes the web-lattice averaging, approximates the normal curve very closely, especially for layers with high μ-s. This fact is also obvious from fig. 2B. The standard deviation of these curves is proportional to $\sqrt{n}$ which corresponds to the square-root of the layer's height in the lattice: μ. For instance, if we take p=q=1/2, we find that the normal curve's center is at k=n/2 and its standard deviation is $\sqrt{n}/2$.

For n-order webs we have similar results. The averaging curves of a 1D third-order web, for example, are obtained by repetitive convolution with a kernel of the shape: [1,1,1]. We receive here the following numbers:

```
                  1
               1   1   1
            1   2   3   2   1
         1   3   6   8   6   3   1
      1   4   9  17  20  17   9   4   1
   1  5  14  30  46  54  46  30  14   5   1
                                    ...etc.
```

Here, also we receive a set of averaging curves that obviously converge to Gaussian curves. We see that the case which applies to DeMoivre-Laplace theorem is a special case that does not apply here.

The 3D webs and lattices supply even more complex averaging functions. Here we have 2D arrays that are generated by repetitive convolution with 2D kernels. For 3D lattice we have the following kernel:

```
1  1
1  1
```

Here we receive the following averaging 2D functions:

$$
\begin{bmatrix} 1 & 1 \\ 1 & 1 \end{bmatrix}
\quad
\begin{bmatrix} 1 & 2 & 1 \\ 2 & 4 & 2 \\ 1 & 2 & 1 \end{bmatrix}
\quad
\begin{bmatrix} 1 & 3 & 3 & 1 \\ 3 & 9 & 9 & 3 \\ 3 & 9 & 9 & 3 \\ 1 & 3 & 3 & 1 \end{bmatrix}
\quad
\begin{bmatrix} 1 & 4 & 6 & 4 & 1 \\ 4 & 16 & 24 & 16 & 4 \\ 6 & 24 & 36 & 24 & 6 \\ 4 & 16 & 24 & 16 & 4 \\ 1 & 4 & 6 & 4 & 1 \end{bmatrix}
$$

For 3D third order web, we apply a kernel of the form:

$$
\begin{matrix} 1 & 1 & 1 \\ 1 & 1 & 1 \\ 1 & 1 & 1 \end{matrix}
$$

To deal with the general web and the multidimensional cases, we have to resort to the central limit theorem. The central limit theorem says roughly [Billingsley 79] that the sum of many independent random variables will be approximately normally (Gaussian) distributed, if each summand has high probability of being small. Let N be a random variable with the standard normal distribution:

$$
P[N\epsilon A] = \frac{1}{\sqrt{2\pi}} \int_A \exp^{\frac{-x^2}{2}} dx \tag{2}
$$

Thus, we shall describe our averaging process in the web-lattice as equivalent to a process of generating a composite distribution of a sum of random variables (RVs). Let us refer first to the 1D case of input arrays. Suppose that we have a set of n independent random variables: $\{y_i; i=1,2,..,r;\}$. Each variable of this set is defined to have a discrete probability distribution that consists of a discrete set of delta functions: $\{1/m \; \delta(x-a_j) \; ; \; j=1..m;\}$. For a second order web, we define the kernel [1,1] as a probability distribution. Hence, m=2 and $a_i = \pm w$. Therefore, the distance between two consecutive locations in the lattice is equal to $2w$. Hence, we define every output of a PE in the first layer of the lattice as a RV: y_i with m=2, $a_1 = h-w$ and $a_2 = h+w$, where h denotes the location of the PE in the lattice. The kernel is also defined as a discrete RV that belongs to the set $\{y_i\}$ with m=2 , $a_1 = -w$, and $a_2 = +w$.

It is well known, that a distribution of a sum of two independent random variables is their convolved distribution. Since every layer's averaging curves are obtained from its next lower layer's curves by convolution with the kernel, we can refer to the averaging curves of every PE in the layer as if they are the combined probability distributions of the sum of the kernel with the previous layer RVs. Thus, if we regard the averaging curves of every layer as discrete probability distributions, and observe that every layer accumulates an additional "RV", we see that the averaging curve of each layer consist of consecutive convolutions with the same kernel, which is equivalent to the consecutive sum of independent RVs. Hence, we can apply the central limit theorem to the averaging curves as if they were probability distributions. The actual averaging curves of every PE, which are derived by convolution with the kernel, completely complies with this analogy. Here, we apply the central limit theorem, and claim that the averaging curves are converging to the normal curve.

This result is also relevant to webs and to the multi-dimensional case. In order to adjust our proof to n-order webs, we just modify the kernel's distribution in accordance with the web's order. In the multi-dimensional case, we are convolving with a multi-dimensional kernel, which can be regarded as a multi-dimensional probability distribution. To prove the convergence of the averaging functions here, we also employ the central limit theorem in its multi-dimensional version.

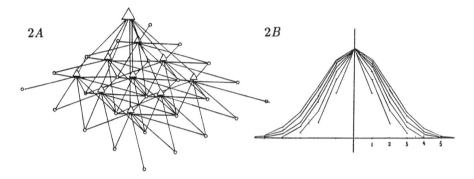

Fig. 2A: Illustrates a second order 3-D web-lattice of 3-order, for Two-dimensional Gaussian Smoothing. Fig. 2B: Describes the progression of the Gaussian averaging curves of a second order web.

III. One dimensional Gaussian Convolution

In order to process 1D arrays, we need a 2D web. In this section, we describe the simplest version of a second order web: a 2D lattice structure, with processing elements (PEs) that have only two inputs. This web processes one dimensional arrays. The web is illustrated in fig. 1A. Each node of the web contains an identical processing element (PE). The PE consists of a two-input analog summer. At each level, the inputs have equal synaptic weights that are denoted by q_μ. The standard PE unit which is used in all the layers is an analog summer that adds up its inputs. The input weights q_μ are calculated so as to normalize the height of the Gaussian curves to a unit value at each layer. The weights for odd and even layers are given by:

$$q_\mu = \frac{\mu+1}{2\mu} \quad for \quad \mu=1,3,5,7, \cdots ,M-2; \tag{3}$$

$$q_\mu = 0.5 \quad for \quad \mu=2,4,6,8, \cdots ,M-1; \tag{4}$$

The input data array resides in the layer that corresponds to level 0 ($\mu=0$) Usually, it is a row or column of photoreceptors (pixels) in the image plane. If we constrain the web outputs only to complete averaging Gaussians, every layer will have one PE less than the preceding layer. Other configurations are described in [Ben-Arie 90c,90e]. Thus, if the basic layer has M elements the next layer has M-1 elements. In this case, the complete lattice consists of M layers (including the receptors layer). Since every layer has one PE less than its preceding one, the top level $\mu=M-1$ has only one PE. Every PE of the first layer ($\mu=1$) is connected to two consecutive pixels. Each PE of the next layers $\mu=2,3,4,...,M-1$ is connected to two neighboring PEs that belong to the layer below.

In the following equations, The horizontal positions of the processing elements of even layers are denoted by even numbers: 2n ,while the locations of the PEs in the odd layers are denoted by odd numbers: 2n+1. The lattice of fig. 1A actually performs one-dimensional hierarchical-recursive filtering operation defined by:

$$Q(\mu,2n)=q_\mu \left[Q(\mu-1,2n-1)+Q(\mu-1,2n+1) \right] \tag{5}$$

$$for \quad \mu=2,4,6,..,M-1;$$

$$Q(\mu,2n+1)=q_\mu \left[Q(\mu-1,2n)+Q(\mu-1,2n+2) \right] \tag{6}$$
$$for \quad \mu=1,3,5,..,M-2;$$

Where Q(a,b) is the PE's output at level a , and b is the PE's horizontal position in the lattice. q_μ is the synaptic weight which is identical for all the PEs at the lattice's layer μ. As claimed in the previous section, we substantiate that any of the outputs $Q(\mu,2n)$ approximates a Gaussian weighted sum of $\mu+1$ receptors:

$$Q(\mu,2n)\approx \sum_{i=n-\mu/2}^{i=n+\mu/2} Q(0,2i)\, e^{-\frac{(2i-2n)^2}{2\sigma^2}} \tag{7}$$

$$for \quad \mu=0,2,..,M-1; \; , \; and \; \mu\leq 2n\leq 2M-2-\mu$$

$$Q\left(\mu,2n\right) \approx e^{\frac{1}{2\sigma^2}} \sum_{i=n-\frac{\mu-1}{2}}^{i=n+\frac{\mu+1}{2}} Q\left(0,2i\right) e^{-\frac{(2i-2n-1)^2}{2\sigma^2}} \tag{8}$$

$$\text{for } \mu=1,3,..,M-2; \text{ and } \mu\leq2n+1\leq2M-2-\mu$$

The standard deviation of the filter σ is proportional to $\sigma\approx0.5\sqrt{\mu}$. Since the standard deviation of the filter is increasing in proportion to the square-root of the layer's height ($\sqrt{\mu}$) , the lattice output may be described as continuous-multi-scaled Gaussian averaging. Higher layers in the web, produce larger scale Gaussian averaging and the scale matches its receptive field. Fig. 2B describes the progression of the Gaussian averaging curves with increasing heights.

IV. Two-Dimensional Gaussian Averaging

To produce two-dimensional Gaussian averaging we introduce a 3D web illustrated in fig. 2A. Here every PE's output $Q(\mu,a,b)$ is defined by a three-dimensional position vector where a and b determine its planar position and μ defines its vertical position (that is equal to the layer's height). With analogy to the 2D web, the 3D web has a basic layer that consists of the input array, but here we have a 2D array instead of a 1D array as in the 2D web-lattice. Higher layers consist of 2D arrays of identical PEs. The overall structure of the 3D web here depends on the requirements. If it is required that all the averaging curves are to be complete Gaussians, then the preferred structure is pyramidal: each layer has one row and one column less than the layer below. Considering the second order web, each PE is an analog adder with four equal weight inputs. These weights denoted by q_μ are equal for all the PEs in the same layer. Every PE is connected to four neighboring PEs of the layer below. In order to normalize to unity the peak height of the averaging 2D Gaussian function at each scale, we determine the synaptic weights at each level according to the following formulae:

$$q_\mu = \left[\frac{\mu+1}{2\mu}\right]^2 \tag{9}$$

$$\text{for } \mu=1,3,5, \cdots ,M-2;$$

and $\qquad q_\mu=1/4 \qquad \text{for } \mu=2,4,6,8, \cdots ,M-1; \tag{10}$

Each PE here performs a hierarchical-recursive filtering operation:

$$Q\left(\mu,2n,2m\right)=q_{\mu}[Q\left(\mu-1,2n-1,2m-1\right)+Q\left(\mu-1,2n+1,2m-1\right)+ \tag{11}$$

$$+Q\left(\mu-1,2n+1,2m+1\right)+Q\left(\mu-1,2n-1,2m+1\right)]$$

for $\mu=2,4,6,..,M-1;$. And for the odd layers:

$$Q\left(\mu,2n+1,2m+1\right)=q_{\mu}[Q\left(\mu-1,2n,2m\right)+Q\left(\mu-1,2n+2,2m\right)+ \tag{12}$$

$$+Q\left(\mu-1,2n+2,2m+2\right)+Q\left(\mu-1,2n,2m+2\right)]$$

for $\mu=1,3,5,..,M-2;$.

For an input array of M x M values denoted by Q(0,2n,2m) where n,m = 0,1,2,... ,M-1; . The network approximates two dimensional Gaussian averaging:

$$Q\left(\mu,2n,2m\right)\approx\sum_{\substack{j=m-\frac{\mu}{2}}}^{j=m+\frac{\mu}{2}}\sum_{\substack{i=n-\frac{\mu}{2}}}^{i=n+\frac{\mu}{2}}Q\left(0,2i,2j\right)\;e^{-\frac{(2i-2n)^{2}+(2j-2m)^{2}}{2\sigma^{2}}} \tag{13}$$

for $\mu=0,2,4,..,M-1;$ and $\mu=<2m\leq2M-2-\mu;\quad\mu\leq2n\leq2M-2-\mu;$.

Similar equation can be obtained for the odd layers.

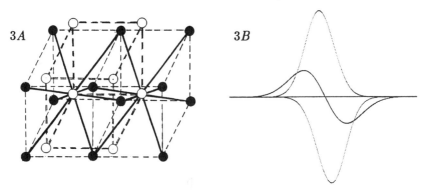

Fig. 3A: Illustrates four-dimensional second order web-lattice. Odd layer PEs are denoted by: black circles, even layers by: white circles. Fig. 3B: Describes the first derivative of a Gaussian approximated as difference of two shifted Gaussians, to form a CED.

V. Three and Higher Dimensional Averaging

Following the basic rules of previous 2D and 3D webs, we describe in this section 3D and higher dimensional Gaussian convolution. For processing of 3D arrays we need a 4D web. A standard PE for a 4D 2-order web has eight equally weighted inputs that are connected to the PE's lower level neighbors. A typical array is illustrated in fig. 3A. The PE is centered in a cube, while lower-level PEs are located at the cube's vertices. The fourth dimension requires identical 3D lattice-structure (like the one illustrated in fig. 3A) for every two consecutive layers.

As with the former lattices the input weights are equal within each level. For the 4D lattice they alternate between $1/8$ for even levels and $[(\mu+1)/2\mu]^3$ for odd ones.

the lattice yields three-dimensional spherical Gaussian averaging that may be used for analysis of image sequences , 3D shapes, etc..

VI. Higher order Webs

In addition to the second order d-dimensional web-lattice which is based on 2^{d-1} inputs for every processing element (PE), we can extend it also to a general lattice structure that we call: **Web-Lattice of order n.** This web has n^{d-1} inputs for every PE. Higher order webs have larger receptive fields and therefore, larger standard deviations of their averaging Gaussians.

For instance, we are describing in figures 1B and 2A, two third-order webs of two and three dimensions. The structure of a third order web (and all the following odd order webs) is more regular than the second order web, discussed in previous sections (and all the following even order webs). The third order web does not have odd and even layers and all the layers have identical structure. Every PE has 3 inputs in the 3-order web that is designed for 1-dimensional array (2D web). The variance of this web is a bit larger than the 2-order web (the regular lattice). A third order web has: $\sigma \approx .75\sqrt{\mu}$. It can be shown that for a fixed number of layers, σ **is proportional to the order n.**

The 3D web intended for 2D arrays, has three dimensional structure like any other order webs. But unlike the 2-order web, it has 9 inputs for every PE, and it sums up the 9 neighbors of a square of 3x3 around the PE's location (including its own location). The 4D Web (for 3D data arrays) of order 3 has 27 inputs and actually sums all the members of the cube of 3x3x3 centered around the PE's location. With direct analogy we can extend the web to higher orders at every dimension. The structures of third order 2D and 3D webs that are designed for 1D and 2D arrays respectively, are illustrated in figs. 1B and 2A .

For the general case of **multidimensional n-th order web-lattice of** dimension d+1 that **performs d-dimensional averaging** , We propose the following structure:

(1) Each PE at level μ is an analog adder that has n^d inputs from level $\mu-1$. The basic level $\mu=0$ consists of the M^d array that is to be smoothed.

(2) The input arrays q_μ for even levels are given according to:

$$q_\mu = \left[\frac{\mu+1}{n\mu}\right]^d \quad for \quad \mu=1,3,5,..,M-2; \tag{14}$$

$$q_\mu = \frac{1}{n^d} \quad for \quad \mu=2,4,6,...,M-1; \tag{15}$$

(3) Each level μ produces d-dimensional Gaussian averaging. The standard deviation of the Gaussian averaging is proportional to $n\sqrt{\mu}$.

VII. Multi-Scale Edge masks

To construct multi-scale square or elongated Gaussian edge detectors all we have to do is to subtract the appropriate outputs of two square or rectangular lattices. This approximates very closely the optimal step edge detectors recommended by [Canny 86]. According to [Canny 86], the optimal mask that detects step edges has a profile that is similar to a Gaussian smoothed step function which is equivalent to the first derivative of a Gaussian curve.

We find that a difference between two identical Gaussians that are σ spaced apart, approximates the first derivative quite accurately:

$$\frac{dG_\sigma(x)}{dx} = \frac{d}{dx}\left[\frac{1}{\sqrt{2\pi}\,\sigma}e^{\frac{-x^2}{2\sigma^2}}\right] = \frac{-x}{\sqrt{2\pi}\,\sigma^3}e^{\frac{-x^2}{2\sigma^2}} \approx G_{\sigma_1}(x+u) - G_{\sigma_2}(x-u) \tag{16}$$

where: $u \approx \sigma/2$ and $\sigma_1 = \sigma_2 \approx \sigma$

The difference in magnitudes between the approximation and the exact derivative is illustrated in fig. 3B. We notice that the difference is so small, it is hardly resolved in the drawing.

To construct a two dimensional edge detector, we can take the difference between two outputs that average two neighboring rectangles or squares. For square edge masks, the mask can be obtained simply by a single subtraction of two PEs that are on the same layer, and have approximately a σ distance in the direction of the desired gradient. For elongated edge masks, we have to subtract two rectangular receptive fields. Here we can use two rectangular smoothing networks that are derived by adding the PE outputs of two elongated regions [Ben-Arie 90].

Different scales and receptive fields may be allocated for the mask just by changing the levels and the groups of outputs to be subtracted. Here we determine the scale and the receptive field just by choosing the appropriate output fields [Ben-Arie 90a].

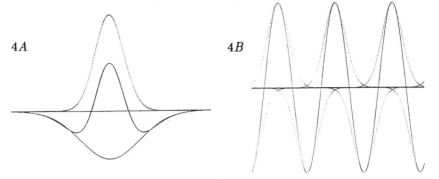

4A

4B

Fig. 4A: Shows the Gaussian-Smoothed-Laplacian (GSL), approximated by a DOG = Difference of Gaussians. The two Gaussians are also displayed. Fig. 4B: Approximation of a sine function as a sum of infinite series of shifted Gaussians (solid line), the actual sine is displayed with broken line, but since the approximation is so close to the actual function, they almost overlap. The Gaussians are drawn with broken lines.

VIII. Deriving the Gaussian-Smoothed-Laplacian

A Gaussian-smoothed-Laplacian (GSL) has the shape of a mexican hat . [Marr 82] suggested the use of the Difference Of Gaussians (DOG) for this purpose. In our web, a difference of Gaussians at different scales is obtained simply by subtracting two PE outputs at the same location but at different layers:

$$L\left(\mu_1,\mu_2,m,n\right)=Q\left(\mu_1,m,n\right)-Q\left(\mu_2,m,n\right) ; \qquad \mu_1>\mu_2 \qquad (17)$$

Where L(.) is the laplacian at planar location (m,n) with scales μ_1,μ_2 . The approximation of the DOG and exact second derivative are displayed in fig. 4A. The 1D Laplacian is expressed by:

$$L\left(x,y,\sigma\right) = [\frac{\partial^2}{\partial x^2}+\frac{\partial^2}{\partial y^2}] \, G_\sigma(x,y) = \frac{1}{\sqrt{2\pi}\,\sigma^3}[\frac{x^2+y^2}{\sigma^2}-2] \, e^{\frac{-[x^2+y^2]}{2\sigma^2}} \qquad (18)$$

$$where: \quad G_\sigma(x,y) = \frac{1}{\sqrt{2\pi}\,\sigma} \, e^{\frac{-[x^2+y^2]}{2\sigma^2}}$$

The DOG approximation is expressed as:

$$L(x,y,\sigma) \approx a G_{\sigma_1}(x,y) - b G_{\sigma_2}(x,y) \tag{19}$$

We find that $a \approx 1$ and *also* $b \approx 1$ and $\sigma_1 \approx 0.816\sigma$; $\sigma_2 \approx 1.15\sigma$. Hence, by a simple linear combination of two web outputs, we can construct the GSL. The GSL scale depends on the two subtracted layers. A simulated example of the GSL is given in section XI.

IX. Generating the Discrete Fourier Transform

Another interesting feature of the web-lattice is its capability to generate the Fourier transform of its input array. First, we construct novel approximations to the required basis functions. We find that a sum of shifted Gaussians with alternating signs can approximate quite closely the sine and cosine functions:

$$\sin(ux) \approx \sum_{i=-\infty}^{\infty} G_\sigma(x - a(2i+1/2)) - G_\sigma(x - a(2i-1/2)) \tag{20}$$

$$\cos(ux) \approx \sum_{i=-\infty}^{\infty} G_\sigma(x - a(2i)) - G_\sigma(x - a(2i-1)) \tag{21}$$

Where: $u = \pi/2a$; $\sigma \approx 0.6a$; The period of the sine and cosine functions is 2a, the amplitude is equal to the magnitude of G_σ at the point x=0. Fig. 4B illustrates the approximation for a sine function. We note that the sum of Gaussians so closely follows the sine function that the approximation and the sine function are completely overlapping !! (actually, the total squared error is in the order of 10^{-12}).

For the practical implementation in 1D lattice, we have to connect to each layer only two summers. One summer, sums up a set of PE outputs with alternating signs, and with spatial translations of $a \approx 1.66\sigma$, and generates the sine function. The other summer sums another set of outputs from different locations (that are shifted in: $0.5a \approx 0.8\sigma$ with respect to the first set) to provide the cosine function. This arrangement is illustrated in fig. 5A. Each layer in the lattice provides a sine and cosine averaging at different frequency. The frequency is inversely proportional to the scale σ of each layer. The real and imaginary parts (denoted here as E(u) and O(u) respectively) of the Discrete Fourier Transform (DFT) is obtained from the the two summing PEs at each layer:

$$O(u) \approx \sum_{x=x_1}^{x_2} \sin(ux)\, f(x) \; ; \qquad E(u) \approx \sum_{x=x_1}^{x_2} \cos(ux)\, f(x) \tag{22}$$

Here f(x) is the 1D input array. The complete DFT is obtained from each layer with level μ at a different frequency: $u_\mu = \pi / 3\sigma \approx 2/\sqrt{\mu}$:

$$F[f(x)] = F(u_\mu) \approx E(u_\mu) + jO(u_\mu) \tag{23}$$

The 1D DFT network is simulated in fig. 5B, with a 1D pulse as an input array. As seen in fig. 5B, the results closely match the analytical curve. Similar method can be applied to obtain higher dimensions of DFTs. Since the DFT is a separable transform, we can separate a 2D DFT into two consecutive 1D transforms. Hence, we use the outputs of a set of web-lattices that produce a set of 1D DFTs, to obtain the complete 2D DFT and higher dimensions as well.

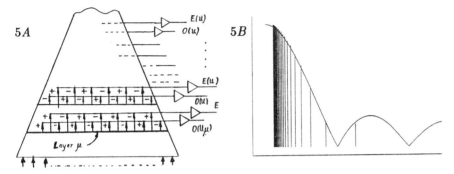

Fig. 5A: Illustrates how to generate a 1D Discrete Fourier transform (DFT) by a web-lattice. Each layer of the web produces the real $E(u_i)$ and the imaginary $O(u_i)$ parts of the DFT. Fig. 5B: Shows the DFT of a pulse, obtained with the simulated web (vertical columns), and the analytical DFT (continuous curve).

X. Gabor Transforms

Following the results of the previous section, in which we derived the Fourier transform by appropriate interlayered connections in the lattice, we can now obtain even more complex transforms such as the Gabor transform. The 2D Gabor filter captures the profiles of 2D cortical receptive fields that were encountered experimentally in mammalians [Hubel 74] [Daugman 80,88].

The general structure of the family of 2D Gabor filters is specified below in terms of the spatial impulse response G(x,y) and its related 2D Fourier transform F(u,v):

$$\tag{24}$$

$$G(x,y) = exp\left[\pi[(x-x_0)^2\alpha^2 + (y-y_0)^2\beta^2]\right] \exp\left[-2\pi i[u_0(x-x_0) + v_0(y-y_0)]\right]$$

$$F(u,v) = exp\left[\pi[\frac{(u-u_0)^2}{\alpha^2} + \frac{(v-v_0)^2}{\beta^2}]\right] \exp\left[-2\pi i[x_0(u-u_0) + y_0(v-v_0)]\right]$$

From the above equation, we note that the Gabor filter has an impulse response with the shape of a sine function that is modulated by a Gaussian. Hence this filter can be implemented in one dimension if we use a Gaussian averaging lattice on top of another lattice that produces a sine averaging like the lattice described in fig. 5A. Such a combined structure is described in fig. 6.

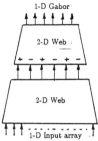

Fig. 6: One Dimensional Gabor transform produced by two 2-D web-lattices. The lower web generates the sine and cosine convolutions, the higher web convolves the result by a set of Gaussians.

XI. Simulation Results

We simulated the 3D lattice (second order web-lattice) with a receptive field of 256x256 pels with an image of matching size. 64 layers of the lattice were simulated. The original image is displayed in fig. 7A . The Gaussian smoothing obtained at layer 64 is displayed in fig. 7B. The CED is simulated by taking the lateral differences of pairs of PEs, either horizontally or vertically. Each layer generates another scale. Fig. 8 illustrates the simulation of layer 8. The GSL was then generated by the subtraction of appropriate layers. The resulting images that correspond to a standard deviation of 3.5 pels, is displayed in fig. 9. These correspond to the difference of layers 64 - 32. The simulation of the DFT is illustrated in fig. 5B.

We can conclude from the experimental results that the lattice yields the expected results quite accurately. Although the computation time of the simulated lattice is not directly related to the actual hardware, the execution time on our computer was much shorter than the time required to perform the same simulation using multi-scale convolution with FFT.

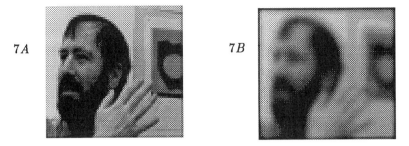

Fig. 7A: The original image. Fig. 7B: Gaussian smoothing of the 32-th web's layer.

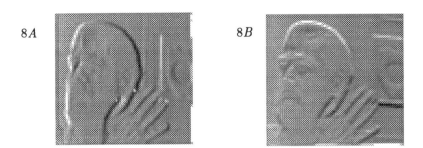

Fig. 8: The Canny Edge Detector derived from the eighth layer of the web, (A) in the horizontal direction, and (B) in the vertical direction.

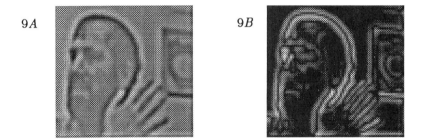

Fig. 9: (A) Shows a result of applying the GSL with $\sigma \approx 3.5$ pels using two layers of the web . (B) is the same GSL but with brightness values that correspond to absolute values of the result. The thin dark lines denote the shape's boundary = zero crossing loci.

XII. Discussion

The major issue of this chapter is a novel artificial neural architecture which has repetitive multilayered structures called web-lattices. In contrast to common neural networks that use non-linear components, our network is completely linear. Every layer of the web-lattice performs only a standard convolution that results in exact multiple-scaled Gaussian averaging. This enables us to derive from the web-lattice, a variety of linear operators, such as: Gaussian averaging, Gaussian-smoothed-Laplacians, Canny edge detectors, Fourier transforms, and Gabor transforms. The inherent multiple-scaled structure of the web-lattice provides all the required scales in parallel. This fact, and the absence of any digitization requirements, constitutes a definite advantage over conventional digital or analog hardware. We also extended the structure of the lattice to include any dimension of data structures without special alterations.

Our webs have obvious advantages over current technology used in speech and image processing. They generate their multiple-scale outputs in parallel, and they directly process the analog data. However, we sense that there must be additional efforts invested to find new directions to use the webs. The ease with which this regular repetitive structure obtains such complex transforms and operators, provides us with new insight to the intricate structure of nature.

We believe that the striking resemblance between the web-lattice's outputs to actual measurements of biological vision systems, also entails a large degree of structural similarity between the two. We argue, that the natural way in which this linear and regular system generates all these results must have severe impact upon current theories, which are mainly based on non-linear models of biological signal processing. We also claim that any shape or texture descriptor, organization and grouping of pictorial features, and even matching of structural descriptions, must be based on such webs. Following these propositions, we developed novel grouping network described in [Ben-Arie 91].

References

[Ben-Arie 90a]: Ben-Arie, J., "Novel Web-Lattice Architectures for parallel multiple-scale and multi-dimensional Gaussian filtering, edge detection, submitted to IEEE Trans. on Neural Networks, Dec. 1990.
[Ben-Arie 90b]: Ben-Arie, J. " Utilizing the Central Limit Theorem for Parallel Multiple-scale Image Processing with Novel Neural Architectures", to appear in SPIE conf. on Stochastic methods in signal Processing, Image Processing and Computer Vision" , San Diego, CA, 1991.
[Ben-Arie 91]: Ben-Arie, J., Huddleston, J., "Aggregation and Description

formation of Curvelinear Image Features by Novel Neural Architecture" submitted to IEEE Trans. on Neural Networks, 1991.

[Billingsley 79] Billingsley ,P., "Probability and Measure", John Wiley, 1979.

[Canny 86]: Canny, J. "A Computational Approach To Edge Detection", IEEE Trans. on Pattern Anal. and Mach. Intell. , Vol. PAMI-8, No.6, Nov. 1986.

[Culhane 89]: Culhane, A.D., Peckerar, M.C., Marian, C.R.K., "A neural net approach to discrete Hartley and Fourier transforms", IEEE Trnas. on Circuits and systems, Vol. 36, No. 5, May 1989, pp.695-702.

[Daugmam 80]: Daugman, J. G. "Two-dimensional spectral analysis of cortical receptive field profile" Vis. Research, vol 20, pp.847-856.

[Daugmam 88]: Daugman, J. G. "Complete Discrete 2D Gabor Transform by Neural Networks for image analysis and compression" IEEE Trans. on ASSP , Vol. 36, No. 7, July 1988, pp. 1169-1179.

[Hubel 74]: Hubel, D., Weisel, T., " Sequence regularity and geometry of orientation columns in the monkey striate cortex" J. Comput. Neurol., vol. 158 pp.267-293, 1974.

[Kobayashi 90]: Kobayashi, H., White, J.L., Abidi, A.A., "An active Resistive mesh for Gaussian convolution of images", submitted to IEEE J. of solid state circuits, 1990.

[Liu 89] Liu, S. , Harris, G. H., "Generalized Smoothing Networks in early Vision" , IEEE CVPR 1898, pp.184-191.

[Marr 82] D. Marr, "Vision", Freeman Publishing Co. , 1982.

[Mead 89] Mead, C. "Analog VLSI and Neural Systems" , Addison Wesley, 1989.

[Papoulis 84] Papoulis, A., "Probability, Random variables, and stochastic processes", McGraw-Hill, 1984.

[Storbach 90]: Storbach, P. "Linear Prediction Theory", Springer Verlag, 1990.

[Tanimoto 80]: Tanimoto, S. and Klinger, A. Eds. "Structured Computer Vision" Academic Press, 1980.

[Tank 86] Tank, D.W., Hopfield, J.J., "Simple neural optimization networks: An A/D conv. , signal decision circuits, and a linear programming circuit", IEEE Trans. on Circuits ans Sys. Vol CAS-36, pp533-546, May 1986.

[White 88]: White, J., Furman, B., Abidi, A.A., Baker, R.L., Mathur, B., Wang, H.T., "Prallel analog architecture for 2D Gaussian convolution of images" , Int. Neural Network Society Conference, Boston, MA, 1988, p.415.

[Witkin 84]: Andrew P. Witkin: "Scale-Space Filtering: A New Approach to Multi-Scale Description", in Image Understanding, S. Ullman, W. Richards Eds.

II.3

ASPECTS OF INVARIANT PATTERN AND OBJECT RECOGNITION

TERRY CAELLI[1],
MARIO FERRARO[2], and
ERHARDT BARTH [1,3]

[1]*Department of Computer Science
The University of Melbourne
Parkville Vic 3052
AUSTRALIA*

[2]*Dipartimento di Fisica Sperimentale
Universita' di Torino
ITALY*

[3]*Supported by the Daimler-Benz Foundation*

I. Introduction

In a fundamental sense the problem of invariance *is* the problem of pattern or object recognition insofar as any system which claims to be capable of recognizing objects or patterns is qualified by its ability to function under, and invariant to, a variety of transformations, whether they be geometric or based on distortions or other types of transformations of data. In this chapter we are concerned with one particular type of invariance, that is, rigid motions, which,

234

in two dimensions (2D), are restricted to planar translations (x, y) and rotations around the z axis (also including zoom-dilation operations). We will also consider the three-dimensional (3D) six-parameter invariance problem, that is, recognition invariant to three dimensional rigid motions of translations (in X, Y, Z directions) and rotations about all three axes (x, y and z).

Needless to say, elegant solutions to the invariant pattern recognition problem centre on developing a representation of both images and objects which enable recognition to occur in what we call the "strong sense". Representations can be "strong" or "weak" in the following ways. Consider a pattern represented by its average intensity. This representation is invariant to rotation and shift, given the pattern was localized for the calculation, but is neither unique nor capable of determining the transformation state. We call this representation "weak". An ideal representation is one which has a component in the representation which enables invariant matching, uniquely defining the pattern and explicitly encoding the transformation states involved. All three ingredients of invariance, uniqueness and transformation state are essential for a "strong" invariant pattern recognition representation. Unfortunately, as we shall show, only until very recently have all three conditions been satisfied in the development of invariant pattern recognition procedures. A second procedural property of "strong" invariant pattern recognition procedures is that they should be fast and efficient. That is, one can imagine representations which have the desired features, though are slow to execute, and procedurally inefficient as, for example, the use of many templates in exhaustive search .

However, it should be noted that the issue of "strong" verses "weak" representations is dependent upon how "patterns" are defined in a specific application. For example, by not requiring metric equivalences and only defining patterns by their topological properties, it is possible to measure the number of connected regions in an image independent of rigid motions. Indeed, Zetzsche and Barth (1990) have recently shown how the well-known Gauss-Bonnet theorem of Differential geometry can be used to obtain such a measure. Such a process remains weak, though, since this theorem does not register the actual transformation states. But the example of topological pattern classes demonstrates that the "uniqueness" criterion for pattern registration is contingent on the representational level.

The difference between three-dimensional object recognition and two-dimensional pattern recognition is not only due to the dimensionality differences and the possible rigid motions (specifically four to six parameter invariance), but also in the very nature of object recognition, in comparison to pattern recognition. Object recognition not only involves the registration of object surfaces but also involves understanding the parameters associated with the transition from view-dependent data to the view-independent object surface information. These extra constraints of rendering and camera calibration further complicate invariant object recognition, particularly from the perspective of the "inverse optics problem": (inferring the existence of view independent objects from two-dimensional view dependent data.

First consider the case where the pattern and data are from the same view. That is, in contrast to the full object recognition problem, both data and patterns have compatible formats: $P(x,y)$ and $I(x,y)$ share the same coordinate systems. For such cases where both pattern and data are specified as functions of the same coordinate system, the available representations fall essentially into two types. One, those based on extended measurements of image domain characteristics, and two, those based on transform techniques, where the representation is determined in a variety of transform domains. We call these techniques *implicit* as they involve the automatic transformation of images without any measurement of image features.

A second type of representation involves the definition of pattern or image data *explicitly* or symbolically. Such representations essentially involve the enumeration of pattern and image parts, the development of predicates which define individual part characteristics (unary predicates), and binary relationships between parts which play a specific role in coding patterns with the required invariance characteristics. Whereas correlation is seen as a predominant matching tool or measure in the implicit representations, graph matching, heuristic search and decision trees play a predominant role in the explicit representation matching procedures.

II. Pattern Recognition

In traditional pattern recognition, that is, the problem of detecting patterns embedded in images invariant to rotations, translations, and dilations of the pattern to be detected, both image and patterns are defined in the same coordinate system, that is, the viewer-dependent image. We divide recognition techniques into implicit and explicit types. By implicit, we simply mean that the pattern and image are defined as real-valued scalar or vector functions of the coordinate system, in contrast to the explicit techniques which define patterns by the extraction of parts, part-labelling and the definition of unary and binary predicates between parts. That is, the difference between implicit and explicit matching processes involves the way in which image parts are indexed - the former by the image (or transform domain) coordinate system, the latter by the parts.

Techniques which have emerged over the last century to enable invariant pattern recognition, where pattern and image data is defined implicitly, further divide into two types. One, those types defined in the image domain itself, that is, representations that are indexed by the image coordinate system. The second type of representation involves the use of transform domains where both patterns and images are transformed into a new coordinate system in which recognition is accomplished. In both cases, however, the matching function is usually considered as correlation, that is, pattern and image regions are matched according to their similarity defined by the correlation between values over the given representation domain.

2.1 Image Domain Techniques

A proper rigid motion in two dimensions is defined by an element of SO^2 - a rotation around the z-axis followed by a translation. However, if dilations are taken into account the transformation is given by:

$$\begin{pmatrix} x' \\ y' \end{pmatrix} = a^{\sigma_0} \begin{pmatrix} \cos\theta_0 & \sin\theta_0 \\ -\sin\theta_0 & \cos\theta_0 \end{pmatrix} \begin{pmatrix} x \\ y \end{pmatrix} + \begin{pmatrix} x_0 \\ y_0 \end{pmatrix} \tag{1}$$

where θ_0, (x_0,y_0) and a^{σ_0} correspond to the rotation, translation and dilation components of the transformation respectively. We use the exponent form of dilation (σ_0) to preserve linearity of the parameter indices (see following), with a base scalar of a (for example a = 2 or e).

It should be noted that in this case the centres of rotations and dilations are common and correspond to the origin: a rotation and dilation followed by a translation. If we consider a translation followed by a rotation and dilation a different transformation will arise:

$$\begin{pmatrix} x' \\ y' \end{pmatrix} = a^{\sigma_0} \begin{pmatrix} \cos\theta_0 & \sin\theta_0 \\ -\sin\theta_0 & \cos\theta_0 \end{pmatrix} \begin{pmatrix} x-x_0 \\ y-y_0 \end{pmatrix} + \begin{pmatrix} x_0 \\ y_0 \end{pmatrix}, \tag{2}$$

that is,

$$\begin{pmatrix} x' \\ y' \end{pmatrix} = a^{\sigma_0} \begin{pmatrix} \cos\theta_0 & \sin\theta_0 \\ -\sin\theta_0 & \cos\theta_0 \end{pmatrix} \begin{pmatrix} x \\ y \end{pmatrix} + \begin{pmatrix} x_0 + a^{\sigma_0}(-x_0\cos\theta_0 + y_0\sin\theta_0) \\ y_0 + a^{\sigma_0}(-x_0\sin\theta_0 - y_0\cos\theta_0) \end{pmatrix}, \tag{3}$$

so rotations and dilations centred at any point P can be reduced to dilations and rotations centred in (0,0) plus a translation which depends on θ_0 and σ_0. In other words given a pattern A, any transformed pattern A' can be obtained by means of a rotation and dilation with centre in (0,0) followed by a suitable translation.

Recently Zetzsche and Caelli (1989) and Jacobson and Wechsler (1990) have shown that for a representation to be strongly invariant (that is, have uniqueness, transformation invariance and transformation registration characteristics) *it must be one whose dimensionality is equal to the number of one-parameter transformations involved.* That is, if one requires a representation that is rotation and shift invariant, only a three-dimensional representation is required. Whereas, rotation, shift and scale invariance requires an image representation in four dimensions (4D). For rotation, scale and shift invariance all transformations can be reduced to translations along the coordinate axis of the

representation. For an image $l(x,y)$ we consider the 4D representation defined by the mapping (Zetzsche and Caelli, 1989):

N: $l(x,y) \rightarrow p(\overline{x}, \overline{y}, \theta, \sigma)$

In this representation the action of a transformation T, denoting collectively translation, rotation and size changes, alters the representation by shifts. That is,

$$T: p(\overline{x}, \overline{y}, \theta, \sigma) \rightarrow p(\overline{x} + \overline{x}_0, \overline{y} + \overline{y}_0, \theta + \theta_0, \sigma + \sigma_0). \qquad (4)$$

This representation can be implemented in a number of ways, the two more common being the multiple template method and the multiple filter method. The multiple template method is based on the simplest form of an invariant representation: the use of multiple versions of the pattern at different transformation states. What makes this method non-trivial is the ability to do this within the minimum number of templates, an issue studied in some detail recently by one of the authors (Caelli and Liu, 1988). Each template has a "trace function" determined by the "generalized auto-correlation function":

$$C(u,v;\sigma,\theta) = \int_y \int_x l(x',y') \cdot l(x + u, y + v)dxdy \qquad (5)$$

where

$$\begin{pmatrix} x' \\ y' \end{pmatrix} = a^\sigma \begin{pmatrix} \cos\theta & \sin\theta \\ -\sin\theta & \cos\theta \end{pmatrix} \begin{pmatrix} x \\ y \end{pmatrix}$$

for the scale (σ) and rotation (θ) transformations. Figure 1 shows such functions for letters and the image of a face.

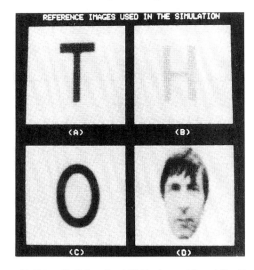

Fig.1(a) Test images (A) letter T, (B) letter H, (C) letter O, and (D) Face image. All are of 64 x 64 and 8-bit in resolution. *

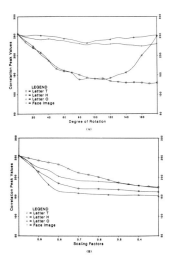

Fig. 1(b). (A) Peak values of the cross-correlation between the images in Fig 1 and their corresponding rotated versions. (B) Peak values of the cross-correlation between the images in Fig. 1 and their corresponding scaled states. As expected, the maxima are related to shapes of objects. *

* (Reprinted with permission from Pergamon Press, Caelli, T. and Liu, Z., *Pattern Recognition*, 21, 3, 205-216, 1988.)

At run time the specified template states are correlated with the new image data and the resultant vectors, in turn, are correlated with each vector of the trace function, in this case a two-dimensional (2D) trace vector (surface σ,θ). The number of states are chosen to guarantee that the comparator (trace vector correlations) remains above a threshold which maximizes hits and minimizes false alarms (see Caelli and Liu, 1988, for more details).

In contrast, the filter method involves the selection of filters indexed for (σ,θ). What Zetzsche and Caelli (1989) showed was that if the outputs of these filters were appropriately normalized, then the resultant 4-dimensional representation satisfies (4). This transformation, corresponding to (1) is:

$$\begin{pmatrix} \bar{x} \\ \bar{y} \end{pmatrix} = a^{-\sigma} \begin{pmatrix} \cos\theta & \sin\theta \\ \sin\theta & \cos\theta \end{pmatrix} \begin{pmatrix} x \\ y \end{pmatrix}. \qquad (6)$$

Figure 2a shows how this multiply representation satisfies (4) in so far as translations, rotations and dilations of the input pattern all correspond to translations in the normalized (6) outputs: allowing invariant matching, in the strong sense, with standard correlation techniques (Figure 2b).

In this implementation we (ibid) used the class of Gabor filters which, being gaussain modulated spatial frequency gratings of the spectral form:

$$H_{ij}(u,v) = \exp\left\{-\pi\ \frac{(u - u_{ij})^2 + (v - v_{ij})^2}{(\frac{2}{3}f_i)^2}\right\} \qquad (7)$$

where

$$u_{ij} = f_i \cos\theta_j$$
$$v_{ij} = f_i \sin\theta_j$$

correspond to the (spectral) filter centre of radial frequency f_i and orientation θ_j. The filters were symmetric (even, zero phase) and had an isotropic band width of one octave. (u,v) correspond to the Fourier transform (spatial frequency) coordinates, and ij index the filter size (scale) and orientation respectively.

Interestingly enough, such filters correspond to the well known receptive field profiles for bar detectors discovered within the vertebrate visual cortex (see Hubel and Wiesel, 1977). That such detectors would be capable of interpreting rotation and scale changes as translations had already been noted by Schwartz (1980) and Cavanagh (1984). However, their representations did not simultaneously contain translation invariance, nor the necessary normalization and matching algorithms.

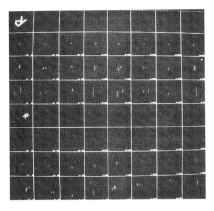

Figure. 2(a) Comparison of responses (rows correspond to different scales and columns to different orientations, see (6) and (7)) for two versions of the letter R differing in scale (by a factor of 2), orientation (by 180°) and position. Note the simple shift in the pattern of responses over the various columns. For example, response (1/0): row 3, column 1 corresponds to (2/180°) : row 8, column 5, etc.

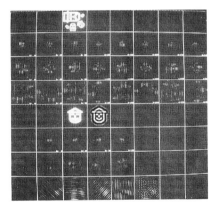

Figure 2(b) *Correlation (or matching) process.* Here we search for the presence of the pattern shown in column 3, of row 5 in the image shown in column 3 of row 1. For illustration purposes we use only one scale ($\sigma = 0$) range to represent the pattern (row 5, column 4). The corresponding 4 orientation filter responses ($\sigma = 0.\pi = 0,45,90,135°$) are shown in normalized coordinates in row 6. These four responses are cross correlated with columns (images) 2 to 5 of row 3 which correspond to the responses of four orientation filters ($\sigma = 1.\pi = 45,90,135,180°$) to the image. These correlations are shown in row 7 in normalized coordinates, and row 8 (columns 2 to 5) in Cartesian coordinates. Column 6 in row 8 shows the total of columns (images) 2 to 5) in Cartesian coordinates. Column 6 row 8 shows the total of columns (images) 2 to 5. Here the output intensity corresponds to the liklihood that the pattern was present at the position reduced in size by a factor of 2 and rotated by 45°. (Reprinted with permission from Academic Press, Zetsche, C. and Caelli, T., *Computer Vision, Graphics and Image Processing*, 45, 251-262, 1989)

2.2   Invariance in Transform Domains

Interest in the use of Fourier methods for invariant pattern recognition originate from the shift theorem for Fourier transforms. That is, given the Fourier transform of a pattern $p(x,y)$ as:

$$F(u,v) = \int_y \int_x p(x,y)\, e^{-2\pi i(ux + vy)}\, dxdy, \qquad (8)$$

in polar form:

$$F(u,v) = A(u,v)\, e^{i\phi(u,v)}, \qquad (9)$$

then, it can be shown that the transformation

$$T: p(x,y) \rightarrow p(x + k, y + l) \qquad (10)$$

changes (9) to:

$$A(u,v) \cdot e^{i[\phi(u,v) + \delta\phi(u,v)]} \qquad (11)$$

where

$$\delta\phi(u,v) = 2\pi(uk + vl) \qquad (12)$$

That is, the amplitude spectrum remains invariant and the phase spectrum encodes the shift. It should be noted, however that this "shift theorem" refers to *global coordinate transformations* and *not* to the non-uniform motions of *individual* patterns. In contrast, rotation and scale changes (via (1)) affect the spectral coordinate systems in so far as:

$$T_{\sigma\theta}: F(u,v) \rightarrow F(u',v') \qquad (13)$$

where (u',v') are defined, relative to (u,v), also in accord with (1), except that:

$$\sigma_{xy} \leftrightarrow \frac{1}{\sigma_{uv}} \text{ and } \theta_{xy} \leftrightarrow -\theta_{uv}$$

The Fourier-Mellin transform was developed to capture all 4 transformations by taking the log-polar transform of the power spectrum. Here, the log-polar transform encodes rotations and dilations as translations, while the phase spectrum encodes translations (see Cavanagh, 1984, for more details). However, as noted above, the two major problems with this representation, for *recognition purposes*, are that: (a) the formulation only applies to transformations of the complete image coordinate system; (b) the power spectrum, alone, is not unique and the extraction of shift from phase involves solving sets of simultaneous equations. Indeed all integral transforms whose coordinate systems are two-dimensional (cartesian or log-polar, see Ferraro and Caelli, 1988), cannot have full rotation, shift and scale invariance-in the strong sense. Further, we (ibid) have shown that in order to have orthogonal transforms which have an invariant amplitude spectrum, and a phase spectrum which encodes the transform, then the transformations need to commute. For example, horizontal and vertical translations commute (cartesian Fourier transform) as do rotations and dilations (log-polar or circular harmonic Fourier transforms).

We have argued here that, independent of whether the pattern representation be in the image or transform domain, the *dimensionality* of the representation must be at least that of the number of transformation parameters involved. Secondly, we have shown that unless the right pair-wise structures are used, and the appropriate normalization factors considered, invariant recognition, in the strong sense, is impossible. However, one of the major problems with these correlational based representational procedures is that they do not permit the types of systematic distortions between pattern parts, or object parts, which are typically required to have a representative definition of "shape". For these reasons, such implicit recognition algorithms are usually restricted to parts of patterns or objects, which are then input into more adaptive or dynamical representations of "shape" based on the part characteristics and their relationships. Such "second-level" or *explicit* representations will be briefly discussed in the following section, since they do involve quite different matching algorithms than the correlation (least-squares) criteria used in implicit representations.

2.3   Patterns Specified Explicitly

The above techniques for invariant pattern recognition are concerned with the problem of recognizing patterns specified exactly as two-dimensional intensity profiles. However, in many pattern and object recognition problems the "shape" is not defined precisely or even if it could be, it would prove to be inefficient to do matching by parallel procedures as implicit in the above representations.

To overcome such limitations, explicit invariant matching procedures are based upon the development of pattern/object representations in terms of partitioning the model and data into parts, deriving unary (individual part properties) and binary (part relationship) features and enacting recognition by graph matching, decision tree or constraint satisfaction procedures. The invariance recognition comes from the development of unary and/or binary features which have specific geometric properties. For example, part colour, area, perimeter are examples of unary features which are invariant to shifts and rotations. Interpart distances and tri-part intersection angles are also invariant to the same transformations, while the latter is also invariant to scale (size) changes. Clearly, the choice of features determines the types of invariances but, it should be noted that, uniqueness and registration of transformation states can only be guaranteed if the pattern can be reconstructed from the feature lists and the features are indexed for the transformation state.

Though this paper is focused upon representational issues, the actual matching procedures, where models and data are specified by parts, are varied and essentially are differentiated by their degree of parallelism. Graph matching techniques, based upon depth-first or breadth-first search, match model to data parts by exhaustively checking the degrees to which unary and binary part features are similar for each model and data part pair. Such a procedure is most inefficient and the comparison time exponentiates with the number of parts. Decision trees differ from direct graph matching in so far as unary and binary features are hierachically organized or ordered into a tree structure where nodes (decision nodes) nearer to the root of the tree are covered by features which differentiate between parts and/or models more acutely. A given model is therefore defined by a complete path in the decision tree, though its actual label occurs at that tree's final leaf. Such decision trees require that features be partitioned in range and so it formally constitutes a computational implementation of step-wise discriminant function analysis (Hand, 1986).

In contrast to such sequential methods, constraint satisfaction approaches to matching, based upon relaxation labelling procedures, involve a parallel update of part labels (that is, the attachment of model parts to data parts) as a function of their compatabilities. Relaxation labeling with n nodes and m labels can be seen as a neural network with $n^2.m^2$ weights which may be trained (or determined) to satisfy specific local or global constraints. That is, relaxation labelling, when required to satisfy compatibility constraints, differs little from neural networks and the main contrast between the representations lies in the "learning" or optimization procedures employed (ibid). The basic algorithm has the following form (Rosenfeld and Kak, 1982):

$$p_i^{t+1}(j) = N \left\{ p_i^t(j) + \sum_{hk} c(i,j; h,k) \cdot p_h^t(k) \right\} \qquad (14)$$

where $p_i^{t+1}(j)$ corresponds to the probability that data part j is labelled with model part i (that is, corresponds to model part i) at time (t+1). N corresponds to response normalization (usually by some logistic transformation) and c(i,j;h,k) corresponds to the "compatibility function" defining the range of consistent and inconsistent relationships, as derived from binary features, or part labels. Again, the *invariance* of such a matching procedure is dependent upon the actual choice of unary and binary features. Such techniques seem to have great potential, particularly where the dynamical system can be distributed over many processors, though it does not take advantage of tree pruning: the deletion of impossible matches, in the early matching stages, so decreasing the number of comparisons required in the implementation of (14).

A final note should be made about whether human pattern recognition is actually invariant to rotations, translations or scale changes. Put simple, results from many experiments show limitations in human pattern recognition under transformations. Factors as the cortical magnification, spatial resolution clearly affect our abilities to recognize patterns under projected retinal position and size (Rentschler and Treutwein, 1985). However, lack of rotation invariance seems to be the more pronounced limitation of human pattern recognition (see Rock, 1973; Caelli and Dodwell, 1984). Fortunately, we have made no claims that anyone of the above techniques represent what humans actually do in pattern recognition, though it is the view of the authors that a combination of explicit and explicit procedures are used by humans in such tasks.

III. Brief Notes in Object Recognition

One way of representing the difference between pattern and object recognition is via the fact that, while, in pattern recognition, the image and model data are adequately represented in the same (view-dependent) coordinate system, objects and image data are not! Indeed, what makes object recognition decidedly more complex than pattern recognition are three major conditions:

(i)   View-dependent data must be matched with view-independent models.

(ii)   Passive/active vision data which result in intensity/depth map images must be adjusted for camera model, rendering conditions including the fusion of lighting, material and surface geometries.

(iii) Rigid motions of objects involve translations in three directions (X, Y, Z) and rotations about three axes - a total of 6 parameters.

To this stage very little is known about how humans solve object recognition problems though some general representations have been considered, including part matching (Biederman, 1985) and full mental registration of objects (Shepard, 1984).

The computational vision literature is vast on object recognition and, here, we only focus on the problem of representing surface patches, or objects, as collections of surfaces, invariant to their rigid motions-as is the topic of this chapter. Here, we adopt the "natural representation" for object recognition: the problem of matching surface depth patches to models composed of many patches both in the view-independent coordinate system (X,Y,Z). That is, we assume that low-level processes which convert intensity $(I(x,y))$ and/or depth $(d(x,y))$ into $P(X,Y,Z)$ are available. The specific question we ask here is as to the available invariant representations? The answer resides in classical Differential Geometry: the mathematical analysis of local surface properties.

Here, surfaces are depicted, at each surface parametric position (u,v), via specific combinations of differential operators. That is, since every surface patch is a (parameterized) two-dimensional manifold, we can study the flow of depth information via the partial derivations.

$$\left\{ \frac{\partial S}{\partial u}, \ \frac{\partial S}{\partial v}, \ \frac{\partial^2 S}{\partial u \partial v}, \ \frac{\partial^2 S}{\partial u^2}, \ \frac{\partial^2 S}{\partial v^2} \right\} \tag{15}$$

for the surface parametric form:

$$S = \{(X(u,v), Y(u,v), Z(u,v)\} \tag{16}$$

where (X,Y,Z) refer to the view-independent coordinate system. It should be noted that, for u=x, v=y, the view-dependent coordinate system, we obtain the data format for object recognition:

$$D (x,y) = \{x, y, z(x,y)\} \tag{17}$$

After a century of analysis we have a number of geometric invariants emergent from (15). Specifically, surfaces are defined by their tangent planes, surface normals and rate of change of the surface normal with respect to its parametric representation. In fact, the fundamental theorem of Differential Geometry shows how the terms in (15) uniquely determine a surface patch up to a rigid motion.

The rate of change of the surface normal $(S_u \times S_v / \|S_u \times S_v\|, S_u = \frac{\partial S}{\partial u})$ defines the principal curvatures of a surface which correspond to the maxima and minima of such a gradient function (k_1, k_2) at a given surface point. The mean (H) and Gaussian (K) curvatures:

$$H = \frac{k_1 + k_2}{2}, \quad \text{and} \quad K = k_1 . k_2$$

are also invariant to rigid motions. However it should be noted that such invariants are indexed by the view-independent coordinate system. That is, although there is an isomorphism between the surface parameterization (u,v) of a surface point and it's 3D coordinates (X,Y,Z), invariance to rigid motion occurs in the latter system. This implies that algorithms to represent *image data* invariant to rigid motions must be transformed into the view-independent system.

In the (computational) object recognition literature, surface patches are typically characterized by H and K (see, for example, Jain and Hoffman, 1988, Fan et al, 1989), and the fundamental derivatives (15) are determined by their appropriate band-pass filters (ibid). However, once these parts are defined in terms of their curvature types, the actual (invariant) recognition algorithms are implemented via graph matching decision trees or constraint satisfaction as in pattern recognition (ibid).

IV. Conclusion

In this chapter we have discussed some representational issues in invariant pattern and object recognition. We have distinguished between *implicit* and *explicit* representations and have pointed to the fact that both forms have been used to develop robust recognition systems. Implicit representational schemes typically use correlation procedures whereas explicit forms use sequential or parallel constraint satisfaction procedures. Further work is particularly required in invariant object recognition systems and the associated investigations of how humans solve such complex problems.

REFERENCES

1. Biederman, I. (1985) Human Image Understanding: Recent Research and a Theory. *Computer Vision, Graphics and Image Processing*, 32, 29-73.
2. Caelli, T.M. and Dodewell, P.C. (1984) Orientation-position coding and invariance characteristics of pattern discrimination. *Perception and Psychophysics*, 36 (2), 159-169.
3. Caelli, T.M. and Liu, Z.Q. (1988) On the minimum number of templates required for shift, rotation and size invariant pattern recognition. *Pattern Recognition*, 21, 3, 205-216.
4. Cavanagh, P (1984) Image Transforms in the Visual System, in P.C. Dodwell and T.M. Caelli (Eds) *Figural Synthesis*, Hillside, N.J. Erlbaum, 185-213.
5. Fan, T. Medioni, G. and Nevatia, R. (1989) Recognizing 3-D Objects Using Surface Descriptions. *IEEE Transactions on Pattern Analysis and Machine Intelligence*, 11, 11, 1140-1156
6. Ferraro, M. and Caelli, T.M. (1988) The relationship between integral transform invariance and Lie Group Theory. *Journal of the Optical Society of America A: Optics and Image Science*, 5, 738-742.
7. Hand, D. (1986) *Discrimination and Classification*. New York, Wiley.
8. Hinton, G (1989) Connectionist Learning Procedures. *Artificial Intelligence*, 40, 185-234.
9. Hubel, D. and Wiesel, T. (1977) Functional architecture of macaque monkey visual cortex. *Proceedings of the Royal Society (London) B*, 198, 1-59.
10. Jacobson, L. and Wechsler, H. (1990) Invariant Architectures for Low-Level Vision (In Press).
11. Jain, A. and Hoffman, R. (1988) Evidence-Based Recognition of 3-D Objects. *IEEE Transactions on Pattern Analysis and Machine Intelligence*, 10, 6, 783-802.
12. Rentschler, I. and Treutwein, B. (1985) Loss of spatial phase relationships in extrafoveal vision. *Nature*, 313 (6000), 308-310.
13. Rock, I. (1973) *Orientation and Form*. New York, Academic Press.
14. Rosenfeld, A. and Kak, A. (1982) *Digital Picture Processing*. New York, Academic Press.
15. Schwartz, E. (1980) Computational Anatomy and Functional Architecture of Striate Cortex: a spatial mapping approach to perceptual coding. *Vision Research*, 20, 645-669.
16. Shepard, R. (1984) Ecological Constraints on Internal Representation. *Psychological Review*, 91 (4), 417-447.
17 Zetzsche, C. and Barth, E. (1990). Image surface predicates and the neural encoding of two-dimensional signal variations. *Proc SPIE*, 1249, Bellingham, Washington, in press.
18. Zetzsche, C. and Caelli, T.M. (1989) Invariant Pattern Recognition Using Multiple filter Image Representations. *Computer Vision, Graphics and Image Processing*, 45, 251-265.

II.4

A NEURAL NETWORK ARCHITECTURE FOR FAST ON-LINE SUPERVISED LEARNING AND PATTERN RECOGNITION

GAIL A. CARPENTER
STEPHEN GROSSBERG
JOHN REYNOLDS

Center for Adaptive Systems and
Graduate Program in Cognitive & Neural Systems
Boston University
111 Cummington Street
Boston, MA 02215

I. Introduction

This chapter describes a new neural network architecture, called ARTMAP (Carpenter, Grossberg, and Reynolds, 1991), that autonomously learns to classify arbitrarily many, arbitrarily ordered vectors into recognition categories based on predictive success. This supervised learning system is built up from a pair of Adaptive Resonance Theory (Carpenter and Grossberg, 1987a, 1987b, 1988, 1990) modules (ART_a and ART_b) that are capable of self-organizing stable recognition categories in response to arbitrary sequences of input patterns (Figure 1). During training, the ART_a module receives a stream $\{a^{(p)}\}$ of input patterns, and ART_b receives a stream $\{b^{(p)}\}$ of input patterns, where $b^{(p)}$ is the correct prediction given $a^{(p)}$. These ART modules are linked by an associative learning network and an internal controller that ensures autonomous system operation in real time. During test trials, the remaining patterns $a^{(p)}$ are presented without $b^{(p)}$, and their predictions at ART_b are compared with $b^{(p)}$.

Tested on a benchmark machine learning database in both on-line and off-line simulations, the ARTMAP system learns orders of magnitude more quickly, efficiently, and accurately than alternative algorithms, and achieves 100% accuracy after training on less than half the input patterns in the database. It achieves these properties by using an internal controller that

248

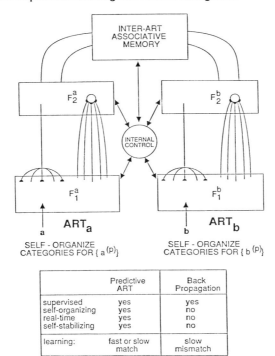

	Predictive ART	Back Propagation
supervised	yes	yes
self-organizing	yes	no
real-time	yes	no
self-stabilizing	yes	no
learning:	fast or slow match	slow mismatch

Figure 1. A Predictive ART, or ARTMAP, system includes two ART modules linked by an inter-ART associative memory. Internal control structures actively regulate learning and information flow. Back Propagation and Predictive ART both carry out supervised learning, but the two systems differ in many respects, as indicated.

conjointly maximizes predictive generalization and minimizes predictive error by linking predictive success to category size on a trial-by-trial basis, using only local operations. This computation increases the vigilance parameter ρ_a of ART_a by the minimal amount needed to correct a predictive error at ART_b. Parameter ρ_a calibrates the minimum confidence that ART_a must have in a category, or hypothesis, activated by an input $\mathbf{a}^{(p)}$ in order for ART_a to accept that category, rather than search for a better one through an automatically controlled process of hypothesis testing. Parameter ρ_a is compared with the degree of match between $\mathbf{a}^{(p)}$ and the top-down learned expectation, or prototype, that is read-out subsequent to activation of an ART_a category. Search occurs if the degree of match is less than ρ_a. ARTMAP is hereby a type of self-organizing expert system that calibrates the selectivity of its hypotheses based upon predictive success. As a result, rare but important events can be quickly and sharply distinguished even if they are similar to frequent events with different consequences. Between input trials ρ_a relaxes to a baseline vigilance $\overline{\rho_a}$. When $\overline{\rho_a}$ is large, the

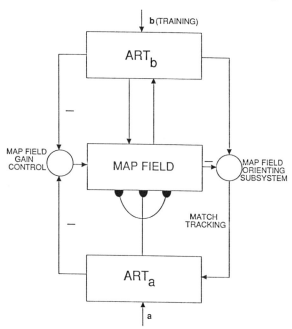

Figure 2. Block diagram of an ARTMAP system. Modules ART_a and ART_b self-organize categories for vector sets **a** and **b**. ART_a and ART_b are connected by an inter-ART module that consists of the Map Field and the control nodes called Map Field gain control and Map Field orienting subsystem. Inhibitory paths are denoted by a minus sign; other paths are excitatory.

system runs in a conservative mode, wherein predictions are made only if the system is confident of the outcome. Very few false-alarm errors then occur at any stage of learning, yet the system reaches asymptote with no loss of speed. Because ARTMAP learning is self-stabilizing, it can continue learning one or more databases, without degrading its corpus of memories, until its full memory capacity is utilized.

II. The ARTMAP System

The main elements of an ARTMAP system are shown in Figure 2. Two modules, ART_a and ART_b, read vector inputs **a** and **b**. If ART_a and ART_b were disconnected, each module would self-organize category groupings for the separate input sets. In the application described below, ART_a and ART_b are fast-learn ART 1 (Carpenter and Grossberg, 1987a) modules coding binary input vectors. ART_a and ART_b are here connected by an inter-ART module that in many ways resembles ART 1.

This inter-ART module includes a *Map Field* that controls the learning of an associative map from ART_a recognition categories to ART_b recognition categories. This map does not directly associate exemplars **a** and **b**, but rather associates the compressed and symbolic representations of families of exemplars **a** and **b**. The Map Field also controls match tracking of the ART_a vigilance parameter. A mismatch at the Map Field between the ART_a category activated by an input **a** and the ART_b category activated by the input **b** increases ART_a vigilance by the minimum amount needed for the system to search for and, if necessary, learn a new ART_a category whose prediction matches the ART_b category.

This inter-ART vigilance resetting signal is a form of "back propagation" of information, but one that differs from the back propagation that occurs in the Back Propagation network (Figure 1). For example, the search initiated by inter-ART reset can shift attention to a novel cluster of visual features that can be incorporated through learning into a new ART_a recognition category. This process is analogous to learning a category for "green bananas" based on "taste" feedback. However, these events do not "back propagate" taste features into the visual representation of the bananas, as can occur using the Back Propagation network. Rather, match tracking reorganizes the way in which visual features are grouped, attended, learned, and recognized for purposes of predicting an expected taste.

The following sections describe ARTMAP simulations using a machine learning benchmark database. For a full specification of the ARTMAP system, and analysis of network dynamics, see Carpenter, Grossberg, and Reynolds (1991).

III. ARTMAP Simulations: Distinguishing Edible and Poisonous Mushrooms

The ARTMAP system was tested on a benchmark machine learning database that partitions a set of vectors **a** into two classes. Each vector **a** characterizes observable features of a mushroom as a binary vector, and each mushroom is classified as edible or poisonous (Schlimmer, 1987a). The database represents the 11 species of genus *Agaricus* and the 12 species of the genus *Lepiota* described in **The Audubon Society Field Guide to North American Mushrooms** (Lincoff, 1981). These two genera constitute most of the mushrooms described in the **Field Guide** from the familiy *Agaricaceae* (order *Agaricales*, class *Hymenomycetes*, subdivision *Basidiomycetes*, division *Eumycota*). All the mushrooms represented in the database are similar to one another: "These mushrooms are placed in a single family on the basis of a correlation of characteristics that include microscopic and and chemical features..." (Lincoff, 1981, p.500).

The **Field Guide** warns that poisonous and edible species can be difficult to distinguish on the basis of their observable features. For example, the poisonous species *Agaricus californicus* is described as a "dead ringer" (p. 504) for the Meadow Mushroom, *Agaricus campestris*, that "may be known better and gathered more than any other wild mushroom in North America" (p. 505). This database thus provides a test of how ARTMAP and other machine learning systems distinguish rare but important events from frequently occurring collections of similar events that lead to different consequences.

The database of 8124 exemplars describes each of 22 observable features of a mushroom, along with its classification as poisonous (48.2%) or edible (51.8%). The 8124 "hypothetical examples" represent ranges of characteristics within each species; for example, both *Agaricus californicus* and *Agaricus campestris* are described as having a "white to brownish cap," so in the database each species has corresponding sets of exemplar vectors representing their range of cap colors. There are 126 different values of the 22 different observable features. A list of the observable features and their possible values is given in Table 1. For example, the observable feature of "cap-shape" has six possible values. Consequently, the vector inputs to ART_a are 126-element binary vectors, each vector having 22 1's and 104 0's, to denote the values of an exemplar's 22 observable features. The ART_b input vectors are $(1,0)$ for poisonous exemplars and $(0,1)$ for edible exemplars.

A. Performance

The ARTMAP system learned to classify test vectors rapidly and accurately, and system performance compares favorably with results of other machine learning algorithms applied to the same database. The STAGGER algorithm reached its maximum performance level of 95% accuracy after exposure to 1000 training inputs (Schlimmer, 1987b). The HILLARY algorithm achieved similar results (Iba, Wogulis, and Langley, 1988). The ARTMAP system consistently achieved over 99% accuracy with 1000 exemplars, even counting "I don't know" responses as errors. Accuracy of 95% was usually achieved with on-line training on 300–400 exemplars and with off-line training on 100–200 exemplars. In this sense, ARTMAP was an order of magnitude more efficient than the alternative systems. In addition, with continued training, ARTMAP predictive accuracy always improved to 100%. These results are elaborated below.

Almost every ARTMAP simulation was completed in under 2 minutes on an IRIS 4D computer, with total time ranging from about 1 minute for small training sets to 2 minutes for large training sets. This is comparable to 2–5 minutes on a SUN 4 computer. Each timed simulation included a

TABLE 1: 22 Observable Features and their 126 Values

Number	Feature	Possible Values
1	cap-shape	bell, conical, convex, flat, knobbed, sunken
2	cap-surface	fibrous, grooves, scaly, smooth
3	cap-color	brown, buff, gray, green, pink, purple, red, white, yellow, cinnamon
4	bruises	bruises, no bruises
5	odor	none, almond, anise, creosote, fishy, foul, musty, pungent, spicy
6	gill-attachment	attached, descending, free, notched
7	gill-spacing	close, crowded, distant
8	gill-size	broad, narrow
9	gill-color	brown, buff, orange, gray, green, pink, purple, red, white, yellow, chocolate, black
10	stalk-shape	enlarging, tapering
11	stalk-root	bulbous, club, cup, equal, rhizomorphs, rooted, missing
12	stalk-surface-above-ring	fibrous, silky, scaly, smooth
13	stalk-surface-below-ring	fibrous, silky, scaly, smooth
14	stalk-color-above-ring	brown, buff, orange, gray, pink, red, white, yellow, cinnamon
15	stalk-color-below-ring	brown, buff, orange, gray, pink, red, white, yellow, cinnamon
16	veil-type	partial, universal
17	veil-color	brown, orange, white, yellow
18	ring-number	none, one, two
19	ring-type	none, cobwebby, evanescent, flaring, large, pendant, sheathing, zone
20	spore-print-color	brown, buff, orange, green, purple, white, yellow, chocolate, black
21	population	abundant, clustered, numerous, scattered, several, solitary
22	habitat	grasses, leaves, meadows, paths, urban, waste, woods

Table 1: 126 values of 22 observable features represented in ART_a input vectors.

total of 8124 training and test samples, run on a time-sharing system with non-optimized code. Each 1–2 minute computation included data read-in and read-out, training, testing, and calculation of multiple simulation indices.

B. On-Line Learning

On-line learning imitates the conditions of a human or machine operating in a natural environment. An input $\mathbf{a}$ arrives, possibly leading to a prediction. If made, the prediction may or may not be confirmed. Learning ensues, depending on the accuracy of the prediction. Information about past inputs is available only through the present state of the system. Simulations of on-line learning by the ARTMAP system use each sample pair $(\mathbf{a}, \mathbf{b})$ as both a test item and a training item. Input $\mathbf{a}$ first makes a prediction that is compared with $\mathbf{b}$. Learning follows as dictated by the internal rules of the ARTMAP architecture.

Four types of on-line simulations were carried out, using two different baseline settings of the ART_a vigilance parameter ρ_a: $\overline{\rho_a} = 0$ (forced choice condition) and $\overline{\rho_a} = 0.7$ (conservative condition); and using sample replacement or no sample replacement. With sample replacement, any one of the 8124 input samples was selected at random for each input presentation. A given sample might thus be repeatedly encountered while others were still unused. With no sample replacement, a sample was removed from the input pool after it was first encountered. The replacement condition had the advantage that repeated encounters tended to boost predictive accuracy. The no-replacement condition had the advantage of having learned from a somewhat larger set of inputs at each point in the simulation. The replacement and no-replacement conditions had similar performance indices, all other things being equal. Each of the 4 conditions was run on 10 independent simulations. With $\overline{\rho_a} = 0$, the system made a prediction in response to every input. Setting $\overline{\rho_a} = 0.7$ increased the number of "I don't know" responses, increased the number of ART_a categories, and decreased the rate of incorrect predictions to nearly 0%, even early in training. The $\overline{\rho_a} = 0.7$ condition generally outperformed the $\overline{\rho_a} = 0$ condition, even when incorrect predictions and "I don't know" responses were both counted as errors. The primary exception occurred very early in training, when a conservative system gives the large majority of its no-prediction responses.

Results are summarized in Table 2. Each entry gives the number of correct predictions over the previous 100 trials (input presentations), averaged over 10 simulations. For example, with $\overline{\rho_a} = 0$ in the no-replacement condition, the system made, on the average, 94.9 correct predictions and 5.1 incorrect predictions on trials 201–300. In all cases a 95% correct-prediction rate was achieved before trial 400. With $\overline{\rho_a} = 0$, a consistent

TABLE 2: On-Line Learning

Average number of correct predictions on previous 100 trials

Trial	$\overline{\rho_a} = 0$ no replace	$\overline{\rho_a} = 0$ replace	$\overline{\rho_a} = 0.7$ no replace	$\overline{\rho_a} = 0.7$ replace
100	82.9	81.9	66.4	67.3
200	89.8	89.6	87.8	87.4
300	94.9	92.6	94.1	93.2
400	95.7	95.9	96.8	95.8
500	97.8	97.1	97.5	97.8
600	98.4	98.2	98.1	98.2
700	97.7	97.9	98.1	99.0
800	98.1	97.7	99.0	99.0
900	98.3	98.6	99.2	99.0
1000	98.9	98.5	99.4	99.0
1100	98.7	98.9	99.2	99.7
1200	99.6	99.1	99.5	99.5
1300	99.3	98.8	99.8	99.8
1400	99.7	99.4	99.5	99.8
1500	99.5	99.0	99.7	99.6
1600	99.4	99.6	99.7	99.8
1700	98.9	99.3	99.8	99.8
1800	99.5	99.2	99.8	99.9
1900	99.8	99.9	99.9	99.9
2000	99.8	99.8	99.8	99.8

Table 2: On-line learning and performance in forced choice ($\overline{\rho_a} = 0$) or conservative ($\overline{\rho_a} = 0.7$) cases, with replacement or no replacement of samples after training.

correct-prediction rate of over 99% was achieved by trial 1400, while with $\overline{\rho_a} = 0.7$ the 99% consistent correct-prediction rate was achieved earlier, by trial 800. Each simulation was continued for 8100 trials. In all four cases, the minimum correct-prediction rate always exceeeded 99.5% by trial 1800 and always exceeded 99.8% by trial 2800. In all cases, across the total of 40 simulations summarized in Table 2, 100% correct prediction was achieved on the last 1300 trials of each run.

Note the relatively low correct-prediction rate for $\overline{\rho_a} = 0.7$ on the first 100 trials. In the conservative mode, a large number of inputs initially make no prediction. With $\overline{\rho_a} = 0.7$ an average total of only 2 *incorrect* predictions were made on each run of 8100 trials. Note too that Table 2 underestimates prediction accuracy at any given time, since performance almost always improves during the 100 trials over which errors are tabulated.

C. Off-Line Learning

In off-line learning, a fixed training set is repeatedly presented to the system until 100% accuracy is achieved on that set. For training sets ranging in size from 1 to 4000 samples, 100% accuracy was almost always achieved after one or two presentations of each training set. System performance was then measured on the test set, which consisted of all 8124 samples not included in the training set. During testing no further learning occurred.

The role of repeated training set presentations was examined by comparing simulations that used the 100% training set accuracy criterion with simulations that used only a single presentation of each input during training. With only a few exceptions, performance was similar. In fact for $\overline{\rho_a} = 0.7$, and for small training sets with $\overline{\rho_a} = 0$, 100% training-set accuracy was achieved with single input presentations, so results were identical. Performance differences were greatest for $\overline{\rho_a} = 0$ simulations with mid-sized training sets (60–500 samples), when 2–3 training set presentations tended to add a few more ART_a learned category nodes. Thus, even a single presentation of training-then-testing inputs, carried out on-line, can be made to work almost as well as off-line training that uses repeated presentations of the training set. This is an important benefit of fast learning controlled by a match tracked search.

1. Off-Line Forced-Choice Learning The simulations summarized in Table 3 illustrate off-line learning with $\overline{\rho_a} = 0$. In this forced choice case, each ART_a input led to a prediction of poisonous or edible. The number of test set errors with small training sets was relatively large, due to the forced choice.

TABLE 3: Off-Line Forced-Choice Learning

Training Set Size	Average % Correct (Test Set)	Average % Incorrect (Test Set)	Number of ART_a Categories
3	65.8	34.2	1–3
5	73.1	26.9	1–5
15	81.6	18.4	2–4
30	87.6	12.4	4–6
60	89.4	10.6	4–10
125	95.6	4.4	5–14
250	97.8	2.2	8–14
500	98.4	1.6	9–22
1000	99.8	0.2	7–18
2000	99.96	0.04	10–16
4000	100	0	11–22

Table 3: Off-line forced choice ($\overline{\rho_a} = 0$) ARTMAP system performance after training on input sets ranging in size from 3 to 4000 exemplars. Each line shows average correct and incorrect test set predictions over 10 independent simulations, plus the range of learned ART_a category numbers.

Table 3 summarizes the average results over 10 simulations at each size training set. For example, with very small, 5-sample training sets, the system established between 1 and 5 ART_a categories, and averaged 73.1% correct responses on the remaining 8119 test patterns. Success rates ranged from chance (51.8%, 1 category) in one instance where all 5 training set exemplars happened to be edible, to surprisingly good (94.2%, 2 categories). The range of success rates for fast-learn training on very small training sets illustrates the statistical nature of the learning process. Intelligent sampling of the training set or, as here, good luck in the selection of representative samples, can dramatically alter early success rates. In addition, the evolution of internal category memory structure, represented by a set of ART_a category nodes and their top-down learned expectations, is influenced by the selection of early exemplars. Nevertheless, despite the individual nature of learning rates and internal representations, all the systems eventually converge to 100% accuracy on test set exemplars using only (approximately) 1/600 as many ART_a categories as there are inputs to classify.

2. Off-Line Conservative Learning As in the case of poisonous mushroom identification, it may be important for a system to be able to respond "I don't know" to a novel input, even if the total number of correct classifications thereby decreases early in learning. For higher values of the baseline vigilance $\overline{\rho_a}$, the ARTMAP system creates more ART_a categories during learning and becomes less able to generalize from prior experience than when $\overline{\rho_a}$ equals 0. During testing, a conservative coding system with $\overline{\rho_a} = 0.7$ makes no prediction in response to inputs that are too novel,

TABLE 4: Off-Line Conservative Learning

Training Set Size	Average % Correct (Test Set)	Average % Incorrect (Test Set)	Average % No-Response (Test Set)	Number of ART$_a$ Categories
3	25.6	0.6	73.8	2–3
5	41.1	0.4	58.5	3–5
15	57.6	1.1	41.3	8–10
30	62.3	0.9	36.8	14–18
60	78.5	0.8	20.8	21–27
125	83.1	0.7	16.1	33–37
250	92.7	0.3	7.0	42–51
500	97.7	0.1	2.1	48–64
1000	99.4	0.04	0.5	53–66
2000	100.0	0.00	0.05	54–69
4000	100.0	0.00	0.02	61–73

Table 4: Off-line conservative ($\overline{\rho_a} = 0.7$) ARTMAP system performance after training on input sets ranging in size from 3 to 4000 exemplars. Each line shows average correct, incorrect, and no-response test set predictions over 10 independent simulations, plus the range of learned ART$_a$ category numbers.

and thus initially has a lower proportion of correct responses. However, the number of incorrect responses is always low with $\overline{\rho_a} = 0.7$, even with very few training samples, and the 99% correct-response rate is achieved for both forced choice ($\overline{\rho_a} = 0$) and conservative ($\overline{\rho_a} = 0.7$) systems with training sets smaller than 1000 exemplars.

Table 4 summarizes simulation results that repeat the conditions of Table 3 except that $\overline{\rho_a} = 0.7$. Here, a test input that does not make a 70% match with any learned expectation makes an "I don't know" prediction. Compared with the $\overline{\rho_a} = 0$ case of Table 3, Table 4 shows that larger training sets are required to achieve a correct prediction rate of over 95%. However, because of the option to make no prediction, the average test set error rate is almost always less than 1%, even when the training set is very small, and is less than .1% after only 500 training trials. Moreover, 100% accuracy is achieved using only (approximately) 1/130 as many ART$_a$ categories as there are inputs to classify.

D. Category Structure

Each ARTMAP category code can be described as a set of ART$_a$ feature values on 1 to 22 observable features, chosen from 126 feature values, that are associated with the ART$_b$ identification as poisonous or edible. During learning, the number of feature values that characterize a given category is monotone decreasing, so that generalization within a given category tends to increase. The total number of classes can, however, also increase, which tends to decrease generalization. Increasing the number of training patterns hereby tends to increase the number of categories and decrease the number of critical feature values of each established category. The balance between these opposing tendencies leads to the final net level of generalization.

Table 5 illustrates the long term memory structure underlying a 125-sample forced-choice simulation. Of the 9 categories established at the end of the training phase, 4 are identified as poisonous (P) and 5 are identified as edible (E). Each ART_a category assigns a feature value to a subset of the 22 observable features. For example, Category 1 (poisonous) specifies values for 5 features, and leaves the remaining 17 features unspecified. The corresponding ART_a weight vector has 5 ones and 121 zeros. Note that the features that characterize category 5 (poisonous) form a subset of the features that characterize category 6 (edible). Recall that this category structure gave 96.4% correct responses on the 7999 test set samples, which are partitioned as shown in the last line of Table 5. When 100% accuracy is achieved, a few categories with a small number of specified features typically code large clusters, while a few categories with many specified features code small clusters of rare samples.

Table 6 illustrates the statistical nature of the coding process, which leads to a variety of category structures when fast learning is used. Test set prediction accuracy of the simulation that generated Table 6 was similar to that of Table 5, and each simulation had a 125-sample training set. However, the simulation of Table 6 produced only 4 ART_a categories, only one of which (category 1) has the same long term memory representation as category 2 in Table 5. Note that, at this stage of coding, certain features are uninformative. For example, no values are specified for features 1, 2, 3, or 22 in Table 5 or Table 6; and feature 16 (veil-type) always has the value "partial." However, performance is still only around 96%. As rare instances form small categories later in the coding process, some of these features may become critical in identifying exemplars of small categories.

IV. Conclusion: Predictive ART

As we move freely through the world, we can attend to both familiar and novel objects, and can rapidly learn to recognize, test hypotheses about, and learn to name novel objects without unselectively disrupting our memories of familiar objects. This chapter has described some properties of a new self-organizing neural network architecture—called a Predictive ART or ARTMAP architecture—that is capable of fast, yet stable, on-line recognition learning, hypothesis testing, and adaptive naming in response to an arbitrary stream of input patterns.

The possibility of stable learning in response to an arbitrary stream of inputs is required by an autonomous learning agent that needs to cope with

TABLE 5

#	Feature	1=P	2=E	3=E	4=E	5=P	6=E	7=P	8=P	9=E
1	cap-shape									
2	cap-surface									
3	cap-color									
4	bruises?							yes	no	yes
5	odor		none				none			
6	gill-attachment	free	free		free	free	free	free	free	free
7	gill-spacing	close			close	close	close	close	close	close
8	gill-size		broad						narrow	broad
9	gill-color								buff	
10	stalk-shape								tapering	enlarged
11	stalk-root								missing	club
12	stalk-surface-above-ring			smooth	smooth	smooth	smooth	smooth	smooth	smooth
13	stalk-surface-below-ring			smooth						smooth
14	stalk-color-above-ring					white	white	white	pink	white
15	stalk-color-below-ring							white		white
16	veil-type	partial	partial	partial	partial	partial	partial	partial	partial	partial
17	veil-color	white	white		white	white	white	white	white	white
18	ring-number	one		one	one		one	one	one	one
19	ring-type			pendant				pendant	evanescent	pendant
20	spore-print-color								white	
21	population					several	several	scattered	several	scattered
22	habitat									
# coded/category:		2367	1257	387	1889	756	373	292	427	251

Table 5: Critical feature values of the 9 category prototypes learned in the 125-sample simulation illustrated in Figure 4c ($\overline{\rho_a} = 0$). Categories 1, 5, 7 and 8 are identified as poisonous (P) and categories 2, 3, 4, 6, and 9 are identified as edible (E). These prototypes yield 96.4% accuracy on test set inputs.

TABLE 6

#	Feature	1=E	2=P	3=P	4=E
1	cap-shape				
2	cap-surface				
3	cap-color				
4	bruises?			no	
5	odor	none			
6	gill-attachment	free	free		
7	gill-spacing			close	close
8	gill-size	broad			broad
9	gill-color				
10	stalk-shape				enlarging
11	stalk-root				
12	stalk-surface-above-ring				smooth
13	stalk-surface-below-ring				
14	stalk-color-above-ring				
15	stalk-color-below-ring		white		
16	veil-type	partial	partial	partial	partial
17	veil-color	white	white	white	
18	ring-number		one		one
19	ring-type				pendant
20	spore-print-color				
21	population				
22	habitat				
	# coded/category:	3099	1820	2197	883

Table 6: Critical feature values of the 4 prototypes learned in a 125-sample simulation with a training set different from the one in Table 6. Prediction accuracy is similar (96.0%), but the ART_a category boundaries are different.

unexpected events in an uncontrolled environment. One cannot *restrict* the agent's ability to process input sequences if one cannot *predict* the environment in which the agent must successfully function. The ability of humans to vividly remember exciting adventure movies is a familiar example of fast learning in an unfamiliar environment.

A. Fast Learning About Rare Events

A successful autonomous agent must be able to learn about rare events that have important consequences, even if these rare events are similar to frequent events with very different consequences. Survival may hereby depend on fast learning in a *nonstationary* environment. Many learning schemes are, in contrast, slow learning models that average over individual event occurrences and are degraded by learning instabilities in a nonstationary environment (Carpenter, 1989; Carpenter and Grossberg, 1988; Grossberg, 1988).

B. Many-To-One and One-To-Many Learning

An efficient recognition system needs to be capable of many-to-one learning. For example, each of the different exemplars of the font for a pre-scribed letter may generate a single compressed representation that serves as a visual recognition category. This exemplar-to-category transforma-tion is a case of many-to-one learning. In addition, many different fonts—including lower case and upper case printed fonts and scripts of various kinds—can all lead to the same verbal name for the letter. This is a second sense in which learning may be many-to-one.

Learning may also be one-to-many, so that a single object can gener-ate many different predictions or names. For example, upon looking at a banana, one may classify it as an oblong object, a fruit, a banana, a yellow banana, and so on. A flexible knowledge system may thus need to repre-sent in its memory many predictions for each object, and to make the best prediction for each different context in which the object is embedded.

C. Control of Hypothesis Testing, Attention, and Learning by Predictive Success

Why does not an autonomous recognition system get trapped into learning only that interpretation of an object which is most salient given the system's initial biases? One factor is the ability of that system to re-organize its recognition, hypothesis testing, and naming operations based upon its predictive success or failure. For example, a person may learn a visual recognition category based upon seeing bananas of various colors and associate that category with a certain taste. Due to the variability of color features compared with those of visual form, this learned recognition category may incorporate form features more strongly than color features. However, the color green may suddenly, and unexpectedly, become an im-portant differential predictor of a banana's taste.

The different taste of a green banana triggers hypothesis testing that shifts the focus of visual attention to give greater weight, or salience, to the banana's color features without negating the importance of the other features that define a banana's form. A new visual recognition category can hereby form for green bananas, and this category can be used to accu-rately predict the different taste of green bananas. The new, finer category can form, moreover, without recoding either the previously learned generic representation of bananas or their taste association.

Future representations may also form that incorporate new knowledge about bananas, without disrupting the representations that are used to predict their different tastes. In this way, predictive feedback provides one means whereby one-to-many recognition and prediction codes can form through time, by using hypothesis testing and attention shifts that support new recognition learning without forcing unselective forgetting of previous knowledge.

D. Self-Organizing Expert System

ARTMAP achieves its combination of desirable properties by acting as a type of self-organizing expert system. It incorporates the basic properties of all ART systems to carry out autonomous hypothesis testing and parallel memory search for appropriate recognition codes. Hypothesis testing terminates in a sustained state of resonance that persists as long as an input remains approximately constant. The resonance generates a focus of attention that selects the bundle of critical features common to the bottom-up input and the top-down expectation, or prototype, that is read-out by the resonating recognition category. Learning of the critical feature pattern occurs in this resonant and attentive state, hence the term *adaptive resonance*.

E. Conjointly Maximizing Generalization and Minimizing Predictive Error

In summary, the ARTMAP system is designed to conjointly *maximize* generalization and *minimize* predictive error under *fast learning* conditions in *real time* in response to an *arbitrary ordering* of input patterns. Remarkably, the network can achieve 100% test set accuracy on a machine learning benchmark database, as described above. Each ARTMAP system learns to make accurate predictions quickly, in the sense of using relatively little computer time; efficiently, in the sense of using relatively few training trials; and flexibly, in the sense that its stable learning permits continuous new learning, on one or more databases, without eroding prior knowledge, until the full memory capacity of the network is exhausted.

Acknowledgements

This research was supported in part by the Air Force Office of Scientific Research (AFOSR 90-0175 and AFOSR 90-0128), the Army Research Office (ARO DAAL-03-88-K0088), BP (98-A-1204), DARPA (AFOSR 90-0083), and the National Science Foundation (NSF IRI-90-00539). The authors wish to thank Cynthia E. Bradford and Carol Y. Jefferson for their valuable assistance in the preparation of the manuscript.

References

1. Carpenter, G.A. (1989). Neural network models for pattern recognition and associative memory. *Neural Networks*, **2**, 243–257.

2. Carpenter, G.A. and Grossberg, S. (1987a). A massively parallel architecture for a self-organizing neural pattern recognition machine. *Computer Vision, Graphics, and Image Processing*, **37**, 54–115.

3. Carpenter, G.A. and Grossberg, S. (1987b). ART 2: Stable self-organization of pattern recognition codes for analog input patterns. *Applied Optics*, **26**, 4919–4930.

4. Carpenter, G.A. and Grossberg, S. (1988). The ART of adaptive pattern recognition by a self-organizing neural network. *Computer*, **21**, 77–88.

5. Carpenter, G.A., and Grossberg, S. (1990). ART 3: Hierarchical search using chemical transmitters in self-organizing pattern recognition architectures. *Neural Networks*, **3**, 129–152.

6. Carpenter, G.A., Grossberg, S., and Reynolds, J.H. (1991). ARTMAP: Supervised real-time learning and classification of nonstationary data by a self-organizing neural network. *IEEE Expert*, **6**.

7. Grossberg, S. (1988). Nonlinear neural networks: Principles, mechanisms, and architectures. *Neural Networks*, **1**, 17–61.

8. Iba, W., Wogulis, J., and Langley, P. (1988). Trading off simplicity and coverage in incremental concept learning. In **Proceedings of the 5th international conference on machine learning**. Ann Arbor, MI: Morgan Kaufmann, 73–79.

9. Lincoff, G.H. (1981). **The Audubon Society field guide to North American mushrooms**. New York: Alfred A. Knopf.

10. Schlimmer, J.S. (1987a). Mushroom database. UCI Repository of Machine Learning Databases. (aha@ics.uci.edu)

11. Schlimmer, J.S. (1987b). Concept acquisition through representational adjustment (Technical Report 87–19). Doctoral dissertation, Department of Information and Computer Science, University of California at Irvine.

II.5

Neural Network Approaches to Color Vision

ANYA C. HURLBERT
Oxford University
Oxford, England

This chapter discusses two approaches to the implementation of color constancy for vision machines, both of which demonstrate the links between neural network and classical techniques of estimation and image reconstruction. These are (1) lightness algorithms synthesized from examples using optimal linear estimation, optimal polynomial estimation and backpropagation on a two-layer artificial neural network and (2) image segmentation algorithms derived from Markov Random Field models.

I. Introduction

The human visual system displays approximate color constancy: colors of objects tend to remain the same under changes in illumination and scene composition. This implies that the visual system is able to extract information about the invariant surface spectral reflectance functions of objects from the varying light signals they send to the retina. Yet the visual system does

265

not achieve perfect color constancy and some scientists have found it more appropriate to emphasize the changes in color under illuminant and scene changes (Helson and Judd, 1936; Buchsbaum (1980)). More recently, Arend and Reeves (1986) have demonstrated that the strength of color constancy depends on the perceptual task required of the observer.

The computational problem of recovering an exact and unvarying description of surface spectral reflectance under changing illumination is insoluble without the imposition of strong constraints. Thus vision machines are as yet also unable to achieve perfect color constancy. Yet the approximate solutions constructed for machine vision help to reveal the constraints under which the human visual system operates.

II. Learning Lightness Algorithms

The solution that lightness algorithms (Blake, 1985; Horn, 1974; Hurlbert, 1986; Land, 1986) implement for the color constancy problem is based on the assumption that color can be obtained by extracting lightness separately and independently in each of three chromatic channels.

Lightness algorithms rely on a simplified model of light reflection, in which the image irradiance equation may be written:

$$S^i(\mathbf{r}) = \log I^i(\mathbf{r}) = \log\left[E^i(\mathbf{r})R^i(\mathbf{r})\right] = \tilde{E}^i(\mathbf{r}) + \tilde{R}^i(\mathbf{r}). \qquad (1)$$

where $S^i(\mathbf{r})$ is the logarithm of the image irradiance $I^i(\mathbf{r})$, $E^i(\mathbf{r})$ is the integrated effective irradiance, and $R^i(\mathbf{r})$ is the integrated surface reflectance, each integrated over the i-th type sensor spectral responsivity in the ith-type channel, as defined by Lee et. al. (1989). $\tilde{R}$ is the logarithm of R; $\tilde{E}$ is the logarithm of E. This equation embodies the assumptions that reflection is everywhere Lambertian, and that the dependence on viewing geometry may be absorbed in the spatial variation of the effective irradiance. Although the equation does not capture the complexity of reflection in the natural world, it nevertheless serves as a good approximation to the image irradiance across local regions away from specularities and where mutual illumination effects are adequately incorporated by the effective irradiance term.

The lightness problem, to recover reflectance from image irradiance in a single chromatic channel, is prototypical of the ill-posed problems of early vision: the information supplied by the image is not sufficient in itself to specify a unique solution (at each image location, $2n$ unknowns must be reconstructed from n sensor responses). The lightness solution be further subdivided into two steps: spatial decomposition, in which the spatial variations in surface reflectance and irradiance are disentangled, and spectral normalization, in which the relative amplitudes of irradiance in the three channels are recovered. Further constraints must be imposed to solve each problem. These may be explicitly crafted from an analysis of the physical properties of surfaces and lights. Yet how might a visual system discover and enforce similar constraints without higher knowledge? How might a vision machine programmed for one environment adapt to changes in those physical properties?

Standard regularization techniques not only provide a way to enforce natural constraints but also suggest one effective learning technique, optimal linear estimation. Here we discuss how regularization may be applied to the spatial decomposition problem.

A. A Regularization Framework for Lightness Algorithms

Equation 1 may be written in the form of an inverse problem:

$$S^i(\mathbf{r}) = A\tilde{R}^i(\mathbf{r}) \tag{2}$$

in which A is a known operator. The problem, to find $\tilde{R}$ given S, admits many solutions and is therefore ill-posed. Standard regularization techniques (Tikhonov, 1977; Poggio, et. al., 1985) restrict the space of acceptable solutions by requiring that the solution minimize an appropriate functional which incorporates physical constraints, e.g.,

$$\|A\tilde{R} - S\|^2 + \lambda\|P\tilde{R}_\|^2. \tag{3}$$

The regularization parameter λ controls the compromise between the degree of regularization of the solution and its closeness to the data, S. Lightness algorithms typically rely on the assumption that the source irradiance varies slowly and smoothly everywhere across the scene, while the surface reflectance function either stays constant within patches of a uniform material, or varies sharply at boundaries. This *spatial regularization* constraint may be enforced on Equation 3 by requiring that its solution minimize the following variational principle:

$$\sum_i [S^i - (\tilde{R}^i + \tilde{E}^i)]^2 + \lambda[\frac{d}{dx}E]^2 + \beta[G * \tilde{R}^i]^2 + \gamma[\frac{d^2}{dx^2}\tilde{R}^i]^2, \tag{4}$$

where G is a gaussian filter with standard deviation σ, and λ, γ and β are parameters controlling the degree of regularization and its closeness to the data.

Solving Equation (4) for its minimum in the Fourier domain reveals how the constraints may be applied in the simple form of a linear filter:

$$\tilde{R}^i(\omega) = \frac{\lambda\omega^2}{\lambda\omega^2 + [1 + \lambda\omega^2][\beta e^{-\omega^2\sigma} + \gamma\omega^4]} S^i(\omega) \tag{5}$$

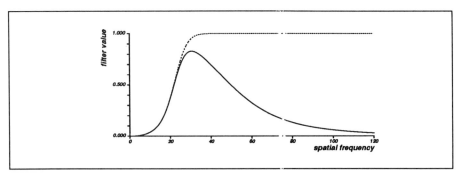

Figure 1: The filter that acts on $S^i(\omega)$ to yield $\tilde{R}^i(\omega)$, derived from Equation (4). (a) Solid line: $\gamma = 1$, $\beta = 10$, $\sigma = 4$, $\lambda = 10$. Dashed line: $\gamma = 0$, $\beta = 10$, $\sigma = 4$, $\lambda = 10$. Note the behavior of the filter when γ goes to zero.

Figure 1 illustrates the behavior of the filter for two values of the parameter γ, clarifying the need for the fourth term of Equation (4). The filter is a bandpass filter that cuts out intermediate spatial frequencies assumed due to the effective irradiance and very high spatial frequencies due to noise, yet retains high spatial frequencies due to reflectance. It filters out the d.c. component, which must be reset by a constant in the spectral normalization step.

In the natural world, changes in reflectance and illumination can occur across various spatial scales. The distribution of spatial frequencies between the two components of image irradiance may therefore vary not only from scene to scene, but also within a scene. A lightness algorithm that strictly classifies image irradiance components in terms of fixed spatial frequency thresholds cannot, therefore, perform as well as one whose thresholds adapt to changing scenes. The dependence of the shape of the filter on the parameters λ, β and γ suggests an inherent adaptiveness of the regularized solution. How a visual system might determine the optimal set of parameters for a given environment, or how it might "learn" lightness solutions from examples, is the topic of the next section.

B. Associative Learning of Standard Regularizing Operators

Minimization of the regularization functional in Equation (4) corresponds to determining a regularizing operator that acts on the input data S and produces as an output the regularized solution $\tilde{R}$. Suppose now that instead of solving for $\tilde{R}$, the task is: given S and its regularized solution $\tilde{R}$, find the operator A that effects the transformation between them. This section demonstrates that the regularizing operator can be synthesized by associative learning from a set of examples. The argument consists of two claims. The first is that the regularizing operator corresponding to a quadratic variational principle is linear. The second is that any linear mapping between two vector spaces may be synthesized by an associative scheme based on the computation of the pseudoinverse of the data.

The discrete form of Equation (3) is, for any two vectors $\mathbf{z}$ and $\mathbf{y}$:

$$\|A\mathbf{z} - \mathbf{y}\|^2 + \lambda \|P\mathbf{z}\|^2, \tag{6}$$

in which A and the Tikhonov stabilizer P are matrices and $\|\cdot\|$ is a norm. A does not depend on the data. The minimum of this functional occurs at its unique stationary point $\mathbf{z}$ found by solving the Euler-Lagrange equations:

$$(A^T A + \lambda P^T P)\mathbf{z} = A^T \mathbf{y}. \tag{7}$$

It follows that the solution $\mathbf{z}$ is a linear transformation of the data $\mathbf{y}$:

$$\mathbf{z} = L\mathbf{y}, \tag{8}$$

where L is the linear regularizing operator. (If the problem were well-posed, L would simply be the inverse of A.) Thus, variational principles of the form of Equation (4) lead to a regularized solution that is a linear transformation of the data.

This observation leads in turn to a powerful technique for synthesizing an adaptive solution to the inverse optics problem. Armed only with the assumption that the mapping between the set of input vectors $\mathbf{y}$ and the regularized solutions $\mathbf{z}$ is linear, we may solve for it using classical estimation techniques. To start, we arrange the sets of vectors $\mathbf{y}$ and $\mathbf{z}$ in two matrices Y and Z. The problem of synthesizing the regularizing operator L is then equivalent to "solving" the following equation for L:

$$Z = LY \tag{9}$$

A general solution to this problem is given by

$$L = ZY^+, \tag{10}$$

where Y^+ is the Moore-Penrose pseudoinverse of Y (Albert, 1972). This is the solution that is most robust against errors, if Equation (9) admits several solutions. It is the optimal solution in the least-squares sense, if no exact solution exists.

These results show that the standard regularizing operator L (parametrized by the lattice of data points) may be synthesized without need of an explicit variational principle, if a sufficient set of correct input-output pairs is available to the system. Note that by supplying as examples the physically correct solutions **z**, one assumes that they are identical to the regularized solutions **z**, and thereby enforces both regularization and correctness on the linear operator obtained.

C. Learning Techniques

1. Optimal Linear Estimation

In section A we derived a regularizing functional for the lightness problem and extracted a linear filter from it. To solve the lightness problem by "learning," we start instead with the single assumption that there exists a linear operator that transforms $S^i(\mathbf{r})$ into $\tilde{R}^i(\mathbf{r})$. Using optimal linear estimation, we may then synthesize a linear operator from examples and examine the constraints it embodies.

To simplify the computation, we restrict it to one dimension. To construct the matrices Y and Z of Equation (9) – note that Y is now the desired output, and Z the input – we construct sets of vectors **p** and **s**, respectively (dropping the superscript i). **s** and **p** may be thought of as vertical scan lines across a pair of two-dimensional Mondrian images (Land, 1986): an input image of a Mondrian under illumination that varies smoothly across space and its desired output image, the Mondrian under uniform, white illumination. Each vector **p** (the discrete version of the function $\tilde{R}(x)$) represents a pattern of step changes across space, corresponding to one column of a (log) reflectance image. The step changes occur at random pixels and are of random amplitude between set minimum and maximum values. Each vector **e** (the discrete version of $E(x)$) represents a smooth gradient across space with a random offset and slope, corresponding to one column of a (log) illumination image. The input "training vectors" **s** (representing the sensor response $S(x)$) are generated by adding together different random **p** and **e** vectors, according to Equation (1). The training vectors **s** and **p** are then arranged as the columns of two matrices S (Z) and R (Y), respectively. The goal is then to compute the optimal solution L of

$$LS = R \qquad (11)$$

where L is a linear operator represented as a matrix.

To avoid a look-up table solution, we overconstrain the problem by using many more training vectors than there are number of pixels in each vector. The operator L computed in this way recovers a good approximation to the correct output vector **p** when given a new **s**, not part of the training set, as input (Hurlbert and Poggio, 1988). The operator also performs well on new test input vectors in which the density and amplitude of the step changes of reflectance differ greatly from those on which it was trained.

Starting from the sole assumption that there exists a linear operator to

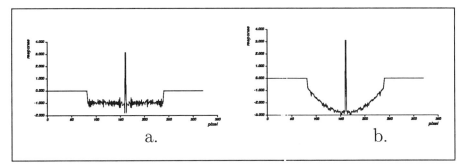

Figure 2: (a) Illustration of the linear operator that best maps, in the least squares sense, irradiance into reflectance, for input Mondrians under linear illumination gradients. See text. (b) The filter estimated from a training set of vectors half of which had linear illumination gradients, the other half sinusoidally varying illumination gradients with random wavelength, phase and amplitude. The peak value of each filter has been scaled by 0.01 for convenience of display.

perform the task of spatial decomposition, we have synthesized one from examples. We may now ask how this compares with one derived from an analysis of physical constraints. What natural constraints does the "learned" linear operator embody? To examine L, we assume that although L is *not* a convolution operator, it should approximate one far from the boundaries of the image. That is, in its central part, the operator should be space-invariant, performing the same action on each point in the image. We may therefore average rows in the center of L, with appropriate shifts, to find the form of L there. The result, shown in Figure 2(a), is a space-invariant filter with a narrow positive peak and a broad, shallow, negative surround. (We do not attempt to find the shape beyond its central space-invariant range. Note that if we were to assume from the start that the optimal linear operator is space-invariant throughout its extent (which it is not), we could considerably simplify the computation by using standard correlation techniques (Albert, 1972). But the resultant operator would probably be less successful.)

The Fourier transform of the filter is approximately a bandpass filter that cuts out low frequencies due to slow gradients of illumination and preserves intermediate frequencies due to step changes in reflectance (see Figure 1). For linear gradients of illumination, which are effectively very low spatial frequencies, the surround is necessarily very broad in the space domain. When the spatial frequencies of illumination are increased, the surround shrinks, as expected (see Figure 2(b)). In contrast, the operator that recovers the illumination, e, takes the form of a low-pass filter.

The form of the space-invariant filter is similar to that derived using regularization theory explicitly to embody the physical constraints on the problem (see Figure 1), which itself is similar to Land's recent retinex operator (Land, 1986). The filter also resembles the solution derived by posing the lightness problem as a Poisson equation (Hurlbert, 1986). The shape of the space-invariant portion of the linear operator, particularly of its large surround, is also suggestive of the non-classical fields that have been found in V4, a cortical area implicated in mechanisms underlying color constancy (Desimone, et. al. 1985; Wild, et. al. 1985; Zeki, 1983).

The shape of the linear lightness operator suggests a way in which simultaneous color (or brightness) contrast might be linked to color constancy. Here the lightness operator is "trained" to discount illumination gradients, the first step towards color constancy (spatial decomposition). Yet what results is an operator whose shape naturally produces simultaneous contrast. The lightness operator trained on a mixture of illumination gradients has a negative surround that weights nearby pixels more heavily than distant ones, and thereby produces local contrast effects. The lightness operator trained on linear gradients, on the other hand, produces global contrast effects of the sort for which lightness algorithms are criticized (Brainard and Wandell, 1986).

Other constraints on the lightness problem may be implemented using standard regularization in a similar way; for example, *spectral* regularization constraints limiting the degrees of freedom in the surface reflectance and irradiance spectra may be applied (Maloney and Wandell, 1986). The technique of associative learning may also be applied to other problems in early vision (Aloimonos and Shulman, 1989).

2. Backpropagation

Because the lightness problem as stated here is a linear problem, perhaps it is not too surprising that the solution provided by optimal linear estimation works so well. In the real world, the recovery of lightness from the image irradiance is not a linear problem, and one would not expect a linear operator to solve it successfully. We therefore explore nonlinear methods of constructing lightness operators from examples, in particular backpropagation and optimal polynomial estimation.

Backpropagation is gradient descent on a "neural" network with nonlinear units arranged in more than one layer (Rumelhart, et. al., 1986). We construct a two-layer backpropagation network with 32 input units, 32 hidden units, and 32 output units. On each trial, each input unit receives the value of one pixel in a 32-pixel input vector. The hidden units and output units have sigmoidal nonlinearities. On each iteration the error between the actual and desired output vectors drives the changes made to the weights on connections. After many passes through a set of training vectors, the weights on the units stabilize to a configuration which, in the ideal case, minimizes the square error between the actual and desired outputs summed over the entire training set. Note that performing gradient descent on a network with *linear* units is equivalent to computing the regularized pseudoinverse. Since the pseudoinverse is the unique best linear approximation in the L_2 norm, a gradient descent method that minimizes the square error between the actual output and desired output of a fully connected linear network is guaranteed to converge to the same global minimum.

The backpropagation network requires an order of magnitude more time to converge to a stable configuration than does the linear estimator for the same set of 10000 32-pixel input vectors with linear gradients of illumination. The network's performance is slightly, yet consistently, better, measured as the root-mean-square error in output, averaged over sets of at least 20000 new input vectors (Set I, Table I). Interestingly, the backpropagation network and the linear estimator seem to err in the same way on the same input vectors. The network and linear operator of Table I were trained on input vectors with edge density 85 % (reflectance edges occur at roughly 85 % of the pixels). Both perform worse when the edge density decreases from 90 to 15. Occasionally, the BP net does much worse than L, when, because it is not minimizing a quadratic functional, it falls into a local minimum during training (Set II, Table I).

	rms error			
percent	Set I		Set II	
edges	BP	lin	BP	lin
15	0.021	0.023	0.41	0.52
50	0.016	0.019	0.41	0.34
90	0.013	0.017	0.35	0.29

Table 1.

Comparison of Linear Estimator and Back-Propagation Net

We might expect the backpropagation network to perform significantly better than the linear estimator on tasks more complicated than the extraction of a linear illumination gradient. But the BP net only slightly outperforms the linear when both are trained on the same set of 10000 input vectors representing Mondrians under *sinusoidally* varying illumination. When both are trained on input vectors representing the *product* of illumination and reflectance (assuming that the logarithmic transformation of Equation (1) is not performed by the light sensors), the linear operator performs slightly but consistently better than the backpropagation net. This result is surprising since the task that the linear operator performs is no longer linear.

3.   Optimal Polynomial Estimation

The natural extension of the optimal linear estimator is the optimal polynomial mapping. The Weierstrass-Stone theorem suggests that polynomial mappings, of which linear mappings are a special case, can approximate arbitrarily well all continuous real functions. We estimate the polynomial mapping of order two between input and output by estimating the optimal linear mapping for input vectors containing the original input components and all pairwise products between them. We compare this polynomial estimator with the BP net trained on the same set of original input vectors, with edge density 85 %. The polynomial estimator outperforms the BP net by a small margin that decreases as the edge density of the input decreases, as illustrated in Table 2.

percent-edges	rms error	
	BP	poly
10	0.016	0.013
50	0.017	0.011
85	0.019	0.010

Table 2.
Comparison of Back-Propagation Net and Optimal Polynomial Estimator

It has been demonstrated that a BP net can represent exactly any polynomial mapping, given polynomial output functions of at least order two for each unit and enough hidden units and layers (Moore and Poggio, 1988). This statement, together with the Weierstrass-Stone theorem, implies that a BP net with sigmoid outputs and enough units and layers can approximate any real-valued continuous function. That the optimal polynomial mapping of order two performs better than does the two-layer BP net suggests that the net might need to be very much larger to approximate closely the lightness transformation. That the linear operator does almost as well as the other two suggests that it captures most of the essential features of that transformation.

D. Limitations of Lightness Algorithms

These algorithms provide good solutions to the lightness problem in the restricted world for which they were designed. Yet lightness solutions cannot solve the full problem of color computation in naturally complicated worlds. They suffer from two serious limitations. The first arises from the fact that the distribution of spatial frequencies between reflectance and illumination is not always ideal. A lightness operator by necessity will confuse shadows and specularities with reflectance edges if the former cause sufficiently sharp image irradiance changes. Additional cues must be exploited to classify the edges properly. One cue that we might use in determining the cause of the shadow edge is the fact that, ideally, hue does not change across it. This is the cue used by the image segmentation algorithms discussed below.

Secondly, lightness algorithms cannot account for certain higher-order phenomena in lightness perception. For example, they cannot reproduce the effects that the higher-level interpretation of luminance edges bear on lightness perception. The Koffka Ring (Koffka, 1935), a uniform gray annulus against a rectangular bipartite background appears to split into two halves of different lightnesses when the midline between the light and dark halves of the background is drawn across the annulus. Whereas our perception of brightness contrast is influenced by the way in which we segment the image into objects, the action of the lightness operator is not. Lightness perception may also be influenced by the apparent depth, orientation and continuity of the surface under view (Gilchrist, 1980). These facts do not preclude the existence of a lightness operator (or its equivalent) in the human visual system, but they suggest that the simple mechanisms it implements must cooperate with higher level processes involved in deriving spatial relationships.

III. Finding Material Boundaries: The Use of Color in Image Segmentation

From a computational point of view, color vision serves two goals: first, to help segment an image into distinct surfaces; and second, to compute surface color labels that stay constant under changes in the illuminant and the scene composition. Both goals are important for object recognition. Lightness algorithms fail to meet the first goal because they identify all sharp changes in the image irradiance as reflectance edges, and hence as material boundaries. In large part, this is because they fail to exploit a fundamental feature of human color vision: color-opponency.

An ideal visual system would transform the responses in the original spectral channels (S^i, S^j, S^k), to create new channels, in which distinct response triplets label distinct surface reflectance properties. Then all a color algorithm need do is detect and enhance edges in the transformed image. Color-opponent channels, which can be interpreted as registering the difference or ratio of signals in the cone channels, come close to satisfying this requirement.

Borrowing from biology, we can construct a marker for surface reflectance that obeys the requirements of an ideal visual system under certain constraints. The main constraint is embodied in the *single source* assumption, which states that all objects in a scene are illuminated by light with the same chromaticity. This assumption requires that the effective irradiance in

Equation (1) separate into the product of two terms:

$$E^i(\mathbf{r}_s) = k^i E(\mathbf{r}_s) \tag{12}$$

so that

$$S^i(\mathbf{r}) = k^i E(\mathbf{r}_s) R^i(\mathbf{r}_s). \tag{13}$$

In other words, the effective irradiance varies in the same way across space for each spectral channel. In general, the assumption is valid when there is a single light source; in particular, illumination changes due to shadows, shading and surface orientation changes usually affect all wavelengths in the same way. Those due to specularities do not. The assumption is clearly violated if there are two spatially and spectrally distinct light sources.

Under the single source assumption, the spatially dependent term of the effective irradiance $E(\mathbf{r})$ will factor out in any ratio of linear combinations of the signals in two distinct channels:

$$h_{ij} = S^i/S^j = \frac{k^i E(\mathbf{r}_1) R^i(\mathbf{r})}{k^j E(\mathbf{r}) R^j(\mathbf{r})} = \frac{k^i R^i(\mathbf{r})}{k^j R^j(\mathbf{r})}. \tag{14}$$

Thus discontinuities in the *hue* h_{ij} will mark discontinuities in the surface spectral reflectance function, or material boundaries. Conversely, image regions across which h_{ij} is constant signify uniform surfaces of single materials.

The idea of taking ratios in spectral bands to factor out spatial variations due to surface irradiance is not new. The CIE chromaticity coordinates perform essentially the same transformation. Rubin and Richards (1982) employ the sign of the ratio of the difference of S^i and S^j to the sum $[(S^i - S^j)/(S^i + S^j)]$ to label materials within regions marked by a previous segmentation step. Other image segmentation algorithms based on taking the ratio have been proposed (e.g. Healey, 1989; Gershon, et. al., 1986). Brill (1990) provides a theoretical framework connecting the idea to other algorithms for color constancy. Here we model how the hue labeling may interact with luminance edges, and the nature of the filling-in mechanism for hue.

By analogy with the physiological color-opponent mechanisms , we choose hue values u and v such that $u = \frac{S^r}{S^r + S^g}$ and $v = \frac{S^b}{S^r + S^g}$.

How well do real images obey the single source assumption? Figure 3(a) shows a digitized image of three fruits taken by a color CCD camera (this, the *luminance* image, is the sum of the red, green, and blue channel images). The lower graph in Figure 3(b) shows a horizontal slice through the pear, revealing the smooth, slow changes due to three-dimensional shading, to be compared with the sharp, fast changes due to specular reflections in the upper graph. Luminance changes would not suffice to segment the image into distinct materials.

Although the scene is illuminated by one light source, mutual reflections between objects strictly violate the single source assumption. Nevertheless the hue values u and v may be used to delimit regions of constant material. They remain roughly constant throughout regions of smooth shading on fruits, as illustrated in the hue (u) image, Figure 4(a). But as the horizontal slice in Figure 4(b) demonstrates, u changes significantly across specularities. Thus, for non-Lambertian surfaces, changes in the hue value alone could not be used reliably to indicate material boundaries.

A. The Role of Luminance Edges

Leaving aside for the moment the problem of specularities, let us turn to another problem in using u as a marker for material boundaries. As Figure (4) illustrates, real hue data are noisy and unreliable. This is because u is the quotient of numbers that are not only noisy themselves but also, at least for biological photosensor spectral sensitivities, very close to one another. The next step is therefore to find a method that enhances discontinuities in the hue values, smoothes the noise and fills in data where they are unreliable. Reasoning from the implications of many psychophysical phenomena, luminance edges are a natural choice for help in enhancing hue discontinuities. For example, isoluminant boundaries are fuzzy; high contrast luminance edges can capture and contain blobs of color even if they do not fall perfectly within the edges, as in impressionistic paintings or color cartoons; luminance edges block the filling-in of color in stabilized image experiments; and, as in the Koffka Ring, luminance edges can create apparent hue discontinuities.

Except in artificial isoluminant images, hue discontinuities rarely occur in the absence of discontinuities in luminance. Therefore the hue edges in an image should form a subset of the set of luminance edges, depending on the parameters used in detecting edges. In the algorithms below, we use luminance edges to activate co-localized hue edges and to block the spreading of uniform hue values.

B. The MRF Approach

One approach to the segmentation problem is to regularize the data using Markov Random Field (MRF) techniques. Similar techniques have been exploited by several authors (Poggio et. al., 1988; Blake and Zisserman, 1987; Geman and Geman, 1984; Marroquin, 1985; Geiger and Girosi, 1989) to solve other surface reconstruction problems in early vision in which the data supplied are sparse and noisy, and where the surface may be defined, for example, by depth, color or motion. MRFs specify the probability distribution of solutions to the surface reconstruction problem by providing an

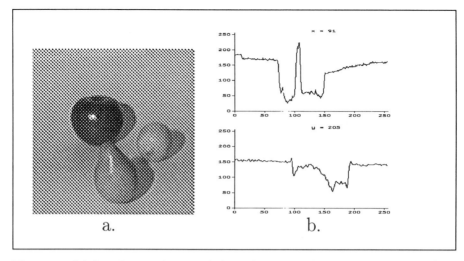

Figure 3: (a) Luminance image of three fruits, made by CCD camera. (b) Upper graph: pixel values along vertical slice through center of specularity (marked by the peak) on apple. Lower graph: Horizontal slice through pear below specularity. The smooth convex curve results from surface shading.

energy associated with each possible solution. The energy function is dependent only on local interactions within the reconstructed surface. That is, the probability that a given point on the surface has a given value is determined solely by the values assigned to its neighbors on the surface.

Formally, the prior probability of a solution field f is given by $P(f) = (1/Z)e^{-E(f)/T}$ where Z is a normalizing constant, $E(f)$ is the energy of the field f and T is the "temperature," a constant. The energy function $E(f)$ is the sum of contributions from each neighborhood in the surface, for which the local energy function has the same form. It typically includes a term that penalizes reconstructed values far from the original data and those far from neighboring values, when a continuous surface is desired. For surfaces in which discontinuities are allowed, the energy function may include a term representing the presence or absence of discontinuities which break the continuity constraint at specific locations (Geman and Geman, 1984; Geiger and Girosi, 1989).

C. A Segmentation Algorithm

A stochastic algorithm based on the MRF formulation selects the most likely surface from a random series of candidates, a procedure that is computationally expensive and biologically unlikely. A deterministic algorithm

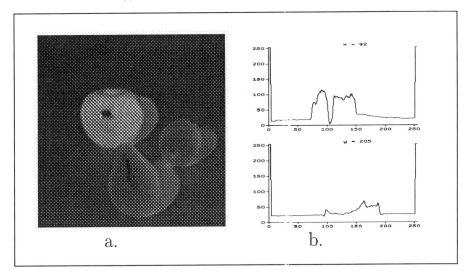

Figure 4: (a) Hue image of three fruits. (b) Upper graph: vertical slice through center of specularity on apple. Lower graph: Horizontal slice through pear below specularity. Note that although the slow changes in luminance due to shading largely disappear, the specularity is still visible.

is in most cases a more efficient and biologically plausible. Here we explore a deterministic approximation to a segmentation algorithm (for a stochastic algorithm, see Poggio, et. al. (1988)).

The main constraint is that the reconstructed hue be piecewise smooth. To implement the smoothness criterion we incorporate it into an energy function that the reconstructed surface should minimize. The full energy function for the point (x, y) is:

$$E^{xy} = (\overline{u}_{xy} - u^o_{xy})^2 + \alpha E^{N_{xy}} + \gamma \sum_{xy \in N_{xy}} E(l_{xy}).$$

u^o_{xy} is the initial hue data, $\overline{u}_{xy}$ the reconstructed hue, N_{xy} the local neighborhood of pixel (x, y) and $E^{N_{xy}}$ the term representing the smoothness criterion. $E(l_{xy})$ is the energy of the line process, which can incorporate both hue and luminance discontinuities and interactions between them.

For the deterministic approximation, we incorporate the term due to the line process into the term $E^{N_{xy}}$ and exclude the first term. Then $E^{N_{xy}}$ becomes equal to the following function:

$$(1 - d_{x+1,y})V(u_{x,y}, u_{x+1,y}) + (1 - d_{x,y+1})V(u_{x,y}, u_{x,y+1})$$
$$+(1 - d_{x-1,y})V(u_{x,y}, u_{x-1,y}) + (1 - d_{x,y-1})V(u_{x,y}, u_{x,y-1}),$$

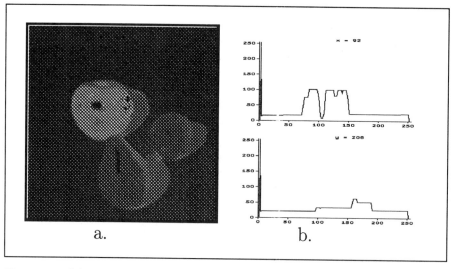

Figure 5: (a) Output of segmentation algorithm acting on hue image of Figure 4. (b) Upper graph: vertical slice through center of specularity on apple. Lower graph: Horizontal slice through pear below specularity. Note that the colored shadow on the right side of the pear is picked out as a distinct region, represented by the narrow plateau at about pixel 150, but that on the left has disappeared.

where $V(u_1, u_2) = V(u_1 - u_2)$ is a quadratic potential around 0 and constant for $|u_1 - u_2|$ above a certain value. (This potential is equivalent to the "weak membrane" energy discussed by Blake and Zisserman, 1987).

The values d_{xy} are explicitly provided at each pixel (x, y) by a binary edge map created by the action of a Canny edge detector (implemented by T. M. Breuel, MIT) on the luminance image. Values in the edge map are either 0 or 1 depending on the absence or presence of an edge at each pixel. Thus, if a valid edge exists at a neighboring pixel (i.e., $d = 1$), the neighborhood interaction term goes to zero and the reconstructed value is exempted from the smoothness criterion. We derive an iterative algorithm by using gradient descent to solve for the stationary value of u. Successive changes in u are governed by the equation $du/dt = -\alpha \frac{\partial E^{N_{xy}}}{\partial u}$.

The result is an algorithm that simply replaces the value of each pixel in the hue image with the average of its local surround, iterating many times over the whole image (for $\alpha = 0.1$, the local surround contains the four nearest neighbors). In practice, the input image is constructed by convolving the hue image with a difference-of-Gaussians operator (DOG), analogously to

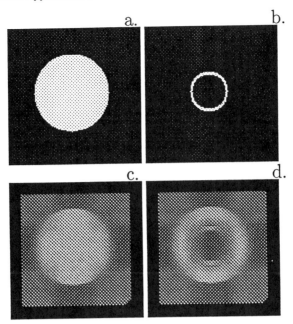

Figure 6: Simulation of filling-in experiment (Paradiso and Nakayama, 1991). (a) The target. (b) The mask. (c) The final output of the segmentation algorithm (50 iterations) when the mask is applied after 40 iterations on the target. (d) The final output when the mask is applied after 10 iterations on the target. The crosses in the background arise from propagated aliasing artifacts. See text.*

the transformation performed by biological center-surround receptive fields. The iterative averaging the algorithm performs is therefore an integration step, similar to the multiple scales solution proposed to the lightness problem (Hurlbert, 1986) and to an algorithm proposed by Grossberg and Todorovic (1988). On each iteration, the value at each pixel in the hue image is replaced by the average of its value and those in its contributing neighborhood. A neighboring pixel is allowed to contribute if (i) it is one of the four pixels sharing a full border with the central pixel (ii) it shares the same edge label with the central pixel in all input edge images (see (iii) its value is non-zero and (iv) its value is within a set range of the central pixel value. The last requirement enables a strong hue discontinuity to veto the absence of a luminance edge.

Figure 5(a) illustrates the result of 7000 iterations of the algorithm on the

DOG-convolved u image of the three fruits in Figure 4, with the Canny edges of Figure 3(a) supplied as the luminance edge map. As illustrated by the lower graph in Figure 5(b), the pear and apple are now defined by constant hues across their surfaces, with the exception of the region of the specularity on the former and the colored shadow rim on the latter. On images with shading but without strong specularities or mutual reflections, the algorithm performs a clean segmentation into regions of different hues.

Results of masking experiments recently reported by Paradiso and Nakayama (1991) suggest that a similar mechanism in humans works to fill in and smoothe brightness within luminance contours. Paradiso and Nakayama found that the brightness in the center of a briefly viewed white disk (the target) was suppressed by a mask consisting of a thin white annulus of smaller radius, viewed briefly after a certain delay. Their results suggest that brightness values propagate from the edges of the target and are blocked by the luminance contours of the mask. Three observations indicate that brightness propagates at a finite speed: the more interior the target area, the more the mask suppresses its brightness; for dichoptic viewing, the shorter the delay between the target and mask presentations, the greater the brightness suppression; and the further the masking contour from the target edge, the longer the target-mask interval at which brightness suppression can still occur. These results emphasize the importance of luminance edges in anchoring region boundaries. It will be interesting to determine whether other discontinuities, e.g. of depth or motion, can similarly block the spreading of hue or brightness.

The segmentation algorithm proposed here reproduces this new filling-in phenomenon. Figure 6 illustrates the action of the algorithm on a uniform white disk against a black background. The initial input to the algorithm is the DOG-convolved target image plus its Canny edge map. After a variable interval, the DOG-convolved mask image is introduced by substituting each zero pixel value in the iterated target image with the corresponding DOG-convolved mask pixel value, on the assumption that already "active" pixels will not react to the new stimulus. The Canny edge map of the mask is introduced in the same way into the existing edge map. Figure 6(c) shows the output of the algorithm when the mask is applied after 40 iterations, which agrees with the percept seen by Paradiso and Nakayama's subjects for long target-mask intervals. When the mask is applied after a short interval, the algorithm's output again agrees with the percept, a disk with a darkened center (Figure 6(d)).

The averaging scheme finds constant hue regions under the single source assumption in a Lambertian world. Weak highlights and slow irradiance gradients average out and disappear from the smoothed hue image. But when the assumption is violated, by strong mutual reflections (visible in the colored shadows cast by one fruit on another) or by strong highlights, the algorithm is less successful. A robust segmentation algorithm for the real world will clearly require means for identifying irradiance edges induced by specular or mutual reflections. Gershon, et. al. demonstrate a method that reclassifies shadow boundaries tainted by mutual reflections by comparing the outputs of lightness-type operators and hue-change detectors. Positive identification of the physical cause of an edge may further entail specialized routines and the interaction between several visual modules. Specular reflections, for example, are characterized by the distinct attributes of colour, form, brightness, relative disparity, and relative motion. Robust identification of a highlight may rely on accumulation of information from all its attributes. Despite its limitations, the simple segmentation algorithm discussed here captures some of the integral features of human vision.

References

1. Albert, A. (1972). *Regression and the Moore-Penrose Pseudoinverse.* Academic Press, New York.
2. Aloimonos, J. and Shulman, D. (1989). "Learning Early-Vision Computations," *Journal of the Optical Society of America*, **6**(6), 908-919.
3. Arend, L.E. and Reeves, A. (1986). "Simultaneous Color Constancy," *Journal of the Optical Society of America*, **3**(10), 1743-1751.
4. Blake, A. (1985). "On Lightness Computation in Mondrian World," in *Central and Peripheral Mechanisms of Colour Vision* (Ottoson, T. and Zeki, S., eds.) Macmillan, London, 45-49.
5. Blake, A. and Zisserman, A. (1987). *Visual Reconstruction.* MIT Press, Cambridge, Mass.
6. Brill, M. H. (1990). "Image Segmentation by Object Color: A Unifying Framework and Connection to Color Constancy," *Journal of the Optical Society of America*, **7**(10), 2041-2047.
7. Buchsbaum, G. (1980). "A Spatial Processor Model for Object Color Perception," *Journal of the Franklin Institute*, **310**, 1-26.
8. Desimone, R., Schein, S. J., Moran, J. and Ungerleider, L. G. (1985). "Contour, Color and Shape Analysis Beyond the Striate Cortex," *Vision Research*, **25**(3), 441-452.
9. Geiger, D. and Girosi, F. (1989). "Mean Field Theory for Surface Reconstruction and Integration," *A. I. Lab. Memo* 1114, MIT, Cambridge, Mass.
10. Geman, S. and Geman, D. (1984). "Stochastic Relaxation, Gibbs Distributions, and the Bayesian Restoration of Images," *IEEE Transactions on Pattern Analysis and Machine Intelligence* **6**, 721-741.
11. Gershon, R. , Jepson, A.D. and Tsotsos, J.K. (1986). "The Effects of Ambient Illumination on the Structure of Shadows in Chromatic Images," *RBCV Technical Report* 86-9, Dept. Computer Science, U. Toronto, Toronto, Ontario.

12. Grossberg, S. and Todorovic, D. (1988). "Neural Dynamics of 1-D and 2-D Brightness Perception: A Unified Model of Classical and Recent Phenomena," *Perception and Psychophysics*, **43**, 241-277.

13. Healey, G. (1989). "Using Color for Geometry-Insensitive Segmentation," *Journal of the Optical Society of America*, **6**(6), 920-937.

14. Helson, H. and Judd, D. B. (1936) "An Experimental and Theoretical Study of Changes in Surface Colors Under Changing Illuminations," *Psychology Bulletin*, **33**, 740-741.

15. Horn, B. K. P. (1974). "On Lightness," *A.I. Lab. Memo* 295, MIT, Cambridge, Mass.

16. Hurlbert, A. C. (1986). "Formal Connections Between Lightness Algorithms," *Journal of the Optical Society of America A*, **3** 1684-1693.

17. Hurlbert, A. C. (1989). "The Computation of Color," *A. I. Lab. Technical Report 1154*, MIT, Cambridge, Mass.

18. Hurlbert, A. C. and Poggio, T. A. (1988). "Synthesizing a Color Algorithm from Examples," *Science*, **239**, 482-485.

19. Koffka, K. (1935) *Principles of Gestalt Psychology*. Harcourt, Brace and Co.

20. Land, E. H. (1986). "An Alternative Technique for the Computation of the Designator in the Retinex Theory of Color Vision," *Proceedings of the National Academy of Science*, **83**, 3078-3080.

21. Land, E. H. and McCann, J. J. (1971). "Lightness and Retinex Theory," *Journal of the Optical Society of America*, **61**. 1-11.

22. Maloney, L. T. and Wandell, B. (1986). "Color Constancy: A Method for Recovering Surface Spectral Reflectance," *Journal of the Optical Society of America*, **3**, 29-33.

23. Marroquin, J. L. (1985). *Probabilistic Solution of Inverse Problems*. PhD thesis, MIT, Cambridge, Mass.

24. Moore, B. and Poggio, T. (1988). "Representation Properties of Multilayer Feedforward Networks," *Abstracts of the First Annual INNS Meeting*, 203.

25. Paradiso, M. and Nakayama, K. (1991). "Brightness Perception and Filling-In," *Vision Research*, to be published.

26. Poggio, T., and staff (1985). "MIT Progress in Understanding Images," *Proceedings of the IU Workshop*, McLean, VA, 25-39.

27. Poggio, T. and staff (1988). "The Vision Machine," *Proceedings of the IU Workshop*, Cambridge, MA.

28. Rubin, J. and Richards, W. (1982). "Color Vision and Image Intensity: When Are Changes Material?" *Biological Cybernetics*, **45**, 215-226.

29. Rumelhart, D. E., Hinton, G. E., and Williams, J. R. (1986). "Learning Representations by Back-Propagating Errors," *Nature*, **323**, 533-536.

30. Tikhonov, A. N. and Arsenin, V. Y. (1977). *Solutions of Ill-Posed Problems*. Winston Sons, Washington, D.C.

31. Wild, H. M., Butler, S. R., Carden, D. and Kulikowski, J. J. (1985). "Primate Cortical Area V4 Important for Colour Constancy But Not Wavelength Discrimination," *Nature*, **313**, 133-135.

32. Zeki, S. M. (1983). "Colour Coding in the Cerebral Cortex: The Responses of Wavelength-Selective and Colour-Coded Cells in Monkey Visual Cortex to Changes in Wavelength Composition," *Neuroscience*, **9**, 767-781.

II.6

Adaptive Sensory-Motor Coordination Through Self-Consistency

MICHAEL KUPERSTEIN

Neurogen Laboratories Inc.

I. Introduction

A. Background

The human brain develops accurate sensory-motor coordination in the face of many unforeseen changes in the dimensions of the body, strength of the muscles and placements of the sensory organs. This is accomplished for the most part without a teacher.

Autonomous robots of the future will have to confront similar constraints if they are to be effective in uncertain environments. They will have to locate, reach and pick up novel payloads, all in real time and be expandable to accommodate many joints and sensors. They will have to learn and maintain accurate performance even after unpredictable changes are made in either the geometrical, mechanical or sensing parameters or from internal parameter changes or damage.

Traditional autonomous robots are controlled by either direct program control, teaching pendants, model reference control or conventional adaptive control techniques. The first two methods are not adaptive. The last two require a model of the robot plant and actuators, which may be difficult to obtain beforehand (Bolles and Roth, 1988). Also, conventional multijoint dy-

Neural Networks for Perception
Volume 1
Human and Machine Perception

285

namic operations require intensive computations which slow down the control process considerably.

The neural network approach appears to be the most promising for addressing the problem of adaptive control in uncertain environments. Progress with this approach will not only become the basis for more adaptive robots but will also guide experimental analysis and understanding of animal and human movement control. Most of the work to date has focused on dynamic motor control and sensory-motor coordination which has recently led to successful implementations in robotics. Some past key milestones include: The first neural controller by Widrow and Smith(1963) who used an adaptive linear element (ADALINE) to balance an inverted broom stick. The controller applied a positive or negative fixed impulse depending on the broom state. Later, Albus (1975) presented the Cerebellar Model Articulation Controller (CMAC) which is essentially an adaptive, distributed table lookup method. Combining the CMAC model with a conventional adaptive controller, Miller (1987, 1989) has implemented a system that learns associations between sensor measurements and desired command signals. Also working on adaptive trajectory tracking, Miyamoto et al (1988)and Kawato et al (1988) have implemented a neural network which generates adaptive inverse kinematics. From a different direction, Grossberg and Kuperstein (1986, 1989) showed how ego-centered coordinates, which can be represented by neural topographies, allow unsupervised adaptive sensory-motor calibrations. Extending this work, Kuperstein (1987, 1988b) and Kuperstein and Rubinstein (1989) have implemented a neural controller in a 5 degree-of-freedom robot to grasp objects in arbitrary positions in 3D space. This controller called IN-FANT learns visual-motor coordination without any knowledge of the geometry of the mechanical system and without a teacher. The INFANT controller is the subject of this review. New work in motor control is now underway in adaptive sequence generation , such as that of Jordon (1989) who uses a recurrent back-propagation method.

In the following review, I present a theory and implementation that suggest how three types of adaptive sensory-motor coordinations might be learned and maintained by animals as well as robot controllers. They are:

1. Locating stationary targets with movable sensors.

2. Reaching arbitrarily positioned and oriented targets in 3D space with multi-joint arms.

3. Positioning an unforeseen payload with accurate and stable movements despite unknown sensor feedback delay.

These three abilities can be tied together by focusing on the overall problem that a human faces in grabbing an object (shown in Figure 1). Here, two moving eyes first have to fixate an object in 3D space. Then what the eyes

Figure 1. Rendering of the mechanical system with two eyes and an arm grasping an object.*

see has to generate a plan for where to reach the cylinder. Finally, the plan has to be performed on an inertial arm to grab the cylinder. Keep in mind, the human does not know the spacing of his eyes, nor the length of his arms, nor the strength of his muscles, nor the feedback delay of his reflexes.

This review describes neural network architectures consisting of large arrays of neural units. The networks combine the constraints of **self-consistency** and **topography** to achieve adaptive sensory-motor coordination without supervision. Together they comprise the INFANT model. The self-consistency hypothesis is an extension of results from developmental studies in coordination behavior. Studies in the kitten (Hein, 1970, 1972, 1974; Hein & Held, 1962; Held and Hein, 1963) show that visually guided behavior develops only when changes in visual stimulation are systematically related to self-produced movement. The hypothesis is also consistent with the motor theory of speech perception (Liberman et. al., 1967; Williams and Nottebohm, 1985).

The INFANT controller's architecture relies on the topography of neural units in a network. Topography is the ordered contiguous representation of inputs or outputs across a surface with possible overlap of neighboring representations. Topographic mappings have been found in most sensory and motor brain structures (Kandel and Schwartz, 1985). In the following neural networks, topography is the universal format for representing, combining and transforming all sensations, plans and movements. The major theme of the following studies is how various geometries of interacting topographic neural fields can satisfy the constraints of adaptive behavior in complete sensory-motor circuits.

In the following sections, I will present the motivations, constraints, experiments, results and interpretations of the INFANT controller. Since all the neural networks are designed to use essentially the same processing and learning rules, they will be summarized in the appendix. Detailed equations can be seen in referenced papers. Alternate processing and learning rules could have been used with similar results. The ones I chose appeared to be the simplest and most convenient for computer processing.

II. Locating Stationary Targets

A. *Defining the problem*

When a target object is perceived in space, its registration on our senses will move, as we move. How then, do we perceive it to be stationary and know where to reach it as we move? Put in different words, how can objects be perceived in their own coordinates when they are sensed in an egocentric frame of reference? For this perception to occur, the representation of the object's spatial location must somehow be invariant with respect to many combinations of the object's sensory registrations. Consider the case of perceiving a target with an eye that is constantly shifting its gaze. There are many combinations of the retinal position of the target and the orbital position of the eye that can be used to view the target. And yet it is perceived as stationary.

An invariant target position map of this kind can be very beneficial for object recognition. When the perceptual system attempts to recognize an object, the association of where an object is, with what an object is, can be more easily made with an invariant target map. Otherwise, the perceptual system would have to reassign the location properties of an object whenever that object is moved relative to the viewer.

What constitutes invariant perception in a neural network? Whatever the internal representation of invariant perception, it is evident that a system has it when its actions are invariant in response to different configurations of an object. But by introspection, a system does not have to respond overtly to an object for the system to have an invariant perception of the object. To satisfy both conditions, an invariant representation can be defined as one that has the potential for invariant action. This definition suggests that at least the representations for action in response to varying presentations of an object are the same. Of course, other prior stages of representation between sensation and action can also be invariant. But the essential element of this definition is that it always ties invariant perception to invariant action.

This definition constrains mechanisms of invariant perception to be concerned with motor performance. In particular, this section shows how spatial targets can be represented by correlating the signals that orient the eye towards those targets, with the visual feedback of those targets. More generally, a space can be represented by signals used to orient in that space or self-consistency.

I present a model for the representation of target positions in the brain that is invariant with respect to combinations of any retinal registration and eye posture (detailed in Kuperstein, 1988a). This model adapts to many sets of parameters that describe the sensory and motor plants as well as variabilities in the internal structure of the model. For focus, the model will be concerned with orientation positions of one eye to targets presented to the peripheral visual field, with the head fixed. Targets used by this model are defined as salient points of light contrasts. The extension of this definition from point targets to real object targets will be addressed later.

The model is designed to be extended to any number of sensory-motor maps used to indicate the position of a target in space by any orienting motor plant. This includes orienting the eye with the head free and orienting the limbs to a visual target.

The goal of the model is to represent the final muscle activation that will orient an eye so that a target will be focused on the fovea. Within this context, invariant representation is defined as the potential for orienting to a stationary target independent of its sensory registration on the retina and the initial posture of the eye in its orbit. Over performance trials, the system's accuracy in computing target position will improve through a simple learning rule which uses the perception of target position error after orientation.

B. Design constraints

Physical constraints on the eye and the retina are the basis for the input representations. The orientation to a visual target by one eye can be computed from the measures of the retinal position of a target and the posture of the eye in its orbit. The dimensionality of these two measures are very different. The retinal coordinates are determined relative to the fovea, while eye position coordinates are determined by either absolute or relative muscle contractions of the six eye muscles. Not only must a target map transcend the difference between coordinate types but it must also yield an invariant representation. Its output for a given target position must be independent of the combination of eye position and retinal position used to generate an orienta-

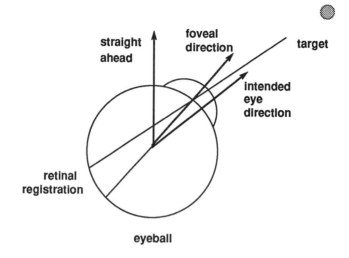

Figure 2. Geometry of the eyeball and target fixation

tion to that target.

Adaptability of the target computation is crucial. Measures of target position made external and internal to the system surely change over time. These include changes in the eye optics and muscle characteristics as well as potential neural damage and developmental changes. The system must be able to recalibrate itself to maintain accurate performance.

Some functional constraints that the eyeball and retina place on orienting to new targets help shape the way retinal and eye position coordinates will be combined. The eye rotates around a point close to the center of the eye ball. The angle of eye ball rotation is monotonically related to eye muscle contraction. As seen in Figure 2, the visual angle of a target is made between a line from the eye lens to the fovea, and a line from the lens to where the target projects on the retina. As a target becomes more eccentric from straight ahead, both measures of visual angle and eye position become monotonically more eccentric, when each measure is made while the other is held constant.

Because of unforeseen physical geometry of the eyeball and eye muscle innervation, a target position is not simply a linear combination of visual angle and eye orbital angle. However, target position is an monotonic function of retinal and eye position. The model crucially depends on this relationship in order to be viable.

C. System design

Now let's consider how these measures can be represented. By considering the computational benefits and drawbacks of both retinal and motor coordinates, I will present a representation that accommodates both coordinates and satisfies all of the constraints for an invariant target position map discussed thus far.

Targets in the model (points of light contrast) are represented as unimodal distributions of neural activity in a visual map. Such a visual map, of course, requires considerable preprocessing of visual inputs to the eye. Details of this preprocessing are outside the scope of the model.

The visual distributions are peaked at locations corresponding to the visual angle of the targets. Thus, the visual map has a typical retinal topography. This includes two hemifields (left-right) of neural units arrayed in two dimensions and spatially ordered by visual angle.

Eye position is determined by the distribution of muscle lengths for the six extraocular eye muscles. In the model, six neural populations, called motor maps, are activated by the contraction of each muscle, respectively. These maps will represent the eye posture during the visual registration of the target. Just like the visual map, the motor maps require considerable preprocessing of proprioceptive inputs from the muscles or corollary discharges of motor outputs to the muscles. Again, details of this preprocessing are outside the scope of the model.

With the sensory representations defined this way, the task of combining representations that yield an invariant target representation is further constrained. Retinal coordinates are in dimensions of relative topographic position, while the motor coordinates are in dimensions of relative activation amplitude.

The visual and motor maps, defined thus far, have complementary ways of representing position information. The visual map is sensitive to the location of a target on a two-dimension plane and insensitive to the intensity amplitude of the target. On the other hand, each motor map is sensitive to the amplitude of muscle length. Defined this way, neither type of map uses the full information potential of a neural network. Activity in a network can be made most informative by using both its amplitude and location in the network.

The system can benefit from the complementary ways in which the two types of maps are used by superimposing the two together into a third type of map, called the target map. In this configuration, muscle representations are interleaved into columns that are spaced periodically across a retinal topography. This architecture is similar to orientation columns in the visual cortex (Hubel and Wiesel, 1962). There, columns spaced periodically across a retinal topography include all orientation specific responses to light con-

Figure 3. Interleaving, columnar architecture of the target
map. One column is shown by the rectangle. The distribution of
muscle representations for the motor inputs are schematized by
arrows that show which directions the muscles pull the eye.
The circles of varying levels of boldness represent three overlapping visual inputs evoked by spot light targets on three different trials. The target map has a global retinal topography.
[Copyright 1988 by the American Psychological Association.
Reprinted with permission from APA, Kuperstein, *Behavioral
Neuroscience*, **102:1**, 148-162]

trasts. Here, shown in Figure 3, the columns include all muscle representations. Within each column, a distribution of activity amplitudes, gated by visual input, locally represent the muscle lengths. Each column is a self-similar structure to the muscles. By interleaving two dimensions of muscle
representations, namely three agonist-antagonist pairs, and superimposing
them with two dimensions of visual representation, four dimensions are
packed into two.

There are two kinds of rules that can be used to combine visual and motor
coordinates. The first uses gating. At every position of the target map, visual inputs gate the motor inputs either on or off. This isolates different visual
pockets of motor inputs for different retinal measures of a target, since the
visual inputs are spread topographically. Within a visual pocket, the amplitude of the motor inputs represent eye position.

The second rule uses the first rule plus addition. This addition rule comes
from the relationships in the measures of target position. As a target becomes more eccentric, either retinal position or the agonist muscle length
alone, will change monotonically. Thus, by adding visual inputs of the target
to agonist motor inputs of initial eye position, elements in the target map

have an activity that is crudely proportional to target position. Visual subtraction occurs for antagonist muscle representations.

By using modifiable input weights together with a local addition / subtraction rule, it becomes possible to generate the appropriate global nonlinearity that is required to describe the relationships of retinal and eye positions to target position. With different weights each target map column locally adds or subtracts visual inputs to motor inputs slightly differently. The architecture becomes piece-wise linear but as a whole, nonlinear. Of the two rules, the second is more accurate according to computer simulations.

Close inspection of this map shows that it has two types of topographies: retinal and muscle. Note that adjacent elements of the target map represent agonist-antagonist muscles. That gives the map its muscle topography. But visual gating of activity also gives it a broad retinal topography. How then do elements of this map get transformed to achieve target position? The real global invariance property is determined by the collective outputs of all active columns. Each muscle representation in every column of the target map outputs to a separate muscle network that corresponds to one of the six muscles. This disentangles the interleaved architecture of muscle representation columns in the target map. The mass convergence of outputs from the target map to the six muscle networks generates the global distribution of motor activity that represents the target position.

Because each muscle network in this final output stage receives an input from many columns, the total activity is relatively insensitive to neuronal noise. The pattern of global activity across the six muscle networks at this stage will be almost identical for the same target as measured from many combinations of retinal and eye positions. This global pattern determines the invariant orientation to the same target as measured with any combination of retinal and eye positions.

The output of the model must then be further processed to control the dynamics of muscle contraction. This is presumably done by a saccade generator. For a discussion of a model for the saccade generator see the study by Grossberg and Kuperstein (1986 and 1989 chapter 7). The present model is designed to interface to a saccade generator by generating a distribution of activity in muscle coordinates that represents the target position.

Learning is crucial to achieving and maintaining the accuracy of the target map. Successful representation of invariant target position depends on the right distribution of weight values for the inputs to the target map. How are these weights to be changed? Fundamentally, the only way the system can be sure whether a target map is correct is to use it for orienting to a target. Since the goal of orienting to a target is to move the eye so that the target lies on the fovea, the truest measure of error is the retinal position of the target relative to the fovea after an attempted orientation.

Other measures of error can come from either proprioceptive feedback or corollary discharge of motor outputs to the muscles. If either of these alternatives are used to correct the modifiable weights directly, then they would have to be first calibrated to the retinal measure of error in order to be reliable.

Once a reliable measure of error is obtained, the system must modify the weights of the inputs to the target map in order to decrease any performance error. Determining which weights to change and by how much presents a problem. Many combinations of retinal and orbital positions can be used for the same target on different trials. Therefore, changing the weights corresponding one set of retinal and eye positions to improve the target position for one target effects many other target positions used on later trials. In particular, there is no guarantee that improving one combination of retinal and eye positions will not hurt another combination and end up in unstable performance. In view of the overlapping nature of the target map, will any learning scheme converge so that all combinations of retinal and eye positions will become accurate?

In order to minimize any negative impact of learning across combinations of different retinal and eye positions, I use an incremental learning scheme. In this scheme, the weights of the current combination of visual and motor inputs to the target map are not modified to achieve perfect accuracy for each trial. Rather, they are modified to achieve accuracy a little at a time. The hope with this scheme is that, over many trials, all the incremental changes will accumulate to give the most parsimonious accuracy for all possible combinations.

Modifications of the input weights for specific target map elements can be mediated by an error map. It first transforms an error registered as the retinal position of a target into motor coordinates after each orientation attempt. This transformation is necessary in order to modify the input weights of the target map, which are organized in columns of muscle representations. One such transformation was presented in the discussion of saccadic error correction by Grossberg and Kuperstein (1986 and 9189 chapter 3). Component sectors of the error map correspond to the six muscle directions. The error map's inputs to the target map follows the interleaved columnar architecture of the target map. The inputs are timed to become active after a measure of performance error is registered. Each of the map's six inputs reaches the corresponding muscle representation in all columns for both hemifields of the target map.

The overall flow of information for eye orientations in one dimension in the model, is shown in Figure 4. It schematizes the processing of only two of

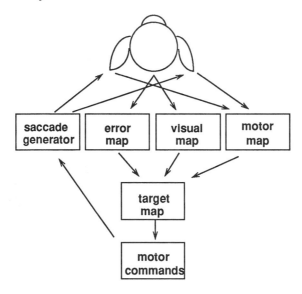

Figure 4. The overall flow of information for two of the
six muscles in the model.

the six muscles in bilaterally symmetric hemifields. First the retinal position
of the target and muscle contractions of the initial eye position are registered
in a visual map and motor map. The two kinds of maps are combined in the
target map with a columnar organization of muscle representations in a global retinal topography. The visual map inputs gate the motor inputs to the
target map. The outputs from the elements of each target map column separate and aggregate into their respective motor command structure. These in
turn activate muscle contraction in each eye muscle for orientation to the target, via a saccade generator. After an attempted orientation, a visual error
registered on the retina activates an error map which modifies the input
weights in the target map for the combination of retinal and eye positions
just used.

D. System performance

Computer simulations of the model were run under various parameter conditions to determine its accuracy, convergence and stability. Figure 5 shows
the activity distributions in the model for one trial. Information flows from
the registration of retinal and eye positions to the visual and motor maps to
the target map and finally to the intended eye position for the target. Values
are in relative units. The visual map hemifield and the 6 motor maps have a

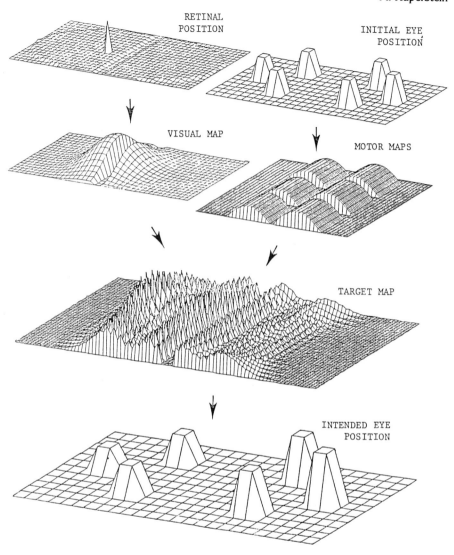

Figure 5. Activity distributions in the model for one trial. [Copyright 1988 by the American Psychological Association. Reprinted with permission from APA, Kuperstein, *Behavioral Neuroscience*, **102:1**, 148-162]

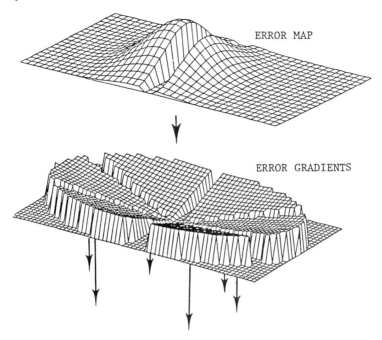

Figure 6. The generation of target map errors from a visual performance error in one trial. [Copyright 1988 by the American Psychological Association. Reprinted with permission from APA, Kuperstein, *Behavioral Neuroscience*, **102:1**, 148-162]

population of 20 x 20 elements each. The target map hemifields have 40 x 60 elements each. In this trial, the initial eye position is .2 unit to the right of center and 0 unit down from middle (in the range 0-1). The light target is .1 unit to the left of center and 0 unit down from middle. Note that the optics invert the image. The registration of initial eye position is represented as levels of contraction for the six eye muscle. The six corresponding motor maps show the recruitment distributions for each contraction level. The motor-visual transformation here is linear so the intended target eye position should be .3 unit to the right. The computed intended eye position for the target generated by the target map is .306 to the right and .08 down which is in error by .6% of the total visual field.

Figure 6 shows the generation of target map errors from a visual performance error in one trial. The visual activity distribution shown on top results from the target being off fovea after an attempted target orientation.

This distribution is multiplied by error gradients for each muscle shown on the bottom. The resulting error components are projected to corresponding motor elements in the target map in order to modify the input weights.

After learning achieves asymptote, the final average performance error for all combinations of retinal and eye positions is about 1% of the total visual field. The model converged in 100,000 trials. Errors made in the model compare favorably with errors made in human saccades (Weber and Daroff, 1972), which range from 3-5% of the visual field.

A model that can map targets invariantly, must show that all combinations of retinal and eye positions for the same target will indeed yield a similar target position. The current model's ability to do this is best exemplified by comparing two trials with the same targets but starting from different combinations of retinal and eye positions. Sampled comparisons of this type yielded an average difference between the intended and actual target positions of less than 1.6% of the visual field.

To test the stability of the model, changes in the following parameters were analyzed: the shape, width, scaling and mirror imaging of the visual map; the shape of the motor maps; the rate of learning; noise in the target map; asymmetric muscle directions; weakened muscles; different muscle scaling; different network size and some network damage. Within a wide range of values for each parameter the model's performance did not significantly change.

The brain structure most closely related to the present model is the posterior parietal cortex. This brain structure "is the most likely location of cells coding the location of visual stimuli in space, since clinical and experimental studies implicate it as essential for accurate spatial orientation and perception" (Critchley, 1982). Recordings of single neurons in this area from behaving monkeys show visual responses that are dependent on the angle of gaze (Sakata, Shibutani and Kawano, 1980; Anderson et al, 1985). In the Anderson et al experiment, monkeys performed a task in which they oriented their eyes to targets at different visual maps starting from various orbital positions of the eye, with head fixed. Visually sensitive neurons in the posterior parietal cortex showed response tuning to target coordinates.

Anderson's group claims that "for many neurons this angle-of-gaze effect can largely be described by gain factors, which are a function of eye position, multiplied by the response profile of the retinal receptive fields." This characterization is similar to the model's formulation where the motor inputs to the model's target map are the product of eye position and visual input.

Moreover, the model predicts columns of visually gated muscle representations in an overall retinal topography. Each column should contain all the eye muscle representations measured in terms of optimal gaze directions. It is important to note that even though the model depicts columns of motor representations, it predicts that only visual responses will be measured because all the motor representations are visually gated. This means that without visual input, the motor inputs will not cause any measurable responses.

All these predictions can be tested experimentally. If a microelectrode is penetrated fairly parallel to the cortical layers, one should find visually-gated, gaze-related neural responses that change in two ways through the penetration. First, neighboring neurons should represent components of gaze in the direction of the six eye muscles. This might occur in some order. Second, this order should cycle over some distance. There should be differences in the relative acitivity observed across cycles. This is due to changes in the topographic position of the visual gating.

So far, discussion of the model has dealt with point targets. How will the model react to a distribution light contrast? First, the visual inputs that reach the target map have already been extensively preprocessed. Not only are they transformed from intensity information to contrast information but they may have already been gated by habituation and processed for subjective saliency. As a result, the original distribution of light intensity may be reduced to a small number of targets. Perhaps the number of targets may range from one up to potentially the limit of short term memory, around seven.

With no further processing, the model will yield the "center of mass" of parallel targets. This is a weighted average of all the target positions, where the weights are determined by the saliency of the contrast information in the visual field. Such a result may have some value in exploring the visual environment, where it is important to orient to new clusters of light contrast that make up new objects.

However, a different use of a target map becomes very beneficial when there is more than just one target to orient to. Consider the problem of orienting to a number of light targets in sequence from a presentation of targets that turns off before any movement. Hallet and Lightstone (1976) presented human subjects with two light targets in sequence before any eye movement. With both lights off, subjects correctly oriented to the spatial locations of the targets in sequence. If only retinal information is used to orient to each light, a problem arises after the first orientation. Because the retina moves in orienting to the first light, the retinal registration for the second light can no longer be used to compute the orientation to that light.

Somehow, appropriate vector combinations of the orbital eye position and the visual maps of the lights are computed for orienting to consecutive lights. The target map yields such a vector computation since it gives an invariant representation of a target independent of the combination of retinal and eye positions used to achieve a target.

There is still the problem of how to manipulate more than one light at a time. The model suggests a way to resolve this problem. If the outputs of the target map could be gated by all the visual distributions of the targets independently, then target positions of each target could be read out one at a time.

The model presented here is designed to be extended in two ways. One extension is to represent targets by combining more sensory maps and the other is to represent targets for more than one joint. The first extension is easily made. The case of more sensory inputs to the target map is exemplified when targets are represented with the freely moving head. Here the invariant representation of a target depends on the retinal position, eye orbital position and head position when the target is registered. The head position is determined either by vestibular or neck muscle inputs.

The target map, as formulated here, can accommodate as many input maps as are needed to determine target position, as long as each input measure is a monotonic function of the target location. Each input map would still be interleaved with all other inputs. The topography would still be globally retinal. Any additional input maps would only change quantitative aspects of the target map . In the case of a free moving head, each column in the target map would contain not only representations from all eye muscles but also all neck muscles and/or all vestibular canals. The system would likely converge through learning for two reasons. First, all individual sensory inputs still have a monotonic relation to target displacement. This ensures that there will not be any ambiguous or contradictory target representation for any combination of inputs. Secondly, the principle of shared incremental learning , previously discussed, applies not only to two inputs but to any number of inputs. The usefulness of this target map may be extended to arm and leg joints as I will describe in the next section.

III. Reaching stationary targets with multiple joints

A. Constraints

This section addresses the problem controlling a multi-joint arm to reach objects in 3D space (detailed in Kuperstein, 1988b; Kuperstein and Rubinstein, 1989).

The design of the neural controller called INFANT that adaptively controls the arm has a number of constraints. First, the controller should contain only minimal information about the physical plant or actuator characteristics. To the extent it can be independent of any physical plant, it can be generically applied to all plants.

The controller must learn the association between the stereo image of a an object and the pattern of motor signals to all the joints. Since an object can be at any location in 3D space and at any orientation, the controller must have some way of processing 3D information from stereo views of the object.

The controller computation must be parallel so that is can be generalized to many joints without increasing processing time.

B. System design

The INFANT controller is designed to learn self-consistency between sensory and motor signals without supervision. In general it operates in two phases in a process called a circular reaction. The current use of circular reaction comes from one of the developmental stages of infant development (Piaget, 1952). In the first phase, sensory-motor relations are learned via correlations between object sensation and self-produced movement signals. In the second phase, the system uses the learned correlations to transform the sensation of an object into a movement that reaches the object.

The schematic diagram in Figure 7 shows the major modules that embody the INFANT controller. During learning in the first phase, a random movement generator first produces random postures of the multijoint arm in space, while the gripper holds an object such as a cylinder. Then the stereo cameras snap an image of the arm holding the object. These images are transformed into neural input maps (left and right visual maps). A third input map (stereo map) is produced as a disparity between the left and right visual maps. The signals coming from the input maps are modulated by a set of weight signals to produce target signals. The weights constitute the global association between all possible images of an object and the arm motor signals.

The target map outputs are compared with the random outputs that generated the arm posture to produce error signals. These error signals are then used to update the weight signals which improves the reaching performance.

During performance in the second phase, the object is located somewhere free in space. The sequence of transformations from the stereo cameras to the target map is reiterated as in the learning phase. The resulting target map outputs then drive the arm actuators. Because of the learned associations between the object images and the arm motor signals, the hand will superimpose on the object.

Control performance is achieved without sensory feedback and with almost no knowledge of the spatial relations of the mechanical system. The controller only knows how many arm joints there are and the limits of their

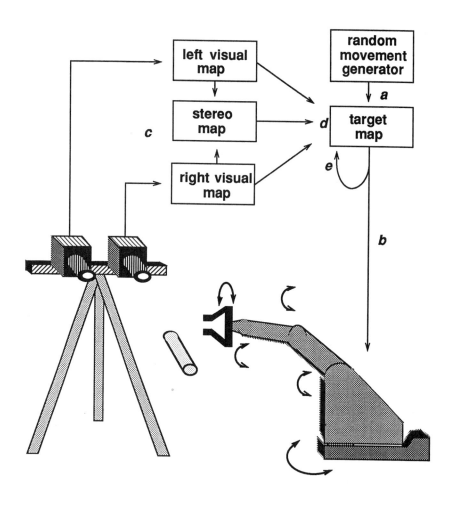

Figure 7. The circular reaction. Self-produced motor signals that manipulate an object target are correlated with target sensation signals. The sequence for training is *a, b, c, d, e*. Correlated learning is done in step *e*. After the correlation is achieved, target sensation signals alone can evoke the associated motor signals to accurately reach the target. The sequence for performance is *c, d, b*.

ranges.

There are a number of methods of transforming visual scenes to neural inputs that will yield similar results. One method is to transform visual scenes into topographic maps like the discussion in last section. Then a stereo disparity map can be computed by the difference between the left and right visual maps that is also gated by both maps. This method is most brain like but requires extensive computer power to implement (Kuperstein, 1988b).

Another method is to transform visual scenes into parameters that summarize the location for the center of mass of visual contrast in each scene along with their disparity. Such parameters can not be used effectively as direct neural inputs because simply attaching neural weights to them would not allow sufficient nonlinearity in the global sensory-motor mapping. Therefore, the parameters can be further transformed into topographic maps in which the peak of a unimodal activity distribution moves across a topographic field in proportion to the parameter's amplitude. Such a transformation was successfully used to achieve accurate reaching performance (Kuperstein and Rubinstein, 1989).

Even after extensive learning and accurate performance, environmental parameters can change in the real world. To maintain accurate performance in the face of unpredictable changes in the geometry of the physical plant, additional learning can occur. This learning is based on errors derived from visual feedback after an attempted grasp.

To illustrate this type of learning, suppose the gripper misses the target in an attempt to grasp a ball. In this case, the visual mismatch between the position of the ball and the position of the gripper is the source of an error. How does a visual source of error generate a motor correction without any prewired sensory-motor transformation? One way is for the visual position of the gripper to get transformed by the current learned sensory-motor map into a new motor target. The difference between the motor target for the ball and the motor target for the gripper results in a motor error which can be used to modify the weights affected by the ball visual input. Such an error changes the weights in the correct direction. The updated weights represent an improved correspondence between the where the ball is seen with where the gripper should move. After the weights are changed, the system can attempt to reach the ball again. This cycle of grasp attempt and weight change repeats until the visual position error between the ball and the gripper lies within a specified accuracy. In practical experiments, the average number of improvement cycles is 2-3 trials.

Such a sensory based learning scheme was considered and rejected as an alternate method for learning the fundamental sensory-motor coordination from the beginning. It would require prior knowledge of the correspondence between sensory errors and motor errors which does not satisfy one of the initial constraints. The self-consistent learning scheme developed from the circular reaction avoids this requirement and thus allows motor learning from any relation between the cameras and the arm. Once a unified, global association between sensation and posture is learned, the association can be used to define the correspondence between sensory errors and motor errors.

C. System performance

An earlier version of the INFANT controller was simulated for the physical plant shown in Figure 1 (Kuperstein, 1988b). This included not only a 5 degree-of-freedom arm but also two movable eyes on a stationary head. In this case the activity from six muscles each on two eyes was included as another neural input to the target map. Reaching accuracy averaged 4% of the arm's length in position and $4°$ of solid angle in orientation.

The INFANT controller has been implemented on an industrial robot arm and stereo cameras and commercial image processing system. The implementation was achieved by developing software that embodies the neural network transformations into an image processor (detailed in Kuperstein and Rubinstein, 1989). The controller was able to accurately reach a cylinder that was arbitrarily positioned anywhere in space within arm's reach. It could not only reach the cylinder that it was trained on, but could also accurately reach many other elongated objects including cylinders of different diameters, lengths and visual contrasts, as well as a piece of paper that was rolled into an irregular elongated form. Performance accuracy for reaching a cylinder target after 1,200 learning trials averaged 3% of the length of the arm. The average angular deviation between intended gripper wrist orientation and the actual cylinder orientation was $6°$ of solid angle.

Stability of the system was tested by relearning whole runs with different arm and camera positions and a range of values for neural parameters including neural map width, learning error rate and normalization constants. The controller showed very similar error convergence for a large range of parameter choices.

There are five key conclusions from this section:

1. The INFANT controller learns about space by associating how the arm moves with what the cameras see. It uses almost no knowledge of the geometry of the mechanical system and there are no inverse computations nor control transfer functions.

2. Learning is achieved without any external source of error correction. This allows the controller to be completely independent of supervision. The learning for one elongated object transfers to any elongated object. Moreover, no calibration for binocular parallax is required.

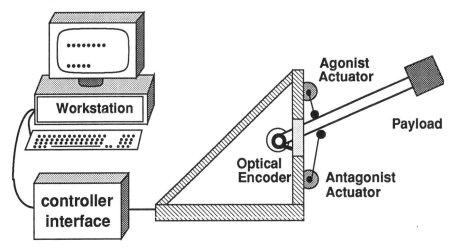

Figure 8. Schematic of the single joint plant. Reprinted with permission from *Neural Networks*, Vol. 4: Kuperstein, "INFANT Neural Controller for Sensory-Motor Coordination" Copyright 1991, Pergamon Press plc.

3. The implementation degrades gracefully to hardware errors.
4. The INFANT controller adapts to unforeseen changes in the geometry of the motor plant.
5. The algorithmic flow of control is both feedforward and parallel during performance, which will ultimately make it fast with parallel hardware.

Further work needs to done in the following areas: perceiving one object from many in a scene; perceiving occluded objects; adaptively reaching moving objects and extending the INFANT controller to multiple limbs and human-like hands.

IV. Dynamic movement control for unforeseen payloads

A. Background

In this section I describe a neural controller that learns to accurately move and position a single joint link carrying an unforeseen payload (Kuperstein, 1991). As shown in Figure 8, this problem is physically implemented with two antagonistic torque motors pulling on a link with tendons.

The standard approach for a controller to move a novel payload is to program a velocity or acceleration ramp at the beginning and end of each movement. The ramp is calibrated to move a worst case payload. This means that movements for most payloads are much slower than they need to be. Such inefficiency is exacerbated by arbitrarily directed movements in 3D space. A neural controller learns the optimal dynamics for moving unforeseen payloads in 3D space.

B. Constraints

There are a number of constraints in this problem that should be satisfied for a generic controller to be useful: First, a lightweight robot should be able to handle the dynamic inertial interactions that it will encounter with real world payloads, especially when the payloads are larger than the mass of the robot links. Payloads can vary considerably between successive movements. A generic controller should be able to measure payload mass indirectly by some uncalibrated means.

To improve positioning performance, kinematic feedback sensors need to measure the length, velocity and acceleration of each actuator tendon. A generic controller should not need these measures to be calibrated, even when they can change over time.

In animals and some robot systems there is some fixed arbitrary delay between torque onset and the effect of sensor feedback on torque generation. In some cases, this feedback delay can be a considerable fraction of the movement duration. These delays can be caused by either slow sensor feedback transmission or slow movement generation. If this delay is not adaptively anticipated, the controller will become unstable. In general, a generic controller should not need to know the phase relationships between output torque dynamics and input sensor dynamics. Although feedback measurements should have accurate repeatability over short time ranges such as hours, they are allowed to drift over longer time ranges such as days and should not need to be calibrated to any objective metric.

A generic controller should learn and maintain accurate performance even after unpredictable changes are made in either the geometrical, mechanical or sensing parameters or from partial internal damage. Learning should be achieved without operator assistance. Changes in the following parameters, which could occur during extended wear, should be accommodated accurately:

1. Transformation of actuator signals to actuator movement.
2. Sensing feedback calibrations from the actuators and payload.
3. Sensor feedback delays.
4. Link lengths.
5. Signal noise.

6. Potential internal processor faults .

C. System design

The design of the neural network that adaptively controls an actuator to move unforeseen payloads has a number of features that satisfy the constraints of a generic controller:

First, it does not contain information about the plant or actuator characteristics, except for the number of inputs, outputs and their range of activation. The less specific information the controller requires about any one plant, the more useful and flexible it will be for many plants.

The neural controller learns to complete a stable movement by the time that the internally generated control signals are complete. This feature is the reverse of the conventional approach. Here , the external movement time course is adapted to the internal control time course instead of vice versa. However, the internal amplitudes of the thrusting burst and braking burst are adapted to the external measures of stability so that there are no oscillations when posture is achieved.

The neural network computation is parallel so that it can be generalized to many joints without increasing processing time.

The implementation of the dynamic neural controller is embodied in a single joint link that is moved by two strings connected to antagonistic torque motors. This muscle analogy was chosen for the implementation to allow variable stiffness during posture. The link is 18 inches long and the motors provide 85 oz-in of torque at 3000 rpm. An optical encoder is attached to the link pivot shaft and is used to provide position and velocity information. A commercial PC-AT controller computer board outputs controls to the motor amplifiers and reads the optical encoder. It resides in a PC-AT computer which hosts the operations and the neural network.

The basic design for the neural controller is shown in Figure 9. It is made to interface with the output of the INFANT controller for adaptive sensory-motor coordination discussed in the last section. The input control commands of initial position, intended position step and measure of payload are first transformed into neural input maps. They are laid out in a 2D topographic input representations. The locations of the peaks of Gaussian distributions in each dimension of the representation vary according to the amplitude of the commands. Thus, for input N_{ij}, the peak index i' is proportional to the initial position and peak index j' is proportional to the desired position step:

$$N_{ij} = \exp[-\lambda \cdot [(i\text{-}i')^2 + (j\text{-}j')^2]] \quad \text{for } i=1,2...I; \quad j=1,2...J \tag{1}$$

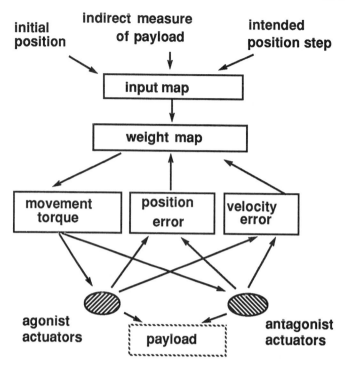

Figure 9. Connection scheme of the neural controller. The input command maps are transformed into outputs of actuator control. Resulting performance errors in joint angular position and velocity are used to modify the weight maps, gated by the input maps. Reprinted with permission from *Neural Networks*, Vol. 4: Kuperstein, "INFANT Neural Controller for Sensory-Motor Coordination" Copyright 1991, Pergamon Press plc.

where λ is a constant for the Gaussian width and I and J are the network population size.

Each neural output torque signal T_k is computed to be the sum of its inputs times their neural weights W_{ijk}:

$$T_k = \Sigma_{ij} N_{ij} \cdot W_{ijk} \quad \text{for i=1,2...I; \ j=1,2...J; k=1,2} \tag{2}$$

where k is the actuator index. The torques operate on the link over time t by combining the neural output T_k, desired position D_k , current position $C_k(t)$ and torque constant α, after some sampling delay Δ:

$$\tau_k(t + \Delta) = \alpha \cdot [\ T_k + D_k - C_k(t)] \tag{3}$$

The antagonistic torques are applied to the link until one of two conditions are reached. If the desired position is reached, the velocity error for each actuator is sensed. If the desired position is not reached within a time limit, the position error for each actuator is sensed. These errors, E_{kn}, (k is actuator index and n is error type) update the modifiable weights. When the movement is finished, antagonistic postural signals P_k are instated:

$$\tau_k(t + \Delta) = \alpha \cdot [\ P_k + D_k - C_k(t)] \tag{4}$$

The weights W_{ijk} associated with the inputs N_{ij} are then changed by the errors E_{kn} gated by a learning rate δ:

$$\Delta W_{ijk} = \delta \cdot N_{ij} \cdot \Sigma_n E_{kn} \tag{5}$$

Even though learning is piece-wise linear the network yields the required emergent nonlinear properties of the transformation as a population.

The control process is achieved without feedback to the network during movement and without knowledge of the actuator characteristics, except for its activation range. Note that in more complicated problems where additional parameters of speed, power or isometric tension are required, more feedforward gains can be applied in parallel. Also in some situations where adaptive compliance is required more sensory feedback circuits would be used.

The payload is assumed to be constant within a single movement, but variable between movements. The measure of payload only needs to be a monotonic function of actual payload weight which can be determined by a number of means. In this implementation, the agonist actuator gradually increased its torque until the unknown payload moved. The final torque is a measure of the payload.

The neural controller is tested for stability by analyzing its performance to unforeseen parameter changes. Unexpected changes in payload and joint viscosity are applied as well as changes in the actuator response characteristics and in the internal parameters of learning.

The errors determine the adaptive goal of the control which in this case is to end the movement at the intended position with no velocity. It is not necessary to exactly calibrate the movement error. The effects of the error signals are incremental and therefore progressively improve the accuracy of the movements. It is only required that the error signal should change the gain in the right direction on a given movement.

D. System performance

Figure 10 shows example performance trials for different initial positions, different intended positions , before and after learning. Note that for this problem, both the agonist and antagonistic torque signals could have flowed to one actuator with a stiff push-pull link. However, the two actuator design was created to prepare for future problems of adaptive compliance and stiffness during posture. Those problems would require different levels of isometric tension from antagonistic actuators.

The average movement achieved its intended position within 5% of the total joint angle range without significant oscillations after about 600 trials. This performance was achieved where each trial had an arbitrary initial position and arbitrary intended position.

Whole learning runs that were done with different link masses, direction of gravity, joint viscosity, nonlinear torque-to-actuator transformations and showed very similar error convergence.

This design concept for the neural controller is generic because it only requires minimal knowledge of the physical plant or actuator characteristics and is designed to be extended to an arbitrarily large number of joints. The overall flow of control is feedforward during movement, which makes it fast. Each new joint in the robot system will require adding new neural input and weight maps to the architecture. The next challenge is to understand how this type of generic architecture will perform with the highly nonlinear coupling that occurs between multiple joints.

The population of units in each weight map is arbitrary and increasing the number should increase the resolution of performance.

This neural controller has three major properties that other dynamic neural controllers do not:

1. It is designed to accurately move an unforeseen payload to arbitrary targets without end-point oscillations, using only one error sample per movement.

2. It can accurately anticipate the effects of large payload inertias and/or delayed sensory feedback. Without anticipation, these effects can cause inappropriate deviations or oscillations during both movement and posture.

3. It is designed to be the basis of incorporating dynamic control for an arbitrary number of joints without changing the structure or slowing the speed of the computation.

All three neural controllers discussed in this review have a number of ap-

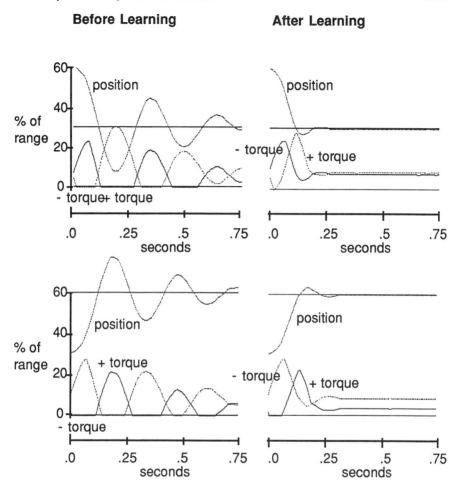

Figure 10. Performance trials for dynamic positioning of arm before and after learning. The horizontal lines show the intended position. The source of the difference is that the braking signal occurs earlier after learning. During learning, one sample per trial of angular position and velocity errors is used to improve subsequent performance by changing the neural weights. Reprinted with permission from *Neural Networks*, Vol. 4: Kuperstein, "INFANT Neural Controller for Sensory-Motor Coordination" Copyright 1991, Pergamon Press plc.

plication benefits. They will deal effectively in novel working environments such as in space because of their ability to deal with unforeseen changes in the mechanical plant and actuators. Their adaptability will allow continuous self-calibration in the face of mechanical wear and its generic design will allow it to be implemented in many different types of robots. The parallel feedforward control architecture will make robot control very fast and the modifiable neural weights with overlapping functionality will allow fault tolerance. This will greatly reduce tooling costs, setup time and task failure in autonomous robot operations.

Hypotheses on neural controllers put forward here can also be tested by researchers for their validity in the brain. Combining both the approaches of brain analysis and machine synthesis will bring us more understanding about human sensory-motor coordination than either approach alone.

V. Summary

The INFANT neural controller learns sensory-motor coordination from its own experience. Three adaptive abilities were discussed: locating stationary targets with movable sensors; grasping arbitrarily positioned and oriented targets in 3D space with multi-joint arms and positioning an unforeseen payload with accurate and stable movements despite unknown sensor feedback delay. INFANT adapts to unforeseen changes in the geometry of the physical motor system, the internal dynamics of the control circuits and to the location, orientation, shape, weight and size of objects. It can learn to accurately grasp an elongated object with almost no information about the geometry of the physical sensory-motor system. This neural controller relies on the self-consistency between sensory and motor signals to achieve unsupervised learning. It is designed to be generalized for coordinating any number of sensory inputs with limbs of any number of joints. The principle theme of this review is how various geometries of interacting topographic neural fields can satisfy the constraints of adaptive behavior in complete sensory-motor circuits.

Appendix

For robustness, all the neural controllers discussed in this review use essentially the same processing and learning rules. Each individual neural output C_j is computed to be either the sum or the multiplication of its inputs N_i via their neural weights W_{ij}. For example:

$$C_j = \Sigma_i N_i \cdot W_{ij} \quad \text{for } i=1,2...I; \quad j=1,2...J \qquad (1)$$

Errors in the system, E_j are typically the difference between the desired or actual outputs, D_j and the computed outputs C_j:

$$E_j = D_j - C_j \qquad (2)$$

The weights W_{ij} associated with the inputs N_i are then changed by the errors E_j gated by a learning rate r:

$$\Delta W_{ij} = r \cdot N_i \cdot E_j \qquad (3)$$

References

1. Albus, J (1975) A New Approach to Manipulator Control: The Cerebellar Model Articulation Controller (CMAC). J. of Dynamic Systems, Measurement and Control, Sept: 220-227

2. Anderson, R.A., Essick, G.K. and Siegel, R.M. (1985) Encoding of Spatial Location by Posterior Parietal Neurons. Science, 230,456-458

3. Bolles, R. and Roth, B. (eds.) (1988) Robotics Research: The Fourth International Symposium. MIT Press, Cambridge, Massachussetts

4. Critchley, M. (1982) The Parietal Lobes. Hafner Press, New York

5. Grossberg, S. and M. Kuperstein (1986) Neural Dynamics of Adaptive Sensory-Motor Control Elsevier/North Holland, Amsterdam (Reprinted by Pergamon Press in 1989).

6. Hallet, P.E. and Lightstone, A.D. (1976) Saccadic eye movements to flashed targets. Vision Research, 16,107-114

7. Hein, A. (1970) Recovering spatial motor coordination after visual cortex lesion. In D.A. Hamburg, K.H. Pribram and A.J. Stunkard (Eds.) Perception and its Disorders, Williams and Wilkins. Baltimore, Md. pp163-175

8. Hein, A. (1972) Acquiring components of visually guided behavior. In A. Pick (Ed), Minnesota Symposia on Child Development,6 University of Minnesota Press, Minneapolis, pp53-68

9. Hein, A. (1974) Prerequisite for development of visually guided reaching in the kitten, Brain Research, 71, 259-263

10. Hein, A. and Held, R. (1962) A neural model for labile sensorimotor coordinations. In E.E. Bernard and M.R. Kare (Eds) Biological Prototypes and Synthetic Systems 1, Plenum Press, New York, pp71-74

11. Held, R. and Hein, A. (1963) Movement-produced stimulation in the development of visually guided behavior , J. Comp. Physiol. Psych. 56, 872.

12. Hubel, D.H. and Wiesel, T.N. (1962) Receptive fields, binocular interaction and functional architecture in the cat's visual cortex. Journal of Physiology, 160,106-154

13. Jordan, M. I. (1989) Generic Constraints on Underspecified Target Trajectories, Internat. Joint Confer. on Neural Networks, June, Washington, DC.

14. Kandel, E. R. and Schwartz, J. H. (1985) Principles of Neural Science (Elsevier Science Publishing).

15. Kawato, M. Uno, Y., Isobe, M. and Suzuki, R. (1988) Hierarchical Neural Network Model for Voluntary Movement with Application to Robotics. IEEE Control Systems Magazine. April: 8-16

16. Kuperstein, M. (1987) Adaptive Visual-Motor Coordination in Multijoint Robots using Parallel Architecture Proc. IEEE Internat. Conf. Automat. Robotics, March, Raleigh, N.C. 1595-1602

17. Kuperstein, M. (1988a) An adaptive neural model for mapping invariant target position. Behav. Neurosci. 102(1):148-162

18. Kuperstein, M. (1988b) Neural Network Model for Adaptive Hand-Eye Coordination for Single Postures Science.239:1308-1311

19. Kuperstein, M. (1991) INFANT Neural Controller for Adaptive Sensory-Motor Coordination, Neural Networks, V4, 131-145

20. Kuperstein, M. and Rubinstein, J. (1989) Implementation of an Adaptive Neural Controller for Sensory Motor Coordination. IEEE Control Systems Magazine. April, V9:3 p.25-30

21. Liberman, A.M., Cooper, F. S., Shankweiler, D. P., Studdert-Kennedy, M. (1967) Perception of the speech code, Psychol. Rev. 74, 431.

22. Luschei, E.S. and Fuchs, A.F. (1972) Activity of brain stem neurons during eye movements of alert monkeys. J. Neurophys, 35, 445-461

23. Miller W.T. (1987) Sensor-based control of robotic manipulators using a general learning algorithm. IEEE J. Robotics and Automation. RA-3:2, 157-165.

24. Miller W.T. (1989) Real-Time Application of Neural Networks for Sensor-Based Control of Robots with Vision. IEEE Trans. Systems, Man Cyber. 19:4, p. 825-831.

25. Miyamoto, H, Kawato, M, Setoyama, T., and Suzuki, R. (1988) Feedback-Error-Learning Neural Network for Trajectory Control of a Robotic Manipulator. Neural Networks 1:3, 251-265.

26. Piaget, J. (1952), The Origins of Intelligence in Children, translated by M.Cook, (International University Press, New York.

27. Sakata, H., Shibutani, H. and Kawano, K. (1980) Spatial properties of visual fixation neurons in posterior parietal association cortex of the monkey. J. Neurophys. 43(6), 1654-1671

28. Weber, R. and Daroff, R. (1972) Corrective movements following refixation saccades, Types, and control system analysis. Vision Research, 12,467-475 .

29. Widrow, B. and Smith, F. (1963) Pattern Recognizing Control Systems.Computer and Information Sciences (COINS) Symposium Proc.Spartan Brooks, Wash. D.C.

30. Williams, H. and Nottebohm, F. (1985), Auditory responses in avian vocal motor neurons: A motor theory for song perception in birds. Science 229, 279.

II.7

Finding Boundaries in Images

JITENDRA MALIK[†] AND
PIETRO PERONA[‡]

[†] *University of California at Berkeley*

[‡] *Università di Padova and Massachusetts Institute of Technology*

I. Introduction

Both human and machine vision start from some visual input, say a binocular pair of spatiotemporal image sequences $I_L(x, y, t)$, $I_R(x, y, t)$ of a given scene, and perform a set of computations which make possible the achievement of certain goals. These goals certainly include (a) the recognition of objects in the scene and (b) determination of spatial relationships in the scene adequate to support motor tasks like manipulation and locomotion.

It has long been recognized that these computations on the visual input must rely on additional assumptions about the nature of the world being imaged. The most basic of these assumptions is that the world consists of a set of piecewise smooth surfaces. While this seems self-evident for manmade objects like cylinders, cubes and spheres, it is interesting to note that we impose this organization as well on natural 'objects' like clouds, treetops and grass fields when they are examined at an appropriate range of scales.

It is reasonable to argue that computed descriptions of a piecewise smooth world should not only represent attributes of surfaces (like depth, orientation, color, texture) but also represent explicitly their boundaries. Indeed, much of the essential information is contained in the boundary curves, as demonstrated by the vivid three-dimensional percept evoked by

Neural Networks for Perception
Volume 1
Human and Machine Perception

315

line drawings. These boundary contours can be very useful for tasks such as object recognition, locomotion (by defining the boundaries of free space), and manipulation.

The determination of these boundaries is also a side product of the determination of the spatial layout of the scene from the visual input. Converging evidence from psychophysics and neurobiology suggests that in primate vision, the early processing of visual information is along parallel, though interacting, pathways [21] specialized for the analysis of cues like color, stereoscopic disparity and motion. Considerable research has been aimed at developing computational models of these. Most of these models make use of weak continuity constraints–enforce smoothness almost always–except along contours which correspond to significant changes. As an example consider stereopsis. Traditional models of global stereopsis such as the Marr-Poggio–Grimson model make use of a smoothness constraint–nearby points have nearly similar values of disparity. If naively applied, this results in smoothing over the depth discontinuities. However, if one makes use of the idea of a line process [27, 9] across which there is no penalty for changes in disparity, one can detect and preserve the disparity discontinuity contours. Similar considerations apply for optical flow.

To conclude, the computation of boundaries is both a goal of early visual analysis as well as a necessary intermediate step. A variety of cues are available in the visual input to support this task. Neighboring surfaces in general position differ in a number of visual attributes: luminance, color, texture, stereoscopic disparity and motion being perhaps the most significant. Our objective in this paper will be to present models of how biological and artificial processors could utilize these cues to provide a parcellation of the visual input. We begin with a review of the biological evidence.

I.1. Boundary detection in biological vision

Psychophysicists have shown that humans can perceive boundary curves defined purely by differences in luminance, color [56], texture [33], stereoscopic disparity [32] and motion [10].

Further insight into the nature and representation of these boundary curves has come from a series of psychophysical experiments. We list some of the more significant observations:

1. Ramachandran, Rao and Vidyasagar[55] have shown that stereopsis can be obtained by fusing a luminance boundary in one eye with a disparate texture boundary or a chromatic boundary in the other eye.

2. Cavanagh, Arguin, von Grunau[17] show that apparent motion can

be seen between two alternating stimuli, even if they are defined with respect to their background by different attributes. This was found to be true for all the combinations studied.

3. It is well known that line drawings convey a vivid three-dimensional percept because of the variety of cues (junctions etc) contained in them. Cavanagh [15] showed that this is also true for Necker cube outline figures defined by color and texture, and also (with some complications due to conflicting depth cues) for cubes defined by stereopsis and motion. However, he also found that the perception of shadows and subjective contours was limited to the luminance pathway.

4. By using a visual search task, Cavanagh, Arguin and Treisman [16] show that popout (i.e. the reaction time as a function of the number of distracters has zero slope) was found for oriented bars with boundaries defined by any of these attributes.

5. Boundaries associated with depth discontinuities are labeled to indicate which of the two regions bordering the boundary is physically attached to the boundary curve [57] .

From these converging lines of psychophysical evidence, one can hypothesize that boundaries can be computed independently from the neural representations of luminance, color, texture, stereoscopic disparity and motion. Also, it is reasonable to assume that there is a common representation for these boundaries. Otherwise the hardware for apparent motion would have to be replicated for all the combinations possible which seems to be a waste in view of how ecologically unlikely these combinations are. There would also need to be replication of the object recognition hardware.

At the present time, we can only speculate on the possible representations of boundaries in the brain. Do the separate modules each have separate boundary representations, or is there a common representation where each module marks the boundaries? Or are there both? Since representations in the extrastriate visual areas such as V2, V3, V4 and MT remain retinotopic there is a plausible physiological substrate for the representation of boundaries at a stage where disparity, motion etc. have been elaborated. There are also ample feedback pathways and horizontal connections among the areas to suggest that different boundary representations could interact.

I.2.   Boundary detection in Machine Vision

Researchers in computational vision have, like psychophysicists, recognized the importance of different pathways such as those for stereopsis or motion. Early work includes that of of Horn on shape-from-shading, Marr and Poggio on stereopsis and Ullman on motion. However, finding boundaries in images has largely been approached as a problem of detecting brightness edges which provide the primary input for the different shape-from-X modules. The dominant framework was most clearly expounded by Marr[45] who argued for the initial computation of a primal sketch–essentially a brightness edge map followed by postprocessing with some local grouping operations. The different modules use the primal sketch as input to compute a common representation of depth and/or surface orientation in viewer centered coordinates known as the 2.5D sketch.

With the benefit of hindsight derived from the last ten years of research, this framework may be critiqued at two levels:

- *Brightness Edges as the basis of the primal sketch.* Marr proposed that brightness edges are detected in the brain by detecting zero-crossings of the retinal image convolved with a Laplacian of Gaussian filter. As a model of biological vision, zero-crossings have not found experimental support from physiology; as a computational theory signal-to-noise ratio arguments [14, 8] support the use of oriented filters instead of the radially symmetric Laplacian of Gaussian filter. However, even if we suppose that the brightness edges are detected by some better method, the important question is whether edge detection is the right preprocessing step for the various modules like stereopsis, texture or motion.

  Marr argued that detection of brightness edges (at multiple scales) was the right first step because they are associated with physical discontinuities. If there existed perfect edge detection mechanisms, this argument would carry a lot of weight. As any one who has run edge-detection programs on real images knows, zero-crossings and their counterparts in other models are often purely due to noise and many real discontinuities are missed. Edge detection at this early stage violates the principle of least commitment; this is particularly so if the texture or stereopsis or motion module is only going to have access to the edges and not to the underlying image. We believe instead that these modules should make use of a much more complete representation of the image–in the next section we argue that the result of convolving the image with a bank of Gaussian derivative filters is much more suitable for this purpose.

- *Separate modules resulting in the 2.5 D sketch.* Considerable research has been done in this paradigm leading to a much better understanding of the constraints which must underly these shape recovery methods. However, we do not yet have robust methods which can work on arbitrary images without handholding. This is particularly true of the monocular shape-from-X methods (texture, contour and shading) where typically more restrictive assumptions have been used. One modification of the framework is to make combined use of cues [2, 41]– but we believe that a more fundamental criticism can be made of the notion of the 2.5D sketch itself. The computation of the 2.5D sketch as a goal may be both excessively ambitious and unnecessary. Information necessary to support the primary goals of vision–object recognition, navigation and manipulation–may be more qualitative in nature.

An alternative to the Marr 'edges-first' framework is to have a first stage of convolving the image with a very redundant bank of linear or quasi-linear filters and to use this representation as the basis for the parallel processing of brightness, color, texture, stereopsis and motion. In each of these pathways, significant discontinuities (boundary curves) can be detected. From signal-to-noise ratio considerations, it is clear that there would be an advantage in having the different modules cooperate in detecting boundaries (this idea has been explored in a Markov Random Field framework by Poggio, Gamble and Little [53]). At the end there is final common representation–a boundary contour sketch–which could be utilized for visual tasks like recognition.

Whether a particular approach to a complicated problem such as early vision will be successful is impossible to say without a collection of circumstantial evidence and experience. Any approach has to be made precise and demonstrated in concrete instances. We believe that now a considerable body of experimentation and some theoretical evidence has been built in favour of the filtering approach to early vision. In the next sections we present first some biological/computational arguments and then some experimental evidence that make us believe that the transition from 'signal' to 'symbols' should happen *after* the early vision modules, rather than *before* as Marr had postulated.

II. Local analysis of image patches by filtering

The filtering approach is loosely inspired by the current understanding of processing in the early stages of the primate visual system. A recent survey may be found in DeValois and DeValois[20].

Hubel and Wiesel in their pioneering work discovered the basic functional architecture of visual cortex area V1–the first stage in the brain for the analysis of visual information. They found that each small region of the visual field (as small as 0.1° in the fovea, larger in the periphery) was analyzed by a large number of neurons (perhaps 100-200K [20]) which responded selectively to spatially localized bars or edges in different orientations, with most neurons being quite selective about the nature of the stimulus (edge or bar) and its orientation. These neurones are groupted in clusters called hypercolumns that are orderly arranged across V1. They were further classified as simple/complex depending on how the response varied as a function of position in the receptive field. Later, more quantitative studies showed that simple cells exhibit considerable linearity of spatial summation. One could regard them as quasilinear devices which compute a weighted sum of the inputs in their receptive fields. This meant that a family of such cells corresponding to the same shape of receptive field, but different locations in cortex (and hence different locations of the visual field) could be regarded as computing the convolution of the retinal image I with f_i the point spread function of some linear filter. This family of cells is referred to as a 'channel' in the psychophysical and physiological literature. It is important to keep in mind that there is a continuum of channels corresponding to the different choices of f_i which will reflect the orientation and size (equivalently, spatial frequency) preferences of the neuron.

To a first approximation, we can classify them into three categories:

1. Cells with radially symmetric receptive fields. The usual choice of f_i is a Difference of Gaussians (DOG) with the two Gaussians having different values of σ. The receptive fields of these cells are similar to those in retinal ganglion cells. Alternatively, these receptive fields can also be modeled as the Laplacian of Gaussian.

2. Oriented oddsymmetric cells whose receptive fields can be modeled as rotated copies of a vertical oddsymmetric receptive field. A suitable point spread function for such a receptive field is $f(x, y) = G'_{\sigma_1}(x)G_{\sigma_2}(y)$ Note that when $\sigma_1 = \sigma_2$, this point spread function

corresponds to directional derivative of a Gaussian which Canny [14] has shown is quite close to being an 'optimal' edge detector.

3. Oriented evensymmetric cells whose receptive fields can be modeled as rotated copies of a vertical evensymmetric receptive field. A suitable point spread function for such a receptive field is $f(x,y) = G''_{\sigma_1}(x)G_{\sigma_2}(y)$. Note that when $\sigma_1 = \sigma_2$, this point spread function corresponds to second directional derivative of a Gaussian which Canny [14] has shown is quite close to being an 'optimal' bar detector.

Receptive fields range over an interval of sizes. In the Gaussian derivative model, this corresponds to a range of choices of σ_1, σ_2. A clear feature of this system is that at any position in the visual field one finds cells that respond to stimuli at any (within the biological limits) orientation and frequncy. It is important to notice that so far we have ignored the time dimension. The temporal properties of the receptive fields of simple cells are less well understood than the purely spatial properties–however it may be noted that an extension of the linear filtering ideas to the spatiotemporal domain can be done [1].

The use of Gaussian derivatives (or equivalently, differences of offset Gaussians) for modeling receptive fields of simple cells is due to Young [61]. Other models include Gabor functions [19] and differences of offset differences of Gaussians [49]. All of these give good fits to the physiological data, so a choice among them is somewhat arbitrary. Our preference for Gaussian derivatives is based on their computational simplicity and their natural interpretation as 'blurred derivatives'[37, 36].

Implicit in the Gaussian derivative model is the assumption that receptive field profiles in the direction perpendicular to their axes are either odd–symmetric or even–symmetric, and not of intermediate phase. While this is suggested by psychophysical studies on phase discrimination[11], electrophysiological mapping of the impulse response function of single cortical simple cells does not support this view [49]. At the cell level there does not seem to be a sharp dichotomy, but rather a continuum between even and odd symmetry. One explanation of this discrepancy could be that the responses of different cells are pooled together in a way that effectively one gets strictly odd or even symmetric mechanisms.

Therefore it appears that, as a first stage of visual processing, the visual system convolves the incoming stream of images with a bank of linear filters where the f_i are of type (1), (2), (3). We will refer to the collection of response images $I * f_i$ as the *hypercolumn transform* of the image.

Why is this useful from a computational point of view? We list here some reasons that we think make this hypercolumn transform an attractive computational strategy:

- The vector of filter outputs $I * f_i(x_0, y_0)$ characterizes the image *patch* centered at x_0, y_0 by a set of values at a *point*. This is similar to characterizing an analytic function by its derivatives at a point-one can use a Taylor series approximation to find the values of the function at neighboring points. As Koenderink and Van Doorn[37] point out, this is more than an analogy, because of the commutativity of the operations of differentiation and convolution, the receptive fields described above are in fact computing 'blurred derivatives'. We recommend the Koenderink papers[37, 36] for a discussion of other advantages of such a representation.

  Therefore the 'hypercolumn transform' makes available at each location of the computational lattice information about a whole neighbourhood of the point.

- Since filters at multiple scales are used in this characterization, the hypercolumn transform provides a natural setting for multiscale analysis. Premature decisions selecting the scale of analysis are not made. Coarse to fine strategies may be employed.

- The outputs of the filters are available in a continuum of scales and orientations. This provides a rotation-invariant and scale-invariant substrate for subsequent computations.

- An impressive fact about the human visual system noted by psychophysicists is that on many pattern detection and discrimination tasks, its performance is fairly close to optimal. The hypercolumn transform provides the right substrate for this ability since it approximates a convolution with a bank of filters 'matched' to the most relevant elementary stimuli. The kernels of these filters–first and second derivatives of Gaussians have been shown by Canny[14] to be fairly close to optimal (for suitably defined performance criteria) for detecting and localizing edges and lines.

- This approach tries to extract maximum mileage from simple, local and parallel computations, making VLSI implementations feasible.

Beyond the general arguments listed above there is evidence that the 'hypercolumn transform' is a good first step for each of the early vision modules. We now discuss how it can be utilized in the different pathways.

- *Brightness.* In computational vision, it is customary to model brightness edges as step edges and to detect them by marking locations corresponding to the maxima of the outputs of odd-symmetric filters at appropriate scales. However, it should be noted that step edges are an inadequate model for the discontinuities in the image that result from the projection of depth or orientation discontinuities in physical scene. Mutual illumination and specularities are quite common and their effects are particularly significant in the neighborhood of convex or concave object edges. In addition, there will typically be a shading gradient on the image regions bordering the edge. As a consequence of these effects, real image edges are not step functions but more typically a combination of steps, peak and roof profiles. In section 3, we will outline how the hypercolumn transform approach can be modified to detect and localize correctly these composite edges. More details may be found in [52].

- *Shape from shading.* A local shape-from-shading analysis [50] can be based on the filter outputs.

- *Texture.* As the hypercolumn transform provides a good local descriptor of image patches, the boundary between differently textured regions may be found by detecting curves across which there is a significant gradient in one or more of the components of the hypercolumn transform. For an elaboration of this approach, see Malik and Perona[44].

- *Stereopsis.* In stereopsis, the primary problem is that of determining the corresponding points in the left and right view. The responses of filters at a given point in an image form a vector that characterizes the local region of the image. Matching can then be based on finding points in the two views for which these vectors are maximally similar. Kass [35] and Jones and Malik [31] have demonstrated this approach on images of both synthetic and natural scenes. More recent work by Jones and Malik has shown that this approach can utilize orientation and spatial frequency disparity between the two views to extract information about surface slant and tilt, instead of regarding it as an annoying source of noise as in the traditional edge-based methods. The detection of disparity discontinuities can also be done in this framework.

- *Motion .* While the problem of computing optical flow has largely been approached by differential methods or by solving the correspondence problem across frames, it can also be studied in the framework of spatiotemporal filtering[1, 29] in a natural generalization of the hypercolumn transform.

II.1.   Efficient computation in the hypercolumn transform

It may be noticed that there is considerable redundancy in the outputs of the family of mechanisms that compute the 'hypercolumn transform'. As discussed in the previous section this redundancy has considerable computational advantages in the implementation of the subsequent visual modules. A computer implementation of these calculations does not need to be redundant and inefficient. One can exploit the fact that the bulk of the computations are linear and perform them in the appropriate 'orthonormal' coordinate systems.

Consider for example the problem of computing the response of a given filter at all orientations in a continuum. Given the kernel $F : \mathbf{R}^2 \to \mathbf{R}^1$, define the family of 'rotated' copies of F as: $F_\theta = F \circ R_\theta$, $\theta \in \mathbf{S}^1$, where $\mathbf{S}^1$ is the circle and R_θ is a rotation. It is possible to express F_θ as

$$F_\theta(\mathbf{x}) = F \circ R_\theta(\mathbf{x}) = \sum_{i=1}^{N} \sigma_i a_i(\mathbf{x}) b_i(\theta) \qquad \forall \theta \in \mathbf{S}^1, \forall \mathbf{x} \in \mathbf{R}^2 \qquad (1)$$

a *finite* linear combination of functions $a_i : \mathbf{R}^2 \to \mathbf{R}^1$ with θ-dependent coefficients $b_i(\theta)$. Then the convolution of the kernel F_θ with an image I is also a finite sum: once n convolutions $S_i = I * a_i$ have been computed, in order to obtain the filter response $S(x, y, \theta)$ at any orientation θ in a continuum we only need to calculate a linear combination of the finite S_i.

One has to be aware of the fact that for most functions F an exact finite decomposition[26] of F_θ as in Eq. (1) is not possible, however good (1% error) approximations typically require few (6-10) components for the kernels used in the hypercolumn transform. The optimal n-approximation can be computed easily by truncating the singular value decomposition of the linear operator associated to the kernel F_θ [51]. The same technique may be applied for approximating more complete families of filters, obtained by scaling and stretching, as well as rotating, a 'template' kernel [51].

Computation of the hypercolumn transform can also be made more efficient by realizing that the components corresponding to the convolution of the image with coarse scale filters f_i (large values of σ_1, σ_2) have high spatial redundancy–the response does not vary much from pixel to pixel. A number of pyramid schemes e.g. [12] have been proposed to exploit this by sampling more coarsely at these scales.

III. Texture Discrimination

Classical theories of texture perception due to Julesz [33, 7] and to Beck [3, 4] attribute preattentive texture discrimination to differences in first-order statistics of stimulus features such as orientation, size and brightness of constituent elements. Experimental results pointing out phenomena not well explained by these theories have been reported [22, 5, 28].

The spirit of these theories is in consonance with the broad outlines of the Marr framework. An edge-detection stage could be used to compute textons–see Voorhees & Poggio [60] for an implementation of this idea.

In this section, we will describe our model of texture perception [44] which is based not on edges but instead on the output of linear filters–the hypercolumn transform approach outlined in the previous section. This model was intended to satisfy the following criteria:

1. *Biological Plausibility:* The stages of the model should be motivated by, and be consistent with known physiological mechanisms of early vision.

2. *Generality:* The model should be general enough that it can be tested on any arbitrary greyscale image.

3. *Quantitative match with psychophysical data:* It should make a *quantitative* prediction about the salience of the boundary between *any* two textured regions. Rank ordering of the discriminability of different texture pairs should agree with that measured psychophysically.

Other research on texture discrimination in this general spirit includes [13, 18, 59, 5, 6, 58, 24].

We outline our model in section III.1.. In section III.2., quantitative predictions from our model are compared with psychophysical data on the discriminability of several texture pairs collected by Gurnsey & Browse [28] and Kröse [39]. Texture boundaries found on several images are also shown.

III.1. A model for texture perception

A schematic view of the model is presented in Figure 1. The first stage is to compute a hypercolumn transform of the image. A bank of linear filters F_k followed by half-wave rectification (we will indicate the positive part with $R^+(x,y) = \max[R(x,y), 0]$ and the negative part with $R^-(x,y) = \max[-R(x,y), 0]$ giving a set of 'neural' responses $R_i(x,y)$ where the index i identifies the orientation-frequency 'channel':

$$R_{2k} = (I * F_k)^+(x,y) \qquad\qquad R_{2k+1} = (I * F_k)^-(x,y) \qquad (2)$$

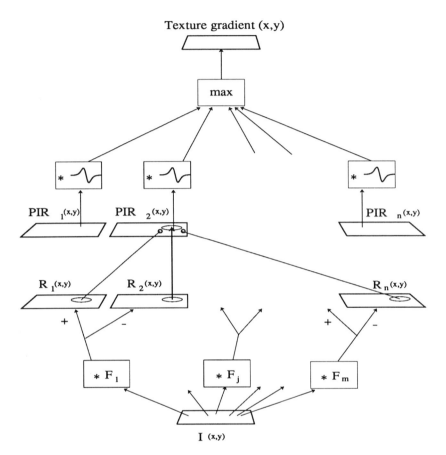

Figure 1: A simplified schematics of our model for texture perception. The image (bottom) is filtered using the kernels $F_1 \ldots F_m$, and half-wave rectified to give the set of "simple-cell" responses $R_1 \ldots R_n$. The post-inhibition responses $PIR_1 \ldots PIR_n$ are computed thresholding the R_i and taking the maximum of the result over small neighbourhoods. The thresholds depend on the activity of all channels. The texture gradient is computed taking the maximum of the responses of wide odd-symmetric filters acting on the post-inhibition responses PIR_i. Reproduced from [43].*

* Reprinted with permission from *Journal of the Optical Society of America* 7 (5), 923–932, May 1990, J. Malik, "Preattentive Texture Discrimination with Early Vision Mechanisms."

Radially symmetric filters (Fig 2-(a),(b)) model non–oriented simple cells. Directionally tuned filters with an even-symmetric cross section perpendicular to their axes (Fig 2-(c)) model bar–sensitive simple cells.

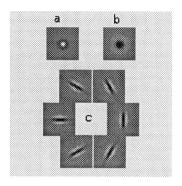

Figure 2: The point-spread functions of some of the filters used in our simulation. The filters were designed after Young [61] summing Gaussian functions (details in [41]) and have zero mean value. (a) DOG2(σ). (b) DOG1(σ). (c) DOOG2(σ,r,θ). In our simulations we used 6 equally spaced orientations θ, a constant aspect ratio $r = 3$, and σ (corresponding to a nominal spatial frequency in c/deg given the viewing distance and size of image) between 3 and 14 c/deg. This gives 96 filters F_i which result in 192 'neural' responses R_i^+, R_i^-. Reproduced from [43].*

The radially symmetric filter classes DOG1(σ) and DOG2(σ) (Fig 2-(a),(b)) model non–oriented simple cells. Directionally tuned filters DOOG2 (σ,r,θ) with an even-symmetric cross section perpendicular to their axes (Fig 2-(c)) model bar–sensitive simple cells. In our simulations we used 6 equally spaced orientations θ and a constant aspect ratio $r = 3$.

The σ parameter of the three filter classes used corresponds to a nominal spatial frequency in c/deg (given the viewing distance and size of image). To sample adequately the mid spatial frequency range around the peak of the luminance contrast sensitivity function, all integer values of the frequency between 3 and 14 c/deg were used. This gives 96 filters F_k which result in 192 'neural' responses R_i. It should be noted that all the filters are zero–mean. Consequently, they have zero response to any image region where the luminance $I(x, y)$ is constant.

Representative examples of these responses for some textures may be found in Fig. 3.

The reader would have noticed that our model incorporates two nonlinearities–half wave rectification and nonlinear inhibition–after the stage corresponding to the computation of the hypercolumn transform.

* Reprinted with permission from *Journal of the Optical Society of America* 7 (5), 923–932, May 1990, J. Malik, "Preattentive Texture Discrimination with Early Vision Mechanisms."

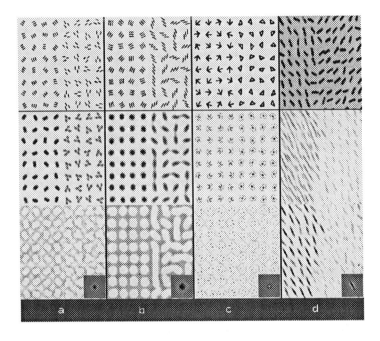

Figure 3: Some textures (top row) and half-wave-rectified response of one of the filters to each (bottom row). The point-spread function of each filter is shown at the bottom-right corner of the response image. The filter shapes are as in Figure 2. Reproduced from [43].*

* Reprinted with permission from *Journal of the Optical Society of America* 7 (5), 923–932, May 1990, J. Malik, "Preattentive Texture Discrimination with Early Vision Mechanisms."

The motivation for this is based on a demonstration that a model based purely on linear mechanisms cannot reproduce human performance. Consider two textures T_1, T_2 which have identical mean brightnesses i.e. identical spatial averages. Convolving them with a linear filter F results in responses $R_{T_1}(x,y)$ and $R_{T_2}(x,y)$ with identical spatial averages. (The value of the power spectra at 0 are identical). Now, we know that humans can preattentively discriminate some textures with identical spatial averages. An example is the even-odd pair from [33], or indeed any discriminable texture pair with identical first order global statistics. A generalization of this observation to n^{th} order statistics and n^{th} order polynomial operators may be found in Kube [39]. Some nonlinearity in the system is therefore necessary for texture perception.

The most obvious choice of nonlinearity is half-wave rectification. V1 cortical cells have low maintained discharge rates and are unable to respond with a decrease in firing rate as required by a negative response. Two different cells are needed (and used) to represent the positive and negative parts of the response belonging respectively to the 'ON' and 'OFF' pathways. We argue in [43] that half-wave rectification is also suitable on computational grounds, and that other proposals like full-wave rectification used by Bergen and Adelson[6] and energy computation used by Sutter, Beck and Graham [58], and by Fogel and Sagi [23] lose essential information.

It turns out however that a second nonlinearity is required. Again we refer the reader to [43] for the justification of our choice of the second nonlinearity–a non-maximum suppression method based losely on a model of intracortical inhibition in V1.

One way to model this inhibition as follows: thresholds $T_i(x_0, y_0)$ for neurons belonging to channel i with retinotopic coordinates x_0, y_0 are computed

$$T_i(x_0, y_0) = \max_j \max_{x,y \in I_{ji}(x_0,y_0)} \alpha_{ji} R_j(x,y) \tag{3}$$

Here I_{ji} is the neighborhood of (x_0, y_0) in which neurons in channel j are able to inhibit neurons in channel i, α_{ji} is a measure of the effectiveness of this inhibition. The post–inhibition response $PIR_i(x_0, y_0)$ is given by

$$PIR_i(x_0, y_0) = \max_{x,y \in S_i(x_0,y_0)} \frac{1}{1 - \alpha_{ii}} [R_i(x,y) - T_i(x,y)]^+ \tag{4}$$

This results in a suppression of responses below the threshold. $S_i(x_0, y_0)$ is a sampling neighborhood from which the strong responses in channel i are selected for subsequent processing.

One way to think about this mechanism is as a 'leaders take most' feedforward network; it is a variant of the 'winner take all' type mechanisms quite popular in the neural network literature.

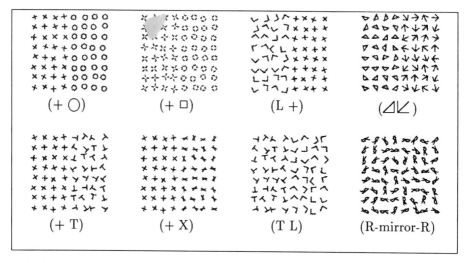

Figure 4: Eight textures used in our experiments. Reproduced from [43].*

We were guided in our choice of I_{ji} and α_{ji} by the design criterion of eliminating 'spurious' responses [43].

The last stage of our model consists of the computation of the texture gradient[47].

The texture gradient we use is defined as $\max_i \nabla(PIR_i * G_{\sigma'})(x,y)$. Biologically, the computation of the gradient of the smoothed post-inhibition response in each channel can be done using odd–symmetric oriented mechanisms similar to the edge–sensitive cells in V1. Of course, the mechanisms responsible for computing the texture gradient have large receptive fields (σ' is a measure of the size) and presumably occur in some extrastriate area. The maximum operation seems a natural way of combining the outputs of the different channels. Texture boundaries may be detected by marking local peaks of the texture gradient magnitude.

III.2. Experimental results

We have compared the *degree* of texture discriminabilty predicted by our algorithm with psychophysical data due to Kröse[38] and Gurnsey and Browse[27]. Figure 4 shows 7 bipartite textures with elements constructed after [38](Section 3.2, pp.34-39), and 1 composed of R's and mirror-image R's (called RR-RL). For two of these textures, the texture gradient ($\sigma' = 12$ pixels, S_i = constant) obtained by our algorithm is plotted as a function of column number (see Figure 5). The texture boundary (column 64) is

* Reprinted with permission from *Journal of the Optical Society of America* 7 (5), 923–932, May 1990, J. Malik, "Preattentive Texture Discrimination with Early Vision Mechanisms."

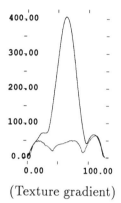

(Texture gradient)

Texture pair	Discriminability		
	Kro	G&B	M&P
+ ○	100(sat)	n.a.	407
+ □	88.1	n.a.	225
L +	68.6	0.736	203
△∠	52.3	0.4–0.55	159
+ T	37.6	0.496	120
+ X	30.3	n.a.	104
T L	30.6	0.421	90*
R-mirror-R	n.a.	n.a.	50*

Figure 5: A comparison of the predictions of our texture segmentation algorithm (M&P) with psychophysical data from Kröse [38, 37] and Gurnsey and Browse [27] (G&B). For the 128x128 textures in Fig. 4 the texture gradient is averaged along the vertical direction on the central middle portion of each column and plotted with respect to the horizontal coordinate. Such plots are shown for the most (L +) and least (R-mirror-R) discriminable textures. The value of the texture gradient at its central peak is taken to be the prediction of our model and is reported in the table for all textures in the (M&P) column. The symbol * indicates that a side peak of the texture gradient was higher than the reported central peak. Because of differences in the scales used, the three columns should be compared only by the rank ordering of discriminability. Reproduced from [43].*

* Reprinted with permission from *Journal of the Optical Society of America* 7 (5), 923–932, May 1990, J. Malik, "Preattentive Texture Discrimination with Early Vision Mechanisms."

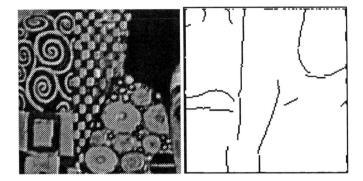

Figure 6: A detail of the portrait of Adele Bloch-Bauer by Gustav Klimt (left) and the texture boundaries found (right). The essential boundaries of the 5 perceived groups have been detected.Reproduced from [43].*

associated with the central peak in the gradient. The value of the gradient associated with this peak is taken to be a measure of the discriminability predicted by our algorithm. In Figure 5, this data is presented in a more easily readable form and compared with Kröse (Table 3.1, pg. 39, SOA=320) and Gurnsey & Browse (pairs 1.1, 1.2, 1.3, 3.1) mean overall discriminability. Note that the rank order of discriminability predicted by our model matches Gurnsey & Browse's ranking exactly, and that of Kröse.

For an example of texture boundaries found by our algorithm, see Fig. 6 and Fig. 7.

This match with the experimental data that we have obtained is surprisingly good–we are not aware of any other model which fits this data. Of course, the usual notes of caution for any model with parameters which are not directly measured from physiology or psychophysics apply. The particular equations and parameters that we have proposed are surely wrong in detail. To have any relevance to biological texture perception, it is important that the model degrade gracefully i.e. roughly similar ideas should work as well and choices of parameters not be too critical. This is explored in [43].

IV. Brightness boundaries

The problem of detecting and localizing discontinuities in greyscale intensity images has traditionally been approached as one of finding step edges. This is true both for the classical linear filtering approaches as well as the more recent approaches based on surface reconstruction.

* Reprinted with permission from *Journal of the Optical Society of America* 7 (5), 923–932, May 1990, J. Malik, "Preattentive Texture Discrimination with Early Vision Mechanisms."

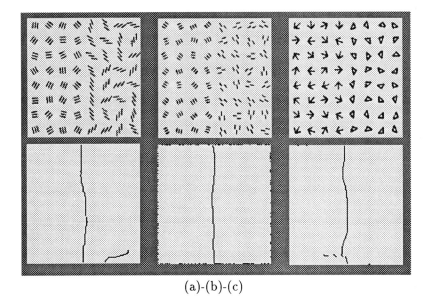

(a)-(b)-(c)

Figure 7: Texture boundaries found by our computational model on a set of images. (a) and (b) Two stimuli constructed after Gurnsey and Browse [27] who used them to criticize the original Julesz texton theory (easily segmentable in spite of identical textons in left and right regions). (c) the triangle-arrow texture pair. In our model, center–surround DOG2 filters contribute most to the segmentation and their responses decrease when the micropatterns are anisotropically stretched explaining the observations of Enns [22].*

* Reprinted with permission from *Journal of the Optical Society of America* 7 (5), 923–932, May 1990, J. Malik, "Preattentive Texture Discrimination with Early Vision Mechanisms."

Unfortunately, step edges are an inadequate model for the discontinuities in the image that result from the projection of depth or orientation discontinuities in physical scene. Mutual illumination and specularities are quite common and their effects are particularly significant in the neighborhood of convex or concave object edges. In addition, there will typically be a shading gradient on the image regions bordering the edge. As a consequence of these effects, real image edges are not step functions but more typically a combination of steps, peak and roof profiles. This had been noted experimentally by Herskovits and Binford back in 1970. Quantitative analyses of the associated physical phenomena have also been provided- Horn[29] and more recently Forsyth and Zisserman [24]. This section addresses the computational problem of detecting and localizing these composite edges.

Most local edge detection methods are based on some decision making stage following a linear filtering stage. Typically one looks for maxima in the filtered image perpendicular to the orientation of the edge. Such an approach (e.g. Canny [14])results in a systematic error in localization whenever there is a composite edge([53](page 9), or [9](Fig. 2. 1)). This problem is not specific to the Gaussian derivative filters used by Canny, but is present whatever the linear filter used. For any such filter there is a systematic localization error for composite edges. Using any (finite) number of linear filters does not help. However, we show here that a *quadratic* filtering approach is adequate. Instead of looking for maxima in $(I * f)$ one looks for maxima in $W = (I * f_1)^2 + (I * f_2)^2$, or more generally $\sum(I * f_i)^2$. A special case of this approach, when two filters which are Hilbert pairs are used, gives the energy based approach due to Morrone, Owens and their colleagues [46, 45].

To detect edges in 2D, we use a Gaussian window to compute the 2D extension of the 1D filter. Rotated copies of the filter are used to (conceptually) compute $W(x, y, \theta)$ for all orientations θ. At each point the locally dominant orientations θ_i which correspond to the local maxima (over θ) are determined. Allowing for multiple orientations enables junctions to be correctly localized without any rounding. Edge points are defined as the points where the directional derivative in the direction perpendicular to a locally dominant orientation is 0. Experimental results are presented.

IV.1.   Dealing with composite edges

We want to detect and localize edges which we choose to model as arbitrary combinations of lines, steps and roofs. For the moment just consider an edges composed of arbitrary combinations of deltas and steps

$I = c_1\delta + c_2\delta^{(-1)}$. The general case involving ramps is considered later. (A word about notation: we will write $f^{(-1)}(x)$ for $\int_{-\infty}^{x} f(t)dt$, and $f^{(-n)}(x) = (f^{(-n+1)})^{(-1)}(x)$. So $\delta^{(-1)}$ will be the step function and $\delta^{(-2)}$ a ramp.)

First we establish a proposition which shows that localizing edges at peaks in the responses of a fixed, finite family of linear filters leads to systematic errors.

Proposition 1 *For any fixed finite family of filters* $\{f_1, f_2, \ldots, f_k\}$, *there exists an image* $I = c_1\delta + c_2\delta^{(-1)}$ *for which none of the filter responses has a maximum at* $x = 0$

Proof.   Edges are declared at the maxima of the response $I * f(x) = c_1 f(x) + c_2 f^{(-1)}(x)$. To ensure correct localization, there should be a maximum at $x = 0$ for any combination of c_1, c_2. For a filter f_i, its response has a maximum at $x = 0$ only if $(I * f_i)'(0) = 0$. Now $(I * f_i)' = c_1 f' + c_2 f$, implying that the vector $[c_1 \ c_2]^T$ is orthogonal to $[f_i'(0) \ f_i(0)]^T$. To establish the proposition, one has only to pick a composite edge for which the vector $[c_1 \ c_2]^T$ is not orthogonal to any of the vectors in the fixed, finite family of the k vectors $[f_i'(0) \ f_i(0)]^T, i = 1, \ldots, k$.

In other words, if we had available to us the outputs of k different filters with a clever strategy which would enable us to pick the 'right' filter f_i whose response should be used to localize the edge, we would still be unable to guarantee zero localization error.

Somehow the problem seems to be that for any particular linear filter we are able to construct a composite edge for which the filter is not matched. This suggests an alternative view–construct a parametrized filter which is a linear combination of an even filter f_e (matched to $\delta(x)$) and an odd filter f_o (matched to $\delta^{(-1)}$) and try to 'adapt' it to the particular composite edge in the image by picking the parameter value that maximizes the filter response at each point.

Call $f_\alpha(x) = \cos \alpha f_e(x) + \sin \alpha f_o(x)$ the filter, $I = c_1\delta + c_2\delta^{(-1)}$ the image, and $U(\alpha, x) = (I * f_\alpha)(x)$ the response. We want to choose $\alpha(\cdot)$ such that at each point x the response is maximized. Define $V(x) = \max_\alpha U(\alpha, x)$ and call $\alpha(x)$ the maximizing parameter (i.e. $V(x) = U(\alpha(x), x)$). Notice that $\alpha(x)$ must satisfy the equation $\frac{\partial}{\partial \alpha} U(\alpha(x), x) = 0$.

We would like the 'maximal' response $V(x)$ to have a maximum in zero, corresponding to the location of the edge: $V'(0) = (U_\alpha \alpha_x + U_x)(\alpha(0), 0) = 0$. Since $U_\alpha(\alpha(x), x) = 0$ then it must be $U_x(\alpha(0), 0) = 0$. Making use of the fact that $f_o(0) = f_e^{(-1)}(0) = 0$ we get the following system of equations:

$$U_x(\alpha(0), 0) = c_1 \sin \alpha f_o'(0) + c_2 \cos \alpha f_e(0) = 0 \qquad (5)$$
$$U_\alpha(\alpha(0), 0) = -c_1 \sin \alpha f_e(0) + c_2 \cos \alpha f_o^{(-1)}(0) = 0 \qquad (6)$$

The maximizing value of α, $\alpha(0)$, can be obtained from Equation 6. Substituting this into Equation 5 gives the following condition:

$$f_e^2(0) = -f_o^{(-1)}(0)f_o'(0) \tag{7}$$

If this normalization condition is satisfied the mixed edge $c_1\delta + c_2\delta^{(-1)}$ will be localized exactly by the maximum of $V(x)$ defined above.

An alternative approach yields the same condition. Define the vector of filters $F(x) = [f_e(x), f_o(x)]^T$. We localize features by looking for local maxima in the norm of the (vector) response to this filter of I. The squared norm of the response, $\mid I * F \mid^2$ is

$$W(x) = \{c_1\delta + c_2\delta^{(-1)} * f_e\}^2 + \{c_1\delta + c_2\delta^{(-1)} * f_o\}^2 \tag{8}$$

Equating the derivative of this expression with respect to x at the origin to 0 gives the condition

$$c_1c_2f_e^2(0) - c_1c_2f_o'(0)f_o^{(-1)}(0) = 0 \tag{9}$$

which is the same as Equation 7

Thus, we have the possibility of getting arbitrarily precise localization of composite edges simply by looking for peaks in the response to a *quadratic* filter, i.e. in $\sum(I * f_i)^2$.

This is similar in form to the approach used by Morrone et al.. While their reasoning was in the Fourier domain and aimed at detecting phase congruency based on a psychophysical definition of a feature, we arrive at a similar formulation purely motivated by a computational criterion of localizing composite edges exactly.

From our formulation it follows that there is nothing particularly sacred about the use of Hilbert filter pairs as done by Morrone, Owens et al. In fact, if the composite edge consists of, say a bar and a step edge at quite different scales, one should probably use f_e and f_o tuned to different widths (scales) and thus not Hilbert pairs. To make a proper choice of these filters, one should instead bring to bear the criteria of having a good signal-to-noise ratio, low stochastic localization error etc. analogous to the approach used by Canny for linear filters. These calculations may be found in [42].

IV.2.   Detecting edges in two dimensions

To detect edges in 2D, a Gaussian window may be used to compute the 2D extension of the filter. Rotated copies of the filter are used to (conceptually) compute $R(x, y, \theta)$. In practice one cannot afford to compute convolutions of the image with filters at an infinity of orientations. It turns out that it is possible to approximate a convolution kernel at all orientations in a continuum using linear combinations of a finite number of functions (this technique is described in [50]). It is therefore possible to compute $R(x, y, \theta)$ on a continuum of orientations (see Fig.8-b).

In a neighbourhood of each edge the filter output 'energy' R will have a maximum at the orientation θ_e parallel to the edge. One can therefore determine at each point the dominant orientations θ_i which corresponding to the local maxima of R over θ. At junctions multiple maxima will be detected due to the co-presence of edges at multiple orientation.

Edge points are defined as the points where the directional derivative in the direction perpendicular to a locally dominant orientation is 0. Fix θ_e and consider $R(x, y, \theta_e)$. Along a line orthogonal to the edge the problem reduces to the 1D case: there will be an energy maximum at the edge. Edges can be found by marking as 'edge points' all the points $p = (x, y, \theta)$ that satisfy:

$$\frac{\partial}{\partial \theta} R(p) = 0 \tag{10}$$

$$\frac{\partial}{\partial \mathbf{v}_\theta} R(p) = 0 \tag{11}$$

where $\mathbf{v}_\theta$ is the unit vector orthogonal to the orientation associated to θ.

The search for the edge points has been implemented as follows:

1. For each image pixel (x, y) the angles $\theta_i(x, y)$ at which the response is maximized are found. For this operation we use Brent's search algorithm (See [54]). The upper bound on the orientation error was set at 0.1 degrees. (See Fig.8-c).

2. The maxima in (x, y) of $R(x, y, \theta_i(x, y))$ are computed with sub-pixel accuracy by fitting a cylindrical paraboloid to $R(x, y, \theta_i)$ in the 3x3 neighbourhood around the pixel.(See Fig.8-d)

The results of the search are shown in figures 10 and 9 compared to the output of a Canny detector using filters of the same scale. The typical number of steps of the Brent algorithm was 2-3. The time spent in the search was always less than the filtering time.

Acknowledgements

This research was supported by NSF Presidential Young Investigator Award No. IRI-8957274 to J.Malik and by Army Research Office grant number

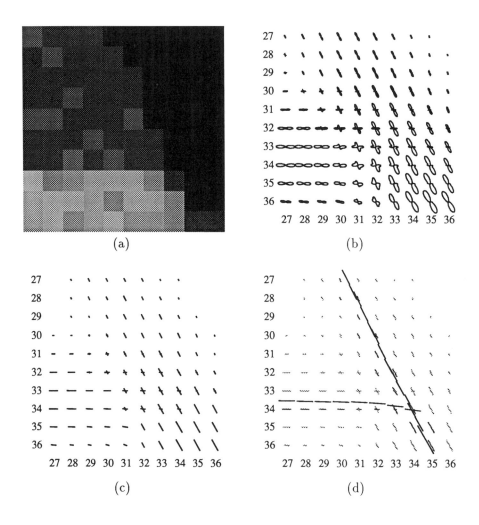

Figure 8: The process of brightness edge detection shown for a detail (a) of the T junction image of Fig. 9. (b) Energies are computed at every pixel as a function $R(x, y, \theta)$. At each pixel the energy is represented by a polar plot; the plots are π-periodic since $R(x, y, \theta)$ does not encode the direction, only the orientation of the edges. Notice that the energies have (c) Maxima in θ are calculated at each pixel. The length of the needles indicates the associated energy. (d) 'Oriented' maxima in (x, y) are computed at subpixel resolution.

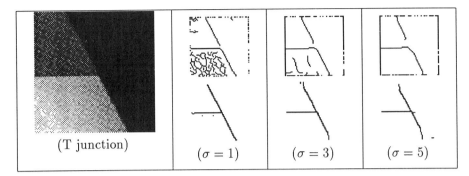

Figure 9: Comparison of the Canny detector (top) and our 2D detector (bottom) at three different scales. Notice the different performance at the junction: the Canny detector misses the junction (despite very low threshold settings) and deforms the remaining corner.

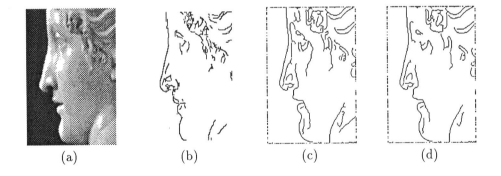

Figure 10: Comparison of the Canny detector and our 2D detector. (a) Original (Paolina Borghese, Canova circa 1800). (b) our detector, sigma = 1, ratio = 2. (c-d) Canny detector with sigma = 1, and thresholds (150,250), and (200,400) respectively.

DAAL 03-86-K-0171. P.Perona conducted part of this research while at the International Computer Science Institute, Berkeley. The experiments reported in this paper have been conducted using Paul Kube's 'viz' image processing package.

References

[1] E. Adelson and J. Bergen. Spatiotemporal energy models for the perception of motion. *Journal of the Optical Society of America*, 2(2):284–299, 1985.

[2] J. Aloimonos and D. Shulman. *Integration of Visual Modules*. Academic Press, 1989.

[3] J. Beck. *Organization and representation in perception*, chapter Textural segmentation. Erlbaum, Hillsdale, NJ, 1982.

[4] J. Beck, K. Prazdny, and A. Rosenfeld. *Human and Machine Vision*, pages 1–38. Academic Press, 1983.

[5] J. Beck, A. Sutter, and R. Ivry. Spatial frequency channels and perceptual grouping in texture segmentation. *Computer Vision, Graphics and Image Processing*, pages 299–325, 1987.

[6] J. Bergen and E. Adelson. Early vision and texture perception. *Nature*, 333:363–364, May 1988.

[7] J. Bergen and B. Julesz. Rapid discrimination of visual patterns. *IEEE Transactions on Systems, Man, and Cybernetics*, 13(5), 1983.

[8] T. Binford. Inferring surfaces from images. *Artificial Intelligence*, 17:205–244, 1981.

[9] A. Blake and A. Zisserman. *Visual reconstruction*. MIT press, 1987.

[10] O. Braddick. A short-range process in apparent motion. *Vision Research*, 14:519–528, 1974.

[11] D. Burr, C. Morrone, and D. Spinelli. Evidence of edge and bar detectors in human vision. *Vision Research*, 29(4):419–431, 1989.

[12] P. Burt and E. Adelson. The laplacian algorithm as a compact image code. *IEEE Transactions on Communications*, 31:532–540, 1983.

[13] T. Caelli. Three processing characteristics of visual texture segmentation. *Spatial Vision*, 1(1):19–30, 1985.

[14] J. Canny. A computational approach to edge detection. *IEEE trans. PAMI*, 8:679–698, 1986.

[15] P. Cavanagh. Reconstructing the third dimension: Interactions between color, texture, motion, binocular disparity, and shape. *Computer Vision, Graphics and Image Processing*, 37:171–195, 1987.

[16] P. Cavanagh, M. Arguin, and A. Treisman. Effect of surface medium on visual search for orientation and size features. *Journal of Experimental Psychology: Human Perception and Performance*, 16(3):479–491, 1990.

[17] P. Cavanagh, M. Arguin, and M. von Grunau. Interattribute apparent motion. *Vision Research*, pages 1197–1203, 1989.

[18] J. Coggins and A. K. Jain. A spatial filtering approach to texture analysis. *Pattern Recognition Letters*, 3:195–203, 1985.

[19] J. D. Daugman. Two dimensional spectral analysis of cortical receptive field profiles. *Vision Research*, 20:847–856, 1980.

[20] R. DeValois and K. DeValois. *Spatial Vision*. Oxford University Press, 1988.

[21] E. DeYoe and D. V. Essen. Concurrent processing streams in monkey visual cortex. *Trends in Neurosciences*, 11:219–226, 1988.

[22] J. Enns. Seeing textons in context. *Perception and Psychophysics*, 39(2):143–147, 1986.

[23] I. Fogel and D. Sagi. Gabor filters as texture discriminators. *Biological Cybernetics*, 61:103–113, 1989.

[24] D. Forsyth and A. Zisserman. Mutual illumination. In *Proceedings of the IEEE CVPR*, pages 466–473, 1989.

[25] W. Freeman and E. Adelson. Steerable filters for image analysis. Technical Report 126, MIT, Media Laboratory, 1990.

[26] S. Geman and D. Geman. Stochastic relaxation, gibbs distributions, and the bayesian restoration of images. *IEEE Transactions on PAMI*, 6:721–741, November 1984.

[27] R. Gurnsey and R. Browse. Micropattern properties and presentation conditions influencing visual texture discrimination. *Perception and Psychophysics*, 41(3):239–252, 1987.

[28] D. Heeger. Optical flow from spatiotemporal filters. In *Proceedings of the First International Conference on Computer Vision*, pages 181–190, 1987.

[29] B. Horn. Image intensity understanding. *Artificial intelligence*, 8(2):201–231, 1977.

[30] D. Jones and J. Malik. Computational stereopsis–beyond zero-crossings. *Invest. Ophtalmol. Vis. Sci. (Supplement)*, 31(4):529, 1990.

[31] B. Julesz. *Foundations of Cyclopean Perception*. University of Chicago Press, 1971.

[32] B. Julesz. Textons, the elements of texture perception and their interactions. *Nature*, 290:91–97, 1981.

[33] B. Julesz, E.N.Gilbert, and J.D.Victor. Visual discrimination of textures with identical third order statistics. *Biological Cybernetics*, 31:137–140, 1978.

[34] M. Kass. Computing visual correspondence. In *Proceedings: Image Understanding Workshop*, pages 54–60, McLean, Virginia, June 1983. Science Applications, Inc.

[35] J. Koenderink. Operational significance of receptive field assemblies. *Biological Cybernetics*, 58:163–171, 1988.

[36] J. Koenderink and A. van Doorn. Representation of local geometry in the visual system. *Biological Cybernetics*, 55:367–375, 1987.

[37] B. Kröse. Local structure analyzers as determinants of preattentive pattern discrimination. *Biological Cybernetics*, 55:289–298, 1987.

[38] B. J. Kröse. *A description of visual structure*. PhD thesis, University of Delft, 1986.

[39] P. R. Kube. *On Image Texture*. PhD thesis, University of California at Berkeley, 1988.

[40] J. Malik and D. Maydan. Recovering three dimensional shape from a single image of curved objects. *IEEE Transactions on Pattern Analysis and Machine Intelligence*, 11(6):555–566, June 1989.

[41] J. Malik and P. Perona. A computational model of texture perception. Technical Report UCB/CSD 89/491, Computer Science Division (EECS), U.C.Berkeley, February 1989.

[42] J. Malik and P. Perona. Detecting and localizing edges composed of steps, peaks and roofs. Technical Report UCB/CSD 90/590, Computer Science Division (EECS), U.C.Berkeley, 1990.

[43] J. Malik and P. Perona. Preattentive texture discrimination with early vision mechanisms. *Journal of the Optical Society of America – A*, 7(5):923–932, 1990.

[44] D. Marr. *Vision*. W.H.Freeman & Co., 1982.

[45] M. Morrone and D. Burr. Feature detection in human vision: a phase dependent energy model. *Proc. R. Soc. Lond. B*, 235:221–245, 1988.

[46] M. Morrone and R. Owens. Feature detection from local energy. *Pattern Recognition Letters*, 6:303–313, 1987.

[47] H. C. Nothdurft. Sensitivity for structure gradient for texture discrimination tasks. *Vision Research*, 25:1957–1968, 1985.

[48] A. Parker and M. J. Hawken. Two-dimensional spatial structure of receptive fields in monkey striate cortex. *Journal of the Optical Society of America A*, 5(4):598–605, 1988.

[49] A. Pentland. Shape information from shading: A theory about human perception. In *Proceedings of Second International· Conference on Computer Vision*, pages 404–413. IEEE Computer Society Press, December 1988.

[50] P. Perona. Finite representation of deformable functions. Technical Report 90-034, International Computer Science Institute, 1947 Center st., Berkeley CA 94704, 1990.

[51] P. Perona and J. Malik. Detecting and localizing edges composed of steps, peaks and roofs. In *Proceedings of the International Conference on Computer Vision*. Osaka, 1990.

[52] T. Poggio, E. Gamble, and J. Little. Parallel integration of vision modules. *Science*, 242:436–440, 1988.

[53] J. Ponce and M. Brady. Towards a surface primal sketch. Technical Report 824, MIT Artificial Intelligence Laboratory, 1985.

[54] W. Press, B. Flannery, S. Teukolsky, and W. Vetterling. *Numerical Recipes in C*. Cambridge University Press, 1988.

[55] V. Ramachandran, V. Rao, and T. Vidyasagar. Apparent movement with subjective contours. *Vision Research*, 13:1399–1401, 1973.

[56] R.L.Gregory. Vision with isoluminant colour contrast: 1. a projection technique and observations. *Perception*, 6:113–119, 1977.

[57] S. Shimojo, G. Silverman, and K. Nakayama. Occlusion and the solution to the aperture problem for motion. *Vision Research*, 29(5):619–626, 1989.

[58] A. Sutter, J. Beck, and N. Graham. Contrast and spatial variables in texture segregation: testing a simple spatial-frequency channels model. *Perception and Psychophysics*, 46:312–332, 1989.

[59] M. Turner. Texture discrimination by gabor functions. *Biological Cybernetics*, 55:71–82, 1986.

[60] H. Voorhees and T. Poggio. Computing texture boundaries from images. *Nature*, 333:364–367, 1988.

[61] R. Young. The gaussian derivative theory of spatial vision: Analysis of cortical cell receptive field line-weighting profiles. Technical Report GMR-4920, General Motors Research, 1985.

II.8

Compression of Remotely Sensed Images using Self Organizing Feature Maps

M. MANOHAR

Universities Space Research Association
Greenbelt, MD

JAMES C. TILTON

NASA Goddard Space Flight Center
Greenbelt, MD

I. Introduction

A. Background

Concerns about environmental degradation, global warming, and other deleterious effects of human activity have led the United States and other countries to organize research efforts to understand the natural and human-induced global changes in the Earth system. NASA's central contribution to the United States Global Change Research Program is the Mission to Planet Earth, with the Earth Observing System (EOS) as the primary component. Current plans call for the launch of the first EOS platform in 1998.

EOS will tremendously increase the volume of data collected from NASA space platforms. It is expected that over its 15 year life, EOS will store and distribute tens of Petabytes of data (1 Petabyte = 1,000 Terabytes; 1 Terabyte = 1,000 Gigabytes; 1 Gigabyte = 1,000 Megabytes). In comparison, the combined total volume of data archived at the Department of the Interior's EROS Data Center from over 18 years of data collection from the Landsat Multispectral Scanner and over 8 years from the Landsat Thematic Mapper currently is approximately 10 Terabytes (Ramapriyan, 1990 and EROS Data Center, 1990).

These large data rates and volumes lead to huge difficulties in data transmission and storage. Optical disk technology promises to be a cost-effective solution to the data storage problem in the near future. However, there does not appear to be such a hardware fix to the data transmission problem, making data transmission bandwidth a precious commodity in both terrestrial network systems and for data transmission from space platforms to earth.

Data compression is one tool that can be used to help overcome data transmission bandwidth limitations. However, for experimental remote sensing data, lossless data compression is required for any data that is to be actually fully analyzed by the researcher utilizing the data. Nonetheless, highly lossy data compression can be used by a researcher who just needs to browse through a large number of data sets, and moderately lossy data compression can be used for the final selection of data sets to be fully analyzed.

As more familiarity is gained with particular data sets, "lossy" data compression algorithms could be designed that give significant compression while loosing only non-essential information (essentially, the "noise"), and retaining all the scientifically significant information. One way this could be accomplished would be by designing the data compression scheme as an integral part of the information extraction process, wherein the data compression is a form of conditioning of the data for analysis.

Among lossy compression techniques there are four important classes:

i.   Predictive coding techniques in which model parameters are estimated and transmitted for reconstruction. Some techniques in this class are Linear Prediction Coding (LPC) used for speech coding, Difference Pulse Code Modulation (DPCM), etc.
ii. Transform techniques in which the original image is transformed into a new coordinate system. Compression is obtained due to the fact that the information is concentrated in relatively few transform coefficients. Some of the transforms used in image coding are Discrete Fourier Transform (DFT), Cosine (DCT), Sine (DST), Hadamard (HT), and Karhunen-Loeve (KLT).
iii. Hybrid coding in which predictive techniques are applied on transform coefficients.
iv. Vector Quantization (VQ) in which data vectors are coded. VQ is motivated by the result of rate-distortion theory (Shannon, 1948) which states that better performance can be achieved by coding vectors rather than scalars.

In this chapter we focus on a Vector Quantization approach that can compress certain NASA images by factors of 10 to 20, at a data rate of approximately 10 Megabits/second.

B. Vector Quantization

Vector Quantization (VQ), as an extension of scalar quantization to higher dimensional space, has proven to be an effective method of compressing speech signals (Gersho and Cuperman, 1983; Buzo, et al, 1980). Recently, these techniques have been applied to images with good results (Gersho and Ramamurthi, 1982; Riskin, 1990; Ramamoorthy, et al, 1989; Nasrabadi and King, 1988). In most of these cases, the algorithm used is some variation of the generalized Lloyd algorithm (GLA) or Linde-Buzo-Gray (LBG) algorithm (Linde, et al, 1975). A good account of Vector Quantization technique and its variants can be found in Gray (1984).

In order to effectively exploit spatial correlations among image pixels in VQ, the image is partitioned into two dimensional cells of fixed size. The pixels in each $k = w_r x w_c$ rectangular cell are scanned in raster scan order and are taken to be a one-dimensional vector of size k (while raster scan order is used here, other scan orders, such as the Z-scan, may be more optimal). As the image is scanned, each vector is compared to standard vectors in a codebook. The address of the standard vector in the codebook that most closely matches the input vector is transmitted or stored as the code for that cell. Compression is obtained because the address bits are much fewer than the number of bits required for representing each vector, and because the number of elements transmitted or stored is less than the original number of pixels by a factor equal to the vector size. Thus, the smaller the codebook size (m), and the larger the vector size (k), the more efficient is the compression (fewer bits are required per pixel).

This relationship of codebook size and vector size to compression efficiency is illustrated by the expression for the number of bits required per pixel, or compression rate (r). The compression rate is calculated as:

$$r = 1/k * \log_2 m \text{ bits/pixel.}$$

A particular rate can be accomplished by several possible pairs of m and k. Selecting small values of the codebook size, m, is not very effective because r changes as logarithm of m. Increasing the vector size is more effective since the rate, r, increase linearly with 1/k. Thus the change in rate, r is more rapid with k than m, implying that large vector dimensions should be used.

In designing a VQ compressor, one must also consider the distortion introduced by the VQ process. The most commonly used distortion measure is the mean squared error between input image and reconstructed image. Although this measure does not necessarily show how close visually the reconstructed image is to the original image, it is used because it is mathematically tractable, and does give some sense of difference between the two images.

Here we use the average mean squared error as a distortion measure for quantifying the performance of the encoder. If X_i, and χ_i are the input vector and reproduced vector respectively, the average distortion, $E(d(X_i, \chi_i))$ is given by

$$d = 1/n \sum (X_i - \chi_i)^2$$

where n is the number of vectors from the input image. For given rate, r (bits/pixel), and given distortion measure d, the vector dimension, k (pixels), and the codebook size, m, can be optimally determined (Lookabaugh and Gray, 1989).

Another common distortion measure is the signal to noise ratio (or signal to quantization noise ratio, Gray (1984)), defined as:

$$SNR = 10 \log(\sigma_x^2/d)$$

where σ_x^2 is the image variance. We will also use this measure to evaluate the performance of our VQ compressor.

As noted earlier, large vector dimensions should be used to achieve low compression rates. Large vector dimensions, however, are difficult to handle even in parallel machines. For a given codebook size, the computational requirements are directly proportional to the vector dimension. Since larger vector dimensions are also recommended to exploit the image spatial correlations effectively, tradeoffs must be made between computational requirements and compression performance (rate and distortion).

The greatest drawback of VQ is that it is computationally very demanding. Using the LGB algorithm, for example, it takes several hours of CPU time to generate a codebook of reasonable size (1024 4x4 codes) for a 512x512 image. In fact, the algorithm that will be presented here takes 5-6 hours for generating the codebook of the above size when run on a sequential computer (a VAX 6000-440). The bulk of the time is consumed performing exhaustive searches of the codebook to find the closest match to a given codeword vector from among those in the candidate set. Different methods of have been developed to speed the search by structuring the codebook, at the cost of lowering the performance of the encoder in terms of compression factor. Parallelization is an obvious solution to this search problem in both codebook generation as well as in data encoding.

C. Neural Net Algorithms

The motivation behind choosing the neural models for developing an image compression system is to achieve speed in performance and fault tolerance (Murali, *et al*, 1990). Neural networks also offer a potential for technology innovation to provide the next-generation of on-board processing capability in space-based systems such as EOS. The most suitable neural net model for VQ is Kohonen's Self Organizing Feature Maps (SOFM).

The following sections describe the model, Vector Quantization using SOFM, and its implementation on a massively parallel computer, the MasPar MP-1. Compression results on NASA image sources are presented, followed by a discussion of the results.

II. Self Organizing Feature Map (SOFM)

A. Background

The Self Organizing Feature Map (SOFM) is a mapping of higher dimensional space onto a two-dimensional discrete lattice. The map is generated by establishing a correspondence between input signals and neurons in a lattice such that topological relationships among the inputs are reflected as faithfully as possible in the arrangement of neurons in the lattice. The values in the cells start out as random numbers and organize themselves to match the events of the input space and also retain the distance relations of the higher dimensional input space in two-dimensional lattice locations of the cells. Thus the spatial location or coordinates of neurons in the network correspond to a particular input pattern. This self organizing property can be exploited as an effective pattern recognition tool in the unsupervised mode (Kohonen, 1982a; Kohonen, 1982b; Kohonen, 1990). Its capability stretches beyond mapping the signal features and effectively maps the semantic relations of the signal (Kohonen, 1989).

The essential function of the training process for generating the SOFM is to localize the neuron activity to a small neighborhood of neurons for every k-dimensional sample presented to the network. The central cell of this neighborhood is the most active cell and is often referred to as the *winner* in the VQ terminology. The second function is to further tune the synaptic weights of these active neurons such that the difference between input vector and weight vector decreases.

The SOFM training process can be conveniently described by assuming an array of cells configured in two-dimensional lattice. This array holds the representative samples to the input set, also called the codebook. The most important function of the SOFM training process is to learn from the input samples the most optimal codebook containing fewer number of samples than the input set.

Let the input event space be represented by

$$\xi = \{X_1, X_2,\ldots, X_i,\ldots, X_n\} \quad \text{where} \quad X_i = (x_{i1}, x_{i2},\ldots, x_{ik})^t$$

and the output space or codebook by

$$\psi = \{Y_1, Y_2,\ldots, Y_j,\ldots, Y_m\} \quad \text{where} \quad Y_j = (y_{j1}, y_{j2},\ldots, y_{jk})^t$$

In all practical situations the codebook size, $m \ll n$ (the number of vectors extracted from the input image). The compression ratio is given by $(n*b)/\log_2 m$, where b is number of bits per vector.

The SOFM training process can be considered to be learning ψ from ξ such that many to one mapping of all the vectors $X_i \in \xi$ onto $Y_j \in \psi$ results in minimum error. The learning starts from some initial state, Y_{j0}, normally taken as set of random numbers. If X_i can be somehow compared simultaneously with all samples in ψ, then the best matching vector, Y_c, is called the *winner*. Now the *winner* Y_c is updated such that X_i and Y_c match even more closely during subsequent iterations. This is called a competitive learning. Using the Euclidean distance measure for matching, the identification of the winner can be mathematically represented as:

$$\| X_i - Y_c \| = \underset{\forall j \le m}{\text{Min}} \| X_i - Y_j \| \tag{1}$$

Y_c is the closest match to the input sample X_i from mean squared error point of view. Alternatively, since minimization of error is also equivalent to maximizing the cross correlation, $\text{Max}\ (Y_j^t X_i);\ \forall j \le m$ can also be used to compute Y_c.

Now Y_c is updated according to the following rule in order to make the match even closer between successive iterations, t and t+1:

$$Y_j(t+1) = Y_j(t) + \alpha(t)(X_i - Y_j(t)) \qquad \text{for } j = c \tag{2}$$

$$Y_j(t+1) = Y(t) \qquad \text{for } j \ne c$$

where $\alpha(t)$ is a monotonically decreasing sequence of scalar values with respect to t, making the error minimization converge locally. When the updating rule of Equation 2 is applied, the error minimizes asymptotically. For every sample presented to the system, a particular entry in the set ψ changes in such a way that the overall error in mapping minimizes. The input sample X_i is selected randomly from the event set ξ.

The above competitive learning is often implemented by accumulating the number of training samples from ξ that map onto same location of the codebook, ψ, based on Equation 1, and then performing the updating operation in a single step by using the mean of the samples that mapped onto each of the codebook locations. This is the K-means algorithm. In K-means, the initial state $Y_i \in \psi$ for all $i \in (1..m)$ is selected from input sample set, ξ, randomly, and then the above two steps of deciding winners and updating are carried out iteratively until convergence.

The K-means algorithm maps input samples onto one of m different codebook vectors. The mapping is done regardless of the index value of, i, of the codebook vector, thereby showing that the m cells act independently. In other words, the input vectors are mapped on the index i in a haphazard order. The impact of this in pattern recognition accuracy is debatable, but it certainly slows the classification speed of incoming features, because of the exhaustive search required to determine the matching pattern in the index range.

This haphazard mapping is contrary to biological cells or neurons, which interact spatially to provide a topologically ordered map of input features. Kohonen's work on SOFM achieves this topological property of the neural systems by modifying the update rule in Equation 2.

Specifically, SOFM training process relates the value of $Y_i \in \psi$ to the index i of the codebook, which is treated as a two-dimensional lattice space ($m = m_r x m_c$). Topological ordering is achieved by allowing lateral interaction among the cells. Thus, the updating rule not only applies to the winner but also to other cells in a neighborhood N_c. However, the degree to which each cell in N_c is affected by this updating varies with the distance of the cell from the winner. The winner is affected most so that the value changes rapidly to match the input sample closer. The nearest neighbors are updated to a higher degree than the farther ones. This updating can be obtained by modifying the Equation 2 in the following way:

$$Y_j(t+1) = Y_j(t) + h_{cj}(t) \, \varepsilon(t) \, (X_i - Y_j(t)) \qquad \text{for } j \in N_c \qquad (3)$$

$$Y_j(t+1) = Y_j(t) \qquad \text{for } j \notin N_c$$

The coefficient $h_{cj}(t)$ is a spatial function which is largest for the most active cell $j = c$, and tapers off exponentially as the distance between c and j increases. Initially the function is selected so that its spatial spread is large enough to enable topological organization on a global scale. The spread of the function should decrease gradually as a function of iteration.

Theoretically, the coefficient $h_{cj}(t)$ can be any function peaking at $j = c$, and tapering of as ‖j - c‖ increases. However, the following function seems to be most appropriate:

$$h_{cj}(t) = h_{cc} \exp(-(c-j)^2/\sigma^2(t)). \qquad (4)$$

where h_{cc} typically equals 0.8. σ^2 is a function of t allowing for localizing the updating of $Y_j(t)$ asymptotically with t to the winner at c. Here $\sigma(t)$ is given by:

$$\sigma(t) = \sigma_0(\sigma_f/\sigma_0)^{t/t_{max}} \qquad (5)$$

From the Equation 5 it is clear that as the number of iterations increases, $\sigma(t)$ decreases, making $h_{cj}(t)$ spatially less spread out. As t approaches t_{max}, the updating becomes localized to c. The initial value, σ_0, and final value, σ_f, are typically selected to be 0.8 and 0.1, respectively.

The coefficient $\varepsilon(t)$ is called the learning rate, which is again a function of iteration. An initially large value of $\varepsilon(t)$, helps in learning the event space much faster. However, as time goes on (for larger iterations) the learning rate should decrease to a smaller value, stabilizing the learning process. The variation of $\varepsilon(t)$ with iteration, t, is given in Equation 5:

$$\varepsilon(t) = \varepsilon_0(\varepsilon_f/\varepsilon_0)^{t/t_{max}} \qquad (6)$$

where, typically, $\varepsilon_f = 0.1$, and $\varepsilon_0 = 0.8$.

B. VQ using SOFM algorithm

The SOFM algorithm can easily be used as an optimal quantizer of the input space, ξ, into an output space, ψ, containing fewer number of samples, using a set of training samples. The neurons are arranged in a rectangular lattice. The size of the lattice can be determined from the rate and distortion specifications of the compression scheme. As per the above algorithm description, each neuron holds a representative vector, or codebook entry, for a set of similar patterns in the input space.

Initially, all lattice locations are given random vectors values. Further, the input image is decomposed into several nonoverlapping two-dimensional windows of size $k = w_r x w_c$. The window position in the image is selected randomly to avoid any order dependency during the training process.

Next, the network is presented with an input pattern. The winner is determined by searching the entire lattice for a vector that matches the input vector closest. This can be obtained by computing the cross correlation between the input vector and the current codebook. The lattice location corresponding to maximum cross correlation is designated as the winner. The winner, and the cells around the winner in the neighborhood specified by Equations 4 and 5 are updated according to Equation 3.

This processes is performed for all vectors in the input image. One pass through the image is called an epoch. The learning is continued for several epochs until the cells do not change their contents appreciably in the consecutive epochs.

After the above training phase comes the coding phase, in which the image is scanned in raster scan mode to extract vectors. For each vector extracted, the location of the cell which holds the vector that most closely matches the input vector is determined by exhaustive search of the codebook. This positional information of the cell or index of codebook is recorded or transmitted as the code for the given input vector. The decoding phase is a simple table lookup process assuming that the codebook is available to the decoder.

Kohonen's SOFM has been used for hierarchical vector quantization in which time series data are quantized in computationally realistic times (Luttrel, 1989a). Essentially the same technique has been extended to images (Luttrell, 1988; Luttrell, 1989b; Mann and Haykin, 1990).

III. MasPar Implementation of Kohonen's SOFM

As just noted, our VQ image compression approach based on Kohonen's SOFM consists of a training phase, coding phase, and decoding phase. The training phase consists of generating a codebook using the SOFM algorithm. This phase will be described here in great detail. The coding phase consists primarily of searching through the codebook for the best match. The decoding phase consists of a straightforward table lookup from the codebook, producing a reconstructed image.

The main drawback of our image compression approach is that the training phase based on SOFM is computationally very intensive. For every sample presented, the entire codebook must be searched to decide the winner, and the codebook must be updated in the winner's location and in the neighborhood of winner. With a naive codebook structure (an array) the algorithm makes an exhaustive search of the codebook as many times as the network is presented with training samples.

On sequential machines, search times may be improved by organizing the entries in efficient tree structures, such as pruned tree (Riskin, 1990) or K-D tree structures (Equitz, 1989). These tree structures reduce the search from O(m) to O(log m), provided the tree is nearly balanced, where m is codebook size. These speedups are obtained by effectively increasing codebook size, thus increasing storage requirements, and decreasing the compression factor. However, on parallel machines, it is straightforward to improve the search time without increasing the codebook size. Recently some attempts have been made to implement this algorithm on some parallel computational models such as Warp Systolic processors (Mann and Haykin, 1990) and transputers (Hodges, *et al*, 1990).

Being readily available in our facility, the MasPar model MP-1 was used as our implementation platform. The MasPar MP-1 is a fine grained SIMD machine with 8192 4-bit processors organized in a 128 row by 64 column array. The codebook size was set to be less than or equal to 128x64, so that each entry of codebook maps on single processor, minimizing the data movement among the processors.

VQ compression using SOFM was implemented on the MasPar MP-1 using a C-like language called MPL (MasPar Language). In MPL, parallel array data is declared as a variable of "plural" data type. A plural variable is actually an array of the processor array size, mapping 1-to-1 directly into each processor. Each element or set of elements of the plural variable is resident in the local memory of the Processing Element (PE). The plural variables can be manipulated like scalars in the sequential code. If variables are not declared as plurals, MPL automatically treats them as scalars.

A. Training

1. Initializing the Codebook. The first steps in the training process are select the codebook and vector sizes, and to initialize the codebook. The codebook size, m, and vector size, k, are normally selected based on the compression factor and distortion specifications for a particular application. However, as we noted earlier, the change in compression rate, r, is more rapid with k than m. Therefore, larger-sized codebooks provide improvement in signal to noise ratio without appreciably affecting compression ratio (doubling the codebook size reduces the compressor rate by only one bit/pixel).

Further, in the MasPar implementation, the computational requirement, T, is unaffected by codebook size as long as it is less than the PE array size. However, when the codebook size is more than PE array size, the computational requirements go up as follows:

$$T = T_0 \lceil m/nproc \rceil \qquad \text{for } m > nproc$$

where nproc is number of PE's in the array (size of PE array), and m is the size of codebook. T_0 is computational requirement for m = nproc.

In light of the above, the best choice for codebook size in the MasPar implementation is an integer multiple of the number of processors in the MasPar, nproc. Further adjustments in compressor rate can be best achieved by varying the vector size, k.

The initial vectors for the codebook can be either random numbers, or randomly selected vectors from the input image. In our experiments we have used random numbers. A plural float array of random numbers between 0 and 1.0 can be generated on MasPar in few machine cycles using an MPL built-in function called p_random as follows:

```
plural float cb[k];

void initcb()
{
    for (i=0; i<k; i++) cb[i] = p_random();
}
```

2. Computing the *winner* for each sample. After the codebook is initialized, the input image pixel values are normalized with respect to maximum pixel value, and the image is decomposed into a set of vectors at randomly chosen locations in the image. The number of vectors extracted is equal to the number of pixels in the image divided by number of pixels in each vector. The vector subimage is usually selected as square, but rectangular blocks differing by a few pixels are not uncommon.

Each of these vectors are broadcast in turn to all PE's in the array, and the Euclidean distance between the input vector and codebook is computed at all locations where the PE's are active. The location where the value is minimum can be found by using the reduction operator which finds the minimum value of the array. Assuming the codebook size, m, is less than or equal to the number of processors, nproc, the MasPar MPL code for computing the winner is as follows:

```
plural float cb[k];              /* plural array codebook of dimension k */
plural unsigned char mask=0;     /* a plural mask to show the active PE's */
plural int ixproc,iyproc,iproc;  /* system variable that have x index,
                                    y index and running indexes of all PE's */
int nxproc,nyproc,nproc;         /* system variables that have values
                                    corresponding to PE array size along x and y
                                    directions and total number respectively */
int mx, my;                      /* size of codebook, m_x columns, m_y rows */
int winner (ipSamp)
float ipSamp[k];                 /* input image vector of dimension k */
{  /* mask is true for all PE's in the codebook of size m=m_x x m_y */
    if ((ixproc < mx) && (iyproc < my)) mask = 1;
    if (mask) {
        for (i = 0; i < k; i++)
            eclDist += (ipSamp[i] - cb[i]) * (ipSamp[i] -cb[i]);
        if (eclDist == reduceMinf(eclDist))
            loc = reduceMin32(iproc);
    } /* end if */
    return(loc);
} /* end winner */
```

The location of the winner for input vector, "ipSamp" is "loc." After updating the codebook (see below), this process is repeated to find the winner for the next input vector.

3. Updating. Once the winner is determined, the codebook is updated in the neighborhood N_c. In the parallel implementation, the neighborhood weights are computed for a given σ and the values are stored in a plural float array, h.

```
plural int ix,iy;
plural float h, cb[k];
plural float eclDist;

void update(σ, ε, loc, ipSamp)
int loc;
float  σ, ε, ipSamp[k];
{
    ix = ixproc - loc % nxproc;    /* compute column and rows from loc */
    iy = iyproc - loc / nxproc;
    h  = fp_exp(((ix*ix + iy*iy)/2)/(σ*σ)); /* exponential func. for plurals */
    for (i=0; i<k; i++)  cb[i] += ε*h*(cb[i] - ipsamp[i]);
}
```

The update function is invoked after the winner is found for each input vector of dimension k, extracted from randomly chosen locations in the input image. The number of different vectors that can be extracted from the input image is equal to the number of image pixels divided by the dimension of the input vector (k). For example, for a 512x512 image and a vector size of 16 (e.g. 4x4), the number of input vectors that can be extracted is 16384. Thus, for this example, the winner is found and the codebook is updated 16384 times for one pass through the image. This one training pass is called an epoch. For a given input image, the codebook is updated until there is no appreciable change in the codebook after. from one epoch to the next. For most practical problems, for error less than 1%, the algorithm converges in 10-15 epochs.

4. Checking for convergence. After each training epoch is completed, the codebook is checked for convergence. This can be easily done as follows.

```
int converge (oldcb, cb)
plural float oldcb[k], cb[k];        /* oldcb is codebook from previous epoch */
{
for (i=0; i<k; i++) if (mask)        /* active PE's corresponding to codebook */
     eclDist += fp_fabs(oldcb[i] - cb[i]); /* absolute function for plurals */
if (reduceMaxf(eclDist) < errval)        /* errval error criterion for
                                             convergence */
     return(1);
else return(0);
}
```

5. Summary of SOFM training procedure. The overall training algorithm can be formally described as follows.

1. Set parameter values (typical values are: $\sigma_0 = 0.8$; $\sigma_f = 0.1$; $\varepsilon_0 = 0.8$; $\varepsilon_f = 0.1$; epochmax = 20; errval = 0.8).

2. Decompose the image into vectors of size k, and load into MasPar   local memory. Let this be plural float ipVect[k].

3. Initialize codebook : initcb

4. Calculate σ and ε: $\sigma = \sigma_0 * (\sigma_f/\sigma_0)^{\text{epoch/epochmax}}$
                                  $\varepsilon = \varepsilon_0 * (\varepsilon_f/\varepsilon_0)^{\text{epoch/epochmax}}$

5. Save a copy of the codebook (oldcb).

6. For every randomly selected sample "ipSamp" of "ipVect":

    compute winner: loc = winner(ipSamp)

    update codebook: update(σ,ε,loc,ipSamp)

7. increment epoch, and if (epoch = epochmax) stop training

8. if not converge(oldcb,cb) repeat steps 4-7

B. Coding

After the training phase, the codebook is frozen and used for coding images of the class whose subset was used for generating the codebook. The coding consists of searching through the codebook for every sample to be coded. Since the codebook is loaded into the PE array's local memory, the computational requirement for exhaustive search is proportional to the size of the vector, and it is independent of the size of the codebook as long as the codebook size is less than or equal to the size of the PE array. In sequential coding this search is proportional to the product of codebook size and vector size. Thus, for this case, the parallel version could be faster than the sequential search by a factor as much as the size of the codebook.

The coding procedure is as follows:

1. Extract a vector of size k from the input image (in raster scan order),

2. broadcast this vector into the local memory of all PE's,

3. compute a distance measure (such as Euclidean distance) between the vector and the codebook at each PE,

4. find the minimum of the Euclidean distance,

5. store or transmit the address bits of the PE where minimum value of the Euclidean measure is obtained.

6. Repeat 1-5 for until the entire image is scanned.

The coding procedure is basically the same as computing the winner in one epoch of the training phase. The difference is in the order in which the vectors are extracted from the image. While in the coding phase the data can be extracted in any convenient order, in the training phase the extraction should be random to avoid introducing an order dependent bias into the codebook.

C. Decoding

Decoding is reconstructing the image from the address bits of each vector. This is a table lookup process in which the codebook vector for each address is substituted for the image data values. This process is sequential and can be carried out on sequential machines more efficiently than parallel machines.

IV. Results and Discussion

The training and coding phases of our SOFM-based VQ image compression approach are computationally intensive, since they involve exhaustive searches through the codebook for every input vector. The MasPar implementation enables training and coding in computationally realistic times.

In our tests, vectors of size 4x4 or 4x8 were extracted at random locations of the image when generating the codebook in the training phase. The number of training samples extracted from the image in each epoch was equal to the number of pixels in the image divided by the vector size.

The codebook generally converged in about 10 epochs (approximately 16000 updates for 512x512 pixel images). The mean squared error (MSE) between the original image and the image reconstructed (coded and decoded) from the codebook was used as the convergence criteria. If the MSE from one epoch to the next did not change by more than given threshold value, convergence was assumed, and the codebook was frozen.

A plot of MSE versus epochs is shown in Figure 1. The MSE asymptotically becomes 15.9 for a compression ratio of 11 for one of the test images. Each epoch takes approximately 40 seconds of MasPar time and so the codebook generation takes as much as 6-7 minutes on the MasPar.

Since training is normally an off-line process, the training timings are not critical. However, the coding of the image is usually required to be carried out in real time. To code an image of 512x512 8-bit pixels, it takes approximately 30 seconds on MasPar, or approximately 14 microseconds per bit.

The Signal Noise Ratio (SNR) improvement of coding as a function of epoch is shown in Figure 2. Both MSE and SNR do not show appreciable improvement beyond 10 epochs.

A vector size of 4x4 with a codebook of size 64x64 corresponds to a compression ratio of $(4*4*8)/\log_2(64*64) \cong 11$, assuming that a pixel has 8 bit gray level resolution. Similarly, a 4x8 vector size with the same codebook size results in compression ratio of approximately 22. The resulting address bit stream can be further compressed using a lossless compression technique such as Lempel-Ziv, giving an additional compression factor of around 1.5. Thus, the results given here correspond to compression ratios of as much as 15 to 30.

Since the size of the codebook is generally very large, one cannot afford to transmit the codebook for every image. Further, a codebook cannot be generated while coding the image. Therefore, our approach is to generate an "optimal" codebook for a class of images and to code all the images belonging to that class. Thus the code/decode scheme should have set of codebooks that are optimized for different classes of images. One question to be addressed is how broad these image classes can be.

Band 4 of set of Landsat Thematic Mapper (TM) images was selected for our compression experiments. The class of images consists of Washington, DC image (urban - Figure 3a.), and an image from west of New Orleans, LA (rural - Figure 3b.). In our experiments the codebook generated by Washington, DC image was used for coding and decoding the New Orleans image and vice versa to validate the codebook for images belonging to this relatively broad class, for both compression ratios.

The codebook generated using the Washington, DC image was used to code itself, giving compression ratios of 11 and 22. The results of the compression are shown in Figure 4 (a-b). Absolute error images (pixel to pixel error), or difference images between the original image and coded and decoded images, are shown in Figure 4 (c-d). As may be expected, the performance of compression is poor at edges or high spatial frequency locations.

The same codebook was also used for coding and decoding New Orleans image. The results of the compression are shown in Figure 5 (a-b) for compression ratios 11 and 22, respectively. The difference images are shown in Figure 5 (c-d).

To substantiate the generality of this compression scheme, band 4 from a set of Thematic Mapper (TM) images of mineralogical interest were selected. The input set consists of 6 subimages of 512x512 images extracted from single frame (Figure 6). The first three images shown in Figure 6 (a-c) were used to generate the codebook and then this codebook was used to code/decode all the images of the set. The results for a compression ratio of 11 are shown in Figure 7 (a-f). Results for a 22 compression ratio are shown in Figure 8 (a-f).

Table 1 gives the MSE and SNR measures for the reconstructed images in Figures 4, 5, 7 and 8. We note that the cases where codebook was not generated from the image that was coded compare favorably with the cases where the codebook was generated from the same image that was coded.

Our experiments lead us to conclude that image compression using Neural Net models has a large potential in space applications for coding images and transmitting them within bandwidth limitations. VLSI implementations, and fault tolerance capabilities of these model, make them very attractive for space applications.

Acknowledgments

This work was supported by the Office of Aeronautics, Exploration and Technology of the National Aeronautics and Space Administration. Thanks also to Raul Garza-Robles for his technical assistance in producing image prints and to Panchapagesan Murali for computer programming support.

References

1. Buzo, A., Gray, A. H., Jr., and Gray, R. M., and Markel, J. D. (1980), "Speech Coding Based upon Vector Quantization," *IEEE Transactions on Acoustics Speech and Signal Processing*, **ASSP-28**, pp. 562-574.
2. Equitz, W. (1989), "A New Vector Quantization Clustering Algorithm," *IEEE Transactions on Acoustics, Speech, and Signal Processing*, **Vol. 37, No. 10**, pp. 1568-1575.
3. EROS Data Center internal report (1990).
4. Gersho, A. and Cuperman, V. (1983), "Vector Quantization: A Pattern-Matching Technique for Speech Coding," *IEEE Communications Magazine*, December 1983.
5. Gersho, A. and Ramamurthi, B. (1982), "Image Coding using Vector Quantization," *Proceedings of the IEEE International Conference on Acoustics Speech and Signal Processing 1*, pp. 428-431, April 1982.
6. Gray, R. M. (1984), "Vector Quantization," *IEEE ASSP Magazine*, pp. 4-28, April 1984.
7. Hodges, R. E., Wu, C.-Hwa, and Wang, C.-J. (1990), "Parallelizing the Self-Organizing Feature Map on Multi-processor System," *Proceedings of the International Joint Conference on Neural Nets*, Jan 15-19, 1990, pp. ii-141-144.
8. Kohonen, T. (1982a), "Clustering Taxonomy, and Topological Maps of Patterns," *Proceedings of the International Conference on Pattern Recognition*, pp. 114-128.
9. Kohonen, T. (1982b), "Self-Organized Formation of Topologically Correct Feature Maps," *Biological Cybernetics*, **Vol. 43**, pp. 59-69.
10. Kohonen, T. (1989), "Self Organizing Semantic Maps," *Biological Cybernetics*, **Vol. 61**, pp. 241-254.
11. Kohonen, T. (1990), "The Self-Organizing Map," *Proceedings of the IEEE*, **Vol. 78, No. 9**, pp. 1464-1480.
12. Linde Y., Buzo, A., and Gray, R. M. (1975), "An Algorithm for Vector Quantizer Design", *IEEE Transactions on Communication*, **Vol. 28, No. 1**, pp. 84-95.
13. Lookabaugh, T. M. and Gray, R. M. (1989), "High Resolution Quantization Theory and the Vector Quantizer Advantage," *IEEE Transactions on Information Theory*, **Vol. 35, No. 5**.
14. Luttrell, S. P. (1988), "Image Compression using A Neural Network," *Proceedings of the Eighth Annual International Geoscience and Remote Sensing Symposium*, Edinburgh, Scotland., pp. 1231-1238.

15. Luttrell, S. P. (1989a), "Hierarchical Vector Quantization," *IEEE Proceedings*, **Vol. 136, No. 6**, pp. 405-413.
16. Luttrell, S. P. (1989b), "Image Compression using a Multilayer Neural Network," *Pattern Recognition Letters*, pp. 1-7.
17. Mann, R. and Haykin, S. (1990), "A parallel Implementation of Kohonen Feature Maps on the Warp Systolic Computer," *Proceedings of the International Joint Conference on Neural Nets*, Jan. 15-19, 1990, pp. ii-84-87.
18. Murali, P., Wechsler, H., and Manohar, M. (1990), "Fault-Tolerance and Learning Performance of the Back-Propagation Algorithm Using Massively Parallel Implementation," *Proceedings of the Third Symposium on the Frontiers of Massively Parallel Computation*, College Park, MD, Oct. 8-10, 1990, pp. 364-367.
19. Nasrabadi, N. and King, R. A. (1988), "Image Coding Using Vector Quantization: A Review," *IEEE Transactions on Communication*, **Vol. 36, No. 8**, pp. 957-971.
20. Ramamoorthy, P. A. and Potu, B., and Tran T. (1989), "Bit-Serial VLSI Implementation Vector Quantizer for Real-Time Image Coding," *IEEE Transactions on Circuits and Systems*, **Vol. 36, No. 10**, pp. 1281-1290.
21. Ramapriyan, H. K. (1990), "The EOS Data and Information System," *AIAA/NASA Second International Symposium on Space Information Systems*, Pasadena, CA, Sept. 17-19, 1990.
22. Riskin, E. A. (1990), "Variable Rate Vector Quantization," A Ph. D. Dissertation submitted to the Electrical Engineering Department, Stanford University, May 1990.
23. Shannon, C. E. (1948), "A Mathematical Theory of Communication," *Bell systems Technical Journal*, **27**, pp. 379-423.

Table 1. MSE and SNR measures between the original and reconstructed images for the reconstructed images in Figures 4, 5, 7 and 8.

Figure	MSE	SNR	Figure	MSE	SNR
4a	15.23	9.40	5a	32.99	22.60
4b	29.83	6.50	5b	79.98	18.79
7a	55.16	14.50	8a	101.69	11.85
7b	31.03	13.35	8b	60.21	10.47
7c	56.28	12.60	8c	100.57	10.12
7d	68.26	16.36	8d	127.51	13.65
7e	31.13	14.64	8e	57.77	11.96
7f	53.09	11.22	8f	102.47	8.36

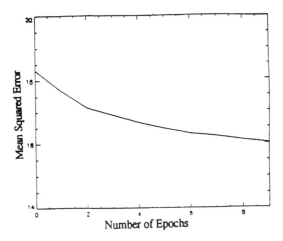

Figure 1. Mean Squared Error plot

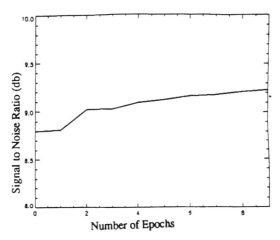

Figure 2. Signal to Noise Ratio plot

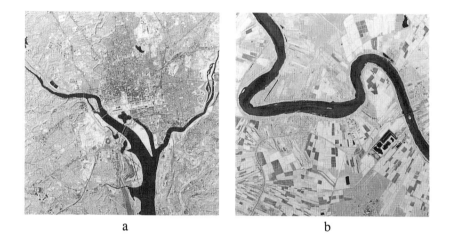

a   b

Figure 3. (a) TM image of Washington, DC image (band4), (b) TM image of New Orleans (band 4).

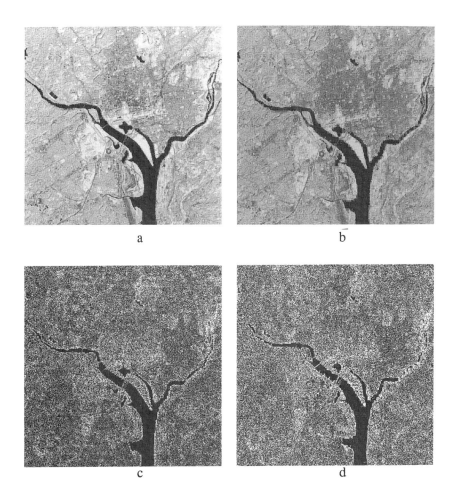

a

b̄

c

d

Figure 4. Compression results for the Washington, DC image using the codebook generated by Washington, DC image. Reconstructed images (a) compression ratio (CR) = 11 (b) CR = 22. Difference images (c) of a (d) of b.

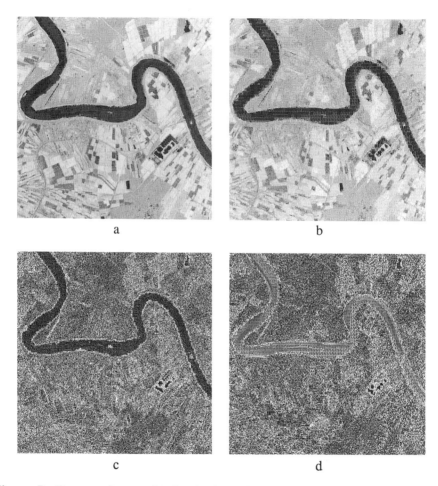

a

b

c

d

Figure 5. Compression results for the New Orleans image using the codebook generated by Washington, DC image. Reconstructed images (a) compression ratio (CR) = 11 (b) CR = 22. Difference images (c) of a (d) of b.

Figure 6. (a-f) Fish Lake images.

Figure 7. Compression results of Fish Lake images for CR = 11. The images shown in Figure 6 (a-c) were used for training and the resulting codebook was used for coding all images.

a   b

c   d

e   f

Figure 8. Compression results of Fish Lake images for CR = 22. The images shown in Figure 6 (a-c) were used for training and the resulting codebook was used for coding all images.

II.9

Self - Organizing
Maps and
Computer Vision

ERKKI OJA

Lappeenranta University of Technology
Lappeenranta, Finland

I. Introduction

A. Machine Vision and Neural Networks

A top-down view of a general-purpose machine vision system is to see it as consisting of consequent layers or levels. The inputs entering at the lowest level are the iconic raw images, which are digitized into discrete arrays of pixels. The final outputs coming out of the uppermost level are descriptions of the contents of the input images, perhaps expressed in verbal form, depending on the application. The same basic formalism applies to other branches of pattern recognition as well. In the modern state-of-the-art (see e.g. Ballard and Brown, 1982), it seems that no single system methodology can solve the entire problem. Many types of technique are needed within these levels.

At the *low level*, dealing directly with the raw sensory data, numerical

368

and statistical methods must be used to perform filtering, transformations, and pattern recognition of basic primitives. At the *high level*, symbolic or AI type processing is almost inevitable. Likewise, the data structures used to represent the relevant contents of the image at different system levels are different: large numerical arrays at low level, and highly compressed and invariant symbolic structures like graphs at high level. The computational requirements influence the kinds of processors and grade of parallelism at various stages. Thus a contemporary machine vision system is a *hybrid* architecture both from the algorithmic, software, and hardware point of view. It consists of a set of parallel and hierarchically organized modules, each having its own task and its own internal data representations and processes.

Between the low level and the high level, there is a region of computation with moderate degree of data parallelism and moderate complexity. It is an open question whether the processing at this *intermediate level* should be symbolic or numerical. In cognitive science, the term *subsymbolic* is often used to describe such intermediate processing, which underlies and implements the symbolic level in the human visual information processing task. Although the artificial machine vision system outlined above is certainly very different from any biological vision, some motivation for using subsymbolic or presymbolic techniques in the intermediate level can be obtained from the study of neural mechanisms underlying human cognitive processes.

Artificial neural networks have been proposed as a new revolutionary kind of computing tool for sensory information processing in pattern recognition systems. Much of the research is centered on individual network models, but it seems that in a complicated engineering task like machine vision, a *system-level view* of neural networks would be highly desirable. Individual artificial neural networks are then seen as components in a larger information processing system which also contains "conventional" modules like filtering or logical inference (see Fig. 1.).

This view is visible in some software efforts (Treleaven, 1989; Koikkalainen and Oja, 1990). The system-level view complies well with the above notion of the hybrid machine vision architecture: some of the modules in the machine vision system could be neural networks. The problem is then what is the most appropriate level for neural network modules.

It is argued here that the *intermediate level of computer vision* is the best place to use neural net modules at present. First, the degree of data parallelism is suitable as compared to low and high levels, respectively. At the lowest level, massive data parallelism but relatively simple instruction streams occur, and $N \times N$ SIMD-type processors are needed in principle

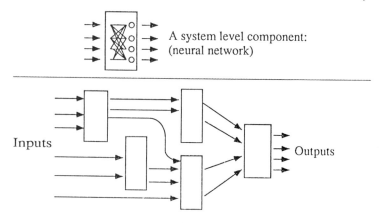

Figure 1. A system level network

to handle an $N \times N$ digital image. This means fine-grained parallelism between very simple processors numbering from a quarter of a million to more than a million. In practice, this is handled by efficient pipeline techniques applied to smaller arrays. At the high level, one powerful serial processor or a coarse-grained net of a few MIMD-type processors are generally used to perform relatively complicated operations like search on highly compressed and structural data representations. The degree of data parallelism in the intermediate level is between these two, perhaps of the order of N. This means that neural networks of a few hundred units could be used, which is computationally feasible in emulations and available in hardware in near future.

Second, the characteristics of the information processing tasks in the intermediate level are most suitable, again relative to the low and high level tasks. In lowest level image processing some central tasks are noise filtering, deblurring, or geometrical transformations, which are often data independent fixed operations to correct the deficiencies of the imaging system. They are followed by operations like histogram equalization, thresholding, and local edge detection. For all of them there exist efficient methods developed over a long time in the domain of digital signal processing. Although neural networks, e.g. Multi-Layer Perceptrons, can now be applied to the same tasks, it is questionable whether they can compete with these conventional standard solutions well enough.

At high level machine vision, state-space search or symbolic processing is needed. Again this is an area that is difficult for neural networks, although connectionist nets and optimization networks like the Boltzmann machine can be applied to some high-level tasks, e.g. matching structured object representations (Xu and Oja, 1990).

In the intermediate level, the central tasks are segmentation, feature extraction, shape analysis, and texture analysis, by which high-level relational structures describing the relevant contents of the image could be automatically formed. These problems involve *learning* of the appropriate features, both local and global, followed by categorization and representation of objects based on these features. Because feature extraction and pattern recognition are the most central application areas of neural networks today, it can be expected that neural nets could be successfully applied to some subproblems at this level.

B. Unsupervised and Supervised Learning

In pattern recognition and machine learning, two basic types of problems are encountered. In *supervised learning*, the learning system is required to form categorizations or other mappings on the space of input patterns based on a training sample: for a set of items in the input space, the correct classification or another desired output value is known, and the system tries to estimate the mapping from inputs to desired outputs based on the sample. In *unsupervised* learning, no desired outputs are known to the system, but learning proceeds driven by the input data alone. A concrete example of unsupervised techniques is *clustering* in which a sample of input items are given and the goal is to divide them into a set of clusters in such a way that some relevant criterion, often related to inter-cluster and intra-cluster variances, is minimized.

Both supervised and unsupervised neural networks have been used in various stages of the computer vision problem. A supervised network can be used for image processing if there exists a training set of corresponding unprocessed and processed images. However, there are some inherent problems.

First, to get the desired outputs, some conventional processing techniques must be used. It is doubtful whether the neural net can learn to produce a better image than the training image, and so replacing the conventional technique by the neural net is questionable. Second, in a modular system consisting of many subsequent processing levels, while the desired overall behavior of the system can be specified, it may not be evident at all what the desired outputs of each given module should be. Especially in feature extraction, it is important to find features that are *independent of the input category*, since the categories are not known at the time when the feature extractors are applied. Thus knowledge of the class of the input pattern is not appropriate as the desired output in the feature extraction phase.

It seems that in many cases unsupervised learning networks are the only available solution for extracting features and image primitives, on which more complicated object representations can be built. This does not mean that supervised techniques would not be needed: at higher levels, when *semantic interpretations* must be given to some primitives in order to use symbolic processing, such names are best given by supervised techniques.

It is the purpose of this chapter to show how an unsupervised neural network, the *Self-Organizing Feature Map* (SOFM) introduced by Kohonen (1982) can be applied to some tasks in intermediate level machine vision. A possible role for the SOFM is outlined, followed by two case studies, originally introduced by the author and his coauthors. They are *texture feature extraction* from textured unsegmented images (Lampinen and Oja, 1989) and *global curve feature extraction* from binary images (Xu, Oja, and Kultanen 1990a). Such features are widely used in machine vision systems to segment digital images and to find compressed representations for regions and boundaries, and many conventional techniques exist for these problems. It is therefore important to find out whether artificial neural networks can be used and how the results obtained with them compare to those of standard non-neural methods. It is also shown that sometimes the insights gained by using neural networks can actually lead to new developments also in the more conventional algorithms.

2. The Self-Organizing Feature Map and Feature Detection

A. Basic Formalism

One of the best-known neural networks in the unsupervised category is the Self-Organizing Feature Map (SOFM) introduced by Kohonen (1982). It belongs to the class of *vector coding* algorithms. In vector coding, the problem is to place optimally a fixed number of vectors, the codewords, into the input space which is usually a high-dimensional real space. Coding facilitates data compression and makes possible postprocessing using the discrete signal codes, e.g. Markov model techniques.

One way to understand the SOFM is to consider it as a neural network implementation of vector coding: each codeword is the weight vector of a neural unit. In the SOFM, the neurons are arranged to a 1-, 2- or multidimensional *lattice* such that each neuron has a set of neighbors. The goal of learning is not only to find the most representative code vectors for the input space in mean square sense, but at the same time to realize a *topological mapping* from the input space to the lattice of neurons. Mathematically, this can be defined as follows.

For any point x in the input space Ω, one or several of the codewords are closest to it. Assume that w_i is the closest among all codewords:

$$\|x - w_i\| = min\|x - w_j\|, j = 1, ..., N \qquad (1)$$

To make the correspondence unique, assume that the codeword with the smallest index is chosen if several codewords happen to be at exactly the minimum distance from x. The unit i having the weight vector w_i is then called the *best-matching unit* for vector x, and index $i = i(x)$ can be considered as the corresponding code value, or *output* of the map. By the above relation, the input space is mapped to the discrete set of neurons.

By a topological mapping the following property is meant: if an arbitrary point $x \in \Omega$ is mapped to unit i, then all points in neighborhoods of x are mapped either to i itself or to one of the units in the neighborhood of i in the lattice. Whether the topological property can hold for all units, however, depends on the dimensionalities of the input space and the neuron lattice. In some earlier works on topologically ordered neuron layers (Amari, 1980), such a mapping was made one-to-one by using a continuum instead of the discrete neuron lattice and by requiring that neighborhoods of points are mapped to neighborhoods. Because no topological maps between two spaces of different dimensions can exist, a two-dimensional neural layer can only follow locally two dimensions of the multidimensional input space. This seems to be the general principle used in sensory areas of the cortex (Amari, 1980; Kohonen, 1982, 1990); biological motivation is also given in (Willshaw and von der Malsburg, 1976).

The fact that the mapping has a topological property has the advantage that it is more error-tolerant: a perturbation of the input may cause the output (the index of the best-matching unit) to jump from the original unit to one of its neighbors, but usually not to an arbitrary position on the lattice, as would be the case if no neighborhood relation existed among the neurons. In a layered neural system in which the next layer "reads" the feature map but does not know the original inputs, such a property is essential to guarantee stable behavior.

The well-known Kohonen algorithm for self-organization of the code vectors is as follows:

1. Choose initial values randomly for the weight vectors w_i of the units i

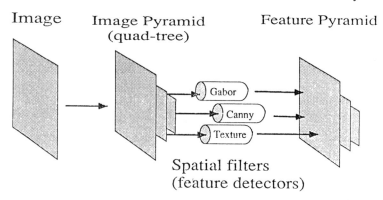

Figure 2. Low-level processing

2. Repeat Steps 3,4 until the algorithm has converged:

3. Draw a sample x from the probability distribution of the input samples and find the best matching unit i according to Eq. (1)

4. Adjust the weight vectors of all units by

$$w_j := w_j + \gamma * h_r * (x - w_j) \tag{2}$$

where γ is a gain factor and h_r is a function of the distance $r = \|i - j\|$ of units i and j measured along the lattice.

(In the original version (Kohonen, 1982), the neighborhood function h_r was equal to 1 for a certain neighborhood of i, and 0 elsewhere. The neighborhood and the gain γ should slowly decrease in time).

The convergence and the mathematical properties of this algorithm have been considered by several authors, e.g. (Kohonen, 1982; Ritter and Schulten, 1989; Luttrell, 1989).

B. Feature Extraction

The role of the SOFM in feature extraction is to construct optimal codewords in abstract feature spaces. Individual feature values can then be replaced by these codes, which results in data compression. Furthermore, hierarchical systems can be built in which the outputs from the maps are again used as input in subsequent layers. The topological property of the feature maps is then essential for low-error performance.

This idea is presented more concretely in Figures 2 and 3. Fig. 2 shows the low-level processing stages of an exemplary machine vision system,

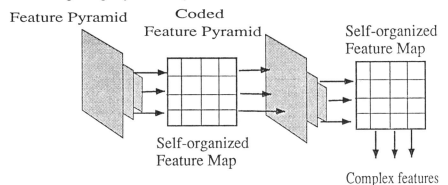

Figure 3. Using the SOFM for feature coding

now under development at the Data Processing Laboratory, Lappeenranta University of Technology. To achieve multiresolution feature extraction, the image (typically of size 512×512) is first presented as a quad-tree. This is a standard technique in which the image at each resolution is obtained from the previous one by combining each 2×2 pixel square into just one pixel, whose gray level is the quantized average of the 4 pixels.

As argued in Section 1, no neural networks are used at the low level, but standard feature extractors like Gabor filters, the Canny edge detector, or some texture window transformations are applied. This results in a *feature pyramid*, in which each pixel in the original image has been replaced by a vector of values given by the feature detectors at that position. This is done at each resolution level independently; feature detectors can be resolution dependent, or the same detectors can be used at all resolution levels.

At the next stage, shown in Fig. 3, the information in the feature vectors must be compressed. This is achieved by vector coding, in which the feature vectors x are compared to a set of predefined code vectors $w_1, \ldots, w_N$ according to Eq. (1) and replaced by their best matching code vectors. When the feature vector at each pixel location in the feature pyramid is replaced by the corresponding code, the *Coded Feature Pyramid* is obtained.

This is a stage where the SOFM is used. During a separate learning phase, the weight vectors of the SOFM neurons develop into code vectors under unsupervised learning in which a representative training set of feature vectors is used. The learning is slow, but it is an "off-line" operation. After the map has been formed, it can be used as such to code images with similar statistical properties with the training images.

Note that it is not necessary to use the values of the codewords, i.e.

weight vectors of the neural units, in the coded feature pyramid; they are used in comparison only, to find the best-matching unit. Some discrete names or values to indicate each unit can be used, e.g. in the case of a 2-dimensional lattice the two indices (i, j) giving the location of the unit will suffice, or a color code can be used in which each unit has its own characteristic color. The codes should have the property, however, that the ordering of the units is preserved by the code, since the codes indicate the positions of the units on the map.

Neither is it necessary at this stage to give any semantic meanings to each unit; it is enough for the subsequent processing stages that the codes are unique in the sense that the same input is always coded in the same way. This is guaranteed by the mathematical mapping from input space to the discrete codes.

At the next stage in Fig. 3, the codes from the coded feature pyramid are combined either spatially or over different resolutions, or both, and such combinations are further used as inputs to another SOFM which gets tuned to characteristic combinations of codes. The vector codes which are formed by the weight vectors of this map represent then more complex features. They are also more general because some variations have been filtered out by the two vector coding steps. This can be followed by more coding steps in which previous features are combined, or by a supervised neural network or other classifier in which the codes are assigned to a priori defined categories.

Exactly the formalism described above was used to find features for some parts of human faces like eyes and mouth in a size and location independent way in (Lampinen and Oja, 1990). The first filtering step was done using Gabor filters. Finally, the features were classified by a simple supervised classifier.

In the following, a subproblem of the above processing system, the formation of image features and the ensuing coded feature image, are explained more concretely in two special cases of practical importance, texture analysis and global curve segment detection. In these experiments, the original image was given at one resolution only but the results could be generalized immediately to the multiresolution case.

3. Texture segmentation by the SOFM

This section follows closely the work of Lampinen and Oja, 1989. Consider the digital 64 × 64 image shown in Figure 4a. This was artificially made from four natural texture images, each occupying one quarter of the image. Such pictures typically arise in applications like remote sensing by satellite, biomedical image analysis, or industrial visual quality control. In this study, we wanted to train a neural network to form features representing different textures, which can be used to segment the image to its component textures; however, we do not give to the training algorithm any information about how many textures there are, where they are in the image, and what they look like. All these must be inferred from this one image only. Evidently, the human visual system is very good in doing this.

The first question concerns the low level feature extraction which is performed with non-neural techniques. Many choices exist for finding class-independent features (Haralick, 1979; Oja and Parkkinen, 1987). We chose to use auto-regressive models which have given excellent results in both texture classification and synthesis (Kashyap, Chellappa and Khotanzad, 1982). Consider a pixel $x_{i,j}$ and some neighborhood $N(i,j)$. A single texture, due to its approximate periodicity, can often be assumed to satisfy the model

$$x_{i,j} = \sum_{(k,l) \in N(i,j)} x_{k,l} \omega_{i,j,k,l} + e_{i,j} \tag{2}$$

with the residual term $e_{i,j}$ small. The model is space-invariant so that the weights $\omega_{i,j,k,l}$ only depend on $|i - k|, |j - l|$. Statistical estimates of the weights can be solved with least mean squares techniques: in the present context, an especially suitable algorithm is the adaptive least mean squares (alms) algorithm of Widrow and Hoff (1960). Let $X_{i,j}$ and W denote vectors consisting of $x_{k,l}$ and $\omega_{i,j,k,l}$, respectively. Note that while the values of pixels in $X_{i,j}$, being in a specific location in the image, depend on the location (i,j), it is assumed that the weights are space invariant. Eq. (2) can be written as

$$x_{i,j} = X_{i,j}^T W + e_{i,j}. \tag{3}$$

In one step in the alms algorithm, a sample pixel with its neighborhood pixels $(x_{i,j}, X_{i,j})$ (in the following called a *sample point*) are drawn from a training image (representing in this case only one texture) and the residual $e_{i,j}$ is computed from Eq. (3) using the current value for the weight vector W. After this, the weight vector is updated according to

$$W := W + \alpha * e_{i,j} * X_{i,j}. \tag{4}$$

This is a sample-based gradient descent algorithm for minimizing $E(e_{i,j}^2)$ which has a single global minimum with respect to W.

How to exactly choose the neighboring pixels in (2) is a question of statistical fit and computational complexity. In the present study, we chose a neighborhood of 8 pixels of which 4 pixels are to the left and 4 pixels are above the current pixel $x_{i,j}$. A better fit could be obtained with a larger neighborhood but then the learning algorithm (4) gets costly computationally.

The crucial difference in the unsupervised approach as compared to the above learning rule is that no training samples are available for each texture. That is where the SOFM can be used. Each unit on the map *represents some texture* in the sense that now the weight vectors $W^{(k)}$ of the units are interpreted as vectors W in the autoregressive models (3). Instead of stating explicitly that a certain sample point $(x_{i,j}, X_{i,j})$ belongs to a given texture, we let the units on the map *compete* over the sample point and the winning (best-matching) unit is assumed to be the one representing the correct texture model for that sample point. The best-matching unit is the one whose weight vector gives the smallest residual for the sample point in Eq. (3).

A modification for this simple competition rule must be done in practice, because natural textures are very noisy and the fit into any autoregressive model of moderate length can be poor. If only the residual for one sample point, $e_{i,j}$ is used, then there is too much randomness in picking the best-matching unit. The fact that texture is not a point property but a region property in the image suggests an improvement: it can be roughly assumed that several neighboring pixels (or rather, the pixels together with their neighborhoods) are likely to belong to the same texture. If the sample points are chosen in an orderly fashion, by taking each pixel in small neighborhoods one at a time, then it is better to base the choice of the best-matching unit not only on the present value of the residual but also on the values obtained at neighboring pixels. The following *smoothed residual* $v^{(k)}$ should be used for unit k at pixel location (i, j):

$$v^{(k)} := [\beta * e_{i,j}^{(k)} + (1 - \beta) * v^{(k)}]/(C + B_{i,j}^{(k)}) \tag{5}$$

where $e_{i,j}^{(k)}$ is the residual for unit k, obtained from Eq. (3) by using the weight vector $W^{(k)}$ of that unit, and $\beta < 1$ is a smoothing parameter. The term $B_{i,j}^{(k)}$ is the number of pixels in the 8-neighborhood of the current pixel $x_{i,j}$ (including the current pixel) such that unit k is the best-matching unit for them, and C is a constant (the value 8 is suitable). The smoothing in Eq. (5) can be started by setting $v^{(k)} = 0$ for all units.

The learning rule for the SOFM is then:

1. Choose some random initial values for the weight vectors $W^{(k)}$

of the units k on the SOFM; set all smoothed residuals $v^{(k)}$ equal to zero.

2. Scan the image point by point, and at each sample point $(x_{i,j}, X_{i,j})$ do steps 3 to 6:

3. For each unit k, compute the residual $e_{i,j}^{(k)}$ from Eq. (3) using $W^{(k)}$.

4. For each unit k, compute the smoothed residual $v^{(k)}$ from Eq. (5).

5. Find the best matching unit that gives the smallest value for $v^{(k)}$.

6. Update the weight vectors of the best-matching unit and its topological neighbors in the map by

$$W^{(k)} := W^{(k)} + \alpha * e_{i,j}^{(k)} * X_{i,j}. \tag{6}$$

As a result, the map will self-organize and some of the units will develop into feature extractors which are tuned to the most prominent textures in the training image.

To show what happens, it is convenient for demonstration purposes to use color codes for the units on the map; a 6×6 map is used, and each of its units is provided at the start with one of 36 colors, as shown in Fig. 4b. Then, to show results of the training algorithm above, each pixel $x_{i,j}$ in the image is colored by the color of the unit that is the best-matching unit for the sample point $(x_{i,j}, X_{i,j})$ in step 5. Fig. 4c shows the outcome after training: most areas of uniform texture are labeled with one color. The edges cause some difficulties due to the neighborhood $X_{i,j}$ that must be used. The other differences with respect to the a priori knowledge (which the learning algorithm never had) are sometimes very natural; e.g. the texture at left-upper corner actually consisted of two slightly different textures, in which the spacing of the dark lines was different, and the method was able to detect that.

Some knowledge of the number of prominent features in the image is revealed if the histogram of the wins scored by all units is computed. There are 4096 pixels in the image, and after training each pixel is allotted to its best-matching unit. The pixels were distributed to the 36 units according to table 1:

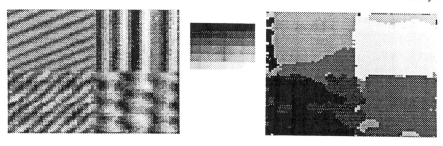

Figure 4. (a), left: the original texture image. (b),middle: the color codes of the 6×6 map. (c), right: the segmentation result after training.

5	1	3	42	95	**582**
0	0	4	38	150	213
2	7	42	**652**	291	37
6	8	21	51	14	**787**
4	2	22	14	**793**	21

Table 1. Distribution of the wins scored by each unit

The table shows rather clearly that there are 4 distinct textures in the image, whose winning units are marked by boldface in Table 1.

The resulting map can be used for segmenting the original image as shown in Fig. 4c. Note that the method is totally unsupervised: there is no a priori knowledge available for the training algorithm about how many textures there are and where they are, and no training samples from known textures could be used. The results show that the SOFM is a powerful tool in feature extraction tasks for problems of realistic scale.

4. Extracting global curve features by the SOFM

Consider now the image in Fig. 5a. When the goal is to recognize or characterize the object in the image, the usual technique is to process the image by edge detection filters to produce the edge image, shown in Fig. 5b. The Canny edge detection operator has been used here. However, since such a filter is of the local type, edges cannot be traced easily. It is an

 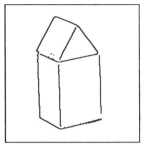 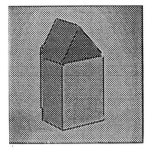

Figure 5. An object (a, left), its local edge points (b, middle) and boundary segments (c,right).*

important task to find the mathematical equations of the curve segments that comprise the edges, like the line segments in Fig. 5c. Using them, the boundary of the object can be expressed in a very compressed way, and different measurements of the object are easy.

Since a curve is defined by a set of parameters (e.g. a line by two parameters), it should be possible to tune a SOFM so that each unit will become a detector for a certain parameter vector, hence to a certain curve in the image (Oja, Xu and Kultanen, 1990; Xu, Oja and Kultanen, 1990a, b; Kultanen, Xu and Oja, 1990).

Consider now a binary edge image like the one in Fig. 5b, with co-ordinates denoted by (x, y). Assume for the moment that (x, y) are continuous. Then a curve is given by $f(a, x, y) = 0$ where $a = (a_1, \ldots, a_m)^T$ is an m-dimensional parameter vector. (For a straight line, $f(a, x, y) = y - a_1 x - a_2 = 0$). To solve for the parameter vector, we need m pixels lying on the curve. The problem is how to find m such pixels lying on the same curve without first knowing the curve segments. Again, here the SOFM can be used.

The algorithm starts by picking m pixels at random from among the edge pixels and by solving the parameter vector a. There are two possibilities: first, the m pixels are actually lying on some true curve segment in the image. Then eventually in the random picking, another set of m pixels will be drawn from the same segment, which results in exactly the same parameter vector a. The parameter vectors of the true curves will be *repeated* in the process of drawing pixel sets and solving the parame-

* (Reprinted with permission from Elsevier Science Publishers, *Pattern Recognition Letters* **11**, 335, 1990.)

ters. Second, the m pixels are not all lying on the same curve segment. The resulting parameter vector defines a nonexisting curve. It is very *unlikely* that exactly the same parameter vector will be repeated later in the process.

Thus, in the space of parameter vectors, which is now the input space to the SOFM, there are some (atomic) points with nonzero probabilities, corresponding to the true curve segments in the image. The rest of the parameter points have in theory zero probability. However, in practice the image coordinates are discrete and thus also the parameter space is discrete; the true curve parameters have relatively high probabilities and the false parameters low probabilities. If vectors from such a distribution are input to a SOFM, the units tend to get tuned to the high probability locations.

The method can be further refined and made much faster by departing from the realm of neural networks and noting a similarity between the above method and a well-known conventional technique developed for the same purpose, the Hough transform (Hough, 1962; Rosenfeld, 1969). Xu, Oja, and Kultanen (1990a) introduced the algorithm called *Randomized Hough Transform, RHT*. In that the SOFM is replaced by a dynamical tree-like data structure of nodes that have a weight vector, like artificial neurons, but once an initial value for the weight vector has been chosen it does not change any more. Instead of updating the weights in learning, the units have a *score parameter* which is used to record the number of times that this unit is the best-matching unit. The algorithm is briefly as follows:

1. Form the set P of all the edge points in the image.

2. Pick a set of m points randomly from the set P.

3. Solve the parameter vector a from the curve equation.

4. Find the best-matching unit (the unit whose weight vector is equal to a found in step 3), and increment its score value by one. If no such unit exists, then create one with weight vector a and score value 1.

5. If the updated score value is equal to a threshold, check from the image if a curve segment has been found, in which case the curve segment parameter vector and end points are recorded, all pixels in the edge image lying on that curve are removed, and all the nodes are deleted. Otherwise, draw another set of m edge points and go to 3.

The matching unit can be found easily by binary searches if the units are arranged in an m-ary tree sorted along each parameter. This ordering is easily achieved when a new node is inserted into the tree at step 4.

More details of the algorithm and its connections with other reported methods can be found in (Xu, Oja and Kultanen, 1990a), and a mathematical analysis of its performance is presented in (Xu, Oja and Kultanen, 1990b). For the edge image in Fig. 5b, the resulting edge segments are shown in Fig. 5c.

The conclusion of the RHT algorithm is that it has several advantages over the conventional Hough transform: due to the way the accumulator array is replaced by a dynamical tree, in which new nodes can be created at will, the parameter resolution and parameter scope is arbitrarily high. Both practical experiments and theoretical analysis reveal that the storage complexity of the algorithm is low, since the threshold in Step 5 can be usually quite small and the dynamical tree is flushed each time a new curve segment has been found. The computation speed is high for the same reason. For the image in Fig. 5, the 12 line segments were found about 20 times faster than with a conventionally implemented Hough transform.

It is also shown in (Xu, Oja and Kultanen, 1990a) that the RHT method is not restricted to line segments, but higher dimensional parameter vectors can be detected by the method, too. Especially for high-dimensional cases, the conventional Hough transform using an accumulator array must accumulate units belonging to hypersurfaces and this can be computationally very heavy, while the RHT method only accumulates individual nodes in all cases.

5. Conclusions

It has been the purpose to emphasize the role of unsupervised learning and self-organization in some stages of a computer vision system. Neural networks can be used in an efficient manner at the intermediate level image processing tasks, especially in global feature extraction. The term global means here that features either are not localized to small pixel neighborhoods spatially, or combine different resolutions, or otherwise represent combinations of the outputs of primary feature detectors. These combinations can be coded by a self-organizing feature map to obtain compressed representations that can be used at later stages.

The use of the SOFM in a typical intermediate level computer vision task, texture feature extraction and texture image segmentation, was demonstrated. It was also shown by an example in curve segment detection that sometimes the central characteristics of neural network learning algorithms, particularly the random sampling from the input space and the mapping of the high-dimensional input space to individual neural units, can give valuable insights in developing efficient non-neural image processing algorithms.

Acknowledgements. The author is grateful to Pasi Koikkalainen for the use of Figures 1, 2 and 3, to Jouko Lampinen for Figure 4 and to Pekka Kultanen for Figure 5. Their contribution, as well as that of Dr. Lei Xu, to the research on which this article is based is also gratefully acknowledged. The work was financed by TEKES under grant 4196/1988 under Finsoft project and the Academy of Finland.

References

Amari, S. (1980). "Topographic organization of nerve fields", *Bull. of Math. Biology 42*, pp. 339 - 364.

Ballard, D. and Brown, C. (1982). *Computer Vision*, Prentice Hall, New Jersey.

Haralick, R. (1979). "Statistical and structural approaches to texture", *Proc. IEEE 67*, pp. 786 - 804.

Hough, P. (1960)."Method and means for recognizing complex patterns". *US Patent 3069654, Dec. 18.*

Kashyap, R., Chellappa, R., Khotanzad (1982). "Texture classification using features derived from random field models", *Pattern Recognition Letters 1*, pp. 43 - 50.

Kohonen, T. (1982). "Self-organized formation of topologically correct feature maps", *Biol. Cyb. 43*, pp. 59 - 69.

Kohonen, T. (1990). "Self-Organizing Feature Map". *Proc. IEEE 78*, pp. 1464 - 1480.

Koikkalainen, P. and Oja, E. (1990). "The Carelia Simulator: a development and specification environment for neural networks". To appear in *Advances in Control Networks and Large Scale Parallel Distributed Processing*, Ablex, New York.

Kultanen, P., Xu. L. and Oja, E. (1990). "Randomized Hough Transform (RHT)". *Proc. 10th Int. Conf. on Pattern recognition*, Atlantic City.

Lampinen, J. and Oja, E. (1989). "Self-organizing maps for spatial and temporal AR models", *Proc. 6th Scand. Conf. on Image Analysis*, Oulu, Finland, pp. 120 - 127.

Lampinen, J. and Oja, E. (1990). "Distortion tolerant feature extraction with Gabor functions and topological coding", *Proc. Int. Neural Network Conf.*, Paris.

Luttrell, S. (1989). "Self-organization: a derivation from first principles of a class of learning algorithms", *Proc. Int. Joint Conf. on Neural Networks*, Washington, D.C., pp. II-495 - II-498.

Oja, E. and Parkkinen, J. (1987). "Texture subspaces". In *Pattern Recognition Theory and Applications*, NATO ASI Series Vol. F30, Springer-Verlag, Berlin, pp. 21 - 33.

Oja, E., Xu, L. and Kultanen, P. (1990). "Curve detection by an extended self-organizing map and the related RHT method", *Proc. Int. Neural Network Conf.*, Paris.

Ritter, H. and Schulten, K. (1989). "Convergence properties of Kohonen's topology conserving maps: fluctuations, stability and dimension selection", *Biol. Cyb. 60*, pp. 59 - 71.

Rosenfeld, A. (1969). *Picture Processing by Computer.* Academic Press, New York.

Treleaven, P. (1989). "Neurocomputers", Research Note 89/9, University College, Department of Computer Science, London.

Widrow, B. and Hoff, M. (1960). "Adaptive switching circuits", *1960 IRE WESCON Convention Record*, New York, pp. 96 - 104.

Willshaw, D. and von der Malsburg, C. (1976). "How patterned neural connections can be set up by self-organization", *Proc. Royal Society, B-194*, pp. 431 - 445.

Xu, L. and Oja, E. (1990). "Improved simulated annealing, Boltzmann machine, and attributed graph matching". In *Springer Lecture Notes in Computer Science 412*, Springer-Verlag, Berlin, pp. 151 - 161.

Xu, L., Oja, E. and Kultanen, P. (1990a). "A new curve detection method: Randomized Hough Transform", *Pattern Recognition Letters 11*, pp. 331 - 338.

Xu, L., Oja, E. and Kultanen, P. (1990b). "Randomized Hough Transform (RHT): theoretical analysis and extensions", *Research Report 18/1990*, *Lappeenranta Univ. of Tech., Dept. of Information Tech.*.

II.10

Region Growing Using Neural Networks

TODD R. REED

Department of Electrical and Computer Engineering
University of California
Davis, California

I. Introduction

Segmentation, the grouping of parts of an image into regions that are homogeneous with respect to one or more characteristics, is an important function in image processing and computer vision. By mapping an image representation, typically at the pixel level, into a description involving regions with common features, segmentation serves as a bridge between low-level and high-level processes.

A more formal definition of picture segmentation [1] is:

Definition 1 *Let X denote the grid of sample points for a given picture. Let Y be a subset of X containing at least two points. Then a uniformity predicate*

Neural Networks for Perception
Volume 1
Human and Machine Perception

386

$P(Y)$ *is one which assigns the value true or false to* Y *depending only on properties of the brightness matrix* $f(i,j)$ *for the points of* Y. *Furthermore, P has the property that if* Z *is a nonempty subset of* Y *then* $P(Y) = true$ *implies* $P(Z) = true$.

Definition 2 *A segmentation of the grid* X *for a uniformity predicate* P *is a partition of* X *into disjoint nonempty subsets* $\{X_i\}$ *such that*

  a) $\cup X_i = X$;

  b) *for all* $1 \leq i \leq n, X_i$ *is connected and* $P(X_i) = true$; *and*

  c) P *is false on the union of any number of adjacent members of the partition.*

It should be noted that the second definition does not imply uniqueness of the segmentation or that the number of regions, n, is as small as possible. In fact, segmentation algorithms examine only a subset of possible partitions. For an image of useful size, an exhaustive search of all possible segmentations is a practical impossibility, since the problem is NP hard. The final segmentation is heavily influenced by the subset examined.

Region growing is one of the main approaches used in segmentation. The goal in region growing is to expand (usually from starting seed points) until the boundaries of the regions are reached. The regions should be filled completely, with as few small, isolated subregions as possible. The most common criterion used in region growing is region homogeneity. Pixels, or groups of pixels, are included in a region only if their characteristics are sufficiently similar to the characteristics of the pixels already in the region. Uniformity of image intensity, color, multispectral data, and range data are all candidates as the basis for region growing [2],[3].

However, when the homogeneity of regions is decided based on the uniformity of the above characteristics, the resulting segmentation is often unsatisfactory [3]. A single, strongly textured surface in an image will be segmented into numerous small regions, rather than the single surface desired. Because textured surfaces are extremely common in natural scenes, this can be a serious difficulty. The desire to segment such scenes into meaningful partitions is the motivation for examining texture for image segmentation.

When textured regions are being considered, homogeneity can be determined using a set of texture features. Examples are features derived by the Spatial Gray Level Dependence method [4], from spatial/spatial-frequency representations such as the Wigner distribution [5], or from banks of Gabor filters [6],[7]. These features can be seen as a mechanism for mapping changes in texture to changes in gray scale. In this way, region growing techniques based on uniformity can be extended to texture segmentation. Based on one or more features, the similarity of each pixel in the image to its neighbors can then be calculated. The resulting similarity values can be considered as assigned to "connections" originating from the respective pixel locations. When the similarity between neighboring pixels is high, they are merged into a common region.

II.   Region Growing Using Neural Networks

When the problem is considered within the framework of weighted connections, a neural network approach is natural. A neuron can be associated with each pixel in the image, with a weighted input for each neighbor. Wherever the connections associated with neighboring pixels are strong (the similarity between pixels is high), the output of the neuron associated with the pixel in question will tend to be high (indicating a region pixel). When pixels are dissimilar, as at the boundaries between regions, the connections are weak and the output of the neuron will tend to be low (indicating a boundary pixel).

The first step in region growing by this method is the definition of neighboring pixels. For simplicity, we define the set of neighbors for each pixel to include only the four nearest neighbors. Extensions to larger neighborhoods are straightforward.

The similarities between each pixel and its neighbors must then be calculated. In this implementation, we have used the normalized inner product of the respective gray values in the image (or in the case of multiple features, images) as the similarity measure. Denoting the similarity between pixel i and pixel j as $S_{i,j}$,

$$S_{i,j} = \frac{1}{N} \sum_{k=1}^{N} \frac{f_k(i) f_k(j)}{max(f_k(i), f_k(j))^2} \qquad (1)$$

where $f_k(i)$ is the value at pixel i in the kth feature image, N is the number of feature images (in the case of simple gray scale region growing, $N = 1$), and $i \neq j$. Other methods could be used for measuring similarity, based on the Euclidean (or some other) distance between the pixels (or pixel vectors, in the case of multiple features), for example.

These similarities can then be used as the weights for a neural network. In this case, a simple perceptron network [8] is used. The weight $T_{i,j}$ of the connection between the neuron corresponding to a pixel i and each of its neighbors j is

$$T_{i,j} = S_{i,j} \qquad (2)$$

with $T_{i,i} = 0$. The total input to the neuron is then

$$\sum_{j \neq i} T_{i,j} I_j \tag{3}$$

where I_j is the input corresponding to neighbor j. The output of the neuron is

$$v_i = g(\sum_{j=1}^{n} T_{i,j} I_j - h_i) \tag{4}$$

where we define

$$g(x) = \begin{cases} 1 & \text{if } x \geq 0 \\ 0 & \text{if } x < 0 \end{cases} \tag{5}$$

and h_i is a threshold.

In the examples that follow, an output of 1 signifies that the pixel location associated with the neuron is part of a region, while 0 signifies a boundary point. The input to the network (which consists of a single layer) is $I_j = 1$ for all j.

It should be noted that all regions are grown simultaneously. Since the selection of seed regions is not required and the thresholds used are not image dependent (depending instead on the degree of homogeneity desired in each region), the method is essentially unsupervised.

III.   Experimental Results

A.   A Simple Two Region Case

To examine the basic behavior of this method, we first consider a simple image with two regions of constant gray value. Shown in Figure 1(a), the image is 64 by 64 pixels in size (as are all the images which follow), with gray values of 200 and 240 (on a scale of 0 to 255) for the left and right regions, respectively. The output of the network is shown in Figure 1(b), using a similarity threshold (h_i) of .475 (as for all the cases that follow, unless otherwise indicated). Pixel locations labelled '1' (indicating region pixels) are shown in white, while locations labelled '0' (boundary pixels) are shown in black. For this simple, ideal case, the results are as expected.

For a slightly more realistic case, uniformly distributed noise with a peak value of 10 (again on a scale of 0 to 255) is added to the previous image, as shown in Figure 2(a). The output of the network is shown in Figure 2(b). While the overall segmentation of the image is correct, some pixels have been incorrectly labelled. This is more prevalent in the low gray value region than in the high value region, since the average similarity is lower in that region.

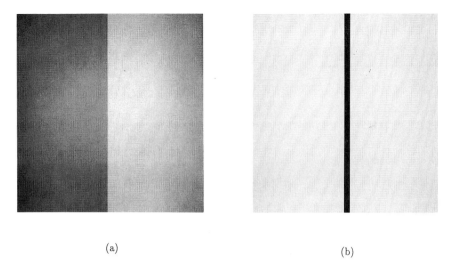

(a)   (b)

Figure 1: (a) A simple image composed of two uniform regions, and (b) the resulting segmentation.

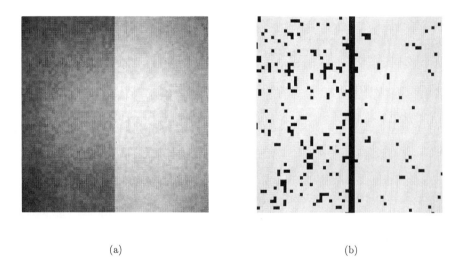

(a)   (b)

Figure 2: (a) The image from Fig. 1(a), with added noise, and (b) the segmentation which results.

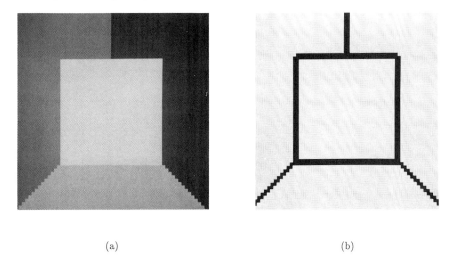

(a)   (b)

Figure 3: (a) An image composed of four uniform regions. (b) The segmented image.

B.   Multiple Regions

A somewhat more complex image, with multiple regions of differing gray values, is shown in Figure 3(a). Counterclockwise from the upper left, these regions have values 120, 160, and 200, with 240 in the center region. The output of the network is shown in Figure 3(b), with regions and boundaries properly labelled. As in the two region case, a similarity threshold of .475 was used.

Adding noise as before (uniformly distributed, with a peak value of 10), the input and output of the network are shown in Figures 4(a) and 4(b). Again the overall segmentation is correct. There is, however, a tendency to mislabel pixels as the region gray value decreases.

C.   Two Regions with a Gradual Transition Region

Since the transitions between regions are not always sharp, the ability of a method to detect distinct regions separated by gradual transitions is also of interest. Two 16 pixel wide, uniform regions, with gray values 80 on the left and 170 on the right, separated by a linear transition region 32 pixels wide, are shown in the image in Figure 5(a). The output of the network, again with a .475 similarity threshold, is shown in Figure 5(b). Because the transition represents a much larger degree of dissimilarity near the low valued region,

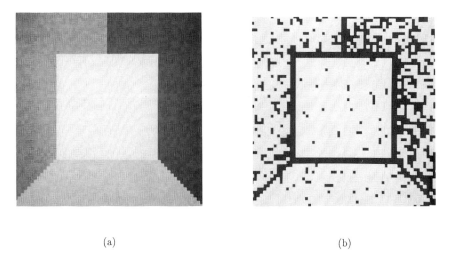

(a)   (b)

Figure 4: (a) The image from Fig. 3(a), with added noise, and (b) the resulting segmentation.

the boundary is detected very close to this region.

D.   Multiple Regions and Multiple Features

Finally, as discussed in the introduction, this method can be applied to texture (and other) segmentation problems through the use of appropriate feature images. Figure 6 shows a set of four idealized feature images, each 64 by 64 pixels in size. Although these are artificially derived images, and as such much more uniform and low-noise than encountered normally, they are similar in nature to those which might be derived based on, e.g., a Gabor filter set applied to a texture mosaic. Each feature consists of a low valued region (with a gray value of 180) and a high valued region (with a gray value of 245). The result of applying the network to this set of feature images (raising the similarity threshold to .485 due to the use of multiple features) is shown in Figure 7. As desired, the information in the individual feature images is integrated to find eight regions, none of which could be found based on a single feature.

Adding noise (uniformly distributed with a peak value of 7.5) to each image, to simulate noisy features, the feature set and segmentation shown in Figures 8 and 9 result. The overall segmentation is as desired, but there are a number of misclassified pixels. The number of these pixels increases as the

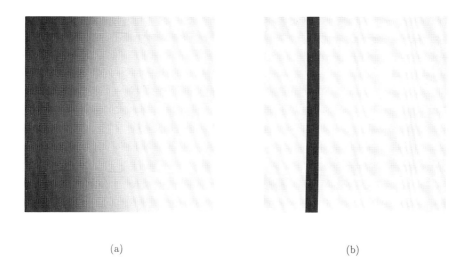

(a)   (b)

Figure 5: (a) An image with two uniform regions, separated by a gradual transition. (b) The segmentation which results.

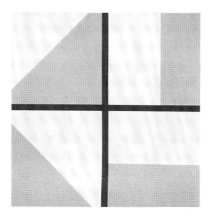

Figure 6: Four simulated feature images.

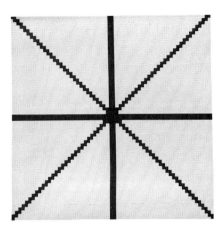

Figure 7: The segmentation produced based on the feature images of Fig. 6.

average gray level (over all feature images) of the region decreases.

IV.   Discussion

Considering the relative simplicity of this scheme, the results obtained above are reasonable. However, it would be desirable to reduce the sensitivity of the method to noise in regions with low gray values. Removing the bias in boundary locations toward regions of low gray value in cases of gradual transitions might also be worthwhile. One solution to these problems may be to adapt the similarity threshold to the average gray value in the neighborhood being considered. In this way, a lower degree of similarity can be required in low gray value regions, suppressing the labelling of pixels as boundary points in these areas.

Another approach which may address these points is the use of the weights derived above in a feedback network, such as a Hopfield [9] neural network. In this case, the total input to the ith neuron is

$$\sum_{j=1}^{n} T_{i,j} v_j(t) + I_i \tag{6}$$

where $T_{i,j}$ is the weight (synaptic interconnection strength) from the output of neuron j to the input of neuron i, $T_{i,i} = 0$ (the neurons have no self

Figure 8: Four feature images with added noise.

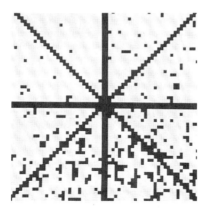

Figure 9: The segmentation based on the noisy feature images.

feedback), $v_j(t)$ is the output of neuron j, and I_i is the direct input to neuron i. The output of the neuron is then

$$v_i = g(\sum_{j=1}^{n} T_{i,j} v_j(t) + I_i - h_i) \qquad (7)$$

where $g(x)$ is as defined previously, and h_i is a threshold.

Because this network includes feedback, all choices of weights (in this case similarity measures) will not guarantee convergence. As stated in [9], if the weights chosen satisfy the requirements $T_{i,j} = T_{j,i}$ and $T_{i,i} = 0$, the network will converge. The weights defined using the similarity measure above (and many other similarity measures, with the additional constraint that $T_{i,i} = 0$) meet these conditions.

V. Summary

In this paper, we have examined image segmentation as performed using a neural network region growing method. This approach proved to be very intuitive when considering the similarities between pixels to be assigned as weights to connections between the pixels within neighborhoods, and neurons associated with each pixel in the image. This method was simulated, and experiments in unsupervised gray scale image segmentation were performed. As shown in the example using multiple feature images, this method could also be extended to texture (or other multiple feature based) segmentation through the use of appropriate features and vector similarity measures.

References

[1] T. Pavlidis. *Structural Pattern Recognition*, chapter 4, pages 68–70. Springer-Verlag, New York, 1977.

[2] R. M. Haralick and L. M. Shapiro. Image segmentation techniques. *Computer Vision, Graphics, and Image Processing*, 29:100–132, 1985.

[3] R. Nevatia. Image segmentation. In T. Y. Young and K. S. Fu, editors, *Handbook of Pattern Recognition and Image Processing*, chapter 9, pages 215–231, Academic Press, New York, 1986.

[4] R. M. Haralick, K. Shanmugam, and I. Dinstein. Textural features for image classification. *IEEE Transactions on Systems, Man, and Cybernetics*, 3(1):610–621, November 1973.

[5] T. R. Reed and H. Wechsler.   Segmentation of textured images and Gestalt organization using spatial/spatial-frequency representations. *IEEE Transactions on Pattern Analysis and Machine Intelligence*, 12(1):1–12, January 1990.

[6] M. Clark, A. C. Bovik, and W. S. Geisler. Texture segmentation using a class of narrowband filters. *Proceedings of International Conference on Acoustics, Speech and Signal Processing*, 14.6.1–14.6.4, April 1987.

[7] J. M. H. du Buf. Towards unsupervised texture segmentation using gabor spectral decomposition. In *Proceedings of the 5th International Conference on Image Analysis and Processing*, pages 65–72, Positano, Italy, September 1989.

[8] M. L. Minsky and S. A. Papert. *Perceptrons (Expanded edition)*. The MIT Press, Cambridge, Massachusetts, 1988.

[9] J. J. Hopfield. Neural networks and physical systems with emergent collective computational abilities. *Proceedings of the National Academy of Sciences*, 79:2554–2558, 1982.

II.11

Vision and Space-Variant Sensing

G. SANDINI and M. TISTARELLI

University of Genoa - DIST
Integrated Laboratory for Advanced Robotics (LIRA - Lab)
Genoa, Italy

Abstract

The advantages of space-variant sensing in a number of visual tasks are discussed and some applications are presented. A prototype space-variant CCD visual sensor is described characterized by a resolution decreasing from the center toward the periphery which resembles the sampling structure of the human retina. Its main advantage is the good balance between resolution and visual field amplitude, allowing data reduction to be performed at the sensor level through visuo-motor coordination (space-variant sensing requires a strong interaction between visual and motor processes to direct the high resolution part over "points of interest").

Several visual modules which exploit the advantages of space-variant sensing are analyzed. They include: target tracking for active gaze control, vergence control, estimation of the *time-to-impact* and recognition of 2D shapes.

Due to the data reduction performed by the retinal sensor and the locality of most pre-attentive visual processes, many tasks can be naturally implemented through neural networks. Examples like ocular movements related to pre-attentive fixation and vergence control are discussed.

398

1. Introduction

In the human visual system the receptors of the retina are distributed in space with increasing density toward the center of the visual field (the fovea) and decreasing density from the fovea toward the periphery. This topology can be simulated, as proposed by Sandini and Tagliasco [34], by means of a discrete distribution of elements whose sampling distance (the distance between neighboring sampling points) increases linearly with eccentricity from the fovea. An interesting feature of the space-variant sampling is the topological transformation of the *retinal image* into the *cortical projection*[1].

This transformation is described as a conformal mapping of the points on the polar (retinal) plane (ρ, η) onto a Cartesian (cortical) plane $(\xi = \log \rho, \gamma = \eta)$, where the values of (ρ, η) can be obtained mapping the Cartesian coordinates (x, y) of each pixel into the corresponding polar coordinates. The resulting cortical projection is invariant, under certain conditions, to linear scalings and rotations of the retinal image. These complex transformations are reduced to simple translations along the coordinate axes of the cortical image. This property is valid if, and only if, the scene and/or the sensor move along (scaling) or around (rotation) the optical axis.

The same properties hold in the case of a simple polar mapping of the image, but a linear dialation around the fovea is transformed into a linear shift along the radial coordinate in the (ρ, η) plane. Meanwhile, the log-polar transformation produces a constant shift along the radial coordinate of the cortical projection.

Beyond the geometric properties of the polar and log-polar mapping, which will be referred to in the following sections, the log-polar transformation performs a relevant data reduction (because the image is not equally sampled throughout the field of view) while preserving a high resolution around the fovea; thus providing a good compromise between resolution and band-limiting needs. This property turns out to be very effective to focus attention on a particular object feature, or to track a moving target (i.e. to stabilize the image of the target in the fovea). Therefore the properties of log-polar mapping has found interesting applications for object and, more specifically, shape recognition and object tracking [25, 31, 48, 47, 32, 42].

The main focus of the paper is, in fact, to stress the peculiarity of this transformation in the computation of *dynamic measurements*. In particular, the main observation is that during the tracking of a moving object the mapping of the stabilized retinal image onto its cortical image deforms in such a way that it is easier to compute those "behavioral variables" useful to control the position of the focus-of-attention or to guide the motion of the sensor. In fact, if the object is perfectly stabilized on the retina, and the shape does not change due to perspective changes (this is a good approximation for images sampled closely in time) the

---

[1]The terms "retinal" and "cortical" derive from the observation that the conformal mapping described here is very similar to the mapping of the retinal image onto the visual cortex of humans [38, 7, 34, 49]

a

b

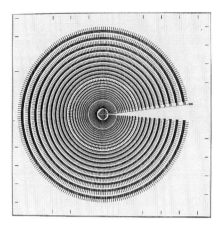

Fig. 1: (a) Structure of the prototype CCD retinal sensor.*(b) Picture of the chip.

component of the velocity field along the $\log \rho$ axis alone measures the "rate of dilation" of the retinal image of the object. This measure can be used to compute the time-to-impact.

1.1.   Structure of the retina-like sensor

A prototype retina-like visual sensor has been designed within a collaborative project involving several partners[2]. In this paper we will refer to the physical characteristics of the prototype sensor when dealing with the log-polar transformation. The results could be easily generalized to any particular log-polar mapping, by modifying the (constant) parameters involved in the transformation.

The retino-cortical mapping is implemented in a circular CCD array [14, 12], using a polar scan of a space-variant sampling structure, characterized by a linear relationship between the sampling period and the eccentricity (the distance from the center of the sensor). The spatial geometry of the receptors is obtained through a square tassellation and a sampling grid formed by concentric circles [14]. The prototype CCD sensor is depicted in Fig. 1[3]. In the experiments the information coming from the fovea is not used.

As for the extra-foveal part of the sensor the retino-cortical transformation is defined by:

---

[2]The institutions involved in the design and fabrication of the retinal CCD sensor are: DIST - University of Genoa, Italy; University of Pennsylvania - Dept. of Electrical Engineering, (PA) - USA; Scuola Superiore "S. Anna" Pisa, Italy. The actual fabrication of the chip was done at IMEC, Leuven, Belgium

[3]Currently the performances of the CCD sensor are being evaluated using a prototype camera. The reported experiments are carried out by re-sampling standard TV images following the geometry of the sampling structure of the sensor.

a

b

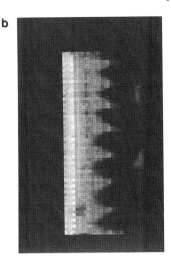

Fig. 2: (a) Synthetized binary image.*(b) Same image of (a) acquired with the prototype CCD retinal sensor. The fovea is centered on the star.

$$\begin{cases} \xi = \log_a \rho - p \\ \gamma = q\,\eta \end{cases} \tag{1}$$

where $(\rho,\ \eta)$ are the polar coordinates of a point on the retinal plane, p, q and a are constants determined by the physical layout of the CCD sensor. In Fig. 2 an image acquired with the prototype CCD retinal sensor is shown.

2. Fixation and space-variant sensing

The role of space-variant vision is to probe the environment at high resolution (with the fovea) and, at the same time, to limit the amount of detailed information (the fovea occupies a small part within the field of view). The processing of foveal data is restricted either to static or stabilized (i.e. tracked objects) visual tasks. In fact, it is not possible to provide detailed information on moving objects[4]. Therefore, a reflex mechanism exists in humans to keep the fixation on the same object point regardless of ego- and/or eco-motion [29, 1], stabilizing the image on the fovea. It is worth noting that the concept of fovea is inherently related to the notion of focus of attention, a classical problem of computer vision [20, 15, 21, 5, 42].

The broad field of view provided by peripheral vision has both alerting and guidance functions. With respect to foveal vision, peripheral vision has enhanced

---

[4]for example, consider the blurring effect perceived on close objects when looking outside a train window.

dynamic performances used for motion detection and for providing the motor control with the information necessary to foveate and track moving objects [8, 3, 2]. Besides these dynamic characteristics, peripheral vision has also a role in the recognition of gross features.

The concepts of foveal and peripheral vision are useless without an efficient motor control capable of directing the fovea toward the desired focus of attention. This function is also important in order to establish the appropriate relations between different locations of the visual field regardless of the actual image feature falling on the fovea. We argue that the active control of fixation is not always driven by cognitive processes, but in most cases this mechanism is activated by task-related parameters. For example, a fast moving object within the field of view, catches ones attention invoking a fast saccadic movement of the eye to *foveate* and track the object. This is also motivated by the fact that, as already mentioned, the detailed analysis of object features *requires* the stabilization of the image. Therefore a pre-attentive, reflex-like process must drive gaze control for fixation.

Similarly we can consider the vergence control of a binocular vision system. In this case we can split the control into two part: the former devoted to the tracking of the object (made by the *dominant eye*), the latter which keeps the vergence of the eyes on the point currently tracked (this is performed by a coordinated control of both eyes). As far as the visual process is concerned, both tracking and vergence control can be achieved by means of low-level processing. This fact further motivates a pre-attentive process.

A problem arising is to determine how to direct attention to a particular point in space.

Gaze control can be driven by three mechanisms:

- Involuntary reflex or reflex-like eye movements. For example when looking outside the window of a moving train the eye movement strategy is characterized by the so-called *optokinetic nystagmus* which is a composed of smooth movements of the eyes (during which the eye track a point of the environment) interrupted by fast saccadic movements which resets the direction of gaze. In this case it is virtually impossible to keep the eyes steady even if the subject is totally uninterested on the scene. The resulting motion strategy maximizes the period during which "useful information" could be analyzed (i.e. information not degraded by motion blurring). This behavior is, again, pre-attentive or, in other words, does not require "high level processing". Another example of this kind is the stabilization of gaze performed during active or passive motion of the head (for example during motion). This eye-head coordination strategy is performed partially through the vestibulo-ocular reflex (which only accounts for the correction of the motion of the head) and partially by active visual tracking (the control of fixation also depends upon the distance of the tracked object which cannot be determined by the vestibular mechanism). It is worth noting that also in this case it is impossible to stabilize the orientation of the visual axis by looking at an "abstract" point in space (if this would happen the visual information would be corrupted by motion blurring).

- Task driven gaze control. A very common example of this kind of control is the strategy adopted during walking. In this case the smooth reflex-like movements described previously are interrupted by saccadic movements which are, in general, directed alternatively on the ground plane (to detect small obstacles and to evaluate the roughness of the floor [17, 16, 9, 37]) and to points far away (used to self orient in space). During this period the peripheral part of the visual field plays a double role: the first, usually limited to the peri-foveal region, is to evaluate image velocity (used to maintain fixation), the second is to detect unexpected changes of the image brightness (or color) distribution. It is worth noting that, also in this case, the direction of gaze does not depend on high-level reasoning process.

- Voluntary fixation control. In this case fixation is directly controlled by high level processes like recognition. For example, wishing to self-orient in a partially known environment, a human moves gaze around, trying to identify some known feature. The direction of gaze is moved toward several points in the scene which exhibit a particular feature, which can facilitate recognition. Doors and windows constitute potential reference objects, therefore fixation can be driven toward vertical edges. Detection of known objects can be performed by moving fixation along relevant features like edges. This approach will be explained in the section on recognition of 2D shapes.

  Also in this case, however, it is possible to design motion control strategies based upon "categorical" features (i.e. features not related to the specific object as a whole but to some of its constituent parts) like corners, luminance or color discontinuities, symmetries, centroids etc.

Within the framework of neurals networks the reflex or reflex-like control of fixation could play a crucial role for many reasons [46]. The major one is, in our opinion, the simple relationship between the input and output signals allowing a reasonable solution with a one or two levels implementation: strictly speaking a visual input, described by two image coordinates and their velocities, should generate a coordinated motor pattern. This is already a sufficiently complex task to fully stress the neural network paradigm without the need of even more complex high-level processes. Another important aspect (which derives directly from the previous one) is the local nature of the visual processing required (like convolutions or correlations) which can be naturally implemented with neural networks organized into receptive fields [35]. Finally a learning mechanism is also necessary to embed in the network also other feature patterns which should activate fixation. For example, experience in performing a given task, like walking or grasping an object, should modify the behavior of the control network, defining more and more precisely *where to look*, to optimize the completion of the task. The alternate change in fixation, in the walking example, should be a pre-programmed behavior but the duration could be varied, while other eye movements could be learnt as well.

A problem arising is the coding of the extracted visual features to generate the inputs for the control network. The relevance of the visual task in the strategy adopted to move fixation enforces the design of a self-organizing network, where the inputs from visual processing are differently weighted, and sometimes discarded, depending on the task to be accomplished.

2.1. Object tracking

The ability to identify and track a moving target is a fundamental aspect of active vision systems [5, 11, 10]. Generally speaking the tracking process can be decomposed in three phases:

- detection;

- foveation;

- and actual tracking.

Each phase has its own computational peculiarities related both to processing and to the constraints imposed on the system.

In the simplest case where the target is a bright spot over a dark background and the sensor is, initially, steady the target is detected by a simple thresholding and the tracking itself is driven by a local computation of retinal velocity (the region where the velocity is non zero is limited to the projection of the target on the retinal plane).

The camera can not translate independently but has two degrees of freedom, which allow a rotation around the x and y axis, relative to the focal point.

At each instant of time, velocity is computed by measuring the displacement of the center of mass in successive images. This measure is used to provide the motor part with the necessary control signal. As soon as a moving target enters the visual field of the sensor, a linear, uniform motion is imposed to the sensor:

$$\begin{cases} x(t) & = & ut + x_0 \\ y(t) & = & vt + y_0 \end{cases} \tag{2}$$

where u and v are the estimated target speeds along the co-ordinate axes and (x_0, y_0) is the sensor initial position. ut and vt represent the displacement of the fovea with respect to the target, on the image plane. This estimate corresponds to an angular displacement for a spherical retina. In order to perform an angular correction of the camera orientation using the two rotational degrees of freedom,

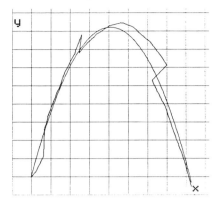

Fig. 3: Tracking of a bright target undergoing a ballistic trajectory. The trajectory of the fovea is superimposed to that of the target. *

we make the approximation of a spherical surface, using the planar displacements as angular correction values. Every time a new image is captured, the measure of the target speed is updated and the camera law of motion is modified consequently. If the object is too far from the fovea, the measured position is used to drive a saccadic movement. The motor strategy of the camera is then an alternation of saccadic and smooth pursuit movements [31], in analogy with the human behavior. A simulation of this procedure using a space-variant sensor is presented in Fig. 3. The target was moving over a trajectory obtained by combining a linear trajectory over the X axis with a parabolic one over the Y axis. In Fig. 3 the X-Y trajectory of the target and the superimposed fovea position are shown. The tracking span a time period of 45 seconds, with the hypothesis of being able to compute target velocity in 300 ms (which seems a reasonable value for our hardware).

It is worth noting that the constraint imposed on the background (i.e. that of being uniform in terms of gray levels) makes the tracking task a lot easier because the motion of the sensor does not need to be measured and subtracted from the motion of the target. Considering the requirements necessary to track a textured object moving over an unconstrained background the detection and the tracking phases are substantially different. In fact while the detection phase must be based on a segmentation process driven "simply" by the computation of the image velocity field, the tracking itself must take into account the component of the optical flow due to the motion of the sensor. If the rotation axis are coincident with the nodal point of the lens this component only involves angular displacement, therefore the motion field does not depend on object distance and can be computed from the known angular displacement of the sensor.

A test image was generated by superimposing a textured pattern on a background from a real image. A sequence of images was obtained by moving the pattern on

* Reprinted with permission from MIT Press, from *Robotics Research, The 5th International Symposium,* Sandini, G., and Dario, P., "Active Vision Based on Space-Variant Sensing." © 1990 MIT Press.

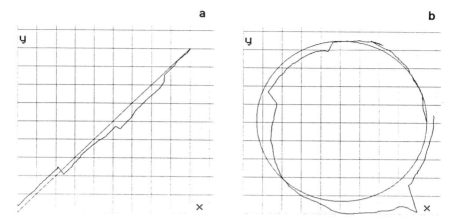

Fig. 4: Tracking of a textured target moving along a linear (a) and circular (b) trajectory. The trajectory of the fovea is superimposed to that of the target.*

the background with a pre-defined motion law. The output of the target tracking is shown in Fig. 4(a) for a linear trajectory and Fig. 4(b) for a circular trajectory of the target.

In this case the optical flow is computed to detect, isolate and foveate the target and then to track it. During this last phase, in order to estimate the tracking error, the expected optical flow, obtained from the known motion of the sensor, is subtracted from the optical flow computed from the sequence of cortical images.

The optical flow is computed by solving an over-determined system of linear equations in the unknown terms $(u, v) = \vec{V}$. The equations impose the constancy of the image brightness over time [19] and the stationarity of the image motion field [44, 13]:

$$\frac{d}{dt} I = 0 \qquad\qquad \frac{d}{dt} \nabla I = \vec{0}$$

where I represents the image intensity of the point (x, y) at time t. The least squares solution of (3) is computed for each point on the cortical plane as:

$$\vec{V}(\xi, \gamma, t) = (A^t A)^{-1} A^t \vec{b} \tag{3}$$

$$A = \begin{bmatrix} \frac{\partial I}{\partial \xi} & \frac{\partial I}{\partial \gamma} \\ \frac{\partial^2 I}{\partial \xi^2} & \frac{\partial^2 I}{\partial \xi \partial \gamma} \\ \frac{\partial^2 I}{\partial \xi \partial \gamma} & \frac{\partial^2 I}{\partial \gamma^2} \end{bmatrix} \qquad \vec{b} = \begin{bmatrix} -\frac{\partial I}{\partial t} \\ -\frac{\partial^2 I}{\partial \xi \partial t} \\ -\frac{\partial^2 I}{\partial \gamma \partial t} \end{bmatrix}$$

where (ξ, γ) represent the point coordinates on the cortical plane.

Let P be a generic point with Cartesian co-ordinates (x, y) with respect to the reference system of the camera, centered on the fovea of the sensor, and corresponding polar co-ordinates $\rho = \sqrt{(x^2 + y^2)}$, $\theta = \arctan\left(\frac{y}{x}\right)$. Given the optical flow due to both sensor and target motion, it is possible to compute the velocity of the target on the image plane:

$$\frac{dx}{dt} = \rho \left(\log_e a \frac{d\hat{u}}{dt} \cos\theta - \frac{\sin\theta}{q} \frac{d\hat{v}}{dt} \right)$$

$$(4)$$

$$\frac{dy}{dt} = \rho \left(\log_e a \frac{d\hat{u}}{dt} \sin\theta + \frac{\cos\theta}{q} \frac{d\hat{v}}{dt} \right)$$

where $\left(\frac{d\hat{u}}{dt}, \frac{d\hat{v}}{dt} \right)$ is the difference between the optic flow extracted from the sequence of cortical images and the velocity field due to camera motion, computed on the cortical plane. By applying these equations, it is possible to identify the points belonging to the target and to estimate their effective speed.

2.2. Binocular vergence control

In binocular systems gaze and fixation control involve keeping the optical axes directed at the point in space currently fixated. This is accomplished through active vergence control.

Olson and Coombs [28] and also Coombs and Brown [10, 11] demonstrated a simple and efficient vergence control system based on cepstral filtering of stereo images. The rationale was the computation of a gross cross-correlation score between the left and right views, the maximum correlation identifying the correct vergence of the cameras.

A similar algorithm has been devised for space-variant stereo images sampled with the retinal sensor. The basic idea is that of computing a pointwise cross-correlation between cortical projections of the left and right views. The vergence between the cameras is varied by moving the *non-dominant* camera, while the cumulative cross-correlation is computed. Even though the cortical images do not differ for a simple translation, like for uniformly sampled, raster images, the global correlation of the images still provide a measure of the displacement between them. When the cameras are almost correctly verged, the global cross-correlation becomes very high. Therefore, if the global cross-correlation decreases, then the non-dominant camera is moved in the opposite direction until the maximum is reached. In Fig. 5(a) a diagram is shown which illustrates the values of the inverse, global cross-correlation (simply computed as the normalized sum of the absolute difference of intensity values between the left and right image) obtained by applying the algorithm to the original, uniformly sampled images. As it can be noticed the outline of the diagrams in Fig. 5(a) and 5(b) is very similar, but the one obtained from the cortical images has a sharper peak at the correct vergence angle. This

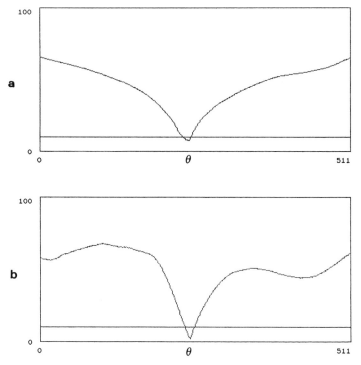

Fig. 5: Inverse, global cross-correlation of uniformly sampled (a) and space-variant (b) images, computed for different vergence angles θ.

fact implies a faster convergence of the algorithm using images sampled with the retinal sensor. It is worth noting that the space variant sampling intrinsically emphasizes the importance of the central part of the image during the cross-correlation procedure. In fact the number of pixels near or inside the fovea is much higher than the pixels on the periphery, therefore the central part of the image weights more than the periphery. As a result the cross-correlation function is much sharper making the vergence control much easier.

In Fig. 6 the images used to obtain the diagrams in Fig. 5 are shown. The image pairs corresponding to the maximum vergence and the correct vergence found using a gradient descent algorithm, together with the pixel-by-pixel inverse cross-correlation of the cortical images, is shown.

2.3. Active shape recognition

As it was demonstrated in [25] two features of the sensor are potentially useful for shape recognition:

a   b

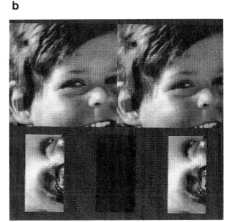

Fig. 6: Results of the vergence control algorithm. On top are the original images, on the bottom are the cortical maps, with the result of the inverse cross-correlation in the middle. (a) Starting vergence. (b) Correct vergence found by the gradient descent algorithm. Notice that the values of the correlation are almost zero.

- the geometry of the sampling structure can be designed so as to optimally sample objects of different sizes (or equivalently observed from different distances);

- the scanning of the sampling points can be performed so as to produce a conformal topological transformation of the input image which is, under achievable conditions, invariant to rotations and scalings of the objects.

A template-matching approach was used for the recognition of two-dimensional shapes independently from their position on the visual field, their spatial orientation, and their distance from the sensing device. This procedure comprises two phases [25, 32]:

- a training phase, during which the objects belonging to the predefined visual world are sampled, moving the fovea over the center of mass of the object, and their cortical mappings are stored into a template file (because of the form-invariance property, only one template is stored for each object irrespective of size and orientation);

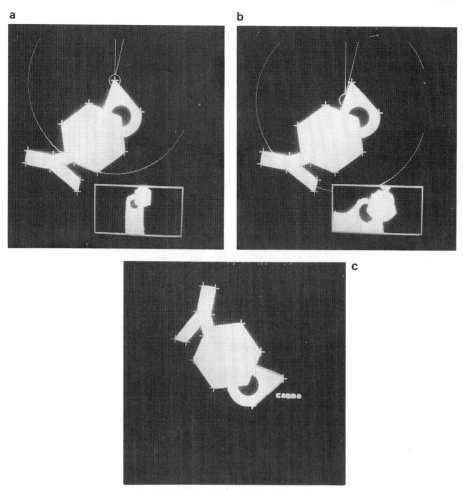

Fig. 7: Recognition of overlapped 2D shapes.* In the small window, on the bottom of each
picture, the retinal sampling applied to the image is presented. (a) Image containing the objects
to be recognized; the fovea is positioned over a peculiar point (all peculiar points are identified
by the small cross). (b) The sensor is scanning the object boundary to identify the features of
the peculiar point. Once the peculiar point has been identified a template matching is performed
with all possible objects (i.e. with all the objects that have such peculiar point). (c) The peculiar
feature has been identified and the object recognized.

- and a recognition phase, where the retinal image is sampled, mapped into
  the cortical plane and segmented so as to separate the various objects; each
  object is then sampled again with the fovea over the center of mass of the
  object. The unknown object is then compared to the templates by computing a similarity score based on the cross correlation between object and
  templates.

The above described procedure has been tested experimentally over a variety of shapes which have been compared successfully with enlarged and rotated instances. The average recognition time for an object out of a set of 50 is about 300 ms on a 68010 machine with C language coded programs.

2.3.1. Recognition of overlapping 2D shapes

The shape recognition algorithm has an obvious limitation in that the recognition is dependent upon the physical separation of the objects. The correct positioning of the fovea, before the template matching, is based on the computation of the center of mass. For ovarlapping 2D shapes the center of mass is no more an invariant feature. For this reason an algorithm has been designed to extend the validity of the approach to overlapping 2D shapes. This has been possible by introducing the concept of *characteristic view*. A characteristic view of an object is the view (shape) of that object obtained by positioning the fovea over "peculiar" features of the objects. Recognition is based on the result of successive template matching computed on characteristic views. In our case, peculiar features are based on the corners along the boundary of the 2D object. An example of such procedure is shown in Fig. 7. Fig. 7(a) shows the scene to be analyzed with the fovea positioned over a peculiar point.

Fig. 7(b) shows an intermediate step during which the sensor scans the border of the object in order to measure the length of the border and, finally, in Fig. 7(c) the result of the recognition is shown.

The exploration strategy, adopted to drive fixation, is of crucial importance. In order to produce a set of useful characteristic views, gaze is sequentially moved over selected object features, in a manner similar to the behavior of the human oculo-motor system when trying to recognize an object (refer to Yarbus [50], for experimental data and also Ballard [5] for an accurate analysis). Unlike the case of non-overlapping shapes, the analysis is not performed *one-shot*, but proceeds in a sequential manner, step by step. Successive fixations can be driven by the position of the feature itself, which can help determining *where to move next*.

2.4. Motion, optical flow and time-to-impact

The ability to quickly detect an obstacle to react in order to avoid it is of vital importance for animates. Passive vision techniques can be beneficially adopted if active movements are performed [5, 4, 26, 18, 3, 32, 33]. A dynamic spatio-temporal representation of the scene, which is the *time-to-impact* with the objects, can be computed from the optical flow which is extracted from monocular image sequences acquired during *tracking* movements of the sensor [5, 36, 29, 39, 45]. The image velocity can be described as function of the camera parameters and split into two terms depending on the rotational and translational components of

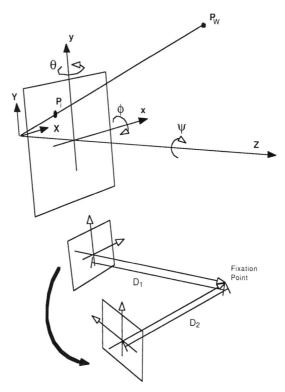

Fig. 8: Diagram of the camera coordinate system, with the dynamic parameters referred in the text.

camera velocity respectively [36]:

$$\vec{V}_r = \left[\begin{array}{c} \dfrac{x\,y\,\phi \;-\; \left[x^2 \;+\; F^2\right]\theta \;+\; F\,y\,\psi}{F} \\[4mm] \dfrac{\left[y^2 \;+\; F^2\right]\phi \;-\; x\,y\,\theta \;-\; F\,x\,\psi}{F} \end{array} \right]^t \qquad (5)$$

$$\vec{V}_t = \left[\begin{array}{c} \dfrac{x\left[D_1 \;-\; D_2\,\cos\phi\,\cos\theta\right] \;-\; F\,D_2\,\cos\phi\,\sin\theta}{Z} \\[4mm] \dfrac{y\left[D_1 \;-\; D_2\,\cos\phi\,\cos\theta\right] \;-\; F\,D_2\,\sin\phi}{Z} \end{array} \right]^t$$

D_1 and D_2 are the distances of the camera from the fixation point in two successive instants of time, ϕ, θ and ψ are the rotations of the camera referred to its coordinate axes, shown in Fig. 8 and Z is the distance of the world point from the image plane. As we are interested in computing the time-to-impact $\frac{W_z}{Z}$, then $\vec{V}_t$ must be derived from the total optical flow.

The optical flow is computed on the (ξ, γ) plane, therefore it is necessary to define an expression to derive $\vec{V}_t$ on the Cartesian plane, given the known velocity on the cortical plane and the motion parameters [42]:

$$
\vec{V}_t = \left[\begin{array}{c} x \dot{\xi} \log_e a - \dfrac{y \dot{\gamma}}{q} - \dfrac{x y \phi - [x^2 + F^2] \theta + F y \psi}{F} \\[2ex] y \dot{\xi} \log_e a + \dfrac{x \dot{\gamma}}{q} - \dfrac{[y^2 + F^2] \phi - x y \theta - F x \psi}{F} \end{array} \right] \tag{6}
$$

$(\dot{\xi}, \dot{\gamma})$ is the velocity field computed from the sequence of cortical images. It is worth noting that, expressing the Cartesian coordinates of a retinal sampling element in microns, the focal length and the retinal velocity $\vec{V}$ are also expressed in the same units.

Adopting the constrained tracking egomotion, the rotational angles are known, as they correspond to the motor control generated by the fixation/tracking system. The time-to-impact of all the image points on the retinal plane can be recovered using a well-known relation [23]:

$$
T_{ti} = \frac{Z}{W_Z} = \frac{D_f}{|\vec{V}_t|} \tag{7}
$$

D_f is the displacement of the considered point from the focus of the translational field on the image plane, and W_Z is the translational component of the sensor velocity along the optical (Z) axis. The ratio on the left-hand side represents the time-to-impact with respect to the considered world point. The location of the FOE is estimated by computing the least squares fitting of the pseudo intersection of the set of straight lines determined by the velocity vectors $\vec{V}_t$ [42].

Even though this algorithm requires few constraints (including the assumption of static environment), they still do not limit the generality of its possible applications. It can be successfully applied, for example, to locate obstacles and detect corridors of free space during robot navigation [43]. The accuracy of the measurements depends on the resolution of the input images, which, for the retinal sensor, is very low. Nevertheless, the hazard map computed with this method can still be exploited for its qualitative properties in visual navigation.

By exploiting further the advantages of the log-polar mapping, all these requirements and constraints will be relaxed in the analysis performed in the remainder of the paper. Our final aim being the estimation of the time-to-impact using only image-derived parameters, in the case of camera *and* object motion.

2.5. Dynamic properties of log-polar mapping

Jain [22, 6] pointed out the advantages of processing the optical flow, due to camera translation, by using a log-polar complex mapping of the images and choosing the

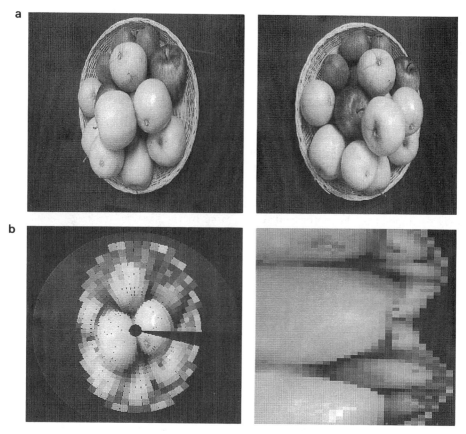

Fig. 9: (a) First and last image of the sequence. (b) Retinal sampling applied to the first image, and simulated output of the retinal CCD sensor, represented in the Cartesian (x, y) and log-polar (ξ, γ) planes.

position of the FOE as the center for the representation.

It is possible to generalize this property to more general and complex kind of motions. Generally, any expansion of the image of an object, due either to the motion of the camera or the object itself, will produce a radial component of velocity on the retinal plane. This intuitive observation can be stated in the following way :

the time-to-impact of a point on the retinal plane, only effects the radial component of the optical flow

we will formally prove this assertion in the remainder of the paper.

This observation lead us to adopt an approach different to the one pursued in the

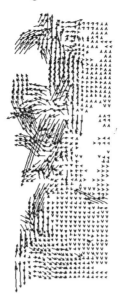

Fig. 10: Optical flow of the sequence in Fig. 9(b), represented in the log-polar (ξ, γ) plane.

previous section, in order to represent the optical flow on the cortical plane. It turns out that the most convenient way of representing and analyzing velocity is in terms of its radial and angular components with respect to the fovea [41].

Let us consider, for the moment, a general motion of the camera both rotational and translational. We will later consider the special case of tracking egomotion, explaining how it simplifies the analysis, and finally dealing also with object motion. The velocity on the image plane along the radial and angular coordinates is:

$$
\begin{cases}
\dot{\rho} = \frac{xu+yv}{\rho} = u\cos\eta + v\sin\eta \\[2mm]
\dot{\eta} = \frac{xv-yu}{\rho^2} = \frac{v\cos\eta - u\sin\eta}{\rho}
\end{cases}
\tag{8}
$$

$(u,v) = (\dot{x}, \dot{y})$ is the retinal velocity with respect to a Cartesian coordinate system centered on the fovea. Plugging in the motion equations for small angular rotations (as from (5)) and expressing the image velocity on the (ξ, γ) plane:

$$\begin{cases} \dot{\xi} = \frac{\dot{\rho}}{\rho}\log_a e \\[2mm] \quad = \left[\frac{1}{Z}\left[W_z - F\left(W_x\cos\frac{\gamma}{q} + W_y\sin\frac{\gamma}{q}\right)\right] + \left(\frac{\rho}{F} + \frac{F}{\rho}\right)\left(\phi\sin\frac{\gamma}{q} - \theta\cos\frac{\gamma}{q}\right)\right]\log_a e \\[2mm] \dot{\gamma} = q\dot{\eta} \\[2mm] \quad = \frac{qF}{\rho}\left[\left(\frac{W_x}{Z} + \theta\right)\sin\frac{\gamma}{q} + \left(\phi - \frac{W_y}{Z}\right)\cos\frac{\gamma}{q}\right] - q\psi \end{cases}$$

$$(9)$$

These equations simply show that, while both components of the optical flow depend upon the depth Z of the objects in space, only the *radial* component $\dot{\xi}$ depends upon the time-to-impact $\frac{Z}{W_z}$. Moreover, only the *angular* component $\dot{\gamma}$ depends upon rotations around the optical axis, while the radial component is invariant with respect to ψ. Notice that up to now we have not made any hypothesis about the motion of the sensor. Therefore equations (9) certainly hold for any kind of camera motion. Even though the analysis has been conducted for a moving camera in a static environment the result obtained in (9) holds for any combination of object **and** camera motion. All the motion parameters are expressed in terms of translational velocities in space (W_x, W_y, W_z) and rotational velocities (ϕ, θ, ψ) referred to a camera-centered Cartesian coordinate system. These velocities have not to be absolute velocities but can represent the relative motion of the camera with respect to the objects, which is the sum of the two velocities.

Equations (9) can be further developed in the case of tracking egomotion. By imposing $\vec{V}(0,0) = \vec{0}$ in the general optical flow equations and substituting the values of W_x and W_y in (13), we obtain:

$$\begin{cases} \dot{\xi} = \left[\frac{W_z}{Z} + \left[\frac{\rho}{F} + \frac{F}{\rho}\left(1 - \frac{D_2}{Z}\right)\right]\left(\phi\sin\frac{\gamma}{q} - \theta\cos\frac{\gamma}{q}\right)\right]\log_a e \\[2mm] \dot{\gamma} = \frac{qF}{\rho}\left(1 - \frac{D_2}{Z}\right)\left(\theta\sin\frac{\gamma}{q} + \phi\cos\frac{\gamma}{q}\right) - q\psi \end{cases}$$

$$(10)$$

D_2 is the distance of the fixation point from the retinal plane measured at the frame time following the one where the optical flow is computed.

The structure of the two equations is very similar. If the rotational velocity of the camera is known, then it is possible to substitute the values for (ϕ, θ, ψ) into (10) to directly obtain $\frac{Z}{D_2}$ from $\dot{\gamma}$ and $\frac{Z}{W_z}$ from the radial component $\dot{\xi}$:

$$\begin{cases} \dfrac{Z}{D_2} = \dfrac{F\left(\phi\cos\frac{\gamma}{q} + \theta\sin\frac{\gamma}{q}\right)}{F\left(\phi\cos\frac{\gamma}{q} + \theta\sin\frac{\gamma}{q}\right) - \rho\left(\frac{\dot{\gamma}}{q} + \psi\right)} \\[4mm] \dfrac{Z}{W_z} = \left[\dot{\xi}\log_e a - \frac{\dot{\gamma}+\psi}{q} - \frac{\rho}{F}\left(\phi\sin\frac{\gamma}{q} - \theta\cos\frac{\gamma}{q}\right)\right]^{-1} \end{cases}$$

$$(11)$$

also the focal length F must be known , while q and a are constant values related to the physical structure of the CCD sensor [14]. It is worth noting the importance of $\frac{Z}{D_2}$ and $\frac{Z}{W_z}$. In fact, they both represent relative measurements of depth which are very important in humans and animals to relate to the environment. The former can be used for manipulation tasks to drive the hand grasping an object which is fixated. The latter has a natural application in visual navigation to determine a safe course avoiding potential obstacle. It is interesting to compare equations (11) with equations (6) and (7). As it can be noticed, equations (11) do not depend on the position of the FOE. Therefore it is not necessary to differentiate the optical flow with respect to the rotational component $\vec{V}_r$ to estimate the translational component $\vec{V}_t$ [30].

A further option is to try to compute the time-to-impact from the partial derivatives of both velocity components:

$$\frac{\partial \dot{\gamma}}{\partial \gamma} = \frac{F}{\rho}\left(\frac{D_2}{Z} - 1\right)\left(\phi\sin\frac{\gamma}{q} - \theta\cos\frac{\gamma}{q}\right)$$

(12)

$$\frac{\partial \dot{\xi}}{\partial \xi} = \left[\frac{\rho}{F} - \frac{F}{\rho}\left(1 - \frac{D_2}{Z}\right)\right]\left(\phi\sin\frac{\gamma}{q} - \theta\cos\frac{\gamma}{q}\right)$$

notice that $\rho = a^{\xi+q}$. By combining these two last equations we obtain:

$$\frac{Z}{W_z} = \left[\dot{\xi}\,\log_e a - \frac{\partial\dot{\xi}}{\partial\xi} + 2\,\frac{\partial\dot{\gamma}}{\partial\gamma}\right]^{-1}$$

(13)

this equation allows the direct computation of the time-to-impact from the images only. Notice that only first order derivatives of the optical flow are required and the pixel position does not appear. The parameters q and a are calibrated constants of the CCD sensor. It is interesting to relate this result to the divergence approach proposed by Thompson [40] and also recently by Nelson and Aloimonos [27]. Equation (13) can be regarded as a formulation of the oriented divergence for the tracking motion, modified to take into account the fact that the sensor is planar and not spherical.

In Fig. 9(a) the first and last image of a sequence of 10 is shown. The images have been acquired at the resolution of 256x256 pixels and then re-sampled performing the log-polar mapping. The motion of the camera was a translation plus a rotation θ around its vertical axis Y. The direction of gaze was controlled so as to keep the fixation on the apple in the center of the basket (which is the object nearest to the observer). The inverse time-to-impact $\frac{W_z}{Z}$, computed by applying equation (13) to the optical flow in Fig. 10 is shown in Fig. 11(a). Despite the low resolution the closest object is correctly located.

a

b

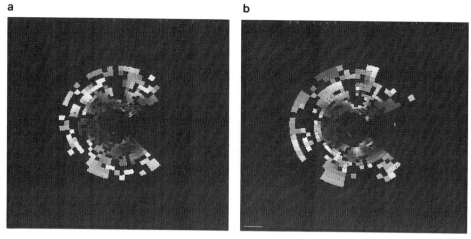

Fig. 11: (a) Time-to-impact of the scene in Fig. 9, computed by applying equation (13) to the optical flow in Fig. 10. (b) Time-to-impact of the scene in Fig. 9, computed by applying equation (14) to the optical flow in Fig. 10. For clarity, data is represented on the retinal plane.

A last equation for the time-to-impact can be obtained by computing the second order partial derivative of $\dot{\xi}$ [41]:

$$\frac{Z}{W_z} = \left[\dot{\xi} \, \log_e a - \frac{\partial^2 \dot{\xi}}{\partial \xi^2} \, \log_a e \right]^{-1} \tag{14}$$

This equation clearly states that the time-to-impact can be computed using only the radial component of velocity with respect to the fovea. Moreover, this formulation does not depend on the motion of the fixated target. In Fig. 11(b) the inverse time-to-impact of the scene in Fig. 9, computed by applying equation (14) to the optical flow in Fig. 10, is shown.

It has been shown that a space-variant velocity representation seems to be best suited to recover the time-to-impact from image sequences. Even though technology has been very conservative in producing only raster CCD arrays and imaging devices (therefore strongly linked to a Cartesian coordinate system), a conformal mapping can be performed in real-time by using commercially available hardware, enforcing the feasibility of the proposed methodology.

3. Conclusion

The application of a space-variant sampling strategy to different static and dynamic visual tasks has been presented. Apart from the advantages or disadvantages related to the use of such a sensor one point is worth stressing, namely the fact that a "traditional" high resolution visual sensor may pose more problems than advantages for visual processing. In fact, if we consider that the optic nerve of the human visual system is composed of about one million fibres (corresponding to a square array of 1000x1000 pixels) and considering that this channel transmit also color information it is evident that the amount of information associated to a "standard" 512x512 image is not far from being, at least quantitatively, the information processed by the human visual system. The basic difference is *where* to sample and not *how much*. It is our opinion that in the recent years much of the research on computer vision has been biased, as far as the sensor is concerned, by the requirements of "image processing" without stressing that in Computer Vision images are to be understood and not transmitted or enhanced. This fact, which has been generally accepted as far as processing is concerned, has been mis-interpreted in relation to visual sensors. Currently available visual cameras are considered a good technological solution and improvements are sought both in terms of resolution and in term of "aperture time". Both these features are, in our opinion, not relevant for vision-based control of autonomous systems. Certainly, the economical implications of developing high resolution sensors are, today, very high (consider, for example the mass production of sensors for home-video cameras) and therefore the major efforts of camera manufacturers are in this direction, but it should be clear this technological trend is not going to solve any of the "important" visual problems, on the contrary, it will make things much harder by sharpening images in space and time. Paradoxically, the latest developments in automatic video-cameras, have originated systems with a built-in fovea. In fact, all the most advanced auto-focusing systems, ask the operator to point a small window, seen through the eyepiece, over the "important" feature he wants to focus on (this is equivalent to a fovea). It is important to note that it would be impossible to perform such operation, independently of the technology used to measure distance, without introducing this sort of foveal mechanism (i.e. it is impossible to focus "everywhere" at the same time). Vergence is another example (the two optical axes are to be oriented toward the same point in space). In this respect it may be said that a fovea is necessary whenever a motor action is involved (and not viceversa as it is generally pointed out)

A further point, which derives from the previous observations, is the misleading meaning which is sometimes given to the concept of *visual attention*. Usually, in fact, visual attention is related to the process of *interpretation* of the visual scene: "if I want to recognize a face I better shift my attention on the eyes and the mouth". Our point is that "attention" has also a very strong *behavioral* basis: "if I want to walk I better look in front of my feet". The major difference between these two different views is that while in the former case an a-priori hypothesis is necessary, based on some high-level processing or expectation, in the latter everything is based on self-generated actions which are, usually, task driven. In the examples given above both focusing and vergence involve the selection of a point in space *before the processing could even start.*

This behavioral connotation is stressed even more during tracking and for the computation of time-to-impact. In fact, if we consider the requirements of a tracking process, the only situation in which this process is not active is when the camera is fixed and looking to a steady environment. In all other situations the need to reduce motion blurring forces the activation of the tracking system which, consequently, cannot be actively suppressed. The alternative, proposed by the current technological trends, is to use high-speed shutters which "freeze" the image by sampling very shortly in time. This certainly avoids motion blurring but still does not prevent the overall system from measuring precise information about egomotion in order to be able to extract useful information from the evolving scene (in particular to separate image velocities generated by ego-motion from those due to objects moving independently on the scene: the case of a moving object tracked by a moving camera). Tracking a point of the environment, on the contrary, gives the system a reference point which does not move in the environment and simplify the computation of time-to-impact [5, 18]. It is worth noting, moreover, that the tracking process is data driven as it is the case for focusing and vergence. The role of high level processing is "limited" to the selection of the target to track which is often based on the behavioral task being executed (think, for instance, to the visuo-motor coordination during walking which has been discussed before). Therefore, the peculiarities of a retina-like space-variant sensor in relation to visual tracking is, in our opinion, the major advantage of this approach. During tracking the high resolution part of the sensor is positioned over the object to track, i.e. where, in the image, the smallest displacements (actually the tracking errors) need to be measured while the low resolution part is sweeping over the background and motion blurring actually filters out the high frequency components of the incoming information.

A last observation is relative to depth and time-to-crash. To this respect the main point presented can be summarized by saying that, from a behavioral view point, depth computation is only necessary within the grasping range of the arm. During manipulative tasks, in fact, the motion of the objects is mainly driven by the arm itself and the "head" can be considered steady. In this situation motion parallax does not provide reliable depth information. As a consequence, during manipulative tasks the major role in depth computation is played by the stereo sub-system. Considering animals, for example, it is not a case that, the position of the eyes on the head, becomes frontal (i.e. maximizing the amplitude of the binocular visual field) as the manipulative ability increases. Very different is the role of motion parallax for the control of ego-motion. The major difference is that, in this case, the motion control system is not really interested in depth computation but in the computation of time-to-crash. In fact, in the case of a steady system (i.e. a system without legs or wheels) the computation of depth outside the range of grasping is entirely useless if one is interested in the role of vision for control and not for interpretation or recognition. On the other hand, as soon as the system starts moving the relevant information is not how far an object is but how long it will take until we reach it. The trajectory used to avoid an obstacle depends more on how fast we are approaching it then on its actual distance. For example, the steering strategy of a driver is very different when parking a car or passing a truck on a highway. Therefore, even if in principle it is possible to compute depth from motion parallax, our opinion is that this is not necessary and that the simpler computation of time-to-crash is a lot more important in these cases. In the paragraph devoted to the use of the retina-like sensor for the computation of this behavioral variable we stressed the unique characteristics of this sampling strategy for the computation of time to crash.

As far as the application of the above concepts to neural networks is concerned, the approach proposed has, at least, two main advantages. The first is directly related to the reduced number of sensitive elements compared to a similar situation using a constant resolution sensor. This feature allows the reduction of the amount of hardware necessary to process visual information. This technological advantage could make the difference between a theoretical implementation and an actually realizable system if we consider that the reduction could be of, at least, one order of magnitude. Locally, the kind of processing performed is not different from what has been proposed in the "low-level" processing literature, but the overall organization does not require a "high-level" process to control the low-level feature extraction (as it is if a *window system* is implemented [20]). The reduction in terms of connections and adaptability of the system is vey large: less hardware is required and not under control of a high level process. The second advantage is due to the fact that the kind of processing envisaged (i.e. active, involuntary, control of fixation) is itself more like a reflex and therefore can be implemented using "hard-wired" connections. We sketch the process of adjusting the weights of the connections as a two-stage process composed of a *genetic* phase and a *learning* phase (much like a biological nervous system). In a reflex, the genetic part can be *pre-wired*, while the learning phase can be used to tune the basic motor actions such as to obtain a more coordinated behavior and adapt to unexpected input patterns (events). The control and maintenance of fixation, for example, even if it requires a very sophisticated visuo-motor coordination and it is per-se a formidable problem to solve, could be implemented following the neural network approach much like the scratch reflex in frogs studied, within this field, by Massone and Bizzi [24]. By applying this kind of processing to the neural network technology, it is possible not only to propose a solution to outstanding problems of computer vision, but also to propose a more realistic model of human functions which can be implemented on the basis of physiological evidence and not implying the simulation of multi-layer structures based on sometimes very weak biological assumptions.

Acknowledgements: The authors thank F. Bosero, F. Bottino and A. Ceccherini for the help in developing the computer simulation environment for the CCD retinal sensor.
This research was supported by the Special Project on Robotics of the Italian National Council of Research.

4. References

[1] J.S. Albus and T.H. Hong. Motion, depth, and image flow. In *Proc. of IEEE Int. Conf. of Robotics & Automation*, pages 1161–1171, Cincinnati, 1990.

[2] J. Aloimonos. Purposive and qualitative active vision. In *Proc. of Int. Workshop on Active Control in Visual Perception*, Antibes (France), 1990.

[3] J. Aloimonos, I. Weiss, and A. Bandyopadhyay. Active vision. *Intern. Journal of Computer Vision*, 1(4):333–356, 1988.

[4] R. K. Bajcsy. Active perception vs passive perception. In *Proc. Third IEEE Workshop on Computer Vision: Representation and Control*, pages 13–16, Bellaire (MI), 1985.

[5] D.H. Ballard, R.C. Nelson, and B. Yamauchi. Animate vision. *Optics News*, 15(5):17–25, 1989.

[6] S.L. Bartlett and R.C. Jain. Depth determination using complex logarithmic mapping. In *SPIE Int. Conf. on Intelligent Robots and Computer Vision IX: Neural, Biological and 3-D Methods*, volume 1382, Boston (MA), 4-9 November 1990.

[7] C. Braccini, G. Gambardella, G. Sandini, and V. Tagliasco. A model of the early stages of the human visual system: Functional and topological transformation performed in the peripheral visual field. *Biological Cybernetics*, 44:47–58, 1982.

[8] P. J. Burt. *Smart Sensing in Machine Vision*. Academic Press, 1988.

[9] S. Carlsson and J.O. Eklundh. Object detection using model based prediction and motion parallax. In *Proc. of first European Conference on Computer Vision*, pages 297–306, Antibes (France), 1990. Springer Verlag.

[10] D.J. Coombs and C.M. Brown. Intelligent gaze control in binocular vision. In *Proc. of the Fifth IEEE International Symposium on Intelligent Control*, Philadelphia, PA, September 1990.

[11] D.J. Coombs, T.J. Olson, and C.M. Brown. Gaze control and segmentation. In *Proc. of the AAAI-90 Workshop on Qualitative Vision*, Boston, MA, July 1990.

[12] I. Debusschere, E. Bronckaers, C. Claeys, G. Kreider, J. Van der Spiegel, P. Bellutti, G. Soncini, P. Dario, F. Fantini, and G. Sandini. A 2d retinal ccd sensor for fast 2d shape recognition and tracking. In *Proc. 5th Int. Solid-State Sensor and Transducers*, Montreux, 1989.

[13] E. DeMicheli, G. Sandini, M. Tistarelli, and V. Torre. Estimation of visual motion and 3d motion parameters from singular points. In *Proc. of IEEE Int. Workshop on Intelligent RObots and Systems*, Tokyo, Japan, 1988.

[14] J. Van der Spiegel, G. Kreider, C. Claeys, I. Debusschere, G. Sandini, P. Dario, F. Fantini, P. Bellutti, and G. Soncini. *Analog VLSI and Neural Network Implementations*. De Kluwer, 1989.

[15] E.D. Dickmanns. 4d-dynamic scene analysis with integral spatio-temporal models. In R. Bolles and B. Roth, editors, *Proc. 5th Int. Symposium on Robotics Research*, Tokyo (Japan), 1988. MIT Press.

[16] W. Enkelmann. Obstacle detection by evaluation of optical flow fields from image sequences. In *Proc. of first European Conference on Computer Vision*, pages 134–138, Antibes (France), 1990. Springer Verlag.

[17] F. Ferrari, E. Grosso, G. Sandini, and M. Magrassi. A stereo vision system for real time obstacle avoidance in unknown environment. In *Proc. of IEEE Int. Workshop on Intelligent RObots and Systems*, pages 703–708, Tsuchiura (Japan), 1990.

[18] E. Grosso, G. Sandini, and M. Tistarelli. 3d object reconstruction using stereo and motion. *IEEE Trans. on Syst. Man and Cybern.*, SMC-19, No. 6, 1989.

[19] B. K. P. Horn and B. G. Schunck. Determining optical flow. *Artificial Intelligence*, 17 No.1-3:185–204, 1981.

[20] H. Inoue, H. Mizoguchi, Y. Murata, and M. Inaba. A robot vision system with flexible multiple attention capability. In *Proceedings of ICAR*, pages 199–205, 1985.

[21] L. Jacobson and H. Wechsler. Joint spatial/spatial-frequency representations for image processing. In *SPIE Int. Conf. on Intelligent Robots and Computer Vision*, Boston (MA), 1985.

[22] R.C. Jain, S.L. Bartlett, and N. O'Brian. Motion stereo using ego-motion complex logarithmic mapping. *IEEE Trans. on PAMI*, PAMI-9, No. 3:356–369, 1987.

[23] D. T. Lawton. Processing translational motion sequences. *CVGIP*, 22:116–144, 1983.

[24] L. Massone and E. Bizzi. A neural network model for limb trajectory formation. In *NATO ARW on Robots and Biological Systems*, Il Ciocco, Tuscany, Italy, 1989. Springer-Verlag.

[25] L. Massone, G. Sandini, and V. Tagliasco. Form-invariant topological mapping strategy for 2-d shape recognition. *CVGIP*, 30 No.2:169–188, 1985.

[26] P. Morasso, G. Sandini, and M. Tistarelli. Active vision: Integration of fixed and mobile cameras. In *NATO ARW on Sensors and Sensory Systems for Advanced Robots*, Berlin Heidelberg, 1986. Springer-Verlag.

[27] R.C. Nelson and J. Aloimonos. Using flow field divergence for obstacle avoidance in visual navigation. *IEEE Trans. on PAMI*, PAMI-11, No. 10, 1989.

[28] T.J. Olson and D.J. Coombs. Real-time vergence control for binocular robots. In *Proc. of the DARPA Image Understanding Workshop*, Pittsburgh, PA, September 1990.

[29] D. Raviv and M. Herman. Towards an understanding of camera fixation. In *Proc. of IEEE Int. Conf. of Robotics & Automation*, pages 28–33, Cincinnati, 1990.

[30] J. H. Rieger and D. T. Lawton. Processing differential image motion. Technical report, COINS Dep., University of Massachusetts, Amherst (MA), 1984.

[31] G. Sandini, F. Bosero, F. Bottino, and A. Ceccherini. The use of an anthropomorphic visual sensor for motion estimation and object tracking. In *Proc. of the OSA Topical Meeting on Image Understanding and Machine Vision*, 1989.

[32] G. Sandini and P. Dario. Active vision based on space-variant sensing. In *Proc. 5th Int. Symposium on Robotics Research*, Tokyo, Japan, 1989. MIT-Press.

[33] G. Sandini, P. Morasso, and M. Tistarelli. Motor and spatial aspects in artificial vision. In *Proc. of 4th Int. Symposium of Robotics Research*, Santa Cruz (CA), 1987. MIT Press.

[34] G. Sandini and V. Tagliasco. An anthropomorphic retina-like structure for scene analysis. *CGIP*, 14 No.3:365–372, 1980.

[35] G. Sandini and M. Tistarelli. Stochastic connectivity in the retinal ganglion cell receptive field: A discrete spatial model. *Neural Networks*, 1, Supp. 1, 1988.

[36] G. Sandini and M. Tistarelli. Active tracking strategy for monocular depth inference over multiple frames. *IEEE Trans. on PAMI*, PAMI-12, No. 1:13–27, 1990.

[37] G. Sandini and M. Tistarelli. Robust obstacle detection using optical flow. In *Proc. of IEEE Int. Workshop on Robust Computer Vision*, pages 396–411, Seattle, (WA), Oct. 1-3, 1990.

[38] E. L. Schwartz. Spatial mapping in the primate sensory projection: Analytic structure and relevance to perception. *Biological Cybernetics*, 25:181–194, 1977.

[39] M.A. Taalebinezhaad. Direct recovery of motion and shape in the general case by fixation. In *Proc. of IEEE Intl. Conference on Computer Vision*, pages 451–455, Osaka (Japan), 1990.

[40] W.B. Thompson and J.K. Kearney. Inexact vision. In *Proc. of IEEE Workshop on Motion: Representation and Analysis*, pages 15–21, Kiawah Island Resort, 1986.

[41] M. Tistarelli and G. Sandini. On the advantages of polar and log-polar mapping for direct estimation of time-to-impact from optical flow. *IEEE Trans. on PAMI, Special Issue on Interpretation of 3D Scenes*, (submitted), 1990.

[42] M. Tistarelli and G. Sandini. On the estimation of depth from motion using a ccd retinal sensor. In *Proc. of first European Conference on Computer Vision*, pages 211–225, Antibes (France), 1990. Springer Verlag.

[43] M. Tistarelli and G. Sandini. Robot navigation using an anthropomorphic visual sensor. In *Proc. of IEEE Int. Conf. of Robotics & Automation*, pages 374–383, Cincinnati, 1990.

[44] S. Uras, F. Girosi, A. Verri, and V. Torre. Computational approach to motion perception. *Biological Cybernetics*, 60:69–87, 1988.

[45] D. Vernon and M. Tistarelli. Using camera motion to estimate range for robotic parts manipualtion. *IEEE Trans. on Robotics & Automation*, RA-6, No. 5:509–521, 1990.

[46] H. Wechsler. *Computational Vision*. Academic Press, San Diego (CA), 1990.

[47] C. F. R. Weiman. Polar exponential sensor arrays unify iconic and hough space representation. In *SPIE Int. Conf. on Intelligent Robots and Computer Vision VIII: Algorithms and Techniques*, volume 1192, pages 832–842, 6-10 November 1990.

[48] C. F. R. Weiman and R. D. Juday. Tracking algorithms using log-polar mapped image coordinates. In *SPIE Int. Conf. on Intelligent Robots and Computer Vision VIII: Algorithms and Techniques*, volume 1192, pages 843–853, Philadelphia (PA), 6-10 November 1990.

[49] C.F.R. Weiman and G. Chaikin. Logarithmic spiral grids for image processing and display. *CGIP*, 11:197–226, 1979.

[50] A.L. Yarbus. *Eye Movements and Vision*. Plenum Press, 1967.

II.12

Learning and Recognizing 3D Objects from Multiple Views in a Neural System

MICHAEL SEIBERT and
ALLEN M. WAXMAN

Machine Intelligence Technology Group
MIT Lincoln Laboratory
Lexington, MA

I   Introduction

Part of designing a machine vision system based on biological and psychophysical observations is to immerse it in an environment with realistic stimuli presented in a realistic manner. Doing so for a machine designed to learn and recognize 3D-objects allows the machine access to a surprising amount of information. Consider an attentive observer watching an object as it moves naturally in his field of view. He may first see the front of the object as it approaches, the transition to a side view, then a profile, the transition to the rear view, and finally the rear view as the object moves beyond him. He experiences not only multiple views of the object, but also sees the relationships between the views unfold in time. He may learn the *views*, the *view transitions*, as well as the *key features* which generalize across

This chapter is based, in part, on studies performed at Lincoln Laboratory, a center for research operated by the Massachusetts Institute of Technology. The work was sponsored by the Department of the Air Force under Contract F19628-85-C-0002.

426

vantage points. He may also use subsequent experiences to refine impressions of previously learned objects, or learn how to explore objects actively for their important features with attentional mechanisms such as directed eye-motions.

This chapter describes a modular neural system implementation of such ideas concerning learning and recognizing 3D objects. Learning of object representations is done in an unsupervised fashion, and recognition is achieved invariant to object position, orientation, scale, foreshortening, and aspect in the visual field. Our system exploits the information in view sequences during both learning and recognition. We believe that the underlying mechanisms described here are plausible for robust 3D-object vision, and have implemented the system described herein.

II Background

We are capable of recognizing familiar, but unexpected views of objects in a fraction of a second. Given the neural latencies of the visual system, it seems unlikely that more than viewer-centered appearance models are employed in such situations. In consideration of the popular machine-vision approaches to recognizing 3D objects, Rosenfeld (1987) notes that there does not seem to be sufficient time to compute the 3D volumes involved in object-centered volumetric models; nor to hypothesize a 3D object (and its 3D position and orientation) and generate the expected 2D appearance, then match the stimulus with the imagined object. Instead of representing an object by its volume or surface, each of which requires complex transformations from the viewer-centered imagery to the object-centered representation, we would like to join with others (e.g., Koenderink & van Doorn, 1979; Underwood & Coates, 1975; Freeman & Chakravarty, 1980) to suggest a viewer-centered representation for 3D objects, and then to propose how such a representation can be learned and used for recognizing objects by an unsupervised machine. Even if a viewer-centered representation is not the final basis of an object-centered representation for 3D objects, it must be a significant avenue for accessing objects in memory.

Important physiological studies support a viewer-centered representation. Perrett and others (Perrett et al, 1985; 1987; 1989) report discovery of cells in the fundus of the anterior superior temporal sulcus (STS) of macaque monkey brain which are selectively responsive to characteristic views of familiar heads and faces in both 3D and 2D (picture) presentations. Different views (e.g., full face, profile, head-up, head-down, back, top) maximally activate different classes of cells. They also found some cells which respond to particular objects (i.e., heads) regardless of view, in essence pooling the particular views together to form a single object representation.

Furthermore, Perrett et al. (1985) also discovered cells which, for example, were not active to either the frontal or profile views, but were active during a dynamic *view transition* from profile to frontal view of the observed head. This suggests that some cells encode the characteristic views and some cells encode the view transitions. Such cells of the latter type could also project onto cells sensitive to the 3D object as a whole in order to provide additional constraints during learning and additional evidence during recognition. These ideas, in part, motivate the *Aspect Network* described later in this chapter.

Among the psychological evidence which supports a view-based approach are the studies of Palmer, Rosch, and Chase (1981) and Edelman, Bülthoff, and Weinshall (1989), which describe recognition performance of humans to objects presented from canonical and unusual vantage points. They found that subjects could recognize objects more quickly from particular vantage points. To show that this effect was not caused by the complexity of the view per se, they also showed that other views could become the most quickly recognized 'canonical' views with practice. Rock and DiVita (1987) described studies where subjects were unable to learn representations independent of viewpoint for certain objects when given a limited number of views. Even in cases of wire-frame objects with depth cues or multiple orthogonal views, which may theoretically provide sufficient information to construct an unambiguous object-centered representation of the 3D objects, subjects seemed unable to recognize the wireframes from some novel vantage points.

III Neural System Architecture

Figure 1 illustrates a machine vision system, based on anatomical, physiological and psychophysical findings. This system learns intermediate 2D representations of an object from images that are largely invariant to the object's apparent position, size, orientation, and perspective effects in the imagery, and uses that invariant 2D information (in conjunction with sequence-information from multiple views) to access previously experienced 3D objects in memory. As shown in Figure 1, the system is implemented as a modular neural vision architecture (Seibert & Waxman 1989; 1990), which is described more fully by Seibert (1991). The early modules of the vision system are arranged primarily in a feedforward manner to extract features, determine attentional cues that drive saccadic and pursuit camera-motions, and learn intermediate representations in memory of 2D shapes that are invariant

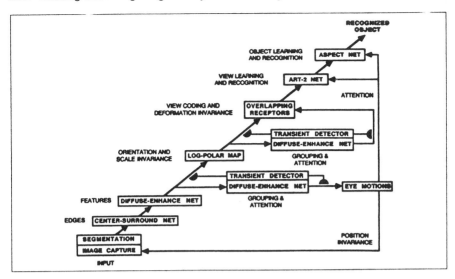

Figure 1: *Neural system architecture for 3D object learning and recognition.*
The early modules employ Diffusion-Enhancement neural-like processing to
extract features, generate attentional cues, and build an intermediate representation of the 2D views. The Aspect Network then combines sequences of
view-categories together into a 3D object representation.

to position, orientation, scale, and small deformation (e.g.,, foreshortening)
on the visual field. We call these 2D representations *aspects*, after the *aspect
graph* concept of Koenderink and van Doorn (1979). The transitions between
aspects which are repeatedly experienced during attentional intervals (maintained by pursuit camera-motions between saccades) manifest themselves as
learned associations in the Aspect Network (Figure 2) representation of a
single object. The learned associations later facilitate evidence accumulation whenever an object is re-experienced. Each object node accumulates
evidence according to how well the present view sequence is consistent with
the previously learned view transitions for its object. The evidence accumulation layer is coupled to an object competition layer, which determines
the node with the maximum evidence, thus indicating the recognized object.
After each attentional reset, triggered during a saccadic camera-motion, the
objects node activities (i.e., evidences) are reset to allow unbiased competition between the stored objects during the new view sequence. The new view
sequence may not match any previously learned objects. If a sufficiently close
match does emerge, then that object representation is refined, otherwise a
representation for the new object begins to crystallize in long-term memory
(LTM). The view transitions learned by our Aspect Network are analogous

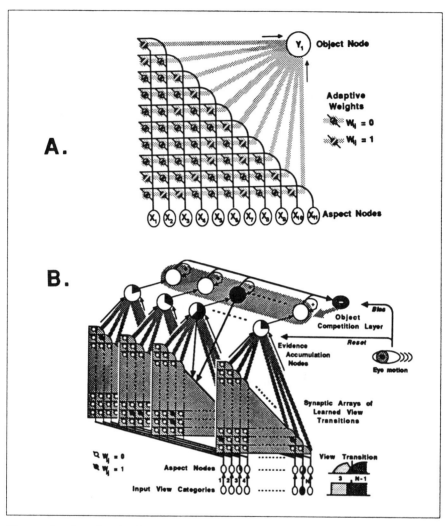

Figure 2: A. *Single-object Aspect Network*. The transitions between sequentially activated aspects are detected and learned by the synapses in the single-object Aspect Network. Each learned synapse is analogous to an arc of the Aspect Graph. The object node accumulates evidence for recognition when the aspects and aspect transitions are re-experienced. B. *Aspect Network*. Evidence for experienced view-trajectories is simultaneously accumulated for all competing objects over time. Recognition emerges at any moment as the maximally activated object node.

to the event-edges of the visual-potential (aspect graph) of Koenderink and van Doorn (1979).

Learning and recognition of objects takes place even when the early modules extract only ambiguous features, because the information contained in the view transitions effectively multiplies the usefulness of the feature set extracted during each view. Recognition emerges via a fusion of evidence from multiple views over time. When designing a machine vision system, one has a choice between two extremes: complex features which alone may provide enough information to locate and identify an object, or simple features which individually provide much less information. We prefer simple features since they are more general, are less expensive to process, do not require a priori knowledge of the environment, and are often more robust.

To provide sufficient constraints in the object search-space for practical 3D object recognition, simple features can either be considered in groups (e.g., the model-based approach of Grimson (1986)) or tracked temporally (e.g., the quantitative 3D surface interpretation method of Waxman and Wohn (1987)). The approach we suggest here, however, is to let each view and view transition of the sequence suggest possible object-hypotheses, and let the evidence for competing hypotheses accumulate over time. The early modules focus attention on individual shapes from the scene, from which features have been extracted. We use a sequence of processing modules to generate an invariant feature vector (Seibert & Waxman, 1989) which becomes the input to an unsupervised view categorizer. ART 2. ART 2 is based on Adaptive Resonance Theory (Carpenter & Grossberg, 1987a; 1987b), and is responsible for assembling all of the features together to choose a view category (i.e., *aspect*) from previous experience, or spawning a new category if a sufficiently close match is not found. Our qualitative approach avoids the cost of pairwise (or n-*ary*) feature-space tree-search, the need for a priori models, and the difficulty of the temporal correspondence problem between features.

Several larger difficulties are also overcome by our method of view sequence processing: noisy presentations, ambiguous representations, and intermittent presentations. When spurious features are detected, or when features drop-out in noisy environments, the appropriate view category may still be close enough to be activated. If not, then the sequence of view categories which is activated during an image sequence may provide sufficient intermittent evidence for the object in the scene. This will result in a weaker object hypothesis, but the hypothesis often remains the maximally activated one. When a view sequence provides evidence for multiple objects, then several hypotheses may be active simultaneously until enough imagery has been experienced to disambiguate them. In addition, initially learned noisy codes

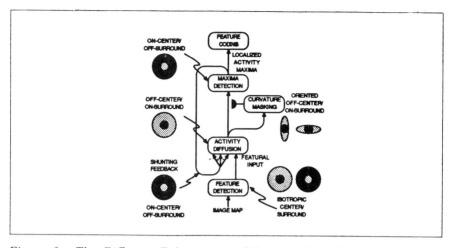

Figure 3: *The Diffusion-Enhancement Bilayer.* The DEB takes featural input and diffuses it over a 2D map as a function of time. Local maxima of activity are detected by the upper level and fed back to the diffusion level via on-center/off-surround connections.

become refined in LTM with experience over time.

IV System Neurodynamics

The first modules of Figure 1 separate object from background based on brightness or temporal change, spatially contrast-enhance them, and extract features of the objects in the image using the Diffusion-Enhancement Bilayer, or DEB (Figure 3). In this case, features are those that can be reliably extracted and grouped to become a feature vector for 2D-shape encoding. The DEB consists primarily of two levels which are coupled through both feedforward and nonlinear feedback connections. Low-level features extracted from the imagery serve as input to the lower level (a two-dimensional map) which, as time progresses, spreads input over larger scales via diffusion. The diffused activity is periodically sampled and passed upward to a contrast-enhancing level which locates local maxima in the terrain of diffuse activity. The periodicity of sampling can be associated with a refractory period of the upper level. It implies that activity spreads a finite distance across the diffusion level for each cycle of the feedback process. The local maxima detected by the upper level are fed back to reinforce the lower diffusion level using shunting dynamics with on-center/off-surround projective fields. The local maxima are also available as outputs of the network, and they may take on a variety of interpretations as a function of the input.

The DEB can be implemented as a 2D field of nodes for each level, indexed by x, y. Each node may have local connections to its neighbors within the level, as well as to the corresponding nodes in the levels above or below. In the following equation, $A(x, y, t)$ represents the activity of a node in the diffusion layer as a function of its position and time, $\delta(\cdot)$ represents input from the feature-detection level, and $G(\cdot)$ represents feedback from the contrast-enhancement level back to the diffusion level.

$$
\begin{aligned}
\frac{\partial A}{\partial t} \;=\;& \kappa \nabla^2 A(x, y, t) - \lambda A(x, y, t) \\
& + (A_{sat} - A(x, y, t)) \overset{inputs}{\underset{i}{\sum}} \delta(X - X_i(t), Y - Y_i(t)) \\
& + (A_{sat} - A(x, y, t)) \overset{maxima}{\underset{m}{\sum}} G_{\sigma_1}(X - X_m(t), Y - Y_m(t)) \\
& - A(x, y, t) \overset{maxima}{\underset{m}{\sum}} G_{\sigma_2}(X - X_m(t), Y - Y_m(t)).
\end{aligned} \tag{1}
$$

Here, κ accounts for the density and conductivity of the region, A_{sat} is the activity saturation value, λ is a passive decay rate, δ is the unit impulse function, and G_{σ_1} and G_{σ_2} are normalized Gaussian functions with spreads σ_1 and σ_2 ($\sigma_1 < \sigma_2$).

Figure 4 plots an activity distribution surface as it spreads by a simple Gaussian diffusion as described above. An interesting and useful result of the diffusive process is that the global activity maximum will settle at the geometric centroid of the features (Seibert & Waxman, 1989). In Figure 4, activity spreads as the time progresses from t_0 until a global activity maximum emerges indicating the geometric centroid of the features. At an intermediate time (Figure 4B) while the spread is still small with respect to the interfeature spacing, separate local maxima can be located, though they have shifted toward a common centroid. The features attract each other on increasing scales with time. When the sloping tail of one Gaussian function is superimposed on the relatively flat peak of another Gaussian function, that peak is biased in the direction of the first Gaussian. As the slope of the tail increases, the biased peak ascends the gradient, until a global maximum emerges at the geometric centroid of the features. The location of the maximum is used as a fixation cue to drive an attentional mechanism, and as a reference location for 2D shape encoding. A variety of early vision applications of the DEB are described by Waxman et al. (1989).

The later modules of the architecture of Figure 1 use the DEB in various modes to help build an intermediate representation of the 2D appearance of

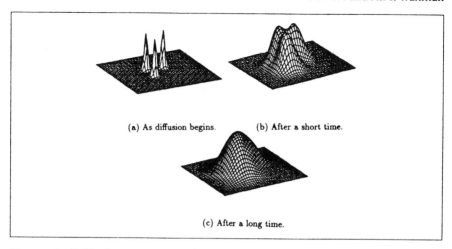

(a) As diffusion begins.   (b) After a short time.

(c) After a long time.

Figure 4: *Diffusing activity surfaces.* The activity distribution of the diffusion level of the DEB (see Figure 3) is plotted in three dimensions at three times: (A) at t_0, as diffusion begins, (B) at t_0^+, after a short time; and much later in (C). In (C), the peak is located at the geometric centroid of the three features shown in (A). No feedback was used in this example.

objects which is invariant to the objects apparent size, orientation, and location on the visual field. Location invariance is accomplished by fixating the centroid of the feature point groups determined by a DEB. Size and orientation effects are also mitigated by the DEB, in conjunction with a log-polar transform. Before applying this second diffusion process, a stable feature cluster in the initial feature map is transformed with respect to its previously determined centroid using a complex logarithmic (*i.e.*, log-polar) transform reminiscent of the mapping from LGN onto the visual cortex (Baron, 1985; Schwartz, 1977, 1980). Points in the image space are denoted using complex notation as $Z = (X - X_c) + i(Y - Y_c)$ or $Z = \rho e^{i\theta}$ where (X_c, Y_c) is the location of the group centroid, $\rho = \|Z\|$, and $\theta = \arg Z$. The conformal mapping, $\ln Z$, has the well-known effect of transforming both rotation and scale effects to translations in transformed-space (Baron, 1985; Schwartz, 1977; 1980; Seibert & Waxman, 1989). The amount of feature group translation in log/polar feature-space indicates the relative size and orientation of the object in the image. The resulting transformed feature set is again grouped by a DEB and shifted by the feature-encoding module so that its new centroid is aligned with the center of the subsequent layer of coding cells. Thus, the data itself can be separated from the effects of scale and rotation for matching.

The feature-set, which has now been processed to eliminate the effects of location, size, and 2D-orientation, is encoded for classification by a set (typically 5 × 5 array) of coarsely tuned, overlapping receptive fields with Gaussian weighted inputs (Seibert & Waxman, 1989). As a result of this encoding architecture, small rotations in depth of the objects can be tolerated during classification, despite the foreshortening and perspective effects induced by such a rotation. This is because the deformations produced by a small rotation in depth do not cause significant change in the activation of the coarse overlapping receptive fields.

A simple example was chosen for Figure 5 to highlight the processing steps described so far. In this example, the final pattern illustrates a feature vector which represents the shape shown in the first frame. The sizes of the disks in the final frame represent the magnitude of the components of the feature vector. The same feature vector is produced regardless of the position, size, or orientation of the original silhouette. Each feature vector produced by the encoding layer is input to the ART module which matches it against the closest stored patterns. If a sufficiently close match emerges, the corresponding aspect category (characteristic view) is refined, otherwise a new aspect category is automatically learned. The aspect categories then individually provide evidence for static views of objects. They also provide evidence for 3D view transitions when considered in sequences by the Aspect Network.

Differential equations govern the dynamics and architecture of the Aspect Network. These shunting equations model cell membrane and synapse dynamics as pioneered by Grossberg (1973; 1988). Input activities to this network are given by equation (2), the learned aspect transitions by equation (3), and the objects recognized from the experienced view sequences by equation (4).

The aspect node activities are governed by:

$$\frac{dx_i}{dt} \equiv \dot{x}_i = I_i - \lambda_x x_i, \tag{2}$$

where λ_x is a passive decay rate, and $I_i = 1$ during the presentation of aspect i and zero otherwise as determined by the output of the ART 2 module in the complete system (Figure 1). This equation assures that the activities of the aspect nodes build and decay in nonzero time (see the timetraces for the input I-nodes and aspect x-nodes in Figure 2B). Whenever an aspect transition occurs, the activity of the previous aspect decays (with rate λ_x) and the activity of the new aspect builds (again with rate λ_x in this case, which is convenient but not necessary). During the transient time when both activities are nonzero, only the synapses between these nodes have both pre- and post-synaptic activities which are significant (i.e., above threshold) and

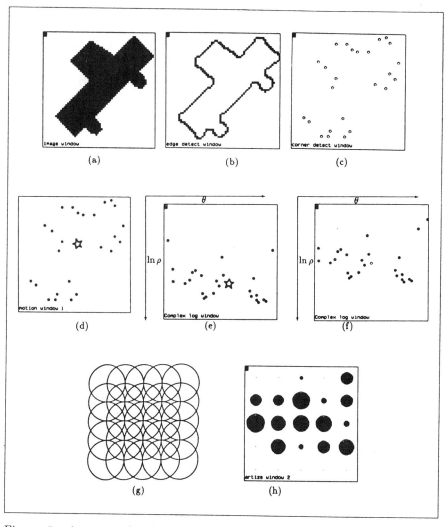

Figure 5: An example of the 2D shape learning and recognition system processing a silhouette:*(a) silhouette; (b) edge feature-map; (c) "interesting" features detected by the DEB; (d) feature-map centroid (star) localized by second DEB; (e) log-polar mapping of features (filled circles), and centroid localized by third DEB (star); (f) log-polar features shifted to center of feature-map; (g) overlapping receptive field pattern used by the feature coding layer to code centered log-polar shape; (h) 25 element feature vector used as input to ART 2.

* Reprinted with permission from *Neural Networks* **2** (1), 9–27, Seibert, M., and Waxman, A.M., "Spreading Activation Layers, Visual Saccades, and Invariant Representations for Neural Pattern Recognition Systems, © 1989, Pergamon Press PLC.

Hebbian associative learning can be supported. The overlap of the pre- and post-synaptic activities is transient, and the extent of the transient is controlled by the selection of λ_x. This is the fundamental parameter for the dynamical behavior of the entire network, since it defines the response time of the aspect nodes to their inputs. As such, nearly every other parameter of the network depends on it.

The aspect transitions that represent objects are realized by synaptic weights on the dendritic trees of object neurons (Figure 2A). Equation (3) defines how the (initially small, positive, and random) weight relating aspect i, aspect j, and object k changes:

$$\frac{dw_{ij}^k}{dt} = \kappa_w \, w_{ij}^k \left(1 - w_{ij}^k\right) \left\{ \Phi_w \left[(x_i + \epsilon)(x_j + \epsilon) \right] - \lambda_w \right\} \Theta_y(\dot{y}_k) \, \Theta_z(z_k). \quad (3)$$

Here, κ_w governs the rate of evolution of the weights relative to the x-node dynamics, and λ_w is the decay rate of the weights. Note that a small "back-ground level" of activity ϵ is added to each x-node activity. This will be discussed in connection with (4) below. $\Phi_w(\gamma)$ is a threshold-linear function; that is: $\Phi_w(\gamma) = \gamma$ if $\gamma > w_{th} > O(\epsilon)$ and zero otherwise. $\Theta_\theta(\gamma)$ is a binary-threshold function of the absolute-value of γ; that is: $\Theta_\theta(\gamma) = 1.0$ if $| \gamma | > \theta_{th}$ and zero otherwise.

Although this equation appears formidable, it can be understood as follows. Whenever simultaneous above-threshold activities arise at node x_i and at node x_j, the Hebbian product $(x_i + \epsilon)(x_j + \epsilon)$ causes $\dot{w}_{ij}^k$ to be positive (since above threshold, $(x_i + \epsilon)(x_j + \epsilon) > \lambda_w$) and the weight w_{ij}^k learns the transition between aspects i and j. By symmetry, w_{ji}^k would also learn, but all other weights decay ($\dot{w} \propto -\lambda_w$). The product of the shunting terms $w_{ij}^k(1 - w_{ij}^k)$ goes to zero (and thus inhibits further weight changes) only when w_{ij}^k approaches either zero or unity. This shunting mechanism limits the range of weights, but also assures that these fixed points are invariant to input-activity magnitudes, decay-rates, or the initial and final network sizes.

The gating terms $\Theta_y(\dot{y}_k)$ and $\Theta_z(z_k)$ modulate the learning of the synaptic arrays w_{ij}^k. As a result of competition between multiple object hypotheses (see Figure 2B above and equation (5) below), only one z_k-node is active at a time. This implies recognition (or initial object neuron assignment) of "Object-k," and so only the synaptic array of Object-k adapts; all other synaptic arrays w_{ij}^l ($l \neq k$) remain unchanged. Moreover, learning occurs only during aspect transitions. While $\dot{y}_k \neq 0$ both learning and forgetting proceed; but while $\dot{y}_k \approx 0$ adaptation ceases though recognition continues (e.g.,, during a long sustained view).

Object nodes y_k accumulate evidence for object hypotheses over time.

Their dynamics are governed by:

$$\frac{dy_k}{dt} \equiv \dot{y}_k = \kappa_y \left\{ \left[\sum_i \sum_{j>i} \Phi_y \left[(x_i + \epsilon) w_{ij}^k (x_j + \epsilon) \right] \right] - \lambda_y y_k \right\}. \qquad (4)$$

Here, κ_y governs the rate of evolution of the object nodes relative to the x-node dynamics, λ_y is the passive decay rate of the object nodes, $\Phi_y(\cdot)$ is a threshold-linear function as above, and ϵ is the same small positive constant as in (3). In this case, however, the threshold is set low enough to allow the $O(\epsilon)$ term of the argument to contribute evidence when only one x-node is active (i.e., during a sustained or static view). The same Hebbian-like product (i.e., $(x_i + \epsilon)(x_j + \epsilon)$) used to learn transitions in (3) is used to detect aspect transitions during recognition in (4) with the addition of the synaptic gating term w_{ij}^k, which produces an axo-axo-dendritic synapse (Seibert & Waxman, 1990). Using this synapse, an aspect transition (or view) must not only be detected, but it must also be a permitted one for Object-k (i.e., $w_{ij}^k > 0$) if it is to contribute activity to the y_k-node.

A "winner-take-all" competition is used to select the maximally active object node. The activity of each evidence accumulation y-node is periodically sampled by a corresponding object competition z-node (see Figure 2B). The sampled activities then compete according to Grossberg's shunted short-term memory model (Grossberg, 1973), leaving only one z-node active at the expense of the activities of the other z-nodes. In addition to signifying the 'recognized' object, outputs of the z-nodes are used to inhibit weight adaptation of those weights which are not associated with the winning object via the $\Theta_z(z_k)$ term in equation (3). The competition is given by a first-order differential equation derived from (Grossberg, 1973):

$$\frac{dz_k}{dt} \equiv \dot{z}_k = \kappa_z \left[f(z_k) - z_k \{ \lambda_z + \sum_l f(z_l) \} \right]. \qquad (5)$$

The function $f(z)$ is chosen to be faster-than-linear (e.g., quadratic). The initial conditions are reset periodically to $z_k(0) = y_k(t)$.

Among the multiple hypotheses activated by a particular image sequence, only the maximally activated hypothesis is able to modify its 3D object representation. The long-term memories of the view sequence (both the view representations and the view-transition representations) continuously adapt during recognition to incorporate current experience with previous experiences. In this way, the expectations always reflect up-to-date perceptions of the object. This allows a greater possibility for finding a match in memory than if a non-adaptive scheme were used. This property is very important when qualitative information is processed, as is the case here.

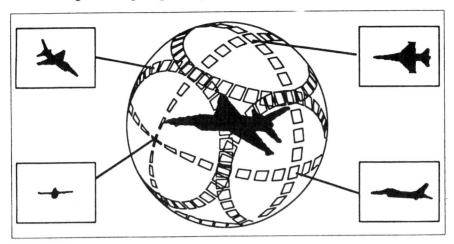

Figure 6: *Viewing sphere of captured view sequences.* View sequences were captured for the test aircraft pitching, yawing, and rolling.

V Demonstration

Figure 6 illustrates the views collected for the model aircraft test objects. The view sequences for an aircraft can be spliced together in different arrangements to provide many different training and test sequences for learning and recognizing the aircraft. There are 22 intersection points on this particular viewing sphere where view sequence segments can be spliced. For training, a sequence of views was constructed for each object which traversed all of the view-sequence segments shown in the figure.

After the 2D-invariant feature vectors are detected by the earlier modules of the vision system, they are used to parcellate the viewing space. Views from nearby vantage points which are similar are collected into a learned aspect which corresponds to an average invariant view from a particular area over the viewing sphere. When an incoming invariant feature vector (generated by the overlapping receptive fields) closely matches a previously learned feature vector (determined by ART 2), it becomes part of that category, and thus also part of the view-space parcel (i.e., aspect) represented by that category. When a view becomes part of an existing aspect category, it helps refine the representation of that category stored on the bottom-up and top-down synaptic weights (LTM traces) in ART. Thus, the potentially infinite number of appearances for an object are collapsed into a finite and manageable set of aspects.

As a demonstration, consider the sequence of views of an aircraft as it pitches along the "prime meridian" of Figure 6 (i.e., views of nose → bottom

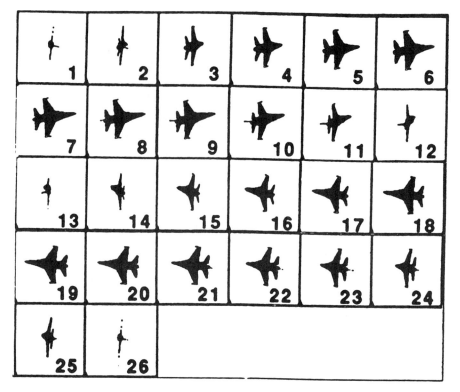

Figure 7: *Aircraft pitch view-sequence*. 26 silhouette views generated as the
aircraft pitches 360 degrees. The numbers indicate the order in which the
views were presented.

→ tail → top → nose) as in Figure 7. Starting with a view of the nose,
this sequence shows an aircraft pitching at a uniform rate. Note that the
silhouette views are ambiguous in the sense that a view of the nose resembles
a view of the tail, and views of the top resemble the views of the bottom.
Such symmetry results in an appearance model which is simpler than the
formal definition of the Aspect Graph of Koenderink and van Doorn (1979).
In this case the reduced complexity may result in a representation which is
more compact and easier to access.

Figure 8 shows the actual graph-like representation learned by the view
categories within ART 2 and the synapses of the Aspect Network, which
are generated by setting the ART 2 vigilance (i.e., matching) parameter
to 0.98, 0.97, and 0.96. The top and bottom views merged into a single

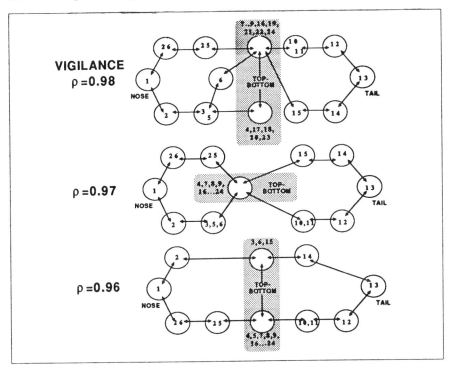

Figure 8: *Learned aspect graphs for aircraft pitch sequence.* View categories (nodes) are learned by the ART 2 network, transitions are learned by the Aspect Network. As expected, decreasing the ART vigilance reduces the number of learned categories. Numbers indicate the views in Figure 7 coded by each category. The shaded "top-bottom" areas indicate aspects which encoded views from both the top and bottom of the aircraft.

aspect category since they are identical in silhouette. The nose and tail views remained separate in this case, however, because there is no view of the tail exactly from the rear so that the tail views never quite match the nose views. With the coarsest categorization in this figure, the 26 views were collected into 10 aspects. Other of our test aircraft appear very similar to this one from a frontal vantage-point, and so share some of the same aspects. This results in views which are ambiguous, from which recognition cannot be made precise without more information. Further views are also sometimes individually ambiguous, but a sequence of (even ambiguous) views which is unique to an object is readily detectable with this system, and so resolves these difficulties (Seibert, 1991).

VI   Conclusion

In this approach to designing a 3D object recognition system, we have taken clues from biology and psychology to develop an architecture which supports the learning of representations for 3D objects from view sequences, and allows subsequent experience to refine the learned representations. The computations are cast as a set of simultaneous coupled differential equations, rather than as algorithmic procedures. The implementation is modular in the sense that the sets of coupled equations (i.e., networks) are interconnected so that information flows from one network to another via feedforward and feedback connections between them. Similar learning principles can be realized by analog electronic devices.

The attributes of an object's appearance which are extracted by the network architecture are increasingly abstract as higher levels of the architecture are activated. The portion of the image which is fixated is first reduced to a feature set, then the effects of position are eliminated, followed by the effects of orientation and scale, followed by the effects of foreshortening and perspective (to some extent), followed by the effects of the particular vantage point. The computational load is distributed throughout the modules.

Many of the ideas discussed here have also been implemented in a real-time system by Baloch and Waxman (1990) and Baloch (1991), who were also concerned with modeling the motivational and emotional drives of an autonomous mobile robot in order to explore issues in behavioral conditioning. They use a simplified version of the object recognition processes described here to process visual stimuli for excitatory and inhibitory conditioning of the robot MAVIN. The robot initially wanders aimlessly about the laboratory. With its binocular visual apparatus, it fixates and tracks the objects it finds during its exploration, learning them so it can later recognize them. The techniques described here are used to insure robust recognition regardless of the position and orientation of the objects in the room. After learning, the stimuli can be temporally paired with certain 'instinctual' responses to demonstrate such effects as primary and secondary conditioning, extinction of conditioned excitors, non-extinction of conditioned inhibitors, and stimulus blocking. The robot learns to avoid objects paired with aversive conditioners by running away. It indicates its preferred objects by approaching them for closer examination. This work is significant because it shows a visually oriented 'organism' interacting in a real environment, and reacting to salient visual stimuli according to its internal drives and past experiences.

References

1. Baloch, A. A., & Waxman, A. M. (1990). A neural system for behavioral conditioning of mobile robots. *Proceedings of the 1990 International Joint Conference on Neural Networks, San Diego.* II-723–II-728.

2. Baloch, A. A. (1991). Neural networks for behavioral conditioning of mobile robots. Ph.D. Thesis, Boston University.

3. Baron, R. J. (1985). Visual memories and mental images. *International Journal of Man-Machine Studies*, **23**, 275-311.

4. Carpenter, G. A., & Grossberg, S. (1987a). ART 2: Self-organization of stable category recognition codes for analog input patterns. *Applied Optics*, **26**(23), 4919-4930.

5. Carpenter, G. A., & Grossberg, S. (1987b). A massively parallel architecture for a self-organizing neural pattern recognition machine *Computer Vision, Graphics, and Image Processing*, **38**, 54-115.

6. Edelman, S., Bülthoff, H., & Weinshall, D. (1989). Stimulus familiarity determines recognition strategy for novel 3D objects. A.I. Memo No. 1138, Artificial Intelligence Laboratory, Massachusetts Institute of Technology.

7. Freeman, H., & Chakravarty, I. (1980). The use of characteristic views in the recognition of three-dimensional objects. In E. S. Gelsema & L. N. Kanal (eds.), **Pattern Recognition in Practice**. New York: North-Holland Publishing Company.

8. Grimson, W. E. L. (1986). The combinatorics of local constraints on model-based recognition. *Journal of the ACM*, **33**(4), 658-686.

9. Grossberg, S. (1988). Nonlinear neural networks: Principles, mechanisms, and architectures. *Neural Networks*, **1**, 17–61.

10. Grossberg, S. (1973). Contour enhancement, short term memory, and constancies in reverberating neural networks. *Studies in Applied Mathematics*, **52**(3), 217-257.

11. Koenderink, J. J., & van Doorn, A. J. (1979). The internal representation of solid shape with respect to vision. *Biological Cybernetics*, **32**, 211-216.

12. Palmer, Rosch, & Chase (1981). Canonical perspective and the perception of objects. In J. Long and A. Baddeley (Eds), **Attention and Performance IX**, Hillsdale, NJ: Erlbaum. 135-151.

13. Perrett, D. I., Harries, M. H., Bevan, R., Thomas, S., Benson, P. J., Mistlin, A. J., Chitty, A. J., Hietanen, J. K., & Ortega, J. E. (1989). Frameworks of analysis for the neural representations of animate objects and actions. *Journal of Experimental Biology*, **146**, 87-113.

14. Perrett, D. I., Mistlin, A. J., & Chitty, A. J. (1987). Visual neurones responsive to faces. *Trends in Neuroscience*, **10**(9), 358-363.

15. Perrett, D. I., Smith, P. A. J., Potter, D. D., Mistlin, A. J., Head, A. S., Milner, A. D., & Jeeves, M. A. (1985). Visual cells in the temporal cortex sensitive to face view and gaze direction. *Proceedings of the Royal Society of London, Series B*, **223**, 293-317.

16. Rock, I., & DiVita, J. (1987). A case of viewer-centered object perception. *Cognitive Psychology*, **19**, 280-293.

17. Rosenfeld, A., (1987). Recognizing unexpected objects: A proposed approach. *International Journal of Pattern Recognition and Artificial Intelligence*, **1**(1), 71-84.

18. Schwartz, E. L. (1977). Spatial mapping in the primate sensory projection: Analytic structure and relevance to perception. *Biological Cybernetics*, **25**, 181-194.

19. Schwartz, E. L. (1980). Computational anatomy and functional architecture of striate cortex: A spatial mapping approach to perceptual coding. *Vision Research*, **20**, 645-669.

20. Seibert, M. (1991). Neural networks for machine vision: Learning three-dimensional object representations. Ph.D. Thesis, Boston University.

21. Seibert, M., & Waxman, A. M. (1990). Learning aspect graph representations from view sequences. In D. S. Touretzky (ed.), **Advances in Neural Information Processing Systems 2**. San Mateo, CA: Morgan Kaufmann. 258-265.

22. Seibert, M., & Waxman, A. M. (1989). Spreading Activation Layers, Visual Saccades, and Invariant Representations for Neural Pattern Recognition Systems. *Neural Networks*, **2**(1), 9-27.

23. Underwood, S. A., & Coates, C. L. (1975). Visual learning from multiple views. *IEEE Transactions on Computers*, **24**(6), 651-661.

24. Waxman, A. M., & Wohn, K. (1987). Image flow theory: A framework for 3-D inference from time-varying imagery. In C. Brown (ed.), **Advances in Computer Vision**, Chapter 3, Hillsdale, NJ: Erlbaum Press. 165-224.

II.13

Hybrid Symbolic-Neural Methods for Improved Recognition Using High-Level Visual Features

GEOFFREY G. TOWELL AND
JUDE W. SHAVLIK

Computer Sciences Department
University of Wisconsin
Madison, WI 53706

I.   Introduction

Suppose that you are tying to teach someone who has never seen some category of objects to recognize arbitrary members of that category. One approach to doing so would be to teach that person how to recognize individual, high-level features common to the category. For instance, in teaching someone how to recognize a coffee mug, you might have that person learn to recognize a handle, notice the ability of hold liquids, and understand the utility of the picture on the side of the mug (i.e., none). Over time, that person would become proficient at recognizing the significant features of a

445

coffee mug. However, proficiency at the recognition of high-level features does not translate to proficiency at distinguishing coffee mugs from pails, bowls, etc. This is because in addition to their features, objects are defined by *relations* between those features. Thus, to teach a person to recognize a class of objects, you must not only provide instruction in the recognition of high-level features, but also in the interaction of those features.

The KBANN (*Knowledge-Based Artificial Neural Networks*) system [11, 14], which we are developing at the University of Wisconsin, investigates the problems that result from giving a computer imperfect instruction in the interactions of high-level features. That is, KBANN learns how to better recognize and more effectively use the high-level features that it already understands, rather than learning to recognize novel features. Instruction to KBANN takes the form of available "rules of thumb," which need be neither complete nor correct. KBANN then uses a set of classified training examples to modify the initially incorrect or incomplete rules so that they perform correctly on the training examples.

Briefly, KBANN is a hybrid learning system, making use of both symbolic and neural learning techniques. The approach taken by KBANN is to create knowledge-based neural networks (KNNs)[1] that initially encode in their units and weights, the information contained in a set of symbolic rules. KNNs are made by establishing a mapping between "domain theories" composed of hierarchical sets of non-recursive, propositional rules and feedforward neural networks. This mapping defines the topology of the KNN as well as its initial link weights. By defining KNNs in this way, problems such as the choice of an initial network topology and the sensitivity of the network to its initial conditions are either eliminated or significantly reduced. Furthermore, unlike ANNs, KNNs have their attention initially focused upon features, and combinations of features, believed to be relevant. Thus, they are less susceptible to spurious correlations in the training data.

While our results show that KBANN is a good method for creating symbolic/neural hybrids, KBANN is not neurologically plausible. Thus, although KBANN has proven to be a good way to provide computers with instruction, it is unlikely to be the way in which people learn.

The following section presents the KBANN algorithm in more detail. The subsequent section describes a set of tests of the algorithm. These tests show that providing a network with instruction, which may be only partially correct, about the interaction of high-level features significantly enhances learning. This enhancement appears both in the ability of the network to correctly generalize to examples not seen during training and in the time

---

[1]For this chapter, ANN refers to any artificial neural network that is not knowledge based. Hence, ANNs and KNNs describe non-intersecting sets of neural networks.

required to train the network. The chapter concludes with discussions of other work involving symbolic/neural hybrids and how our approach can be viewed as bridging the gap between low and high-level vision.

II.   The KBANN Algorithm

KBANN uses a knowledge base of domain-specific inference rules in the form of PROLOG-like clauses to define what is initially known about a topic. The knowledge base need be neither complete nor correct; it need only support approximately correct explanations. KBANN translates the knowledge base into an KNN in which units and links in the KNN correspond to parts of the knowledge base, as described in Table 1. The first subsection presents the approach KBANN uses to translate rules into neural networks. This is followed by a small example of the translation of a set of rules into a KNN. Subsequent subsections provide details of the KBANN algorithm. A final part of this section describes a recent enhancement to KBANN that further tightens the link between symbolic and neural learning.

Table 1. Knowledge Base – ANN Correspondences.

Knowledge Base	Neural Network
Final Conclusions	Output Units
Supporting Facts	Input Units
Intermediate Conclusions	Hidden Units
Dependencies	Weighted Connections

II.A.   Translation of Rules into KNNs

This section describes how KBANN translates rules containing the logical connectives AND, OR, and NOT into a KNN. Rules are assumed to be conjunctive, nonrecursive, and variable-free; disjuncts are encoded as multiple rules. (To simplify discussion in this section, only binary-valued features are assumed to exist. Handling of non-binary features is described in Section II.D.)

   The KBANN method sets weights on links and biases of units so that units have significant activation only when the corresponding deduction could be made using the knowledge base. For example, assume there exists a rule in the knowledge base with M *mandatory* antecedents (i.e., antecedents which must be true) and P *prohibitory* antecedents (i.e., antecedents which must not be true). The system sets weights on links in the KNN corresponding to the mandatory and prohibitory dependencies of the rule to ω and $-\omega$, respectively. The bias on the unit corresponding to the rule's consequent is set to $M * \omega - \phi$. ϕ is a parameter chosen so that units are active (i.e., have *activation* ≈ 1.0) when their antecedents are satisfied and are inactive (i.e., *activation* ≈ 0.0) otherwise.[2]

As illustrated in the example of the following section, this mapping procedure is sufficient only for a purely conjunctive knowledge base. Disjuncts cannot be handled because there is no way to set the bias of a unit that can be "deduced" in multiple ways such that no unintended combinations are allowed. For example, assume there exists a consequent Υ which can be proven by two rules, R_1 and R_2. Further assume, that there are seven antecedents (labeled to 0, ..., 6) to Υ and that antecedents [0 1 2] are mandatory for R_1 while antecedents [3 4 5 6] are mandatory for R_2. If the antecedents of R_1 and R_2 are all connected to Υ such that either [0 1 2] or [3 4 5 6] can activate Υ, then there is no way to set the bias of Υ such that unwanted combinations (e.g., [0 1 3 4]) cannot also activate Υ.

KBANN handles disjuncts by creating units Υ_1 and Υ_2, which correspond to R_1 and R_2, using the approach for conjunctive rules described above. These units will only be active when their corresponding rule is true. KBANN then connects Υ_1 and Υ_2 to Υ by a link of weight ω and sets the bias of Υ to $\omega - \phi$. Hence, Υ will be active when either Υ_1 or Υ_2 is active.

II.B.   Example of the Algorithm

As an example of the KBANN method, consider the artificial knowledge base in Figure 1a, which defines membership in category A. Figure 1b represents the hierarchical structure of these rules: solid and dotted lines represent necessary and prohibitory dependencies, respectively. Figure 1c represents the KNN that results from the translation into a neural network of this knowledge base. Units B1 and B2 in Figure 1c are introduced into the KNN to handle the disjunction in the rule set. Otherwise, each unit in the KNN corresponds to a consequent or an antecedent in the knowledge base. The thick lines in Figure 1c represent heavily-weighted links in the KNN that correspond to dependencies in the domain theory. The thin lines represent the links added to the network to allow refinement of the knowledge base.

As this example illustrates, the use of KBANN to initialize KNNs has two principal benefits. First, it indicates the input features that are believed to be important to an example's classification. Second, it specifies important

---

[2]Currently, we use $\omega = 4.0$ and $\phi = 2.0$, values empirically found to work well on several domains.

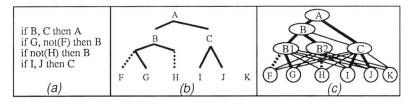

Figure 1. Translation of a Knowledge Base into a KNN.

derived features, thereby guiding the choice of the number and interconnectivity of *hidden units* in the KNN.

II.C.   Algorithm Specification

Three additional steps are required to complete ANN following the initial translation of the knowledge base. First, input units corresponding to features of the environment that do not appear as an antecedent of any rule must be added to the network. These units are necessary because an approximately-correct knowledge base may not have used some features that are necessary to accurately express a concept. Second, links must be added to the network to give existing rules access to items not mentioned in the knowledge base. These links initially have weight equal to zero. They are placed by grouping units according to their maximum path length from an input unit and adding links between all units in successive groups. Third, the network must be perturbed by adding random numbers within ϵ of zero to all link weights and biases to avoid symmetry breaking problems [10].[3]

The KBANN algorithm is summarized in Table 2. Once the network is produced, it is refined by providing training examples which are processed using backpropagation [10].

Table 2. Overview of the KBANN Algorithm.

1.	Translate rules to set initial network structure.
2.	Add input units not specified by translation.
3.	Add links not specified by translation.
4.	Perturb the network by adding near-zero random numbers to all link weights and biases.

[3]We currently use $\epsilon = 0.01$.

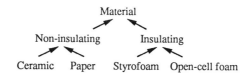

Figure 2. A Hierarchy of Cup Materials.

II.D.   Handling Non-Binary Features

Currently, the system can handle three types of features: *nominal, linear* and *hierarchical.* Discussions of the exact approach used to handle these feature types, and the added information they require, follows.

II.D.1.   Nominal

Nominally valued features are features whose possible values can be listed and have no structure. They are handled by assigning one input unit to each value of the feature. To do this, KBANN must be given a list of the possible values a feature can have. For example, if the feature color is stated to have three values: *red, green* and *blue*, then three input units: *color-is-blue, color-is-red* and *color-is-green*, will be created.

II.D.2.   Hierarchical

Hierarchical features are features that exist within an "ISA" hierarchy (e.g., a robin "is a" bird). They are handled, with one exception, as if a set of rules defined the ISA hierarchy. The exception is that whenever a rule in the knowledge base refers to an element in a hierarchy, in addition to the high-weight link from that element, low-weight links are created from all ancestors and descendants of the element. So, looking at Figure 2, if a rule contains *non-insulating* as an antecedent, the unit corresponding to the consequent of this rule would be given low weight links to *material, paper* and *ceramic*. In this way, the network is given the capability to specialize or generalize the initial rule according to the hierarchy.

II.D.3.   Ordered

Ordered features are a special type of nominal features for which the values are totally ordered. For example, *size* is typically represented using a totally ordered set of values similar to { *tiny small medium large huge* }. Like nominal features, ordered features are handled by creating one input unit for each value. However, ordered features cannot be treated like simple nominal features because the boundaries between subsequent values in the ordering are typically indistinct. Therefore, when an object is described as having *medium* size equally correctly be described as being either *large* or *small*. To account for the fuzziness inherent in ordered features, we activate all values of an ordered feature according to their distance from the given value using the following formula:

$$activation = \frac{1}{2}^{distance\_from\_given\_value}$$

Thus, when an object is described as *small*, the unit corresponding to small would have an activation of 1.0 while the units corresponding to *tiny* and *medium* would have activations of 0.5. The activations of *large* and *huge* would be 0.25 and 0.125 respectively.

II.E. KBANN-DAID

KNNs of the sort created by KBANN are difficult to train using backprop- agation because the weight-change algorithm of backpropagation implicitly assumes that networks are initially randomly weighted (see [10], pg. 300). KNNs violate this assumption. As a result, backpropagation can be ineffec- tive at correcting errors in the initial set of rules. Alternate error functions, like the *cross-entropy* function suggested by Hinton [6] ease this problem but do not eliminate it.

Therefore, we have developed the DAID (*Directed Activation Identifi- cation and Descent*) algorithm to enhance the ability of standard neural learning mechanisms to learn effectively and efficiently using KNNs. DAID acts a symbolic pre-processing phase for a KNN, making changes to KNNs based upon a set of examples and the information contained in the hierar- chical structure of the rules upon which the KNN is based. This attention to structure allows the DAID algorithm to make changes to parts of the net- works which require modifications while leaving unchanged those parts of the network that are correct. Thus, the DAID algorithm tightens further the links between symbolic and connectionist learning in the hybrid KBANN system.

Table 3 contains psuedocode for the KBANN-DAID algorithm. Briefly, the algorithm operates by presenting each example to a newly created KNN. If the KNN misclassifies the example, then the desired activation of that example is propagated to the parts of the network responsible for the errors. Rather than making changes based on a single example, the suggestions for change of every misclassified example are collected and changes are made which reflect the most common suggestions. While the changes are very

Table 3. The KBANN-DAID algorithm.

___

Translate the roughly correct set of rules into an KNN
For each example in the training set
   Classify using the KNN
   If the classification is incorrect then propagate desired activation
      through the network
   Collect suggestions resulting from the example
      When the desired activation reaches the input units
         call the suggestions *strong*
      Call all other suggestions *weak*
With collected suggestions
   Find the most common receiving unit (call it ϕ)
      While there exists strong suggestions to ϕ
         Find the most mentioned link among the specific suggestions
         Make the suggested change
         Remove suggestions to ϕ from examples corrected by the change
With remaining weak suggestions make small changes to the link weights
Train the KNN using backpropagation

___

likely good, they are not guaranteed to be correct nor are they guaranteed to be all the changes required by the network. Thus, as a final step of KBANN-DAID, the KNN is trained using backpropagation and the complete set of training examples.

The DAID algorithm is explained in more detail in [13].

III.   Empirical Tests of KBANN-DAID

This section presents a set of experiments which demonstrate the utility of symbolic/neural hybrids for learning to recognize objects using high-level features. For these experiments we use two domains, the recognition of cups and the recognition of chairs. These domains are defined in the next section. Our experiments, described in the following section, test the learning characteristics of neural networks over training sets of linearly increasing size. These tests show that using KBANN to provide a set of initial instructions about the interaction of the high-level features significantly enhances generalization ability of neural networks. Further tightening the link between symbolic and neural learning by using KBANN-DAID improves generalization over standard KNNs. The experiments also show that symbolic/neural hybrids can reduce the amount of training required by neural networks.

III.A. Datasets

The cup recognition studied studied in this paper is derived from [9]. The particular implementation of the cup problem, as well as the chair problem, is very similar to one previously used for testing KBANN [11].

For both of these datasets we formed a pool of training examples by first locating every combination of high-level features (Tables 4 and 7) that are categorized as positive examples by the "ideal" rule sets (Tables 6 and 9) for each problem domain. We then formed sets of negative examples by finding all examples not members of the set of positive examples that differ from a positive example by a single high-level feature. Thus, the set of negative examples contains only near-misses of the concept.

III.A.1. Cup Recognition

The cups dataset consists of three sets of information. First, a description of the information available about objects. This information, summarized in Table 4, contains the features used to describe objects and the values that those features may have. Second, a roughly-correct set of rules (Table 5) that describes an initial guess at what it means to be a cup in terms of the features in Table 4. Third, an "ideal" rule set (e.g., a set of rules that correctly label items drawn from the general population) in Table 6. The ideal set is never seen by the learning system; it serves as a reference point for the experiments. Thus, the learning problem is to adjust the initial rules so that they mimic the ideal. In Table 6 describing the cup ideal, *ADD* indicates a rule added to the initial rule set while *DROP* indicates a rule dropped from the initial rule set.

Given the high-level features describing cups (Table 4) and the set of ideal rules (Table 6), there are 16 positive examples. The initial set of rules provided to the KNN classifies 12 (75%) of these examples correctly. There are 112 examples in the set of negative examples that differ by one feature from the concept. The initial rules correctly classify 88 (79%) of these examples. Overall the initial rule set has a diagnostic significance of 0.58.[4]

---

[4]Diagnostic significance is a statistical score used to describing the combined effect of false positive and false negative guesses. It is defined by the following equation:
$$diagnostic\ significance = \frac{correct\ positives}{total\ positives} * \frac{correct\ negatives}{total\ negatives}.$$
In a two-category domain, random guessing has a diagnostic significance of 0.25.

Table 4. High-Level Features of Cups .

Features	Values	Features	Values
Has Handle	yes, no	Handle on Top	yes, no
Handle on Side	yes, no	Bottom is Flat	yes, no
Has Concavity	yes, no	Concavity Points Up	yes, no
Light	yes, no	Fragile	yes, no
Expensive	yes, no		
Made of	Ceramic, Paper, Styrofoam		

Table 5. Roughly-Correct Rules for Recognizing Cups .

Cup	:-	Stable, Liftable, Open-Vessel.
Stable	:-	Flat-Bottom.
Liftable	:-	Graspable, Light.
Graspable	:-	Has-Handle.
Open-vessel	:-	Has-Concavity, Concavity-Points-Up.

Table 6. Changes to Initial Cup Rules to Create the Ideal.

ADD	Graspable	:-	Handle-on-Side.
ADD	Graspable	:-	Made-of-Styrofoam, (NOT Handle-on-Top).
DROP	Graspable	:-	Has-Handle.

III.A.2.   Chair Recognition

Like the cups dataset, the chair recognition dataset consists of three sets of information: [1] a set of high-level features used to describe objects (Table 7), [2] a roughly-correct set of rules that describes what it means to be a chair (Table 8), and [3] an "ideal" rule set (Table 9). Notation in these tables follows that of the cup domain.

As in the cup domain, there are 16 positive examples of chairs. The initial set of rules provided to the KNN classifies 4 (25%) of these examples correctly. There are 120 negative examples of which 116 (97%) are correctly classified by the initial rules. Overall, the initial rules correctly classify 88% of these examples but have a diagnostic significance of 0.24, less than that of random guessing.

III.B.   The Efficacy of Symbolic/Neural Hybrids

This section presents tests of the ability of three neural learning systems to generalize, from training on sets of examples of increasing size, to correct classification of sets of examples not seen during training (e.g., testing sets). The three learning systems, presented in increasing order of symbolic/neural

Table 7. High-Level Features of Chairs.

Features	Values	Features	Values
Horizontal Seat	yes, no	Seat Hieght	medium, other
Seat Size	medium, other	Has Back	yes, no
Number of Legs	three, four, other	Leg Lengths	equal, not equal
smooth seat	yes, no	padded seat	yes, no
Has Arms	yes, no	Has Wheels	yes, no
Supports Load	yes, no		

Table 8. Roughly-Correct Rules for Recognizing Chairs.

Chair	:-	Stable, Comfortable, Can-Support.
Can-Support	:-	Supports-Bottom, has-back.
Supports-Bottom	:-	has-horizontal-seat, medium-sized-seat,
	:-	medium-height-seat.
Stable	:-	four-legs, equal-length-legs.
Comfortable	:-	has-smooth-seat, has-padded-seat.

Table 9. Changes to Initial Chair Rules to Create the Ideal.

DROP	Supports-Bottom	:-	has-horizontal-seat, medium-sized-seat,
		:-	medium-height-seat.
DROP	Can-Support	:-	Supports-Bottom, has-back.
ADD	Can-Support	:-	Supports-Bottom.
ADD	Stable	:-	three-legs, equal-length-legs.
ADD	Supports-Bottom	:-	has-horizontal-seat, medium-sized-seat
		:-	medium-height-seat, can-support-load.

hybridization, are standard ANNs, KNNs, and KNNs trained using KBANN-DAID.

Training consisted of randomly selecting N positive and $3 * N$ negative examples from the pool of examples. This collection of examples was then used to train each of the learning systems. Networks were trained with backpropagation [10] using the *cross-entropy* error function [6] by presenting examples to the network until the activation of the output unit was within 0.25 of the correct answer for every training example. Examples were presented using a pick-and-replace methodology biased to preferentially select examples which were incorrectly classified on their previous presentation. After training, every example in the pool that was not a member of the training set was used for testing. Examples in the test set were considered correctly classified when the difference between the actual output activation and the correct output activation was less than 0.5.

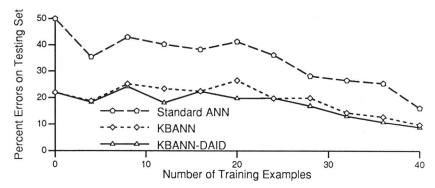

Figure 3. Error Rates in the Cup Domain.

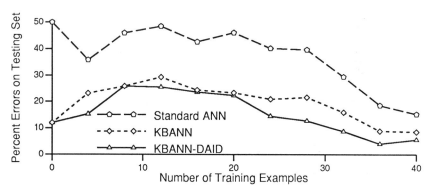

Figure 4. Error Rates in the Chair Domain.

III.B.1.   Error Rates on Testing Examples

Figures 3 and 4 present the average error rate as training set size increases for **cups** and **chairs**, respectively. Over both domains and all training set sizes, networks trained using KBANN-DAID had lower error rates than either of the other systems. Standard ANNs consistently had the highest error rates. A statistical analysis of these results indicates that KNNs, using both standard KBANN and KBANN-DAID, are significantly superior to standard ANNs. Further, KBANN-DAID often significantly improves, and never significantly harms, generalization by KNNs.

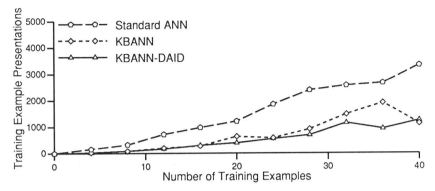

Figure 5. Examples Required for Training in the Cup Domain.

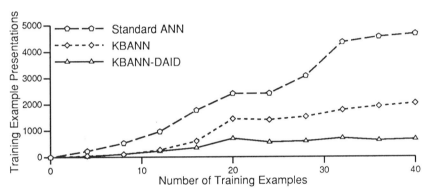

Figure 6. Examples Required for Training in the Chair Domain.

III.B.2. Training Required by Networks

Figures 5 and 6 present the median number of training example presentations as a function of training set size for cups and chairs, respectively.[5] Over both domains and all training set sizes, KNN required much less training than standard ANNs. As for error rates, statistical analysis shows that networks trained using KBANN-DAID were never significantly slower than standard KNNs and were often significantly faster. Also, standard ANNs took significantly more time to train than KNNs.

---

[5] We use median here to avoid distortions resulting from occasional, extremely long training times.

IV. Discussion

The results provide strong evidence that symbolic/neural hybrids, such as KBANN, are effective for learning how to recognize objects when provided with high-level features. Tests of the KBANN-DAID algorithm indicate that tightening the links between symbolic and neural learning beyond that of KBANN can result in further improvements.

Beyond the anticipated result that increasing the strength of the symbolic/neural hybrid improves learning, there is one significant pattern in the data. Specifically, the error rate for KNNs both with and without DAID initially increases in the chairs domain. This increase occurs because on small training sets the network improves its ability to correctly categorize positive examples at the expense of additional errors on the negative examples. Thus, the diagnostic significance of the trained network improves although its accuracy declines. As the size of the training set increases the error rate falls, eventually reaching levels superior to the initial rule set. At the largest size training set, the error rate for KBANN-DAID is less than half of the initial error and the diagnostic significance has improved from 0.24 to 0.91.

By contrast, on the cups domain diagnostic significance is initially high because the error rates on positive and negative examples are approximately equal. Thus, training with small set of examples has little effect on either the diagnostic significance or the error rate. With more than 20 examples in the training set for cups, the error rate declines steadily and the diagnostic significance of the trained KNN increases. Final diagnostic significance for KBANN-DAID is 0.82, a major increase from the 0.58 of the initial rules.

Notice that each of the high-level features that we use as inputs could itself be the output of a network designed to recognize that particular feature. That is, there could be trainable networks for the recognition of handles, wheels or arms, the differentiation between types of construction material, the determination that a chair seat is padded, etc. Thus, the hybrid networks that we propose can be pictured as sitting at the top of a hierarchy of networks. At the lowest level of this hierarchary would be networks that recognize very small features directly from images.

The important part of this hierarchy is that many of its parts are independently trainable. Thus, like the person in the introduction who is taught to recognize a coffee mug by recognizing its parts, lower-level networks could be trained separately. Then, hybrid networks such as those discussed in this chapter could be created to relate features already known to the system.

V.   Related Work

Little work has been done on the use of symbolic/neural hybrids for the improvement of existing knowledge as described in this chapter. Several systems have been described for implementing rule-based reasoning in ANNs [4, 12]. However, these systems do not learn; ra her they use ANNs as an approach to parallel implementations of production systems. On the other end of the spectrum are approaches to building ANNs from scratch using neural learning techniques that have been adapted to produce networks that are symbolically interpretable throughout learning [2, 5]. These systems receive no initial instruction, hence they may generalize no better than a standard ANN. However, they have an advantage over a standard ANN in that the information contained in the networks is in a human-comprehensible form.

The approach to symbolic/neural hybrids taken by the KBANN system falls somewhere between these extremes. Also falling between these extremes are systems by Fu [3] and Katz [8]. Both of these systems are learning systems that use a set of initial knowledge to define the structure and weights of an ANN. However, the approaches taken by the these systems are quite different from KBANN. Katz' system [8] focuses on improving the execution speed of the network by learning new new connections that bypass hidden layers in its initial network. Thus, his algorithm is similar in spirit to explanation-based learning, a field of symbolic machine learning that explores the problems of learning to use knowledge efficiently [1, 9].

Fu's system [3] is, perhaps, the most similar to KBANN. However, while we were very careful to use only differentiable functions to form KNNs, Fu's system requires non-differentiable functions. Therefore, his system is unable to use standard neural-learning mechanisms like backpropagation. To skirt this problem, he uses two mechanisms to propagate error through networks, one for differentiable, and one for non-differentiable, units. By carefully controlling modifications, the network can add or delete rules and rule antecedents until it performs correctly on a training set. However, this control appears to be expensive, as it may require checking every training example to make a single change to the network. While the system was shown to correctly repair rule sets to which low levels of noise were added, no results were reported for its ability to generalize to examples not seen during training.

VI. Conclusions

In this chapter we have described the KBANN system, which is a hybrid of symbolic and connection learning procedures. Our experimental results indicate that KBANN can be used to improve roughly-correct information about the recognition of objects given high-level features. Our results further indicate that while this roughly-correct information can result in initial performance that is worse than random guessing, its use as a basis for learning can significantly improve generalization by trained networks while reducing the time required for training.

While we make no claims about neurological plausibility, we expect that the approach characterized by KBANN will prove useful in interpreting the information derived by low-level vision systems [7]. Thus, our approach may point the way to computer-based systems for object recognition based wholly upon artificial neural networks.

Acknowledgement

This research was partially supported by Office of Naval Research Grant N00014-90-J-1941 and National Science Foundation Grant IRI-9002413.

References

[1] G. F. DeJong and R. F. Mooney. Explanation-based learning: An alternative view. *Machine Learning*, 1:145–176, 1986.

[2] J. Diederich. Knowledge-intensive recruitment learning. Technical Report ICSI-TR-88-010, International Computer Science Institute, Berkeley, CA, 1988.

[3] Li-Min Fu. Integration of neural heuristics into knowledge-based inference. *Connection Science*, 1:325–340, 1989.

[4] S. I. Gallant. Connectionist expert systems. *Communications of the ACM*, 31:152–169, 1988.

[5] L. O. Hall and S. G. Romaniuk. A hubrid connectionist, symbolic learning system. In *Proceedings of the Eighth National Conference on Artificial Intelligence*, pages 783–788, Boston, MA, August 1990.

[6] G. E. Hinton. Connectionist learning procedures. *Artificial Intelligence*, 40:185–234, 1989.

[7] P. Kanerva. Countour-map encoding of shape for early vision. In *Advances in Neural Information Processing Systems*, volume 2, pages 282–289, Denver, CO, 1989. Morgan Kaufmann.

[8] B. F. Katz. EBL and SBL: A neural network synthesis. In *Proceedings of the Eleventh Annual Conference of the Cognitive Science Society*, pages 683–689, Ann Arbor, MI, August 1989.

[9] T. M. Mitchell, R. Keller, and S. Kedar-Cabelli. Explanation-based generalization: A unifying view. *Machine Learning*, 1:47–80, 1986.

[10] D. E. Rumelhart, G. E. Hinton, and R. J. Williams. Learning internal representations by error propagation. In D. E. Rumelhart and J. L. McClelland, editors, *Parallel Distributed Processing: Explorations in the microstructure of cognition. Volume 1: Foundations*, pages 318–363. MIT Press, Cambridge, MA, 1986.

[11] J. W. Shavlik and G. G. Towell. An approach to combining explanation-based and neural learning algorithms. *Connection Science*, 1:233–255, 1989.

[12] D. S. Touretsky and G. E. Hinton. A distributed connectionist production system. *Cognitive Science*, 12:423–466, 1988.

[13] G. G. Towell and J. W. Shavlik. Directed propagation of training signals through knowledge-based neural networks. Technical Report 989, University of Wisconsin, Computer Sciences Department, Madison, WI, 1990.

[14] G. G. Towell, J. W. Shavlik, and M. O. Noordewier. Refinement of approximately correct domain theories by knowledge-based neural networks. In *Proceedings of the Eighth National Conference on Artificial Intelligence*, pages 861–866, Boston, MA, 1990.

II.14

Multiscale and Distributed Visual Representations and Mappings for Invariant Low-Level Perception

HARRY WECHSLER

Dept. of Computer Science
George Mason University
Fairfax, VA

I. Introduction

The underlying challenge for computational vision is that the sheer complexity of the visual task has been mostly ignored by current approaches. Most visual tasks are complex because they are underconstrained--or in mathematical terms are ill-posed; however, the human visual system displays robustness despite stringent constraints on what can be accomplished and with relatively limited computational resources. As a consequence, one can argue for an integrated goal-driven theory of distributed computation over space, time and function (Wechsler, 1990). Distributed computation goes beyond mere processing to include image representations and strategies.

Distributed strategies represent active perception and the symbiotic link to the environment. They are functional if flexible processing is allowed, or exploratory when we engage the environment to interpret it better. Exploratory behavior, which mediates between sensory inputs and exploratory and performatory motor actions, could be encoded as the links of aspect graphs known as visual potentials (Koenderink and van Doorn, 1979). Note that many of those affordances are ecologically motivated and correspond to the niche we have built for ourselves during evolution. The functional aspect of active perception amounts to top-down modeling priming the operation and integration of modular processes towards image interpretation and analysis.

The visual system casts most visual tasks as minimization problems and solves them using distributed computation and enforcing nonaccidental, natural constraints. The constraints are either prewired or evolve through system adaptation and learning. Computational vision (CV) amounts then to

$$CV = PDC$$

$$= PDR + PDP + PDS$$

$$= PDR + PDP + AP$$

$$= PDR + PDP + (FAP + EAP)$$

where the abbreviations stand for parallel distributed computation (PDC), parallel distributed representations (PDR), parallel and distributed processing (PDP), parallel distributed strategies (PDS), active perception (AP), functional active perception (FAP), and exploratory active perception (EAP). A multilevel architecture, which implements such a computational vision theory, has been suggested recently (Wechsler, 1990).

The organization of the human visual system (HVS) is retinotopic and as a consequence the relative positioning of the receptive fields (RF) preserves the input's spatial topology. The research done by Hubel and Wiesel (1962) has uncovered a regular pattern of interconnections for the early visual processing stages. Their suggested pattern, or cytoarchitecture, has as its main processing unit a 3D hypercolumn whose coordinate axes are those of RF position, orientation, and size. The functionality of such an architecture, originally thought to detect edges, has been challenged and instead the possibility that such an architecture derives conjoint spatial/spatial-frequency image representations has emerged. The evolvement of such conjoint image representations parallels the development and use of multiresolution image representations (Rosenfeld, 1984) such as the pyramidal structures and/or the wavelets.

Conjoint spatial/spatial-frequency representations are primarily useful because they improve pattern separability relative to pure spatial or spatial-frequency representations and offer enhanced localization. Representational separability is a central problem in pattern recognition and signal detection theory, and not surprising, it should be an important component of texture and shape representations. The spatial separability offered by conjoint representations extends to the temporal dimension as well and can be exploited towards optical flow derivation, depth and depth of field computation, and shape from texture estimation. The derivation of conjoint (spectral) representations, in terms of their coefficients, can be done using parallel and distributed processing. Both supervised and unsupervised neural learning algorithms can be used towards that end and in addition to the separability mentioned above one also achieves a significant degree of adaptive (localized) data compression.

According to Herbert Simon, all mathematical derivation can be viewed simply as a change of representation, making evident what was previously true but obscure. This view can be extended to all of problem-solving. Solving a problem amounts to representing and transforming it so as to make the solution transparent. To paraphrase the last sentence, information has to be made explicit if and when needed. Perception is a sequence of transformations or mappings whose goal is to capture some invariant aspect of the world surrounding us. The invariance is needed for both recognition and us moving around and performing safely despite image variability. A basic issue underlying self-organization is that of determining what principles, if any, lead to the development of neural circuitry. Linsker (1988) has considered multi-layered networks with feed-forward connections, linear summation response and Hebbian (classical conditioning) learning in order to derive optimization principles leading to the development of cortical cells. The development of such cells is predicated on the preservation of information when signals are transformed at each processing stage. Such information preserving mappings could account for the development of a hypercolumnar architecture made up of cells whose sensitivity is with respect to contrast and orientation.

Spatial cognition and purposeful behavior depends largely on detection, tracking and recognition. To accomplish such goals, the visual system needs to permanently map retinal-centered representations into both head-centered and canonical object-based representations. The eye and retinal coordinates can be used by backpropagation (gradient-descent) neural learning to determine the head-centered coordinates as needed for motor coordination under visual guidance. Mapping between viewer-centered representations and canonical representations is essential for object recognition. Another strategy for recognition could involve the permanent upgrading of maps keeping in registration viewer-oriented representations as subsumed by visual potentials and (retinal) viewer-centered image representations. The last possibility is related to the concepts of directed and active perception.

Directed perception (Cutting, 1986) implements a many(information)-to-one(object properties) mapping. Thus, there is the possibility of being selective about which information source one can use. Different invariants, based on their specific information efficacy, can then be selected and used for different tasks. Directed and active perception underspecify process but overspecify interpretation. The perceiver has the choice of what information to pick up, and both adaptation and task functionality can further enhance the ultimate visual performance. Exploration, which is characteristic of active perception, is clearly an essential ingredient, because it allows the observer to attend to only those affordances most likely to be successful in sifting through the information available in the optical array. As a consequence directed perception provides a mobile and intelligent observer with the capability to decide what and how much one needs to be exposed to, and from that experience what and how much information to "intelligently" pick up and process, so it can correctly interpret the surrounding world. Directed perception, builds upon low-level invariants and mappings to be described later on, and is the model-driven counterpart of the data-driven multiscale and distributed low-level visual representations.

The scope of this chapter is then to present a multiscale and distributed visual architecture across both the spatial and temporal dimensions and to describe its invariant characteristics with respect to the geometry of the image formation process. The architecture lends itself to the mappings needed to align between retinal images and head-centered coordinates and/or between viewer-oriented and canonical object or viewer-centered image representations. The resulting cytoarchitecture leads to compact image representations and data compression, facilitates alignment, and helps with the derivation of middle-level intrinsic image representations such as optical flow, depth and depth of focus, and 3D structure (shape) from shade or texture information. Memory models can be learned and implemented using similar concepts of parallel distributed computation (PDC). As a result the multiscale and distributed visual representation and mappings characteristic of invariant low-level vision provide a cytoarchitecture that facilitates image analysis and understanding using bottom-up and top-down processes suitable for the traditional analysis & synthesis (prediction) interpretation cycle.

II. Multiscale and Distributed Image Representations

Conjoint spatial/spatial-frequency representations (s/sf) are based on image representations indicating the spectral contents in localized regions in the spatial domain. As a consequence these methods overcome the shortcomings of traditional Fourier-based techniques and can achieve high resolution in both the spatial and spatial-frequency domain. High resolution, an indication of the degree of localization, is achieved through the distributed aspect of image representations. Furthermore, the capability to derive high resolution spectral information makes available multiscale information as well. As a result the conjoint spatial/spatial-frequency representations yield highly effective multiscale and distributed image representations. A detailed discussion of such image representation and their usefulness for computational vision is provided by Jacobson and Wechsler (1988). Many empirical studies have suggested that conjoint s/sf representations are fundamental to the encoding of visual information in the cortex of all mammals including our own human species (Pollen and Ronner, 1983).

The class of conjoint s/sf image representations includes the spectrogram, the difference of Gaussians (DOG), the Gabor (power spectrum) and the Wigner distribution (WD). The search for multiscale and distributed image representations permeates much of computer vision research and one should note that fractals (Mandelbrot, 1982) and especially the wavelets (Mallat, 1989), which are classes of localized and recursively defined expansion function in terms of dilation, translation, and rotation parameters, are conceptually related to the conjoint s/sf representations. Daugman (1990) has shown that the class of 2D Gabor elementary functions can be derived from a single basic generator by dilations, translations, and rotations, using the concept of wavelets, while the relationship between fractals and wavelets is discussed by Holschneider (1988).

A key issue in comparing conjoint s/sf image representations is the resolution that can be attained simultaneously in the two domains (s & sf). Often referred to as uncertainty, this topic has been addressed first by Wilson and Granlund (1984) and Daugman (1985). As an example, Daugman has examined the class of Gabor filters and found that they achieve the lower bound of uncertainty as measured by the product of effective widths corresponding to the spatial and spectral domains. The uncertainty, related to entropy, is measured separately along each dimension of the joint s/sf representation.

Jacobson and Wechsler (1988) probed further into the resolution/uncertainty issue and came to the following two conclusions. First, the uncertainty of conjoint s/sf image representations should be derived from the Cartesian ($s \times sf$) domain rather than be measured over two independent dimensions, those of s and sf. Second, the spectrogram, the DOG, and Gabor power spectrum representations are smoothed versions of the Wigner distribution. The smoothing results from convolving the WD with various kernels. As a consequence no conjoint s/sf image representation can achieve better resolution than the Wigner distribution.

Conjoint s/sf image representations have become a major tool for texture analysis. Malik and Perona (1989) have developed a computational model of human texture perception based on the use of radial and directional Gaussian derivatives (and DOG) and targeted on texture segmentation. Rentschler et al (1988) and Bovik et al (1990) have used Gabor filters for texture analysis, while Reed and Wechsler (1990) have employed the Wigner distribution for texture segmentation and Gestalt clustering.

The actual derivation of conjoint s/sf image representations illustrates the relationship between parallel distributed representations (PDR) and their computation using parallel distributed processing (PDP). As an example, Daugman (1988) has shown how to derive the coefficients of the 2D Gabor transform using a three-layer neural network and minimization of energy landscapes. (Gradient-descent type) minimization using additive neural models (Cohen and Grossberg, 1983; Hopfield, 1984) is employed. Neural computing of the discrete Gabor transform is of interest because the corresponding base is not orthogonal and because the set of coefficients can be quite useful for data compression applications. Another example where PDP cab be used for the derivation of a conjoint s/sf representations is the computation of the DOG. Specifically, Szu and Messner (1986) have used the distributed associative memory (DAM) as correlation learning (outer product) (Kohonen, 1987) to model the connecting network as a negative-feedback system. The multichannel system corresponding to the DOG can then be derived if the coupling matrix of the negative-feedback system is modelled by a Gaussian and it implements a modulation transfer function (MTF).

The domain of applicability of conjoint s/sf image representations can be extended to the derivation of intrinsic image representations. The temporal dimension can then be included as well and the concept is supported among other things by stroboscopic apparent motion studies that can be explained in terms of spatiotemporal frequency (STF) bandpass channels (Watson and Ahumada, 1983). STF methods for deriving optical flow have been suggested first by Jacobson and Wechsler (1987) and Hegger (1987) using the Wigner distribution and the Gabor power spectrum for the underlying RF, respectively, and by Fleet and Jepson (1989) using local phase information.

The extension of conjoint s/sf representations to stereoscopic computation was done by Jepson and Jenkin (1988). Their work makes a compelling case "against the extraction of complex monocular features such as zero-crossings, against the use of inhibiting surface constraints and against the use of global stereopsis to produce a single-valued retinotopic depth map." Such comments are closely related to the ones espoused earlier by Jenkin and Kolers (1986) in the context of optical flow derivation. Disparity is related to the local phase difference between bandpass versions of the stereo pair. No complex token extraction or feature correspondence is needed, and the spatial and temporal properties of the disparity measurement allow the construction of filter detectors that are tuned to surfaces with particular 3D orientations and of specific 3D trajectories. The approach is conceptually similar to the STF method mentioned earlier and reaffirms that intrinsic images, characteristic of middle-level vision can be derived using conjoint (multiscale and distributed) s/sf image representations.

Optical flow and stereoscopic computation suggest a massive cytoarchitecture of spatiotemporal filters starting from low-level vision and extending throughout middle-level vision as well. The same cytoarchitecture also leads to compact image representations and data compression and facilitates the recovery of 3D structure (shape) from shade or texture information. As an example, Pentland (1988) approach for shape from shading discards the usual assumptions about surface smoothness and advances instead the use of multiscale and distributed representations in terms of orientation, spatial-frequency, and phase. Spectral information is obtained using Gabor filters and yields localized measurements of sine and cosine phase frequency contents. Krumm and Shafer (1990) have used the spectrogram, another example of a conjoint s/sf representation to develop algorithms for shape from texture and for dealiasing image data. They suggest that conjoint s/sf representations "should be the key aid in untangling the complex interaction of phenomena in images, allowing automatic understanding of real-world scenes", and that the resulting "sense of vision" would be a prerequisite for a robot to function in an unstructured environment.

III. Invariance

One of the reasons for the high degree of computational complexity of perception lies in the inherent variability of the input. Such variability can be the result of noise, incomplete (or missing) data, and geometric or topological changes. Machine vision systems must not only perceive the identity of objects despite such variability but they must also explicitly characterize it because the variability in the image formation process, particularly that due to geometric distortions, inherently carries valuable information about the scene.

The variability aspect could also be very harmful, if not appropriately handled, because the recognition system would then need to deal with a possible infinite number of image occurrences. Since there are many viewpoints this would lead to searching a multidimensional parameter space, a quite expensive computational proposition. To deal with such viewpoint variability one must rather define and capture image invariants and such an approach is related to James Gibson's pioneering work in the psychophysics of perception. Gibson (1950, 1966, 1979) has emphasized throughout his career the important role of geometric and topological invariants. Gibson's approach, sometimes coined as direct perception, suggests the derivation of image invariants, and it is feasible for a visual system employing parallel and distributed processing to resonate to such invariants (Wechsler, 1990).

Ecological optics as defined by Gibson (1979) refers to that human ability of perceiving a stable and consistent world using a systemic approach consisting of optics, perspective geometry, and environmental information. According to Gibson "the basis of the so-called perception of space is the projection of its objects and elements as an image, and the consequent graduate changes of size and density in the image as the objects and elements recede from the observer. Multiscale and distributed visual representations as discussed earlier are the foundation necessary to capture the image contents in terms of size and density such that one can then "consider, one by one, these various so-called cues for distance perception when they are reformulated as gradients of the retinal image. The hypothesis is that constant perception depends on the ability of the individual to detect the invariants, and that he ordinarily pays no attention whatever to the flux of changing sensations."

Image invariants are crucial for robust and efficient perception in terms of performance and resources. As stated by Gibson (1966) "beside the changes in stimuli from place to place and from time to time, it can also be shown that certain higher-order variables of stimulus energy--ratios and proportions, for example--do *not* change. They remain invariant with movements of the observer and with changes in the intensity of the stimulation, and they constitute, therefore, information about the permanent environment." As a consequence there is a need for both spatiotemporal conjoint visual representations and invariants. The remaining of this section considers such invariants in terms of their spatial and temporal characteristics and suggests an architecture built in terms of distributed and localized spatiotemporal filters.

A. Spatial Invariance

We discuss first spatial invariance to linear transformation given in terms of scale, rotation, and translation. One technique useful to achieve invariance to rotation and scale changes is the conformal mapping. The conformal mapping, also known as the complex-logarithmic (CL) or log-polar transformation , maps logarithmically spaced concentric rings and radials of uniform angular spacing into uniformly spaced straight lines. After CL mapping, rotation and scaling about the origin in the Cartesian (x, y) domain become linear shifts in the log-polar $[\ln(r), \theta]$ domain. CL mapping has also been conjectured as an important cortical function by neurophysiological research (Schwartz, 1977). Following the CL mapping one can use correlation techniques to detect invariance to (scale and rotation) within a linear shift (WALS) between objects.

Both the Wigner and Gabor representations can be subject to log-polar mappings. As an example, Jacobson and Wechsler have shown how the 4D conformally mapped Wigner distribution (WD) is WALS-invariant to scale and rotation about some fixation point such as the origin (0, 0) (Wechsler, 1990), while the spectral self-similarity of the 2D Gabor primitives becomes apparent in the 2D Fourier plane when using the polar wavelet code (Daugman, 1990)

The next question is how to achieve also shift invariance. One can take the CL concept and achieve shift (translation) invariance as well using the Mellin transform (MT) (Bracewell, 1978) at the price of discarding phase information thought to be necessary for faithful image representation and recognition (Oppenheim and Lim, 1981). Note that the magnitude of the MT is the same as the magnitude of the Fourier transform (FT) evaluated using an exponentially sampled grid. Such a sampling grid is similar to that employed by the human retina, and yields high resolution in the fovea and low resolution in the preattentive periphery. Another alternative, that of multi-positional conformal mappings, which is more in line with an active perceptual system design to detect and track visual targets, would have the fixation point (i.e., the origin) sequentially moved about, at the cost of adding two additional dimensions to the parametrized 4D conformally mapped WD. The schemes fall within the framework of active perception and they are computationally less expensive to implement than a full 6D WALS-invariant WD as suggested earlier. Large misalignments due to translation could be accounted for by gaze control. Another possibility for achieving full invariance to linear transformations (LT) (translation included) within a distributed filter architecture in presented next.

Zetsche and Caelli (1989) suggest a 4D perceptual representation, which is "encapsulated in a set of filtered images, each containing the original Cartesian coordinates of the image and indexed in terms of the orientation and scale-specific filters used to produce them. The result of this scheme is that a change in position, scale, or orientation of the input pattern has the effect of shifting the distribution of filters outputs within (position) and between (orientation and scale) columns." Such a distributed representational scheme is implemented through filters defined in terms of specific scale and orientation characteristics. The corresponding FT of such filters are Gaussian, are sufficient to reconstruct the input image, and their spectral position and bandwidth define the scale and orientation sensitivity range.

Having dealt with invariance to linear transformations (LT) we turn now our attention to projection invariance. One solution considered by Jacobson and Wechsler (1991) is to apply to a given image all possible reprojective transformations in terms of slant and tilt (σ, τ) pairs. The important observation to make is that every planar form in the scene that produced the original image will appear in frontoparallel view within one of the reprojected images and that the inverse projection mapping finds the object plane coordinates only to within a scale factor, proportional to the distance from the viewpoint to the intersection between the object plane and the line of sight. Conjoint s/sf visual representations can then be geometrically reprojected back to multiple, distal surface coordinate reference frames. Such a concept is supported by McLean-Palmer et al (1985), who have reported that simple cells exhibit a spatial receptive field (RF) skew ranging from 10 to 43 degrees between the main axis of the RF envelope and the axis of RF modulation, and is also consistent with zero-skew Gabor functions seen in perspective views.

We have shown above that conjoint s/sf visual representations can be augmented to include invariance with respect to linear transformations (LT) and projection. The use of LT and/or reprojection filters amounts to the availability of a massive cytoarchitecture whose responsibility is to achieve geometrical invariance within a linear shift. Such an architecture is also well-suited to implement fault-tolerant and robust visual behavior with respect to noise and/or occlusion. The invariant conjoint representations are analog and could help with the derivation of intrinsic images and/or could interface directly with the visual memory for recognition purposes

B. Temporal Invariance

Algebraic considerations can be used to derive temporal invariants and to implement qualitative motion interpretation. Hoffman (1977) and Dodwell (1983) have suggested the Lie transformation group (LTG) model "to represent and explain how the locally smooth processes observed in the visual field, and their integration into the global field of visual phenomena, are consequences of special properties of the underlying neuronal complex. The LTG model seeks to relate microgenetic processes in the visual field, which are reflected in strictly localized activities within the nervous system to more macroscopic aspects of both the visual scene and the neural activities which underlie pattern processing." The LTG model could establish "resonance" relationships between a given LTG operator and the trajectory/orbit which it generates. Conversely, if the result of applying the operator to a given trajectory is identically zero then the operator is the one that generated that trajectory.

As an example consider the case of landing on a surface, which corresponds to an optical flow whose pattern is one of dilation, and for whom the corresponding LTG operator is $L = [x\partial/\partial x + y\partial/\partial y]$. Other examples include LTG (invariant) operators such as $(L_x, L_y, L_t) = (\partial/\partial x, \partial/\partial y, \partial/\partial t)$ whose orbits are (horizontal, vertical, straight lines parallel to the t-axis in the x-y-t space) and achieve shape constancy under translation and/or time. Perceptual invariance to rotation changes is achieved using $L = -y\partial/\partial x + x\partial/\partial y$ whose orbits are concentric circles. Translation at constant depth can be detected by looking for an above threshold average flow $\mathbf{v} = (v_x, v_y)$. Constant horizontal or vertical translation is detected by detecting flow fields for whom $\partial v_x/\partial x = 0$ or $\partial v_y/\partial y = 0$. Translation and rotation in depth correspond to shrinking or dilation patterns and concentric circles and can be detected using the operators L_s and L_r defined as $L_s(\mathbf{v}) = x\partial\mathbf{v}/\partial x + y\partial\mathbf{v}/\partial y$ and $L_r(\mathbf{v}) = -y\partial\mathbf{v}/\partial x + x\partial\mathbf{v}/\partial y$. The shrinking and dilation patterns correspond to focus of dilation (FOD) and expansion (FOE) characteristic to taking off or landing. Impeding collision can be detected if $L_s(\mathbf{v}) < \varepsilon$ and $\partial\mathbf{v} = 0$.

LTG operators could account for a fast response in critical situations, such as collision avoidance, and their implementation would be in terms of resonance to that specific invariant. Papathomas and Julesz (1988) have surveyed the LTG model in neurophysiology (LTG/NP) and the psychophysical evidence associated to known phenomena of constancy. They have shown that an LTG model might provide a unifying theory to identify images that obey affine transformations. The underlying computation is mostly local and could be easily implemented using single instructions multiple data (SIMD) type of parallel and distributed architectures.

The qualitative interpretation of optical flow has been extended by Eagleson (1987) to the interpretation of general 3D motion in terms of perceptual invariants and the corresponding spatiotemporal filters needed to capture them. 3D motion is factored out into localized 2D horizontal and vertical translations, divergence, curl, and 2D shear optical flows. The flow fields correspond to specific motion deformations and a 6D TLG, which consists of six orthogonal multiscale and distributed convolution kernels, can resonate to these specific types of motion. The optical flows can be estimated using the phase shifts of spatiotemporal filters rather than slope measurements based on the intensity function. The localized deformations and the resonators are related through exponential conformal mappings.

The 6D LTG consists of $<L_x, L_y, L_s, L_r, L_b, L_B>$, where the first two operators resonate to horizontal and vertical translation, the next two (divergence and curl) to dilation and rotation patterns, and the last two operators resonate to shear. Assuming that projected motion, i.e., optical flow $\mathbf{v}$ is defined as $\mathbf{v} = (v_x, v_y)$ then the (spatial derivatives) LTG operators are defined as *divergence* $= v_{xx} + v_{yy}$, *curl* $= v_{xy} - v_{yx}$, *shear (b)* $= v_{xx} - v_{yy}$, *shear (B)* $= v_{xy} + v_{yx}$. The operators estimate the spatial derivatives of optical flow in terms of filter-based kernels. Resonance to 3D motion is accomplished by estimating the 6D LTG group from 2D bandpass spatial frequency filters. The factorization of 3D motion and the corresponding 6D TLG points out to the strong relationship between multiscale and distributed conjoint visual representations, conformal mappings, perceptual invariance, and resonance.

IV. Mappings

We discussed earlier specific mappings, such as the conformal mapping, whose role is to undo the geometrical changes involved in the image formation process and to make available canonical visual representations suitable for invariant image recognition. We consider next distributed mappings whose goal is to provide invariances appropriate for sensorimotor control and orientation.

The retinal image undergoes continuous deformations whenever the head moves, but the visual world remains stable. The only objective perception is the subject's own locomotion. Changes in retinal images are modeled as projective transformations, where point-to-point and line-to-line correspondence is preserved but shape changes. The geometry of transformations is of considerable importance for vision and according to Gibson (1950) "it is conceivable that the clue to the whole problem of pattern perception might be found here. The transformations of a given pattern, mathematically defined, does not simply destroy the pattern as one might at first suppose. A transformation is a regular and lawful event which leaves certain properties of the pattern invariant. Moreover, a series of transformations can be endlessly and gradually applied to a pattern without affecting its invariant properties. The features that are preserved may be the mediators of a stable world and the features not preserved the mediators of the visual impression of motion."

A basic question of interest is related to the computations needed to implement coordinate transformations which map sensory inputs to motor outputs. As discussed by Zipser and Andersen (1988) "visual inputs are collected in the coordinate frame of the retina on which the visual environment is imaged, but motor movements such a such as reaching are made to locations in external space. Changes in eye position will alter the retinal locations of targets while their spatial locations remain constant. As a result, visual inputs must be transformed from retinal coordinates to coordinates that specify the location of visual objects with respect to the body to perform accurately directed movements." Neurophysiological studies carried out by Zipser and Andersen seem to suggest that the neural area responsible for such spatial transformations is the area 7a of the posterior parietal cortex. The neurons encode both the retinal (grid) location of the visual stimulus and the position of the eyes (within the orbit) for subsequent processing responsible to compute the spatial location of external targets. A connectionist model, implemented using back-propagation (BP) learning, was able to map the spatial information available in area 7a neurons and could account for their observed response properties. Mappings as reported above together with well-known behavioral adaptation shown by fast recalibration for space distortions (such as those caused by wearing prisms) suggest that the perceptual system is quite plastic. Learning, possibly of the parallel and distributed (PDP) type, is then crucial for mapping the environment into purposeful and successful behavior.

There have been additional neorophysiological studies concerned with the mappings involved in purposeful motor behavior. As an example, Grobstein (1990) considers directed movement and spatial representation in the frog. The study rejects the hypothesis that the sensorimotor interface can be implemented using table look-up mapping for the simple reason that there is a dimensionality mismatch between the (2D) retinal projection and the orienting movements to be performed in the 3D Euclidean space. The conclusions reached by Grobstein suggest that "the linkage between a sensory map and the circuitry responsible for the elaboration of ballistic movement is not itself map-like but instead involves an activity-gated divergence, and that an apparently general, non map-like form of spatial representation is involved in the linking circuitry." The "activity-gated divergent network" stands for a neural architecture "in which activity at a given location in the nervous system may have any of a variety of outcomes, depending on the pattern of some other contemporaneous activity." Such a characteristic is reminiscent of the mapping considered by Zipser and Andersen (1988) and discussed earlier, and leads to machine vision tasks such as data fusion and/or multisensory data integration. One concludes that distributed mappings are most appropriate for fault-tolerant (to lesions) and robust (to environmental changes) sensorimotor linkages.

Motion analysis provides many clues for image interpretation while at the same time leads to major computational problems such as blur and perceptual stability. Van Essen and Anderson (1990) suggest that "the cortical representations of moving images may be transformed from absolute retinal coordinates into a relativistic coordinate frame using local motion information intrinsic to the retinal image." Dynamic remappings, crucial for a mobile observer, have to permanently update and maintain faithful world visual representations and seem to be implemented "using a dynamic but relativistic reference frame for motion analysis that is linked to the local velocity field, so that common (reference) image motion is subtracted out during visual processing." The most likely solution suggested by van Essen and Anderson (1990) to achieve both deblur and perceptual stability seems to employ relativistic velocity fields, which are "narrowly tuned for velocity, but whose optimum velocity can be dynamically changed to match the local velocity field." The intrinsic spatiotemporal conjoint optical flow representations discussed earlier support such velocity channels and could account for the trade-offs involved in orientation, position, and spatial-frequency uncertainty (Marcelja, 1980). Shifter circuits, the hardware likely to implement such relativistic coordinate transformations, could also be responsible for some of the characteristics of directed perceptions leading to adaptively controlled resolution.

Spatial cognition depends largely on detection, tracking, and recognition. As discussed before any visual system needs to permanently update the transformations mapping the memory contents into the continuously changing view of the world. Wechsler and Zimmerman (1988, 1989) have shown how resonance to geometrical invariants can be achieved through the use of distributed associative memory (DAM). Ballard (1988) relates active vision to the transformations involved to maintain object-centered frames (OCF) and their relationships. The transformations sought map the OCF into views dynamically established as fixation-point frames (FPF). Such mappings, similar to the Hough transform, emerge when enough supporting evidence supporting a particular transformation has accrued as a result of matching the OCF and FPF representations. Hinton and Parsons (1988) bring supporting evidence in favor of scene-based representations (SBR) based on mental-rotation-like experiments. The paradigm they suggest maps retina-based representations (RBR), which are viewer centered, into canonical object-based representations (OBR). The mappings discussed and their robust and efficient implementation using parallel and distributed processing (PDP) is crucial for the further development of intelligent robotics and autonomous navigation.

V. Conclusions

We have shown that multiscale and distributed visual representations and mappings permeate much of low-level vision and that they are responsible for later stages of visual processing such as the derivation of intrinsic images and object recognition. Conjoint spatial/spatial-frequency (s/sf) visual representations invariant to linear transformations and projective distortions are feasible and they can be realized through the use of a massive architecture of bandpass filters.

The resulting bandpass cytoarchitecture leads to compact image representations and data compression, facilitates alignment, and helps with the derivation of middle-level intrinsic image representations such as optical flow, depth and depth of focus, and 3D structure (shape) from shade or texture information. Memory models can be learned and implemented using similar concepts of parallel distributed computation (PDC) and they facilitate fast and robust indexing capabilities. As a result the multiscale and distributed visual representation and mappings, characteristic of invariant low-level vision, provide a cytoarchitecture that facilitates image analysis and understanding using bottom-up and top-down processes suitable for the traditional analysis & synthesis (prediction) interpretation cycle. Directed perception, building upon low-level invariants and mappings, is the model-driven counterpart of the data-driven multiscale and distributed low-level visual representations.

The emergence of conjoint visual representations, motivated by Linsker (1988) from an information theory viewpoint, leads according to Daugman (1990) to advantageous "coding criteria such as decorrelation, completeness, compression, extraction of redundancy, minimization of conjoint 2D spatial/spectral uncertainty, self-similarity of primitives, and sensitivity to anisotropic statistics in image structure." Known relationship between spectral and statistical information support the fundamental role such conjoint representations can play in texture segmentation and Gestalt clustering.

An example of a machine vision system implementing the analysis & synthesis interpretation cycle is ZEEL (Zimmerman and Wechsler, 1990). The system recognizes 3D objects from their 2D perspective projections. The approach taken is to search for information which remains invariant with respect to certain metric and non-metric transformations produced by viewpoint change. The distributed associative memory (DAM) stores invariant (to scale and rotation) characteristic 2D views (as those employed by visual potentials) and can actively adjust the system parameters. As a consequence both the interpretation of spatial layout and object recognition could be accomplished simultaneously. This is an example of functional visual perception (FAP) discussed earlier and the goal is guide the formation of the (intrinsic) depth map used for recognition.

Invariants should play a crucial role in perception because they correspond to fixed principles of causality, space, and time. Such ethological principles, consistent within our own ecological niche rather than learning, impose organization and structure on visual perception. Such a view is also consistent with Gestalt psychology, which asserts that visual characteristics are holistic and that perception of components is determined by their relationship to the whole. Resonance models, as those suggested by the Lie Transformation Group (LTG), and implemented using parallel and distributed processing (PDP) models such as connectionism (and back-propagation) and distributed associative memory (DAM), can be easily coupled to conjoint s/sf low-level image representations and are characteristic of the upper levels of perception and cognition.

Such principles as espoused above are consistent with the methodology suggested earlier by Witkin and Tenenbaum (1983) who stated that "perceptual organization is a primitive level of inference, the basis for which lies in the relation between structural and causal unit. The appearance of spatiotemporal coherence or regularity is so unlikely to arise by chance interaction of independent entities that such regular structure when observed, almost certainly denotes some underlying unified cause or process. This will be shown to have broad implications for computational theories of vision, providing a unifying framework for many current techniques of early and intermediate vision, and enabling a style of interpretation more in keeping with the qualitative and holistic character of human vision."

References

1. Ballard, D. H. (1988), Eye Fixation and Early Vision: Kinetic Depth, *Int. Conf. Computer Vision (ICCV)*, Tampa, Florida, 524-531.

2. Bovik, A. C., Clark. M, and Geisler, W. S. (1990), Multichannel Texture Analysis Using Localized Spatial Filters, *IEEE Trans. Pattern Analysis and Machine Intelligence*, **12**(1), 55-73.

3. Bracewell, R. (1978), *The Fourier Transform and its Applications*, McGraw-Hill.

4. Cohen, M. A., and Grossberg, S. (1983), Absolute Stability of Global Pattern Formation and Parallel Memory Storage by competitive Neural Networks, *IEEE Trans. Systems, Man, Cybernetics*, **13**(5), 815-825.

5. Cutting, J. E. (1986), *Perception with an Eye for Motion*, MIT Press.

6. Daugman, J. G. (1985), Uncertainty Relation for Resolution in Space, Spatial Frequency, and Orientation Optimized by Two-Dimensional Visual Cortical Filters, *J. of the Optical society of America (JOSA)*, **2**, 1160-1169.

7. Daugman, J. G. (1988), Complete Discrete 2-D Gabor Transform by Neural Networks for image Analysis and Compression, *IEEE Trans. Acoustics, Speech, and Signal Processing*, **36**(7), 1169-1179.

8. Daugman, J. G. (1990), An Information-Theoretic View of Analog Representation in Striate Cortex, in E. Schwartz (Ed.), *Computational Neoroscience*, MIT Press, 403-423.

9. Dodwell, P. C. (1983), The Lie Transformation Group Model of Visual Perception, *Perception and Psychophysics*, **34**(1), 1-16.

10. Eagleson, R. (1987), Estimating 3D Motion Parameters from the Changing Responses of 2D Bandpass Spatial Frequency Filters, *IEEE Montreal Technologies Conference: Compint '87*, 102-105.

11. Fleet, D. F., and Jepson, A. D. (1989), Computation of Normal Velocity from Local Phase Information, *Conf. Computer Vision and Pattern Recognition*, San Diego, CA, 379-386.

12. Gibson, J. (1950), *The Perception of the Visual World*, Houghton-Mifflin.

13. Gibson, J. (1966), *The Senses Considered as Perceptual Systems*, Houghton-Mifflin.

14. Gibson, J. (1979), *The Ecological Approach to Visual Perception*, Houghton-Mufflin.

15. Grobstein, P. (1990), Strategies for Analyzing Complex Organization in the Nervous System. II. A Case Study: Directed Movement and Spatial Representation in the Frog, in E. Schwartz (Ed.), *Computational Neuroscience*, MIT Press, 242-255.

16. Heeger, D. J. (1987), Optical Flow from Spatiotemporal Filters, *Int. Conference Computer Vision (ICCV)*, London, UK, 181-190.

17. Hinton, G. E., and Parsons, L. M. (1988), Scene-Based and Viewer-Centered Representations for Comparing Shapes, *Cognition*, **30**, 1-35.

18. Hoffman, W. C. (1977), An Informal historical description of the "LTG/NP", *Cahiers de Psychologie*, **20**, 139-150.

19. Holschneider, M. (1988), On the Wavelet Transformation of Fractal Objects, *Journal of Statistical Physics*, **50**(5/6), 963-993.

20. Hopfield, J. J. (1984), Neurons with Graded Responses Have Collective Computational Properties like those of Two-States Neurons, *Proc. Natl. Acad. Sci. USA*, **81**, 3058-3092.

21. Hubel, D. H., and Wiesel, T. N. (1962), Receptive Fields, Binocular Interaction and Functional Architecture in the Cat's Visual Cortex, *J. Physiology*, **160**, 106-154.

22. Jacobson, L., and Wechsler, H. (1988), Joint Spatial/Spatial-Frequency Representations, *Signal Processing*, **14**, 37-68.

23. Jacobson, L., and Wechsler, H. (1987), Derivation of Optical Flow Using a Spatiotemporal-Frequency approach, *Computer Vision, Graphics, and Image Processing*, **38**, 29-65.

24. Jacobson, L., and Wechsler, H. (1991), Invariant Architectures for Low-Level Vision, *Computer Vision, Graphics, and Image Processing* (special issue) (to appear).

25. Jain, A. K., and Farrokhnia, F. (1990), Unsupervised Texture Segmentation Using Gabor Filters, *IEEE Conf. Systems, Man, and Cybernetics*, Los Angeles, CA.

26. Jenkin, M., and Kolers, P. A. (11986), Some Problems with Correspondence, RBCV-TR-86-10, Computer Science Dept , University of Toronto.

27. Jepson, A. D., and Jenkin, M. 91989), The Fast Computation of Disparity from Phase Differences, *Conf. Computer Vision and Pattern Recognition,* San Diego, CA, 386-398.

28. Koenderink, J. J., and van Doorn, A. J. (1979), The Internal Representation of Solid Shape with respect to Vision, *BiolCyb*, **32**, 211-216.

29. Kohonen, T. (1987), *Self-Organization and Associative Memories* (2nd ed), Springer-Verlag.

30. Krumm, J., and Shafer, S. A. (1990), Local Spatial Frequency Analysis for Computer Vision, CMU-RI-TR-90-11, Robotics Institute, Carnegie Mellon University.

31. Linsker, R. (1988), Self-Organization in a Perceptual Network, *Computer*, **21**(3), 105-117.

32. Malik, J., and Perona, P. (1989), A Computational Model of Texture Segmentation, *IEEE Conf. Computer Vision and Pattern Recognition*, San Diego, CA, 326-331.

33. Mallat, S. (1990), A Theory for Multiresolution Signal Decomposition : the Wavelet Representation, *IEEE Trans. Pattern Analysis and Machine Intelligence*, **11**(7), 674-693.

34. Mandelbrot, B.B. (1982), *The Fractal Geometry of Nature*, W. H. Freeman.

35. Marcelja, J. (1980), Mathematical Description of the Responses of Simple Cortical Cells, *J. Opt. Soc. Am. (JOSA)*, **70**, 1297-1300.

36. McLean-Palmer, J., Jones., J., and Palmer, J. (1985), New Degrees of Freedom in the Structure of Simple Receptive Fields, in *Investigative Opthalmology and Visual Science Supplement (ARVO)*, **265**.

37. Oppenheim, A. V., and Lim, J. S. (1981), The Importance of Phase in Signals, *Proc. IEEE*, **69**, 529-541.

38. Papathomas, T., and Julesz, B. (1988), Lie Differential Operators in Animal and Machine Vision, *NATO Conf. From Pixels to Features*, Bonas, France.

39. Pentland, A. (1988), Shape Information from Shading: A Theory About Human Perception, *Int. Conference Computer Vision (ICCV)*, Tampa, FL, 404-413.

40. Pollen, D. A., and Ronner, S. F. (1983), Visual cortical neurons as localized spatial frequency filters, *IEEE Trans. Systems, Man, Cybernetics*, **13**(5), 907-915.

41. Reed, T. R., and Wechsler, H. (1990), Segmentation of Textured Images and Gestalt Organization Using Spatial/Spatial-Frequency Representations, *IEEE Trans. Pattern Analysis and Machine Intelligence*, **12**(1), 1-12.

42. Rentschler, I., Hubner, M., and Caelli, T. (1988), On the Discrimination of Compound Gabor Signals and Textures, *Vision Research*, **28**(2), 279-291.

43. Rosenfeld, A. (Ed.) (1984), Multiresolution Image Processing and Analysis, Springer-Verlag.

44. Schwartz, E. L. (1977), Spatial Mapping in the Primate Sensory Projection: Analytic Structure and Relevance to Perception, *BiolCyb*, **25**, 181-194.

45. Szu, H., and Messner, R. P. (1986), Adaptive Invariant Novelty Filters, *Proc. IEEE*, **74**(3), 518-519.

46. Van Essen, D. C., and Anderson, C. H. (1990), Reference Frames and Dynamic Remapping Processes in Vision, in E. Schwartz (Ed.), *Computational Neoroscience*, MIT Press, 278-294.

47. Watson, A. B., and Ahumada, A. J., Jr., (1983), A Look at Motion in the Frequency Domain, *SIGRAPH/SIGART Interdisciplinary Workshop, Motion : Representation and Perception*.

48. Wechsler, H. (1990), *Computational Vision*, Academic Press.

49. Wechsler, H., and Zimmerman, L. (1988), 2D Invariant Object Recognition Using Distributed Associative Memories, *IEEE Trans. Pattern Analysis and Machine Intelligence*, **10**(6), 811-821.

50. Wechsler, H., and Zimmerman, L. (1989), Distributed Associative Memory for Bin-Picking, *IEEE Trans. Pattern Analysis and Machine Intelligence*, **11**(8), 814-822.

51. Wilson, R., and Granlund, G. H. (1984), The Uncertainty Principle in Image Processing, *IEEE Trans. Pattern Analysis and Machine Intelligence*, **6**(6), 758-767.

52. Witkin, A., and Tenenbaum, J. M. (1983), On the Role of Structure in Vision, in J. Beck, B. Hope and A. Rosenfeld (Eds.), *Representation and Understanding*, Academic Press, 35-82.

53. Zetzche, C., and Caelli, T. (1989), Invariant Pattern Recognition Using Multiple Filter Image Representations, *Computer Vision, Graphics, and Image Processing*, **45**, 251-262.

54. Zimmerman, L., and Wechsler, H. (1990), 3D Recognition Through Equal Area Reprojection and Rotation/Scale Invariant Classification, *IEEE Trans. Pattern Analysis and Machine Intelligence* (under review).

55. Zipser, D., and Andersen, R. A. (1988), A Back-Propagation Programmed Network that Simulates Response Properties of a Subset of Posterior Parietal Neurons, *Nature*, **331**(6158), 679-684.

II.15

Symmetry: a context free Cue for Foveated Vision

YEHEZKEL YESHURUN
DANIEL REISFELD
HAIM WOLFSON

Dept. of Computer Science
Tel Aviv University
Tel Aviv, Israel

1 Introduction

The amount of visual information that is gathered by humans from a field of view that subtends over 200 degrees is enormous. In order to analyze this input in a plausible time frame, some data compression must be applied. The solution that is suggested by primate vision is based on foveated vision: the resolution of the retina decreases as we go from the fovea to the periphery, and computational resources are selectively directed towards a set of *fixation points*, forming a "scan path". A fixation point is projected on the fovea where it is sampled with the highest resolution, while the rest of the image is sampled by a decreasing number of "processors" (photoreceptors, ganglion cells and cortical cells) in the periphery. These points are natural *attention points*, and the visual information that is gathered when the eye is directed towards these points provide a basis for a more thorough investigation by higher processes. Numereous experimental results indicate this type of processing; when a primate focuses his attention on a spatial location, events occurring at that point are responded to more rapidly, give rise to enhanced electrical activity, and can be reported at a lower threshold (Posner adn Peterson 1990). While there is no obvious algorithmic definition of the scan path for primates, it is clear that fixation points are not chosen at random, but rather selected by some "Interest Detection" operator. We will use this term to describe the hypothetical operator that receives an image as an input and assigns an "interest"" value to each location in the image. A fixation point is selected according to the peaks of these interest values, and the scan path is the route defined by successive fixation points. It is clear that the actual mechanism in primates is highly context dependent and hard to define, but we will show that it is possible to construct a non trivial interest operator by using only low level, context free visual data. In this chapter we suggest an operator based on the intuitive notion

Neural Networks for Perception
Volume 1
Human and Machine Perception

477

of symmetry, which effectively locates interest point of a picture in real time, can be incorporated in passive, as well as active, visual systems, and can be naturally implemented by a neural network. The results of its operation are consistent with psychophysical evidence that suggest that symmetry plays a role in the selection of fixation points, and can be applied successfully without a priori knowledge of the world. For machine vision tasks, combining the operator with some predefined conceptions about the input images can provide a powerful tool for finding features in intricate natural scenes. We demonstrate, for example, the localization of faces and facial features in real time on detailed and noisy pictures.

Natural objects often give rise to the human sensation of symmetry. Consider, for example, the fact that a stereotypical drawing of a tree or a mountain is highly symmetric. Our sense of symmetry is so strong that most man-made objects are symmetric. It is thus clear why the Gestalt school considered symmetry as a fundamental principle of perception (Kohler 1929). This symmetry is , however, more generalized than the strict mathematical notion of symmetry. For instance, an image of a human face would be considered highly symmetric by most human observers, but is not symmetric in the mathematical sense. The operator we suggest is inspired by the intuitive notion of symmetry, and assigns a "symmetry value" to every point in a picture, based on data that can be extracted at a very low level vision stage. In this respect, points with high symmetry value are natural interest points.

The most general definition of an interest point use the observation that it is often the spatial location where the "unexpected" happens (Ullman 1984). This view can be specified in terms of various image dimensions, such as edges, texture and colour. For example, interest points are regarded by many as points of high curvature (e.g. (Attneave 1954;Kaufman and Richards 1969; Yeshurun and Schwartz 1989) , and, indeed, if we expect edges and their derivatives to be continuous, points of high curvature are unexpected. Others suggest to measure edge density, designated as "busyness" – the smoothed absolute value of the Laplacian of the data (Peleg et al. 1987), or rapid changes in the gray levels (Sorek and Zeevi 1988). We argue that symmetry is a more general and powerful concept, since it more closely fits psychophysical evidence, and it is more useful in detecting interesting features in complex scenes.

Symmetry is being widely used in computer vision (Atallah 1985; Blum and Nagel 1978; Brady and Asada 1984; Bookstein 1979; Freidberg 1986; Ho and Dyer 1986; Nalwa 1989; Nevatia and Binford 1977; Marula 1989; Xia 1989; Yuen 1989) (additional comprehensive bibliography can be found in (Xia 1989; Uen 1989). However, it is used as a mean of convenient representation, characterization, shape simplification, or approximation of objects, whose existence is already assumed. A typical vision task consists of edge detection, followed by segmentation, followed by recognition. A symmetry operator is usually applied after the segmentation stage. Our symmetry operator can be applied immediately after the stage of edge detection, where there is absolutely no knowledge regarding the objects in the scene. Moreover, the output of the symmetry operator can be used effectively to direct higher level processes, such as segmentation and recognition, and can serve as a guide for locating the interesting objects.

The symmetry operator lends itself to a very natural implementation by neural networks. If we assume the existence of orientation selective elements with an elongated receptive fields, the symmetry operator can be implemented by a small number of neural maps that process the input of the orientation selective layers and produce a spatial map where centers of symmetry are marked by peaks in neural activity.

2   Defining the Operator

In the usual mathematical notion, an object is regarded as symmetric if the application of certain transformations, called symmetry operations, leaves it unchanged while permuting its parts. In order to use these symmetry operations it is necessary to know the shape of an object before we can predicate whether it is symmetric or not. However, the process of finding interest points must precede complex processes of detecting the objects in the scene. Even if the objects' shapes are known, truly symmetric objects are rare in natural scenes, and therefore any attempt to formulate an interest operator based on the strict mathematical notion of symmetry is doomed to fail.

In this section we define a symmetry measure for each point and direction. Let $p_k = (x_k, y_k)$ be any point $(k = 1, \ldots, K)$, and denote by $\nabla p_k = \left(\frac{\partial}{\partial_x} p_k, \frac{\partial}{\partial_y} p_k \right)$ the gradient of the intensity at point p_k. We assume that a vector $v_k = (r_k, \theta_k)$ is associated with each p_k such that $r_k = \log \left(1 + \| \nabla p_k \| \right)$ and $\theta_k = \arctan \left(\frac{\partial}{\partial_y} p_k / \frac{\partial}{\partial_x} p_k \right)$. For each two points p_i and p_j, we denote by l the line passing through them, and by α_{ij} the angle counterclockwise between l and the horizon. (See Figure 1).

We define the set $\Gamma(p, \psi)$, a distance weight function $D_\sigma(i, j)$, and a phase weight function $P(i, j)$ as

$$\Gamma(p, \psi) = \left\{ (i, j) \, \middle| \, \frac{p_i + p_j}{2} = p \, , \, \frac{\theta_i + \theta_j}{2} = \psi \right\}$$

$$D_\sigma(i, j) = \frac{1}{\sqrt{2\pi}\sigma} e^{-\frac{\| p_i - p_j \|}{2\sigma}}$$

$$P(i, j) = \left(1 - \cos \left(\theta_i + \theta_j - 2\alpha_{ij} \right) \right) \left(1 - \cos \left(\theta_i - \theta_j \right) \right)$$

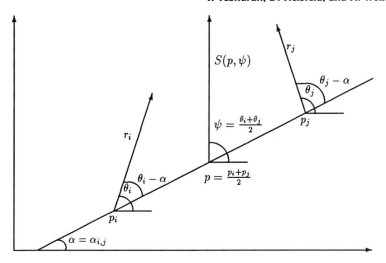

Figure 1: The contribution to symmetry of the gradients at p_i and p_j.

The symmetry measure $S_\sigma(p, \psi)$ of each point p in direction ψ is defined as

$$S_\sigma(p, \psi) = \sum_{(i,j) \in \Gamma(p,\psi)} D_\sigma(i,j) P(i,j) r_i r_j$$

The rationale of this formula can be understood by decomposition and explanation of the operands:

$D_\sigma(i,j)$: The symmetry induced by two points decreases as their distance increases, thus the operator has a local nature. Different values for σ enable different scales.

$r_i r_j$: This term is high when there is a good correlation between two large gradients. We use gradients rather than intensities since meaningful information is usually connected with changes of intensity. For instance, a uniform intensity wall is highly symmetric but probably not very interesting. In natural scenes we prefer to use the logarithm of magnitude instead of the magnitude itself, since it reduces the differences between high gradients, and therefore the correlation measure is less sensitive to very strong edges.

$1 - \cos(\theta_i + \theta_j - 2\alpha_{ij})$: A maximum symmetry measure is achieved when $(\theta_i - \alpha_{ij}) + (\theta_j - \alpha_{ij}) = \pi$, i.e. when the gradients at p_i and p_j are oriented in the same direction towards each other. This is consistent with the intuitive notion of

Figure 2: Two opposite situations with the same symmetry value.

symmetry. The expression $1 - \cos(\theta_i + \theta_j - 2\alpha_{ij})$ decreases continuously as the situation deviates from the ideal one. Notice that the same measure is achieved when the gradients are oriented towards each other or against each other. The first situation corresponds to symmetry within a dark object on a light background, and the second corresponds to symmetry within a light object on a dark background. It is easy to distinguish between the two cases. (See Figure 2).

$1 - \cos(\theta_i - \theta_j)$: The previous expression attains its maximum whenever $(\theta_i - \alpha_{ij}) + (\theta_j - \alpha_{ij}) = \pi$, and includes the case $\theta_i - \alpha_{ij} = \theta_j - \alpha_{ij} = \pi/2$, which occures on a straight edge, which we do not regard as interesting. The current expression compensates for this situation.

S_σ can be implemented either as an array of a fixed number of discrete angle bins (typically $n = 1, 2, 4, 8$ or 16) or as a dynamic data structure containing all the nonzero symmetry value directions. Representing in a discrete number of bins is faster and has a natural interpretation. We shall denote by S_n the symmetry operator implemented by using n bins as follows:

$$S_n(p, i) = \int_{\psi \in bin(i)} S_\sigma(p, \psi)\, d\psi$$

where $bin(i)$ is defined for $i = 1, \ldots, n$ as

$$bin(i) = \bigcup_{k=0,1} \left[k\pi + \frac{(i-1)\pi}{n} - \frac{\pi}{2n}, \; k\pi + \frac{i\pi}{n} - \frac{\pi}{2n} \right)$$

An important special case is S_1:

$$S_1(p, 1) = \int_0^{2\pi} S_\sigma(p, \psi)\, d\psi$$

which is the isotropic symmetry operator. It is interesting to note, in that regard, that if the image is considered to be the cotangent field of the intensity image, then the isotropic operator will detect the singularities of the principle direction fields (Sander and Zucker 1988). $S_2(p, i)$, for example, classifies symmetry points as horizontal – $S_2(p, 1)$ and vertical symmetry points – $S_2(p, 2)$. Its bins are drawn in Figure 3.

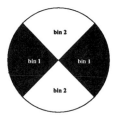

Figure 3: The angle bins of $S_2(p, 2)$.

Sometimes it is necessary to detect points that are highly symmetric in several distinct directions. We call such a symmetry a *circular symmetry* – $CS(p)$ and its value can be evaluated using the formula:

$$CS_\sigma(p) = \iint_{\zeta < \eta} S_\sigma(p, \zeta) S_\sigma(p, \eta) \sin\left(\frac{\eta - \zeta}{2}\right) d\zeta \, d\eta$$

Note that the term $\sin\left(\frac{\eta-\zeta}{2}\right)$ reaches its peak when η and ζ are in opposite directions, and decreases monotonically until they are identical.

If the operator is implemented in a small number of discrete bins, a simpler definition for circular symmetry suffices:

$$CS_n(p) = \prod_{i=1}^{n} (1 + S_n(p, i))$$

3   Operation on Natural scenes

The symmetry operator can be applied successfully on intricate natural scenes. Figure 4 depicts three people on a noisy background. The strongest peaks of $CS_8(p)$ are marked by crosses and are located on the three faces in one of the images. In the other one, two faces are marked, but the third one (with the gas mask) seems to be merged with the square above it (which is marked). This case demonstrate one of the drawbacks of the operator: in order to use only low level analysis, occluded objects that are not separated by marked edges might be merged. However, one should bear in mind that the interest operator is used to specify an area where additional analysis is required rather than locate an object.

Another intricate scene is demonstrated in Figure 5. The location of the strongest peaks of $CS_8(p)$ are marked by crosses and are located on the eyes.

Combination of semantics with the symmetry operator can serve for feature detection. An example is facial feature detection. We have already demonstrated that

Figure 4: The strongest peaks of $CS_8\,(p)$ are marked by crosses on the original picture.

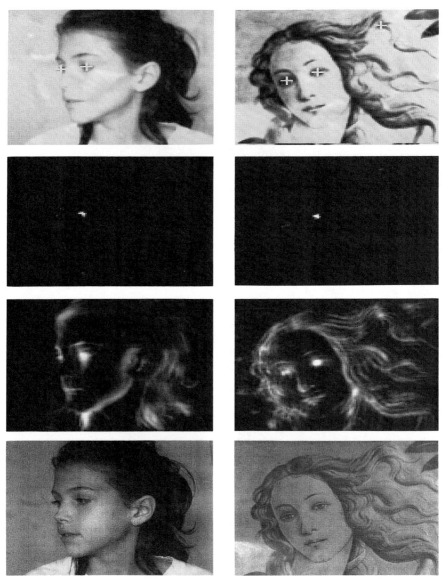

Figure 5: Interest points on human faces. for each of the two faces, we show (bottom to top) the original image, $S_8(p)$, highest peaks of $CS_8(p)$, and superposition of the peaks on the original images).

$CS_8(p)$ applied to a face attains high peaks at the eyes, since the eyes are symmetric along various directions and scales. In addition, various facial features have high symmetry values along vertical lines, and therefore we expect $S_8(p, 1)$ to highly respond to the eyes, mouth and nose. Figure 5 shows the result of the application of $S_8(p, 1)$ on a face image.

4 Psychophysical Correlates

Symmetry is considered to be a powerful organizing principle by the Gestalt theory (Kohler 1929). This is not a surprising result, considering the fact that many natural and man-made objects are symmetric, and that symmetry can be used as a very efficient data compression cue. There are many psychophysical works investigating humans ability to detect bilateral symmetry (For example (Bruce and Morgan 1975)). It is accepted that human are able to detect mirror symmetry and that symmetry detection has a local nature. However, there is no link suggested between these capabilities and the choosing of attention points. Some relations between symmetry and fixational mechanisms might be hinted upon by Kaufman and Richards (1969). In a psychophysical experiment, they presented small line drawings (subtending less than 5° on the retina) to subjects, and traced the scan path that was elicited.

Figure 6 shows the fixation points superimposed on some of the stimuli used. It can be seen that most of the fixation points are in intriguing agreement with the results of applying the symmetry operator to a similar image – the operator $S_1(p, 1)$ attains its peaks at the same points for all the figures reported. Another finding of this experiment shows that the fixation points tend to be more scattered as the size of the drawings increases, thus supporting the assumption that symmetry detection can be partly attributed to local mechanisms.

Symmetry in nature (as projected on the retina) does not follow the exact mathematical formulation of symmetry. Retinal projections of objects is skewed, occluded and noisy. Some results (Barlow and Reeves 1979) suggest that there is a certain degree of tolerance to deviations from exact symmetry. In this exeepriment humnas were presented Random Dot Displays that consist of varying degree of symmetry, and asked whether the display is symmetric. It was found that the placing of symmetrical pairs need not be exact in order to perceive it as symmetrical, and can be compensated up to a displacement of 24 arc minutes. These results are also in agreement with our operator, since it responds to a more generalized type of symmetry, and can accomodate a considerable deviation from exact symmetry.

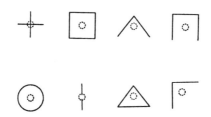

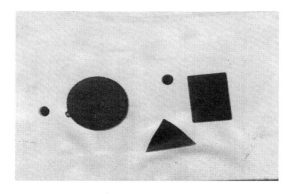

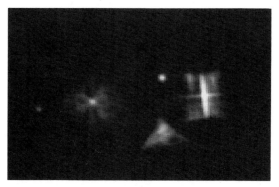

Figure 6: Top: Mean spontaneous fixation positions for various figures, each subtending on the retina about 2° visual angle, reported by Kaufman and Richards. The small dotted circles indicate the region in which 86% of the fixations occurs. Middle: Dark geometrical objects. Bottom: application of $CS_8\,(p)$ to the image.

5 Implementation by Neural Networks

The symmetry operator we suggest operates on an edge map, and produces an intensity map, where intensity represents the probability of a point being an "interesting" foveation target.

While we do not suggest here that this symmetry operator is actually implemented in the primate visual pathway, we claim that our operator can be realized by a system whose architecture shares many typical building blocks with the biological visual system. The symmetry operator involves two main principles: local detection of edges in a preferred configuration of spatial orientation, and summation of responses of cells to such a spatial configuration in various distances, with weighting factors that decreases by the distance. These principles are highly accepted as biologically plausible, and are assumed to exist in virtually every computational model of the visual system.

The network we suggest for implementing the symmetry operator consists of two main layers: orientation selective layers and integration layers. An orientation selective layer consists of a retinotopical organized cells map, where all the cells response to edges in their receptive fields, with the maximum response achieved at a given edge orientation for a given layer. Different layers differ in their preferred orientation (and possibly in the size of their receptive fields - though this attribute is not necessary for a simple implementation of the operator). There are as many layers as primary orientations in the operator, namely, n layers if $CS_n(p)$ is implemented. It should be noted, however, that for primates, there exists about 20 main orientations in each ocular dominance column, and this number can be regarded as an upper bound for n.

The integration layers consists of cells that are also retinotopically organized, and are connected to the orientation selective layers such that a given cell in the integration layer receives its inputs from cells in the orientation selective layers whose preferred orientations correspond; for example, in the case of $CS_2(p)$, a given cell in the integration layer is connected to orientation cells whose preferred orientations are orthogonal. In Figure 7 a schematic network is depicted. Cells in layers C and D have orthogonally oriented receptive fields. Cells in B are performing the AND operation on the orientation selective cells they are connected to, and cells in layer A perform OR on layer B cells. Thus, a cell in layer A is activated if its receptive field (defined by the corresponding receptive fields in layers B, C and D) contains edges whose relative orientations are similar to the situation depicted in Figure 2

The Gaussian distance factor (as defined in the formulation of the operator) can be implemented in several ways. It is possible to implement it by having several integration layers, each retinotopically organized, and each cell connected to cells in the orientation selective layers that have the same corrresponding orientations, but

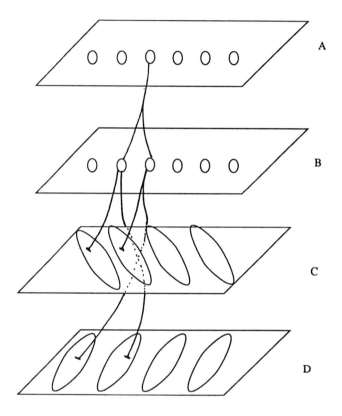

Figure 7: Schematic represntation of the network. Cells in the integration layers (A and B) receive input from the orientation selective layers (C and D). The receiving cell in A is increasingly activated as it becomes the center of symmetry - see text.

are located in an increasing distance from the integrator cell. Assigning a decreasing synaptic weights to increasing distances and summing the activities of all integration cells in a given retinotopical position will yield the required result. Another possibility involves the use of multiple representation of a given orientation by cells with increasing receptive fields sizes (which amounts to using multiple spatial frequency channels). Thus, symmetric edges at larger distance from a given point are responded to by cells with a larger receptive fields, and edges having the same size would elicit a response that decreases with distance.

6 Conclusion

The symmetry operator can be used as an efficient low level process for indexing attention to the regions that are likely to be of high interest in a picture. Other processes can then move the attention to these regions and interpret the data in them. The symmetry operator value is high in the vicinity of high curvature and multiple edges, and thus is a generalization of these two common machine vision approaches to the indexing problem. The symmetry operator agrees with some psychophysical data and can be further investigated to find its relations to models of attention indexing in biological vision, such as the models used by Posner and Peterson (Posner and Peterson 1990) and Ullman (1984). We do not claim that the suggested symmetry operator is being actually used in biological visual systems, but we have demonstrated that a simple feed forward network of orientation selective cells and layers of AND/OR cells can be used to implement the operator.

In this chapter, we have introduced a low level operator that can be used to locate regions of high "symmetry value", and use them as fixation cues. However, a powerful tool for object recognition can be designed using semantics in combination with the symmetry operators. For example, we can locate a face using the circular symmetry operator, $CS_n(p)$ applied to a rough resolution of the picture, and then apply both circular symmetry, $CS_n(p)$, and symmetry along horizontal lines, $S_n(p,1)$, on smaller focused regions of the picture in higher resolution. Recent object recognition paradigms (Lamdan et al 1988; Thompson and Mundy 1987; Huttenlocher and Ullman 1987) have shown that recognition can be performed using interest points in unsegmented scenes. Such paradigms may use as input the symmetry operator output. Moreover, the symmetry operator produces more than interest points. One may view the computation of the symmetry measure $S(p, \psi)$ as a "symmetry edge" extraction procedure, where the response in given directions is computed for all the points. consequence of this approach is in the observation that one may apply most of the standard (e.g Hough Transform, edge linking) computer vision operations to this map exactly in the same way that we apply it to a standard edge map, thus enabling the extraction of more complex symmetry lines and symmetry curves.

References

[1] M. J. Atallah. On symmetry detection. *IEEE Trans. Comput.*, C-34:663–666, 1985.

[2] F. Attneave. Informational aspects of visual perception. *Psychological Review*, 61:183–193, 1954.

[3] H. B. Barlow and B. C. Reeves. The versatility and absolute efficiency of detecting mirror symmetry in random dot displays. *Vision Research*, 19:783–793, 1979.

[4] H. Blum and R. N. Nagel. Shape description using weighted symmetric axis features. *Pattern Recognition*, 10:167–180, 1978.

[5] F. L. Bookstein. The line-skeleton. *Comput. Graphics Image Processing*, 11:123–137, 1979.

[6] M. Brady and H. Asada. Smoothed local symmetries and their implementation. *The International Journal of Robotics Research*, 3(3):36–61, 1984.

[7] V. G. Bruce and M. J. Morgan. Violation of symmetry and repetition in visual patterns. *Perception*, 4:239–249, 1975.

[8] S. A. Freidberg. Finding axis of skewed symmetry. *Comput. Vision, Graphics, Image Processing*, 34:138–155, 1986.

[9] S. B. Ho and C. R. Dyer. Shape smoothing using medial axis properties. *IEEE Trans. Pattern Anal. Machine Intell*, PAMI-8(4):512–520, 1986.

[10] D. P. Huttenlocher and S. Ullman. Object recognition using allighnment. In *Proc. of the 1'st int. conf. on computer vision*, pages 102–111, London, 1987.

[11] L. Kaufman and W. Richards. Spontaneous fixation tendencies for visual forms. *Perception & Psychophysics*, 5(2):85–88, 1969.

[12] Y. Lamdan, J. T. Schwartz, and H. Wolfson. On recognition of 3-d objects from 2-d images. In *IEEE int. conf. on Robotics and Automation*, pages 1407–1413, April 1988.

[13] G. Marola. On the detection of the axis of symmetry of symmetric and almost symmetric plannar images. *IEEE Trans. Pattern Anal. Machine Intell*, 11(1):104–108, 1989.

[14] V. S. Nalwa. Line-drawing interpretation: bilateral symmetry. *IEEE Trans. Pattern Anal. Machine Intell*, 11(10):1117–1120, 1989.

[15] R. Nevatia and T. O. Binford. Description and recognition of curved objects. *Artificial Intelligence*, 8:77–98, 1977.

[16] S. Peleg, O. Federbush, and R. Hummel. Custom made pyramids. In L. Uhr, editor, *Parallel Computer Vision*, pages 125–146. Academic Press, NY, 1987.

[17] M. L. Posner and S. E. Peterson. The attention system of the human brain. *Annu. Rev. Neurosci.*, 13:25–42, 1990.

[18] P. T. Sander and S. W. Zucker. Singularities of principal directions fields from 3d images. Technical Report CIM-88-15, McRCIM, McGill University, 1988.

[19] N. Sorek and Y. Y. Zeevi. Online visual data compression along a one dimensional scan. *SPIE*, 1001 Visual Communication and Image Processing:764–770, 1988.

[20] D. W. Thompson and J. L. Mundy. Three dimensional model matching from an unconstrained viewpoint. In *IEEE int. conf. on Robotics and Automation*, pages 208–220, Raleigh, North Carolaina, 1987.

[21] S. Ullman. Visual routines. *Cognition*, 18:97–15997–159, 1984.

[22] W. Köhler. *Gestalt psychology*. Liveright, New York, 1929.

[23] Y. Xia. Skeletonization via the realization of the fire front's propagation and extinction in digital binary shapes. *IEEE Trans. Pattern Anal. Machine Intell*, 11(10):1076–1089, 1989.

[24] Y. Yeshurun and E. L. Schwartz. Shape description with a space-variant sensor: Algorithm for scan-path, fusion, and convergence over multiple scans. *IEEE Trans. Pattern Anal. Machine Intell*, 11(11):1217–1222, 1989.

[25] Shiu-Yin Kelvin Yuen. Shape from contour using symmetries. Technical Report 141, Univ. of Sussex, 1989.

II.16

A Neural Network for Motion Processing

Y. T. ZHOU

HNC, INC.
San Diego, CA

R. CHELLAPPA

University of Southern California
Los Angeles, CA

Abstract

A locally connected artificial neural network based on physiological and anatomical findings in the visual system is presented for motion processing. A set of velocity selective binary neurons is used for each point in the image. Motion processing is carried out by neuron evaluation using a parallel updating scheme. A deterministic decision rule is used to ensure quick convergence of network to probably a local minimum. In view of high parallelism and local connectivity, this network is suitable for VLSI implementation.

Both batch and recursive algorithms based on this network are presented for computing optical flow and recovering depth from a sequence of monocular images. The batch algorithm simultaneously integrates information from all images by embedding them into the bias inputs of the network, while the recursive algorithm uses a recursive least squares (RLS) method to update the bias inputs of the network. Detection rules are also used to find the oc-

492

cluding elements. Based on information on the detected occluding elements, the network can automatically locate motion and depth discontinuities. Both these algorithms need to compute optical flow at most twice and depth only once. Hence, less computations are needed and the recursive algorithm is amenable for real time applications.

1. Introduction

Recently, based on physiological and anatomical findings in the visual system [1, 2, 3] we have developed a discrete, parallel, deterministic and locally connected artificial neural network for motion perception. Motion perception is one of the most prominent features in the visual system. Once motion information enters the visual system through the retina, interpretation is performed in parallel to construct the velocity (optical flow) and depth in the visual cortex. Our network is able to compute optical flow and recover depth from a sequence of monocular images. We also expect the network to be able to handle binocular image sequences. A similar network has also been proposed by Bülthoff, Little and Poggio [4] for computing optical flow based on edges or filtered intensity values. They showed that the algorithm based on such a network is consistent with several perceptual effects.

The network used in our work has several important features. First, it uses the principle curvatures and image intensity values as measurement primitives for computing optical flow, and first order derivatives and Chamfer distance values for recovering depth. As the principle curvatures and image intensity values are dense and rotation invariant, our network can detect not only translations but also rotations [1] and give a dense flow field. Second, it can accurately locate motion and depth discontinuities. Usually, a smoothness constraint is used for obtaining a smooth optical flow and depth fields. Using a smoothness constraint may blur surface boundaries and hence motion and depth discontinuities may not be detected. Since motion discontinuities contain rich information about the surface boundaries and the spatial arrangement of the objects, attempts have been made to detect them by using a line process [5]. However, without exactly knowing where the occluding elements are, the discontinuities detected by the line process may be shifted. Our approch first detects the occluding elements from the initial motion measurements and embeds them in the bias inputs, then lets the network locate the discontinuities automatically. For the purpose of real time implementation, both neurons and lines are updated in a parallel fashion. Third, it can handle multiple image frames. Natural images are often degraded by the imaging system. Based on such imperfect observations, it is difficult to accurately compute the optical flow and depth, especially near motion depth discontinuities. To improve the accuracy of the solution, multiple frames are used. Two algorithms, batch and recursive, are presented. The batch algorithm simultaneously integrates information from all images by embedding them into the bias inputs of the network, while the recursive algorithm uses a recursive least squares (RLS) method to update the bias inputs of the network. Both these methods need to compute optical flow at most twice and depth only once. Hence, less computations are needed and the recursive algorithm is amenable for real time applications.

2. A Neural Network

Microelectrode studies in cats and monkeys indicate that the visual cortex is organized in a topographic, laminar and columnar fashion [6, 7]. The image on the retina is first projected to the lateral geniculate bodies and then from there to the visual cortex in a strict topographical manner The neurons in the visual cortex are arranged in layers and grouped according to several stimulus parameters such as eye dominance, receptive field orientation and receptive field position. The groupings take the form of vertically arranged parallel slabs spanning the full cortical thickness. The optical nerve fibres arriving from the lateral geniculate bodies mostly terminate in layer 4 of visual area 17, yielding a cortical representation of retina. From area 17 the visual signals pass to adjacent area 18 and other higher visual areas such as middle temporal (MT), each with a complete topographic map of the visual field. Neurons with similarly orientation- and direction-selectivities are stacked in discrete columns which are perpendicular to the cortical surface. All the neurons such as simple, complex and hypercomplex within a column have the same receptive field axis orientation. For instance, if an electrode is penetrated into the cortex in a direction perpendicular to the cortex surface, all the neurons encountered shows the same axis orientation. If the electrode goes in a direction parallel to the cortex surface, there occurs a regular shift in the axis orientation, about $5 - 10°$ for every advance of $25 - 50$ μm. Over a distance of about 1 mm, there is roughly a full complete of rotation (180°). A set of orientation columns representing a full rotation of 180° together with an intersecting pair of ocular dominance columns forms a hypercolumn. Each hypercolumn as an elementary unit of the visual cortex is responsible for a certain small area of the visual field and encode a complete feature description of the area by the activity of neurons. Advancing more than 1 mm produces a displacement in the visual field, out of the area where one started and into an entirely new area. The simple neuron is orientation-selective and the complex neuron is direction-selective. The simple neuron responds best to a stationary line which is oriented with the axis of the receptive field. For the complex

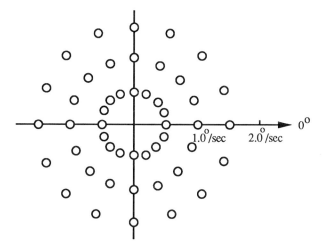

Figure 1. A 2-D grouping pattern for the neurons within a hypercolumn.

neurons, not only the orientation of the line but also the stimulus speed and motion direction are important. A oriented line produces strong responses to a complex neuron if it moves at an optimal speed in a direction perpendicular to the receptive field axis orientation within the receptive field. About half of the complex neurons responds only to one direction of movement. If the speed is less or greater than the optimum, the neuron's firing frequency tends to fall off sharply. The optimal speed varies from neuron to neuron. For instance, in cats it varies from about 0.1°/sec up to about 20°/sec [6]. Hence, the complex neurons are direction- and speed-selective, i.e., velocity-selective. We assume that the complex neurons within a column can be further grouped according to their speed selectivity. Figure 1 shows a possible 2-D grouping pattern of the complex neurons within hypercolumn. Neurons are arranged according to their direction and speed selectivity. Each circle represents one or more neurons since several neurons may have the same velocity selectivity. The coordinates of the circle indicate the velocity selectivity of the neurons.

MT is also known as a "motion area". Neurons in MT are predominantly direction-selective, about 90% show some direction selectivity and 80% are highly selective, and are arranged in columns according to direction selectivity [8, 9, 10]. Area 17 projects to area MT in a very unique way: (1) the projection only happens between the columns with similar directionality; (2) neurons projecting from a given location in area 17 diverge to several periodically spaced locations in MT, and several locations in area 17 converge upon a given location in MT. These properties probably play very important rule in maintaining axis and direction selectivity and forcing the neighboring receptive fields to have the same directional preference.

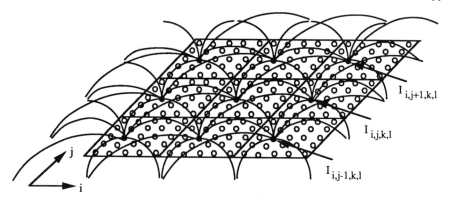

Figure 2. An artificial neuron network.

As images are digitized, and computing optical flow and depth is essentially to find the conjugate points in images and compute their displacements, for implementation purposes, we assume that the neurons in a hypercolumn are uniformly distributed over a 2-D Cartesian plane. The conjugate point can be found by checking every image pixel within a neighborhood in the successive frame based on the measurement primitives. The maximum search range, i.e., the maximum displacement can be determined by the maximum optimal speed.

Each hypercolumn represents a single image pixel or subpixel (if the image is subsampled). Let the maximum displacement be D, about $(2D+1)^2$ mutually exclusive neurons are needed for each pixel and a total number of $N_r \times N_c \times (2D+1)^2$ neurons are required for a $N_r \times N_c$ image. Since two objects cannot occupy the same place at the same time, only one velocity value can be assigned to each pixel. Therefore, in each hypercolumn, only one neuron is in active state. The velocity value can be determined according to its direction selectivity. Figure 2 shows such a network with the small frames for the hypercolumns and the circles for the neurons. The neurons in a hypercolumn are uniformly distributed on a plane. Each neuron receives inputs from itself and other similar directionally selective neurons at the neighboring points, and a bias input from outside world.

In fact, each small frame contains many neurons. For simplicity, only a few neurons are present in each frame. Each neuron receives a bias input from outside world. The bias input may consist of several different types of measurement primitives, such as the raw image data, filtered image data including their derivatives, edges, lines, corners etc. As the neighboring receptive fields are forced to have the same directional preference, we assume that neurons with similar velocity selectivity in the neighboring hypercolumns

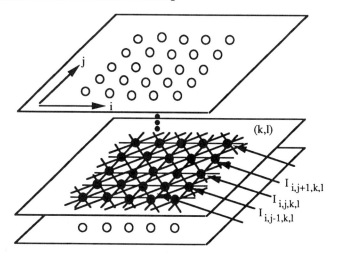

Figure 3. An equivalent multi-layer network.

tend to affect each other through receiving inputs from each other as shown in Figure 2. This feature implies the smoothness constraint which can be seen more clearly if the network is organized in a multi-layer fashion. Figure 3 shows a multi-layer network which is equivalent to the original one. The neurons are arranged in layers according to their velocity selectivity. In our notation, i and j denote the image coordinates and k and l denote the velocity coordinates. The network consists of $(2D_k + 1) \times (2D_l + 1)$ layers. Each layer corresponds to a different velocity and contains $N_r \times N_c$ neurons. Each neuron receives excitatory and inhibitory inputs from itself and other neurons in a neighborhood in the same layer. For each point, only the neuron that has the maximum excitation among all neurons in the other layers is on and the others are off. When the neuron at the point (i, j) in the kth and lth layers is 1, this means that the velocities in k and l directions at the point (i, j) are $k\,W$ and $l\,W$, respectively.

Let $V = \{v_{i,j,k,l}, 1 \le i \le N_r, 1 \le j \le N_c, -D_k \le k \le D_k, -D_l \le l \le D_l\}$ be a binary state set of the neural network with $v_{i,j,k,l}$ denoting the state of the (i, j, k, l)th neuron which is located at point (i, j) in the (k, l)th layer, $T_{i,j,k,l;m,n,k,l}$ the synaptic interconnection strength from neuron (i, j, k, l) to neuron (m, n, k, l) and $I_{i,j,k,l}$ the bias input. Each neuron (i, j, k, l) is assumed synchronously to receive inputs from itself and neighboring neurons and a bias input

$$u_{i,j,k,l} = \sum_{(m-i, n-j) \in S_0} T_{i,j,k,l;m,n,k,l} v_{m,n,k,l} + I_{i,j,k,l} \tag{1}$$

where S_0 is an index set for all neighbors in a $\Gamma \times \Gamma$ window centered at point (i, j). The potential of the neuron, $u_{i,j,k,l}$, is then fed back to corresponding neurons after maximum evolution

$$v_{i,j,k,l} = g(u_{i,j,k,l}) \tag{2}$$

where $g(x_{i,j,k,l})$ is a maximum evolution function (it is also called winner-take-all function)

$$g(x_{i,j,k,l}) = \begin{cases} 1 & if \ x_{i,j,k,l} = \max_{p,q}\{x_{i,j,p,q}\}. \\ 0 & otherwise. \end{cases} \tag{3}$$

The neuron evaluation will be terminated if the network converges, i.e., the energy function of the network defined by

$$E = -\frac{1}{2} \sum_{i,j,k,l} (\sum_{(m-i,n-j)\in S_0} T_{i,j,k,l;m,n,k,l} \, v_{i,j,k,l} \, v_{m,n,k,l} + I_{i,j,k,l} \, v_{i,j,k,l}). \tag{4}$$

reaches a minimum. Two important features of the network should be noted: (1) The synaptic interconnection strength between neurons in different layers are zero since only the neurons in the same layer are connected. (2) A maximum evolution function is used to ensure that only one neuron can be on at each point.

3. Computing Optical Flow

Optical flow is the distribution of instantaneous apparent velocities of motion brightness patterns in an image/retina. Except for some special cases [11], optical flow corresponds to the motion field.

A. Neural Network Formulation

Without adding any physical constraints to the solution, optical flow computed from a pair of image frames usually is noisy and inaccurate. For instance, the correlation method may provide a solution based on the local match without any smoothness constraint, but the resulting optical flow is not accurate and the local error is undetectable. In our method, a smoothness constraint is used for obtaining a smooth optical flow field and a line process is employed for detecting motion discontinuities. The line process consists of vertical and horizontal lines, L^v and L^h. Each line can be in either one of two states: 1 for acting and 0 for resting. The error function for computing the optical flow can be properly expressed as

$$E = \sum_{i=1}^{N_r}\sum_{j=1}^{N_c} \sum_{k=-D_k}^{D_k} \sum_{l=-D_l}^{D_l} \{[A\,(k_{11}(i,j) - k_{21}(i+k,j+l))^2$$

$$+A\left(k_{12}(i,j)-k_{22}(i+k,j+l)\right)^2+(g_1(i,j)-g_2(i+k,j+l))^2]v_{i,j,k,l}$$
$$+\frac{B}{2}\sum_{s\in S}(v_{i,j,k,l}-v_{(i,j)+s,k,l})^2+\frac{C}{2}[(v_{i,j,k,l}-v_{i+1,j,k,l})^2(1-L^h_{i,j,k,l})$$
$$+(v_{i,j,k,l}-v_{i,j+1,k,l})^2(1-L^v_{i,j,k,l})]\} \tag{5}$$

where $k_{11}(i,j)$ and $k_{12}(i+k,j+l)$ are the principle curvatures of the first image, $k_{21}(i,j)$ and $k_{22}(i+k,j+l)$ are the principle curvatures of the second image, $\{g_1(i,j)\}$ and $\{g_2(i+k,j+l)\}$ are the intensity values of the first and second images, respectively, $S=S_0-(0,0)$ is an index set excluding $(0,0)$, A, B and C are constants. The first term in (5) is to seek velocity values such that all points of two images are matched as closely as possible in a least squares sense. The second term weighted by B is the smoothness constraint on the solution and the third term weighted by C is a line process to weaken the smoothness constraint and to detect motion discontinuities. The constant A in the first term determines the relative importance of the intensity values and their principle curvatures to achieve the best results.

By choosing the interconnection strengths and bias inputs as

$$\begin{aligned}
T_{i,j,k,l;m,n,k,l} = & -[48B+C(4-L^h_{i,j,k,l}-L^h_{i,j-1,k,l}-L^v_{i,j,k,l}\\
& -L^v_{i-1,j,k,l})]\delta_{i,m}\delta_{j,n}+C[(1-L^h_{i,j,k,l})\delta_{i,m}\delta_{j+1,n}+(1\\
& -L^h_{i,j-1,k,l})\delta_{i,m}\delta_{j-1,n}+(1-L^v_{i,j,k,l})\delta_{i+1,m}\delta_{j,n}+(1\\
& -L^v_{i-1,j,k,l})\delta_{i-1,m}\delta_{j,n}]+2B\sum_{s\in S}\delta_{(i,j),(m,n)+s} \tag{6}
\end{aligned}$$

and

$$\begin{aligned}
I_{i,j,k,l} = & -A[(k_{11}(i,j)-k_{21}(i+k,j+l))^2+(k_{12}(i,j)\\
& -k_{22}(i+k,j+l))^2]-(g_1(i,j)-g_2(i+k,j+l))^2 \tag{7}
\end{aligned}$$

where $\delta_{a,b}$ is the Dirac delta function, the error function (5) is transformed into the energy function (3) of the neural network. Note that the interconnection strengths consist of constants and line process only. The bias inputs contain all information from the images. This is why we like to call $I_{i,j,k,l}$ bias input instead of threshold, because the neurons receive the information from outside through the bias inputs. Equation (7) also gives us a hint to develop multiple frame algorithms. Computation of optical flow is carried out by neuron evaluation. When the network reaches a stable state, the optical flow field is determined by the neuron states. The size of the smoothing window used in (6) is 5×5. As the first and second terms in (5) do not contain line process, line process and the neurons can be independently updated. The initial state of the neurons is determined by the bias inputs, only the information from outside world. It is set as

$$v_{i,j,k,l} = \begin{cases} 1 & if \ \ I_{i,j,k,l} = max(I_{i,j,p,q}; -D_k \leq p \leq D_k, -D_l \leq q \leq D_l). \\ 0 & otherwise \end{cases} \quad (8)$$

where $I_{i,j,k,l}$ is the bias input. If there are two maximal bias inputs at point (i,j), then only the neuron corresponding to the smallest velocity is initially set at 1 and the other one is set at 0. This is consistent with the minimal mapping theory [12]. In the updating scheme, we also use the minimal mapping theory to handle the case of two neurons having the same largest inputs.

Since each neuron has self-feedback i.e., receives input from itself, the interconnection strength $T_{i,j,k,l;i,j,k,l}$ is nonzero. The self–feedback may increase the energy function E after a transition. To enforce the energy function to decrease, a deterministic decision rule is used for updating the neuron states, i.e., a new state is taken if the energy change is less than zero. Using the deterministic decision rule helps the network to converge to a minimum very fast. But it may be a local minimum. To reach a global minimum, a stochastic decision rule [13] employing simulated annealing techniques can be used. However, only a careful choice of the temperature schedule and the parameters may result in a good solution. Otherwise, a local minimum is inevitable [14].

B. *Detection of Motion Discontinuities*

Motion discontinuities in optical flow often result from occluding contours of moving objects. In this case, the moving objects are projected into image plane as adjacent surfaces and their boundaries are undergoing either split or fusion motion. These motion situations give rise to discontinuities along their boundaries. To overcome such difficulties and to locate the discontinuities more accurately, the occluding elements are detected first based on the initial motion measurements. Then all the information about the occluding elements are embedded into the bias inputs such that the network can automatically take care of motion discontinuities during the updating procedure.

To formalize the analysis, we have to distinguish split motion and fusion motion. As explained in [12], the split motion occurs when a single element is replaced by multiple elements, i.e. in two successive frames the single element is shown first followed by multiple elements, while the fusion motion results when multiple elements are presented first followed by a single element. An example is given in Figure 4 to illustrate fusion motion. Figure 4(a) is composed of two frames and each frame contains two surfaces moving towards each other, one in front and the another in back. For the first frame, the elements of the surfaces in the front and back are denoted by A_1, B_1, C_1, D_1 and X_1, Y_1, Z_1, respectively. For the second frame, A_2, B_2, C_2, D_2 and

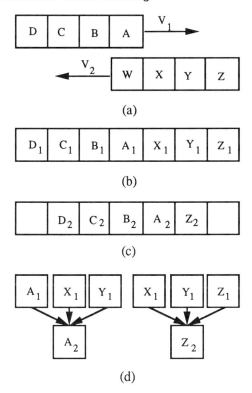

Figure 4. Fusion motion.

X_2, Y_2, Z_2 denote the elements of the surfaces in front and back, respectively. The elements can be either image pixels or lines. The elements X and Y of the surface in back are visible in the first frame as shown in Figure 4(b), while in the second frame they are occluded by the front surface as shown in Figure 4(c). Hence, the elements A_1, X_1 and Y_1 (or X_1, Y_1 and Z_1) are replaced by the element A_2 (or Z_2), and a fusion motion is observed. While computing the optical flow, the fusion motion usually causes problem but the split motion does not. As shown in Figure 4(d), in the fusion motion case only one of three elements can find correspondence. The optical flow at the two unmatched points is undetermined. Unlike the fusion motion, split motion has only one element to be matched with one of many elements. Hence optical flow at a point can be determined according to the measurement primitive. If the optical flow is perfectly determined, then the line process can successfully and correctly locate motion discontinuities. Thus we will concentrate on the fusion motion case for detecting the occluding elements.

Suppose that the surfaces are translating with constant velocities. Let us

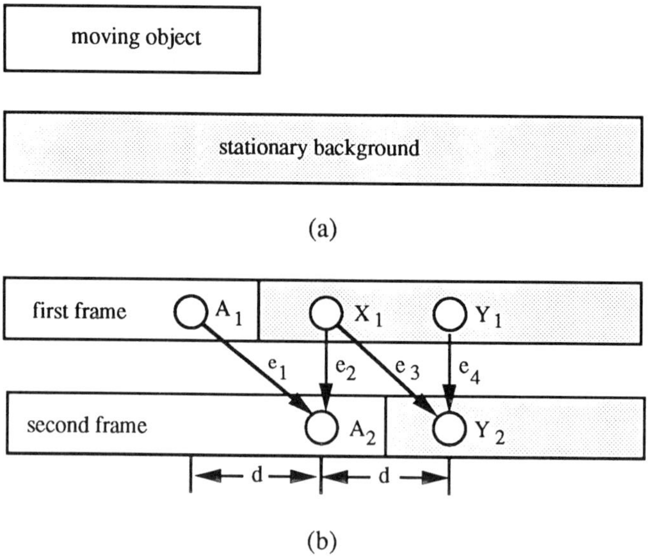

Figure 5. Detection of the occluding element.

consider the case in which a surface is moving against a stationary background as shown in Figure 5(a). Let X_1 denote the occluding element, A_2 and X_2 the corresponding elements of A_1 and X_1, respectively. Let (i, j) be the coordinates of element A_1, d_i and d_j the i and j components of optical flow at (i, j), respectively. We assume that X_1 and Y_1 are located at $(i+d_i, j+d_j)$ and $(i + 2 \times d_i, j + 2 \times d_j)$ respectively. By defining the match errors

$$e_1(i, j) = -I_{i,j,d_i,d_j}$$

$$e_2(i, j) = -I_{i+d_i,j+d_j,0,0}$$

$$e_3(i, j) = -I_{i+d_i,j+d_j,d_i,d_j}$$

$$e_4(i, j) = -I_{i+2\times d_i,j+2\times d_j,0,0}$$

where $I_{.,.,.,.}$ are bias inputs given in (7), the following relations (as shown in Figure 5(b)) hold under orthographic or perspective projection for the case when there is no motion along the optical axis,

$$e_1(i, j) \leq e_2(i, j)$$
$$e_4(i, j) \leq e_3(i, j). \tag{9}$$

Note that if the above relations do not hold then the element X_1 is not an occluding element. Hence, it is natural to use (9) for detecting the occluding elements.

Detection rule: An occluding element is detected at $(i + d_i, j + d_j)$ if the optical flow has nonzero values at (i, j) and

$$\bar{e}_2(i.j) - \bar{e}_1(i,j) > T$$
$$\bar{e}_4(i.j) - \bar{e}_3(i,j) > T \tag{10}$$

where the theshold T is a nonnegative number and $\bar{e}_k(i,j)$ are the average values of the matching errors within a $\Gamma_T \times \Gamma_T$ window S_T

$$\bar{e}_k(i,j) = \frac{1}{\Gamma_T^2} \sum_{s \in S_T} \bar{e}_k((i,j) + s)$$

$$for \quad k = 1, 2, 3, \ and \ 4.$$

For digitized natural images, T usually takes a nonzero value to reduce the effects of quantization error and noise. Using a large value for T can eliminate false occluding elements but may miss the true ones. Since optical flow at an occluding point has zero values, the *a priori* knowledge about the occluding elements can be embedded in the bias inputs by setting, (for instance at point $(i + d_i, j + d_j)$)

$$I_{i+d_i,j+d_j,0,0} = min(I_{i+d_i,j+d_j,k,l}; \ -D_k \leq k \leq D_k, -D_l \leq l \leq D_l). \tag{11}$$

Accordingly, the neural network will prefer zero optical flow at these points and therefore the line process can precisely locate motion discontinuities. The complete algorithm is then
1. Compute optical flow.
2. Detect occluding elements and reset bias inputs accordingly.
3. Compute optical flow with new bias inputs.

C. Multiple Frame Approaches

When image quality is poor, measurement primitives estimated from these images are not accurate and reliable. For instance, if the images are blurred by motion, then the local features are smeared and much of the information is lost. Especially, the object boundaries become wide and the derivatives of the intensity function become small at the boundaries. Based on these low quality measurements, motion discontinuities can not be correctly located and hence optical flow can not be accurately computed. To improve the accuracy, one way is to improve the image quality by using some image restoration techniques to remove degradations. However, without *a priori* knowledge of the degradations, such as blur function, an image can not be restored perfectly. When the blur is ill conditioned, it is still difficult to restore the image even if the blur function is given. An alternative is to compute optical flow over a long time interval, i.e. using multiple frames. In this section, two algorithms, batch and recursive, using more than two frames of images are presented.

1. Batch Algorithm

Assume that the objects in the scene are moving with a constant velocity translational motion. It is interesting to note that in the two frame case the bias inputs (7) contain nothing but the measurement primitives, the intensity values and principle curvatures, which are estimated from images. The bias inputs of the network are completely determined by the observations, i.e. the images, while the interconnection strengths (6) do not contain any observations. All these facts suggest that any information from outside world can be included in the bias inputs. The network learns all information directly from the inputs. Hence, it is natural to extend the two frame approach to multiple frames by adding more observations to the bias inputs. Assuming M frames of images are available, the bias inputs are given by

$$
\begin{aligned}
I_{i,j,k,l} = & -\sum_{r=1}^{M-1}\{A[(k_{r1}(i+(r-1)k,j+(r-1)l)-k_{(r+1)1}(i+rk,j+rl))^2 \\
& +(k_{r2}(i+(r-1)k,j+(r-1)l)-k_{(r+1)2}(i+rk,j+rl))^2] \\
& +(g_r(i+(r-1)k,j+(r-1)l)-g_{r+1}(i+rk,j+rl))^2\}.
\end{aligned}
\tag{12}
$$

Accordingly, the initial state of the neurons (8) is set by using these new bias inputs. The two frame algorithm presented in section 2.2 can be used without any modifications for the multiple frame case.

2. Recursive Algorithm

If all the images are not available at the same time or if one wants to compute the optical flow in real time, a recursive algorithm can be used. The recursive algorithm uses an RLS algorithm to update the bias inputs. First, the initial condition for the bias inputs is set to zero, i.e.

$$
I_{i,j,k,l}(0) = 0.
\tag{13}
$$

This is reasonable, because there is no information available at the beginning. Then, whenever a new frame becomes available, the bias inputs can be updated by

$$
I_{i,j,k,l}(r) = I_{i,j,k,l}(r-1) + \frac{1}{r}(\tilde{I}_{i,j,k,l}(r) - I_{i,j,k,l}(r-1))
\tag{14}
$$

$$
for \quad 2 \le r \le M
$$

Figure 6. The first frame of pick-up truck images.

where $\tilde{I}_{i,j,k,l}(r)$ is a new observation given by

$$
\begin{aligned}
\tilde{I}_{i,j,k,l}(r) = {} & -A[(k_{r1}(i + (r-1)k, j + (r-1)l) - k_{(r+1)1}(i + rk, j + rl))^2 \\
& + (k_{r2}(i + (r-1)k, j + (r-1)l) - k_{(r+1)2}(i + rk, j + rl))^2] \\
& + (g_r(i + (r-1)k, j + (r-1)l) - g_{r+1}(i + rk, j + rl))^2. \quad (15)
\end{aligned}
$$

In fact, this RLS algorithm is equivalent to the batch algorithm. If the intermediate results are not required, optical flow can be computed after all images are received. As one can see, the RLS algorithm is parallel in nature and very few computations are required at each step. Hence this algorithm is extremely fast and can be implemented in real time. Since the number of occluding elements dramatically increases as more image frames are involved, special attention has to be paid to this problem. With minor modifications, the detection criterion used for the two frames can be extended to multiple frames [15].

The multiple frame based algorithms can be summarized as

1. Compute optical flow from the first two frames.
2. Update bias inputs.
3. Detect occluding elements and reset bias inputs accordingly. For the recursive algorithm, go back to step 2 if the incoming frame is not the last one; otherwise, go to step 4.
4. Compute optical flow with updated bias inputs.

Figure 7. The fourth frame of pick-up truck images.

D. *Results*

Figures 6 and 7 show the first and fourth frame of a sequence of images, a pick-up truck moving from right to left against a stationary background. The images are of size 480×480. As the rear part of the truck is missing in the first frame, we reversed the order of image sequence so that there is a complete truck image in the first frame. Accordingly, the direction of the computed optical flow should be reversed. For the two frame approach, we used the fourth frame as the first frame and the third frame as the second frame. For reducing computations, the image size was reduced to 120×120 by subsampling. For each point, we use two memories in the range $-D_k$ to D_k and $-D_l$ to D_l to represent velocities in i and j directions, respectively, instead of using $(2D_k + 1)$ and $(2D_l + 1)$ neurons. Due to local connectivity, the potential of the neuron is computed only within a small window. By setting $A = 2$, $B = 250$, $C = 50$, $D_k = 7$, and $D_l = 1$, the optical flow was obtained after 36 iterations. A 48×113 sample of the computed optical flow corresponding to the part framed by black lines in Figure 6(b) is given in Figure 8. Since the shutter speed was low, the truck was heavily blurred by the motion. The motion blur smeared the edges and erased local features, especially the features on the wheel. Hence, it is difficult to detect the rotation of the wheels. Also note that although most of the boundary locations are correct, the boundaries due to the fusion motion such as the rear part of the truck and the driver's cab are shifted by the line process.

The occluding pixels were detected at $T = 100$ based on the initially com-

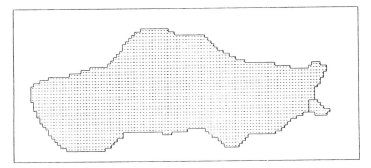

Figure 8. Optical flow computed from two frame.*

puted optical flow of Figure 8. By embedding the information about the occluding pixels into the bias inputs, using the initially computed optical flow as the initial conditions and choosing $A = 2$, $B = 188$, $C = 200$, $D_k = 7$ and $D_l = 1$ the final result shown in Figure 9 was obtained after 13 iterations. The accuracy of boundary location is significantly improved.

For the multiple frame approaches, we used four image frames. Theoretically there is no limit to the number of frames that can be used in the batch approach. For the same reason mentioned before, the fourth frame was taken as the first frame, the third frame as the second frame, etc. Since the batch and recursive algorithms are similar in spirit, a set of identical parameters was used for both algorithms in this experiment and same results were obtained. The occluding pixels were detected at $T = 100$ from four frames. Figure 10 shows the optical flow computed from four frames using the occluding pixel information. The parameters used were $A = 4$, $B = 850$, $C = 80$, $D_k = 7$ and

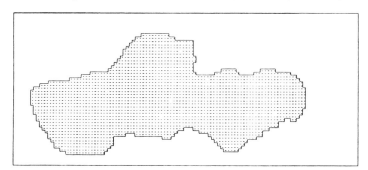

Figure 9. Optical flow computed from two frames using the occluding element information.*

* Reprinted with permission from The Institute of Electrical and Electronics Engineers, Inc., Y.T. Zhou and R. Chellappa/IEEE Neural Networks Council, *Proceedings of International Joint Conference on Neural Networks* **II**, 869–884. © 1990 IEEE

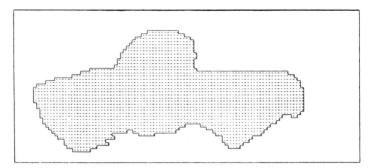

Figure 10. Optical flow computed from four frames using the occluding element information.*

$D_l = 1$, and 12 iterations were required. As expected, the output is much cleaner and the boundaries are more accurate than that of the two frame based approach. The number of iterations is also reduced.

4. Recovering Depth

Recovering depth is a problem of the third dimensional perception. Physiological studies show that depth can be recovered based on either monocular cues or binocular cues. Deriving depth information from a moving camera through a stationary 3-D environment is also known as motion stereo. Since motion stereo uses more than two image frames, it usually gives more accurate depth measurements than static stereo which uses only two image frames.

A. Depth from Motion

It is assumed that a sequence of images is taken by a camera moving along with a constant velocity from right to left along a straight line, as shown in Figure 11. Several assumptions are made to simplify the problem. First, we assume that the optical axis of the camera is perpendicular to the moving direction and the horizontal axes of the image planes are parallel to the moving direction. The constraint imposed on the camera configuration is to restrict the search within the horizontal direction only, the so called epipolar constraint. Secondly, we assume that the camera takes pictures exactly every t seconds apart. Thus, all images are equally separated, i.e. each successive image pairs has the same baseline.

Let $OXYZ$ be the world coordinate system with Z axis directing along the camera optical axis and $o_i x_i y_i$ be the pth image plane coordinate system. The origin of the pth image system is located at $(0, -(p-1)vt, f)$ of the world

* Reprinted with permission from The Institute of Electrical and Electronics Engineers, Inc., Y.T. Zhou and R. Chellappa/IEEE Neural Networks Council, *Proceedings of International Joint Conference on Neural Networks* **II**, 869–884. © 1990 IEEE

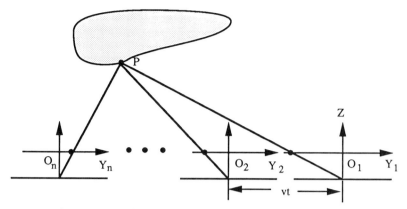

Figure 11. Camera geometry for motion stereo.

system, where v is the velocity of camera, vt is the distance between two successive images and f is the focal length of the lens which takes a positive value in the world system. Under perspective projection, a point in the world, (X_o, Y_o, Z_o), projects into the pth image plane at

$$(x_i, y_i) = (\frac{f\ X_0}{Z_o}, \frac{f\ (Y_o + (p-1)\ v\ t)}{Z_o}) \qquad (16)$$

The disparity D_o can be derived from any two successive image frames

$$D_o = y_p - y_{p-1} \qquad (17)$$

and the depth Z_o can then be recovered by

$$Z_o = f\ d\ \frac{1}{D_o} \qquad (18)$$

where $d = v\ t$ is the baseline. Since the depth values can be computed from the disparity values without any difficulty, usually only disparity values are required to be estimated.

B. *Estimation of Pixel Positions*

Let (i, j) be the position of the (i, j)th pixel in the first frame. In the successive frames, due to camera motion, the position of all pixels are shifted to the right by vt. Under the epipolar constraint, the shift happens only in the horizontal direction. For example, the (i, j)th pixel moves from position (i, j) in the first frame to position $(i, j + \frac{fvt}{Z_{i,j}})$ in the second frame. Let $S_{i,j}(p)$ be the total shift of pixel (i, j) from the first to the pth frame. Thus

$$
\begin{aligned}
S_{i,j}(p) &= (p-1)\frac{fvt}{Z_{i,j}} \\
&= (p-1)\,d_{i,j}
\end{aligned}
\tag{19}
$$

where $d_{i,j}$ is the true disparity value for pixel (i, j). Note that the shift $S_{i,j}(p)$ is continuous due to the continuous variable $d_{i,j}$. A rounding operation has to be applied to $S_{i,j}(p)$ for locating the (i, j)th pixel in the subsampled image. After rounding, the position of the (i, j)th pixel in the pth frame is given by

$$
(i, j + [\frac{S_{i,j}(p)}{W}]W).
\tag{20}
$$

where $[\ ]$ is a rounding operator. It can be simply written as

$$
(i, j + kW)
\tag{21}
$$

where

$$
k = [\frac{S_{i,j}(p)}{W}].
$$

C. Neural Network Formulation

As the camera moves in one direction, all the neurons corresponding to other directions will not be stimulated. For implementation purposes, we use only $(D+1)$ mutually exclusive binary neurons $\{v_{i,j,0}, v_{i,j,1}, ..., v_{i,j,D}\}$ for each pixel to represent the disparity value, if the maximum disparity is DW. We assume that the disparity range is sampled using bins of size W. When $v_{i,j,k}$ is 1, this means that the disparity value is kW at the pixel (i, j). The network consists of $N_r \times N_c \times (D+1)$ neurons, where N_r and N_c are the image row and column sizes, respectively. Suppose that M image frames are used for matching, the error function for the batch algorithm can be written as

$$
\begin{aligned}
E = {} & \frac{1}{M-1}\sum_{i=1}^{N_r}\sum_{j=1}^{N_c}\sum_{k=0}^{D}\sum_{p=1}^{M-1}\{[(g'_p(i, j + (p-1)kW) \\
& - g'_{p+1}(i, j + pkW))^2 + \kappa(f_p(i, j + (p-1)kW) \\
& - f_{p+1}(i, j + pkW))^2]\,v_{i,j,k} + \frac{\lambda}{2}\sum_{s\in S}(v_{i,j,k} - v_{(i,j)+s,k})^2\}
\end{aligned}
\tag{22}
$$

where $\{g'_p(\cdot)\}$ and $\{f_p(\cdot)\}$ denote the intensity derivatives and the Chamfer distance values at $(\cdot)$ of the pth frame, respectively, S is an index set excluding

$(0,0)$ for all the neighbors in a $\Gamma \times \Gamma$ window centered at point (i,j), λ and κ are constants. The chamfer distance value is defined as the distance from the non-edge pixel to the nearest edge pixel [16]. We used a parallel algorithm to estimate chamfer distance values [2].

Accordingly, the interconnection strengths and bias inputs are

$$T_{i,j,k;l,m,n} = -48\lambda\delta_{i,l}\delta_{j,m}\delta_{k,n} + 2\lambda \sum_{s \in S} \delta_{(i,j),(l,m)+s}\delta_{k,n} \tag{23}$$

and

$$
\begin{aligned}
I_{i,j,k} \;=\; & -\frac{1}{M-1} \sum_{p=1}^{M-1} [(g'_p(i,j+(p-1)kW) \\
& -g'_{p+1}(i,j+pkW))^2 + \kappa(f_p(i,j+(p-1)kW) \\
& -f_{p+1}(i,j+pkW))^2]
\end{aligned}
\tag{24}
$$

where $\delta_{a,b}$ is the Dirac delta function. The size of the smoothing window used in (23) is 5.

Since the bias inputs (24) consist of the measurement primitives only, a recursive algorithm similar to (14) and (15) can be constructed by using the RLS algorithm [2]. For the recursive algorithm, we do not have to implement the matching algorithm for every recursion if the intermediate result are not required. The conventional algorithms [17] implement matching procedure many times requiring a lot of computations. For example, if there are M image frames, the matching procedure has to be implemented $(M-1)$ times to obtain $(M-1)$ disparity measurements for each pixel. To obtain a good estimate of disparity value from these measurements, usually a filtering procedure is required. Instead of doing matching $(M-1)$ times, our batch and recursive algorithms implement the matching algorithm only once and need no interpolation procedure so that computational complexity is greatly reduced. Since the neural network can be run in parallel and the RLS algorithm can be implemented on line, the recursive algorithm is extremely fast and hence useful for real time robot vision applications.

D. Detection of Occlusions

Detection of occluding pixels is an important issue in motion stereo. When a smoothness constraint is used, although the matching algorithm always assigns some values to the occluding pixels, the discontinuities of the disparity field may be shifted. As the number of frames increases, the number of occluding pixels will dramatically increase too. For instance, if only two object points are occluded for the second image, then about ten points are occluded for the sixth image which gives a ten pixel wide occluding region in

Figure 12. The first frame of tree images.

the first image plane. However, in some cases the number of occluding pixels does not increase as the number of frames increases [2].

To prevent the algorithm from updating the bias input at the location of occluding pixels, the following detection rule is used.

Detection rule: An occluding pixel at location (i, j) is detected if

$$min(I_{i,j,k}|_{\kappa=0}; \; 0 \leq k \leq D) >$$

$$max(\mathbf{E}\{error(i,j)_k\}; \; 0 \leq k \leq D) + b \qquad (25)$$

where $\mathbf{E}\{error(i,j)_k\}$ is the mean of matching error given in [2] and $b \geq 0$ is a constant for raising the threshold. To estimate the mean of matching error, the variance of noise and the second order derivatives of the intensity funtion are needed. When the noise variance is unknown, one can use a constant threshold instead of the mean error.

For the recursive algorithm, once an occluding pixel is detected, the bias inputs of neurons at such locations will not be updated anymore. But during the first iteration, the bias inputs of neurons at the locations of occluding pixels are first updated and then corrected accordingly. The correction procedure is as follows. The width of the occluding region, i.e. the number of the occluding pixels is approximately given by

$$\hat{\Delta}_{i,j} = [\frac{D_{i,j-1} - D_{i,j+\Delta_{i,j}}}{W}] \qquad (26)$$

where [ ] is a rounding operator, (i, j) denotes the location of the left most occluding pixel, $\Delta_{i,j}$ is the true width, $\hat{\Delta}_{i,j}$ is a estimate of the width, and $D_{i,j-1}$

and $D_{i,j+\Delta_{i,j}}$ are the disparity values of the nearest left and right nonocclud-ing pixels, respectively. Since a smoothness constraint is used, the occluding pixel usually takes either a high disparity value $D_{i,j-1}$ or a low disparity value $D_{i,j+\Delta_{i,j}}$. The discontinuities of the disparity field can be detected by checking the disparity values in the y_1 direction if there is a transition from the high value to the low value. Starting with the discontinuity pixel, we check all the left and right neighboring pixels. The search procedure will not be stopped until a $\hat{\Delta}_{i,j}$ wide or less occluding region including the discontinuity pixel is found. Then, for all occluding pixels the bias input of the $\Delta_{i,j}$th neuron is corrected by

$$I_{i,l,D_{i,j+\Delta_{i,j}}}(1) = min(I_{i,l,k}(1); \; k = 0, 1, ..., D). \tag{27}$$

For the batch algorithm, the bias inputs at occluding pixels are estimated using only the first two image frames.

E. Results

We arbitrarily chose five successive frames for testing, although there is no limit to the number of frames that can be used. The images are of size 256×233. Figure 12 shows the first frame. No alignment in the vertical direction was made and the maximum disparity, about 2 pixels, was measured by hand. Same parameters were chosen for both the algorithms. The subpixel width W was set at 0.2 and hence $D = 10$. The parameter λ and κ were set at 20 and 5, respectively. The threshold for occluding pixel detection was set at 150 because the noise variance is unknown.

Figure 13 shows the batch result after 45 iterations. The disparity map is represented as an intensity image with the brightest value denoting the max-imum disparity value. The recursive result is shown in Figure 14. Twenty iterations were needed to obtain the recursive solution. Since at occlud-ing regions we still use the measurement primitives extracted from the first two image frames for matching, the algorithms might generate some isolated points or regions (at most $[WD]$ pixels wide) due to the incorrect information caused by occlusions. To remove such points and regions, a median filter is used in our experiments.

5. Discussion

We have presented a parallel deterministic network for computing optical flow and depth. For optical flow, we made no assumptions or requirements on the solutions except smoothness in the two frame case. For the multiple frames, we assumed that the object is undergoing a pure translational motion and

Figure 13. Disparity map of tree images, batch results.

two algorithms, batch and recursive, were used. Experimental results show that principle curvatures are useful for matching and our approaches based on such measurement primitives work very well especially for some low quality natural images such as the truck images. The algorithm for detecting motion discontinuities also works very well.

For computing depth, two algorithms, batch and recursive, have been presented. Both algorithms need to implement the matching procedure only once. Unlike the existing recursive algorithms, the disparity field obtained by our algorithm is smooth and dense. Also no batch results are needed for setting the initial states of the neurons. Both batch and recursive methods gave very good results in comparison to Barnard's approach [18]. Experimental results show that the recursive algorithm needs fewer iterations than the batch algorithm. This is because the recursive algorithm uses a better bias input updating scheme, especially for the occluding pixels. The good estimate of the bias inputs makes the network converge fast, although the updating step for bias inputs takes more computations. In view of parallelism and fast convergence, the recursive algorithm is useful for real time implementation, such as in a robot vision system. In our experiment, the threshold used was 150 which seems a little bit conservative. However, the maximum disparity is only about 2 pixels which means that the width of the occluding region is less than 2 pixels for two frames and there are only a few occluding pixels along the right boundaries of the trees. Hence the occluding pixels do not cause a serious problem in this experiment. This is also why the iteration number does not reduce a lot. We believe that if the maximum disparity is

Figure 14. Disparity map of tree images, recursive results.

large and a long sequence of images is used, then the improvement on the occluding pixel detection will greatly reduce the number of iterations. Also note that since our algorithms locate occluding pixels accurately, using more image frames does not increase the number of the undeterminable pixels. Instead it gives information on the occluding pixels which can be used to locate the discontinuities of the depth map.

References

[1] Y. T. Zhou and R. Chellappa. "Computation of Optical Flow Using a Neural Network". In *Proc. IEEE Intl. Conf. on Neural Networks*, vol. 2, pp. 71–78, San Diego, CA, July 1988.

[2] Y. T. Zhou and R. Chellappa. "Neural Network Algorithms for Motion Stereo". In *Proc. Intl. Joint Conf. on Neural Networks*, vol. 2, pp. 251–258, Washington D.C., June 1989.

[3] Y. T. Zhou and R. Chellappa. "A Network for Motion Perception". In *Proc. Intl. Joint Conf. on Neural Networks*, vol. 2, pp. 875–884, San Diego, CA., June 1990.

[4] H. Bülthoff, J. Little, and T. Poggio. "A Parallel Algorithm for Real-Time Computation of Optical Flow". *Nature*, vol. 337, pp.549–554, Feb. 1989.

[5] C. Koch. "Analog Neuronal Networks for Real-Time Vision Systems". In *Proc. Workshop on Neural Network Devices and Applications*, Los Angeles, CA, February 1987.

[6] D. H. Hubel and T. N. Wiesel. "Receptive Fields and Functional Architecture in Two Nonstriate Visual Areas (18 and 19) of the Cat". *J. Neurophysiol.*, vol. 128, pp.229–289, 1965.

[7] D. H. Hubel and T. N. Wiesel. "Functional Architecture of Macaque Monkey Visual Cortex". *Proc. R. Soc. Lond. Ser. B*, vol. 198, pp.1–59, 1977.

[8] V. M. Montero. "Patterns of Connections from Striate Cortex to Cortical Visual Area in Superior Temporal Sulcus of Macaque and Middle Temporal Gyrus of Owl Monkey". *J. Comp. Neurol.*, vol. 189, pp.45–59, 1980.

[9] S. Lin C, R. E. Weller, and J. H. Kaas. "Cortical Connections of Striate Cortex in the Owl Monkey". *J. Comp. Neurol.*, vol. 211, pp.165–176, 1982.

[10] T. D. Albright, R. Desimone, and C. G. Gross. "Columnar Organization of Directionally Selective Cells in Visual Area MT of the Macaque". *J. Neurophysiol.*, vol. 51, pp.16–31, 1984.

[11] B. K. P. Horn. *Robot Vision*. The MIT Press, Cambridge, Massachusetts, 1986.

[12] S. Ullman. *The Interpretation of Visual Motion*. M.I.T. Press, Cambridge, MA, 1979.

[13] Y. T. Zhou, R. Chellappa, A. Vaid, and B. K. Jenkins. "Image Restoration Using a Neural Network". *IEEE Trans. Acoust,Speech,Signal Processing*, vol. 36, pp.1141–1151, July 1988.

[14] D. M. Greig, B. T. Porteous, and A. H. Seheult. "Exact Maximum *A Posteriori* Estimation for Binary Images". *J. Royal Statist. Soc. B*, vol. 51(2), pp.271–279, 1989.

[15] Y. T. Zhou. *"Artificial Neural Network Algorithms for Some Computer Vision Problems"*. PhD thesis, University of Southern California, Los Angeles, CA, November 1988.

[16] H. G. Barrow, J. M. Tenenbaum, R.C. Bolles, and H. C. Wolf. "Parametric Correspondence and Chamfer Matching: Two New Techniques for Image Matching". In *Proc. Fifth International Joint Conf. on Artificial Intelligence*, Cambridge, MA, 1977.

[17] L. Matthies, R. Szeliski, and T Kanade. "Kalman Filter-Based Algorithms for Estimating Depth from Image Sequences". In *Proc. DARPA Image Understanding Workshop*, pp. 199–213, Cambridge, MA, April 1988.

[18] S. T. Barnard. "A Stochastic Approach to Stereo Vision". In *Proc. Fifth National Conf. on Artificial Intelligence*, Philadelphia, PA, August 1986.

Index

A

Adaptive resonance theory (ART), 249, 427
  ARTMAP, 250–251
Alignment, 469, *see also* Recognition, 3D;
  Reprojection
Architecture
  columnar, *see* Cytoarchitecture
  distributed, *see* Cytoarchitecture
Aspect, 27–28, 427
  graphs, 425–427
  transition network (ATN), 427, 433–436
Associative memory (AM), *see* Memory
Attention, 262–263, 401–402, 417

B

Background, 151
Backpropagation (BP), *see* Learning
Binding problem, 42, *see also* Cortical,
  integration; Data fusion
Boundary contour system, (BCS)
  motion, 65
    oriented contrast filter (MOC), 65, 69,
      76–82
  static, 45, 65–66
    cooperative-competitive (CC) feedback
      network loop, 66
    oriented contrast-sensitive filter (SOC),
      66–68
Boundary detection, 315–318, 329–333,
  379–382

C

Central limit theorem (CLT), 215
Characteristic view, *see* Aspect
CL (complex-logarithmic) mapping, *see*
  Mapping, conformal

Classical conditioning, *see* Hebbian
  mechanism
Closure, *see* Contour, subjective
Collision detection, *see* Navigation
Color, 265, 275–277
Conjunction of localized features (CLF)
  model, 31–33, 36–37
Constancy
  of color, 265–266
  of shape, 467
  of size, 183
Contour
  subjective, 43–45, 67, 75–76, 153–159, *see*
    also Kanitza triangle
Control
  gaze, 401–402
  vergence, 406–407
Coordinate transformation, *see* Mapping
Cortex
  MT, 52–53, 64–65, 74, 494
  V1, 44, 64–65, 74, 319–320
  V2, 44, 64–65, 74
  visual, 8–9
Cortical
  areas, 41–42
  integration, 42, 115–116, 180, *see also* Data
    fusion; Reentrant and cortical
    integration
Cytoarchitecture, 120, 290–291, 319–321, 462,
  494

D

Data compression, 345, *see also* Vector
  Quantization
Data fusion, *see also* Cortical, integration;
  Markov random field
  FACADE theory, 97–99

reentrant cortical integration (RCI) model,
    45–48
Depth, 506
    from motion, 506–509
    map, 187–188
Diffusion, 430–432
Disparity, see Optical flow; Stereopsis
DOG (difference of Gaussians), 226–227,
    319, 463–464
Dominance columns
    ocular (ODC), 133–138
    orientation, 120–121
DOOG (difference of offset Gaussians), 320

E

Ecological optics, 465
Edge detection, 226–227, 316, 317–318,
    333–336, see also DOG; Motion,
    discontinuities; Zero crossings
Energy function, 188
Estimate
    optimal linear (LMS), 183, 270
    optimal polynomial, 274

F

FACADE theory, see Data fusion
Fault-tolerance, see Memory
Feature
    contour system (FCS), 70
    detection, 115–116, 373–375, 379–382,
        481–484
    high-level, 371–373, 444
Figure, see Foreground
Fixation point, 401–402, 475–476
Focus of
    attention, 262, 400
    expansion (FOE), 411–413, 467
Footprints, 33–34
Foreground, 151
Fovea, 177–178, 398–400
FT (Fourier transform), 183
    DFT (discrete Fourier transform), 228–229

G

Gabor transform, 229–230, 464
Gaussian
    convolution, 214, 218–224
    curvature, 246
    filter, 317

smoothed-Laplacian, 227–228
Generalization
    anisotropic, 29–31, see also View, point,
        dependency
    RAM, 205–206
Generalized inverse (GI), see Moore-Penrose
    inverse
Gestalt symmetry, 483
Ground, see Background

H

Hamiltonian, 126, 129–130
Hand-eye coordination, 285–286, 468–469,
    see also Mapping
Hebbian mechanism, 119
Hypercolumn transform, 320–323

I

Image
    intrinsic, 464
Invariance, 234–236
    filters, 240–241
        to linear transformations, 237–238
        to projection, 466
        to rigid motion, 246
    templates, 238–239

K

Kanitza triangle, 43, 49, 67
Knowledge-based
    artificial neural network (KBANN),
        444–449
    neural network (KNN), 444–447

L

Laplacian, 183, 317
Lateral geniculate nucleus (LGN), 13–15,
    19–20
Learning
    associative, 268–269
    backpropagation (BP), 272–273, 449, 468
    correlation, 464
    directed activation identification and
        descent (DAID), 449
    hybrid, 444
    supervised, 370
    unsupervised, see Adaptive resonance
        theory; Self-organization, feature map

Lightness, 266
  recovery
    backpropagation, 272-273
    linear estimation, 268-272, *see also*
      Memory, DAM
    regularization, 266-268
LTG (Lie transformation group), 467-468
Lyapunov functional, 129-130

M

Mapping
  conformal, 179, 183-184, 398, 411-416,
    432, 465-466
  reprojection, 184-187
  retinotopic, 461, 485
  sensory (visual) - motor, 290-294, 468-469
  visual, 180, 290
Markov random field (MRF), 277-288
Mean field theory, 15-19
Mellin transform, 466
Memory
  associative (AM), 212, 248-249, *see also*
    WISARD
  DAM (distributed associative), 183, *see
    also* Moore-Penrose inverse
  fault-tolerance, 205
Mental rotation, 28-29
Monocular deprivation (MD), 19-21
Moore-Penrose inverse, 269
Motion, 75-76
  apparent, 82-88
  curl, 468
  discontinuities, 498-501
  divergence, 468
  invariance, 467, *see also* LTG
  segmentation, 55-58
  shear, 468
  2D, 464
  3D, 467
Multiplex filter hypothesis (MFH), 111-113

N

Navigation
  collision detection, 409-416, 467
  tracking, 299-303, 403-406
Network
  cortical, 11-13, 19-21
  lattice, 217-218
  probabilistic, 203-204
  pyramid, 210-211, 217

RAM, 203-204
topography, 286-287
web-lattice, 214, 218-221, 225-226
winner-take-all (WTA), 437
Neural controller, 299-308
Neuron
  Bienenstock, Cooper, and Munro (BCM),
    11-12
  cortical, 10
  McCullough-Pitts, 207
  probabilistic, 203-204
  RAM, 203-204
Neuronal code, 104-105, *see also* Multiplex
    filter hypothesis
NMDA receptor, 22

O

Occlusion detection, 48-52, 510-512
Optical flow
  derivation, 409-411, 464, 494-498
  multiframe, 501-506
  STF (spatiotemporal-frequency), 464

P

PDC (parallel and distributed computation),
    461
PDR (parallel and distributed
    representations), 461
Perception
  active, 460, *see also* Attention
  categorical, 437-439, 450-455
  direct, 465
  directed, 462, 470
  exploratory, 461
Polar coordinates, *see* Mapping, conformal
Potts spin, 125-126
Power spectrum, 183
  magnitude, 183
  phase, 183
Problem ill-posed, 266-267, *see also*
    Regularization
Pseudoinverse matrix, *see* Moore-Penrose
    inverse

R

Receptive field (RF), 127-129, 132-133
Recognition
  alignment, 31, 182, *see also* Reprojection
  human, 27-31

object, 26–39, 408–409, 451–452
  2D, 183, 408–409
  3D, 31–38, 181–189, 425
Reentrant cortical integration (RCI) model,
    see Data fusion
Reflectance, see Lightness
Region growing, 387–388, 391–395
Regularization, 267–268
Remote sensing, 344, 357
Representation
  conjoint (spatial and spatial-frequency),
      463–465
  multiscale, 463
Reprojection, 184–187
Resolution, 463
  conjoint, 463–464
Restoration, see Markov random field;
    Regularization
Retinal ganglion cells (RGC), 139–140
Retinex theory, see Color

S

Scale space, 215–216, 323
Segmentation, 275–283, 385–386. see
    also Boundary detection;
    Diffusion; Edge detection; Region
    growing; Texture
Self-organization, 121–126, 129–133, 462
  feature map (SOFM), 348–350,
      371–373
    implementation (MASPAR), 351–356
Sensor
  fusion, see Data fusion
  retinal, 399–400
Sensory-motor coordination, 468, see
    also Mapping
Sketch
  primal, 317
  2.5D, 318
Space-variant sampling, 179, 398
Spatial fill-in, 162–170
Stable state, see Aspect
Stereopsis, 322, 465
Strategy
  analysis and synthesis, 462, 470

bottom-up, 462
top-down, 462
Symmetry, 475–476
  form-motion (FM) principle, 71–72,
      91–93
  operator, 477–480
Synapse
  GABAergic, 19
  modification, 11–13, 22, 122
  stability, 122–126

T

Textons, 147–148, 171–172
Texture, see also Contour, subjective
  assymetry, 151–152, 160–170
  discrimination, 146, 171–174, 324–329
    linearity, 148–149
    non-linearity, 149–150, 324–329
  preattentive, 147
  segmentation, 375–379
Thin membrane, 188
Tracking, see Navigation

V

Vector quantization (VQ), 346–347,
      350–351. see also
          Self-organization, feature map
View
  canonical, 27–28
  centered, 246, 426, 463
  oriented, 463
  point, 26–27
    dependency, 31
Visual potential, see Aspect, graphs

W

Wigner distribution (WD), 463, 466
WISARD, 206–209

Z

Zero crossings, 317